# Lecture Notes in Computer Science 907

Edited by G. Goos, J. Hartmanis and J. van Leeuwen

Advisory Board: W. Brauer    D. Gries    J. Stoer

Takayasu Ito   Akinori Yonezawa (Eds.)

# Theory and Practice of Parallel Programming

International Workshop TPPP '94
Sendai, Japan, November 7-9, 1994
Proceedings

Springer

Series Editors

Gerhard Goos
Universität Karlsruhe
Vincenz-Priessnitz-Straße 3, D-76128 Karlsruhe, Germany

Juris Hartmanis
Department of Computer Science, Cornell University
4130 Upson Hall, Ithaca, NY 14853, USA

Jan van Leeuwen
Department of Computer Science, Utrecht University
Padualaan 14, 3584 CH Utrecht, The Netherlands


Volume Editors

Takayasu Ito
Department of Computer and Mathematical Sciences
Graduate School of Information Sciences, Tohoku University
Sendai 980, Japan

Akinori Yonezawa
Department of Information Science, University of Tokyo
7-3-1 Hongo, Bunkyo-ku, Tokyo 113, Japan

CR Subject Classification (1991): C.1.2, C.4, D.1-3, F.3, F.1

ISBN 3-540-59172-9 Springer-Verlag Berlin Heidelberg New York

CIP data applied for

© Springer-Verlag Berlin Heidelberg 1995
Printed in Germany

Typesetting: Camera-ready by author
SPIN: 10485561        06/3142-543210 - Printed on acid-free paper

# Preface

Parallel Programming is now the major field in computer science in both theoretical and practical aspects. Virtually all researchers and practitioners in programming issues related to parallel/concurrent/distributed programming.

TPPP'94 is the first International Workshop on Theory and Practice of Parallel Programming, held at Gonryo-Kaikan, Tohoku University, Sendai, Japan, November 7, 8 and 9, 1994. It focused on theoretical foundations of parallel languages and parallel programming, their implementation issues, and practices of parallel programming. Specific topics included: models of computation, logic, proof, specification of programs, semantics of languages, implementation issues of languages and systems, and architectual support for parallelism and massively parallel computation.

The workshop program consisted of 9 invited lectures and 15 contributed talks with extensive discussions. The invited speakers were:

Vaughan Pratt (Stanford University)
Manfred Broy (Technische Universität München)
Benjamin Pierce (Edinburgh University, now at Cambridge University)
Robert H. Halstead, Jr. (DEC Cambridge Research Lab)
Christian Queinnec (Ecole Polytechnique)
John H. Reppy (AT&T Bell Laboratories)
Suresh Jagannathan (NEC Princeton Research Institute)
Naoki Kobayashi (University of Tokyo)
Taiichi Yusasa (Toyohashi University of Technology).

This volume contains all the invited speakers' papers as well as those of contributors, each of which is an improved/updated version of one prepared for the preliminary proceedings of the workshop, reflecting comments and discussions during the workshop. The following people helped with additional reviewing comments for the contributed papers: Manfred Broy, Robert H. Halstead, Jr., Christian Queinnec, Naoki Kobayashi, Satoshi Matsuoka, Atsushi Ohori, Taiichi Yuasa. We would like to express our sincere gratitude to them and to all the authors for submitting their papers to this volume.

The invited speakers of TPPP'94 were partially supported by the invitation programs of Ministry of Education and Culture (Mombusho) and International Information Science Foundation (IISF) and the research projects on parallel programming conducted by the workshop organizers. Special thanks go to Masahiko Ohtomo (the workshop secretary), Noriko Kusama, Shin-ichi Kawamoto, Kenji Takahashi, Tomohito Uchida, and all those who helped organize, and participated in, the workshop for their invaluable contributions. Finally, we thank Alfred Hofmann of Springer-Verlag for his assistance in this book's publication.

February 1995

Takayasu Ito
Akinori Yonezawa
Workshop Co-Organizers
TPPP'94

# Contents

# Time and Information in Sequential and Concurrent Computation

Vaughan Pratt*
Stanford University

### Abstract

Time can be understood as dual to information in extant models of both sequential and concurrent computation. The basis for this duality is phase space, coordinatized by time and information, whose axes are oriented respectively horizontally and vertically. We fit various basic phenomena of computation, and of behavior in general, to the phase space perspective. The extant two-dimensional logics of sequential behavior, the van Glabbeek map of branching time and true concurrency, event-state duality and schedule-automaton duality, and Chu spaces, all fit the phase space perspective well, in every case confirming our choice of orientation.

## 1 Introduction

Our recent research has emphasized a basic duality between time and information in concurrent computation. In this paper we return to our earlier work on sequential computation and point out that a very similar duality is present there also. Our main goal here will be to compare concurrent and sequential computation in terms of this duality.

First, we have previously analyzed a number of extant logics of sequential behavior under the general heading of two-dimensional logic [Pra90, Pra94c]. Here we fit the individual models of such logics to the information-time phase space framework of this paper.

*This work was supported by ONR under grant number N00014-92-J-1974

Second, R. van Glabbeek has developed a comprehensive classification of the basic models of concurrent behavior, which we here dub the "van Glabbeek map." The key feature of this classification is that it plots degrees of concreteness along two roughly independent axes. One axis is associated with the passage from linear time to branching time, which adds to the basic model information about the timing of decisions, whether a given decision is made earlier or later relative to the events being decided between. Here we fit the whole van Glabbeek classification to the phase space framework.

Third, sequential nonbranching computation can be understand as the alternation of events and states, like the alternation of moves of a game. We fit this simplistic linear notion of behavior to our phase-space framework and obtain the basic notions of *automaton* and *schedule*, as respectively the *imperative* and *declarative* views of programs, by projection of phase space trajectories onto respectively the information and time axes.

Fourth, the passage to concurrent and branching computation can be understood as the relaxing of the linear structure on each of the axes of phase space to something weaker. (In fact all structure can be dropped, and recovered later from the phase space itself.) In this way we arrive at the notion of Chu space as a basic notion of behavior. Chu spaces are mathematically universal in that they realize all relational structures, from which we infer that there is unlikely to be a more general basic notion of behavior.

## 2 Background

This section reviews some basic extant models of behavior. This will provide some of the necessary background, and hopefully will also serve to orient the reader's perspective to align it with ours.

### 2.1 Sequential Behavior

Two basic widely used models of sequential behavior are binary relations and formal languages.

The binary relation model begins with a set $W$ of *states* or *possible worlds* and associates with each program or activity $\alpha$ a set $a$ of pairs $(u, v)$ of states. These pairs denote the *possible* state transitions of the program: the pair $(u, v)$ indicates that whenever the program is started in state $u$, the possibility exists, at least when it starts, that it will eventually terminate, and that on that termination it will be in state $v$.

The total interpretation is that for every $u$ such that there exists at least one $v$ for which $(u, v) \in a$, the program is guaranteed to eventually reach some state $v'$ such that $(u, v') \in a$. This is the natural interpretation when *identifying* the pairs with the possible computations or *runs* of $\alpha$.

The more natural interpretation however is the partial one, whereby there also exists the possibility of failure to reach any final state. In this interpretation every pair $(u, v)$ *reflects* a run (defined somehow, but other than as merely a pair of states) which starts in state $u$ and terminates in state $v$. Here more than one run may give rise to a given pair, and, of greater concern, some runs may lack a final state (or conceivably a starting state depending on the exact definition of "run").

There is no natural encoding of this possibility in a binary relations on ordinary states, but it may be accommodated by adding a fictitious "bottom " state $\perp$. The presence of the pair $(u, \perp)$ in $a$ indicates the possibility that when started in state $u$, program $a$ will fail to reach a final state. A further distinction may be drawn here between two types of failure to terminate, namely blocking and divergence. One convenient basis for this distinction is whether the run is finite or infinite. When a nonterminating run is finite it is said to *block*, and when it is infinite it is said to *diverge*. This further distinction may be represented in a binary relation by replacing the single state $\perp$ with two states $\beta$ and $\delta$ indicating a blocked run and a diverging run respectively. Then $(u, \beta)$ and $(u, \delta)$ indicate the respective possibilities of blocking and diverging when started in state $u$. when started in state $u$. A natural restriction is that $(\beta, v)$ is only permitted as a transition when $v = \beta$, and similarly $(\delta, v)$ requires $v = \delta$; this ensures that if $a$ fails to terminate then so does $a; b$, and via the same size of run.

The formal language model begins with a set or *alphabet* Act (sometimes $\Sigma$) of *actions*, and interprets each program as a set of strings or *traces* $u \in \text{Act}^*$. Each such trace denotes one of the *possible* sequences of actions the program may perform.

Corresponding to the divergent state of the partial interpretation of binary relations, the possibility of infinite traces may be permitted, achieved by extending $\text{Act}^*$ to $\text{Act}^\infty$ defined as $\text{Act}^* \cup \text{Act}^\omega$. Just as a finite string of length $n$ may be defined as a function from the initial segment $0, 1, \ldots, n - 1$ of the natural numbers to Act, collectively forming $\text{Act}^*$, so may an infinite string may be defined as a function from the set $\omega$ of all natural numbers to Act, collectively forming $\text{Act}^\omega$ (following the usual convention by which $A^B$ denotes the set of all functions from $B$ to $A$).

The advantage of the formal language model over the binary relation model is that they admit various operations of *parallel composition*, none of which are meaningfully definable for binary relations.

The basic such operation is independent or *asynchronous* parallel composition, realized by the *shuffle* or *interleaving* operation $a\|b$. We define $a\|b$ to be the set of all traces $u_1v_1\ldots u_nv_n$, $n \geq 0$, for which $u_1\ldots u_n \in a$ and $v_1\ldots v_n \in b$ and $u_i, v_i \in \text{Act}^*$. That is, the $u_i$'s and $v_i$'s are not actions but rather possibly empty finite traces of actions (otherwise this would be the *perfect* shuffle, with $a$ going first). We imagine a scheduler first letting $a$ run for a while (not just one step), then $b$, these two turns being called a *ply* in game parlance. The scheduler grants a total of $n$ plies.

Whereas asynchronous parallel composition minimizes interaction, *synchronous* parallel composition maximizes it by defining $a\|b$ to be simply the intersection $a \cap b$, in the case that the programs have a common action set Act. This is the appropriate operation for the case when the two programs are run in lock step performing the same actions.

Typical concurrent execution lies somewhere in between these two extremes. A natural blend of the two operations is obtained when $a$ and $b$ have their own action sets, respectively $\text{Act}_a$ and $\text{Act}_b$. In this case $a\|b$ behaves synchronously on the common actions $\text{Act}_a \cap \text{Act}_b$ and asynchronously on the rest. Formally, $a\|b$ consists of those traces $u$ for which $u \cap \text{Act}_a^* \in a$ and $u \cap \text{Act}_b^* \in b$.

## 2.2 Concurrent Behavior

It is natural to regard sequential behavior as the special case of concurrent behavior in which exactly one agent is behaving. This has proved to be harder to formalize than it sounds. Our diagnosis is the the prior lack of appreciation for the independent roles of time and information in this generalization.

The crucial issue for both time and information is locality of each. In modelling a computation as the set of its possible traces, information resides in the choice of the trace while time is indicated by the position within the trace. In this model there is no connection between runs, whence we say that the information is global; creating connections localizes choice information by associating it with a particular point in a run. Dually there is complete connection within runs (i.e. they are linearly ordered), making the associated time global; relaxing linear orders to partial localizes time by dropping the premise that all pairs of events have a well-defined temporal order.

We note in passing that we may refine this model by equipping the set of traces with a real-valued probability measure, and by suitably timestamping the events of each run with a real-valued time relative to the start of the trace. This particular type of refinement does not change the global nature of either the time or the information.

The oldest model of concurrency, Petri nets [Pet62], made both time and information local, at a time when there was very little modeling of even sequential behavior in computer science.

Setting Petri nets to one side for the moment, the progression from sequential to concurrent behavior began with the basic step of replacing binary relations, as sets of state transitions (as used by Park and Hitchcock [HD73], DeBakker and deRoever [dBdR72], Pratt [Pra76], etc.), by processes as sets of traces [HL74]. This refinement permits the definition of concurrent composition as the interleaving or shuffle of traces. However this model is global as noted above with respect to both information and time.

The passage from sequential to concurrent behavior appears to have set off warning bells for some about the unsuitability of the extant sequential models for concurrent behavior. As is clear today there are two basic limitations of sets of traces. In the beginning this was much less clear, and each objector tended to focus on just one of these limitations. We now describe each of these types of objection.

## 2.3  Branching Time as Local Information

Milner [Mil80] was the first to spell out a notion of local information, which soon became known as branching time to distinguish it from the linear time of the trace model. Milner proposed synchronization trees as a model of behavior more concrete than sets of traces in that it fails to validate $ab + ac = a(b + c)$. A rigid synchronization tree is a rooted directed (away from the root) unoriented tree whose edges are labeled with actions from Act. Omitting "rigid" connotes a partial labeling, with the unlabeled edges understood equivalently as labeled with a "silent action" $\tau \notin$ Act. Whereas $ab + ac$ denotes a 4-edge tree branching at the root, i.e. having two $a$-labeled edges leaving the root, $a(b + c)$ denotes a 3-edge tree branching only after $a$.

While the passage from linear to branching time can be understood as generalizing a single linear order to a tree by permitting it to branch, this view misses the point that a general behavior is not a single trace but a set of traces. The passage is better understood as generalizing a set of linear orders to a synchronization tree by permitting similarly labeled initial segments to be identified. Such identifications localize choice information to the branch points of the resulting trees. With disconnected traces no information can be communicated about the timing of a choice: one may choose to understand all choices as being made at the beginning of time, or dually at the last possible moment, but no natural encoding of either a mixture of these or of intermediate timings has been proposed for sets of traces by themselves. The possibility of identifying initial segments of traces creates a degree of freedom that can be used to indicate when during the behavior a particular choice was made. Connecting only at the start means the choice is made at the start, connecting along some initial segment means that the choice is made at the end of that segment.

## 2.4   True Concurrency as Local Time

The dual of local information is local time, popularly called true concurrency in Europe starting around 1987. Local time was addressed early on by Mazurkiewicz [Maz77], who realized it in the form of a symmetric binary relation on the alphabet Act indicating *causal independence* of occurrences of those actions. This relation induces a congruence (with respect to Kleene's regular operations plus shuffle) on Act$^*$, and more generally on Act$^\infty$, whereby two traces are congruent when they may be obtained from each other by interchanging adjacent occurrences of independent actions. Mazurkiewicz called the quotient of Act$^*$ by this congruence a *partial monoid*; here partiality is understood to relax the ordering of traces, now understood to be partial in contrast to Act$^*$'s linear traces, rather than restricting the domain of concatenation as the term "partial monoid" might lead one to expect.

Mazurkiewicz traces, as the elements of such a partial monoid have come to be called, associate the independence information with the action alphabet Act. A stronger notion of true concurrency associates it instead with the *action occurrences* or *events* of a particular behavior. Viewing traces as *linearly* ordered sets of events in which each event is labeled with the action of which it is an occurrence, one relaxes this linear order to a partial order to arrive at what has been called a *partial word* [Gra81] and a *partially ordered multiset* [Pra82] or pomset, the term now used.

In a pomset with two occurrences of action $a$, an occurrence of $b$ may be comparable with one of the $a$'s and incomparable with the other, not possible with Mazurkiewicz traces as originally formulated (Mazurkiewicz subsequently extended his notion to multitraces to achieve this effect). If for example $a$ is the action of writing a 1 into a memory and $b$ that of reading 1, then a given occurrence of $b$ should be comparable with the responsible occurrence of $a$, but not with subsequent occurrences of $a$, which having no causal relationship to that occurrence of $b$ can be performed independently of it. This distinction must be expressible in order to distinguish a simple memory whose reads and writes are interleaved, with the read returning the most recently written value, from a more sophisticated one that permits simultaneous reading and writing with the expectation that the read will return a previously written value.

## 3   Two-Dimensional Logic

We recently [Pra94c] defined a general notion of two-dimensional logic, into which various logics of action could be fitted. The significance of two-dimensional logics for the present paper is that their disjunction and conjunction operations are the natural operations of accumulation for respectively information and time. We return to this point after a walk around the domain of two-dimensional logics to familiarize ourselves with the scope of such logics.

The following picture of the main two-dimensional logics should be understood as a cube with appendages.

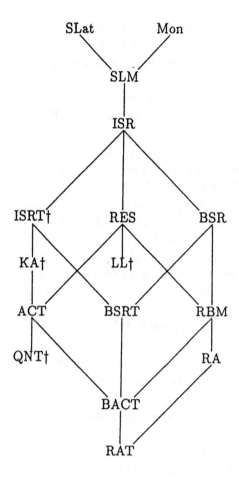

Starting from the top of this diagram, a *semilattice* is a set $A$ with an associative commutative idempotent binary operation $a + b$; **SLat** denotes the class thereof. We write $a \leq b$ for $a + b = b$, a binary relation that can be shown to be partially order $A$. Semilattices form the models of a basic logic of *disjunction*.

A *monoid* is a set $A$ with an associative binary operation $ab$ and a constant 1 as that operation's unit or neutral element, $a1 = a = 1a$; the associated class is **Mon**. We shall use general monoids to model *noncommutative conjunction*.

A set with both these operations and satisfying a two-sided distributivity principle $a(b + c) = ab + ac$ and $(a + b)c = ac + bc$ is called an *idempotent semiring*, forming the class **ISR**. This combines conjunction and disjunction in the one logic.

The three axes of the cube having **ISR** at its apex correspond to the following constraints on ISR's. The subclass **ISRT** of **ISR** consists of those ISR's in which for every element $a$ there exists a least reflexive $(1 \leq a)$ transitive $(aa \leq a)$ element $a^*$ such that $a \leq a^*$. Logics with such an operation cater to *iterated conjunction* or repetition.

The subclass **RES** of residuated ISR's consists of those ISR's in which for all elements $a, b$ there exists a greatest element $a \rightarrow b$ such that $a(a \rightarrow b) \leq b$, and dually a greatest element $b \leftarrow a$ such that $b(b \leftarrow a) \leq a$; $a \rightarrow b$ is called the *right residual* of $b$ by $a$, while $b \leftarrow a$ is dually called the *left residual* of $b$ by $a$. Such logics add implication to the language. These are the Ajdukiewicz monoids [Ajd37], brought to greater prominence two decades later by Lambek [Lam58]. The term residuation was coined by Ward and Dilworth [WD39]. That the binary relations on a set formed a residuated ISR was first observed, as "Theorem K," by De Morgan [DM60].

The subclass **BSR** of Boolean semirings has the property that the semilattice structure forms a Boolean algebra; for this it suffices for an antimonotone operation of negation $\neg a$ to exist and satisfy $\neg\neg a = a$. This yields classical logic with a second conjunction $\neg(\neg a + \neg b)$ distinct (in general) from the main conjunction $ab$; pure Boolean logic obtains when these operations coincide.

The remaining classes **ACT**, **BSRT**, and **RBM** combine these conditions pairwise, and **BACT** imposes all three conditions, see [Pra90, Pra94c] for details.

The class **QNT** of quantales consists of ISR's for which the semilattice is complete (has all suprema or joins $\Sigma_i a_i$ including the empty supremum 0 and infinite suprema). Residuals and transitive closures always exist in quantales, being expressible as respectively infinite infima and infinite suprema.

The Jonsson-Tarski class **RA** of *relation algebras* is obtained from **RBM** by identifying the left and right residuals of the Boolean complement 0' of 1 by any given value $a$: $a \rightarrow 0' = 0' \leftarrow a$. This class together with transitive closure, **RAT**, was the subject of Judith Ng's thesis [NT77, Ng84].

There are two basic models of two-dimensional logic that pervade computer science, formal languages as sets of strings, and binary relations as sets of pairs. For both, $a + b$ is union. For languages, $ab$ is concatenation, while for binary relations it is composition or relative product. For a fixed set $X$, the algebra of all binary relations on $X$, i.e. all subsets of $X^2$, under $a + b$ and $ab$, belongs to both **QNT** and **RAT**. Likewise so does the algebra of all languages on $X$ treated as an alphabet, i.e. all subsets of the set $X^*$ of all finite strings on $X$.

Sometimes one does not want all languages or all binary relations but only certain ones, which collectively then may not form an RAT or a quantale but may nevertheless belong to one of the larger classes in the above classification. In addition other structures closed under operations $a + b$ and $ab$ suitably interpreted may satisfy enough conditions to locate them collectively in one or another of these classes.

Now let us turn to the connection with information and time. Our intuitions as to how each of these accumulate are nicely captured by the two basic operations of two-dimensional logic.

We understand information from an information theoretic perspective. Here information is measured not by number of facts but by variety of choices. When there is only one option no information can be conveyed by indicating that it is the option. Two options permit one bit, four two bits, etc. The operation $a + b$ is taken to denote accumulation of choices. The order in which two choices are presented does not matter, expressed by the commutativity of $a + b$. Being presented with the same choice twice does not increase our options, expressed by idempotence $a + a = a$.

We think of $ab$ as the *temporal* conjunction $a$ *and then* $b$, as in "open the door and then walk through it." This operation accumulates not facts but rather events. Like $a + b$ it is associative. However it is not commutative, witness walking through the door and then opening it. Nor is it idempotent, witness the action of paying a dollar, which when repeated becomes the action of paying two dollars. This in contrast to *factual* conjunction, where two facts may be learned in either order (commutativity), and having learned a fact one learns nothing new by learning it again (idempotence).

An ordered monoid in ISR may be understood as a monoidal category, and as such, as a one-object 2-category. A 2-category has two compositions, conventionally called horizontal (composing the 1-cells) and vertical (composing the 2-cells). These compositions correspond to respectively the monoid conjunction and the semilattice disjunction. 2-cells are then naturally drawn with the orientation as typified by the following diagram illustrating the interchange law for 2-categories.

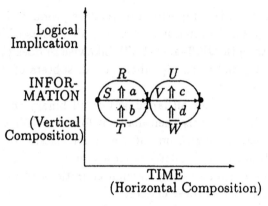

Figure 1. 2D Logic

This is the first of what will be four situations all fitting the same basic information-time phase diagram. In all four cases the conventions that have emerged favor orienting information vertically and time horizontally.

## 4   The van Glabbeek Map

In the previous section the individual logics were two-dimensional, forming a landscape that was not itself two-dimensional. We pass now to the landscape of concurrency models studied in the thesis of our colleague R. van Glabbeek. Here the landscape itself is a two-dimensional logic. Van Glabbeek's original landscape, which he chose to orient as here, contained some 36 models of concurrency; here we have cut it down for simplicity to an incompletely filled 3 × 3 array of a mere half dozen models.

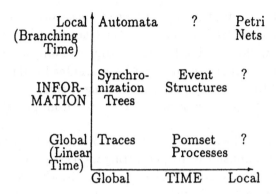

Figure 2. A Van Glabbeek Map.

In the previous section the two axes measured respectively increasing number of options (no choices at the bottom, many choices at the top) and increasing time (early on the left, late on the right). Here the axes measure *expressiveness*. The information axis measures the precision with which the timing of a branch may be specified. At the bottom no information is conveyed as to when a decision is made. At the synchronization tree level $ab + ac$ can be distinguished from $a(b + c)$, which we associate with respectively early and late commitment to the choice of $b$ or $c$. At neither of these levels can it be specified when the information represented by these choices is subsequently forgotten; it would seem that all choices are remembered forever. At the automaton level we can distinguish between $ac + bc$ and $(a + b)c$ as respectively long and short memory. The former remembers the choice longer until after $c$, while the latter forgets it before $c$, a distinction drawn by conventional (finite) state automata as well as by Boudol's flow event structures [Bou90].

The vertical axis therefore indicates the passage from global choice, where choice commitment and forgetting has no specific location in the computation, to local choice, that is, localized to specific points in the computation.

The time axis measures the precision with which we may distinguish the truly concurrent execution $a\|b$ of $a$ and $b$ from the "false concurrency" or mutual exclusion $ab + ba$. Traces fail to draw this distinction, for which Grabowski [Gra81] and Pratt [Pra82] introduced pomsets, as labeled *partial* orders generalizing the notion of trace as a labeled *linear* order. Indicating time by a single global clock leads naturally to the trace model, in which all pairs of events have a well-defined order. When time can only be measured by local clocks, this linear order can no longer be guaranteed and it becomes natural to understand time as only partially ordering events.

The horizontal axis therefore indicates the passage from global time to local time.

Petri nets achieve more locality in these two coordinates than any competing model. They accomplish this by permitting in-degree and out-degree greater than one at both places (state-holders) and transitions (event-holders). The branching, both in and out, is disjunctive at places and conjunctive at transitions. Branching at places increases the expressiveness of Petri nets in the information domain while branching at transitions increases expressiveness in the time domain.

An ordinary sequential automaton may be understood as a Petri net with no branching at transitions, either in or out, only at places. In the "token game" standardly used to equip Petri nets with a semantics, an automaton can neither create nor destroy tokens. Sequential computation can then be understood as the trajectory of a single token through the net.

A pomset process, as a set of pomsets analogous to a trace process as a set of traces, may be understood as a Petri net with no branching at places.

## 5   Linear Automata and Schedules

We turn now to a point of view we developed recently [Pra92] as a simple setting in which time and information were dual. There we gave up all branching in both the time and information domains to reduce this duality to its simplest form. The essence of this duality reduced to the self-duality of suitable categories of chains, which we illustrated there with the category of finite chains with bottom and their monotone functions; certain other categories of chains are also self-dual.

Persisting with our two-dimensional phase space, we return to our original understanding of the horizontal axis as indicating increasing time. We take the vertical axis however to be *decreasing* options, whence we associate upwards motion with learning as the process of narrowing the possible alternatives. For simplicity we suppose that both axes order their respective domains linearly.

We now view computation, and more generally any behavior, as alternately changing state and passing time, like a chess player making a move and then awaiting her opponent's move. Thus behavior may be depicted as a monotonically increasing trajectory as follows.

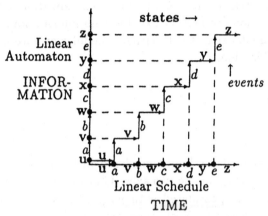

Figure 3. A Linear Phase Space.

The horizontal moves are *states*, in which time passes while information remains fixed. We use $u - z$ to denote states, which we suppose are drawn from a set $X$ of states.

The vertical moves are *events*, which holds time fixed (events are ephemeral) while changing information. We use $a - e$ to denote events, drawn from an event set $A$.

A trajectory in phase space constitutes a neutral view of behavior. We take sides by projecting the trajectory onto one or the other axis. Projecting it onto the information axis sends the states to points while preserving the spatial extent of the events. The resulting graph can then be seen to be an *automaton*, of the straightline kind one necessarily associated with a completely nonbranching behavior.

Dually, projecting the trajectory onto the time axis sends events to points and states to lines, recognizable as a *schedule*, again linearly ordered as with the automaton.

Because the trajectory is simply a staircase, only the number of steps matters. Since this can be recovered from either the automaton or the schedule (taking suitable care at the endpoints not to lose information), either one suffices as our view of this admittedly very simple behavior.

We have represented the trajectory as a line, but it may equivalently be understood as a partition of phase space into an upper and lower part, representable by a function from phase space to $\{0, 1\}$. We may then recover the trajectory as the common boundary of the two blocks of this partition of phase space. This point of view leads naturally into the Chu space generalization of linear computation. This generalization will retain the property that projection onto either axis loses no information. That is, we can program general Chu spaces with either schedules or automata with equal precision of specification.

# 6 Chu Spaces

## 6.1 Concept

A Chu space is a structure of the kind considered in the previous section, less the assumption of linearity for the two axes. Chu spaces are particularly simple in that their axes are postulated with *no* particular structure, that is, they are taken to be pure sets $X$ of states (the vertical axis) and $A$ of events (the horizontal axis). In place of a trajectory of alternating states and events through phase space, we associate with each pair $(x, a)$ a value which may be interpreting as either the *truth* of $a$ in $x$ (an information-theoretic view), or the *time* of $a$ relative to $x$ (when in state $x$, how long ago did $a$ happen?).

The simplest nontrivial Chu spaces have binary entries. A 1 at location $(x, a)$ may read as either that $a$ is true in possible world $x$ (the modal logic viewpoint), or that in state $x$, $a$ has already happened (the dynamic viewpoint). There is no identifiable notion of "$a$ happening during $x$," in each state $a$ either has or has not happened.

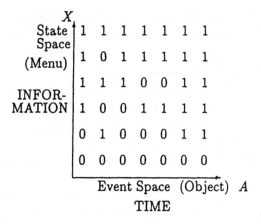

Figure 4. A Chu Space.

## 6.2 Example: Sets of Traces

It will be helpful to see how traditional formal languages as sets of strings
fit in here. To begin with, these Chu spaces are to formal languages as the
real plane is to the Mona Lisa: only the canvas is represented, the paint
is omitted. For languages this means that we regard an *occurrence* of a
symbol in a string as a point somewhere along the string, and the symbol
of which it is an occurrence as a mere label on that point indicating the
"color" it has been painted, our palette being the alphabet $\Sigma$. Our theory
neglects these labels or colors and treats the underlying geometry of the
behavior of automata rather than the full notion of behavior corresponding
to a finished work of art. In this respect it is just like Hilbert space as it
arises in quantum mechanics, which makes no attempt to label either its
dimensions or its points with anything concrete, this being left to operators
for extracting physical quantities from wavefunctions defined as points of
Hilbert space.

A formal language is then understood as just a set of anonymous finite
strings, the only feature of which that now matters is its length. The set
$A$ of events is taken to be the set of all occurrences of symbols in strings,
equivalently the disjoint union of the strings, together with one additional
point called $\infty$ (this point is added for the sake of a nice duality property of
formal languages that does not obtain in general for arbitrary Chu spaces). If

two distinct strings of the same language have the same length, they remain distinguished in $A$. In particular if language $L$ consists of two strings both of length three, e.g. $abc$ and $aba$, $A$ will consist of seven points, namely the six occurrences of symbols in $L$ together with $\infty$.

We take the set $X$ of states to be $A$, reflecting the above-mentioned peculiarity of formal languages that they are self-dual. We define $x \models a$ to be 1 (true) just when $x$ and $a$ are in the same string and $x$ follows $a$ (including the case when $x$ *is* $a$). Otherwise it is 0, the case when $x$ and $a$ come from different strings, or from the same string but with $x$ strictly preceding $a$, or when either is $\infty$.

The underlying geometry of $L$ can be recovered from this construction of $(X, A, \models)$ by defining an equivalence relation on $A$ which makes two points equivalent just when one precedes or equals the other. The strings are then the equivalence classes, and $\infty$ is the element that is not related to any element, even itself. The restriction of $\models$ to a string linearly orders that string, allowing us to reconstruct the position of each occurrence in its containing string. This construction works even for languages with infinitely many strings, including the duality property, which however does not hold in general in the presence of infinitely long strings. This completes the account of how a language consisting of finite strings can be represented as a Chu space.

## 6.3   Schedules and Automaton

We observed that in the linear case no information was lost in the projection of a trajectory onto either axis. With suitable care in the definition of projection we may accomplish the same for *biextensional* Chu spaces, namely those having no repeated rows or columns, via a process we have previously described [GP93], which we sketch briefly here.

We project onto the information axis to yield an automaton in two steps. First close the rows of the Chu space under arbitrary union and intersection (OR and AND of the rows as bit-vectors), by adding new rows as needed. Now draw the poset of all resulting rows ordered by inclusion, and color the elements black or white according to whether they were originally present or not. This poset turns out to be a profinite distributive lattice, that is, a complete distributive lattice (one having all meets and joins including the empty and infinite ones) whose maximal chains are nowhere dense: between any two distinct points of the chain lie two distinct points with no other point between them. We recover $A$ as those elements of this lattice not the join of the lattice elements strictly below them, $X$ as the set of black points of the lattice, and $x \models a$ as the relation $a \le x$. The theorem [GP93] is that recovered space is isomorphic to the originally projected space.

This construction works equally well when "row" and "column" are interchanged everywhere, dealing immediately with the case of projection onto the time axis, yielding a schedule.

That these objects are recognizable automata and schedules respectively (with loops and disjunctive confluences unfolded) can be appreciated from the examples in [Gup93, GP93, Pra93b, Gup94, Pra94a].

## 6.4  Universality of Chu Spaces

The categories $\mathbf{Str}_\kappa$ of $\kappa$-ary relational structures and their homomorphisms where $\kappa$ is any ordinal are universal categories for mathematics to the extent that they *realize* many familiar categories: groups, lattices, and Boolean algebras when $\kappa = 3$, rings, fields, and categories when $\kappa = 4$, etc. We say that a concrete category $D$ *realizes* a concrete category $C$ when there exists a functor $F : C \to D$ that is full and faithful and which commutes with the respective underlying-set functors of $C$ and $D$.

Elsewhere [Pra93b, pp.153-4] we proved that the self-dual category $\mathbf{Chu}_{2^\kappa}$ of Chu spaces over the power set of $\kappa = \{0, 1, \ldots, \kappa - 1\}$ realizes $\mathbf{Str}_\kappa$. Relational structures being universal, this makes Chu spaces at least as universal. The embedding being "sparse," there are many other Chu spaces besides those representing relational structures; in particular those Chu spaces dual to some relational structure may prove as useful as that structure itself. We have more recently streamlined our original argument, and it is presently available by anonymous ftp as /pub/uni.tex.Z from boole.stanford.edu.

When a model of behavior at the same time forms a universal category for mathematics, it is reasonable to infer that a more general model is not possible. The one flaw in this argument is in the amount of structure preserved by the functor doing the modeling. For the functor to destroy essential structure constitutes an "incompleteness" in the universality of the model, in turn weakening the claim to being a universal model of computation. This situation could be resolved either way: Chu spaces could turn out to capture all the structure that matters, or the category of Chu spaces over $K$ as a whole may turn out to lack essential structure that can be recovered only by giving up the appealing self-duality of the category, or its completeness or cocompleteness, etc. This issue most certainly deserves to be pursued further.

## 6.5 Duality

The duality of time and information is reflected for Chu spaces in a variety of ways. Mathematically it is represented by how Chu spaces transform. A Chu transform from $(A, X, \models)$ to $(A', X', \models')$ consists of a pair $(f, g)$ of functions $f : A \to A'$, $g : X' \to X$, satisfying $g(x) \models a = x \models' f(a)$ for all $a \in A$ and $x \in X'$. These have the evident composition as $(f, g)(f', g') = (ff', g'g)$ with evident identies and thus constitute the morphisms of the category $\mathbf{Chu(Set, 2)}$ of Chu spaces over the two-element set $2 = \{0, 1\}$. Chu spaces have an equally evident duality obtained by transposition, which has the side effect of reversing the direction of the Chu transforms. As noticed by Barr [Bar91] and further developed by several authors [dP89, BG90, LS91, BGdP91, Pra93b], Chu spaces provide a straightforward interpretation of full linear logic; the fact that **Set** (as well as **Pos** and other even larger cartesian closed categories) is comonadic (cotripleable) in **Chu** gives a straightforward interpretation of Girard's "bang" operation $!A$ as the functor of that comonad.

For those who are put off by the transformational view of duality, it is possible to appreciate the duality of Chu spaces in entirely noncategorical terms.

The interpretation of each row of a Chu space as one of the *possible* "paintings" of the underlying set $A$ of points of the space is in agreement with the basic theme of this paper, that the vertical axis of the information-time phase diagram denotes a *disjunctive* space, and thereby constitute a *menu. The basic feature of a menu is that its entries are selected one at a time.*

Likewise each column of a Chu space as the "identifier" of a point makes the horizontal axis conjunctive: this point is identified in this way *and* that point is identified in that way and so on. The points of the space coexist, and thereby constitute an *object. The basic feature of an object is that its points coexist.*

With regard to orientation, menus normally list their selections vertically, while the elements of an object such as a Lisp list or an APL array are usually listed horizontally.

A set (of points), as a set transforming by functions, is a pure body or *object*. An antiset (of states), as a set transforming by antifunctions (the converse of a function), is a pure mind or *menu*. A Chu space $(A, X, \models)$, as a binary relation $\models$ from an antiset $X$ to a set $A$, denotes a more or less fruitful blend of mind and body. The extremal Chu spaces are $(A, 2^A, \ni)$

and $(2^X, X, \in)$, denoting respectively the object or pure body $A$ and the menu or pure mind $X$.

The idea that a menu is mental is reinforced by the observation that the category of sets and antifunctions is equivalent to the category of complete atomic Boolean algebras and their complete homomorphisms. Boolean logic is the purest possible logic in that it has the maximum possible equations for its signature: adding just one more equation to the equational theory of Boolean algebras leads to inconsistency in the sense that $x = y$ can be proved for all terms $x$ and $y$.

Menus and objects are analogous to your moves and your opponent's moves. The former are your opportunities, one of which you must select from, the latter are your risks, all of which must be guarded against since any one might happen.

Computer scientists are chided by some mathematicians for their preference for logic over algebra. Yet this preference is more deeply rooted than generally appreciated. Algebra transforms via *functions*, which up to isomorphism serve to *identify* (not all functions are injective) and *adjoin* (not all functions are surjective). Dually, *antifunctions* serve respectively to *copy* and *delete*. But in computer science the natural operations are copy and delete, which are easily implemented. Identification of existing elements and adjoining new elements are more sophisticated operations that each require some effort to implement.

This bias makes antifunctions, alias complete Boolean homomorphisms but more naturally understood as copy and delete operations, the natural side of the set-antiset duality for computer scientists to gravitate towards. Mathematicians on the other hand are above mere copying and deleting of individual points and prefer to operate on whole spaces. This moves them "up one exponential," and their concern is therefore not surprisingly with the dual space.

We close by mentioning two striking similarities with quantum mechanics. First, the rows and columns of a Chu space interfere in essentially the same way that conjugate variables of a quantum mechanical system interfere to limit their joint precision according to Heisenberg's inequality $\Delta p.\Delta q \geq \hbar$ expressing the celebrated uncertainty principle of quantum mechanics. Second, residuation of Chu spaces, from which the associated state transition matrix (which makes no reference to events) may be recovered, amounts to their inner product when binary relations are understood as the points of a sort of "logician's Hilbert space." Furthermore the progression from automata to Chu spaces recapitulates the progression from Langrangian mechanics retaining even some of the essential properties of the Legendre transform by which this passage is standardly accomplished. Some of these connections are developed in [Pra93a, Pra94b], although the details of this second point of contact have only become clear to us since then.

These connections get considerably closer to the essence of quantum mechanics than does quantum logic [BvN36], which abstracts away from complementarity to capture just the underlying projective geometry of quantum mechanics. Quantum logic is to Chu spaces as nonconstructive methods of mathematics are to constructive, e.g. deciding whether one can get somewhere vs. exhibiting a route. Nonconstructivity confines itself to the "pure mind" extreme of mathematics, in the neighborhood of Boolean algebras and antisets. The full gamut of mathematics, from pure body to pure mind, can only be spanned constructively.

I believe that with due care computer science and physics can be made to look more like each other, and like mathematics, than they presently appear. Such connections would then broaden the role of constructivity to make it equally essential for all three subjects. For computer science at least, the least surprised by this will be the humble programmer, who would have great difficulty imagining that much good could come of purely nonconstructive software that indicated the end but not the means.

# References

[Ajd37]  K. Ajdukewicz. Die syntaktische konnexität. *Studia Philosophica*, I:1–27, 1937. English translation in S. McCall, Polish Logic 1920-1939, Clarendon Press, Oxford, 1967.

[Bar91]  M. Barr. ∗-Autonomous categories and linear logic. *Math Structures in Comp. Sci.*, 1(2), 1991.

[BG90]  C. Brown and D. Gurr. A categorical linear framework for Petri nets. In J. Mitchell, editor, *Logic in Computer Science*, pages 208–218. IEEE Computer Society, June 1990.

[BGdP91]  C. Brown, D. Gurr, and V. de Paiva. A linear specification language for Petri nets. Technical Report DAIMI PB-363, Computer Science Department, Aarhus University, October 1991.

[Bou90]    G. Boudol. Computations of distributed systems, part 1: flow event structures and flow nets, 1990. Report INRIA Sophia Antipolis, in preparation.

[BvN36]    G. Birkhoff and J. von Neumann. The logic of quantum mechanics. *Annals of Mathematics*, 37:823–843, 1936.

[dBdR72]  J.W. de Bakker and W.P. de Roever. A calculus for recursive program schemes. In M. Nivat, editor, *Automata, Languages and Programming*, pages 167–196. North Holland, 1972.

[DM60]    A. De Morgan. On the syllogism, no. IV, and on the logic of relations. *Trans. Cambridge Phil. Soc.*, 10:331–358, 1860.

[dP89]    V. de Paiva. A dialectica-like model of linear logic. In *Proc. Conf. on Category Theory and Computer Science, LNCS 389*, pages 341–356, Manchester, September 1989. Springer-Verlag.

[GP93]    V. Gupta and V.R. Pratt. Gates accept concurrent behavior. In *Proc. 34th Ann. IEEE Symp. on Foundations of Comp. Sci.*, pages 62–71, November 1993.

[Gra81]    J. Grabowski. On partial languages. *Fundamenta Informaticae*, IV.2:427–498, 1981.

[Gup93]    V. Gupta. Concurrent kripke structures. In *Proceedings of the North American Process Algebra Workshop, Cornell CS-TR-93-1369*, August 1993.

[Gup94]    V. Gupta. *Chu Spaces: A Model of Concurrency*. PhD thesis, Stanford University, September 1994. Tech. Report, available as ftp://boole.stanford.edu/pub/gupthes.ps.Z.

[HD73]    P. Hitchcock and Park D. Induction rules and termination proofs. In M. Nivat, editor, *Automata, Languages and Programming*. North-Holland, 1973.

[HL74]    C.A.R. Hoare and P.E. Lauer. Consistent and complementary formal theories of the semantics of programming languages. *Acta Informatica*, 3:135–153, 1974.

[Lam58]    J. Lambek. The mathematics of sentence structure. *American Math. Monthly*, 65(3):154–170, 1958.

[LS91]     Y. Lafont and T. Streicher. Games semantics for linear logic. In *Proc. 6th Annual IEEE Symp. on Logic in Computer Science*, pages 43–49, Amsterdam, July 1991.

[Maz77]    A. Mazurkiewicz. Concurrent program schemas and their interpretation. In *Proc. Aarhus Workshop on Verification of Parallel Programs*, 1977.

[Mil80]    R. Milner. *A Calculus of Communicating Systems, LNCS 92*. Springer-Verlag, 1980.

[Ng84]     K.C. Ng. *Relation Algebras with Transitive Closure*. PhD thesis, University of California, Berkeley, 1984. 157+iv pp.

[NT77]     K.C. Ng and A. Tarski. Relation algebras with transitive closure, Abstract 742-02-09. *Notices Amer. Math. Soc.*, 24:A29–A30, 1977.

[Pet62]    C.A. Petri. Fundamentals of a theory of asynchronous information flow. In *Proc. IFIP Congress 62*, pages 386–390, Munich, 1962. North-Holland, Amsterdam.

[Pra76]    V.R. Pratt. Semantical considerations on Floyd-Hoare logic. In *Proc. 17th Ann. IEEE Symp. on Foundations of Comp. Sci.*, pages 109–121, October 1976.

[Pra82]    V.R. Pratt. On the composition of processes. In *Proceedings of the Ninth Annual ACM Symposium on Principles of Programming Languages*, January 1982.

[Pra90]    V.R. Pratt. Action logic and pure induction. In J. van Eijck, editor, *Logics in AI: European Workshop JELIA '90, LNCS 478*, pages 97–120, Amsterdam, NL, September 1990. Springer-Verlag.

[Pra92]    V.R. Pratt. The duality of time and information. In *Proc. of CONCUR'92, LNCS 630*, pages 237–253, Stonybrook, New York, August 1992. Springer-Verlag.

[Pra93a]   V.R. Pratt. Linear logic for generalized quantum mechanics. In *Proc. Workshop on Physics and Computation (PhysComp'92)*, pages 166–180, Dallas, 1993. IEEE.

[Pra93b]   V.R. Pratt. The second calculus of binary relations. In *Proceedings of MFCS'93*, pages 142–155, Gdańsk, Poland, 1993. Springer-Verlag.

[Pra94a]   V. Pratt. Chu spaces: complementarity and uncertainty in rational mechanics. Technical report, TEMPUS Summer School, Budapest, July 1994. Manuscript available as pub/bud.tex.Z by anonymous FTP from Boole.Stanford.EDU.

[Pra94b]   V.R. Pratt. Chu spaces: Automata with quantum aspects. In *Proc. Workshop on Physics and Computation (PhysComp'94)*, Dallas, 1994. IEEE.

[Pra94c]   V.R. Pratt. A roadmap of some two-dimensional logics. In J. Van Eijck and A. Visser, editors, *Logic and Information Flow (Amsterdam 1992)*, pages 149–162, Cambridge, MA, 1994. MIT Press.

[WD39]   M. Ward and R.P. Dilworth. Residuated lattices. *Trans. AMS*, 45:335–354, 1939.

# NOTES ON P-ALGEBRA 1: PROCESS STRUCTURE

KOHEI HONDA

Department of Computer Science, Keio University

3-14-1 Hiyoshi, Kohoku-ku, Yokohama, 223, Japan

ABSTRACT. We develop an elementary theory of *process structure*, a mathematical object which is intended to capture a basic aspect of concurrent processes in a simple way. It has two kinds of presentations, one underlying many extant process theories and another with a more geometric flavour, which are shown to be essentially equivalent. The theory forms a basis of P-algebra, a general semantic structure for concurrent processes.

## 1. Introduction

The aim of the present notes is to develop an elementary theory of *process structure*, a mathematical object which is intended to capture a basic aspect of concurrent processes in a simple way. It has two kinds of presentations, one underlying many extant process theories and another with a more geometric flavour, which are shown to be essentially equivalent. The theory forms a basis of P-algebra, a general semantic structure for concurrent processes, to be developed in the sequels to these notes.

While we leave discussions on the overall motivations underlying the study of process structures and P-algebra to elsewhere, let us comment briefly on what *this* exposition achieves. Processes in process algebras usually arise as (congruence classes of) terms in some term algebra, and, there, the idea of names, either for communication ports or for actions, play an important role. So here are two entities, *processes* and *names*. We first form a simple class of algebras based on only these two elements, and dig out some structures hidden under their simple outlook. The observations now lead to another presentation of the same notion, simpler and more intuitive, which somehow dispenses with names. Theory of nameless processes is then developed, which can do the same thing as the original one, though with a quite different outlook. We finally prove equivalence of two theories in terms of both individual objects and their ambient categorical universes.

The study in the present notes can be regarded as part of our trial to delineate the notion of processes as a pure mathematical object, and to develop a general theory around it. The subsequent expositions will hopefully clarify what can be done in this vein. In the rest of the paper, Section 2 studies "rooted" process structures, i.e. the presentation which use names. Section 3 studies the non-rooted, or proper, process structures, and shows that it is equivalent to the first presentation.

Thanks to the participants of TPPP'94 for discussions, to the anonymous reviewer for useful suggestions, and to Nobuko Yoshida for her work on process graphs. The author is partially supported by JSPS Fellowships for Japanese Junior Scientists, for which he is grateful.

One idea from group theory is extensively used in the notes, which we list in the following for reference.

**Definition.** Let $G$ be a group with unit $e$ and $X$ be a set. Then a *group action of $G$ on $X$* is a function $* : G \times X \to X$ such that:

    (i) $*(e, x) = x$ for any $x \in X$.

    (ii) $*(g_1 g_2, x) = *(g_1, *(g_2, x))$ for any $g_1, g_2 \in G$ and for any $x \in X$.

We often write $gx$ instead of $*(g, x)$, and say $X$ is a *$G$-set* under the group action.

Said differently, a group action is an algebra over $X$ with operations from the elements of a group $G$ such that $ex = x$ and $(g_1 g_2)x = g_1(g_2 x)$ for any $g_1, g_2 \in G$ and $x \in X$. Yet another way of saying the same thing is that a group action is a homomorphism from a group $G$ to the group of permutations over $X$.

Other related notions will be introduced as we go on.

## 2.     Rooted Process Structure

Rooted process structures are a class of algebras which we can more or less directly extract from many extant process algebras, acting as a bridge from the essentially syntactic notion of processes to the one developed in Section 3. After reviewing basic algebraic elements, the idea of symmetry of processes is studied, which anticipates the construction in Section 3.

**2.1. Definition.** (rooted process structures) Given a countable set $\mathcal{N}$ of names, ranged over by $a, b, c, \ldots$, an *$\mathcal{N}$-rooted process structure* or just a *rooted process structure* is given by a set $\mathcal{P}$ of rooted processes, ranged over by $P, Q, R, \ldots$, together with the following data:

    (i) An operation $[\sigma] : \mathcal{P} \to \mathcal{P}$, written postfix, for each bijection $\sigma$ over $\mathcal{N}$. $[\sigma]$ is called *name permutation by $\sigma$*.

    (ii) A function $\mathcal{FN} : \mathcal{P} \to 2^{\mathcal{N}}$, assuming $\mathcal{F}(P)$ is always finite. $\mathcal{FN}(P)$ is called *free names* of $P$.

    (iii) Equations:

        1. $P[\sigma][\sigma'] = P[\sigma' \circ \sigma]$ (here $\circ$ is a functional composition).

        2. $(a \in \mathcal{FN}(P) \ \Rightarrow \ \sigma(a) = a) \ \Rightarrow \ P[\sigma] = P$.

        3. $\mathcal{FN}(P[\sigma]) = \sigma(\mathcal{FN}(P))$.

We usually fix some $\mathcal{N}$, and let $A, A', \ldots$ or $A_{\mathcal{P}}, A'_{\mathcal{P}'}, \ldots$ range over rooted process structures.

In other words, a rooted process structure $A_{\mathcal{P}}$ is a group action of the group of permutations over $\mathcal{N}$ on $\mathcal{P}$, equipped with an extra function $\mathcal{FN}(\cdot)$, relating $S_{\mathcal{N}}$ and $\mathcal{P}$. Note, as an algebra, $\mathcal{N}$ is *not* a constituent of a rooted process structure, but rather its prerequisite, since the signature depends on $\mathcal{N}$.

Some remarks on Definition 2.1:

## 2.2. Discussions.

    (1) A rooted process $P$ denotes an entity having several interface points with the outside, which are connected to (or *rooted to*) names, given by $\mathcal{FN}(P)$. Such a structure is often implicit in process algebras, in some ways or others, and notions like dynamics of interaction and process composition are formulated

on its basis. We will see that this structure is worth studying as a separate mathematical object.

(2) Explicit introduction of *bijective renaming* as operation, in combination with *free name function*, is essential. It acts on processes and relate them by name correspondence. The idea should be strictly differentiated from non-injective renaming (such as usual substitution), whose introduction necessitates another level of mathematical abstraction, essentially P-algebra itself.

(3) The free name function makes the range of names definite which a process is rooted to and which, therefore, bijective renaming has real effect on. This has a far reaching consequence in representation of rooted processes as will be studied in this section. We note that other formulations of the idea are possible, cf. 2.4 (iii).

## 2.3. Examples.

(i) Terms of CCS [10], possibly modulo strong bisimilarity, give such a structure, forgetting various constructors for process composition and augmented with $[\sigma]$ (defined syntactically) and $\mathcal{FN}(P)$ (using the static/dynamic sorts). It would be better to assume that $\bar{a}.P$ denotes a constructor which is distinct from $a.P$ but using the same name $a$ (instead of having a single prefix for a name and its coname), thus e.g. $a.0$ and $\bar{a}.0$ have the same set of free names, $\{a\}$.

(ii) Terms of $\pi$-calculus [13] or $\nu$-calculus [6] modulo $\alpha$-convertibility, or better, modulo structural equality [1, 12], augmented with $[\sigma]$ and $\mathcal{FN}(P)$. In fact a prototypical example of a rooted process structure is the combinatory representation of these calculi studied in [7, 8].

(iii) Another example is the set of terms in the pure $\lambda$-calculus modulo $\alpha$-convertibility, where we understand the variables occurring free in a term as its free names.

We now present some immediate consequences of Definition 2.1.

**2.4. Notations.** By $S_\mathcal{N}$ we mean the group of permutations over $\mathcal{N}$, where the group operation is given by permutation multiplication, written $\sigma \circ \sigma'$ etc. We write $id_\mathcal{N}$ for the unit of $S_\mathcal{N}$, and $\sigma^{-1}$ for the inverse of $\sigma$.

**2.5. Proposition.**

(i) *A process structure $A_P$ forms a group action of $S_\mathcal{N}$ on $\mathcal{P}$.*

(ii) *With $A \subset \mathcal{N}$, let $\sigma \restriction A$ denote a function restricted to the domain $A$. Then for any $P$, $\sigma_1$ and $\sigma_2$, we have:*

$$\sigma_1 \restriction A = \sigma_2 \restriction A \wedge \mathcal{FN}(P) \subset A \quad \Rightarrow \quad P[\sigma_1] = P[\sigma_2] \ .$$

(iii) *Call $A \subset \mathcal{N}$ a base of $P$ if, for any $\sigma_1$ and $\sigma_2$,*

$$\sigma_1 \restriction A = \sigma_2 \restriction A \quad \Rightarrow \quad P[\sigma_1] = P[\sigma_2] \ .$$

*Then $\bigcap \{A | A \text{ is a base of } P\} = \mathcal{FN}(P)$.*

PROOF: (i) follows from Definition 2.1.(iii)-1 and $P[id_\mathcal{N}] = P$ the latter being a consequence of Definition 2.1.(iii)-2. For (ii), note if $a \in A$ then $\sigma_2^{-1} \circ \sigma_1 (a) = a$, hence $P[\sigma_1] \circ [\sigma_2^{-1}] = P$ by Definition 2.1 (iii)-2, which is equivalent to $P[\sigma_1] = P[\sigma_2]$, as required. But this says $\mathcal{FN}(P)$ itself is a base of $P$, thus (iii) holds. $\square$

Note (iii) suggests an alternative way of formulating the idea of free names (we further require that an arbitrary intersection of bases is again a base).

As any study of algebraic structure, we start with relations and maps over rooted processes.

**2.6. Definition.** (compatible relations and homomorphisms) A *compatible relation* from $A_{\mathcal{P}}$ to $A'_{\mathcal{P}'}$ is the one so with respect to operations $\{[\sigma]\}$, i.e. a relation $\mathcal{R}$ from $\mathcal{P}$ to $\mathcal{P}'$ such that $P\mathcal{R}Q \;\Rightarrow\; P[\sigma]\mathcal{R}Q[\sigma]$ for any $[\sigma]$. A compatible relation which is also an equivalence relation is a *congruence*. A compatible relation which is also a function is a *homomorphism*. *Isomorphisms* are bijective o homomorphisms. We write $A \simeq A'$ if there is an isomorphism between $A$ and $A'$.

**2.7. Discussions.** (compatible relation) Relations closed under name permutation are omnipresent in process algebra, e.g. bisimilarities and other standard equivalences/preorders, reduction relation over process terms, and, with a slight extension, labeled transition relation, etc. More deeply, this is because the essential use of names in relating processes lies in *specification of structural correspondence on interface points between processes*. Take an example of CCS, $a.b.0 + b.a.0 \sim a.0|b.0$, with $\sim$ being a strong bisimilarity. Here $a$ and $b$ are significant precisely because they specify how these two processes are structurally related. So *as far as the same correspondence is maintained*, we can permute names freely, e.g. $l.m.0 + m.l.0 \sim l.0|m.0$ holds again.

As in usual algebra (cf. [2]), compatible relations and quotient sets can be considered as assuming the same structure as the underlying object.

**2.8. Proposition.**

(i) *Given a compatible relation* $\mathcal{R} \stackrel{def}{=} \{\langle P, Q\rangle\}$, *take* $\mathcal{R}$ *itself as the set of processes and define:* (a) $\langle P, Q\rangle[\sigma] \stackrel{def}{=} \langle P[\sigma], Q[\sigma]\rangle$ *and* (b) $\mathcal{FN}(\langle P, Q\rangle) = \mathcal{FN}(P) \cup \mathcal{FN}(Q)$. *Then* $\mathcal{R}$ *forms a rooted process structure.*

(ii) *Given a congruence* $\sim$ *on* $A$, *write* $[P]_\sim$ *for an equivalence class by* $\sim$. *Define:* (a) $[P]_\sim[\sigma] \stackrel{def}{=} [P\sigma]_\sim$ *and* (b) $\mathcal{FN}([P]_\sim) \stackrel{def}{=} \bigcap_{P'\sim P} \mathcal{FN}(P')$. *Then* $\mathcal{P}/\sim$ *forms a rooted process structure. We call this structure the* quotient *of* $A$ *by* $\sim$ *and write it* $A/\sim$.

PROOF: In both (i) and (ii), the property as algebra is standard, so we check consistency of the definition of free names with equations 2 and 3 of Definition 2.1.(iii). For tuples, suppose, for $\sigma$, $a \in \mathcal{FN}(\langle P, Q\rangle)$ implies $\sigma(a) = a$. Then it is identity on both $\mathcal{FN}(P)$ and $\mathcal{FN}(Q)$, hence $\langle P, Q\rangle[\sigma] = \langle P, Q\rangle$, therefore the second equation is satisfied. As to the third equation, $\mathcal{FN}(\langle P, Q\rangle[\sigma]) = \mathcal{FN}(P[\sigma]) \cup \mathcal{FN}(Q[\sigma]) = \sigma(\mathcal{FN}(P)) \cup \sigma(\mathcal{FN}(Q)) = \sigma(\mathcal{FN}(P) \cup \mathcal{FN}(Q))$, hence done.

For equivalence classes, let $A = \bigcap\{\mathcal{FN}(P')|P' \in [P]_\mathcal{R}\}$. Suppose $\sigma_1 \upharpoonright A = \sigma_2 A$. Then we get: $P[\sigma_1] = P \; \Pi_{1\leq i\leq n}[\binom{\sigma_2(x_i)\sigma_1(b_i)}{\sigma_2(x_i)\sigma_1(b_i)}] \circ [\sigma_2] \circ \Pi_{1\leq i\leq n}[\binom{\sigma_2(x_i)}{x_i}]$ where $\{b_i\} = \mathcal{FN}(P)\backslash A$ and $\{x_i\}$ are taken fresh. If, now, $\{b_i\}$ is *not* empty, there is a name $b_1$ which is *not* in $\mathcal{FN}(P')$ for some $P' \in [P]_\mathcal{R}$. By compatibility and because we have $P'[\binom{b_i x_i}{x_i b_i}] = P'$ for such $P'$, we have:

$$P[\rho] \quad \mathcal{R} \quad P' \; \Pi_{1\leq i\leq n}[\binom{\sigma_2(x_i)\sigma_1(b_i)}{\sigma_2(x_i)\sigma_1(b_i)}] \circ [\sigma_2] \circ \Pi_{2\leq i\leq n}[\binom{b_i x_i}{x_i b_i}]$$
$$= \quad P' \; \Pi_{1\leq i\leq n}[\binom{\sigma_2(x_i)\sigma_1(b_i)}{\sigma_2(x_i)\sigma_1(b_i)}] \circ [\sigma_2] \circ \Pi_{2\leq i\leq n}[\binom{b_i x_i}{x_i b_i}].$$

Repeating the procedure and using transitivity of $\mathcal{R}$, we finally get $P[\sigma_1]\mathcal{R}P[\sigma_2]$, i.e. $[P]_{\mathcal{R}}[\sigma_1] = [P]_{\mathcal{R}}[\sigma_2]$, as a consequence of $\sigma_1 \upharpoonright A = \sigma_2 \upharpoonright A$. Therefore, if for any $a \in \bigcap\{\mathcal{FN}(P')|P' \in [P]_{\mathcal{R}}\}$, $\sigma(a) = a$ holds, then the above discussions show $[P]_{\mathcal{R}}[\sigma] = [P]_{\mathcal{R}}[id_{\mathcal{N}}] = [P]_{\mathcal{R}}$. Regarding the third equation, it holds since $\mathcal{FN}([P]_{\mathcal{R}}[\sigma]) = \bigcap\{\sigma(\mathcal{FN}(P'))|P' \in [P]_{\mathcal{R}}\} = \sigma(\mathcal{FN}([P]_{\mathcal{R}}))$, hence done. $\square$

Next we turn to homomorphisms. In Definition 2.6, a homomorphism only considers operations $\{[\sigma]\}$, not the free name function (so it is just a group action morphism between $S_{\mathcal{N}}$-sets). The following shows that we can somehow recover the information a posteriori.

**2.9. Proposition.** *Given a homomorphism $\mathcal{F}$, suppose $Q$ is in its image. Then we have:* $\mathcal{FN}(Q) = \bigcap_{Q=\mathcal{F}(P')} \mathcal{FN}(P')$.

PROOF: Suppose $Q = \mathcal{F}(P)$. If $a \in \mathcal{FN}(Q)\backslash\mathcal{FN}(P)$ then $\mathcal{FN}(Q[\binom{af}{fa}]) \neq \mathcal{FN}(Q)$ ($f$ fresh) by Definition 2.1 (here $\binom{af}{fa}$ is understood as its *extension*, i.e. a permutation over $\mathcal{N}$ which includes $\binom{af}{fa}$ and is identity other than $\{a, f\}$), but $Q[\binom{af}{fa}] = \mathcal{F}(P[\binom{af}{fa}]) = \mathcal{F}(P) = Q$, contradiction. But if $a \in \mathcal{FN}(P)\backslash\mathcal{FN}(Q)$ then $\mathcal{F}(P[\binom{af}{fa}]) = Q[\binom{af}{fa}] = Q$ ($f$ fresh) with $a \notin P[\binom{af}{fa}]$ hence done. $\square$

Note how the above result is consistent with the definition of free names for the quotient construction in 2.8 (ii). This assures a natural map from $A$ to $A/\sim$ to be a homomorphism, and, conversely, any homomorphic image of $A$ to be isomorphic to a certain quotient of $A$, making, as a whole, a coherent algebraic theory.

For isomorphisms, we can have a stronger statement.

**2.10. Corollary.** *If $\mathcal{F}$ is an isomorphism, we have $\mathcal{FN}(P) = \mathcal{FN}(\mathcal{F}(P))$.*

PROOF: Immediate from Proposition 2.9. $\square$

By the corollary, we know isomorphisms determine not only how group action operates on processes but also free names they own (later we show they further determine another essential internal structure of rooted processes, called symmetries). So in most imaginable purposes treating rooted process structures modulo isomorphisms is enough, and it is technically convenient that these properties are automatically ensured by establishing only group action isomorphisms.

We also mention one characterisation of a homomorphism, suggestive to its alternative presentation in Section 3. It roughly says that in which way you may look at the source process, a homomorphism will map it in a coherent way.

**2.11. Proposition.** *A compatible relation $\mathcal{R}$ is a homomorphism if and only if $P\mathcal{R}Q$ and $P[\sigma]\mathcal{R}Q'$ implies $Q' = Q[\sigma]$.*

PROOF: Take $\sigma = id_{\mathcal{N}}$ for "if" direction, while "only if" part comes from existence of inverse of $\sigma$. $\square$

We now move to the study of deeper mathematical structure of rooted processes. For the purpose, several group theoretic notions are essential, which we briefly summarise in the following.

**2.12. Definition.** Below let $G$ be a group and $X$ be a set, and consider a group action of $G$ on $X$. We write $gx$ for the action of $g$ on $x$.

(i) (morphism) Given two $G$-sets $X$ and $Y$, a *morphism* from $X$ to $Y$ is a function $F : X \to Y$ such that $F(gx) = g(Fx)$ for any $g \in G$ and $x \in X$. A morphism is an *isomorphism* if it is bijective.

(ii) (orbits) A maximal subset $Y$ of $X$ such that, for any $y_1, y_2 \in Y$, we have $y_2 = gy_1$ for some $g$, is called an *orbit* of $Y$. Orbits partition $X$ and thus induce an equivalence relation.

(iii) (transitive $G$-set) A $G$-set $X$ is *transitive* if for any $x_1, x_2 \in X$, we can write $x_2 = gx_1$. So, in (ii), each orbit is a transitive $G$-set, and $X$ as a whole is a disjoint union of these transitive $G$-sets.

(iv) (conjugate) Given a subgroup $G'$ of $G$, $G'' = gG'g^{-1}$ ($= \{gg'g^{-1}|g' \in G'\}$) is another subgroup of $G$. Then we say $G'$ and $G''$ are *conjugate*. Note conjugate subgroups are isomorphic.

(v) (isotropy) Let $G_x$ be $\{g \mid g \in G \text{ s.t. } gx = x\}$. Then $G_x$ forms a subgroup for each $x \in X$, called *isotropy subgroup* of $x$. Note if $y = gx$ we have $G_y = gG_xg^{-1}$, i.e. $G_x$ and $G_{gx}$ are always conjugate.

For us the following result regarding isotropy is essential.

**2.13. Proposition.** *Two $G$-sets $X$ and $Y$ are isomorphic if and only if the following holds: there is a bijective correspondence between their orbits and, moreover, in each pair of orbits $\langle X_i, Y_j \rangle$ under this correspondence, we have $G_x = gG_yg^{-1}$ for some $x \in X_i, y \in Y_j$ and $g \in G$.*

PROOF: Suppose $X'$ and $Y'$ are transitive $G$-sets, and for some $x' \in X'$ and $y' \in Y'$, we have $G_x = g \cdot G_y \cdot g^1$. It is standard that if $y'' = gy' \in Y'$ then $G_{y''} = g \cdot G_y \cdot g^1 = G_x$, so that, for any $g$, we have $G_{gx'} = G_{gy''}$ by Definition 2.12 (iii). Now construct a function $F$ s.t. $F(gx') = g(Fx')$ and $F(x') = y''$ for any $g$. This is well-defined, because: if $g_1x' = g_2x'$ then $g_1x' = (g_2g_1^{-1}g_1)x'$ so that $g_2g_1^{-1} \in G_{g_1x'} = G_{g_1y''}$, therefore

$$F(g_1x') = g_1y'' = (g_2g_1^{-1}g_1)(y'') = g_2y''.$$

So $F$ defines a map, and indeed a morphism. But if $F(g_1x') = F(g_2x')$ then $g_2g_1^{-1} \in G_{g_1y''} = G_{g_1x'}$ so that $g_1x' = (g_2g_1^{-1}g_1)(x') = g_2x'$, so that $F$ is bijective hence an isomorphism. Returning to Proposition above, since each orbit is transitive, the bijective correspondence in the statement of the above proposition induces isomorphisms between respective orbits, which together form an isomorphism as a whole, hence done. $\square$

**2.14. Notations.**

(i) In a rooted process structure, we write $P \overset{N}{\sim} Q$ if $P$ and $Q$ are in the same orbit, i.e. if $P = Q[\sigma]$ for some $\sigma \in S_N$. So the equivalence classes from $\overset{N}{\sim}$ are orbits in $\mathcal{P}$ under $S_N$.

(ii) In a rooted process structure, the isotropy group of $P$ under $S_N$ is written $S_N(P)$. Note, as noted above, if $\rho \in S_N(P)$, $S_N(P[\rho])$ is given by $\rho \cdot S_N(P) \cdot \rho^{-1}$, which is isomorphic to $S_N(P)$.

Now we introduce the key notion for our study of rooted process structures.

**2.15. Definition.** (symmetries) A *symmetry of* $P$ is a permutation of $\mathcal{FN}(P)$ which, seen as an element of $S_{\mathcal{N}}$ by extension, is in $S_{\mathcal{N}\langle P\rangle}$. The set of symmetries of $P$ form a group denoted by $sym(P)$.

Symmetry arises inevitably in processes:

**2.16. Examples.**

(1) In CCS, a permutation $\binom{ab}{ba}$ is a symmetry of a process "$a.0|b.0$," seen modulo strong bisimilarity.

(2) Similarly, "$a(x).(\bar{b}x|\bar{c}x)$" in $\pi$-calculus modulo structural equality has a symmetry $\binom{abc}{acb}$. As seen, symmetry in processes typically occurs when an agent contains a subterm of the form $P|(P\sigma)$ modulo commutative monoid law, cf. Berry and Boudol [1]. In contrast, $\lambda$-terms (viewed as processes, cf. Examples 2.3) only own trivial symmetry; the non-commutative nature of applicative structure is well known.

(3) Not being mentioned explicitly as such, the significance of symmetry in reasoning about processes *was* indeed perceived in the literature. See e.g. Section 4 of [11] where it is used to reduce the size of a bisimulation.

One useful fact about isotropy and symmetry follows.

**2.17. Proposition.** *Given any isotropy $\rho \in S_{\mathcal{N}\langle P\rangle}$, its restriction (of the domain) to $\mathcal{FN}(P)$ gives a permutation of $\mathcal{FN}(P)$, which is indeed a symmetry of $P$.*

PROOF: But if $\rho$ is not a bijection over $\mathcal{FN}(P)$, then $\rho(\mathcal{FN}(P)) \neq \mathcal{FN}(P)$, contradiction. Then use Proposition 2.4 (ii). □

Symmetries give essential insights about our algebraic constructions we already presented.

**2.18. Proposition.**

(i) Let $\mathcal{R}$ be a compatible relation. By Proposition 2.8, $\mathcal{R}$ is a rooted process structure. Now suppose $\langle P, Q\rangle \in \mathcal{R}$. Then $sym(\langle P, Q\rangle) = \{\sigma \upharpoonright \mathcal{FN}(\langle P, Q\rangle) \mid \sigma(P) = P \wedge \sigma(Q) = Q)\}$.

(ii) Let $\sim$ be a congruence and let $\mathcal{P}/\sim$ be the corresponding quotient, seen as rooted processes as in Proposition 2.8. Then the symmetries of processes are given by: $sym([P]_\sim) \overset{\text{def}}{=} \{\sigma \upharpoonright \mathcal{FN}([P]_\sim) \mid \sigma(P) \sim P\}$.

(iii) *Let $\mathcal{F}$ be a homomorphism. Then $Q = \mathcal{F}(P)$ and $\rho \in sym(P)$ implies $\rho \upharpoonright \mathcal{FN}(Q) \in sym(Q)$. If, moreover, $\mathcal{F}$ is an isomorphism, we have $sym(P) = sym(Q)$.*

PROOF: By Proposition 2.17, we only check that specified permutations are isotropies. In (i), given such $\sigma$, we have $\langle P, Q\rangle[\sigma] = \langle P[\sigma], Q[\sigma]\rangle = \langle P, Q\rangle$. For (ii), if $P[\sigma] \sim P$, then $[P]_\sim$ and $[P]_\sim[\sigma] \overset{\text{def}}{=} [P[\sigma]]_\sim$ define the same set, hence done. For (iii), note we already know $\mathcal{FN}(Q) \subset \mathcal{FN}(P)$ by Proposition 2.9. But if $\rho \in sym(P)$ we have $Q[\rho] = \mathcal{F}(P[\rho]) = \mathcal{F}(P) = Q$ (here $\rho$ is taken as its extension), therefore, by Proposition 2.17, it includes the symmetry of $Q$. Finally if $\mathcal{F}$ is an isomorphism, Proposition 2.10 tells us $\mathcal{FN}(P) = \mathcal{FN}(Q)$, hence $sym(P) \supset sym(Q)$. By taking $\mathcal{F}^{-1}$ we know $sym(P) \subset sym(Q)$. □

Note:

(i) In (i), a symmetry of $\langle P, Q \rangle$ should come from one symmetry of $P$ and another of $Q$ whose values should coincide at names $\mathcal{FN}(P) \cap \mathcal{FN}(Q)$. In this case, therefore, symmetries decrease in general. case.

(ii) In contrast, in (ii) above, notice that we only require $P$ and $P[\sigma]$ is equal up to the congruence. So even if no symmetry except identity exists originally, new symmetry would arise after quotienting. Thus *quotient construction may increase symmetries of processes.*[1]

(iii) In (iii), we know homomorphisms generally increase symmetries (in accordance with its close connection to quotient constructions) In addition, we now know that isomorphisms completely characterise symmetries in addition to group actions and free names, cf. 2.5.

Having seen how symmetries arise in rooted processes, we ask the following question: can symmetries completely replace isotropies, the power of the latter is already known by Proposition 2.13? The free name function works.

**2.19. Lemma.** (representation of isotropy) $S_{\mathcal{N}\langle P\rangle} = S_{\mathcal{N}\langle Q\rangle}$ *if and only if* $sym(P) = sym(Q)$.

PROOF: From Proposition 2.17, "if" direction is immediate. For "only if" direction, if we know that $S_{\mathcal{N}\langle P\rangle} = S_{\mathcal{N}\langle Q\rangle}$ implies $\mathcal{FN}(P) = \mathcal{FN}(Q)$, again by Proposition 2.17, we are done. But suppose not, i.e. for some $a$ we have e.g. $a \in \mathcal{FN}(P) \backslash \mathcal{FN}(Q)$. Take $f$ fresh, then $\binom{a\,f}{f\,a}$ is in $S_{\mathcal{N}\langle Q\rangle}$ but not in $S_{\mathcal{N}\langle P\rangle}$ by Definition 2.1 (iii)-3, which is a contradiction, hence done. $\square$

The main message of the Lemma is that, in rooted process structure, *symmetries characterise everything* (up to isomorphism). Thus, as the main result of the present section, we arrive at:

**2.20. Proposition.** (representation of a rooted process structure by symmetries) *Given $A_{\mathcal{P}}$, let $I = \mathcal{P}/ \overset{N}{\sim}$, the set of orbits in $\mathcal{P}$. Then a symmetry presentation of $A_{\mathcal{P}}$, denoted by $\alpha$, $\beta$, etc. is an $I$-indexed family of symmetries, say $\{sym(P_i)\}_{i \in I}$, such that we have $P_i \in i$ for all $i \in I$. Then $\alpha$ and $\beta$, possibly from two different rooted process structures, are* isomorphic *when there is a bijection $F$ between them such that:*

$$F(\alpha_i) = \sigma \cdot \alpha_i \cdot \sigma^{-1}$$

*where $\alpha_i$ denotes $i$'th member of $\alpha$. Then $\leftrightarrow$ is an equivalence relation. Moreover:*

(i) *If $\alpha$ and $\beta$ come from the same rooted process structure, then always $\alpha \leftrightarrow \beta$.*

(ii) *By (i), write $A \leftrightarrow A'$ when a pair of symmetry presentations of $A$ and $A'$ are isomorphic. Then we have $A \leftrightarrow A'$ if and only if $A \simeq A'$.*

---

[1] Since the quotient may in general "cut off" unrelated names (typically in process theories those which are semantically insignificant), the sheer number of symmetries may decrease; however the original symmetries are all inherited within the reduced set of names.

PROOF: Since $P \overset{N}{\sim} Q$ implies $S_{\mathcal{N}(P)}$ and $S_{\mathcal{N}(Q)}$ are conjugate, and, by Lemma 2.19, this implies the conjugacy of $sym(P)$ and $sym(Q)$ again, (i) follows. For (ii), "only if" direction follows from Proposition 2.13 and Lemma 2.19. For "if" direction, suppose $A_P \simeq A'_{P'}$, i.e. there is an isomorphism $\mathcal{F} : \mathcal{P} \to \mathcal{P}'$. Clearly each orbit in $\mathcal{P}$ is one-one mapped to an orbit in $\mathcal{P}'$, and, by Proposition 2.18 (iii), this map preserves symmetries, hence done. $\square$

For our later purpose, it is convenient to formulate the ambient universes of algebra of rooted processes as categorical structures. When dealing with relations, we also would like to preserve essential relational operations, which let us map not only relations themselves but also relational reasoning to another domain.

**2.21. Definition.** A *complete boolean allegory* (cf. [3]) is a category in which, for each pair of objects $A$ and $B$, we have:

(i) $hom(A, B)$ forms a complete boolean algebra, with operations $\bigcup, \cap, (\cdot)^c$, the first two of which are compatible with categorical composition $\circ$, i.e. $(\bigcup_i R_i) \circ S = \bigcup_i (R_i \circ S)$ and $S \circ (\bigcup_i R_i) = \bigcup_i (S \circ R_i)$, similarly for $\cap$.

(ii) There is an operation $(\cdot)^{-1}$ which sends each element of $hom(A, B)$ to $hom(B, A)$ bijectively, for which we have:

$$(R_1 \circ R_2)^{-1} = R_2^{-1} \circ R_1^{-1} \qquad (\bigcup_i R_i)^{-1} = \bigcup_i (R_i^{-1}) \qquad (R^c)^{-1} = (R^{-1})^c$$

*Functors* between two complete boolean allegories are those between the underlying categories which also preserve these operations. Two complete boolean allegories are *equivalent as allegories* when they are categorically equivalent involving functors in the above sense.

Note $(\bigcap_i R_i)^{-1} = \bigcap_i (R_i^{-1})$ is derivable from other equations.

**2.22. Proposition.** (RPS$_{rel}$ and RPS) *Fix some $\mathcal{N}$. Then the set of rooted process structures and name compatible relations between them form a complete boolean allegory. This allegory (as a category) contains the category of the same set and homomorphisms as its subcategory. We call these two structures, RPS$_{rel}$ and RPS, respectively. Note isomorphisms coincide in RPS$_{rel}$ and RPS.*

PROOF: For RPS$_{rel}$, we only take relational composition, inverse, and set union/intersection for the corresponding operations. $\square$

Some discussions on RPS and RPS$_{rel}$:

(1) Remember we take $\mathcal{N}$ as countable. Under this condition, usage of different sets of names only result in isomorphic allegories and categories. Thus it suffices to think of one pair of category and allegory.

(2) Clearly RPS is a full subcategory of all $S_{\mathcal{N}}$-sets and their morphisms, similarly for RPS$_{rel}$. This suggests a certain (but not much) generalisation of our results in these notes, though our present interest lies in these specific structures.

(3) In RPS, products are given by the set-theoretic products (seen as a rooted process structure as in Proposition 2.8), co-products by disjoint unions, the initial object by the empty set, and the final objects by structures with one element $P$ such that $\mathcal{FN}(P) = \emptyset$. Note each object is given by a co-product of (a possibly infinite number of) structures each having only a single orbit.

**2.23. Question.** (leading to the next section) We already know that rooted processes have concise representation by a family of symmetries, cf. Proposition 2.20. These symmetry presentations are even equipped with an idea of isomorphism, but that is all, so we have not much other than the objects part of the corresponding categories above. What notions correspond to the *arrow parts* of $RPS_{rel}$ and $RPS$? That is, how can we think of relations and maps between processes in the presentation by symmetries?

## 3. Process Structure and Equivalence Theorem

In the following we present a theory of processes which is essentially equivalent to what we have seen in the preceding section but is based on more concise and direct constructs, exposing basic ideas of processes. In our study in the subsequent expositions, it will be shown how this presentation allows generalisation of various elements of process theories not possible or at least not amenable in the traditional formulations. Though having a close relationship to our development in Section 2 and remembering the question posed in the last question, we rather start with presenting the theory without referring to the preceding development, to make basic ideas come out as succinctly as possible. Later we will come back to the question on how two theories are related.

The following is the primary object of study in this section.

**3.1. Definition.** (process structure) *A (non-rooted) process structure, or a p-structure,* is a triple $\langle \mathbf{P}, \mathcal{H}, \mathcal{S} \rangle$ where:

(i) $\mathbf{P}$ is the set of *(non-rooted) processes*, ranged over by $p, q, r, \dots$.

(ii) $\mathcal{H}$ assigns, to each $p$, a set called *handles* of $p$. A handle is denoted by $h, h', \dots$.

(iii) $\mathcal{S}$ assigns, to each $p$, a subgroup of $S_{\mathcal{H}(p)}$ (the group of permutations over $\mathcal{H}(p)$), called *symmetry on $p$*.

A *substructure* of a process structure is a subset of processes together with two assignments inherited from the original structure. The *arity* of a process, written $ar(p)$, is given by $|\mathcal{H}(p)|$, which we assume finite in the present paper. We sometimes write $p^{(n)}$ to denote the arity of $p$. Often the underlying set $\mathbf{P}$ denotes a process structure.

We can think of a process as a geometric object with multiple discrete points of connection and interaction:

FIGURE 1. A Process

While such an object seems not to have been studied as such so far, some examples inducing similar structures can nevertheless be found.

**3.2. Examples.**

(1) Girard's Proof Nets [4], as well as Lafont's Interaction Nets [9], can be considered as forming process structures, regarding their "free edges" as handles.

(2) An important example is *process graphs* in [14], a graphical presentation of concurrent combinators [7, 8] (discussed in 2.3) In fact process graphs are the prototypical example of process structures, and form certain free objects in the universe of nameless processes. Symmetry comes from the one inherent in graphs.

In many senses, a process structure can be regarded as a generalisation of a set: instead of a collection of elements, we have a collection of processes, and the essential point is that we deal with a process considering its internal structures, i.e. its handles and symmetries. In essence, this comes from our foremost concern, i.e. to build a basic stratum of general process theory where we naturally have to consider dynamics and (in)equality among processes each of which has multiple interface points and interact with the outside through them. As a stratum, the present theory has no notion of composition of processes nor does it include direct formulation of such ideas as dynamics of process interaction and behavioural semantics. However it *does* provide the basic elements which would be essentially used for these purposes, such as theory of maps, relations, and quotients, each of which, in spite of quite different content, go surprisingly parallel to those counterparts in theory of sets and elements. We start with one general idea of how we can relate two processes. Soon we will be content with its less general variant, but if we remember only one way to relate two *elements* (in a set) is by forming a tuple, the following should be instructive.

**3.3. Definition.** (web) A *web from $p_1$ to $p_2$* is a triple $\langle p_1,\ \delta,\ p_2 \rangle$, where $\delta$ is a relation from $\mathcal{H}(p_1)$ and $\mathcal{H}(p_2)$ such that, if $\delta : h \mapsto h_1$, $\delta : h \mapsto h_1$ and $\delta : h' \mapsto h_2$ then we always have $\delta : h \mapsto h_2$.

A web relates two processes by mapping handles collection by collection, where each collection forms a partial partition of handles of each party. Note composable webs are composed to make another web and the inverse of a web is again such. Generality of webs in relating processes allows us to treat many interesting phenomena in concurrent processes. We however leave theory of webs to the subsequent exposition and concentrate on its special case, called *correspondences*, where in mapping a collection of handles to another collection, we restrict them to singletons, since this suffices for our present purpose.

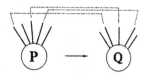

FIGURE 2. A Correspondence

**3.4. Definition.** (correspondence, cf. Figure 2)

(i) A *correspondence* is a web $\langle p_1,\ \delta,\ p_2 \rangle$ in which $\delta$ is injective but not necessarily total. By abuse of notation, we let $\delta, \delta, \ldots$ range over correspondences. $\mathrm{dom}(\delta)$ and $\mathrm{cod}(\delta)$ denote the source process and the target process, respectively. Then $\mathrm{im}(\delta)$ is the image of the component function in the handles of the target.

(ii) We say $\langle p, \delta, q \rangle$ and $\langle p, \delta', q \rangle$ are *essentially equivalent*, written $\delta \sim \delta'$, if, for some $\rho \in S(p)$ and $\rho' \in S(q)$, we have $\rho' \circ \pi_1 \circ \rho = \pi_2$. A correspondence is *surjective* (resp. *total*) if its component function is surjective (resp. total). $\mathrm{id}_p$ denotes an identity map on $\mathcal{H}(p)$.

(iii) Let $\langle p, \delta_1, q \rangle$ and $\langle q, \delta_2, r \rangle$ be correspondences. Then their *composition* is another correspondence $\langle p, \delta_2 \circ \delta_1, r \rangle$. The *inverse* of a correspondence $\langle p, \delta, q \rangle$ is $\langle q, \delta^{-1}, p \rangle$.

Correspondences are like *tuples*: then their collection forms what may be regarded as *relation* in the present setting.

## 3.5. Definition. (p-relation)

(i) A *p-relation* $\mathfrak{R}$ *from* $\mathbf{P}_1$ *to* $\mathbf{P}_2$ is a set of correspondences with domains in $\mathbf{P}_1$ and codomains in $\mathbf{P}_2$ such that if $\delta \in \mathfrak{R}$ and $\delta' \sim \delta$, then $\delta' \in \mathfrak{R}$ again. We write $p \mathfrak{R}_\delta q$ to mean $p$ is related to $q$ in $\mathfrak{R}$ by $\delta$.

(ii) Given $\mathfrak{R}_1$ from $\mathbf{P}$ to $\mathbf{Q}$ and $\mathfrak{R}_2$ from $\mathbf{Q}$ to $\mathbf{R}$, their *composition*, written $\mathfrak{R}_2 \circ \mathfrak{R}_1$, is a p-relation from $\mathbf{P}$ to $\mathbf{R}$ given by: $\{\delta_2 \circ \delta_1 \mid \delta_1 \in \mathfrak{R}_1 \wedge \delta_2 \in \mathfrak{R}_2 \wedge \mathrm{dom}(\delta_2) = \mathrm{cod}(\delta_1)\}$. The *inverse* of $\mathfrak{R}$, written $\mathfrak{R}^{-1}$, is the set of inverse correspondences of the original one, again forming a p-relation. Given an arbitrary family $\{\mathfrak{R}_i\}_{i \in I}$ of p-relations all from $\mathbf{P}$ to $\mathbf{Q}$, their set-theoretic intersection and union are again p-relations, just written $\bigcap\{\mathfrak{R}_i\}_{i \in I}$ and $\bigcup\{\mathfrak{R}_i\}_{i \in I}$. Similarly for two p-relations sharing domain and codomain, their difference is again a p-relation, denoted by $\mathfrak{R} \setminus \mathfrak{R}'$.

(iii) The *product* of $\mathbf{P}_1$ and $\mathbf{P}_2$, written $\mathbf{P}_1 \times \mathbf{P}_2$, is the set of all correspondences between $\mathbf{P}_1$ and $\mathbf{P}_2$. The *identity p-relation* on $\mathbf{P}$ is the set of all symmetries (as correspondences) on processes of $\mathbf{P}$, written $\mathbf{ID}_{\mathbf{P}}$. A p-relation $\mathfrak{R}$ on $\mathbf{P}$ is *reflexive* if $\mathbf{ID}_{\mathbf{P}} \subset \mathfrak{R}$, *transitive* if $\mathfrak{R} \circ \mathfrak{R} \subset \mathfrak{R}$, and *symmetric* if $\mathfrak{R}^{-1} = \mathfrak{R}$. If the three hold together, $\mathfrak{R}$ is an *equivalence p-relation*.

**3.6. Discussions.** (abstract correspondence) A basic building block of a p-relation is a correspondence modulo $\sim$ rather than a correspondence itself. Call such a correspondence an *abstract correspondence*: formally a p-relation is an abstract correspondence if it is non-empty and whenever $\delta$ and $\delta'$ are its elements we have $\delta \sim \delta'$.

However there is a subtle point in treating abstract correspondences: composition of two abstract correspondences may *not* form another (single) abstract correspondence. To see this, given $p[h]$, $q[i_1, i_2]$, and $r[j]$ (here $[h]$ etc. shows handles a process owns) with $S(q) = \{\binom{i_1 i_2}{i_2 i_1}\}$, as well as symmetries from identity permutations. Now if we compose $\{\langle p, \{h \mapsto i_1\}, q \rangle, \langle p, \{h \mapsto i_2\}, q \rangle\}$ and $\{\langle q, \{i_1 \mapsto j\}, r \rangle, \langle q, \{i_2 \mapsto j\}, r \rangle\}$, both being abstract correspondences, then we get: $\{\langle p, \{h \mapsto i\}, q \rangle, \langle p, \emptyset, q \rangle\}$, which is the union of *two* abstract correspondences. This shows that composition of p-relations needs to be understood with care.

The point we just noted is especially pertinent when we formulate function-like p-relations, as follows.

**3.7. Definition.** (p-map) A correspondence $\langle p, \delta, q \rangle$ is *symmetry preserving* when, if $\rho \in S(p)$, for some $\rho' \in S(q)$, we have $\delta \circ \rho = \rho' \circ \delta$. Then a *p-map* is a p-relation $\mathfrak{R}$ such that: (1) $\mathfrak{R}$ contains, for each process in the source, a set of correspondences any two of which are equated by $\sim$, and (2) $\delta \in \mathfrak{R}$ implies $\delta$ is surjective and symmetric preserving. A p-map whose inverse is also a p-map is called an *isomorphism*. By the *image* of a p-map $\mathfrak{R}$, we mean a sub process structure of $\mathrm{cod}(\mathfrak{R})$ given by $\{q \mid \exists p.\ p\mathfrak{R}_\delta q\}$.

Note a p-map consists of a collection of abstract correspondences one for each process in the domain, in the sense of 3.6. Note also we define isomorphisms as stronger than bijective homomorphisms. By imposing conditions as given above, p-maps indeed behave like functions between sets. For example, symmetry preservation has the following important consequence:

**3.8. Proposition.** *Given two p-maps composable as p-relations, their composition is again a p-map.*

PROOF: Let $\mathfrak{R}_1$ and $\mathfrak{R}_2$ be p-maps composable as p-relations. Then immediately $\mathfrak{R}_2 \circ \mathfrak{R}_1$ is a p-relation, its correspondences are all surjective, and it is everywhere defined in its source. Moreover if $\delta_2 \circ \delta_1$ is a composed correspondence and if $\rho_1$ is a symmetry of $\mathrm{dom}(\delta_1)$, then $\delta_2 \circ \delta_1 \circ \rho_1 = \delta_2 \circ \rho_2 \circ \delta_1 = \rho_3 \circ \delta_2 \circ \delta_1$ where $\rho_2 \in S(\mathrm{cod}(\delta_1)) = S(\mathrm{dom}(\delta_2))$ and $\rho_3 \in S(\mathrm{cod}(\delta_2))$, hence it is symmetry preserving. The rest is the uniqueness of the value modulo $\sim$. Suppose $\delta_2' \circ \delta_1'$ as well as $\delta_2 \circ \delta_1$ is in $\mathfrak{R}_2 \circ \mathfrak{R}_1$, whose domain coincides. But this means $\delta_1 \sim \delta_1'$ hence $\delta_2 \sim \delta_2'$, so we can write $\delta_1' = \rho_2 \circ \delta_1 \circ \rho_1$ and $\delta_2' = \pi_3 \circ \delta_1 \circ \pi_2$ where $\rho_{1,2}$ and $\pi_{1,2}$ are symmetries of respective processes. But using symmetry preservation, for an appropriate symmetry $\pi_3'$:

$$\delta_2' \circ \delta_1' \overset{\mathrm{def}}{=} \pi_3 \circ \delta_2 \circ \pi_2 \circ \rho_2 \circ \delta_1 \circ \rho_1$$
$$= \pi_3 \circ \pi_3' \circ \delta_2 \circ \delta_1 \circ \rho_1 \quad \sim \delta_2 \circ \delta_1$$

hence done. $\square$

Next we show how isomorphisms deserve their name, a consequence of surjectivity of correspondences in p-maps.

**3.9. Proposition.** (isomorphisms)

(i) *Let $\mathfrak{R}$ be an isomorphism. Then $\mathfrak{R}$ is bijective on processes. If $\delta \in \mathfrak{R}$, then $\delta$ is also bijective.*

(ii) *Let let $\mathfrak{R}$ be an isomorphism and $\langle p,\ \delta,\ q \rangle \in \mathfrak{R}$. Then $S(p)$ and $S(q)$ are isomorphic in the way:*

(3.1) $$S(q) = \delta \cdot S(p) \cdot \delta^{-1}.$$

(iii) **P** *and* **Q** *are isomorphic if and only if there is a bijective correspondence between processes which induce, for each pair $\langle p,\ q \rangle$, a bijection on handles $\delta$ such that the equation (3.1) holds.*

PROOF: (i) is immediate from the function-like characters of p-maps and surjectivity of correspondences in isomorphisms. (ii) follows from that, by (i) above, $\delta$ is a bijection and that symmetry preservation should be both-way in isomorphisms. Finally "only if" of (iii) is immediate, while, if there is a bijection $\delta$ between $\mathcal{H}(p)$ and $\mathcal{H}(q)$ as specified, then we can write, for any $\rho \in S(p)$, $\rho = \delta^{-1} \circ \rho' \circ \delta$, that is, $\delta \circ \rho = \rho' \circ \delta$ for some $\rho' \in S(q)$, that is, $\delta$ is symmetric preserving. Similarly any bijection of the form $\rho_2 \circ \delta \circ \rho_1$ where $\rho_1 \in S(p)$ and $\rho_2 \in S(q)$ is symmetry preserving. Collect all these bijections for each process, and the result is the required isomorphism. ☐

By (i) and (ii), isomorphisms preserve all essential information in process structures. Note, without the condition on surjectivity, (i) (hence (ii)) does not hold. At the same time, one may notice there is some interests in studying non-surjective p-maps since, e.g. Proposition 3.8 does not depend on surjectivity. At any rate, surjectivity does result in a simpler theory, see how its combination with symmetry preservation results in a coherent notion of natural p-map later.

Relations can be treated as sets, and thus relational reasoning includes set operations, which is useful. Just like that, a p-relation is another process structure.

**3.10. Proposition.** (relation as a process structure) *Given a p-relation $\mathfrak{R}$, take it as a set of processes and define:*

(i) $\mathcal{H}(\langle p,\ \delta,\ q \rangle) \overset{\text{def}}{=} (\mathcal{H}(p) \backslash \mathrm{im}(\delta^{-1})) \cup \delta \cup (\mathcal{H}(q) \backslash \mathrm{im}(\delta))$.

(ii) $S(\langle p,\ \delta,\ q \rangle) \overset{\text{def}}{=} \{\langle \rho_1,\ \rho_2 \rangle \mid \rho_2^{-1} \circ \delta \circ \rho_1 = \delta\}$

*then $\mathfrak{R}$ defines a process structure.*

PROOF: The only point to check is whether $S(\langle p,\ \delta,\ q \rangle)$ really defines a symmetry, i.e. whether it forms a subgroup of $S_{\mathcal{H}(\langle p,\ \delta,\ q \rangle)}$. Now how a tuple $\langle \rho_1,\ \rho_2 \rangle$ given as (ii) operate on $\mathcal{H}(\langle p,\ \delta,\ q \rangle)$ given as (i)? At $\langle h_1,\ h_2 \rangle \in \delta$, we take $\langle \rho_1(h_1),\ \rho_2(h_2) \rangle$. By (ii) we have $\delta(\rho_1(h_1)) = \rho_2(\delta(h_1))$ so $\langle \rho_1(h_1),\ \rho_2(h_2) \rangle \in \delta$, and the map is obviously injective, so it gives a permutation over $\delta$. This also tells us that an orbit of $\rho_1$ containing $h \in \mathcal{H}(p) \backslash \mathrm{im}(\delta^{-1})$ can never intersect with $\mathrm{im}(\delta^{-1})$, similarly for $\rho_2$. So just take $\rho_1$ and $\rho_2$ itself for these cases, then the operation as a whole becomes a permutation over $\mathcal{H}(\langle p,\ \delta,\ q \rangle)$. Since the unit and the inverse can easily be defined, we conclude that the symmetry is well-defined. ☐

How can we know that this definition, which is surely consistent, really "works"? The following shows one place where it does function well.

**3.11. Proposition.** (universality of product) *Given $\mathbf{P}_1$ and $\mathbf{P}_2$, define two p-maps $\Pi_1 : \mathbf{P}_1 \times \mathbf{P}_2 \rightarrow \mathbf{P}_1$ and $\Pi_2 : \mathbf{P}_1 \times \mathbf{P}_2 \rightarrow \mathbf{P}_2$ such that:*

(i) *if $\langle \langle p_1,\ \delta,\ p_2 \rangle,\ \pi,\ p_1 \rangle \in \Pi_1$, we have $\pi : h \mapsto h$ for $h \in \mathcal{H}(p_1) \backslash \mathrm{im}(\delta^{-1})$ and $\pi : (h_1 \mapsto h_2) \mapsto h_1$ for $(h_1 \mapsto h_2) \in \delta$, else undefined.*

(ii) *Similarly for $\Pi_2$.*

*Then whenever we have two p-maps $\mathfrak{R}_1 : \mathbf{P}' \rightarrow \mathbf{P}_1$ and $\mathfrak{R}_2 : \mathbf{P}' \rightarrow \mathbf{P}_2$ for some $\mathbf{P}'$, then there is a unique p-map $\Psi$ such that $\mathfrak{R}_1 = \Pi_1 \circ \Psi$ and $\mathfrak{R}_2 = \Pi_2 \circ \Psi$.*

PROOF: That $\Pi_1$ and $\Pi_2$ are p-maps are easy (note by the definition of $S(\langle p,\ \delta,\ q \rangle)$ in Proposition 3.10 both are obviously symmetry preserving). We leave the construction of $\Gamma$ to the reader (hint: in the case $\langle p',\ \delta_1,\ p_1 \rangle \in \mathfrak{R}_1$ and $\langle p',\ \delta_2,\ q_1 \rangle \in \mathfrak{R}_2$, say $\langle p_1,\ \delta,\ p_2 \rangle$ is *consistent* with $\delta_1$ and $\delta_2$ when

$$\delta : h_1 \mapsto h_2 \quad \Leftrightarrow \quad \exists h' \in \mathcal{H}(p').\ (\delta_1 : h' \mapsto h \wedge \delta_2 : h' \mapsto h_2).$$

Construct a correspondence from $p'$ to the above correspondence (as a process) as a component of $\Gamma$. Show that if another map is composed with $\Pi_1$ and $\Pi_2$, the required property cannot hold). ☐

There are other consistency conditions which the construction of Proposition 3.10 satisfies, which we do not discuss. Now we move to the quotient construction. We need the following notions: Given an equivalence $\Re$, the set of $\Re$-*effective handles*, written $\mathcal{H}(p)|\Re$, is a set of elements of $\mathcal{H}(p)$ which are in $\text{im}(\delta)$ for any $\delta \in \Re$ with $\text{cod}(\delta) = p$. Note:

**3.12. Fact.** *If $\Re$ is an equivalence, then $p\Re_\delta q$ implies $\sharp(\mathcal{H}(p)|\Re) = \sharp(\mathcal{H}(q)|\Re)$ where $\sharp(A)$ denotes the cardinality of $A$.*

This is because, if not, any partial injection from a smaller one to a larger one cannot cover the latter. The quotient construction follows.

**3.13. Definition.** (quotient)

    (i) Given an equivalence p-relation $\Re$ on $\mathbf{P}$, the *equivalence class* of a process $p$ with respect to $\Re$ is defined as:

$$[p]_\Re \overset{\text{def}}{=} \{Q \mid \exists \delta.\ \langle p,\ \delta,\ q \rangle \in \Re\}.$$

    (ii) A *quotient* of $\mathbf{P}$ with respect to $\Re$ is given by the following data:
- The set $\{[p]_\Re \mid p \in \mathbf{P}\}$.
- The function $\mathcal{H}$ which assigns, to each $[p]_\Re$, $\mathcal{H}(p)|\Re$.
- The function $\mathcal{S}$ which assigns, to each $[p]_\Re$, a set of permutations $\mathcal{S}([p]_\Re)$ over $\mathcal{H}([p]_\Re)$, such that:

$$s \in \mathcal{S}([p]_\Re) \quad \Leftrightarrow \quad \exists \delta.\ \langle p,\ \delta,\ p \rangle \in \Re$$

    i.e. we take restriction of reflexive correspondences on $\mathcal{H}(p)|\Re$.

Instead of taking a specific $p$ in the concerned equivalence class, one can use more elaborate construction which is more deterministic and hence which would be more satisfactory. Here we are content with the intuitive and tractable treatment in the above, since the following shows that not much is lost:

**3.14. Proposition.** *The above quotient defines a process structure. Moreover if we have two quotients of $\mathbf{P}$ with respect to $\Re$, then they are isomorphic.*

PROOF: We first show that $\mathcal{S}([p]_\Re)$ forms a group. We note that any $\langle p,\ \delta,\ p \rangle \in \Re$ should includes permutation of $\mathcal{H}(p)|\Re$ (since $\delta^{-1} \in \Re$ this should be the case). Then $id_p \in \Re$ since $\Re$ is reflexive, so the unit exists, the inverse always exists since $\Re$ is symmetric, and finally if two permutations are in $\mathcal{S}([p]_\Re)$, then their composition is also in it by transitivity of $\Re$. Hence it forms a group.

Suppose there are two quotients from $\Re$. Then construct a p-map so that, for each $[p]_\Re$, there are correspondences such that: if the first quotient takes $\mathcal{H}(q_1)|\Re$ for $\mathcal{H}([p]_\Re)$ and the second $\mathcal{H}(q_2)|\Re$ for the same, then $\langle [p]_\Re,\ \delta,\ [p]_\Re \rangle$ if and only if $q_1 \Re_\delta q_2$ with $\text{im}(\delta) = \mathcal{H}(q_2)|\Re$. We leave it to the reader to check such a map is really symmetry preserving. $\square$

Now we show that how p-maps relates to this quotient construction.

### 3.15. Proposition.

(i) *Given an equivalence $\mathfrak{R}$ over $P$, a natural map $\eta_{\mathfrak{R}}$ is the set of correspondences from $P$ to $P/\mathfrak{R}$ such that, for $q \in [p]_{\mathfrak{R}}$, we have a correspondence $\langle q, \delta, [p]_{\mathfrak{R}}\rangle$ if and only if $q\mathfrak{R}_{\delta}p$ with $im(\delta) = \mathcal{H}(p)|\mathfrak{R}$, assuming $\mathcal{H}(p)|\mathfrak{R}$ is used for $\mathcal{H}([p]_{\mathfrak{R}})$. Then $\eta_{\mathfrak{R}}$ is a p-map surjective on processes.*

(ii) *Suppose a p-map $\mathfrak{R} : P \to Q$ covers all processes in $Q$. Define a set of correspondences $\sim'$ over $P$ by setting $p \sim'_{\delta} p'$ if and only if, for some $q$, $\pi_1$ and $\pi_2$, we have:*

$$p\mathfrak{R}_{\pi_1}q \;\wedge\; p'\mathfrak{R}_{\pi_2}q \;\wedge\; \delta = \pi_2^{-1}\circ\pi_1 \;.$$

*Then $\sim = \sim' \cup \mathrm{ID_P}$ is an equivalence p-relation. Moreover, there is an isomorphism $\mathfrak{R}'$ from $P_{\sim}$ to $Q$ such that $\mathfrak{R} = \mathfrak{R}' \circ \eta_{\sim}$.*

PROOF:

(i) We only have to show $\eta_{\mathfrak{R}}$ indeed defines a p-map, since surjectivity (on processes) is obvious from the definition. First, that $\eta_{\mathfrak{R}}$ really gives a p-relation is not so difficult: since $\mathfrak{R}$ itself is a p-relation, whenever $\langle q, \delta, p\rangle \in \mathfrak{R}$ with $im(\delta) = \mathcal{H}(p)|\mathfrak{R}$ and $\rho_q$ and $\rho_p$ are some symmetries, we always have $\langle q, \rho_q \circ \delta \circ \rho_p, p\rangle\mathfrak{R}$ and $im(\rho_q \circ \delta \circ \rho_p) = \mathcal{H}(p)|\mathfrak{R}$ again. The essence lies in uniqueness, since originally diverse correspondences can be found in $\mathfrak{R}$. This becomes possible due to the definition of symmetry for $[p]_{\mathfrak{R}}$. Suppose $\langle q, \delta, p\rangle\mathfrak{R}$ and $\langle q, \delta', p\rangle\mathfrak{R}$ with both having images in $\mathcal{H}(p)|\mathfrak{R}$. Then we can write

$$\delta' = (\delta \circ \delta^{-1}) \circ \delta'$$

But, by definition, $\delta \circ \delta^{-1} \in \mathcal{S}([p]_{\mathfrak{R}})$, hence done.

(ii) That $\sim'$ (hence $\sim$) is a p-relation and that $\sim$ is an equivalence are both easy. To show that there is an isomorphism $\mathfrak{R}'$, we should show three things: (1) there is a bijection at the level of processes, (2) it induces bijection at the level of handles, and (3) it gives the isomorphism of symmetries as specified in Proposition 3.9. Constructing a map from $P/\sim$ to $Q$ in the way so that $[p]_{\sim}$ is mapped to $q$ by $\delta$ iff $p\mathfrak{R}_{\delta}q$ (remember $[p]_{\sim}$ is essentially $\mathcal{H}(p)|\mathfrak{R}$), (1) and (2) are not difficult. The essential point is (3). By symmetry preservation, we already know that, if $p\mathfrak{R}_{\pi}q$, the symmetries in processes of $[p]_{\sim}$ can be already found in $q$. On the other hand, let us assume $s \in \mathcal{S}(q)$. If $p\mathfrak{R}_{\pi}q$, then $p\mathfrak{R}_{p\circ s}q$, hence $p \sim_{\pi^{-1}\circ s\circ\pi} p$. In this way all symmetries are reflected conjugately in $\sim$. Thus (3) is shown and we are done. $\square$

Note that the above shows how both p-map and quotient drop some information (by cutting off handles and adding symmetries) and, thus, raise the abstraction level.

Having been through the basic constructions for process structures, it is time to clarify how the theory in this section corresponds to the one in Section 2. Let us first go back to Proposition 2.20, where we know a symmetry presentation of a rooted process structure maintains all essential information of the original structure. But we already know such a presentation is nothing but a process structure itself!

### 3.16. Proposition. *Suppose $\alpha$ is a symmetry presentation of some rooted process structure, i.e. a family $\{sym(P_i)\}_{i\in I}$ where $I$ being the equivalence classes by $\overset{N}{\sim}$ and $P_i \in i$ for each $i$. Then this defines a process structure with the following data:*

(i) *Processes are given by the indices $\{i\}$.*

(ii) Handles are given by $\mathcal{H}(i) = \mathcal{FN}(P_i)$.

(iii) Symmetry is given by $\mathcal{S}(i) = sym(P_i)$.

*Moreover we have $\alpha \leftrightarrow \beta$ if and only if $\alpha \simeq \beta$.*

PROOF: That $\alpha$ is a process structure is immediate. For isomorphisms, clearly if there is an isomorphism in the sense of process structure, then they are isomorphic as symmetry presentations. Conversely, Proposition 3.9 (iii) shows that isomorphism between symmetry presentations is enough for generating an isomorphism as a p-map, hence done. □

Thus, given any rooted process structure, if we take any one of its symmetry presentations, it is already a corresponding process structure. Moreover, from isomorphic *rooted* process structures, we always get isomorphic *non-rooted* process structures, by Proposition 2.20 and above.

As expected, there is also a way which does the converse. This needs some construction, but it also enjoys a virtue that, for any process structure, we can always get a canonical rooted version. We fix some $\mathcal{N}$ as always.

**3.17. Proposition.** *Given a process structure $P$, we form an algebra by the following data:*

(i) *The set of all injections from $\mathcal{H}(p)$ to $\mathcal{N}$ for each $p \in P$, each written $\langle \Psi,\ p \rangle$ etc. and collectively as $\{\langle \Psi,\ p \rangle\}$.*

(ii) *Operations $[\sigma]$ defined as: $\langle \Psi,\ p \rangle[\rho] \overset{\text{def}}{=} \langle \rho \circ \Psi,\ p \rangle$ (well defined since $\rho \circ \Psi$ is again an injection from $\mathcal{H}(p)$ to $\mathcal{N}$), and a function $\mathcal{FN}(\cdot)$ defined as: $\mathcal{FN}(\langle \Psi,\ p \rangle) \overset{\text{def}}{=} \text{im}(\Psi)$.*

(iii) *Relation $\approx$ over $\{\langle \Psi,\ p \rangle\}$ defined as:*

$$\langle \Psi,\ p \rangle \approx \langle \Psi',\ p \rangle \quad \Leftrightarrow \quad \Psi' = \Psi \circ s \ \text{ for some } s \in \mathcal{S}(p).$$

*Then $\approx$ is a congruence over $\{\langle \Psi,\ p \rangle\}$, and $\{\langle \Psi,\ p \rangle\}/\approx$ defines a rooted process structure. Moreover, writing $[\![P]\!]$ for the resulting rooted process structure, we have, for any $P$ and $Q$, $P \simeq Q$ if and only if $[\![P]\!] \simeq [\![Q]\!]$.*

PROOF: If $\langle \Psi,\ p \rangle \approx \langle \Psi',\ p \rangle$, i.e. $\Psi' = \Psi \circ s$ for some $s \in \mathcal{S}(p)$, then

$$\langle \Psi,\ p \rangle[\rho] = \langle \rho \circ \Psi,\ p \rangle \approx \langle \rho \circ \Psi \circ s,\ p \rangle = \langle \Psi',\ p \rangle[\rho]$$

and

$$\mathcal{FN}(\langle \Psi \circ s,\ p \rangle) = \text{im}(\Psi \circ s) = \text{im}(\Psi) = \mathcal{FN}(\langle \Psi,\ p \rangle)$$

So $[\sigma]$ and $\mathcal{FN}(\cdot)$ are well-defined over $\{\langle \Psi,\ p \rangle\}/\approx$. Moving to equations of Definition 2.1, associativity of $[\sigma]$ holds easily, while if $\rho$ does not change names in $\text{im}(\Psi)$, then $\sigma \circ \Psi = \Psi$, hence the second equation holds. Finally $\mathcal{FN}(\langle \Psi,\ p \rangle[\sigma]) = \text{im}(\sigma \circ \Psi) = \sigma \mathcal{FN}(\langle \Psi,\ p \rangle)$, hence the third equation holds, so that we know it forms a rooted process structure. For isomorphisms, check that, for any $p \in P$, the set of all rooted processes of the form $[\langle \Psi,\ p \rangle]_\approx$ is an orbit and, for any process in this orbit, say $P$, $sym(P)$ and $\mathcal{S}(p)$ are conjugately related by some bijection between $\mathcal{FN}(P)$ and $\mathcal{H}(p)$. Using these data, construct an isomorphism in one domain from the one in another domain in each turn, whose exact construction we leave to the reader. □

Let us assume a function $\langle\!\langle \cdot \rangle\!\rangle$ which, to each rooted process structure, gives one of its symmetry presentations definitely. Whatever the choice we may take for $\langle\!\langle \cdot \rangle\!\rangle$, $[\![ \cdot ]\!]$ and $\langle\!\langle \cdot \rangle\!\rangle$ are inverse to each other, in the following sense:

### 3.18. Proposition.

(i) *For any rooted process structure $A$, we have*  $[\![ \langle\!\langle A \rangle\!\rangle ]\!] \simeq A$.

(ii) *For any process structure $\mathbf{P}$, we have*  $\langle\!\langle [\![ \mathbf{P} ]\!] \rangle\!\rangle \simeq \mathbf{P}$.

PROOF: We prove only (ii), since, by Propositions 3.16 and 3.17, we know (i) and (ii) are equivalent. Given process structures $\mathbf{P}$ and $\langle\!\langle [\![ \mathbf{P} ]\!] \rangle\!\rangle$, we construct a bijection between processes which induce a conjugate isomorphism for each pair, then use Proposition 3.9 (iii). But this is easy since, first, by $[\![ \cdot ]\!]$, each $p \in \mathbf{P}$ is mapped to a single orbit which includes $P = [\langle \Psi, p \rangle]_{\approx}$, for which $S(p)$ and $sym(P)$ are conjugate by $\Psi$, then by $\langle\!\langle \cdot \rangle\!\rangle$ this is mapped, essentially speaking, to $sym(P)$ itself, so that we already have the required map. This concludes the proof. $\square$

Since we have accumulated enough knowledge about how each object in one form can be mapped to the one in another without losing essential information, our next task is to show there are similar exact correspondence in their ambient universes. In rooted process structures, our choice was a natural one, $RPS_{rel}$ for relations and RPS for homomorphisms. For process structures, the only possibility would be to take p-relations and p-maps.

### 3.19. Proposition. *The set of process structures and p-relations among them forms a complete boolean allegory and includes, as its subcategory, the category of process structures and p-maps. The former is called $PS_{rel}$, while the latter is called PS.*

We devote the rest of the section to the outline of the proof of:

### 3.20. Theorem. $RPS_{rel}$ *and* $PS_{rel}$ *are equivalent as allegories, where involved functors induce categorical equivalence between RPS and PS.*

### 3.21. Definition. (Relational Mappings)

(i) Given $\mathcal{R} : A \to A'$, we define $\mathcal{R}^\circ$ as the minimum set of correspondences from $\langle\!\langle A \rangle\!\rangle$ to $\langle\!\langle A' \rangle\!\rangle$ satisfying:

$$\langle P, Q \rangle \in \mathcal{R} \quad \Rightarrow \quad \langle p, \pi \circ \rho^{-1}, q \rangle \in \mathcal{R}^\circ \text{ where } p \in sym(P[\rho]) \text{ and } q \in sym(Q[\pi]).$$

Above we are assuming that, from $P$'s orbit, $\langle\!\langle \cdot \rangle\!\rangle$ selects $sym(P[\rho])$ as a symmetry presentation.

(ii) Given $\Re : \mathbf{P}_1 \to \mathbf{P}_2$, we define $\Re^*$ as the minimum relation from $[\![ \mathbf{P}_1 ]\!]$ to $[\![ \mathbf{P}_2 ]\!]$ satisfying:

$$\langle p, \delta, q \rangle \in \Re \quad \Rightarrow \quad \langle [\langle \Psi_1, p \rangle]_{\approx}, [\langle \Psi_2, q \rangle]_{\approx} \rangle \in \Re^*$$

such that $\delta = {\Psi_2'}^{-1} \circ \Psi_1'$ with $\Psi_i' \approx \Psi_i$, $i = 1, 2$.

**3.22. Proposition.**

(i) *If $\mathcal{R}$ is a compatible relation, then $\mathcal{R}^\circ$ is a p-relation. In particular:*

    (1) $\emptyset^\circ = \emptyset$.

    (2) *If $\mathcal{R}$ is the compatible closure of a single tuple, then $\mathcal{R}^\circ$ is an abstract correspondence (cf. 3.6).*

    (3) $(\bigcup_i \mathcal{R}_i)^\circ = \bigcup_i (\mathcal{R}_i^\circ)$.

(ii) *If $\Re$ is a p-relation, then $\Re^*$ is a compatible relation. In particular:*

    (1) $\emptyset^* = \emptyset$.

    (2) *If $\Re$ is an abstract correspondence, then $\Re^*$ is the compatible closure of a single tuple.*

    (3) $(\bigcup_i \Re_i)^* = \bigcup_i (\Re_i^*)$.

(iii) *For a compatible relation $\mathcal{R}$, we have $\mathcal{F}_1 \circ \mathcal{R}^{\circ *} \circ \mathcal{F}_2 = \mathcal{R}$ where $\mathcal{F}_{1,2}$ are isomorphisms. Similarly for a p-relation $\Re$, we have $\Re_1 \circ \Re^{* \circ} \circ \Re_2 = \Re$ where $\Re_{1,2}$ are isomorphisms.*

PROOF: For (i), we should show that the resulting set of correspondences is closed under $\sim$. It is easy to know that, without loss of generality, we can set:

$$\delta = \langle sym(P[\rho]),\ \pi \circ \rho^{-1},\ sym(Q[\pi]) \rangle \in \mathcal{R}^\circ$$

which comes from $\langle P, Q \rangle \in [\![R]\!]$. Now if $\rho' \in sym(P[\rho])$, by compatibility and observing $\rho'^{-1} \in sym(P[\rho])$ too, we have $\langle P[\rho][\rho'^{-1}], Q[\rho][\rho'^{-1}] \rangle \in \mathcal{R}$ so that, finally, $\langle P[\rho], Q[\pi][pi^{-1}][\rho][\rho'] \rangle \in \mathcal{R}$ from which (by definition) we know $\langle p, \pi \circ \rho^{-1} \circ \rho', q \rangle \in \mathcal{R}^\circ$. Similarly for the case when we take a symmetry of $Q[\pi]$.

Next we should show that if $\mathcal{R} = \{\langle P[\rho], Q[\rho] \rangle\}$ for some $P$ and $Q$, then $\mathcal{R}^\circ$ is an abstract correspondence. From the above discussions, and due to the form of the mapping, we only have to consider the case for $\langle sym(P), \delta, sym(Q) \rangle$, which comes from $\langle P, Q \rangle \in \mathcal{R}$. But we can easily see that the correspondences from $sym(P)$ to $sym(Q)$ are all generated from tuples of the form $\langle P[\rho], Q[\sigma] \rangle$ for some $\pi \in sym(P)$ and $\rho \in sym(Q)$, and in these cases what we have is $\langle p, \pi^{-1} \circ \delta \circ \rho, q \rangle$, which is essentially equivalent to the original correspondence, hence done.

Finally that the union operation commutes with the map is easy from the definition.

For (ii), the only non-trivial reasoning is whether the resulting relation is compatible or not. Suppose, w.l.o.g., $\langle [\langle \Psi_1, p \rangle]_\approx, [\langle \Psi_2, q \rangle]_\approx \rangle \in \Re^*$, which comes from $\langle p, \delta, q \rangle$, so that we have $\delta = \Psi_2 \circ \Psi_1$. But then for any $\sigma$ we have $\delta = \Psi_2 \circ \rho^{-1} \circ \rho \circ \Psi_1$, so that we know $\langle [\langle \rho \circ \Psi_1, p \rangle]_\approx, [\langle \rho \circ \Psi_2, q \rangle]_\approx \rangle \in \Re^*$, as required.

Now the above reasoning and the proof of 3.18, as well as the construction of relational mappings themselves, show how we can compose mappings to form an isomorphism from $\mathcal{R}$ to $\mathcal{R}^{\circ *}$ and the one from $\Re$ to $\Re^{* \circ}$. We leave the concrete construction of the isomorphisms to the reader. $\square$

While this suffices for "allegorical" correspondences (take the isomorphisms in (iii) above as natural isomorphisms for the equivalence), we should also show the following:

**3.23. Proposition.**

(i) *If $\mathcal{R}$ is a homomorphism (of rooted process structures), then $\mathcal{R}^\circ$ is a p-map.*

(ii) *If $\Re$ is a p-map (of process structures), then $\Re^*$ is a homomorphism.*

PROOF: For (i), suppose $\mathcal{R}$ is a homomorphism. We should derive three conditions for p-maps, i.e. uniqueness, surjectivity, and symmetry preservation, from the property of $\mathcal{R}$. Now we can easily verify that uniqueness (up to $\sim$) is derived from Proposition 2.11 (which says that if one process in an orbit in the source is mapped to an orbit in the target, then whatever process in the former orbit is always mapped to the same orbit), and surjectivity of correspondences is a direct consequence of Proposition 2.9, and symmetry preservation also directly follows from Proposition 2.18, hence done. For (ii), what we should know is that how three properties we just established can yield the property of being a function, i.e. uniqueness and everywhere-definedness, since compatibility is not a question any longer. But everywhere-definedness just comes from surjectivity of p-maps (on processes), so that the uniqueness as functions is the only remaining concern. The essential fact is that we need *both* uniqueness as p-maps *and* symmetry preservation to ensure the property in the resulting relation, used one by one. Firstly, the uniqueness in the sense of p-maps lets us have a constraint in the resulting compatible relation so that, if $\Re$ is a p-map, and $P\Re^*Q$ and $P\Re^*Q'$ holds, then $Q' = Q[\rho]$ should hold for some $\rho \in sym(P)$. So we have uniqueness up to symmetries of $P$. Next, the symmetry-preservation property of a p-map lets us have, whenever $P\Re^*Q$ holds, for any $\rho \in sym(P)$, we have $\rho \upharpoonright \mathcal{FN}(Q) \in sym(Q)$. Therefore we know that "$Q$ may vary up to the symmetry of $P$" just means "$Q$ may vary up to the symmetry of $Q$," that is, if $P$ is decided $Q$ is decided too (i.e. $Q = Q'$ in the above). Note, in this way, we can observe two clearly separated elements in homomorphisms, even within the realm of rooted process structures. Thus $\Re^*$ is not only compatible but also everywhere-defined and single-valued, which, by definition, says that it is a homomorphism, hence done. $\square$

This establishes Theorem 3.20 and answers to the question we posed at the end of the preceding section.

### References

1. Berry, G. and Boudol, G., The Chemical Abstract Machine. *Theoretical Computer Science*, vol 96, pp. 217–248, 1992.
2. Cohn, P.M., *Universal Algebra*, D.Reidel, 1981.
3. Freyd, P.J. and Scedrov, A., *Categories and Allegories*, North-Holland, 1990.
4. Girard, J.-Y., Linear Logic, *Theoretical Computer Science*, Vol. 50, pp.1–102, 1987.
5. Honda, K. *Presenting Processes*. Under preparation.
6. Honda, K. and Yoshida, N., On Reduction-Based Process Semantics, *13th. FST/TCS*, LNCS 761, pp.371–387, Springer-Verlag, 1993.
7. Honda, K. and Yoshida, N., Combinatory Representation of Mobile Processes, *POPL'94*, pp.348–360, ACM press, 1994.
8. Honda, K. and Yoshida, N., Replication in Concurrent Combinators, *TACS'94*, LNCS 789, pp.786–805, Springer-Verlag, 1994.
9. Lafont, Y., Interaction Nets, *POPL'90*, pp. 95–108, ACM press, 1990.
10. Milner, R., *A Calculus of Communicating Systems*, LNCS 76, Springer-Verlag, 1980.
11. Milner, R., *Communication and Concurrency*, Prentice Hall, 1989.
12. Milner, R., Functions as Processes. *Mathematical Structure in Computer Science*, 2(2), pp.119–146, 1992.
13. Milner, R., Parrow, J.G. and Walker, D.J., A Calculus of Mobile Processes, *Information and Computation* 100(1), pp.1–77, 1992.
14. Yoshida, N., *Graph Notation for Concurrent Combinators*, in this volume.

# Simulating Guarded Programs in Linear Logic

Max I. Kanovich

Department of Computer and Mathematical Sciences
Graduate School of Information Sciences
Tohoku University
Sendai 980, Japan
and
Russian Humanities State University
Moscow, Russia
email: maxk@ito.ecei.tohoku.ac.jp

**Abstract.** *Petri Nets* are one of the most basic formal models for the representations and analysis of concurrent programming. Combining *finite automata* with *non-deterministic Petri net,* we introduce a new paradigm of *Non-Deterministic Petri Nets with States* in order to grasp the non-deterministic cases that can occur within concurrent processes. *Linear Logic* was introduced by Girard as a *resource-sensitive* refinement of classical logic. The *guarded commands* approach to *non-deterministic* and *parallel programming* was introduced by Dijkstra. Based on our (*Petri Nets* $\Leftrightarrow$ *Linear Logic*) correspondence, we prove that programs built up of *guarded commands* can be simulated directly within the framework of Horn Linear Logic.

## 1 Introduction and Summary

*Petri Nets* are one of the most fundamental formal models for the representations and analysis of concurrent programming [20]. With the help of those models, we can control the dynamic *resource-sensitive* behaviour of interacting parallel processes. Involving *non-determinacy* in consideration, we generalize these concepts [18] so that *non-deterministic Petri nets* can include:

- *Ordinary transitions.*
  The *firing* of such a transition yields **deterministic** rearrangement of the current *marking* (the distribution of resources) on the given Petri net.
- *Non-deterministic transitions.*
  The *firing* of a non-deterministic transition involves development of our concurrent processes in one of several *alternative directions.*

In this paper, by combining *finite automata* with *non-deterministic Petri net,* we introduce a new paradigm of *Non-Deterministic Petri Nets with States* that allows us to distinguish the following two aspects in the behaviour of the system under consideration:

- Information.

– Resources.

In particular, *configurations* of the system are represented by pairs

*(state,  distribution-of-resources)*

where the first component is controlled in the finite automaton manner, while we can control the use of resources in the second component.

The difference between *ordinary* and *non-deterministic* transitions can be perceived as follows:
When we *fire* a certain transition, we make thereby **our own choice** from the given set of possible transitions.

– If we choose an *ordinary* transition to be fired, we know the result of this firing to be **deterministic.**
– On the contrary, having chosen a *non-deterministic* transition to be fired, we meet with the following **non-deterministic** situation.
  Actually we have put a certain question to the *Net Oracle* to be being pondered. And we do not know *in advance* what action from the set of the alternative ones will be allowed to be performed in a given case. Only after having got his response, we will know what we may do.

The *reachability* problem for Petri nets consists of deciding, given a Petri net $\mathcal{P}$ and markings $\overline{m}_0$ and $\overline{m}$, whether $\overline{m}$ can be reached from $\overline{m}_0$. It is well known, that many other problems of Concurrency Theory can be reduced to the *reachability* problem for Petri nets.

Linear Logic was introduced by Girard [9] as a *resource-sensitive* refinement of classical logic. Based on our **direct** simulation of Petri nets in terms of Linear Logic developed in [15, 16], we prove the equivalence of the following problems:

– The reachability problem for *Non-Deterministic Petri Nets with States.*
– The derivability problem for *Horn-like* sequents in Linear Logic.

Moreover, we establish the exact correlation between *derivations* in Horn Linear Logic and *computations* performed by Non-Deterministic Petri Nets with States.

The *guarded commands* approach to *non-deterministic* and *parallel programming* was introduced by Dijkstra [5, 6].

*Guarded commands* are introduced as building blocks for *sequential, alternative* and *repetitive constructs.*

A *program semantics* is defined by means of *predicate transformer wp:*
"We use the notation $wp(S, R)$, where $S$ denotes a *statement* and $R$ some *condition* on the state of the system, to denote the **weakest precondition** for the *initial* state $\kappa$ of the system such that activation of $S$ is **guaranteed** to lead to a properly terminating activity leaving the system in a *final* state $\zeta$ satisfying the *postcondition R* (even in the case of possibly *non-deterministic* behavior)." [5]

In this paper we introduce a natural semantics **behind** the Dijkstra's semantics.

The main idea is to conceive of each of possibly *non-deterministic* statements $S$ as a *multi-valued* mapping from *initial* program states $\kappa$ to *final* states $\zeta$:

$$S : \kappa \to S[\kappa]$$

where $S[\kappa]$ is the set of all *final* states $\zeta$ to which $S$ can lead from $\kappa$.

Now the Dijkstra's *predicate transformer* $wp$ can be defined in the natural way:

$$wp(S, R)(\kappa) \equiv \text{``}S[\kappa] \text{ is } \textbf{non-empty} \text{ and } \forall\zeta\Big(\big((\zeta \in S[\kappa]) \to R(\zeta)\big)\Big)\text{''}$$

The justification for our proposal is that all formal definitions declared in [5, 6] can be converted to theorems.

Indeed, Dijkstra's language is extremely powerful.

In particular, any **propositional** logical system can be readily simulated within its framework.

As to the opposite directions, we will show that, contrary to what might be expected, we can prove that all programs built up of *guarded commands* are simulated directly within the framework of Horn Linear Logic.

Namely, based on our (*Petri Nets* ⇔ *Linear Logic*) correspondence, for any *construct $S$ built up of Dijkstra's guarded commands,* we assemble a multiset of Horn-like formulas $\widetilde{T_S}$ such that, whatever *initial* state $\kappa$ we take,

$$S[\kappa] = \{\zeta_1, \zeta_2, \ldots, \zeta_k\}$$

**if and only if** the a Horn-like sequent of the form [1]

$$\widetilde{q_1}, \widetilde{\kappa}, !\widetilde{T_S} \vdash \big(\widetilde{q_0} \oplus (\widetilde{q_2} \otimes (\widetilde{\zeta_1} \oplus \widetilde{\zeta_2} \oplus \cdots \oplus \widetilde{\zeta_k}))\big)$$

is derivable in Linear Logic.

Moreover, together with the foregoing simulation of the non-deterministic results of the execution of $S$, actually we simulate completely the non-deterministic behaviour of $S$:

*there is an* **exact** *correspondence between cut-free derivations of the above sequent and terminated computations of $S$ leading from $\kappa$ to $\{\zeta_1, \zeta_2, .., \zeta_k\}$.*

## 2  Guarded Commands Programming

The *guarded commands* approach to *non-deterministic* and *parallel programming* was introduced by Dijkstra [5, 6].

---

[1] Where states $\kappa, \zeta_1, \ldots, \zeta_k$ are represented by certain tensor products of propositional literals $\widetilde{\kappa}, \widetilde{\zeta_1}, \ldots, \widetilde{\zeta_k}$, respectively.

## 2.1 Guarded Commands Language

Within the Dijkstra's approach, *elementary statements* can be specified in rather a free manner. This means that we are only interested in those peculiarities of this approach that provide us with a model of the system behaviour modulo the expressiveness of *elementary statements*. The effect is that we can confine ourselves to the following simplified version of the Dijkstra's approach.

We will assume that we deal with *registers,* more precisely, *counters,*

$$register_1, \ register_2, \ \ldots, \ register_m, \ \ldots$$

that can contain *non-negative integers.*

The current value of an $m$-th register will be represented by the variable $x_m$.

Any *state* $\kappa$ of the system will be described by a linearly ordered sequence of non-negative integers contained in the registers:

$$\kappa = (k_1, \ k_2, \ \ldots, \ k_m, \ \ldots)$$

As for *elementary statements,* we will consider only counter *assignment* statements of one of the following three forms:

$$x_m := c$$
$$x_m := x_m + c$$
$$x_m := x_m - c$$

where $c$ is a non-negative integer constant.

*Guarded commands* are introduced as building blocks for *sequential, alternative* and *repetitive constructs.*

**Definition 1. A guarded command** is an expression of the following form

$$[] \ \langle guard \rangle \ \rightarrow \ \langle guarded \ statement \rangle$$

where

(a) $\langle guard \rangle$ is a Boolean expression of the form [2]

$$(x_i \leq x_j)$$

(b) $\langle guarded \ statement \rangle$ is defined by induction:
  $\langle guarded \ statement \rangle$ is to be
  (b1) either an *elementary statement,*
  (b2) or a *sequential construct,*
  (b3) or an *alternative construct,*
  (b4) or a *repetitive construct.*

---

[2] Any Boolean combinations of equalities and inequalities might be used.

**Definition 2.** A *sequential construct* is defined in the standard way:

$$
\begin{array}{c}
\textbf{begin} \\
S_1; \\
S_2; \\
\cdots \\
S_n; \\
\textbf{end}
\end{array}
$$

The semicolons in *sequential constructs* have the usual *naive* meaning:
  The *guarded statements* $S_i$ should be executed *successively* in the natural order.

**Definition 3.** An *alternative construct* is written in the following form:

$$
\begin{array}{ll}
\textbf{if} & \\
[] \ B_1 & \rightarrow \ S_1 \\
[] \ B_2 & \rightarrow \ S_2 \\
\cdots & \\
[] \ B_n & \rightarrow \ S_n \\
\textbf{fi} &
\end{array}
$$

According [5, 6], the *naive* semantics of our *alternative construct* is as follows:

(a) If in the current state each of the *guards* is **false,** the program will **abort.**
(b) Otherwise, an **arbitrary** *guarded statement* $S_i$ with the **true** *guard* $B_i$ is allowed to be selected for execution.

**Definition 4.** A *repetitive construct* is defined as follows:

$$
\begin{array}{ll}
\textbf{do} & \\
[] \ B_1 & \rightarrow \ S_1 \\
[] \ B_2 & \rightarrow \ S_2 \\
\cdots & \\
[] \ B_n & \rightarrow \ S_n \\
\textbf{od} &
\end{array}
$$

(a) Here a situation in which each of the *guards* is **false** means proper **termination.**
(b) Otherwise, a new choice of some *guarded statement* $S_i$ with the **true** *guard* $B_i$ should be made.
(c) After the selected *guarded statement* $S_i$ having been executed, we come back to the entry of our *repetitive construct* and **repeat** the foregoing procedure.

*Example 1.* The following *guarded* program $S_0$ illustrates that not only the computation but also the final state is not necessarily *deterministic* .

For given $x_1$ and $x_2$, the program $S_0$ determines a position $x_3$ of the maximum $\max\{x_1, x_2\}$ in the pair $(x_1, x_2)$:

$$S_0 = \begin{cases} \textbf{if} \\ \quad [] \, (x_1 \leq x_2) \;\rightarrow\; x_3 := 2 \\ \quad [] \, (x_2 \leq x_1) \;\rightarrow\; x_3 := 1 \\ \textbf{fi} \end{cases}$$

## 2.2  Formal Semantics

In [5, 6] a *program semantics* is defined by means of *predicate transformer wp*:

**Definition 5.** According to [5], "We use the notation $wp(S, R)$, where $S$ denotes a *statement* and $R$ some *condition* on the state of the system, to denote the **weakest precondition** for the *initial* state $\kappa$ of the system such that activation of $S$ is **guaranteed** to lead to a properly terminating activity leaving the system in a *final* state $\zeta$ satisfying the *postcondition* $R$ (even in the case of possibly *non-deterministic* behavior)."

To make this definition precise, Dijkstra associated a certain formal definition of $wp(S, R)$ with each of the basic *constructs*.

In this paper we introduce a natural semantics **behind** the Dijkstra's semantics and show that all formal definitions of Dijkstra can be converted to theorems.

The main idea is to conceive of each of possibly *non-deterministic* statements $S$ as a *multi-valued* mapping from *initial* program states $\kappa$ to *final* states $\zeta$:

$$S : \kappa \rightarrow S[\kappa].$$

Let $\kappa$

$$\kappa = (k_1, \; k_2, \; \ldots, \; k_m, \; \ldots)$$

be a state of our system.

The set of all *final* states $\zeta$ to which $S$ can lead from $\kappa$ is denoted by $S[\kappa]$ and defined as follows.

**Definition 6.** For any *assignment* statement $S$ of the form

$$x_m := x_m - c,$$

if $k_m \geq c$ then we define:
$$S[\kappa] = \{\zeta\}$$

where

$$\zeta = (k_1, \; k_2, \; \ldots, \; k_m - c, \; \ldots).$$

Otherwise, $S[\kappa]$ is declared to be **empty**.

The remaining cases of *elementary statements* are handled similarly.

**Definition 7.** For any *sequential construct* $S$ of the form

$$S = \begin{cases} \text{begin} \\ \quad\quad S_1; \\ \quad\quad S_2; \\ \text{end} \end{cases}$$

if $S_1[\kappa]$ is **non-empty** and for **every** state $\rho$ from $S_1[\kappa]$ the set $S_2[\rho]$ is also **non-empty**, then

$$S[\kappa] = \bigcup_{\rho \,\in\, S_1[\kappa]} S_2[\rho].$$

Otherwise, $S[\kappa]$ is declared to be **empty**.

The general case of *sequential constructs* where $n > 2$ is handled by induction.

**Definition 8.** For any *alternative construct* $S$ of the form

$$S = \begin{cases} \text{if} \\ \quad [] \ B_1 \ \rightarrow \ S_1 \\ \quad [] \ B_2 \ \rightarrow \ S_2 \\ \quad \cdots \\ \quad [] \ B_n \ \rightarrow \ S_n \\ \text{fi} \end{cases}$$

if at least one of *guards* $B_i$ is **true** and for **every** true $B_i$ the set $S_i[\kappa]$ is **non-empty**, then

$$S[\kappa] = \bigcup_{B_i \text{ is true}} S_i[\kappa].$$

Otherwise, $S[\kappa]$ is declared to be **empty**.

**Definition 9.** For any *repetitive construct* $S$ of the form

$$S = \begin{cases} \text{do} \\ \quad [] \ B_1 \ \rightarrow \ S_1 \\ \quad [] \ B_2 \ \rightarrow \ S_2 \\ \quad \cdots \\ \quad [] \ B_n \ \rightarrow \ S_n \\ \text{od} \end{cases}$$

$S[\kappa]$ is defined to be **non-empty** if and only if there exists a finite rooted tree built up of states of our system such that

(a) The root is defined to be $\kappa$.
(b) For each of terminal vertices $\zeta$ all *guards* $B_i$ are **false**.
   In addition, the set of all terminal vertices $\zeta$ forms exactly our set $S[\kappa]$.

(c) For each of non-terminal vertices $\rho$, at least one of *guards* $B_i$ is **true** and the set of all sons of this vertex $\rho$ coincides exactly with $S'[\rho]$ where $S'$ denotes the following *"one-step" instance* of $S$:

$$S' = \begin{cases} \textbf{if} \\ \quad [] \; B_1 \; \rightarrow \; S_1 \\ \quad [] \; B_2 \; \rightarrow \; S_2 \\ \quad \cdots \\ \quad [] \; B_n \; \rightarrow \; S_n \\ \textbf{fi} \end{cases}$$

*Example 2.* E.g., in Example 1 we have

$$S_0[(8,8,0)] = \{(8,8,2),\, (8,8,1)\}.$$

The *naive* Definition 5 is reformulated as follows:

**Definition 10.** Let $R$ be any *condition* on states of the system.
For a given statement $S$, we define the **weakest precondition** $wp(S, R)$ by the following:

$$wp(S, R)(\kappa) \equiv \text{"}S[\kappa] \text{ is } \textbf{non-empty} \text{ and } \forall \zeta \Big( (\zeta \in S[\kappa]) \rightarrow R(\zeta) \Big) \text{"}$$

We can justify our approach by the following theorem:

**Theorem 11.** *All properties of the Dijkstra's* **predicate transformer** *wp* **de-clared** *in [5, 6] can be* **proved** *within the framework of Definition 10.*

## 3 Branching Resource-Sensitive Horn Computations Performed by Finite-State Machines

We will use the concept of *Non-Deterministic Petri Nets with States (NPNS)* which is equivalent to *Non-Deterministic Petri Nets* introduced in [18].

An **NPNS** $\mathcal{P}$ can be defined as a product of a *finite automaton* and a *non-deterministic Petri net*.

**Definition 12.** A **Non-Deterministic Petri Net with States (NPNS)** $\mathcal{P}$ is defined by a tuple

$$\mathcal{P} = (\mathcal{Q},\, q_1,\, \mathcal{Q}_0,\, \mathcal{T})$$

where $\mathcal{Q}$ is a finite set of *states*,
$q_1$ is an *initial* state,
$\mathcal{Q}_0$ is a finite set of *final* states,
$\mathcal{T}$ is a finite set of *transitions*.

We suppose that we deal with a set of *places* $S$

$$S = \{s_1,\, s_2,\, \ldots,\, s_n\},$$

each place $s_i$ can contain *tokens* of the corresponding $i$-th sort.

**Definition 13.** A *configuration* is a pair:

$$(q, \bar{a})$$

where $q$ is the current *state*, and the non-negative[3] $n$-dimensional integer vector $\bar{a}$

$$\bar{a} = (a_1, \ a_2, \ldots, a_n)$$

represents the current distribution of tokens (the so-called *marking*) on our Petri net: for each place $s_i$, **exactly** $a_i$ tokens are available at this place $s_i$.

**Definition 14.** We will use transitions of two kinds:

(a) **ordinary** transitions $\tau$ of the form

$$\tau = \left( q, \bar{x} \rightarrow q', \bar{y} \right)$$

where non-negative $n$-dimensional integer vectors $\bar{x}$ and $\bar{y}$ represent *preconditions* and *postconditions* of $\tau$, resp.,[4] and

(b) **non-deterministic**, or **branching**, transitions $\tau$ of the form

$$\tau = \left( q \rightarrow (r_1 \vee r_2 \vee \cdots \vee r_n) \right)$$

Here $q, q', r_1, r_2, \ldots r_n$ are *states* from $\mathcal{Q}$.

**Definition 15.** A *computation* performed by a given NPNS $\mathcal{P}$ is a finite rooted tree built up of configurations such that each edge of the tree is labelled by a transition from $\mathcal{T}$:

(a) If a vertex $(q, \bar{a})$ has exactly one son $(q', \bar{b})$ then its outgoing edge

$$\left( (q, \bar{a}), (q', \bar{b}) \right)$$

should be labelled by an ordinary transition $\tau$ of the form

$$\tau = \left( q, \bar{x} \rightarrow q', \bar{y} \right)$$

such that the vector $(\bar{a} - \bar{x})$ is **non-negative** and

$$\bar{b} = (\bar{a} - \bar{x}) + \bar{y}$$

---

[3] An integer vector is said to be *non-negative* if all its components are *non-negative* integers.

[4] While *firing* this transition, $\bar{x}$ indicates the number of tokens that should be removed from, $\bar{y}$ indicates the number of tokens that should be added to the corresponding places.

(b) Let $(q, \bar{a})$ be a branching vertex with exactly $n$ sons. Then all these sons should be of the form

$$(r_1, \bar{a}), \ (r_2, \bar{a}), \ \ldots, \ (r_n, \bar{a})$$

(with just the same $\bar{a}$) and each of $n$ edges outgoing from $(q, \bar{a})$ should be labelled by one and the same branching transition $\tau$:

$$\tau = \left( q \rightarrow (r_1 \vee r_2 \vee \cdots \vee r_n) \right)$$

(c) Finally, any vertex of the form $(q, \bar{a})$ is *terminal* if and only if $q$ is a *final* state of $\mathcal{P}$.

**Definition 16.** For a given NPNS $\mathcal{P}$:

$$\mathcal{P} = (\mathcal{Q}, \ q_1, \ \mathcal{Q}_0, \ \mathcal{T}),$$

we will say that

$$\mathcal{P}(\bar{m}) = \bar{z}$$

if there exists a computation performed by NPNS $\mathcal{P}$ such that

(i) The *root* of it is of the form
$$(q_1, \bar{m})$$

where $q_1$ is the *initial* state of $\mathcal{P}$.

(ii) Each of *terminal* vertices of our computation is of the form

$$(q_0, \bar{z})$$

where $q_0$ is a *final* state of $\mathcal{P}$.

# 4 Horn-like Fragments of Linear Logic

Here we will use only *Horn-like* formulas of Linear Logic that are built up of **positive** *elementary propositions (literals)*:

$$p_1, \ p_2, \ \ldots, \ p_n, \ \ldots,$$

by the following connectives:

$$\{\otimes, \ \multimap, \ \oplus, \ !\}.$$

**Definition 17.** The tensor product of a *positive* number of positive literals is called **a simple product**. A single literal $p$ is also called **a simple product**.

Here (and henceforth) simple products will be denoted by $X, Y, Y_1, Y_2, \ldots, Y_m, U, V, W, Z$, etc.

**Definition 18.** Horn-like formulas are introduced by the following:

(a) A **Horn implication** is a formula of the form

$$\left( X \multimap Y \right).$$

(b) A ⊕-**Horn implication** is a formula of the form

$$\left( X \multimap \left( Y_1 \oplus Y_2 \oplus \cdots \oplus Y_m \right) \right).$$

**Definition 19.** Let a multiset $\Gamma$ consist of *Horn implications* and ⊕-*Horn implications*.
Then a sequent of the form[5]

$$W, !\Gamma \vdash Z$$

will be called a (!,⊕)-**Horn sequent.**
We will also consider (!,⊕)-Horn sequents of the following form:

$$W, !\Gamma \vdash (Z_1 \oplus Z_2 \oplus \cdots Z_k).$$

We can reveal **the intuitionistic nature** of the Horn fragments of Linear Logic:

**Lemma 20.** *Any* (!,⊕)-*Horn sequent is derivable in Linear Logic* **if and only if** *it is derivable in Intuitionistic Linear Logic (its rules are listed in Table 1).*

# 5   NPNS ⟺ HLL

It is well known that Linear Logic provides us with natural encodings of ordinary Petri net problems [3, 4, 8, 23]. As for *Non-Deterministic Petri Nets with States,* we demonstrate that the reachability problem for such Petri nets is **exactly** equivalent to the derivability problem for *Horn Linear Logic.*
We encode our Petri nets into Linear Logic as follows.

**Definition 21.** Each place $s_i$ from $S$ will be associated with literal $p_i$. Each state $q$ from $Q$ will be represented by a certain literal $\tilde{q}$.
Any pair of the form $(q, \bar{a})$ where

$$\bar{a} = (a_1, a_2, \ldots, a_n)$$

will be represented by the following simple tensor product [6]

$$\widetilde{(q, \bar{a})} = (\tilde{q} \otimes (p_1^{a_1} \otimes p_2^{a_2} \otimes \cdots \otimes p_n^{a_n})).$$

---

[5] Where $!\Gamma$ stands for the multiset resulting from putting the *modal storage* operator $!$ before each formula in $\Gamma$.

[6] Here, and henceforth, $G^0 = 1$, $G^k = \underbrace{(G \otimes G \otimes \cdots \otimes G)}_{k \text{ times}}$.

$$
\textbf{I} \quad \frac{}{A \vdash A} \qquad\qquad \textbf{P} \quad \frac{\Sigma_1, A, B, \Sigma_2 \vdash C}{\Sigma_1, B, A, \Sigma_2 \vdash C}
$$

$$
\textbf{L}\!\multimap \quad \frac{\Sigma_1 \vdash A \qquad B, \Sigma_2 \vdash C}{\Sigma_1, \left(A \multimap B\right), \Sigma_2 \vdash C} \qquad \textbf{R}\!\multimap \quad \frac{\Sigma, A \vdash B}{\Sigma \vdash \left(A \multimap B\right)}
$$

$$
\textbf{L}\!\otimes \quad \frac{\Sigma, A, B \vdash C}{\Sigma, (A \otimes B) \vdash C} \qquad \textbf{R}\!\otimes \quad \frac{\Sigma_1 \vdash A \qquad \Sigma_2 \vdash B}{\Sigma_1, \Sigma_2 \vdash (A \otimes B)}
$$

$$
\textbf{L}\!\oplus \quad \frac{\Sigma, A \vdash C \quad \Sigma, B \vdash C}{\Sigma, (A \oplus B) \vdash C} \qquad \textbf{R}\!\oplus \quad \frac{\Sigma \vdash A \qquad\qquad \Sigma \vdash B}{\Sigma \vdash (A \oplus B) \quad \Sigma \vdash (A \oplus B)}
$$

$$
\textbf{L!} \quad \frac{\Sigma, A \vdash C}{\Sigma, !A \vdash C} \qquad\qquad \textbf{R!} \quad \frac{!\Sigma \vdash C}{!\Sigma \vdash !C}
$$

$$
\textbf{W!} \quad \frac{\Sigma \vdash C}{\Sigma, !A \vdash C} \qquad\qquad \textbf{C!} \quad \frac{\Sigma, !A, !A \vdash C}{\Sigma, !A \vdash C}
$$

$$
\textbf{L1} \quad \frac{\Sigma \vdash C}{\Sigma, 1 \vdash C} \qquad\qquad \textbf{R1} \quad \frac{}{\vdash 1}
$$

**Table 1.** The Inference Rules of Intuitionistic Linear Logic.

**Definition 22.** (a) An ordinary transition

$$
\tau = \left(q, \overline{x} \rightarrow q', \overline{y}\right)
$$

is axiomatized by the Horn implication

$$
\tilde{\tau} = \left(\widetilde{(q, \overline{x})} \multimap \widetilde{(q', \overline{y})}\right).
$$

(b) A non-deterministic transition

$$
\tau = \left(q \rightarrow (r_1 \vee r_2 \vee \cdots \vee r_n)\right)
$$

is axiomatized by the $\oplus$-Horn implication

$$
\tilde{\tau} = \left(\tilde{q} \multimap \left(\tilde{r}_1 \oplus \tilde{r}_2 \oplus \cdots \oplus \tilde{r}_n\right)\right).
$$

**Theorem 23. (Completeness)** *For a given Non-Deterministic Petri Net with States $\mathcal{P}$:*

$$
\mathcal{P} = (Q, q_1, \{q_0\}, \mathcal{T}),
$$

*any* (!,⊕)-*Horn sequent of the form*

$$(\widetilde{q_1, \overline{m}}), \, !\widetilde{\mathcal{T}} \vdash (\widetilde{q_0, \overline{z}})$$

*is derivable in (Horn) Linear Logic* **if and only if**

$$\mathcal{P}(\overline{m}) = \overline{z}.$$

*Moreover, there is an* **exact** *correspondence between computations performed by* $\mathcal{P}$ *leading from the* initial *marking* $\overline{m}$ *to the target marking* $\overline{z}$ *and cut-free derivations of the* (!,⊕)-*Horn sequent under consideration.*

*Proof.* We can generalize a proof from [15, 16] where a slightly different version of *resource-sensitive* Horn computations is considered. □

# 6 Guarded Commands ⟹ HLL

The Dijkstra's language of *guarded commands* is extremely powerful.

In particular, the full Linear Logic, as well as any **propositional** logical system, can be readily simulated within its framework.

Contrary to what might be expected, we will show that all programs built up of *guarded commands* can be simulated directly within the framework of Horn Linear Logic.

Similarly to the previous sections, we use the following encoding of the *Guarded Commands* language:

**Definition 24.** Each register $register_i$ that we are dealing with will be associated with literal $p_i$.

Any *state* $\kappa$ of the system

$$\kappa = (k_1, \, k_2, \, \ldots, \, k_m, \, \ldots)$$

will be represented by the following simple tensor product

$$\widetilde{\kappa} = (p_1^{k_1} \otimes p_2^{k_2} \otimes \cdots \otimes p_m^{k_m} \otimes \cdots).$$

Taking into account the foregoing correspondence:

$$(Petri\ Nets \Leftrightarrow Linear\ Logic),$$

we prove the following:

**Theorem 25.** *For any* construct $S$ *built up of* guarded commands *which uses* $n$ registers, *we can construct an NPNS* $\mathcal{P}_S$

$$\mathcal{P}_S = (\mathcal{Q}, \, q_1, \, \{q_0, q_2\}, \, \mathcal{T}_S)$$

*such that, whatever state of the system* $\kappa$

$$\kappa = (k_1, \, k_2, \, \ldots, \, k_n)$$

*we take,*

"$S[\kappa]$ *is non-empty*"

**if and only if** *there exists a computation performed by* $\mathcal{P}_S$ *such that*

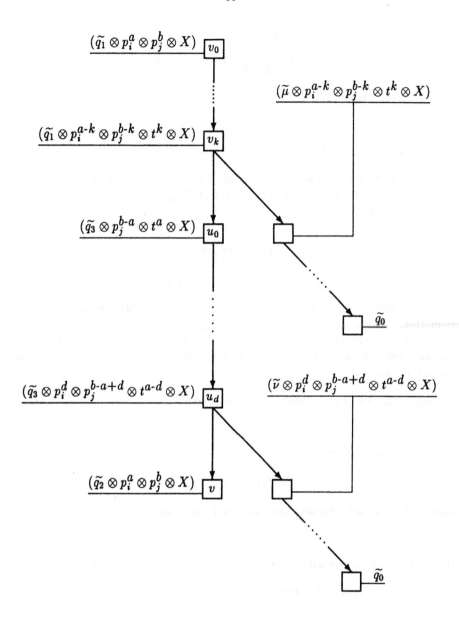

**Fig. 1.** Simulation of the *guard* $(x_i \le x_j)$.

(a) *The root of it is of the form*

$$(\tilde{q_1} \otimes (p_1^{k_1} \otimes p_2^{k_2} \otimes \cdots \otimes p_n^{k_n})).$$

(b) *For every terminal vertex of the form*

$$(\tilde{q_0} \otimes Y),$$

$Y$ *is equivalent to* **1**.

*Moreover, whatever computation performed by* $\mathcal{P}_S$ *satisfying the above conditions we take,* $S[\kappa]$ *coincides exactly with the set of all* $\zeta$:

$$\zeta = (z_1, \ z_2, \ \ldots, \ z_n),$$

*such that there is a terminal vertex of the form*

$$(\tilde{q_2} \otimes (p_1^{z_1} \otimes p_2^{z_2} \otimes \cdots \otimes p_n^{z_n})).$$

*Proof.* Following the *inductive* Definition 1, we will assemble the desired $\mathcal{P}_S$ by induction.

To begin with, we simulate *guards* by the following lemma that actually is the **key technical point** in our simulation of *guarded commands* by Linear Logic formulas:

**Lemma 25.i** *For a given guard B of the form*

$$(x_i \leq x_j),$$

*we can construct an NPNS* $\mathcal{P}_B$

$$\mathcal{P}_B = (\mathcal{Q}, q_1, \{q_0, q_2\}, \mathcal{T}_B)$$

*such that, whatever non-negative integers a and b we take,*

$$a \leq b$$

**if and only if** *there exists a computation performed by* $\mathcal{P}_B$ *such that*

(a) *The root of it is of the form*

$$(\tilde{q_1} \otimes p_i^a \otimes p_j^b \otimes X)$$

   *where X is a tensor product of literals* $p_k$ *except for* $p_i$ *and* $p_j$.

(b) *For every terminal vertex of the form*

$$(\tilde{q_0} \otimes Y),$$

$Y$ *is equivalent to* **1**.

*Moreover, whatever computation performed by* $\mathcal{P}_B$ *satisfying the above conditions we take,*

(i) *one of its* terminal *vertices*[7] *is of the form*

$$(\widetilde{q_2} \otimes p_i^a \otimes p_j^b \otimes X),$$

(ii) *and each of remaining its* terminal *vertices is of the form*

$$(\widetilde{q_0} \otimes \mathbf{1}).$$

*Proof.* As $\widetilde{T_B}$ we define the set consisting of the following transitions:

(i) $\left((\widetilde{q_1} \otimes p_i \otimes p_j) \multimap (\widetilde{q_1} \otimes t)\right)$
where $t$ is a temporary literal,

(ii) $\left(\widetilde{q_1} \multimap \left(\widetilde{q_3} \oplus \widetilde{\mu}\right)\right)$
where $\mu$ will be used to *kill* all literals except for $p_i$,

(iii) $\left((\widetilde{\mu} \otimes x) \multimap \widetilde{\mu}\right)$
where $x$ ranges over all literals $p_1, p_2, \ldots,$ and $t$ except for $p_i$.

(iv) $\left(\widetilde{\mu} \multimap \widetilde{q_0}\right),$

(v) $\left((\widetilde{q_3} \otimes t) \multimap (\widetilde{q_3} \otimes p_i \otimes p_j)\right),$

(vi) $\left(\widetilde{q_3} \multimap \left(\widetilde{q_2} \oplus \widetilde{\nu}\right)\right)$
where $\nu$ will be used to *kill* all literals except for $t$,

(vii) $\left((\widetilde{\nu} \otimes x) \multimap \widetilde{\nu}\right)$
where $x$ ranges over all literals $p_1, p_2, \ldots,$ (except for $t$).

(viii) and $\left(\widetilde{\nu} \multimap \widetilde{q_0}\right).$

Let us consider the case where

$$(a \leq b).$$

Starting from the initial configuration:

$$(\widetilde{q_1} \otimes p_i^a \otimes p_j^b \otimes X),$$

the desired computation is constructed in the following way (See Figure 1):

(i) First, we create a chain of $a$ edges and label each of these edges by one and the same ordinary transition

$$\left((\widetilde{q_1} \otimes p_i \otimes p_j) \multimap (\widetilde{q_1} \otimes t)\right)$$

to get the configuration

$$(\widetilde{q_1} \otimes p_i^{a-a} \otimes p_j^{b-a} \otimes t^a \otimes X).$$

---

[7] We will call it the *main terminal*.

(ii) Then, we create two outgoing edges and label these new edges by the branching transition

$$\left(\tilde{q}_1 \multimap \left(\tilde{q}_3 \oplus \tilde{\mu}\right)\right)$$

to produce the following son configurations:

$$(\tilde{q}_3 \otimes p_j^{b-a} \otimes t^a \otimes X)$$

and

$$(\tilde{\mu} \otimes p_j^{b-a} \otimes t^a \otimes X)$$

(iii) The next step is, with the help of *killing* transitions

$$\left((\tilde{\mu} \otimes x) \multimap \tilde{\mu}\right),$$

to get the following configuration on the $\mu$-line:

$$(\tilde{\mu} \otimes \mathbf{1}).$$

(iv) Our $\mu$-line is eventually ended at the configuration

$$(\tilde{q}_0 \otimes \mathbf{1})$$

by firing the transition

$$\left(\tilde{\mu} \multimap \tilde{q}_0\right).$$

(v) As for the *main* branch, by repeatedly applying

$$\left((\tilde{q}_3 \otimes t) \multimap (\tilde{q}_3 \otimes p_i \otimes p_j)\right),$$

we restore the initial marking:

$$(\tilde{q}_3 \otimes p_i^a \otimes p_j^b \otimes X).$$

(vi) In its turn, we create two outgoing edges and label these new edges by the branching transition

$$\left(\tilde{q}_3 \multimap \left(\tilde{q}_2 \oplus \tilde{\nu}\right)\right)$$

to get the desired configuration on the *main* branch:

$$(\tilde{q}_2 \otimes p_i^a \otimes p_j^b \otimes X)$$

and the starting configuration of a $\nu$-line:

$$(\tilde{\nu} \otimes p_i^a \otimes p_j^b \otimes X)$$

(vii) On the $\nu$-line, by repeatedly applying

$$\left((\tilde{\nu} \otimes x) \multimap \tilde{\nu}\right),$$

we kill all undesired literals getting the configuration

$$(\tilde{\nu} \otimes \mathbf{1}).$$

(viii) Then we eventually finish at the configuration

$$(\tilde{q}_0 \otimes \mathbf{1})$$

by firing the transition

$$\left(\tilde{\nu} \multimap \tilde{q}_0\right).$$

In the opposite direction, we prove that an arbitrary computation performed by $\mathcal{P}_B$ cannot be but of the form described above (See Figure 1), and, hence,

$$a \leq b.$$

For a given computation, let $k$ be the maximum length of non-branching segment, starting from the initial configuration:

$$(\tilde{q}_1 \otimes p_i^a \otimes p_j^b \otimes X).$$

It means that at $k$-th step we get the following configuration

$$(\tilde{q}_1 \otimes p_i^{a-k} \otimes p_j^{b-k} \otimes t^k \otimes X)$$

that should be the father of two sons:

$$(\tilde{q}_3 \otimes p_i^{a-k} \otimes p_j^{b-k} \otimes t^k \otimes X)$$

and

$$(\tilde{\mu} \otimes p_i^{a-k} \otimes p_j^{b-k} \otimes t^k \otimes X).$$

Let us examine the descendants of the latter son.

Taking into account the definability conditions, we can conclude that all its *terminal* descendants must be of the form

$$(\tilde{q}_0 \otimes p_i^{a-k}).$$

Recalling the hypotheses of the lemma, we have

$$a-k = 0,$$

and, hence,

$$b \geq k = a.$$

Now, let $d$ be the maximum length of non-branching segment, starting from the configuration:

$$(\tilde{q}_3 \otimes p_j^{b-k} \otimes t^k \otimes X).$$

It implies that we can get the following configuration

$$(\tilde{q}_3 \otimes p_i^d \otimes p_j^{b-k+d} \otimes t^{k-d} \otimes X),$$

the father of two sons:

$$(\tilde{q}_2 \otimes p_i^d \otimes p_j^{b-k+d} \otimes t^{k-d} \otimes X)$$

and

$$(\tilde{\nu} \otimes p_i^d \otimes p_j^{b\text{-}k+d} \otimes t^{k\text{-}d} \otimes X).$$

Reproducing arguments from the previous branching case, we can prove that

$$k\text{-}d = 0$$

and the *main* branch ends at the desired configuration

$$(\tilde{q}_2 \otimes p_i^a \otimes p_j^b \otimes X).$$

□

We can prove a symmetrical form of Lemma 25.i as well.

**Lemma 25.ii** *For a given guard $B$ of the form*

$$(x_i \le x_j),$$

*we can construct an NPNS $\mathcal{P}_B$*

$$\mathcal{P}_B = (\mathcal{Q}, q_1, \{q_0, q_2, q_5\}, \mathcal{T}_B)$$

*such that, whatever non-negative integers $a$ and $b$ we take, there exists a computation performed by $\mathcal{P}_B$ such that*

(a) *The root of it is of the form*

$$(\tilde{q}_1 \otimes p_i^a \otimes p_j^b \otimes X).$$

(b) *All terminal vertices except for one vertex are of the form*

$$(\tilde{q}_0 \otimes \mathbf{1}).$$

*Moreover, whatever computation performed by $\mathcal{P}_B$ satisfying the above conditions we take, one of its terminal vertices is of the form*

$$(\tilde{q}' \otimes p_i^a \otimes p_j^b \otimes X)$$

*where*

(A) *$q' = q_2$, if $a \le b$,*
(B) *$q' = q_5$, if $a > b$.*

*Proof.* Similarly to Lemma 25.i. □

As a corollary, we get the following **complete** simulation of any Boolean combination of *guards*.

**Lemma 25.iii** *Let*

$$B(x_1, x_2, \ldots, x_n)$$

*be a Boolean combination of* guards.
*Then we can construct an NPNS* $\mathcal{P}_B$

$$\mathcal{P}_B = (\mathcal{Q}, q_1, \{q_0, q_2, q_5\}, \mathcal{T}_B)$$

*such that, whatever state of the system* $\kappa$

$$\kappa = (k_1, k_2, \ldots, k_n)$$

*we take,*

(1) *There exists a computation performed by* $\mathcal{P}_B$ *such that*
  (1a) *The root of it is of the form*

$$(\tilde{q_1} \otimes (p_1^{k_1} \otimes p_2^{k_2} \otimes \cdots \otimes p_n^{k_n})).$$

  (1b) *For every terminal vertex of the form*

$$(\tilde{q_0} \otimes Y),$$

  $Y$ *is equivalent to* **1**.
(2) *Whatever computation performed by* $\mathcal{P}_B$ *satisfying the above conditions we take,*
  (2a) *One of its terminal vertices is of the form*

$$(\tilde{q'} \otimes (p_1^{k_1} \otimes p_2^{k_2} \otimes \cdots \otimes p_n^{k_n})).$$

  (2b) *For all its terminal vertices of the form*

$$(\tilde{q'} \otimes Y)$$

  *where* $q'$ *is equal either to* $q_2$ *or to* $q_5$, *the following holds:*

$$Y \equiv (p_1^{k_1} \otimes p_2^{k_2} \otimes \cdots \otimes p_n^{k_n})$$

  *and*
  (A) $q' = q_2$, *if* $B(k_1, k_2, .., k_n)$ *is* **true**,
  (B) $q' = q_5$, *if* $B(k_1, k_2, .., k_n)$ *is* **false**.

*Elementary statements are simulated as follows:*

**Lemma 25.iv** *For a given* assignment statement $S$, *we can construct an NPNS* $\mathcal{P}_S$

$$\mathcal{P}_S = (\mathcal{Q}, q_1, \{q_0, q_2\}, \mathcal{T}_S)$$

*such that, whatever state of the system* $\kappa$

$$\kappa = (k_1, k_2, \ldots, k_n)$$

*we take,*

$$\text{``}S[\kappa] \text{ is non-empty''}$$

**if and only if** *there exists a computation performed by* $\mathcal{P}_S$ *such that*

(a) *The root of it is of the form*

$$(\tilde{q_1} \otimes (p_1^{k_1} \otimes p_2^{k_2} \otimes \cdots \otimes p_n^{k_n})).$$

(b) *For every terminal vertex of the form*

$$(\tilde{q_0} \otimes Y),$$

$Y$ *is equivalent to* **1**.

*In addition, whatever computation performed by $\mathcal{P}_S$ satisfying the above conditions we take,*

(i) *one of its terminal vertices is of the form*

$$(\tilde{q_2} \otimes (p_1^{z_1} \otimes p_2^{z_2} \otimes \cdots \otimes p_n^{z_n}))$$

*where*

$$S[\kappa] = \{(z_1, \ z_2, \ldots, z_n)\},$$

(ii) *and each of remaining its terminal vertices is of the form*

$$(\tilde{q_0} \otimes \mathbf{1}).$$

*Proof.* The most complicated and non-trivial case where an *assignment statement $S$* is of the form

$$x_m := c,$$

is handled similarly to Lemma 25.i.
*Assignment statements $S$* of one of the following two forms

$$x_m := x_m + c$$
$$x_m := x_m - c$$

are readily simulated by transitions

$$\left(\tilde{q_1} \multimap (\tilde{q_2} \otimes p_m^c)\right),$$

$$\left((\tilde{q_1} \otimes p_m^c) \multimap \tilde{q_2}\right)$$

respectively. □

In order to simulate *sequential, alternative* and *repetitive constructs.* we can use just the same technique of Lemma 25.i as well.

Now, bringing together all the cases considered, we can complete Theorem 25. □

**Corollary 26.** *For any* construct $S$ *built up of* guarded commands *which uses* $n$ *registers, we can construct an NPNS* $\mathcal{P}_S$

$$\mathcal{P}_S = (\mathcal{Q},\, q_1,\, \{q_0, q_2\},\, \mathcal{T}_S)$$

*such that, whatever state of the system* $\kappa$

$$\kappa = (k_1,\ k_2,\ \ldots,\ k_n)$$

*we take,*

*"$S[\kappa]$ is non-empty"*

**if and only if** *a Horn-like sequent of the form*

$$\tilde{q_1}, \tilde{\kappa}, !\widetilde{\mathcal{T}_S} \vdash (\tilde{q_0} \oplus (\tilde{q_2} \otimes (\tilde{\zeta_1} \oplus \tilde{\zeta_2} \oplus \cdots \oplus \tilde{\zeta_k})))$$

*is derivable in Linear Logic.*
*Moreover, if a Horn-like sequent of the form*

$$\tilde{q_1}, \tilde{\kappa}, !\widetilde{\mathcal{T}_S} \vdash (\tilde{q_0} \oplus (\tilde{q_2} \otimes (\tilde{\zeta_1} \oplus \tilde{\zeta_2} \oplus \cdots \oplus \tilde{\zeta_k})))$$

*is derivable in Linear Logic then*

$$S[\kappa] = \{\zeta_1, \zeta_2, \ldots, \zeta_k\}$$

*and there is an* **exact** *correspondence between cut-free derivations of this sequent and terminated computations of* $S$ *leading from* $\kappa$ *to* $\{\zeta_1, \zeta_2, .., \zeta_k\}$.

*Proof.* It follows from Theorem 25. $\qquad\qquad\qquad\qquad\qquad\qquad\qquad\Box$

# 7   Concluding Remarks

Here we have focused on the study of a number of basic concepts related to different branches of Computer Science:

(a) *Non-Deterministic Petri Nets with States,*
(b) *Resource-Sensitive Horn Computations,*
(c) *Guarded Commands Programming,*

putting them into correlation with some *natural* fragments of Linear Logic within the well-known paradigm:

$$Derivations \Longleftrightarrow Computations.$$

We have demonstrated natural simulations of each system of basic concepts in terms of each of the others.

As a corollary, we can obtain a full computational characterization of the above concepts.
E.g., we can prove that:

- There exists a non-deterministic Petri net such that its reachability problem is undecidable.
- For ordinary Petri nets, their reachability problem has been proved to be decidable [25, 21].
- For non-deterministic Petri nets each of whose transitions is allowed to be fired **only once,** their reachability problem is $PSPACE$-complete.
- On the other hand, for non-deterministic Petri nets each of whose transitions must be fired **once and exactly once,** their reachability problem is $NP$-complete.
- For ordinary Petri nets each of whose transitions is allowed to be fired **only once,** their reachability problem is $NP$-complete.
- For ordinary Petri nets each of whose transitions must be fired **once and exactly once,** their reachability problem is also $NP$-complete.

Contrary to the case of *ordinary* Petri nets, the foregoing **complete correspondence** between all concepts under consideration has allowed us to establish the *highest* expressive power for *non-deterministic* Petri nets and the Horn fragment of Linear Logic:
All programs built up of Dijkstra's *guarded commands* can be simulated directly

- within the framework of *non-deterministic* Petri nets,
- and within the Horn framework of Linear Logic.

## Acknowledgements

I am very much obliged to P.Lincoln, J.Mitchell, V.Pratt, A.Scedrov, and N.Shankar for their inspiring introduction to the problems related to Linear Logic and fruitful discussions on it.

I owe special thanks to J.-Y.Girard, Y.Lafont, and L.Regnier for providing supportive and stimulating environment to discuss all these new concepts during my stay in Laboratoire de Mathématiques Discrètes.

I am greatly indebted to S.Artemov and his Seminar on Logical Methods in Computer Science at the Moscow State University for the opportunity of developing and clarifying my results.

I am also grateful to Takayasu Ito for insightful comments and suggestions related to the *guarded commands* approach that encouraged me to establish new connections between *Linear Logic* and *Non-Deterministic Programming.*

## References

1. S.Abramsky. Computational interpretation of linear logic. Imperial College Research Report DOC 90/20, 1990.
2. S.Abramsky, Computational Interpretations of Linear Logic, *Theoretical Computer Science*, v.111, 1992, p.3–57. (Special Issue on the 1990 Workshop on Math. Found. Prog. Semantics.)

3. A.Asperti, G.-L.Ferrari, and R.Gorrieri. Implicative formulae in the 'proofs as computations' analogy. In *Proc. 17-th ACM Symposium on Principles of Programming Languages, San-Francisco,* January 1990, p.59-71

4. A.Brown. Relating Petri Nets to Formulas of Linear Logic. Technical Report. LFCS, Edinburgh, 1989.

5. E.W.Dijkstra. A Discipline of Programming. 1976.

6. E.W.Dijkstra. Guarded Commands, Nondeterminacy and Formal Derivation of Programs. In *Current Trends in Programming Methodology, Volume 1, Software Specification and Design* 1977, p.233–242.

7. M.R.Garey and D.S.Johnson. Computers and Intractability: A Guide to the Theory of $NP$-Completeness. 1979.

8. V.Gehlot and C.A.Gunter. Normal process representatives. In *Proc. 5-th Annual IEEE Symposium on Logic in Computer Science, Philadelphia,* June 1990.

9. J.-Y.Girard. Linear logic. *Theoretical Computer Science,* 50:1, 1987, pp.1–102.

10. J.-Y.Girard and Y.Lafont. Linear logic and lazy computation, *Proceedings of TAPSOFT 87,* Springer Lecture Notes in Computer Science n°257, 1987, pp.52–66.

11. J.-Y.Girard, A.Scedrov, and P.J.Scott, Bounded Linear Logic: A Modular Approach to Polynomial Time Computability, *Theoretical Computer Science,* 97, 1992, pp.1–66.

12. J.-Y.Girard. Linear logic : a survey, *Logic & Algebra of Specification,* NATO ASI Series F, 94, eds. Bauer & al., Springer Verlag, 1993.

13. C.A.Gunter and V.Gehlot. Nets as Tensor Theories. In *Proc. 10-th International Conference on Application and Theory of Petri Nets, Bonn,* 1989, p.174-191

14. J.Hopcroft and J.Pansiot, On the reachability problem for 5-dimensional vector addition systems, *Theoretical Computer Science,* 8, 1979, pp.135–159

15. M.I.Kanovich. Horn Programming in Linear Logic is NP-complete. In *Proc. 7-th Annual IEEE Symposium on Logic in Computer Science, Santa Cruz,* June 1992, pp.200-210

16. M.I.Kanovich. Linear logic as a logic of computations, *Annals Pure Appl. Logic,* 67 (1994) p.183–212

17. M.I.Kanovich. The complexity of Horn Fragments of Linear Logic, *Annals Pure Appl. Logic,* 69 (1994) p.195–241. (Special Issue on LICS'92)

18. M.I.Kanovich. Petri Nets, Horn Programs, Linear Logic, and Vector Games. Proceedings of the International Symposium Theoretical Aspects of Computer Software, TACS'94, Sendai, Japan, April 1994. In *Lecture Notes in Computer Science, (ed. M.Hagiya and J.Mitchell),* 1994, 789, p.642-666

19. M.I.Kanovich. Computational and Concurrency Aspects of Linear Logic. Proceedings of the IFIP 13th World Computer Congress, Hamburg, Germany, 28 August - 2 September, 1994. In *Technology and Foundations, Information Processing '94,* Volume 1, (ed. B.Pehrson and I.Simon) 1994, pp. 336–341

20. R.M.Karp and R.E.Miller. Parallel Program Schemata. *Journal of Computer and System Sciences,* 3 (1969), pp. 147–195.

21. R.S.Kosaraju. Decidability of reachability in vector addition systems. In *Proc. 14-th Annual Symposium on Theory of Computing,* 267–281, 1982. Preliminary Version.

22. P.Lincoln, J.Mitchell, A.Scedrov, and N.Shankar. Decision Problems for Propositional Linear Logic. Technical Report SRI-CSL-90-08, CSL, SRI International, August 1990. *Annals Pure Appl. Logic,* 56 (1992) pp. 239–311.

23. N.Marti-Oliet and J.Mesequer. From Petri Nets to Linear Logic. In: Springer LNCS 389, ed. by D.R.Pitt et al., 1989, p.313-340

24. E.Mayr and A.Meyer. The complexity of the word problems for commutative semi-groups and polynomial ideals. *Advances in Mathematics*, 46, 305–329, 1982.

25. E.Mayr, An algorithm for the general Petri net reachability problem. SIAM J.Comput., 13, N 3, 441–460, 1984.

26. T.Murata. Petri Nets: Properties, Analysis, and Applications. *Proceedings of the IEEE*, vol.77, No.4, p.541–580, 1989.

27. V.R.Pratt, Event spaces and their linear logic, In *AMAST'91: Algebraic Methodology and Software Technology, Iowa City, 1991,* Workshops in Computing, 1-23, Springer-Verlag, 1992.

28. A.S.Troelstra, *Lectures on Linear Logic,* CSLI Lecture Notes No. 29, Center for the Study of Language and Information, Stanford University, 1992.

# Sharing Mutable Objects
# and Controlling Groups of Tasks
# in a Concurrent and Distributed Language

Christian Queinnec*

École Polytechnique & INRIA-Rocquencourt

**Abstract.** This paper presents: *(i)* an operational semantics, based on a functional framework, for a concurrent and distributed extension of the Scheme programming language, *(ii)* a coherency protocol taking care of shared mutable objects, *(iii)* a new coherency protocol to imperatively control hierarchical groups of cooperating tasks. These two protocols do not require broadcast, nor FIFO communications, nor a centralized machine; they allow to manage an unbound number of shared mutable values and groups of tasks. This paper also advocates for the use of a functional continuation-based presentation for these protocols.

The omnipresence of interconnected networks exacerbates the need for high level languages allowing to express and control widely distributed computations. Much network services such as **news**, **finger**, **archie**, **netfind** etc. [ODL93] basically manage a set of informations which is accessed and enriched on a world-distributed basis. We think that it will become more and more necessary for these services as well as future ones to offer causal coherency. In the case of the **news** system for instance, to receive answers before questions would not be possible.

We have been designing an extension of the Scheme programming language, a Lisp dialect called ICSLAS, allowing to write such applications. We do not expect whole applications to be written in our language but rather wish to offer the ideal glue to tie together sequential sub-applications. It will act as a kind of "shell" offering high level constructs and built-in causal coherency. Therefore the ICSLAS language has not been designed for speed-up but for expressiveness.

Being a member of the Lisp family of dialects, the ICSLAS language is highly dynamic and supported by a garbage collector (GC). This distributed GC is described in [LQP92]. Causal coherency is usually studied independently of any language and often limits the number of shared mutable values or requires broadcast (or multicast) to be achieved. Since ICSLAS allows to create at run-time as many shared mutable values as wanted (within memory constraints) and since communication delays through networks as well as computer failures make broadcast difficult, our coherency protocols circumvent these two problems.

It is often the case that one wants to control the progress of distributed computations and possibly suspends or resumes them. The ICSLAS language does not

---

* Laboratoire d'Informatique de l'École Polytechnique (URA 1439), 91128 Palaiseau Cedex, France – Email: queinnec@polytechnique.fr This work has been partially funded by GDR-PRC de Programmation du CNRS.

offer first-class tasks (since they pose semantical problems with respect to first-class continuations) nor UNIX[2]-based **signal** machinery but rather offers the concept of groups of tasks. A program (or more generally an expression) can be sponsored by a first-class *group* object which allows to control this evaluation as a whole. Groups can be dynamically created and may be hierarchically embedded. To suspend a group implicitly suspends all its subgroups which can be resumed independently. We propose a coherency protocol to achieve the distributed management of these groups.

Section 1 informally presents the essential features of the ICSLAS language, already described in more details in [Que92, QD93, Que94]. The basic operational machinery we use to define the language appears in Section 2. We also exercise it to define the functional kernel and the concurrent features of the language. Distribution aspects as well as the protocol to manage shared mutable objects are dealt with in Section 3. Controlling groups of task is handled in Section 4. Related works is considered at the end of each of these sections.

# 1 An essential concurrent and distributed language

This section informally describes the main features of a concurrent and distributed toy functional language. This language (see figure 1) is based on Scheme [CR91] and is an essential version of the language described with examples in [Que92, QD93, Que94].

| | | | |
|---|---|---|---|
| $\nu$ | (quote $\varepsilon$) | (lambda ($\nu$...) $\pi$) | ($\pi$ $\pi$...) |
| (if $\pi_1$ $\pi_2$ $\pi_3$) | (begin $\pi_1$ $\pi_2$) | (new-box $\pi$) | (box-ref $\pi$) |
| (box-set! $\pi_1$ $\pi_2$) | (fork $\pi_1$ $\pi_2$) | (suicide) | (remote $\pi_1$ $\pi_2$) |
| (sponsor $\pi$) | (pause! $\pi$) | (awake! $\pi$) | |

**Fig. 1.** Syntax of the essential language

The value of a variable is obtained via its name ($\nu$). Constants values ($\varepsilon$) can be cited with **quote**. Closures are created by abstractions, identified by **lambda**, and can be applied with combinations ($\pi$ $\pi$...). These previous features form the kernel of the language giving it the power of a sugared applied $\lambda$-calculus. Alternatives and sequences are identified with **if** or **begin** keywords.

Variables are immutable: there is no assignment. Side-effects can nevertheless be performed through boxes that are similar to ML references. Three predefined functions exist to create boxes with an initial content (**new-box**), to read the content of a box (**box-ref**) or to alter the content of a box (**box-set!**). This last function is an atomic exchange i.e., it atomically writes a value in a box while returning as result the former value the box was holding. Mutable variables and other mutable values can easily be simulated by boxes [KKR+86].

---

[2] UNIX is a registered trademark of UNIX Systems Laboratories, Inc. in the USA and other countries.

The (fork $\pi_1$ $\pi_2$) special form kills the current task while creating two new independent tasks, one evaluating $\pi_1$ and another one evaluating $\pi_2$. If $\pi_1$ yields a value, this value is also yielded by the initial fork form, and similarly for $\pi_2$. Technically speaking, $\pi_1$ and $\pi_2$ have the same continuation: the very continuation of the fork form. Thus, our model allows a form to return multiply as for the generators of Icon-like languages [MH90]. The fork special form is the only form that creates tasks. Conversely a task can explicitly terminates itself with suicide. An important characteristic of our language is that tasks are not first-class values, they have no identity therefore they cannot be sent signals à la UNIX.

Distribution is introduced through the (remote $\pi_1$ $\pi_2$) special form. The first term $\pi_1$ is evaluated and must return a *site*. The second term $\pi_2$ is then evaluated on that site. A site is a first-class value that represents an independent machine or, an independent process on the same machine with a separate data space. From an implementational point of view, sites can only exchange messages. If $\pi_2$ yields a value, this value is also yielded by the original remote form on the very site. Our essential language supports the distributed shared memory (DSM) model i.e., remote forms are transparent wrt sites.

Tasks can be controlled by the sponsor function. When invoked, as in (sponsor $\varphi$), sponsor creates a new object called a *group* and applies its argument (the unary function $\varphi$) on it. The body of function $\varphi$ may perform arbitrary computations which can involve a number of tasks on a number of sites. This computation can be controlled as a whole through the *group* object (received by $\varphi$ as argument) and two new imperative functions. The pause! function when applied on a group, suspends (all the tasks cooperating to perform) the associated computation while the awake! function resumes it. When a task makes the sponsor call to yield a value, this task exits from the associated group of tasks: it is no longer a member of that group. Technically, tasks belong to a group while they are in the dynamic extent of the sponsor function that created that group.

```
(lambda (thunk)
  ((lambda (barrier)
    ((lambda (group+result)
      (if (box-set! barrier #t)
          (suicide)
          (begin (pause! (car group+result))
                 (cdr group+result) ) ) )
    (sponsor (lambda (g)
                (cons g (fork (remote site1 (thunk))
                              (remote site2 (thunk)) ) ) )) ) )
  (new-box #f) ) )
```

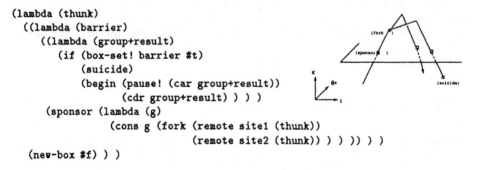

**Fig. 2.** A program example

The program of figure 2 illustrates nearly all the features of our essential language. We assume the usual car, cdr and cons functions to be predefined and cons to only create immutable pairs. The shown function receives a computation encoded as a thunk (a closure based on an abstraction without variables), it then creates a mutable box to hold a boolean flag (initially false #f), binds it to the barrier (immutable) variable, and starts a sponsor-ed computation concurrently invoking the received thunk on two different sites (held in variables site1 and site2). As soon as one of these thunks yields a value, this value is paired with its sponsoring group object and is bound to the group+result variable. The boolean held in the barrier box is then changed to true (#t). The mutation operator box-set! returns the former content of the barrier box so two cases are possible. If the former content was true then the task commits suicide since it is not the first one that mutates the barrier box. Conversely, if the former content was false then the group is paused i.e., any task on any site which is still running under the sponsorship of that group is suspended; the result is then returned as the value of the function.

The right part of figure 2 may help to visualize the main steps. It is a 3D-approximation of the behavior of the above example. The first axis represents time ($t$), the second axis shows the various tasks ($\theta^*$) and the third axis approximates the depth of continuations ($\kappa$) i.e., recursion stack. A plan is associated to the invocation of sponsor showing the dynamic extent of the group: tasks belong to that group while above this plan. Entry in the group is marked by a black square, exit with a white square. The invocation to fork (marked by a black circle) creates two tasks, one of which commits suicide (marked by a white circle) after exiting the sponsor form

Roughly stated, the example spawns two similar computations on two different sites, returns the value of the first one to complete and disposes of the remaining spawned task[3]. A paused group that becomes unreachable is collected by the Garbage Collector (GC), but the paper will not emphasize the connection to the GC. The previous example exhibits a poor-man's implementation of fault tolerance where the burden of making thunk insensitive to the fact that it is concurrently invoked is entirely on the shoulders of the programmer.

This concludes the informal description of our essential language. Around a pure functional kernel, it offers orthogonal features such as side-effects, concurrency, distribution and groups of tasks. These new features are added as functions or special forms as felt convenient to express their semantics below. Examples of the fully-fledged version of this essential language as well as a comparison with related work may be found in [Que92, QD93, Que94].

## 2 The functional abstract machine

This section presents an operational semantics describing our language. The protocols that manage coherency of boxes and groups are parts of the definitions. These definitions can also be viewed as the specification of an abstract machine with transitions between states. We assume some familiarity with denotational semantics [Sto77, Sch86] or at least higher order functional programming [Hen80, FWH92]. To improve the legibility of definitions, we adopt a syntax close to that of a programming language. We expect these denotations to be self explanatory.

---

[3] There can be more than one task if (thunk) forks new tasks

The language runs on a network of heterogeneous workstations. A site is represented by a regular UNIX process. A site has a copy of the runtime library of the language, it runs a local scheduler which chooses which task to run in its local queue of tasks. Tasks can only be preempted in well defined places ascribed by the semantics of the language that is why tasks are composed of a succession of uninterruptible but short computation steps. When a box or a group is created, it remains on its birth site. If there are $n$ sites, then any site has $n$ clocks, one of which is its proper clock and is incremented any time a local box (resp. a group) is mutated (resp. paused or awakened). The other clocks represent what the site believes the other proper clocks to be, these clocks are updated any time messages are received [Fid88, Mat88].

The abstract machine has a *state* made of four components: *(i)* a set of threads, *(ii)* a store, *(iii)* a time, *(iv)* and, a list of already produced answers.

$$\textbf{State} = \mathbb{P}(\textbf{Thread}) \times \textbf{Store} \times \textbf{Time} \times \textbf{Value}^*$$

A *thread* represents an atomic computation step within a task. When a thread is run, it performs some action and generally yields a new thread (representing the work the task has still to do) that is incorporated back in the set of threads. The inner structure of a thread will be detailed below.

The *store* represents the shared memory seen by all sites. The store associates to any site and any box (resp. group), its content (resp. group status) as perceived by this site. The store is therefore represented by a function mapping a site and a box or group onto a value or a cached-value or a constant saying that no associated information is locally available.

$$\textbf{Store} = (\textbf{Site} \times (\textbf{Box} + \textbf{Group})) \rightarrow (\textbf{Value} + \textbf{CachedValue} + \{\textit{not-here}\})$$

Each site of a distributed shared memory has some clocks. One of these clocks is the proper clock of the site, the others hold what the site thinks the other proper clocks to be. This is represented by the *time* function which associates to a site $\mu_1$ and a site $\mu_2$ the value of the proper clock of $\mu_2$ as perceived by $\mu_1$. Clock values i.e., dates, belong to the **Date** domain and can be seen as natural numbers. For a site $\mu$ and a time function $\tau$, the proper time of the site is $\tau(\mu, \mu)$.

$$\textbf{Time} = (\textbf{Site} \times \textbf{Site}) \rightarrow \textbf{Date}$$

A cached value is a tuple made of a value and a date that indicates the proper time of the site when and where the value was remotely fetched.

$$\textbf{CachedValue} = \textbf{Date} \times \textbf{Value}$$

Due to the **fork** construct, a program may have multiple answers. Therefore the state of the machine accumulates the sequence of already answered values in its fourth component. The **Value** domain contains at least closures, boolean values, boxes, groups and sites which are necessary for our essential language. It may also contain pairs, numbers, etc.

We suppose some sites to exist and to be represented by elements of the **Site** domain. We also suppose the constant *all-sites* to be the finite sequence of all sites:

this constant does not need to be visible from the programmer. The only information attached to a box is its birth site. To any group is not only attached its birth site but also its supergroup i.e., the group that was in control when created. Groups form a tree rooted by $\gamma_{init}$. Birth-sites (resp. supergroups) can be known with the *site* (resp. *super*) function.

$$site : (\mathbf{Box} + \mathbf{Group}) \rightarrow \mathbf{Site}$$

$$super : \mathbf{Group} \rightarrow \mathbf{Group}$$

We can now return to the denotation of a thread. Being the first computation step of a task, a thread expresses that some computation is performed on a site and under the control of a group. The various possibilities for computations will be unveiled in the next sections.

$$\mathbf{Thread} = \mathbf{Computation} \times \mathbf{Site} \times \mathbf{Group}$$

Following the great tradition of denotational semantics, all variables are represented by Greek letters making their types explicit. The chosen notations appear on figure 3.

| | | | |
|---|---|---|---|
| $\pi$ : **Program** | $\nu$ : **Identifier** | $\varepsilon$ : **Value** | $\varphi$ : **Function** |
| $\epsilon$ : **CachedValue** | $\gamma$ : **Group** | $\beta$ : **Box** | $\sigma$ : **Store** |
| $\theta$ : **Thread** | $\mu$ : **Site** | $\chi$ : **Computation** | $\kappa$ : **Continuation** |
| $\rho$ : **Environment** | $\tau$ : **Time** | $\Sigma$ : **State** | |

| | | | |
|---|---|---|---|
| < STATE: _, _, _, _ > : | **State** | < GROUPSTATUS: _, _, _ > : | **GroupStatus** |
| ☐ : | **Computation** | ⟨⟨_, _, _⟩⟩ : | **Thread** |
| < CACHEDVALUE: _, _ > : | **CachedValue** | <...> : | **Continuation** |

**Fig. 3.** Denotational notations

## 2.1 Denotation of the kernel

This section describes the semantics of the functional kernel of the language in terms of elements of **Computation**. The presentation of the scheduler is delayed to section 4.2 but it informally works as follows: if the current state is < STATE: $\theta^*, \sigma, \tau, \varepsilon^*$ >, and if there is a thread among $\theta^*$ that can be run, say $\theta = \langle\langle \chi, \mu, \gamma \rangle\rangle$, then the scheduler invokes:

$$step\ \chi(\mu, \gamma)(\theta^* - \{\theta\}, \sigma, \tau, \varepsilon^*) = < \text{STATE: } \theta^{*\prime}, \sigma', \tau', \varepsilon^{*\prime} >$$

The *step* function performs the computation $\chi$ on site $\mu$ and under sponsorship of $\gamma$. It also receives the set of the remaining threads $\theta^* - \{\theta\}$, the store $\sigma$, the time $\tau$ and the sequence of already returned answers $\varepsilon^*$. The result is a new state on which the scheduler is applied again until no task can be run.

For the functional kernel, a thread just yields another thread. To conveniently express that, we introduce the *adjoin* utility function which takes a computation and adjoins it (properly wrapped into a thread on the current site and under the sponsorship of the current group) to the current set of threads.

$$adjoin \ \chi = \lambda\mu\gamma.\lambda\theta^{*}\sigma\tau\varepsilon^{*}. <\text{STATE: } \{\langle\!\langle\chi,\mu,\gamma\rangle\!\rangle\} \cup \theta^{*}, \sigma, \tau, \varepsilon^{*} >$$

To shorten space, we limit the semantics of functions and combinations to the unary case, we also suppose programs to be correct and error-free. To improve readability, computations are typeset inside (typographic) boxes and start with a curly letter identifying their nature. A computation can be an evaluation (marked as $\boxed{\mathcal{E}[\![\pi]\!]\rho\kappa}$) of a program $\pi$ within lexical environment $\rho$ and continuation $\kappa$. A computation can also be the return of a value $\varepsilon$ to a continuation $\kappa$ (marked as $\boxed{\mathcal{R}\kappa\varepsilon}$). Here follow the denotations of the functional kernel of our language:

$$step \ \boxed{\mathcal{E}[\![\nu]\!]\rho\kappa} = adjoin \ \boxed{\mathcal{R}\kappa\rho(\nu)}$$

$$step \ \boxed{\mathcal{E}[\![(\texttt{lambda } (\nu) \ \pi)]\!]\rho\kappa} = adjoin \ \boxed{\mathcal{R}\kappa\lambda\kappa'\varepsilon.adjoin \ \boxed{\mathcal{E}[\![\pi]\!]\rho[\nu \rightarrow \varepsilon]\kappa'}}$$

$$step \ \boxed{\mathcal{E}[\![(\pi \ \pi')]\!]\rho\kappa} = adjoin \ \boxed{\mathcal{E}[\![\pi]\!]\rho\texttt{<arg0 } \kappa \ \rho \ \pi'\texttt{>}}$$

$$step \ \boxed{\mathcal{R}\texttt{<arg0 } \kappa \ \rho \ \pi\texttt{>}\varphi} = adjoin \ \boxed{\mathcal{E}[\![\pi]\!]\rho\texttt{<apply1 } \kappa \ \varphi\texttt{>}}$$

$$step \ \boxed{\mathcal{R}\texttt{<apply1 } \kappa \ \varphi\texttt{>}\varepsilon} = \varphi(\kappa, \varepsilon)$$

The semantics of the unary combination $(\pi \ \pi')$ is the most complex. First, the functional term $\pi$ (which is in functional position) is evaluated with a new continuation identified by `<arg0...>`. When this continuation receives the value $\varphi$ of the functional term, it evaluates the second term of the original combination but with a new continuation, identified by `<apply1...>`, memorizing the received function. Finally when this `<apply1...>` continuation receives a value $\varepsilon$, it applies the memorized function $\varphi$ on $\varepsilon$ and the result is given back to the original continuation of the combination.

The semantics of the unary abstraction is to create a closure on this abstraction and to return it immediately to the continuation. When the closure is invoked, for instance with the above `apply1` rule, it will create a new thread that will evaluate the body of the abstraction in the appropriate environment. The notation $\rho[\nu \rightarrow \varepsilon]$ returns a new environment similar to $\rho$ except on point $\nu$ where it now yields $\varepsilon$.

These denotations form the $\lambda$-calculus-like kernel of our language. The computation is expressed as a succession of transition steps i.e., calls to the *step* function. Some scheduling may occur between these steps i.e., computation steps are interleaved to simulate concurrency.

## 2.2   Task birth and death

In the initial state, the initial store contains nothing, the initial time function sets all clocks from all sites to zero, no answer is already produced and a single thread exists which has to evaluate the initial program $\pi$ within the predefined lexical environment and the initial continuation <result>.

$$\Sigma_{init} = < \text{STATE: } \{ \langle\!\langle \boxed{\mathcal{E}[\![\pi]\!]\rho_{init}\text{<result>}}, \mu_{init}, \gamma_{init} \rangle\!\rangle \}, \sigma_{init}, \tau_{init}, <>>$$

When a value is returned to the <result> continuation, it is appended ($\varepsilon^* \S < \varepsilon >$) to the sequence of already produced answers and the current task is terminated.

$$step \boxed{\mathcal{R}\text{<result>}\varepsilon} = \lambda\mu\gamma.\lambda\theta^*\sigma\tau\varepsilon^*. < \text{STATE: } \theta^*, \sigma, \tau, \varepsilon^* \S < \varepsilon >>$$

A task can be prematurely terminated by the (suicide) special form. New tasks can be created by the fork special form, they are evaluated with the same lexical environment and continuation. Once created, tasks are independent and can only exchange informations through the store.

$$step \boxed{\mathcal{E}[\![\text{(suicide)}]\!]\rho\kappa} = \lambda\mu\gamma.\lambda\theta^*\sigma\tau\varepsilon^*. < \text{STATE: } \theta^*, \sigma, \tau, \varepsilon^* >$$

$$step \boxed{\mathcal{E}[\![\text{(fork } \pi \ \pi')]\!]\rho\kappa} =$$
$$\lambda\mu\gamma.\lambda\theta^*\sigma\tau\varepsilon^*. < \text{STATE: } \{ \langle\!\langle \boxed{\mathcal{E}[\![\pi]\!]\rho\kappa}, \mu, \gamma \rangle\!\rangle \} \cup \{ \langle\!\langle \boxed{\mathcal{E}[\![\pi']\!]\rho\kappa}, \mu, \gamma \rangle\!\rangle \} \cup \theta^*, \sigma, \tau, \varepsilon^* >$$

Task birth or death do not affect store or time, they are purely functional.

## 2.3   Discussion

The semantics of the above abstract machine improves on the denotational semantics given in [Que92] by its simplicity. It uses interleaving to express concurrency. Although the scheduler apparently sequentializes all threads, this order can only be perceived by the program through side-effects on boxes. The semantics of our abstract machine is rather similar to the semantics of actors language [AMST92] except that our language is more complex due to the presence of closures that shares bindings i.e. accesses to the store.

Other differences with respect to other formalisms are   *(i)* the various perceptions of store and time are now explicit,   *(ii)* sites are not sequential processes but have multitasking capacity.

## 3   Boxes and the remote special form

This section describes the distribution aspects and mainly the remote special form and the box coherency machinery.

## 3.1 Migration

A computation can migrate as specified by the `remote` special form. This form evaluates its first term with a continuation (identified by `<migrate...>`) which waits for a site. When receiving a site, this continuation remotely adjoins the evaluation of the second term on that site (instead of the current one if they are different) but with a new `return` continuation that will migrate the resulting value back to the original site. The `return` continuation might be called a "geographic" continuation whose sole rôle is to migrate a value from one site to another.

$$step \boxed{\mathcal{E}[\![\text{(remote } \pi\ \pi')]\!]\rho\kappa} = adjoin \boxed{\mathcal{E}[\![\pi]\!]\rho\text{<migrate } \kappa\ \rho\ \pi'\text{>}}$$

$$step \boxed{\mathcal{R}\text{<migrate } \kappa\ \rho\ \pi\text{>}\mu} =$$
$$\lambda\mu'\gamma.\ \text{if } \mu' = \mu$$
$$\quad \text{then } adjoin \boxed{\mathcal{E}[\![\pi]\!]\rho\kappa}\ (\mu',\gamma)$$
$$\quad \text{else } remote\text{-}adjoin\ \mu \boxed{\mathcal{E}[\![\pi]\!]\rho\text{<return } \kappa\ \mu'\text{>}}\ (\mu',\gamma)$$
$$\quad \text{endif}$$

$$step \boxed{\mathcal{R}\text{<return } \kappa\ \mu\text{>}\varepsilon} = remote\text{-}adjoin\ \mu \boxed{\mathcal{R}\kappa\varepsilon}$$

Communications use the *remote-adjoin* function that takes a site and a computation, creates a new thread within the current group but on the given site and adjoins this new thread to the set of runnable threads. Although the communication seems instantaneous, the migrated thread has to wait to be scheduled: this is equivalent to safe communications (no message loss and no duplication of messages) with bounded transmission delays provided the scheduler is fair. Observe that messages are not ordered and communications are not FIFO either.

As in many coherency protocols, communications i.e., threads sent by *remote-adjoin*, are accompanied by some time informations to make clock progress. This time update is represented by $\boxed{T\chi\mu\tau}$: the emitting site $\mu$ sends the computation $\chi$, its own identity $\mu$ and the current time function $\tau$ containing its perception of time. At the other end, when the message is processed, the clocks of the receiving site are updated i.e., every clock of the receiving site is set to the higher value it had on the receiving or the emitting site. This is achieved by the *update-time* function. We note $\tau[\mu_1 \times \mu_2 \rightarrow t]$, the new time function that is entirely similar to $\tau$ except that site $\mu_1$ now believes that the proper clock of site $\mu_2$ is now $t$. After updating clocks of the receiving site, the computation $\chi$ is wrapped into a thread that is added to the set of runnable threads.

$$remote\text{-}adjoin\ \mu\chi = \lambda\mu_1\gamma.\lambda\theta^*\sigma\tau\varepsilon^*.\ <\text{STATE: } \{\langle\!\langle\boxed{T\chi\mu_1\tau},\mu,\gamma\rangle\!\rangle\} \cup \theta^*, \sigma, \tau, \varepsilon^* >$$

$$step \boxed{T\chi\mu\tau} =$$
$$\lambda\mu_1\gamma.\lambda\theta^*\sigma\tau_1\varepsilon^*.\ <\text{STATE: } \{\langle\!\langle\chi,\mu_1,\gamma\rangle\!\rangle\} \cup \theta^*, \sigma, update\text{-}time(\mu_1,\tau_1,\mu,\tau_1), \varepsilon^* >$$

$$update\text{-}time(\mu,\tau,\mu_1,\tau_1) =$$
$$\text{let } \tau_2 = reduce(\lambda\tau_2\mu_2.\ \text{let } t = \tau_2(\mu,\mu_2)$$
$$\qquad\qquad\qquad\qquad \text{and } t_1 = \tau_1(\mu_1,\mu_2)$$
$$\qquad\qquad\qquad\qquad \text{in if } t_1 > t$$

$$\text{then } \tau_2[\mu \times \mu_2 \rightarrow t_1]$$
$$\text{else } \tau_2$$
$$\text{endif} \quad , \tau, \text{ all sites})$$

in $\tau_2$

whererec $reduce(\Phi, \tau_2, \mu^*) =$
$$\text{if } \mu^* = <>$$
$$\text{then } \tau_2$$
$$\text{else } reduce(\Phi, \Phi(\tau_2, \mu^* \downarrow_1), \mu^* \uparrow 1)$$
$$\text{endif}$$

We now introduce the box machinery which requires time consideration for its coherency. All box-related features are implemented as functions. They thus have the interface of unary or binary functions.

## 3.2 Box creation

The new-box function allocates a box and returns it to its continuation along with a modified store recording, on the current site, the initial content of this box. The notation $\sigma_1[\mu \times \beta \rightarrow \varepsilon]$ returns a store function identical to $\sigma_1$ except that, on site $\mu$, the box $\beta$ now contains $\varepsilon$. The creation of a box does not change the time function: a box creation is not a side effect wrt time. The *allocate-a-box* function is implementation dependent (it encapsulates the GC aspects), it allocates, in store $\sigma$, a box whose birth site is $\mu$ such that $site(\beta) = \mu$. The modified store and the box itself are given to the third argument of *allocate-a-box* as $\sigma_1$ and $\beta$.

$\rho[\![\text{new-box}]\!] =$
$\lambda \kappa \epsilon . \lambda \mu \gamma . \lambda \theta^* \sigma \tau \epsilon^* . allocate\text{-}a\text{-}box(\sigma, \mu, \lambda \sigma_1 \beta . adjoin \boxed{\mathcal{R} \kappa \beta} (\mu, \gamma)(\theta^*, \sigma_1[\mu \times \beta \rightarrow \epsilon], \tau, \epsilon^*))$

## 3.3 Box modification

Writing in a box is simpler than reading it (as far as denotation is concerned). The box-set! function is defined by the utility function *perform-box-update* which recognizes two cases. If the box is local i.e., was created on the current site, then the box is modified (the store function is updated and the proper clock is incremented) then the old content of the box is returned to the continuation. Since these actions are done within a single computation step they form an atomic sequence of actions. If the box is not local then a message is sent to the birth site of the box. The message, a box write request identified by $\boxed{\mathcal{B}_W \text{<return } \kappa \ \mu \text{>} \beta \epsilon}$, will perform the mutation and will return the result back to the current site.

$\rho[\![\text{box-set!}]\!] = perform\text{-}box\text{-}update$

$step \boxed{\mathcal{B}_W \kappa \beta \epsilon} = perform\text{-}box\text{-}update(\kappa, \beta, \epsilon)$

$perform\text{-}box\text{-}update =$
$\lambda \kappa \beta \epsilon . \lambda \mu \gamma . \lambda \theta^* \sigma \tau \epsilon^* .$
$$\text{if } \mu = site(\beta)$$

then let $\epsilon_1 = \sigma(\mu, \beta)$

    in *adjoin* $\boxed{\mathcal{R}\kappa\epsilon_1}$ $(\mu, \gamma)(\theta^*, \sigma[\mu \times \beta \to \epsilon], \tau[\mu \times \mu \to 1 + \tau(\mu,\mu)], \epsilon^*)$

else *remote-adjoin site*$(\beta)$ $\boxed{\mathcal{B}_W \texttt{<return } \kappa \, \mu \texttt{>} \beta \epsilon}$ $(\mu, \gamma)(\theta^*, \sigma, \tau, \epsilon^*)$

endif

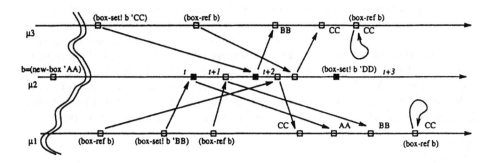

**Fig. 4.** Box at work

Roughly speaking, all modifications to a box $\beta$ are migrated towards its birth site i.e. *site*$(\beta)$ where they are sequentialized. For example in figure 4, the original site of the box is $\mu_2$ and all **box-set!** operations migrate towards $\mu_2$ where they are sequentialized.

## 3.4 Reading box

As many other protocols, sites locally cache non local boxes to avoid communication delays and speed up multiple readings. But to cache boxes requires to invalidate them when the content of the original boxes change. Instead of eagerly broadcasting an invalidation message, we lazily propagate the invalidation information through messages; the validity of cached boxes is checked when read.

When a box is locally cached, its value is time-stamped with the proper time of the original site when remotely read. For instance on figure 4, the first (**box-ref** b) request from $\mu_3$ returns a cached value $(t + 2, CC)$. The cached value of a box is valid, up to date, if its time-stamp is equal to the time the birth site of the box is believed to be. For instance still on figure 4, while $\mu_3$ believes $\mu_2$ to be at time $t + 2$, the cached value $CC$ is valid so the second **box-ref** on $\mu_3$ is immediately evaluated. When a box is modified on its birth site, the proper clock of the birth site is incremented and this naturally invalidates all the caches that perceives this time incrementation.

As for writing in boxes, two cases are distinguished whether the box is local or not. If it is local, the box is read and its content is returned to the continuation. If the box is not local then two new cases are recognized. If the box is validly cached then the cached value is extracted and returned to the continuation. Otherwise a

<u>box</u> <u>reading</u> message (identified as $\boxed{B_R\kappa\beta}$) is emitted towards the birth site of the box. When this message is processed on the birth site of the box, the content of the box is time-stamped with the proper current time of the birth site to form a cached value that is returned to the continuation. The continuation of a $B_R$ message is a composed continuation since not only it has to migrate back the cached value towards the requesting site but it also has to locally cache the fetched value to improve future reading on that site, this effect is achieved by the `<box-cache...>` continuation which is run on the requesting site. Due to transmission or scheduling delay, the `<box-cache...>` continuation may be activated so late that it is no longer possible to cache the value since it is already obsolete. This is the case in figure 4 on site $\mu_1$ when the second (`box-ref b`) request returns $(t+1, BB)$. This value is obsolete and must not be cached since it is already known by site $\mu_1$ that site $\mu_2$ has a proper clock at least equal to $t+2$. Moreover, there is already an up to date value in the cache, $CC$, which was brought back by the first (`box-ref b`) on site $\mu_1$. However, due to the semantics of `box-ref`, $BB$ is still returned to the continuation.

$\rho[\text{box-ref}] =$
$\lambda\kappa\beta.\lambda\mu\gamma.\lambda\theta^*\sigma\tau\varepsilon^*. \text{ if }\mu = site(\beta)$

   $\qquad\text{then } adjoin\;\boxed{\mathcal{R}\kappa\sigma(\mu,\beta)}\;(\mu,\gamma)(\theta^*,\sigma,\tau,\varepsilon^*)$

   $\qquad\text{else let }\varepsilon = \sigma(\mu,\beta)$

   $\qquad\qquad\text{in if }\varepsilon \in \text{CachedValue}$

   $\qquad\qquad\qquad\text{then let } <\text{CACHEDVALUE}:\; t,\varepsilon> = \varepsilon$

   $\qquad\qquad\qquad\qquad\text{in if } t = \tau(\mu, site(\beta))$

   $\qquad\qquad\qquad\qquad\qquad\text{then } adjoin\;\boxed{\mathcal{R}\kappa\varepsilon}\;(\mu,\gamma)(\theta^*,\sigma,\tau,\varepsilon^*)$

   $\qquad\qquad\qquad\qquad\qquad\text{else } remote\text{-}adjoin\; site(\beta)$

   $\qquad\qquad\qquad\qquad\qquad\boxed{B_R\text{<return <box-cache `\kappa` }\beta> \mu>\beta}\;(\mu,\gamma)(\theta^*,\sigma,\tau,\varepsilon^*)$

   $\qquad\qquad\qquad\qquad\text{endif}$

   $\qquad\qquad\qquad\text{else } remote\text{-}adjoin\; site(\beta)$

   $\qquad\qquad\qquad\boxed{B_R\text{<return <box-cache }\kappa\; \beta> \mu>\beta}\;(\mu,\gamma)(\theta^*,\sigma,\tau,\varepsilon^*)$

   $\qquad\qquad\text{endif}$

   $\qquad\text{endif}$

$step\;\boxed{B_R\kappa\beta}\; =$
$\lambda\mu\gamma.\lambda\theta^*\sigma\tau\varepsilon^*.adjoin\;\boxed{\mathcal{R}\kappa <\text{CACHEDVALUE}:\; \tau(\mu,\mu), \sigma(\mu,\beta) >}\;(\mu,\gamma)(\theta^*,\sigma,\tau,\varepsilon^*)$

$step\;\boxed{\mathcal{R}\text{<box-cache }\kappa\;\beta>\varepsilon}\; =$
$\lambda\mu\gamma.\lambda\theta^*\sigma\tau\varepsilon^*.\text{ let } <\text{CACHEDVALUE}:\; t,\varepsilon> = \varepsilon$

   $\qquad\text{in } adjoin\;\boxed{\mathcal{R}\kappa\varepsilon}\;(\mu,\gamma)(\theta^*,\text{ if } t = \tau(\mu, site(\beta))$

   $\qquad\qquad\qquad\qquad\qquad\qquad\quad\text{then } \sigma[\mu \times \beta \rightarrow \varepsilon]$

   $\qquad\qquad\qquad\qquad\qquad\qquad\quad\text{else } \sigma$

   $\qquad\qquad\qquad\qquad\qquad\qquad\quad\text{endif}\;, \tau, \varepsilon^*)$

## 3.5 Discussion

The above coherency protocol is supported by the following principles:

- A side effect perceived by a thread cannot be ignored by the threads in its continuation. This does not depend on the sites where these threads are run.

— A site can be viewed as an entity within which threads share clocks i.e., a similar perception of time. In other words, a side effect perceived by a thread on a site cannot be ignored by the threads of the same site if they are scheduled after.

The first principle is related to causality i.e., the natural sequentiality present in our language, while the second reflects what sharing clocks is all about.

The above protocol for boxes coherency ensures soundness: modification of boxes are coherently perceived, but this does not ensure liveness. If a site never receives messages then it ignores boxes that may have changed and thus prevents computations to usefully progress if these changes were known. This is the case on the right of figure 4 where box b is modified and sites $\mu_1$ and $\mu_3$ did not perceive it yet. This is coherent since it is as if the threads of $\mu_1$ and $\mu_3$ were scheduled on $\mu_3$ before $t + 3$. To ensure liveness, one may program a "worm" that passes regularly trough all sites in order to propagate clocks.

When a box is changed on a site then the proper clock is incremented and this makes obsolete all cached boxes from that site. This may be considered as too strong but can be alleviated by the use of more clocks. Suppose for instance that a site has more than one proper clock, suppose also that it is possible to know to which clock is associated a box, then any time a box is changed only its related clock is incremented, therefore only boxes associated to that same clock will be invalidated. To handle an unbound number of boxes while bounding the size of messages introduces some imprecision. However if a box is of considerable value, it can have its own proper clock (the protocol then resembles that of [MSRN92]). Of course to augment the number of clocks also augments the size of messages that have to carry all these clock values (but see 5.2).

The protocol is rather naïve and not very efficient but it only expresses the essence of the protocol. For instance, a remote box writing can also return the new value to update the local cache. Remote box read requests can be shared to spare bandwidth. Another source of improvement is to only increment clocks if the new value is different from the former value.

Our protocol describes how shared mutable boxes are "migrated". More complex mutable objects can be constructed with our boxes using indirections. if they are to be migrated, immutable values such as numbers, booleans, characters and even closures are simply copied from one site to another. The traditional difference of Lisp between physical equality (eq?) and structural equality (equal?) vanishes for immutable objects.

To sum up, our protocol (the *lazy invalidation propagation*) innovates on several points:

1. it is specified in a denotational-like style. The description makes use of functions and continuations expressing atomic computation steps and communications. It has a higher level compared to descriptions using messages, automata and side-effects. Related sequential computations are naturally expressed via continuations.
2. it can handle an arbitrary number of boxes,
3. it does not require communications to be FIFO,
4. it does not require a centralized controller,

5. it does not require broadcast technology but favors instead a lazy propagation of invalidation information. This takes naturally into account bounded communication breakdown provided no message is lost.

# 4 Groups of tasks

This section exposes the coherency protocol used to control hierarchically embedded groups of tasks that can be paused or awakened. Groups of tasks are created via the **sponsor** function. Groups can be arbitrarily embedded, they form a tree. When created, groups are running. They can be suspended (resp. resumed) with the **pause!** (resp. **awake!**) imperative primitive. These functions pose many problems to be defined and implemented.

The first problem comes from their semantics. Very roughly said, to **pause!** a group is similar to set the running status of the given group to false. At that time and on every site, the tasks that belong to the group must be suspended. When this is finished, **pause!** returns to its caller the former running status of the now paused group. Suspending tasks thus seems to impose a sort of global synchronization among all sites. The following protocol avoids this global synchronization and uses instead (once again) a lazy propagation of pausing or awakening information.

If **pause!** (resp. **awake!**) is to return immediately then non local tasks have to be paused (resp. awakened) lazily. It must be ensured that there is no still running task in the group that may alter the behavior of the caller of **pause!**. In other words, if a task pauses a group (and does not belong to this same group otherwise it would be also paused) then it cannot be later affected by the tasks that are supposed to be suspended from its point of view. For example, on figure 5, site $\mu_2$ knows that group g is paused, it thus cannot accept to run a thread coming from $\mu_1$ and belonging to that very group: when received on $\mu_2$, this thread is automatically paused.

To each group is associated a box that holds its running status, a boolean stating if the group is running or not i.e., awakened or paused. The box coherency protocol is used to manage these boxes but groups are more complex objects since they form a tree that must be kept coherent. Pausing a group also means pausing all the subgroups it contains etc. The second problem, see figure 6, is that a task can require to pause a group while another task requires to awake one of its subgroup. This contention problem has only two exclusive solutions: or all tasks belonging to g are paused even those of sg or, all tasks belonging to g are paused except those belonging to sg. The choice between the two solutions depends on whether pausing g is perceived after or before awakening sg from the point of view of the birth site of sg.

The essence of the protocol is to ensure that no decision or action is taken on a group with an uncertain running status. Each site maintains up to date the running status of all the groups to which its local threads belong. Sites know the running

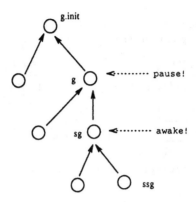

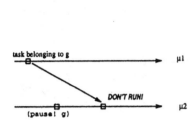

Figure 5: Altering the continuation of pause!

Figure 6: Concurrent pause! and awake!

status of all their local groups and cache the running status of all their non local groups. If the running status of a group is obsolete or unknown then the site asks for it, meanwhile its local scheduler defers running any threads belonging to that group. When the status of a non local group changes then this new status has to be recursively propagated to the local groups. These mutations of running status of local groups are simple boxes mutations that regularly increment the proper clock of the site. The regular box machinery will propagate these mutations and will force other sites to ask again for the running status of these groups. A group status change is therefore propagated top-down in the tree of groups. An important point is that groups know their supergroups but there is no link from groups to their subgroups since it would be difficult to maintain such a dynamic cyclic structure that will unnecessarily augments the burden of the GC. It is therefore of the duty of groups to ensure that they are aware of the running status of their parentage.

This organization is not sufficient to solve the second problem cited above. For that it must be possible to order all operations on hierarchy of groups. We therefore associate to each group a box containing its group status. This group status not only contains its running status (a boolean) but also the last date when this group status changed as well as the date of the last perceived change in the super-group, see figure 7. These two dates are expressed wrt the proper clocks of the birth site of the group and supergroup. The running status of a group is certain as soon as its group status is known i.e., is local or validly cached, and up to date wrt the group hierarchy i.e., perceived changes on any of its supergroups are not ignored.

## 4.1 The group protocol

This section details the underlying algorithms of the protocol. The sponsor function receives a function $\varphi$, allocates a group object (whose supergroup is the current group) on the current site and in the current store, augments the continuation with a <group...> continuation then invokes the received function $\varphi$ under the control of

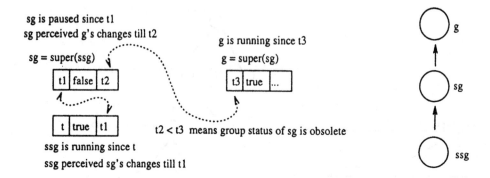

**Fig. 7.** Group status coherency

this new group. The created group is running i.e., its running status is true. The time function is not changed by this allocation: it is not a side-effect. The <group...> continuation is needed to restaure the correct group sponsorship when the function $\varphi$ returns a value. The group status is a triple. Its first component is the last date it was changed, the second is its running status (a boolean) and its third component is the date of the last perceived supergroup's change. This first component can be extracted from a group by the *group-last-change-date* utility function which recognizes the top-group $\gamma_{init}$ as a special case to avoid infinite regression.

$\rho[\![\text{sponsor}]\!] =$
$\lambda\kappa\varphi.\lambda\mu\gamma.\lambda\theta^*\sigma\tau\varepsilon^*.\text{allocate-a-group}(\sigma,\mu,\gamma,$
$\quad\quad \lambda\sigma_1\gamma_1.\text{ let } \sigma_2 = \sigma_1[\mu\times\gamma_1\rightarrow<\text{GROUPSTATUS: } \tau(\mu,\mu),$
$\quad\quad\quad\quad\quad\quad\quad\quad\quad\quad\quad\quad\quad\quad\quad\quad\quad \text{true},$
$\quad\quad\quad\quad\quad\quad\quad\quad\quad\quad\quad\quad\quad\quad\quad\quad\quad \text{group-last-change-date}(\gamma,\mu,\sigma_1) >]$
$\quad\quad\quad\quad \text{in adjoin}\; \boxed{\mathcal{R}\text{<apply1 <group } \kappa \text{ } \gamma\text{> } \varphi\text{>}\gamma_1}\; (\mu,\gamma_1)(\theta^*,\sigma_2,\tau,\varepsilon^*) )$

$\text{group-last-change-date}(\gamma,\mu,\sigma) =$
$\quad \text{if } \gamma = \gamma_{init}$
$\quad \text{then } 0$
$\quad \text{else } \text{if } \mu = \text{site}(\gamma)$
$\quad\quad\quad \text{then let } <\text{GROUPSTATUS: } t,\varepsilon,t_1 >= \sigma(\mu,\gamma)$
$\quad\quad\quad\quad\quad \text{in } t$
$\quad\quad\quad \text{else let } <\text{CACHEDVALUE: } t,\varepsilon >= \sigma(\mu,\gamma)$
$\quad\quad\quad\quad\quad \text{in let } <\text{GROUPSTATUS: } t_1,\varepsilon_1,t_2 >= \varepsilon$
$\quad\quad\quad\quad\quad\quad \text{in } t_1$
$\quad\quad\quad \text{endif}$
$\quad \text{endif}$

$\text{step}\; \boxed{\mathcal{R}\text{<group } \kappa \text{ } \gamma\text{>}\varepsilon}\; = \lambda\mu\gamma_1.\text{adjoin}\; \boxed{\mathcal{R}\kappa\varepsilon}\; (\mu,\gamma)$

The **pause!** and **awake!** functions are symmetrical: they just call the *perform-status-change* function to set the running status of the group to **true** or **false**. As usual, the *perform-status-change* function recognizes two cases whether the group object is local or not. If the group is not local then a message (a group write request, identified by $\mathcal{G}_W$) is sent to run *perform-status-change* on the birth site of the group with a `<return>` continuation that will bring back the result.

If the group is local and its group status certain then its running status is changed and the proper clock is incremented.

$$\rho[\![\text{pause!}]\!] = \lambda\kappa\gamma.\textit{perform-status-change}(\kappa, \gamma, \text{false})$$

$$\rho[\![\text{awake!}]\!] = \lambda\kappa\gamma.\textit{perform-status-change}(\kappa, \gamma, \text{true})$$

$$\textit{step}\;\boxed{\mathcal{G}_W\kappa\gamma\varepsilon}\; = \textit{perform-status-change}(\kappa, \gamma, \varepsilon)$$

$\textit{perform-status-change} =$
$\lambda\kappa\gamma\varepsilon.\lambda\mu\gamma_1.\lambda\theta^*\sigma\tau\varepsilon^*.$
    if $\mu = \textit{site}(\gamma)$
    then  if $\textit{group-parentage-known}?(\gamma, \mu, \sigma, \tau)$
         then let $\epsilon = \sigma(\mu, \gamma)$
             and $t = 1 + \tau(\mu, \mu)$
             in let $< \text{GROUPSTATUS: } t_1, \varepsilon_1, t_2 >= \epsilon$
                in let $\varepsilon_2 =< \text{GROUPSTATUS: } t, \varepsilon, t_2 >$
                   in adjoin $\boxed{\mathcal{R}\kappa\varepsilon_1}\,(\mu, \gamma_1)(\theta^*, \sigma[\mu \times \gamma \to \varepsilon_2], \tau[\mu \times \mu \to t], \varepsilon^*)$
        else $\textit{ensure-parentage}(\gamma, \boxed{\mathcal{G}_W\kappa\gamma\varepsilon})(\mu, \gamma_1)(\theta^*, \sigma, \tau, \varepsilon^*)$
        endif
    else $\textit{remote-adjoin site}(\gamma)\boxed{\mathcal{G}_W\texttt{<return } \kappa\ \mu\texttt{>}\gamma\varepsilon}\,(\mu, \gamma_1)(\theta^*, \sigma, \tau, \varepsilon^*)$
    endif

Two new functions were introduced in the previous definition: *group-parentage-known?* and *ensure-parentage*. The first one checks whether a group status is certain i.e., known for sure on a site. The second is called whenever the first answers false, it then tries to remedy to this situation before restarting the actual computation, more on it below.

The function *group-parentage-known?* checks whether a group has a perfectly known status on a site in a given store and at a precise time. The initial group $\gamma_{init}$ is always perfectly known to be running since it is a value that the program cannot grab and therefore cannot mutate. A group status is certain if it is local or validly cached, if it is coherent with its supergroup and if its supergroup status is also certain. This is the case if the date of the last change it perceived from its supergroup is not less than the date of the last change as recorded in the group status of the supergroup, see again figure 7.

$\textit{group-parentage-known}?(\gamma, \mu, \sigma, \tau) =$
$\textit{check}(\gamma)\textbf{whererec}\ \textit{check} =$
    $\lambda\gamma_1.$ if $\gamma_1 = \gamma_{init}$
        then true
        else $\textit{check}(\textit{super}(\gamma_1)) \wedge$
            if $\mu = \textit{site}(\gamma_1)$
            then let $< \text{GROUPSTATUS: } t, \varepsilon, t_1 >= \sigma(\mu, \gamma_1)$
               in $t_1 \geq \textit{group-last-change-date}(\textit{super}(\gamma_1), \mu, \sigma)$
            else let $\epsilon = \sigma(\mu, \gamma_1)$

   in if $\epsilon \in$ CachedValue
    then let $<$ CACHEDVALUE: $t, \varepsilon > = \epsilon$
     in $t = \tau(\mu, site(\gamma_1)) \wedge$
      let $<$ GROUPSTATUS: $t_1, \varepsilon_1, t_2 > = \varepsilon$
      in $t_2 \geq$ group-last-change-date$(super(\gamma_1), \mu, \sigma)$
   else false
   endif
  endif
 endif

If some group status is uncertain then the current computation is suspended while this group status and its consequences are established. The *ensure-parentage* is the most complex function of this paper since it has to deal with multiple cases. It first looks for the first uncertain group starting from top to bottom. If the uncertain group is local, two more cases are recognized whether the known supergroup is also local or not. In both cases, the running status of the supergroup has to be propagated to the current group, this is achieved by fetching the status of the supergroup (with a group read request identified as $\mathcal{G}_R$) with a continuation that will propagate this running status to the uncertain group.

$ensure\text{-}parentage(\gamma, \chi) =$
$\lambda \mu \gamma_1. \lambda \theta^* \sigma \tau \epsilon^*. climb(\gamma, super(\gamma)) \text{whererec } climb =$
 $\lambda \gamma_2 \gamma_3.$ if group-parentage-known?$(\gamma_3, \mu, \sigma, \tau)$
  then if $\mu = site(\gamma_2)$
   then if $\mu = site(\gamma_3)$
    then *adjoin* $\boxed{\mathcal{G}_R\text{<propagate } \gamma_2 \ \chi \ \gamma_1\text{>}\gamma_3} \ (\mu, \gamma_{init})(\theta^*, \sigma, \tau, \epsilon^*)$
    else *remote-adjoin* $site(\gamma_3)$
     $\boxed{\mathcal{G}_R\text{<return <propagate } \gamma_2 \ \chi \ \gamma_1\text{> } \mu\text{>}\gamma_3} \ (\mu, \gamma_{init})(\theta^*, \sigma, \tau, \epsilon^*)$
   endif
  else let $\epsilon = \sigma(\mu, \gamma_2)$
   in if $\epsilon \in$ CachedValue
    then let $<$ CACHEDVALUE: $t, \varepsilon > = \epsilon$
     in if $t = \tau(\mu, site(\gamma_2))$
      then
let $\theta = $<propagate $\gamma_2$ $\boxed{\mathcal{G}_R\text{<return <group-cache } \gamma_2 \ \chi \ \gamma_1\text{> } \mu\text{>}\gamma_2}$ $\gamma_{init}$>
in *remote-adjoin* $site(\gamma_3)$ $\boxed{\mathcal{G}_R\text{<return } \theta \ site(\gamma_2)\text{>}\gamma_3} \ (\mu, \gamma_{init})(\theta^*, \sigma, \tau, \epsilon^*)$
      else *remote-adjoin* $site(\gamma_2)$
     $\boxed{\mathcal{G}_R\text{<return <group-cache } \gamma_2 \ \chi \ \gamma_1\text{> } \mu\text{>}\gamma_2} \ (\mu, \gamma_{init})(\theta^*, \sigma, \tau, \epsilon^*)$
     endif
    else *remote-adjoin* $site(\gamma_2)$
    $\boxed{\mathcal{G}_R\text{<return <group-cache } \gamma_2 \ \chi \ \gamma_1\text{> } \mu\text{>}\gamma_2} \ (\mu, \gamma_{init})(\theta^*, \sigma, \tau, \epsilon^*)$
    endif
   endif
 else $climb(\gamma_3, super(\gamma_3))$
 endif

If the uncertain group is not local then its cached group status might be obsolete or unknown. In that case we simply emit towards its birth site a request to read the uncertain group status with a new continuation that will try to cache this group status when coming back (and if still up to date). This behavior is similar to the behavior of boxes as previously seen.

$$step \boxed{\mathcal{R}\text{<group-cache } \gamma \times \gamma_1 \text{>}\epsilon} =$$
$$\lambda\mu\gamma_2.\lambda\theta^*\sigma\tau\epsilon^*. \text{ let } <\text{CACHEDVALUE: } t, \epsilon > = \epsilon$$
$$\text{in } <\text{STATE: } \{\langle\!\langle \chi, \mu, \gamma_1 \rangle\!\rangle\} \cup \theta^*, \text{ if } t = \tau(\mu, site(\gamma))$$
$$\text{then } \sigma[\mu \times \gamma \to \epsilon]$$
$$\text{else } \sigma$$
$$\text{endif }, \tau, \epsilon^* >$$

If the uncertain group is not local and if its cached group status is valid then that means that it is incoherent wrt its supergroup i.e., it perceived a modification of the running status of its supergroup it has still not propagated. The action to take there is complex since the current site emits a request to the birth site of the group asking it to update itself with respect to its supergroup. In this case, a remote site perceives that a group is incoherent before the birth site of that group.

When a site receives a $\mathcal{G}_\mathcal{R}$ request, it has to return the actual group status of a specified group. It can only do that if the group status is certain otherwise the request is suspended while *ensure-parentage* is run.

$$step \boxed{\mathcal{G}_{R\kappa}\gamma} =$$
$$\lambda\mu\gamma_1.\lambda\theta^*\sigma\tau\epsilon^*. \text{ if } group\text{-}parentage\text{-}known?(\gamma, \mu, \sigma, \tau)$$
$$\text{then } adjoin \boxed{\mathcal{R}\kappa <\text{CACHEDVALUE: } \tau(\mu, \mu), \sigma(\mu, \gamma) >} (\mu, \gamma_1)(\theta^*, \sigma, \tau, \epsilon^*)$$
$$\text{else } ensure\text{-}parentage(\gamma, \boxed{\mathcal{G}_{R\kappa}\gamma})(\mu, \gamma)(\theta^*, \sigma, \tau, \epsilon^*)$$
$$\text{endif}$$

Finally the propagation of the running status from a supergroup to a group just accounts to mutate accordingly the running status of the group provided all its parentage is up to date. When this is ensured and the incoherency is still present then the running status is propagated otherwise it is now superseded by already made new group mutations and simply forgotten.

$$step \boxed{\mathcal{R}\text{<propagate } \gamma \times \gamma_1 \text{>}\epsilon} =$$
$$\lambda\mu\gamma_2.\lambda\theta^*\sigma\tau\epsilon^*.$$
$$\text{let } <\text{CACHEDVALUE: } t, \epsilon > = \epsilon$$
$$\text{in let } <\text{GROUPSTATUS: } t_1, \epsilon_1, t_2 > = \epsilon$$
$$\text{in let } \gamma_3 = super(\gamma)$$
$$\text{in let } \sigma_1 = \text{ if } \mu \neq site(\gamma_3) \wedge$$
$$t = \tau(\mu, site(\gamma_3))$$
$$\text{then } \sigma[\mu \times \gamma_3 \to \epsilon]$$
$$\text{else } \sigma$$
$$\text{endif}$$
$$\text{in if } group\text{-}parentage\text{-}known?(\gamma_3, \mu, \sigma_1, \tau)$$
$$\text{then if let } <\text{GROUPSTATUS: } t_3, \epsilon_2, t_4 > = \sigma_1(\mu, \gamma)$$
$$\text{in } t_4 \geq group\text{-}last\text{-}change\text{-}date(\gamma_3, \mu, \sigma_1)$$
$$\text{then } <\text{STATE: } \{\langle\!\langle \chi, \mu, \gamma_1 \rangle\!\rangle\} \cup \theta^*, \sigma_1, \tau, \epsilon^* >$$
$$\text{else let } t_3 = 1 + \tau(\mu, \mu)$$
$$\text{in let } \epsilon_2 = <\text{GROUPSTATUS: } t_3, \epsilon_1, t_1 >$$

$$\text{in } <\text{STATE: } \{\langle\!\langle \chi, \mu, \gamma_1 \rangle\!\rangle\} \cup \theta^*,$$
$$\sigma_1[\mu \times \gamma \to \epsilon_2],$$
$$\tau[\mu \times \mu \to t_3],$$
$$\epsilon^* >$$

> endif
>
> else $<\text{STATE: } \{\langle\!\langle \chi, \mu, \gamma_1 \rangle\!\rangle\} \cup \theta^*, \sigma_1, \tau, \epsilon^* >$
>
> endif

## 4.2 Scheduler

It is now possible to explicit the scheduler. A thread can only be run if all the groups it belongs to are running. If it is not the case then the missing informations are asked for and the thread is temporarily suspended meanwhile i.e., it is wrapped into a new type of computation: the execution, marked as $\boxed{\mathcal{X}_{\chi\gamma}}$, of computation $\chi$ under sponsorship of $\gamma$.

Among the whole set of threads, the scheduler just *try* one of them, obtain a new state and reiterates the process until all threads are *not-runnable* thus ending the whole program. In fact, a thread can be run if the first group to which it belongs is certain and running. This is sufficient since *group-parentage-known?* implies that all supergroups are running.

Observe that missing informations on groups are asked for under the sponsorship of $\gamma_{init}$ which cannot be suspended.

$try(\theta) =$
$\lambda\theta^*\sigma\tau\epsilon^*.$ let $\langle\!\langle \chi, \mu, \gamma \rangle\!\rangle = \theta$
     in if $group\text{-}parentage\text{-}known?(\gamma, \mu, \sigma, \tau)$
       then if $group\text{-}running?(\gamma, \mu, \sigma, \tau)$
         then $step\ \chi(\mu, \gamma)(\theta^*, \sigma, \tau, \epsilon^*)$
         else $not\text{-}runnable$
         endif
       else $ensure\text{-}parentage(\gamma, \boxed{\mathcal{X}_{\chi\gamma}})(\mu, \gamma)(\theta^*, \sigma, \tau, \epsilon^*)$
       endif

$group\text{-}running?(\gamma, \mu, \sigma, \tau) =$
$\gamma = \gamma_{init} \lor$ if $\mu = site(\gamma)$
       then let $<\text{GROUPSTATUS: } t, \epsilon, t_1 >= \sigma(\mu, \gamma)$
         in $\epsilon$
       else let $<\text{CACHEDVALUE: } t, \epsilon >= \sigma(\mu, \gamma)$
         in let $<\text{GROUPSTATUS: } t_1, \epsilon_1, t_2 >= \epsilon$
           in $\epsilon_1$
       endif

$step\ \boxed{\mathcal{X}_{\chi\gamma}} = \lambda\mu\gamma_1.adjoin\ \chi(\mu, \gamma)$

## 4.3 Discussion

The above group coherency protocol is supported by the previous box protocol. The information on groups is propagated lazily but with an additional constraint related to the tree shape of groups. Any action on a group (scheduling, reading or mutating its running status) is preceded by a check verifying whether the information on that group is up to date. This check ensures a sequentialization of mutations in case of simultaneous **pause!** or **awake!** on embedded groups.

Due to their importance, groups are examples of objects which can be associated to dedicated clocks. To have on each site a second clock recording mutations on local groups independently of local boxes is more efficient since group mutation are more rare and because a box mutation will not invalidate the local groups and thus does not affect the scheduler.

This protocol is rather naïve and may be improved: time-updates messages as encapsulated within *remote-adjoin* are actually run under the sponsorship of a group. If the group is uncertain, then the time-update is deferred instead of being immediately processed. This can be optimized. As for boxes, information on an uncertain group may be asked more than once and would gain if shared. This has to be done in a real implementation to spare bandwidth.

Our implementation of protocols supposes that caches have an arbitrary size since they are never flushed. This would require to abandon the functional representation of the store since it is not possible to inspect the domain of a function in a denotational framework.

# 5  Extensions

The ICSLAS language tries to offer a convenient framework to express distributed computations. This section sketches two new techniques to manage increasing numbers of sites.

## 5.1  Adding sites

Messages carry the set of clocks expressing the perception the emitting site had of all proper clocks. It is rather simple to adjoin a new site to the net of already existing sites. When a site $\mu$ decides to involve a new site $\mu'$ into the computation it participates in, it only has to mention the new clock of $\mu'$ in all the messages it emits. When a third site hears about the existence of $\mu'$, it simply adds it to the set of sites it is aware of and it then propagates the existence of $\mu'$ (through $\mu'$'s clock) in all the messages it now emits.

When a message is emitted, the emitting site pairs all the sites it knows with the clock value it thinks they are. These pairs are appended to the content of the message and transmitted. When a message is received and as pairs (site, clock) are decoded, the existence of new sites is lazily propagated.

If FIFO channels (say TCP connections) were used between two sites then those sites may avoid to exchange any stale clock. A simple trick to achieve this is to time-stamp (with another clock, private to the emitting site and never exchanged) every clock update and to record, associated to the connection, the last time-stamp associated to the clocks sent through this connection. Only clocks incremented after that time-stamp need then to be exchanged. This reduces message size but requires FIFOness.

The problem of removing a site from a computation is much much complex since all the data held by this site have to be saved or migrated towards elsewhere. We do not have actually a good solution for this problem.

## 5.2   Clustering sites

Message size suffers from the number of clocks that have to be propagated. To limit this number, it is possible to gather sites within clusters. Suppose that there exists a single gateway that intercepts all the messages that are emitted by the sites from the cluster to the sites out of the cluster; the gateway does not have to be aware of the internal messages exchanged by sites inside the cluster. Suppose also, to simplify, that this gateway holds a single clock which represents the perception the gateway has of the sum of all the clocks of all the internal sites. Whenever a message is issued from the cluster to the outside, the gateway updates the perception it has of the internal clocks, increments its proper clock to reflect the sum of all the internal clocks; it then removes these clocks from the message, replaces them with its single proper clock and resumes the transmission of the message. In a way, internal clocks are folded into a single one for the exclusive view of the outside of the cluster: a cluster is viewed as a regular site from the outside.

A single change inside the cluster increments the gateway's clock and therefore invalidates all the cached boxes outside the cluster. It is, of course, possible to let the gateway possess more than one clock to limit the invalidations. There again a good mapping from mutable data to their associated clocks is necessary to achieve good performances.

This idea was developed conjunctly with José Piquer.

# 6   Conclusion

Besides the lazy invalidation protocol already presented in [Que94], this paper proposes some original results:

- a functional specification of an abstract machine for an essential applicative, concurrent and distributed language,
- a protocol for the imperative control of groups of cooperating tasks.
- some new ideas to manage greater number of sites.

Although the definitions given above have a strong functional flavor, they can help to figure out how they can be implemented. For instance, distribution is entirely encapsulated within *remote-adjoin* while concurrency is private to *adjoin*. The rest of the definitions do not need to bother about these aspects.

Allied to the GC technique described in [LQP92] and the indirect reference count technique of [Piq91], we expect to release soon a first version of the ICSLAS language. Due to the avoidance of broadcast technology, it seems adapted to the niche of loosely coupled computers, the laziness of its protocols allows it to easily cope with short-term communication failures provided no message is lost. Since ICSLAS belong to the Lisp family of dialects, it has all its usual features: macros, high-order functions, dynamic evaluation, objects and classes [Que93], interactive debugging tools written in Lisp etc.

# Bibliography

[AMST92] Gul Agha, Ian Mason, Scott Smith, and Carolyn Talcott. Towards a theory of actor computation. In W R Cleaveland, editor, *CONCUR '92 – Proceedings of the Third International Conference on Concurrency Theory*, LNCS630, pages 565–579. Springer-Verlag, 1992.

[CR91] William Clinger and Jonathan A Rees. The revised[4] report on the algorithmic language scheme. *Lisp Pointer*, 4(3), 1991.

[Fid88] J. Fidge. Timestamps in message passing systems that preserve the partial ordering. In *Proc. 11th. Australian Computer Science Conference*, pages 55–66, 1988.

[FWH92] Daniel P Friedman, Mitchell Wand, and Christopher Haynes. *Essentials of Programming Languages*. MIT Press, Cambridge MA and McGraw-Hill, 1992.

[Hen80] Peter Henderson. *Functional Programming, Application and Implementation*. International Series in Computer Science. Prentice-Hall, 1980.

[KKR+86] David Kranz, Richard Kelsey, Jonathan A. Rees, Paul Hudak, James Philbin, and Norman I. Adams. Orbit: an optimizing compiler for scheme. In *Proceedings of the SIGPLAN '86 Symposium on Compiler Construction*, pages 219–233. ACM, June 1986.

[LQP92] Bernard Lang, Christian Queinnec, and José Piquer. Garbage collecting the world. In *POPL '92 – Nineteenth Annual ACM symposium on Principles of Programming Languages*, pages 39–50, Albuquerque (New Mexico, USA), January 1992.

[Mat88] F. Mattern. Virtual time and global states of distributed systems. In *Parallel and Distributed Algorithms*, pages 215–226. North-Holland, 1988.

[MH90] Thanasis Mitsolides and Malcolm Harrison. Generators and the replicator control structure in the parallel environment of alloy. In *PLDI '90 –ACM SIGPLAN Programming Languages Design and Implementation*, pages 189–196, White Plains (New-York USA), 1990.

[MSRN92] Masaaki Mizuno, Gurdip Singh, Michel Raynal, and Mitchell L Neilsen. Communication efficient distributed shared memories. Research Report 1817, INRIA, December 1992.

[ODL93] Katia Obraczka, Peter B Danzig, and Shih-Hao Li. Internet resource discovery services. *Computer*, 26(9):8–24, September 1993.

[Piq91] José Miguel Piquer. Indirect reference counting: A distributed garbage collection algorithm. In *PARLE '91 – Parallel Architectures and Languages Europe*, pages 150–165. Lecture Notes in Computer Science 505, Springer-Verlag, June 1991.

[QD93] Christian Queinnec and David De Roure. Design of a concurrent and distributed language. In Robert H Halstead Jr and Takayasu Ito, editors, *Parallel Symbolic Computing: Languages, Systems, and Applications, (US/Japan Workshop Proceedings)*, volume Lecture Notes in Computer Science 748, pages 234–259, Boston (Massachussetts USA), October 1993.

[Que92] Christian Queinnec. A concurrent and distributed extension to scheme. In D. Etiemble and J-C. Syre, editors, *PARLE '92 – Parallel Architectures and Languages Europe*, pages 431–446, Paris (France), June 1992. Lecture Notes in Computer Science 605, Springer-Verlag.

[Que93] Christian Queinnec. Designing MEROON v3. In Christian Rathke, Jürgen Kopp, Hubertus Hohl, and Harry Bretthauer, editors, *Object-Oriented Programming in Lisp: Languages and Applications. A Report on the ECOOP'93 Workshop*, number 788, Sankt Augustin (Germany), September 1993.

[Que94]  Christian Queinnec. Locality, causality and continuations. In *LFP '94 – ACM Symposium on Lisp and Functional Programming*, pages 91–102, Orlando (Florida, USA), June 1994. ACM Press.

[Sch86]  David A Schmidt. *Denotational Semantics, a Methodology for Language Development.* Allyn and Bacon, 1986.

[Sto77]  Joseph E Stoy. *Denotational Semantics: The Scott-Strachey Approach to Programming Language Theory.* MIT Press, Cambridge Massachussetts USA, 1977.

# Multi-threaded PaiLisp with Granularity Adaptive Parallel Execution

Shin-ichi Kawamoto and Takayasu Ito
{kawamoto, ito}@ito.ecei.tohoku.ac.jp

Department of Computer and Mathematical Sciences
Graduate School of Information Sciences
Tohoku University
Sendai 980, Japan

**Abstract.** This paper describes a new implementation of PaiLisp interpreter PaiLisp/MT on a multi-thread architecture. A P-continuation based PaiLisp interpreter called PaiLisp/FX is implemented on Alliant FX/80 [ItoS93]. PaiLisp/FX executes any PaiLisp programs under a non-preemptive scheduling policy and a static task partitioning method called eager task creation(ETC). PaiLisp/MT can be used as an experimental system of granularity adaptive parallel execution of PaiLisp programs to select multiple evaluation strategies. The granularity of programs is estimated by an average execution time and standard deviation of distributions of their execution time according to the granularity of target programs. In case of coarse-grained programs, PaiLisp/MT can execute them under a preemptive scheduling policy and the lazy task creation(LTC). In case of fine-grained programs it can execute them under a non-preemptive scheduling policy and LTC. This kind of adaptation of evaluation strategies can be done according to the granularity of programs and the number of executable processes. Experimental results show that the lazy task creation under the non-preemptive scheduling is very effective for a wide range of parallel programs but the granularity adaptation is useful when a program creates with various degree of granularity.

## 1 Introduction

PaiLisp is a parallelized Scheme based on shared memory architecture. PaiLisp has rich parallel constructs including **future**, an exclusive function closure, a construct to support parallel continuation called P-continuation, parallel-and, parallel-or, etc. Lisp program segments defined by parallel constructs create PaiLisp processes. A P-continuation based PaiLisp interpreter called PaiLisp/FX [ItoS93] is implemented on Alliant FX/80. There are two problems with PaiLisp/FX as follows.

(1) PaiLisp/FX executes all the PaiLisp processes under a non-preemptive scheduling policy. In case of non-preemptive scheduling there is no overhead of context-switching in scheduling PaiLisp processes, since a process will be allocated to a processor in a fixed manner until its completion. However in this case we may have some idle processors which wait completion of executions of processes running on some other processors. This phenomena incur considerable overhead in executions of coarse-grained programs.

(2) The implementation of parallel constructs in PaiLisp/FX is based on a static task partitioning method called eager task creation (ETC), which creates new PaiLisp processes whenever a parallel construct is evaluated. In case of fine-grained programs ETC incurs considerable overhead caused by excessive creation of processes.

For the problem (1) PaiLisp/MT is designed to use a preemptive scheduling policy on the Mach multi-thread mechanism instead of non-preemptive scheduling, to reduce the idling time of processors. For the problem (2) PaiLisp/MT is designed to use a dynamic task partitioning method based on lazy task creation (LTC) [MoKH91] to suppress excessive creation of PaiLisp processes. Thus, our new implementation PaiLisp/MT can be used as an experimental system of granularity adaptive parallel execution of PaiLisp programs to select multiple evaluation strategies. The granularity of programs is estimated by an average execution time and standard deviation of distributions of their execution time according to the granularity of target programs. In case of coarse-grained programs PaiLisp/MT executes them using a preemptive scheduling policy with LTC. In case of fine-grained programs it executes them using a non-preemptive scheduling policy with LTC.

PaiLisp/MT is currently implemented on a shared memory parallel machine with four processors that supports the Mach multi-thread mechanism. The preemptive scheduling of PaiLisp/MT is implemented using the multi-thread mechanism of Mach OS. Each PaiLisp process is executed on one thread of control, and the preemption of a PaiLisp process is realized by context-switching of thread. The method of implementing LTC in PaiLisp/MT adopts a method of implementing LTC in Multilisp so as to handle P-continuation properly.

Section 2 explains PaiLisp and its interpreter PaiLisp/FX, and we point out some problems of the evaluation strategies of PaiLisp/FX. Section 3 discusses the preemptive scheduling, the lazy task creation in PaiLisp environments and granularity adaptive parallel execution in PaiLisp/MT. Section 4 explains the current implementation of PaiLisp/MT. Section 5 explains some experimental results with a set of benchmark programs.

## 2  PaiLisp and its interpreter

In 2.1 we give an outline of PaiLisp and its kernel language PaiLisp-Kernel. In 2.2 we explain an outline of PaiLisp/FX, a PaiLisp interpreter implemented on Alliant FX/80, and we point out some problems of the evaluation strategies of PaiLisp/FX.

### 2.1  PaiLisp

PaiLisp is a parallelized Scheme based on shared memory architecture. PaiLisp-Kernel is a small kernel language of PaiLisp, and it is defined as below:

PaiLisp-Kernel = Scheme + {**spawn, suspend, call/cc, exlambda**}

The four concurrency constructs of PaiLisp-Kernel have the following meanings:

**(spawn** *e*) **spawn** creates a process to compute *e*.

**(suspend) suspend** suspends the execution of a process being executed.

**(call/cc** *e*) **call/cc** of PaiLisp is an extension of Scheme's **call/cc** into concurrency. **call/cc** creates a pair of procedure of one argument to denote its current continuation and the process-id that captured its continuation, and it applies the procedure *e* of one argument to the current continuation. This current continuation with its process-id is called P-continuation. When a P-continuation is invoked, the process which captured it executes the rest of the computation.

**(exlambda** $(x_1 \cdots x_n)$ $e_1 \cdots e_n$**) exlambda** creates an exclusive function closure that is executed exclusively.

In [ItoM90] PaiLisp-Kernel is shown to be universal in the sense that the meanings of all the PaiLisp constructs can be described by PaiLisp-Kernel. Roughly speaking PaiLisp is defined as PaiLisp-Kernel plus some parallel constructs.

$$\text{PaiLisp} = \text{PaiLisp-Kernel} + \{\textbf{pcall}, \textbf{par}, \textbf{future}, \textbf{par-and}, \cdots \}$$

, where **pcall**, **par**, **future** and **par-and** have the following meanings.

**(pcall** *f* $e_1 \cdots e_n$**) pcall** supports a parallel evaluation of functional form. After completion of parallel execution of $e_1, \cdots, e_n$ the expression *f* is evaluated and then its resulting value will be applied to the values of $e_1, \cdots, e_n$.

**(par** $e_1 \cdots e_n$**) par** is a structured concurrency construct and creates the child processes which compute $e_1, \cdots, e_n$ in parallel, and it terminates when the executions of all the child processes terminate.

**(future** *e*) **future** is a construct introduced by Halstead[Hals84b] in Multilisp. **future** returns a special virtual value for *e*, called the future-value, and it creates concurrently a new process which computes *e*. The parent process continues its execution using the future-value for *e*. When an operation on the future-value for *e* requires the true value it will be suspended until the true value of *e* is obtained. The action to obtain the true value for the future-value is called **force**.

**(par-and** $e_1 \cdots e_n$**) par-and** executes $e_1, \cdots, e_n$ in parallel and if one of them $e_k$ yields false then the result of the **par-and** statement becomes false, terminating all the executions of other running processes among $e_1, \cdots, e_n$. If none of $e_1, \cdots, e_n$ yields false then the value of $e_n$ is returned as the value of this statement.

The other concurrency constructs and their meanings are described in [ItoM90].

## 2.2 PaiLisp/FX

A P-continuation based PaiLisp interpreter called PaiLisp/FX [ItoS93] is implemented on a shared-memory parallel machine Alliant FX/80 with eight processors, running under Concentrix OS. In PaiLisp/FX a PaiLisp process is interpreted by the Abelson-Sussman's Register Machine [AbeS85]. Each register machine (RM) is realized as a unix process on Alliant FX/80, being executed in parallel. The organization of PaiLisp/FX is illustrated in Fig. 1. RM evaluates PaiLisp expressions calling the system internal function named eval_dispatch.

eval_dispatch is a function to sort PaiLisp expressions and to call a specific internal routine. eval_dispatch is called whenver a PaiLis expression is evaluated.

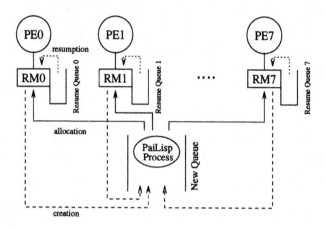

**Fig. 1.** Organization of PaiLisp/FX

Each RM has a LIFO queue called the resume queue. The RMs share a FIFO queue called the new queue. These queues are used to schedule executions of PaiLisp processes. A PaiLisp process takes one of four different states, *queued, running, killed,* and *suspended.* A new PaiLisp process created by evaluation of a parallel construct is stored in the new queue with *queued.* If a PaiLisp process is suspended by **suspend** or **exlambda**, it becomes *suspended.* When a suspended PaiLisp process is resumed for execution it must be stored into the resume queue of the RM. If a PaiLisp process is terminated, it falls into *killed.* When a PaiLisp process becomes *killed* or *suspended* the RM checks its own resume queue and new queue in this order to see if there exists any PaiLisp process. If there is any the RM takes it and executes it. If there exists no PaiLisp process in these queues, the RM repeats to check them. Once a RM initiates the execution of a PaiLisp process, its execution will be continued until the PaiLisp process becomes *suspended* or *killed.* This fixed scheduling policy is called the *non-preemptive scheduling.*

**On non-preemptive scheduling**

In case of non-preemptive scheduling a process will be allocated to a processor in a fixed manner until its completion(that is, until it falls into *killed* or *suspended*), so that there is no overhead of context-switching in scheduling PaiLisp processes. However it will be not efficient to execute coarse-grained programs with non-preemptive scheduling, since we do not fully utilize the computing power of the parallel machine. Consider an execution of

$$(\textbf{par } A \ B \ C \ D \ E)$$

under non-preemptive scheduling with four processors. For simplicity, we assume that the arguments $A, \cdots, E$ are coarse-grained and independent each other, and they consume the same execution time $T$ with the cost of process creation $\delta t$. Fig. 2 illustrates an example of executing the processes created by the expression, using four processors PE0, PE1, PE2 and PE3. The four arguments $A, B, C, D$ are allocated and executed in parallel with the processors PE0, PE1, PE2, PE3, respectively. After completion of execution of $A$, the remaining $E$ will be allocated and executed on PE0. Because of non-preemptive scheduling and the meaning of the **par** statement three processors (PE1,PE2,PE3) will become idle until completion of the execution of $E$. In order to reduce the idling time of processors we introduce a preemptive scheduling policy.

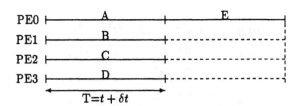

**Fig. 2.** Execution of (**par** $A$ $B$ $C$ $D$ $E$) in non-preemptive scheduling

### On Eager Task Creation

In PaiLisp/FX the implementation of parallel constructs such as **spawn**, **par**, **pcall** and **future** are based on eager task creation(ETC), which creates new Pai-Lisp processes whenever a parallel construct is evaluated. Eager task creation is a straightforward implementation method for concurrency constructs. However, ETC may incur considerable overhead caused by process creation in case of fine-grained programs that create many PaiLisp processes with small execution time. In order to reduce these overheads we introduce the dynamic task partitioning method called the lazy task creation (LTC)[MoKH91].

## 3   Design of PaiLisp/MT

PaiLisp/MT is designed to support an adaptive strategy of parallel executions of PaiLisp programs according to the granularity of programs on a shared-memory parallel architecture with the multi-thread mechanism. The parallel architecture with the multi-thread mechanism allows us to implement **preemptive scheduling** in addition to **non-preemptive scheduling**, and in order to execute parallel constructs we can introduce two task partitioning methods, **eager task creation (ETC)** and **lazy task creation (LTC)**. Combining these scheduling strategies and task partitioning methods we give multiple evaluation strategies of PaiLisp processes created by PaiLisp program segments. The granularity adaptive parallelization of PaiLisp/MT is realized as a system to select these multiple evaluation strategies according to the granularity of programs and the number of executable processes. In 3.1 we explain the preemptive scheduling based on a multi-thread mechanism. In 3.2 we explain how to introduce LTC into PaiLisp/MT. In 3.3 we explain our basic ideas to realize the granularity adaptive parallel execution integrating these scheduling policies and task partitioning methods.

## 3.1 Preemptive scheduling based on the multi-thread mechanism

PaiLisp/FX uses a non-preemptive scheduling that may not be efficient for coarse-grained parallel programs, as was explained in the previous section. In order to execute coarse-grained programs efficiently we introduce a preemptive scheduling into PaiLisp/MT. The preemptive scheduling of PaiLisp/MT is a scheduling policy in which PaiLisp processes are executed for a certain time-slice called time quantum one after another. An example of executing the previous expression (**par** *A B C D E*) under the preemptive scheduling with four processors is shown in Fig. 3.

$$T_q = T/4$$

**Fig. 3.** Example of executing (**par** *A B C D E*) under preemptive scheduling

In this example the PaiLisp processes $A, B, C, D$ and $E$ will be chopped into small pieces of processes. With this preemptive scheduling we can reduce the idling time of processors. But, the preemptive scheduling may incur some overhead of context-switchings of PaiLisp processes which are indicated as $o$ in Fig. 3. Also PaiLisp process migrations caused by context-switchings cost some amount of overhead, since when a processor executes another PaiLisp process the information about that process may not exist on the cache of that processor. Therefore we have to consider carefully about the following points to minimize a context-switching overhead, the number of context-switching, and PaiLisp process migrations.

1. How to implement context-switchings of PaiLisp processes.
2. How to allocate pieces of PaiLisp processes to processors.

The preemptive scheduling of PaiLisp/MT is realized using the multi-thread mechanism of Mach OS. Mach OS supports a preemptive scheduling of threads, performing their context-switchings. In Mach OS [Blac90] when a processor begins to run a thread, that thread is assigned a time slice called a time quantum. Periodic clock interrupts decrement this quantum. When the quantum expires the thread scheduler causes a context switch if there is another runnable thread with higher priority, otherwise the original thread continues running with a new quantum. The cost of context-switching of threads is usually much smaller than that of context-switching of UNIX processes. And Mach attempts to minimize the number of context switchings of threads using time quanta. Fig. 3 is drawn taking into account this kind of behaviors of the Mach OS.

In such implementation there are two limitations of applying preemptive scheduling to target programs for efficient execution.

1. The number of context-switchings of PaiLisp processes increases as the number of PaiLisp processes increases. The execution time of a program which creates many PaiLisp processes under preemptive scheduling will exceed that under non-preemptive scheduling. Therefore a preemptive scheduling is applicable to programs which create a small amount of PaiLisp processes with relatively large execution time.

2. The time quantum assigned by the Mach OS of the machine used for PaiLisp/MT is about 100 [msec]. If the execution time of PaiLisp processes are smaller than 100 [msec], those processes should be executed under non-preemptive scheduling with context-switching of threads. Therefore a preemptive scheduling is applicable to programs which create PaiLisp processes with execution time longer than 100 [msec].

### On implementation of the preemptive scheduling

In our model of PaiLisp interpreter a register machine RM executes PaiLisp processes. Therefore the preemptive scheduling by use of context-switchings of threads is realized by allocating each register machine to a thread, and we create the RMs (which are realized by threads) with the same number of the PaiLisp processes. By a preemptive scheduling of threads in Mach OS, the RMs will be executed under preemptive scheduling, and PaiLisp processes on each RM will be executed piece by piece.

When the number of PaiLisp processes is smaller than the number of RM, the RMs with no allocated processes tries to get PaiLisp processes from the resume queue and the new queue repeatedly. This excessive repetitive actions create another overhead. In order to reduce this overhead we need to terminate the RMs which perform these excessive repetitive actions. Thus the RMs should be implemented as follows:

1. if there exists any PaiLisp process in the resume queue it will be executed and then go to 1,
2. if there exists any PaiLisp process in the new queue it will be executed and then go to 1,
3. terminate the RM.

A terminated RM will be re-started when a new PaiLisp process is created and it is registered at the new queue.

### 3.2   Dynamic partitioning of PaiLisp processes

The eager task creation ETC used in PaiLisp/FX is not an efficient method in executing fine-grained programs because of high cost of creating many fine-grained processes, as was explained in the previous section. It is well known[Hals90] [MoKH91] [Feel93a] [WeeP90] that in case of fine-grained programs the dynamic task partitioning methods ( load based partitioning and lazy task creation ) are superior to a static task partitioning method like ETC. The load based partitioning (LBP) is simple to implement and efficient for many programs, but LBP falls into deadlock for some programs. The lazy task creation (LTC) is slightly harder to implement, but it is deadlock-free and more efficient than LBP for almost all programs. Thus, we use LTC as the dynamic task partitioning method in PaiLisp/MT.

## Lazy task creation in PaiLisp/MT

The lazy task creation LTC introduced in Multilisp[MoKH91] is a dynamic task partitioning method for **future** to execute fine-grained programs efficiently. Consider the execution of $(f$ (**future** $e))$. According to LTC in Multilisp [MoKH91] this expression means "Start evaluating $e$ in the current task, but save enough information so that its continuation $f$ can be moved to a separate task if another processor becomes idle". An idle processor and busy processor will be called a thief and victim, respectively. We would like to introduce this clever dynamic task partitioning method into PaiLisp/MT. However, in order to introduce this idea of lazy task creation into PaiLisp/MT we need to modify the implementation procedure of Multilisp, since the notion of **continuation** is different in two systems. That is, Multilisp uses the Scheme continuation, while PaiLisp uses its own continuation called P-continuation, an extension of Scheme continuation into concurrency. In the rest of this paragraph we explain how to modify and extend LTC for its implementation in PaiLisp.

## P-continuation and LTC

Unlike Scheme continuation a P-continuation is defined for each process, and a P-continuation of a process is a package of its process-id and the continuation. Thus when a P-continuation is invoked the process to execute the rest of computation is the process that captured the P-continuation[ItoM90][ItoS92]. Consider the following program:

```
(K (call/cc (lambda (resume)
              (begin (future (resume (f x)))        ···(1)
                     (suspend))))))
```

**call/cc** captures the P-continuation which is the rest of the computation K with its process-id, and it applies the lambda closure to this P-continuation. The application of the lambda closure binds this P-continuation to the variable **resume**, and the body of the closure will be evaluated under the new environment after this binding. In ETC a new PaiLisp process to compute (**resume** (**f x**)) will be created, and its execution will be suspended by **suspend**. When the execution of (**f x**) is finished by another processor, it invokes its P-continuation with the value of (**f x**). This invocation of P-continuation resumes the suspended parent process executing the computation K with the value of (**f x**). This situation is illustrated in Fig. 4 (a). In LTC the body part of **future** will be executed by the parent process, and the continuation (parent task) stolen by an idle processor will be created as another process. The P-continuation captured before the execution of **future** is the rest of computation of the parent task, so that its application must be executed on the newly-created process of the continuation (parent task). This is illustrated in Fig. 4 (b).

## On implementation of LTC in PaiLisp/MT

P-continuation is realized as a pair of a pointer to a copy of the stack of the process captured it and a pointer to process-id. Upon application of P-continuation the invoked process must be executed with the process denoted by **process-id** using the contents of the copied stack. For correct implementation of LTC under

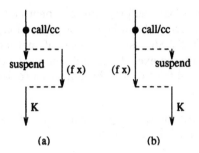

**Fig. 4. future** and invocation of P-continuation

PaiLisp environments with P-continuation we must keep consistency of **process-id** during the course of stealing of the rest of computation, since the process-ids will change during the stealing actions. A simple method is as follows:

- identify the body-part of **future** by a new process-id, and save the old process-id together with the rest of computation.
- the rest of computation will be executed, recovering the old process-id.
- when the rest of computation is stolen, it will be executed with the (saved) old process-id on the thief processor.

### 3.3 Granularity adaptive parallel execution

#### On granularity adaptive parallelization
PaiLisp/MT is designed as a system of granularity adaptive parallel execution of PaiLisp programs to select multiple evaluation strategies based on two scheduling policies and two task partitioning methods according to the granularity of processes and the number of executable processes. Before discussing the granularity adaptation in PaiLisp/MT we briefly explain what is being done in **granularity adaptive parallelization** of parallel programs.

The granularity adaptive parallelization in executing parallel programs is known to be one of the most interesting yet difficult topics in parallel programming. According to our knowledge there is no precise definition nor definite framework of the granularity adaptive parallelization of parallel programs yet. However there are several attempts related to this topics:

1. to give efficient methods of parallel programs, depending upon granularity of parallel programs.
   The load based partitioning and lazy task creation in the previous paragraph are such methods in fine-grained parallel Lisp programs, and the load-balancing method is a well-known and commonly used method in various situations.
2. to estimate granularity of functional programs and logic programs for parallel evaluation.
   The dynamic granularity estimation relative to thread-creation costs and degree of parallelization has been attempted in [HuLA94] and [DeLH90].
3. to analyze and estimate execution time of Lisp programs and functional programs.

The time-complexity of parallel programs can be used to estimate the granularity of programs in terms of symbolic cost expressions to denote execution time of programs. [ItTW86] uses this kind of method to give theoretical comparisons of interpreted executions and compiled executions of pure Lisp programs, and [ReiG94] tries to use this approach to dynamic parallelization of functional programs.

To develop the granularity adaptive parallelization of parallel programs it is hoped to clarify and explore the following:

1. how to define granularity of programs
2. how to estimate granularity of programs
3. how to decide and design methods of evaluating programs in terms of their granularity
4. how to implement various evaluation strategies efficiently
5. how to adjust adaptively parameters and knowledge bases to select various evaluation strategies
6. how to transform a parallel program into an effectively-executable one, using the granularity information of processes to be created by the program.
7. how to integrate multiple evaluation strategies and adaptation mechanisms to form a good adaptive system on a given parallel machine.

This assumes the existence and availability of parallel machines good for the purpose. So we need to explore good parallel machines to realize granularity adaptive parallelization.

Generally speaking the granularity adaptive parallelization of parallel programs is a method to extract and utilize full processing power of a parallel machine by adaptive application of optimal evaluation strategies and by an optimal transformation of programs according to granularity of programs, and if the machine configuration is adjustable the adaptive capability should be extended to cope with optimal adaptive re-configuration of the machine organization.

The current granularity adaptive parallel execution of PaiLisp/MT is only an infant step toward an ideal granularity adaptive parallelization of parallel programs.

**Granularity adaptive parallel execution in PaiLisp/MT**
PaiLisp/MT is designed as an experimental system of granularity adaptive parallel execution of PaiLisp programs to select multiple evaluation strategies according to the granularity of processes and the number of executable processes. In order to design and implement such a system we have to give

- a method of estimating granularity of parallel programs
- a method of adaptive selection method of evaluation strategies according to the granularity of processes.

In general the granularity of a program will be defined or decided in terms of

- execution steps by its computation
- memory size used in its computation ,

both of which depend on the size and structure of input data for the program. In case of parallel programs we must take into account the number of executable processes relative to the number of available processors. As was mentioned in the above paragraph there are at least a number of methods to estimate granularity of programs. However it is not an easy task to give a good estimate of granularity of parallel programs.

### On estimation of granularity of parallel programs

In case of PaiLisp/MT the granularity of parallel programs is determined by distributions of execution time of executable processes. It will be interesting to apply theory-based yet practical methods of estimating execution steps used in [ItTW86] and [ReiG94]. However, the current PaiLisp/MT uses the following simple and easy way to estimate the granularity of parallel programs, based on average execution time and the number of executable processes. First, we prepare a set of benchmark parallel programs to estimate their granularity. We actually execute these benchmark programs and calculate

- the average execution time of processes created by the programs

and

- the number of executable processes created by the programs

, changing the size of their input data. We can visualize their distributions on the (execution time)-(number of processes) coordinate, which will be called the eT-nP coordinate. Notice that a parallel program will usually create many processes with various degree of granularity. Instead of using these distributions we calculate an average and standard deviation for each of these distributions for each input data. At this point we can think of a region determined by the average and standard deviation, and we can draw the traces of these regions, changing input data for the programs, to see a profile of behaviors of the programs. When a parallel program is given, there will be the following cases:

(1) static case

Let us assume that it is possible to execute the parallel program to calculate its approximate granularity identified by its average and standard deviation of execution time of processes together with the number of processes created. In this case we can easily see

- where the granularity of the program is located in the eT-nP coordinate

and

- which benchmark program is the nearest to the given program in its granularity.

Using these information we can determine an appropriate evaluation strategy, as will be discussed below. In actual executions of parallel programs they create executable processes dynamically, so that we will be able to draw a dynamic profile of creation of processes using the traces of the average and standard deviation of execution time. These dynamic profiles will be more useful to see the dynamic nature of granularity of processes.

(2) dynamic case

Let us assume that the given program cannot be run repeatedly. In this case we have to estimate the granularity of the given program dynamically. As the executions of the given program proceed, they will create executable processes, and they will be actually executed. Concurrently with these executions the average execution time and the number of processes will be calculated periodically with a certain time interval. In this case, for example, during the first stage (determined by the time intervals) the granularity of the first segment of the program may be coarse-grained, but as the executions of the program proceed the granularity of the program may change to fine-grained. This kind of situations often occur, since a parallel program creates many sub-processes with various degree of granularity. In this dynamic case it will happen that we have to change evaluation strategies during the course of executions of a program.

The number of executable processes can be easily determined by counting the number of processes created by a parallel program. However, in order to estimate an execution time of each process we need some technique to calculate it, since we cannot use the system timer to estimate an execution time of fine-grained processes with a small amount of execution time. In case of PaiLisp/MT every evaluation of a PaiLisp expression is done under `eval_dispatch`. To estimate an execution time of a program we can use the number of calls to `eval_dispatch` during a course of executions of the program. According to the current implementation of PaiLisp/MT one call to `eval_dispatch` corresponds to about 1/75000 sec.

### On granularity adaptation
According to the discussions in 3.1 and 3.2 we can observe the following phenomena.

- It is obvious that when the number of executable processes is smaller than the number of processors the ETC under NPS is more effective than any other execution strategies, since there exists no overhead caused by this fixed evaluation mode.
- It is known that for fine-grained programs with a large number of processes the lazy task creation (LTC) is more effective than the eager task creation.
- For coarse-grained programs with a small number of processes, the preemptive scheduling (PS) is more effective than non-preemptive scheduling (NPS). Under this circumstance we can expect that LTC is more effective than ETC according to the efficient inlining in LTC.

We can think of the following evaluation strategies:

**NPS+ETC**, which means the use of ETC under NPS.

**NPS+LTC**, which means the use of LTC under NPS.

**PS+LTC**, which means the use of LTC under PS.

The granularity adaptation of PaiLisp/MT is to select one of

$$\{NPS+ETC, NPS+LTC, PS+LTC\}$$

according to the estimate of granularity of programs and the number of executable processes. Again, we work on a set of benchmark programs to see which benchmark programs are better to be executed in which evaluation strategies. When a program is given we estimate its granularity using the average execution time and standard deviation or their dynamic profile in the eT-nP coordinate. With these information we determine which evaluation strategy is better for the given program, comparing to the results for the benchmark programs.

# 4 Implementation of PaiLisp/MT

In 4.1 we explain an outline of PaiLisp/MT. In 4.2 we describe an implementation of schedulings using the multi-thread mechanism of Mach OS. In 4.3 we explain an implementation of lazy task creation in the PaiLisp environments. In 4.4 we describe our current implementation of granularity adaptive parallel execution in PaiLisp/MT.

## 4.1 Outline of PaiLisp/MT

PaiLisp/MT is implemented on a multi-thread parallel machine OMRON LUNA88K with four MC88100 processors, running under Mach2.5 OS. We used C-thread library of Mach2.5 to handle threads. PaiLisp/MT is a multi-threaded version of PaiLisp interpreter based on PaiLisp/FX for the study of granularity adaptive parallel execution, so that PaiLisp processes are interpreted on Abelson-Sussman's Register Machine (RM). Each RM is executed on a thread. The organization of PaiLisp/MT is illustrated in Fig. 5. RM evaluates PaiLisp expressions calling the system internal function named eval_dispatch. eval_dispatch is a function to be used for sorting PaiLisp expressions, and it is called whenever a PaiLisp expression is evaluated.

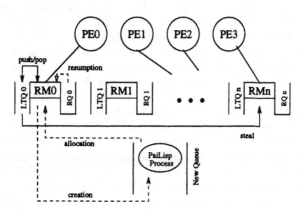

**Fig. 5.** Organization of PaiLisp/MT

The system creates several threads, the number of which is the same as the process threshold *PT* mentioned below, and on these threads the register machine RMs are executable. Each RM has its own *resume queue*(RQ), and the RMs share a *new queue*(NQ). Moreover each RM has its own double-ended queue named *lazy task queue* (LTQ) for selective inlining of LTC.

## 4.2 Implementation of scheduling using multi-thread mechanism

The preemptive scheduling of PaiLisp/MT is implemented using context-switchings of threads under Mach OS. PaiLisp/MT creates several threads, and RM will be executed on each thread. There is a flag named `rm_sleep_flag` which controls the termination of RM. If this flag is false all of the RMs will be executed, namely PaiLisp processes will be executed with preemptive scheduling (PS). If this flag becomes true several RMs which exceed the number of processors will be terminated with `condition_wait` C-thread library function. Therefore each running RM will be allocated to a processor in a fixed manner, and PaiLisp processes are executed under non-preemptive scheduling (NPS). So, it is possible to change the scheduling policy of PaiLisp/MT changing the status flag `rm_sleep_flag`.

As we described in 3.1, a repetitive action of RM under a preemptive scheduling causes overhead. To reduce this overhead, a RM which has no executable PaiLisp process will be terminated using `condition_wait` C-thread library function. If a new PaiLisp process is stored into the new queue or a rest of the computation is stored into LTQ, all terminated RMs are re-started using `condition_broadcast` C-thread library function.

## 4.3 Implementation of lazy task creation

We modified the Mohr's implementation of LTC called SM protocol [MoKH91] [Feel93a] to handle P-continuation properly. In the current PaiLisp/MT only a **future** construct is implemented using LTC.

Each register machine (RM) has a double-ended queue named lazy task queue (LTQ) in addition to the resume queue (RQ). When a **future** is evaluated on the register machine RM0, a new process-id will be created and the current process-id will be exchanged for it. Then a pair of the old process-id and a stack pointer which represents the rest of the computation of the **future** will be pushed into the LTQ tail of RM0. Namely the rest of the computation of the **future** is stored with its process-id, and the **future**'s body part will be executed with a new process-id. After completion of the **future**'s body part, RM0 pops a pair of process-id and a stack pointer from its own LTQ tail, and RM0 restores an extracted process-id and stack pointer, and then it executes the rest of the computation. When another register machine RM1 becomes idle, it searches other RM's LTQ. If there are some pairs of process-id and stack pointer on RM0's LTQ, RM1 extracts one of them from its LTQ head, and it copies a part of RM0's stack which is indicated by the extracted stack pointer. After then RM1 attaches the extracted process-id on the body part of RM1's process, and it executes the rest of the computation of a **future** using the copied stack and extracted process-id. In such implementation the rest of the computation of a **future**, namely the **future**'s parent process, has a fixed process-id, and a P-continuation will be executed on a proper process.

Consider that the PaiLisp program (1) mentioned in 3.2 is executed on RM0 with the process-id p0. The evaluation of the **call/cc** creates a P-continuation PC0 which contains the rest of the computation K and a pointer to the process-id p0. When the **future** is evaluated RM0 pushes a pointer to the **future**'s continuation which includes **suspend** with the process-id p0 on LTQ tail, creating its new process-id p1. This situation is illustrated in Fig. 6(a). When the RM1 steals a **future**'s continuation from the RM0's LTQ head, the contents of the stack A indicated in Fig. 6 are transferred to the RM1's stack, and the process-id p0 is attached to the process body of RM1 as is illustrated in Fig. 6(b). Therefore RM1 executes the rest of the computation identified by the process-id p0. Since

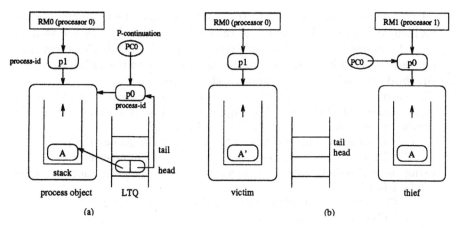

**Fig. 6.** Implementation of LTC in PaiLisp/MT

the P-continuation PC0 has the process-id p0, its invocation leads to the correct execution of K on RM1.

In this implementation of LTC in PaiLisp/MT, a process-id is created whenever a **future** is evaluated. Its creation gives some amount of cost, but according to our experiments this overhead is small.

### 4.4 Implementation of granularity adaptive parallel execution

In order to realize an simple mechanism of granularity adaptive parallel execution mentioned in 3.3, we installed the following mechanisms in PaiLisp/MT:

**(1) multiple evaluation strategies based on {NPS, PS} and {ETC, LTC}**

We already explained
- what NSP, PS, ETC and LTC are
- how to implement them
- how they are implemented.

In the current implementation we can choose any combination from {NPS, PS} and {ETC, LTC}, although only NPS+LTC and PS+LTC have practical significances according to the current granularity adaptation in PaiLisp/MT.

**(2) methods of estimating granularity of programs**

The granularity of processes created by programs will be estimated by calculating an average execution time of processes in the current system. Since an execution time of a fine-grained process is too small to be counted by the system timer of the machine we use an approximate yet sufficient method to count up the number of calls to the **eval_dispatch** routine to estimate an average execution time. It is experimentally known that one call to **eval_dispatch** corresponds to 1/75000 sec.

**eval_dispatch** is a function to be used for sorting PaiLisp expressions in PaiLisp/MT, and it is called whenever a PaiLisp expression is evaluated. Thus the number of calls to **eval_dispatch** in execution of a process is considered to be proportional to the execution time of the process. In the PaiLisp/MT system the number of calls will be counted up in the variable *gcount* equipped in each PaiLisp process. Also, the number of executable processes created by programs will be counted up into the variable *pcount*.

**(3) methods of switching evaluation strategies**

The current methods of selecting and switching evaluation strategies are quite simple and premature. We employ the following simple methods the current system. We have two threshold values:

$GT$: Granularity threshold (a threshold value for granularity)

$PT$: Process threshold(a threshold value for the number of processes)

Using these threshold values we select and switch the evaluation strategies by the following rule:

PS+LTC    when *gcount* > $GT$ and *pcount* < $PT$,

NPS+LTC   otherwise

Since the NPS+LTC mode has a good applicability for a wide range of programs we use the following execution mode as a current standard in the system:

- an evaluation starts with the NPS+LTC mode, and the number of calls to **eval_dispatch** and the number of executable processes will be counted by *gcount* and *pcount*, respectively.

- when *gcount* > $GT$ and *pcount* < $PT$ are satisfied the evaluation strategy will be switched from NPS+LTC to PS+LTC, and when it happens that this condition is not satisfied in the progress of computation the evaluation strategy will be switched to NPS+LTC, again.

How to determine $GT$ and $PT$ adaptively are being examined together with some experiments. Also, the use of the standard deviation of distributions and the dynamic profile of process behaviors is being contemplated, with some preliminary experiments.

# 5    Experimental results of PaiLisp/MT

PaiLisp/MT has been implemented on a parallel machine OMRON LUNA88K with four processors running under the Mach 2.5 OS, as is explained in the previous section. We performed some preliminary experiments of PaiLisp/MT using several benchmark programs. In 5.1 we explain preliminary results on granularity of PaiLisp programs and multiple evaluation strategies based on {NPS, PS} and {ETC, LTC} for a set of benchmark programs. In 5.2 we show some experimental results to see dynamic natures of behaviors of parallel programs for future extension and exploration of granularity adaptive parallel execution in PaiLisp/MT.

## 5.1    Experiments on program granularity and evaluation strategies

In order to see the relationship between program granularity and evaluation strategies we performed some experiments of running PaiLisp/MT for a set of benchmark programs.

The following seven benchmark programs were used in our experiments [1]
```
        fib  tarai  queen  qsort  prolog  tsp  fatwalk
```
The program texts of these programs are available by anonymous ftp
from
```
                    ftp.ito.ecei.tohoku.ac.jp
```
on directory
```
                    /pub/pailisp/benchmark
```
, and the program texts of fib, tarai, queen, qsort and fatwalk are also given
in APPENDIX I.
Our experimental environments are as follows:

**System:** PaiLisp/MT on OMRON LUNA88K under the Mach 2.5 OS
**Number of threads for the RMs (= _PT_):** 16
**Evaluation Strategies:** NSP+ETC, NPS+LTC, PS+ETC, PS+LTC
**Granularity measure:** Number of calls to eval_dispatch,
where 1 call to eval_dispatch corresponds to about 1/75000 sec.
**Actual benchmark programs with the input data:**
tarai940 = (tarai 9 4 0)
fib20 = (fib 20)
queen8 = (queen 8)
qsort2000 = (qsort list-of-2000-data)
prologq4 = (prolog test-program-queen4)
tsp11 = (tsp c11)
fatwalk9 = (fatwalk 9)
where prolog is a Pure Prolog interpreter written in PaiLisp, tsp is a PaiLisp
program of traveling salesman problem, and the meanings of other programs
are obvious from the program texts in APPENDIX I. (Some additional explanations are available from the *anonymous ftp* mentioned above.)

Table 1 shows an experimental result for the benchmark programs, when we fix
the evaluation strategies to one of {NPS+ETC, NPS+LTC, PS+ETC, PS+LTC}
for each of the benchmark programs. In this table,

- #-executable processes means the total number of processes created by the
  corresponding programs.
- $T_e$ and $\sigma_e$ means the average execution time and the standard deviation
  expressed by the number of calls to eval_dispatch of each program, respectively. $T_t$ and $\sigma_t$ are calculated from $T_e$ and $\sigma_e$, respectively, assuming that
  1 call to eval_dispatch is 1/75000 sec.

We can observe the following from the results of Table 1

1. tarai940 and fib20 create many fine-grained processes with the small average
   execution time $T_e$ and the small standard deviation $\sigma_e$. They are considered
   as fine-grained programs, and NPS+LTC is the most effective evaluation
   strategy for these programs, as is expected.
2. tsp11 and fatwalk9 create a small number of processes with fairly long average execution time $T_e$, although their standard deviations are different

---

[1] The function **tarai** is often called the **tak** function in the literatures outside Japanese
Lisp community.

**Table 1.** Granularity of benchmark programs and their execution times under four
evaluation strategies

| program | tarai940 | fib20 | queen8 | qsort2000 | prologq4 | tsp11 | fatwalk9 |
|---|---|---|---|---|---|---|---|
| # of executable processes | 27613 | 10944 | 5507 | 2000 | 135 | 11 | 9 |
| $T_e$ | 27 | 27 | 145 | 534 | 11608 | 45631 | 104512 |
| $T_t$ [msec] | 0.36 | 0.36 | 1.93 | 7.12 | 155 | 608 | 1390 |
| $\sigma_e$ | 23 | 25 | 92 | 2708 | 4296 | 28423 | 0 |
| $\sigma_t$ | 0.31 | 0.33 | 1.23 | 36.11 | 57.28 | 378.97 | 0 |
| NPS+ETC [sec] | 5.85 | 2.04 | 3.29 | 5.25 | 12.04 | 4.92 | 3.48 |
| NPS+LTC [sec] | 2.67 | 0.86 | 2.81 | 4.96 | 11.89 | 4.43 | 3.44 |
| PS+ETC [sec] | 8.29 | 2.88 | 3.47 | 5.36 | 12.59 | 4.03 | 3.07 |
| PS+LTC [sec] | 3.43 | 1.03 | 3.15 | 5.24 | 13.61 | 3.32 | 2.96 |

(that is, very small in fatwalk9 but very big in tsp11). These programs are
considered as coarse-grained, and PS+LTC is the most effective evaluation
strategy for these programs, as is expected.

3. According to this experiment queen8 may be considered as a fine-grained program, so that NPS+LTC is the effective evaluation strategy for this program.
qsort2000 and prologq4 may be considered as a kind of medium-grained
programs, since they are located at an intermediate position between fine-
grained and coarse-grained according to their average execution time and
the number of processes created by them. But this experimental results tell
that even for these programs NPS+LTC is the most effective according to
Table 1. That is, we may say that NPS+LTC is very effective for a wide
range of granularity of parallel programs except for a class of apparently
coarse-grained programs.

These observations tell that LTC (which reduces the idling time of processors by inlining and stealing) is an efficient method. Also, we can estimate the
overhead of process creation from this experiment in the following way.

**On estimation of overhead of process creation**
Analyzing the execution time of ETC and LTC evaluations under NPS we can
estimate the overhead of a process creation. Let us consider the NPS+ETC and
NPS+LTC evaluations for tarai940 and fib20.

- In case of NPS+ETC mode the execution times of tarai940 and fib20 are
    5.85 [sec],
    2.04 [sec]
, respectively, according to Table 1. Since four processors are used for computation we can say that the total computation time is about
    5.85 [sec] × 4 = 23.40 [sec]    for tarai940
    2.04 [sec] × 4 = 8.16 [sec]     for fib20.
In this case the number of created processes are
    27613    for tarai940
    10944    for fib20
- In case of NPS+LTC mode we can say that the total computation time is
about

$$2.67 \ [\text{sec}] \times 4 = 10.68 \ [\text{sec}] \qquad \text{for tarai940}$$
$$0.86 \ [\text{sec}] \times 4 = 3.44 \ [\text{sec}] \qquad \text{for fib20.}$$

In this case the number of created processes (which is significantly reduced by LTC) are

|  |  |
|---|---|
| 90 | for tarai940 |
| 30 | for fib20 |

If we consider that the execution overhead in the NPS+ETC mode for the programs is caused by excessive creation of processes we can say that

$$(23.40 - 10.68) \ / \ (27613 - 90) = 0.46 \ [\text{msec}] \qquad \text{for tarai940}$$
$$(8.16 - 3.44) \ / \ (10944 - 30) = 0.42 \ [\text{msec}] \qquad \text{for fib20}$$

are the estimates for the overhead of process creation per process.

Thus we may say that the overhead of a process creation in PaiLisp/MT will be about 0.50 [msec].

## On effect of switching evaluation strategies

As was mentioned in 4.4 the current PaiLisp/MT uses a simple and easy adaptive method to switch the evaluation strategies. When an evaluation starts the system always employs the NPS+LTC mode. However, in case of tsp11 and fatwalk9 the results of Table 1 show that the evaluation mode should be switched to the PS+LTC mode when the number of processes reaches to the process threshold $PT$. Since $PT = 16$ under the current situation (see the above assumption) the current PaiLisp/MT switches its evaluation strategy from NPS+LTC to PS+LTC automatically in case of tsp11 and fatwalk9. In this case we obtained an experimental result shown in Table 2.

**Table 2.** Results of tsp11 and fatwalk9 in PaiLisp/MT

| system | tsp11 | fatwalk9 |
|---|---|---|
| NPS+ETC [sec] | 4.43 | 3.44 |
| MT(16,7500) [sec] | 3.36 | 2.94 |
| MT(16,30000) [sec] | 3.38 | 2.98 |

In Table 2

- NPS+LTC means that the evaluation is fixed to NPS+LTC as in the case of Table 1.
- MT($pt$, $gt$) means that the evaluation should be changed with the process threshold value $pt$ and the granularity threshold value $gt$ according to the rule explained in 4.4.

This result shows an evidence that the way of switching the evaluation strategies in PaiLisp/MT will be useful. However, in order to claim this fact more strongly we need more experiments on various programs ranging from coarse-grained to medium-grained. Moreover we have to give some reliable method of determining the threshold values $PT$ and $GT$. Since a parallel program creates processes with various degree of granularity we may have even the following case:

Evaluation starts with NPS+LTC
⇒ Program creates several coarse-grained processes with big granularity
    [→ Evaluation strategy will be changed to PS+LTC]
⇒ After creating dozens of coarse-grained processes the program starts to
    create many fine-grained processes
    [→ Evaluation strategy will be changed to NPS+LTC]
⇒ ···
    ···

This kind of dynamic switchings of evaluation strategies will be required in practice. The experimental results in the next section will tell that these dynamic behaviors of process creation will actually occur in many practical cases. The threshold values of $PT$ and $GT$ should be decided with considerable experiments on this kind of dynamical situations.

## 5.2 On distributions of granularity and dynamic behaviors of processes

The granularity of processes created by a program forms a distribution of execution time. The current PaiLisp/MT employs an easy and simple-minded way of using only the average execution time and standard deviation of distributions of granularity of created processes. They are effective in some simple experiments on a set of benchmark programs according to the results explained in 5.1. However, it will be useful to see actual distributions of granularity for further exploration of granularity adaptive parallel execution. Fig. 7 and Fig. 9 show the histograms of execution time for fib20 and queen8, respectively. In case of Fig. 7 the peak values of histograms are located within the interval $[m - \sigma, m + \sigma]$; this means that the average and standard deviation capture well the nature of the distribution of granularity of processes in this case. However, in case of Fig. 9 the peak values of histograms are located outside of the interval $[m' - \sigma, m' + \sigma]$; this means that the nature of the distribution of granularity of processes are not captured by the average and standard deviation. In APPENDIX II we gave similar histograms for tarai940, qsort2000 and prologq4, all of which show that the average and standard deviation do not capture the nature of distributions well. These results tell that it will be hard to expect that the average and standard deviation of distributions of granularity capture well the nature of the distributions of granularity of parallel processes.

Also, if we know the distribution like Fig. 9 we may work to find some methods to reduce processes whose granularity exceeds $m' + \sigma'$, transforming programs of this region into more fine-grained programs; this transformation may be said a method to decrease process granularity. This kind of transformation will be often possible, utilizing concurrency constructs like **future** and **pcall**. After decreasing program granularity we can apply the LTC under NPS efficiently.

However these static observations may not be sufficient in case of dynamic granularity adaptation process, since the process of creating parallel processes is quite dynamic in general. Fig. 8 and Fig. 10 show an example to tell how process creation proceeds dynamically. Fig. 8 and Fig. 10 should be read as follows. They illustrate the dynamic behaviors of process creation, showing the timings of process creation and durations of execution for each created process. In the figures *execution time of a process* means the duration of execution of a process. Each ♦-mark denotes a creation of a process, and the timing value (in the horizontal axis) tells the birth-time of the process and its duration of execution (namely, the life-time of the process) can be read from the value of the vertical axis. Because of this kind of dynamic behaviors of process creation we will actually encounter the cases to require dynamic switchings of evaluation strategies mentioned at the end of 5.1. In order to explore some effective procedure of dynamic granularity adaptive parallelization we need more experiments to see dynamic behaviors of processes created by various programs together with the effect of transforming programs to decrease process granularity.

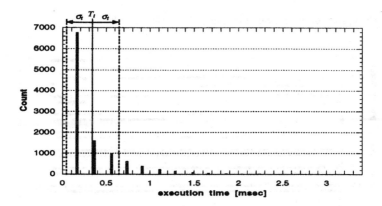

**Fig. 7.** Histogram of execution time per process on fib20

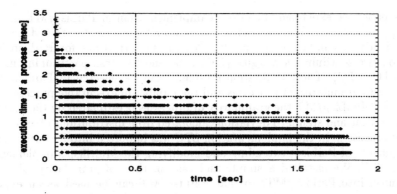

**Fig. 8.** Dynamic behavior of fib20

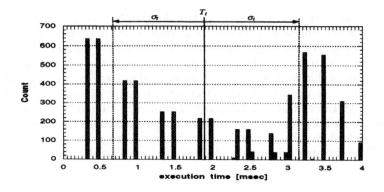

**Fig. 9.** Histogram of execution time per process on queen8

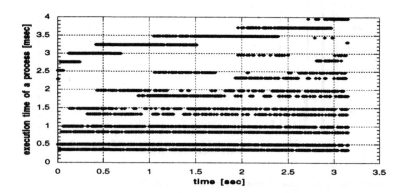

**Fig. 10.** Dynamic behavior of queen8

## 6   Conclusion

In this paper we explained the current implementation of PaiLisp/MT, a new PaiLisp interpreter using the multi-thread architecture under the Mach OS. We designed and implemented multiple evaluation strategies for PaiLisp/MT based on two scheduling strategies {NPS, PS} and two task partitioning methods {ETC, LTC}. These evaluation strategies can be selected in PaiLisp/MT according to granularity of processes and the number of executable processes. In the current PaiLisp/MT the granularity of processes is estimated by the average execution time and standard deviation calculated from distributions of execution time of processes. In the implementation LTC was imported into P-continuation environments of PaiLisp, extending and modifying the Multilisp's implementation of LTC. We installed a simple and easy method of granularity adaptive mechanism into PaiLisp/MT, so that PaiLisp/MT can be used as an experimental system of granularity adaptive parallel execution of parallel programs. According to our preliminary experiment the LTC under NPS works effectively for a wide range of parallel programs, but the LTC under PS must be used to a class of apparently coarse-grained programs for more efficient execution than the LTC under NPS. This kind of switching of evaluation strategies can be done automatically even in the current premature implementation of PaiLisp/MT. This shows an evidence of usefulness of granularity adaptive parallel execution of parallel programs. Also, PaiLisp/MT was used to see dynamic behaviors of process creation by parallel programs. This preliminary results suggest that we have to explore more dedicated methods for granularity adaptive parallelization of parallel programs, including the use of

- theory-based step evaluators based on [ItTW86] and [ReiG94],

- a method of decreasing granularity of processes by transforming parallel programs to expand applicability of the LTC under NPS.

The current PaiLisp/MT is an interpreter. It is desired to implement a complier for PaiLisp/MT to explore and widen its practical applications. In case of a compiler-based implementation a process creation overhead will be less than half of the current interpreter, and a compiler-based evaluation of PaiLisp program segments will be at least 10 times faster than an interpreter-based evaluation in most practical cases. Thus we can expect that in case of a compiler-based system the LTC under NPS will become more effective for a wider range of parallel programs than the LTC under PS, since the overhead of context switchings under PS will incur more degradation for the total execution time.

## Acknowledgements

We would like to express our thanks to discussions of the TPPP'94 participants. We would like to express our special thanks to Robert Halstead, Jr., Christian Queinnec, Suresh Jagannathan, John Reppy and Naoki Kobayashi for various discussions and comments that helped refine the ideas presented in the preliminary draft of this paper.

## References

[AbeS85] H.Abelson, G.Sussman. Structure and Interpretation of Computer Programs. The MIT Press, 1985.

[Blac90] David L. Black. Scheduling support for concurrency and parallelism in the Mach operating system. CMU Technical Report CMU-CS-90-125, April 1990

[DeLH90] S.K.Debray, N.W.Lin, M.Hermenegildo. Task granularity analysis in logic programs. Conference Record of Programming Language Design and Implementation, 174-188, 1990

[Feel93a] Marc Feeley. A message passing implementation of lazy task creation. "Parallel Symbolic Computing: Languages, Systems, and Applications, US/Japan Workshop", Springer LNCS 748, 94-107, 1993.

[Feel93b] Marc Feeley. An efficient and general implementation of futures on large scale shared-memory multiprocessors. Dissertation presented to the Faculty of the Graduate School of Arts and Sciences Brandeis University Department of Computer Science. 1993.

[GabM84] R.Gabriel, J.McCarthy. Queue-based multiprocessing Lisp. Conference Record of 1984 ACM Symposium on Lisp and Functional Programming, 25-44, 1984.

[Hals84a] R.Halstead,Jr. Implementation of Multilisp: Lisp on a multiprocessor. Conference Record of 1984 ACM Symposium on Lisp and Functional Programming, 9-17, 1984.

[Hals84b] R.Halstead,Jr. Multilisp: A language for concurrent symbolic computation. ACM Trans. on Programming Languages and Systems, Vol.4, No.7, 501-538, 1985.

[Hals90] R.Halstead,Jr. New ideas in parallel lisp: language design, implementation, and programming tools. "Parallel Lisp: Languages and Systems, US/Japan Workshop on Parallel Lisp", Springer LNCS 441, 2-57, 1990.

[HalI93] R.Halstead,Jr., T.Ito. "Parallel Symbolic Computing: Language, Systems and Applications, US/Japan Workshop", Springer LNCS 748, 1993.

[HuLA94] L.Huelsbergen, J.R.Larus, A.Aiken. Using the run-time sizes of data structures to guide parallel-thread creation. Proc. ACM Conf. Lisp and Functional Languages, 79-90, 1994.

[ItTW86] T.Ito, T.Tamura, S.Wada. Theoretical comparisons of interpreted/compiled executions of Lisp on sequential and parallel machine models. Information Processing 86, Proceedings of IFIP Congress 86, 349-354, 1986.

[ItoH90] T.Ito, R.Halstead,Jr. "Parallel Lisp: Languages and systems, US/Japan Workshop on Parallel Lisp", Springer LNCS 441, 1990.

[ItoM90] T.Ito, M.Matsui. A parallel lisp language PaiLisp and its kernel specification. "Parallel Lisp: Languages and Systems, US/Japan Workshop on Parallel Lisp", Springer LNCS 441, 58-100, 1990.

[ItoS92] T.Ito, T.Seino. On PaiLisp continuation and its implementation. Proceedings of ACM Workshop on Continuations (ed. O.Danvy & C.Talcott), Stanford, 73-90, 1992.

[ItoS93] T.Ito, T.Seino. P-continuation based implementation of PaiLisp interpreter. "Parallel Symbolic Computing: Languages, Systems, and Applications, US/Japan Workshop", Springer LNCS 748, 108-154, 1993.

[MoKH91] E.Mohr, D.A.Kranz, R.Halstead,Jr. Lazy task creation: A technique for increasing the granularity of parallel programs. IEEE Trans. Parallel and Distributed Systems, Vol.2, No.3, 264-280, 1991.

[ReiG94] B.Reistad, D.K.Gifford. Static dependent costs for estimating execution time. Proc. ACM Conf. Lisp and Functional Languages, 65-78, 1994

[WeeP90] J.S.Weening, J.D.Pehoushek. Low-cost process creation and dynamic partitioning in Qlisp. "Parallel Lisp: Languages and Systems, US/Japan Workshop on Parallel Lisp", Springer LNCS 441, 182-199, 1989.

**N.B.**

# APPENDIX I: benchmark programs

## fib

```
(define (fib n)
  (if (< n 2)
      n
      (+ (future (fib (- n 2)))
         (fib (- n 1)))))
```

## tarai

```
(define (tarai x y z)
  (if (>= y x)
      y
      (tarai (future (tarai (- x 1) y z))
             (future (tarai (- y 1) z x))
             (tarai (- z 1) x y))))
```

## queen

```
(define (queen n)
  (define (1-to n)
    (do ((i n (- i 1))
         (l '() (cons i l)))
        ((zero? i) l)))
  (define (try x y z)
    (if (null? x)
        (if (null? y) 1 0)
        (+ (future (if (ok? (car x) 1 z)
                       (try (append (cdr x) y) '() (cons (car x) z))
                       0))
           (try (cdr x) (cons (car x) y) z))))
  (define (ok? row dist placed)
    (if (null? placed)
        #t
        (and (not (= (car placed) (+ row dist)))
             (not (= (car placed) (- row dist)))
             (ok? row (+ dist 1) (cdr placed)))))
  (try (1-to n) '() '()))
```

## qsort

```
(define (qsort lst)
  (define (qs lst tail)
    (if (pair? lst)
        (let ((pivot (car lst))
              (other (cdr lst)))
          (let ((sorted-larger
                  (future (qs (filter (lambda (x) (not (< x pivot)))
                                      other)
                              tail))))
            (qs (filter (lambda (x) (< x pivot)) other)
                (cons pivot sorted-larger))))
        tail))
  (define (filter keep? lst)
    (define (filter-iter lst)
      (if (null? lst)
          '()
          (let ((head (car lst)))
            (if (keep? head)
                (cons head (filter-iter (cdr lst)))
```

```
                (filter-iter (cdr lst))))))
      (filter-iter lst))
   (qs lst '()))
```

## fatwalk

```
(define (fatwalk n)
  (map force
       (map (lambda (arg) (future (f arg)))
            (do ((i n (- i 1))
                 (l '() (cons 18 l)))
                ((zero? i) l)))))
```

# APPENDIX II: histograms of execution time of benchmark programs

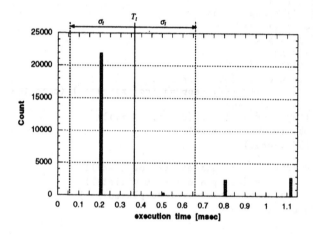

**Fig. 11.** tarai940

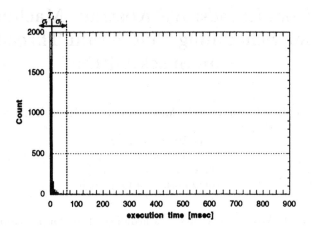

**Fig. 12.** qsort2000

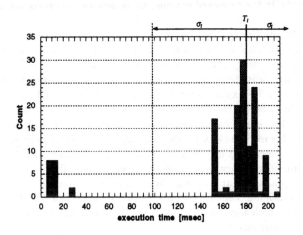

**Fig. 13.** prologq4

## N.B.

In case of qsort2000 there are a small number of processes with big execution time (for examples, 2 processes with 940 [msec]) which may incur considerable effect in evaluation, although their distributions are invisible in Fig. 12. This kind of phenomena occur in many other cases.

# *StackThreads*: An Abstract Machine for Scheduling Fine-Grain Threads on Stock CPUs

Kenjiro Taura, Satoshi Matsuoka, and Akinori Yonezawa

The University of Tokyo
tau@is.s.u-tokyo.ac.jp
matsu@ipl.t.u-tokyo.ac.jp
yonezawa@is.s.u-tokyo.ac.jp

**Abstract.** We present a software scheduling scheme for *fine-grain* threads, typical granularity of which is a single procedure invocation. Such fine-grain threads appear in many language implementations such as Multilisp and concurrent object-oriented languages in which an asynchronous procedure/method invocation is a building block of parallel programs. An implementation is described in terms of our abstract machine *Stack-Threads*. In the proposed scheme, an asynchronous procedure invocation (a procedure call attached with a thread creation) is performed in less than 10 additional RISC instructions to normal procedure calls in traditional sequential languages such as C, as long as the thread terminates without blocking. *StackThreads* unifies asynchronous and synchronous procedure calls, deriving a synchronous call by a combination of an asynchronous call + explicit synchronization between the caller and the callee. Therefore, each thread does not have to have its own stack for intra-thread procedure calls, simplifying management of activation records. *StackThreads* serves as a compiler target for general purpose languages such as concurrent object-oriented languages or functional languages on distributed memory multicomputers where the efficiency of intra-node thread management is crucial. We also give benchmark results of our implementation of concurrent object-oriented language ABCL/*f*, the compiler of which uses *StackThreads* as the intermediate representation of source programs.

## 1 Introduction

One of the most crucial issues in implementations of general purpose parallel languages is how to manage *intra-node* parallelism efficiently. The runtime system must have a mechanism which is able to schedule an *arbitrary number of* threads, each of which may perform *arbitrarily deep* procedure calls. Instances of general purpose parallel programming languages are ABCL[11, 10], Concurrent Aggregates[2], Multilisp[2] and CC++[1]. One of the most challenging implementation issues for such languages is how to support efficient multithreading without sacrificing sequential performance.

The problem is critical especially on *distributed memory parallel computers* where the presence of remote pointers makes typical computation granurality smaller and unpredictable at compile-time. To illustrate the problem, consider a parallel recursive tree summation program in Figure 1, which sums up all the leaf values in a given tree whose nodes may be scattered across processors (Figure 2). We want to perform recursive calls in parallel if they are located on different processors. We assume locations of nodes are not known at compile time. In distributed memory parallel computers, a computation is blocked when a child node is located on a remote node and we have to schedule other computation. Consequently, a recursive call to the left child has to fork a new thread so that we are able to resume the parent thread when the computation on the left child is blocked. Notice that we should create a thread even when the left child is on the same node as the parent node, because the child thread may be blocked during its subsequent recursion. The resulting number of created threads is $2^N$ where $N$ is the depth of the tree, even though the exploited parallelism is at best the number of the processors!

This simple example prohibits us from adopting a naive implementation where every recursive call to the left child creates a thread with a private stack assigned to it. In Figure 2, we observe that the created parallelism is useless if the thread performs only local computation. In general, a created parallelism turns out to be useless if *the created thread terminates without blocking.* Since whether or not a given thread terminates without blocking depends on data location, which is, in general, unknown at compile time, what is required is some *runtime mechanism* where the cost of non-blocking thread is extremely low, while the cost of blocking thread is reasonably small.

```
(define (tree-sum tree)
   (if (leafp tree)
       (value-of tree)
       ;; two recursive (parallel) calls
       (let ((s (tree-sum (lchild tree))))
          (+ (tree-sum (rchild tree)) (touch s)))))
```

**Fig. 1.** Parallel Tree Summation: When the computation on lchild is blocked, the parent process should be resumed, so that the computation on rchild can take place.

This paper proposes a method which satisfies the above requirement. In the proposed scheduling method, a thread creation provisionally allocates its context (*i.e., activation frame*) on the stack, which is similar to a procedure call in traditional sequential languages. Upon blocking, the thread lazily allocates a heap frame, releasing the stack frame. In this way, the overhead of a thread creation is kept small as long as the thread is not blocked. We also propose an efficient mechanism which communicates reply values between caller threads and callee threads. Since the context of a caller thread does not necessarily reside directly under that of the callee thread (assuming the stack expands upwards), the traditional procedure call/return mechanism does not work well. This work

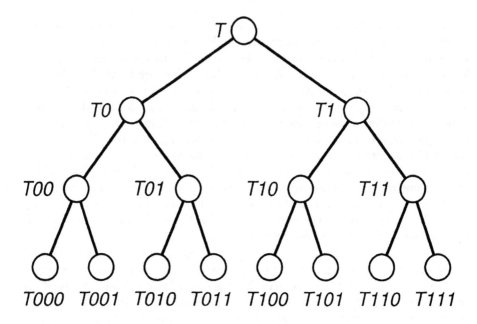

**Fig. 2.** An Example of a Tree: Nodes scatter over processors.

extends and generalizes our previous work in [9], by proposing an efficient reply protocol and by describing our idea in terms of an abstract machine.

The rest of the paper is organized as follows: Section 2 briefly introduces our setting in which the problem and our solution are stated more clearly. Sections 3 and 4 explain details of our implementation. Section 5 demonstrates how the presented solution works using an example. Section 6 outlines our portable code generation based on *StackThreads*. Section 7 shows some benchmark results. After discussing some related work in Section 8, we conclude in Section 9.

## 2 Computation Model

To make our discussion as concrete as possible, this section informally explains our computation model and introduces a tiny language which embodies the model, and also serves as an *intermediate language* of various parallel language implementations. Later sections then describe how to map the intermediate language onto conventional CPUs.

A computation consists of multiple threads, each of which performs any sequential operations such as register arithmetics, memory operations, and branches.[1] In addition, each thread may create another thread in the following way:

(**fork** *code* ( *arg0 ... argn*) *reply-dest*)

---

[1] Unlike definitions of a thread appearing in some literatures, a thread may be blocked by waiting for certain values.

This invokes a parallel thread which evaluates the body of *code*, with (*arg0* ... *argn*) as arguments. *Reply-dest* specifies a placeholder, or a *reply box* from which the caller receives a reply value, and is called *reply destination* of the invocation. Although the number of words representing a reply box varies depending on the type of the reply value and is typically two or three words, it is written in one word in *StackThreads* instructions. (The details are described in Section 4.) There is also **remote fork** instruction which is the same as **fork** except that it creates a new thread on the specified processor.

A new (empty) reply box is created by:

**(make-reply-box** *dest-var*).

where the new reply box is bound to *dest-var*. Extracting the value from a reply box is done by:

**(recv** *reply-box var*)

where *reply-box* gives a reply box and the extracted value goes to *var*. Again, their sizes depend on the types of the reply values. If the reply box has not yet received any values, the thread becomes blocked until a value arrives. Finally, sending a value to a reply box is done by:

**(reply** *value reply-box*)

where *value* and *reply-box* have obvious meanings. Although the operation is called 'reply' because its primary usage is replying a result value of an invocation, its usage is not limited to it; we can construct arbitrary complex synchronization patterns by waiting on/replying to reply boxes (i.e., reply boxes are first class citizens). This model does not ensure any properties about the number of replies; multiple replies may arrive, or there are even cases where no value arrives. Here we assume that the second or later replies are just ignored, for its treatment does not affect the following discussion,

We first note that a normal procedure call is actually realized by a thread fork followed by receiving a reply value immediately after the fork. For instance, a procedure call (f x y) can be done by:

**(make-reply-box** rb) ; *create a reply box*
**(fork** f (x y) rb)
**(recv** rb r) ; *r gets the reply*

In this way, we unify normal procedure invocation and creation of an asynchronous thread. More specifically, what we should consider is how to represent a reply box at runtime, thereby deriving implementations of **fork**, **recv**, and **reply**.

This unification simplifies implementation significantly; each thread does not have to have its own local stack. The reader might argue that this unification sacrifices the efficiency of frequently occurring cases, that is, synchronous procedure calls. A plausible optimization is to adopt two separate calling sequences, one for asynchronous calls which use a reply box and the other for local synchronous calls which behave just like procedure calls. The reason why we did not adopt this approach is that it has to duplicate all the procedures that are called both asynchronously and synchronously. Another reason is that since *StackThreads* computation model allows the callee to continue computation even after replying a value, synchronous calls and asynchronous calls cannot be distinguished solely by examining call-sites. As we will see in later sections, we optimize creation of reply boxes and threads in a general way and performance degradation caused by the unification is not significant enough to justify the code duplication.

Figure 3 shows a parallel recursive Fibonacci function which **forks** two subtasks recursively, followed by two recvs. In the example, variables and labels are written symbolically for readability. The presented abstract machine, called *StackThreads*, was primarily designed and is being implemented as an intermediate representation for implementation of our concurrent object-oriented language ABCL on stock multicomputers[9]. More comprehensive description of ABCL can be found in [11, 8, 10] and more about *StackThreads* in [8]. In the implementation, both inter-object method invocation and intra-object procedure call correspond to a thread creation in *StackThreads*. The frontend, which takes ABCL/*f* program as inputs and generates *StackThreads* instructions, does not care about complicated thread management, which is handled efficiently by the code generator from *StackThreads*. We believe implementations of other languages can benefit from the *StackThreads* backend as well.

```
 1:  ;; declare parameter and reply destination
 2:  (code "fib" (n) rd
 3:     (bl n 2 L0)              ; if n < 2 goto L0
 4:     (add n -1 t0)            ; t0 := n - 1
 5:     (make-reply-box t1)
 6:     (fork "fib" (t0) t1)     ; recurse
 7:     (add n -2 t2)            ; t2 := n - 2
 8:     (make-reply-box t3)
 9:     (fork "fib" (t2) t3)     ; another fork
10:     (recv t1 t4)             ; get 1st result
11:     (recv t3 t5)             ; get 2nd result
12:     (add t4 t5 t6)           ; add results
13:     (reply t6 rd)            ; reply the sum
14:     (ba L1)                  ; branch always
15:  (label L0)                  ; label L0
16:     (reply 1 rd)             ; reply 1
17:  (label L1))                 ; label L1
```

**Fig. 3.** A Parallel Fibonacci Example: Lines 4–9 make two recursive calls and lines 10–11 join them.

# 3   Management of Activation Frames

This section gives the reader a rough overview of how the entire scheduling mechanism works. In particular, this section ignores how threads communicate via **recv** and **reply**, focusing on how a thread is forked and what happens when a thread becomes blocked.

Since a thread may become blocked in the course of computation, it is natural to allocate activation frames from heap, rather than from a stack, so that we can schedule runnable thread in any sequence. This increases the overhead of **fork**, however—recall that our **fork** is used for procedure calls, hence should be as fast as possible.

Our implementation of **fork** is just a procedure invocation in traditional sequential languages (i.e., grow stack, pass arguments via registers, and jumps to the procedure body) without any heap allocation. This scheme performs excellently for tree of local procedure calls because it is based on 'callee-first' strategy where the caller is likely to have already received a reply at the first **recv** after it has resumed. A difficulty arises when a thread becomes blocked; since the thread occupies the topmost portion of the stack, we have to somehow 'free' it for allowing another thread to run. This is done by allocating a frame from the heap and storing necessary values from registers (or possibly from stack if registers have spilled) into the heap-frame. When the thread later becomes unblocked, these stored values are reloaded into registers (or stack). The heap-frame is kept until the thread terminates (i.e., Heap allocation occurs at most once per each thread). Blocking inside a deep procedure call does not have to be treated specially: the topmost frame is first removed, resuming the next frame which will try to receive a reply value. If it finds no reply value has arrived yet, it is immediately blocked, which will in turn cause the third frame to be removed, and so forth. This unwinding continues until the control reaches some runnable thread. Section 5 shows an example scenario.

Our scheme can be viewed as a lazy allocation of heap-frames. A thread begins to run without a heap-frame. It hopefully terminates without blocking (this will typically be the case for local procedure calls), hence without heap-frame allocation. When a thread is blocked for the first time, it *lazily* allocates a heap-frame which serves as a 'backing store' of the context.

Notice that this method works on any stock CPU, provided that a (sequential) procedure calling convention is defined. In other words, our fork is implemented on top of a sequential procedure call. In particular, it does not preclude the use of register window; as a matter of fact, our method will perform best with register windows where small procedure calls are done very quickly. On a more conventional CPUs without register windows, it is still advantageous because it saves heap-frame allocation and explicit linking from the callee frame to the caller frame.

# 4   Communication via Reply Boxes

It is not enough to avoid heap-frame allocation and pass arguments via registers. To make our procedure call performance truly close to that of sequential programming languages, we should be able to pass a *reply value* through a register with neither heap allocation nor memory read/write. This is far from trivial because replying a value is done via a reply box, which will normally be implemented by a pointer to a memory location.

In order to address this problem, a similar lazy allocation technique is applied for representing a reply box. A reply box has dual representations, either *boxed* or *unboxed*, which are switched between these two. A boxed reply box is a pointer to a (possibly remote) memory location which keeps track of all the information such as full/empty flag, replied value, and waiting thread queue. An unboxed reply box is represented by two words, one for the full/empty flag and the other for the value. Another one bit flag (the *boxity bit*) is necessary to distinguish these two representations. Assuming that the representation of a remote pointer is a pair (node_id, machine_address) and the lowest two bits of machine addresses are zero, the representation of a reply box is either:

- boxed:
     node_id + { addr + boxity bit } or,
- unboxed:
     value + { full/empty bit + boxity bit }

where { ... } indicates that the contents are packed in one word. When the value is an integer, the total number of words for representing a reply box is two words because the node_id and the value share a same word. If the value is a double-precision real number, for instance, a reply box is represented by two integer registers plus one floating point register. The following discussion assumes the type of the value to be an integer.

A reply box is initially created as an unboxed representation. Thus creating a reply box requires just one instruction (on many RISCs), loading a small immediate into a register. **Reply** and **recv** on a reply box first perform a boxity check followed by appropriate operations (which are obvious). **Reply**ing a value to an unboxed reply box takes 4 instructions in a case the reply box has not yet received any reply. **Recv**ing a value from an unboxed one consumes 3 instructions in a case a value has already arrived.

A less trivial problem is how threads communicate via unboxed reply boxes. When multiple threads share a reply box (with unboxed representation) and a thread replies a value to the reply box, how does the replier notify all the other threads of the reply value? More precisely speaking, when the state of a reply box changes (by replying a value, or switching to the boxed representation), how do we properly update *all* the references[2] to it? There must be some protocol to

---

[2] Although it sounds strange to use the term 'reference' for unboxed representations because it does not actually reference any memory location, we could not think of better terminology.

properly update all the copies and some invariant for unboxed representations to work.

The representation of a reply box remains unboxed as long as:

1. all the copies of the reference appear in stack frames of a processor, and
2. its reference has been copied only via the reply destination field.

Given invariant 1, when we change a state of a reply box, all the copies of the reference exist below the stack frame of the currently running thread. In order to update other references, when the current thread resumes the next thread, it notifies the caller thread of the current state of the reply destination by putting the representation on some registers. This protocol is akin to the procedure return mechanism in traditional sequential languages where the return value is put in a register when a procedure call exits. Invariant 2 precludes threads from copying a reference to other threads via normal arguments, whose state change does not consistently propagate otherwise. It also prevents a single thread from having multiple references to a reply box so that when we change a state of a reply box, other variables are not affected.

Invariant 2 is rarely violated in "normal" local computation where reply boxes are used only for receiving a reply value of procedure calls. "First class operations" such as creating a list of reply boxes or storing a reference to a data structure make representation boxed. Invariant 1 is, on the other hand, violated when a thread becomes blocked, because references to reply boxes escape from stack frame, being stored into a heap frame.

## 5   Example

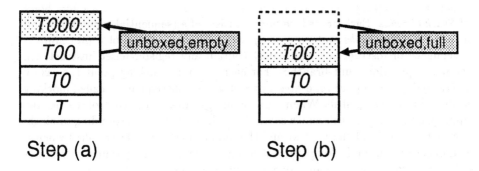

Step (a)          Step (b)

**Fig. 4.** An Example of Scheduling

We show how our scheme works using the example introduced in Section 1, which computes summation of leaf values of a tree in parallel. An example tree is shown in Figure 2. Each node and leaf is labeled with a name.

First, let us consider a situation where the entire tree is located in one node. It works as if it were written in some traditional sequential languages, except for replying/receiving protocol. To see how a reply is returned, let us examine the leaf call made by $T00$ to $T000$ (Here we identify a node name with the thread which deals with the node and call the reply destination of $Txxx$ $Rxxx$). $T00$ creates an empty and unboxed reply box ($R000$), and passes it to $T000$ (Step (a) in Figure 4). When $T000$ replies the value and exits, it notifies $T00$ of the current state of $R000$ (which is, unboxed and full) using some registers. $T00$ regains control, updates $R000$, and finds that the reply has arrived (Step (b) in Figure 4). In this way, all reply boxes remain unboxed.

To see what happens on blocking, suppose only $T000$ happens to be located on a remote node, hence the corresponding call becomes a remote procedure call. When $T00$ makes the remote procedure call, the reply destination $R000$ is made boxed and passed to the remote node. After the remote procedure call, $T00$ forks the right child ($T001$) and eventually becomes blocked because the result from the left child has not arrived, resuming the caller ($T0$). When $T00$ blocks, it makes its reply destination ($R00$) boxed (as $R00$ escapes from stack) and resumes the caller, notifying the caller of the representation of $R00$, which has been made boxed. When $T0$ begins to run, it updates the representation of $R00$.

Similarly, $T0$ and $T$ also fork their right child and will eventually be blocked because the result from the left child will have not arrived. When the result from $T000$ eventually arrives, it replies the value to $R000$ which resumes the suspended thread, which is $T00$. $T00$ replies the summation to $R00$, resuming $T0$, which then resumes $T$.

## 6 Code Generation Issues

It is relatively straightforward to generate machine code from a procedure body of *StackThreads*. Each procedure body consists of a (sequential) main body and a set of *blocking stubs* and *unblocking stubs*. The main body of a procedure is a sequence of instructions which may contain any register-based instructions, memory operations and branches. For each possible blocking point (i.e., **recv** operation), the compiler generates a pair of small code sequences, called blocking stub and unblocking stub. When a procedure is blocked, the control reaches the appropriate blocking stub which saves the address of the corresponding unblocking stub as a part of the context and the unblocking stub is later called when it is unblocked. An unblocking stub takes a heap-frame as the parameter, restores saved context from the heap-frame and jumps to the blocked location.

We are also interested in generating C code both for portability and for taking advantage of machine-dependent optimization performed by C compilers. Translating *StackThreads* into C code is, however, not as straightforward as into assembly language basically because C functions can have only one entry point. Since we do not know how the C compiler allocates registers for variables, unblocking stubs must be written in the same function as the main body. Consequently, a single C function must serve both as the main body and blocking/unblocking stubs. A single *StackThreads* procedure is translated into a single C function, which takes an additional parameter *fr* which represents the heap-frame of the running thread. *Fr* is zero when the heap-frame has not been allocated. A blocking point is represented by a small integer (rather than a code address) and the number is stored into the heap-frame when the thread is blocked. Upon unblocking, the C function is called with the thread's heap-frame as the argument. The thread first checks if *fr* is non-zero and if it is, performs switch-case on the blocking point number, restores the appropriate context and goes to the blocking point. Resulting C functions have a non-zero check on *fr*, followed by a large switch-case statement for the non-zero case at the top of the function. Each case of the switch-case statement is a list of loading values from *fr* to variables, followed by a goto which jumps to the blocking point. A skeleton of a generated C code is shown in Figure 5. To improve performance, we can generate multiple versions from a given procedure body; one may generate a version for a blocking point or, what will be particularly worthy is to generate two versions, one for the case *fr* is zero and the other for non-zero case. It removes the overhead which is otherwise paid at every procedure call.

```
foo (fr, x, y, r0, r1)
{
  if (fr) {
    switch (fr->block_point) {
      case 1: restore context; goto L1;
      case 2: restore context; goto L2;
        ...
    }
  }
  /* begin procedure body */
  L1:   ...
  L2:   ...
}
```

**Fig. 5.** Skeleton of a C Code Generated from a *StackThreads* Procedure: Each label corresponds to a potential blocking point. fr is a pointer to the heap-frame (zero if it has not been allocated).

## 7 Performance Evaluation

As for node-local scheduling, what is particularly important is procedure invocation cost, which consists of (a) creating a reply box, (b) forking a new thread, (c) replying a value to the reply box, (d) receiving the value from the reply box. In *StackThreads*, when a callee is not blocked, the scheduling cost for such typical combinations of fork/receive is quite small, approaching the cost of normal procedure calls in sequential languages. When the callee happens to be blocked, the scheduling cost increases since it requires heap-frame allocation, saving live variables etc. This cost depends on the amount of context (i.e., live variables).

## 7.1   Future and Procedure Invocation

Table 1 shows instruction counts (in Sparc) of a leaf procedure call, which takes no arguments and replies a constant integer. A possible *StackThreads* code sequence is shown in Figure 6 (a). Since the procedure is not blocked, the reply box created at line 9 remains unboxed representation and **recv** instruction at line 11 successfully gets the result value to **v**. Totally 13 instructions are required none of which accesses memory. A comparable C function call (Figure 6 (b)) requires 5 instructions. $13 - 5 = 8$ instructions is the additional overhead which are resulted from checking tag (full/empty bit, boxity bit) of the reply box and passing additional arguments (the reply box) at the fork. Notice that this is the *general* calling sequence in *StackThreads*—caller assumes neither non-blocking property of the procedure nor presence of the reply value at the **recv** instruction, and we by no means prohibit compile-time optimizations such as inlining or inference of the non-blocking property. Also notice that this overhead remains nearly constant, independently from the invoked procedure. Hence, the larger the procedure body, the smaller the overhead relative to the procedure body.

```
 1:  (code
 2:   "leaf" () r
 3:     ;; a leaf procedure
 4:   ((reply (10) r)))
 5:
 6:  (code
 7:    "call-leaf" () r
 8:      ;; the caller of "leaf"
 9:   ((make-reply-box t)
10:    (fork "leaf" () t)
11:    (recv t v)))
```

(a) *StackThreads*.

```
1: int leaf ()
2: {
3:      return 10;
4: }
5:
6: void call_leaf ()
7: {
8:      int t = leaf ();
9: }
```

(b) C.

**Fig. 6.** A Leaf Procedure Call in *StackThreads* (a) and C (b): Both procedures immediately return 10.

| | # of instructions |
|---|---|
| Create a reply box | 1 |
| Fork | 3 |
| Prologue/epilogue | 3 |
| Reply (in the callee) | 3 |
| Recv | 3 |
| Total: | 13 |
| (Comparable C function) | 5 |

**Table 1.** Instruction Counts for a Tiny Leaf Procedure Call: 8 RISC instructions are added to C function call.

## 7.2 Application Benchmark

To demonstrate the impact of our scheduling methods, we performed several sequential benchmark programs on a single node of AP1000, which is a Sparc processor running at 25Mhz with 16MB of local memory. The programs are written in ABCL/$f$, our newly designed concurrent object-oriented language. ABCL/$f$ provides an extension of the *future* which originated from Multilisp[4]. Both future invocations and synchronous invocations are translated into a combination of **make-reply-box**, **fork**, and **recv** instructions in *StackThreads*. The benchmark programs are described in Table 2.

| | Description | N |
|---|---|---|
| Qsort | Quicksort $N$ elements list | 40,000 |
| Nqueen | # of solutions of $N$ queen | 13 |
| Prime | Generate all primes less than $N$ | 200,000 |
| Nbody2 | Naive $N$ body simulation ($O(N^2)$) | 1,300 |
| Nbody | Barnes and Hut $N$ body simulation ($O(N \log N)$) | 1,300 |

**Table 2.** Benchmark Programs: All programs run on a single node of AP1000 (Sparc 25Mhz, 16MB memory)

For each benchmark, we wrote an ABCL/$f$ program and a comparable C program. We also tested two versions of *StackThreads* → C code generator; the one presented in this paper and a simpler code generator, the generated code of which always allocates reply boxes from heap.

Since our code generator is still in the early stage of development, we manually assisted the code generator in some benchmarks: (1) In Qsort, we inline-expanded small primitives such as **cons, car, cdr**, or **null**. This optimization is also done in the C version. (2) In the force-calculation phase of the Nbody program, we reused the registers for reply boxes which have been used for previous procedure calls. What the optimization (1) saves is obvious; it eliminates a creation of a reply box, argument marshalling, forward and backward jumps, a flag check on the reply box, and a register-to-register move to obtain the result. The reason why (2) achieves better performance is less obvious. Since our code generator generates C code without any register allocation, it naively maps a local variable in *StackThreads* to a local variable in C, leaving the task of register allocation to the C compiler. The resulting code tends to have a large number of local variables, especially if it performs many procedure calls, because a procedure call typically creates a new reply box, which is represented by several words. Although there is no theoretical reason why a C compiler cannot reuse registers for the reply boxes (in sequential programs, their live ranges are naturally disjoint), too many local variables and labels introduced by unblocking stubs seems to confuse C compilers. This manual optimization achieved 40% improvement in the Nbody.

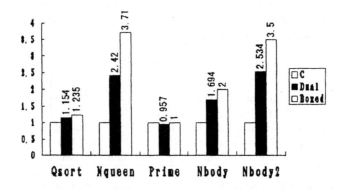

**Fig. 7.** The Results of Benchmarks

Figure 7 shows the elapsed time normalized to C. Higher bars indicate slower execution time. While we observe nearly the same or even better speed compared to C in some benchmarks (Prime, Qsort), others add non-negligible overhead (Nqueen, Nbody, Nbody2). Although our experience on the code generator is not extensive enough to conclude the source of the inefficiencies, we expect they are partly due to the apparent complexity of the generated code, which include unusually large number of local variables and goes to which jump *inside* a block, etc. We expect their performance will be improved if a register allocation is done so that several *StackThreads* variables share a single C variable, and smarter and well-structured C code which C compilers like is generated.

# 8  Related Work

Any parallel implementation of general purpose languages encounters the same problem: "How to manage activation frames of concurrent threads". The problem arises regardless whether the language has an explicit notion of concurrent threads—while in concurrent object-oriented languages, an asynchronous method invocation explicitly creates a thread, the compilers for implicitly parallel functional languages determine where a thread is created (typically a loop and a function body corresponds to a thread). Our work shares the goal with several recent attempts to this problem.

TAM[3] is Threaded Abstract Machine which is intended to be mapped on conventional multicomputers, and whose primary usage is the intermediate representation of a non-strict functional language Id[7]. TAM has a very efficient scheduling mechanism for logically related threads, but the efficient mechanism is applied only for threads *which are related at compile time*. Consequently, the mechanism is primarily used to manage parallelism *inside function/loop bodies*. While this plays a crucial role for implementation of languages such as Id where their non-strict semantics substantially decreases the average granularity, the original problem still remains: how to manage *function-level* parallelism more efficiently.[3] TAM has no runtime mechanism to improve scheduling cost for this level of parallelism; a function-invocation in TAM always requires a frame allocation, followed by writing arguments into the frame, and linking between the callee and the caller.

Concert[5], which is a runtime for COOP languages, recognizes the cost hierarchy of method invocations. In particular it uses stack allocation for *non-blocking* methods. This approach is similar to ours, but the faster invocation mechanism is applied only for methods which are *proved to be non-blocking at compile-time*. Our method, on the other hand, relies only on runtime information; the cheaper scheduling cost (i.e., stack) is applied whenever the method happens to be non-blocking at runtime. Since the non-blocking nature of an invocation is highly dependent on runtime state, especially on whether or not necessary data are located on the same node, we believe our method has more chances for optimization.

The spirit of our work is the most similar to that of Lazy Task Creation (LTC)[6] for implementing the *future* construct of Multilisp[4], though the main platform of LTC is shared-memory machines. In Multilisp, each future call creates a logically parallel thread, hence naive implementation schemes of Multilisp are either to create a separate stack for each future call or to have a heap-frame for each function call. In LTC, a future call provisionally allocates an activation frame on stack. When a thread blocks, it splits the stack at the topmost

---

[3] Quanta-level parallelism, in terminologies of TAM.

fork point (where the most recent future call was made) whereby resuming the continuation of the future call. *StackThreads* has a similar strategy for frame allocation and deadlock avoidance. Both are based on the same point: we do not have to create threads, unless the current thread becomes blocked. The difference between the scheduling mechanism of *StackThreads* and LTC is that *StackThreads* has first class placeholders (reply boxes) we can use to construct various synchronization patterns. Even an intra-thread procedure call is derived by combining a thread creation and a communication via a reply box. The efficiency of intra-thread procedure calls is preserved by the dual representation of reply boxes. This unification of thread creations and procedure calls is useful both for portability and efficiency; since a blocked thread simply resumes the thread directly under itself, a stack is, unlike LTC, never split. This ensures *StackThreads* is easily implemented on any CPU including ones that have register windows, provided that traditional stack-based languages are implemented, and allows optimizations such as callee-save registers where contexts of threads are not necessarily saved on stack.

## 9   Conclusion

A runtime scheme which provides both fast thread creations and procedure calls has been presented. It achieves local procedure calls which is as fast as the counterpart in traditional sequential languages in the presence of multiple concurrent threads which may be blocked in the middle of the execution. Roughly speaking, the method is based on 'lazy' allocation of frames and reply boxes. Implementation has been described in terms of simple and general abstract machine, which is an intermediate representation for parallel implementation of languages on distributed memory machines.

## References

1. K. Mani Chandy and Carl Kesselman. CC++: A declarative concurrent object-oriented programming notation. In Gul Agha, Peter Wegner, and Akinori Yonezawa, editors, *Research Directions in Concurrent Object-Oriented Programming*, chapter 11, pages 281–313. The MIT Press, 1993.
2. Andrew A. Chien. *Concurrent Aggregates (CA)*. PhD thesis, MIT, 1991.
3. David E. Culler, Anurag Sah, Klaus Erik Schauser, Thorsten von Eicken, and John Wawrzynek. Fine-grain parallelism with minimal hardware support: A compiler-controlled threaded abstract machine. In *ASPLOS*, pages 166–175, 1991.
4. Robert Halstead, Jr. Multilisp: A language for concurrent symbolic computation. *ACM Transactions on Programming Languages and Systems*, 7(4):501–538, April 1985.
5. Vijay Karamcheti and Andrew Chien. Concert—efficient runtime support for concurrent object-oriented programming languages on stock hardware. In *Supercomputing*, pages 598–607, 1993.
6. Eric Mohr, David A. Kranz, and Robert Halstead, Jr. Lazy task creation: A techinque for increasing the granularity of parallel programs. *IEEE Transactions on Parallel and Distributed Systems*, 2(3):264–280, July 1991.

7. R. S. Nikhil and Arvind. Id: a language with implicit parallelism. Technical report, MIT, 1990.

8. Kenjiro Taura. Design and implementation of concurrent object-oriented programming languages on stock multicomputers. Master's thesis, The University of Tokyo, Tokyo, February 1994.

9. Kenjiro Taura, Satoshi Matsuoka, and Akinori Yonezawa. An efficient implementation scheme of concurrent object-oriented languages on stock multicomputers. In *ACM PPOPP*, pages 218–228, San Diego, California, May 1993.

10. Kenjiro Taura, Satoshi Matsuoka, and Akinori Yonezawa. ABCL/$f$: A future-based polymorphic typed concurrent object-oriented language - its design and implementation -. In G. Blelloch, M. Chandy, and S. Jagannathan, editors, *Proceedings of the DIMACS workshop on Specification of Parallel Algorithms*, 1994. (to appear).

11. Akinori Yonezawa. *ABCL: An Object-Oriented Concurrent System — Theory, Language, Programming, Implementation and Application*. The MIT Press, 1990.

# Higher-Order Concurrent Linear Logic Programming

Naoki Kobayashi and Akinori Yonezawa

Department of Information Science
University of Tokyo
7-3-1 Hongo, Bunkyo-ku, Tokyo, 113 Japan
{koba, yonezawa}@is.s.u-tokyo.ac.jp

**Abstract.** We propose a typed, higher-order, concurrent linear logic programming called *higher-order ACL*, which uniformly integrates a variety of mechanisms for concurrent computation based on asynchronous message passing. Higher-order ACL is based on a proof search paradigm according to the principle, *proofs as computations, formulas as processes* in linear logic. In higher-order ACL, processes as well as functions, and other values can be communicated via messages, which provides high modularity of concurrent programs. Higher-order ACL can be viewed as an asynchronous counterpart of Milner's higher-order, polyadic $\pi$-calculus. Moreover, higher-order ACL is equipped with an elegant ML-style type system that ensures (1) well typed programs can never cause type mismatch errors, and (2) there is a type inference algorithm which computes a most general typing for an untyped term. We also demonstrate a power of higher-order ACL by showing several examples of "higher-order concurrent programming."

## 1 Introduction

In logic programming, computation is often regarded as a *controlled deduction*. By changing the underlying logic, we can obtain a variety of programming languages. Recently, linear logic programming, whose underlying logic is Girard's linear logic[6], has been drawing great attentions. Several linear logic languages[8] were proposed as refinements of traditional logic programming languages, while others were proposed as novel concurrent programming languages[2][13]. In the previous papers[13][11], we proposed an asynchronous concurrent linear logic language called ACL. While traditional concurrent logic programming models stream-based communication, concurrent linear logic programming naturally models message-passing style asynchronous communication. Further difference comes from the fact that in concurrent linear logic programming, messages as well as processes are represented in terms of propositions[13]. This gives rise to an elegant abstract interpretation technique for linear logic languages[3].

The purpose of this paper is to further extend a concurrent linear logic language ACL and give a more powerful and elegant framework called *Higher-Order ACL* (in short, HACL), for asynchronous concurrent programming languages.

We extend ACL in the following two significant ways. First, we replace the first-order linear logic with *higher-order linear logic*. This enables processes to pass processes as well as functions and basic values as arguments of messages, just as functions can take functions as arguments in functional programming. More importantly, processes can be parameterized by other processes and communication interfaces (i.e., messages), which provides a high modularity of concurrent programs and enhances code reuse. Higher-order processes are useful for defining a large process by composing smaller subprocesses. This mechanism contributes to *structuring* concurrent programs and exploiting *intra-process* concurrency, by which separating *abstraction* and *granularity* of concurrent programs. On the other hand, this separation does not exist in the first-order concurrent language including most of the existing concurrent object-oriented languages. Therefore, if a programmer wants to obtain more concurrency from his program, he must change abstraction of the program by dividing some processes into smaller processes, or completely restructuring the program. Another relevant advantage of higher-order processes in HACL is that we can easily make *communication topologies* between multiple processes by using higher-order processes. For example, we can define a higher-order process which takes a list of processes as arguments, and connects them in a ring structure or a mesh structure.[1]

Second, we introduce a natural and elegant ML-style static, polymorphic type system into HACL. Since computation in HACL can be viewed as a deduction in higher-order linear logic, the notion of *well-typed processes* in HACL corresponds to that of *well-formed formulas* of higher-order linear logic. For example, a process which take an integer as an argument is assigned a type $int \rightarrow o$, where $o$ is the distinguished type of propositions. A *message predicate* (which is viewed as a *communication channel* or a *port name*) that takes an argument of type $\tau$ is assigned a type $\tau \rightarrow o$. Since each message predicate is consistently typed in its scope, no type mismatch error occurs in message passing. An operator of parallel composition $\otimes$ is assigned a type $o \rightarrow o \rightarrow o$. Such formulation of type systems is found in other higher-order logic programming languages such as $\lambda$Prolog[16]. The basic type system for HACL obtained in this manner is exactly the same as Damas-Milner type system[4] for ML. An important observation from this fact is that we can easily enrich the basic type system with extensions of ML-type system such as subtyping, recursive typing, polymorphic records, and bounded polymorphism, which have been well-investigated in the communities of functional/object-oriented/logic programming. As a specific application, we show in [14] that polymorphic record extensions of higher-order ACL can be a powerful basis for accounting for typed concurrent object-oriented programming with inheritance and method overriding. Although type systems for concurrent calculi have been recently investigated by many researchers[5][9][19][24][25], we believe that our formulation is one of the most elegant ones. The basic type system of HACL ensures that no type mismatch error occurs, liberates program-

---

[1] From our experience in programming using concurrent object-oriented language ABCL[26], we have long recognized that it is very cumbersome to make such topologies between concurrent objects using only *first-order* concurrent objects.

mers from complex type declarations, and also provides for useful compiling information. For example, type information need not be embedded in messages at runtime, which reduces both the size of messages and the cost of message handling. We also give several simple refinements of the basic type system to get more precise information such as input/output modes of messages. The refined type system is useful for the detection of orphan messages, dead-code elimination, etc.

The general motivation of our research on HACL is to give a foundation for asynchronous concurrent programming languages including concurrent object-oriented languages, through which we aim at

1. development of type systems and program analysis techniques,
2. systematic design of asynchronous concurrent languages, and
3. discussion of optimization/compilation techniques,

just as $\lambda$-calculus has been used as a foundation of functional programming languages.

In Section 2, we present the syntax and operational semantics of HACL. Section 3 demonstrates the power of higher-order concurrent linear logic programming. In Section 4, we refine the type system given in Section 2. Section 5 compares related work, and Section 6 concludes this paper. For those who are not familiar with linear logic and concurrent linear logic programming, Appendix A gives a brief introduction to concurrent linear logic programming. Appendix B gives a rough correspondence between HACL and Milner's higher-order, polyadic $\pi$-calculus. In Appendix C, we give inference rules of higher-order linear logic.

# 2  Syntax and Operational Semantics of Higher-Order ACL

This section introduces the syntax, operational semantics and the basic type system of Higher-order ACL.

## 2.1  Overview

As in the first-order ACL[13][11], computation in Higher-order ACL (in short, HACL) is described in terms of bottom-up *proof search* in Girard's (higher-order) linear logic[6]. Each formula of (a fragment of) higher-order linear logic is viewed as a process, while each sequent, a multiset of formulas, is regarded as a certain state of the entire processes. A message is represented by an atomic formula, whose predicate is called a *message predicate*. The whole syntax of HACL process expressions is summarized in Figure 2. The first column shows textual notations for process expressions. The second column shows corresponding formulas of linear logic. In the figure, $x$ ranges over variables, $P$ over process expressions, and $R$ over process expressions of the form $x(x_1, \ldots, x_n)$=>$P$.

A behavior of each process is naturally derived from inference rules of linear logic. For example, from the inference shown in the Figure 1, we can regard a formula $\exists x_1 \cdots \exists x_n.(x(x_1,\ldots,x_n)^\perp \otimes P)$ as a process which receives a message $x(v_1,\ldots,v_n)$ and then behaves like $P[v_1/x_1,\ldots,v_n/x_n]$. For instance,

$$\cfrac{\cfrac{\vdash x(v_1,\ldots,v_n), x(v_1,\ldots,v_n)^\perp \qquad \vdash P[v_1/x_1,\ldots,v_n/x_n], \Gamma}{\vdash x(v_1,\ldots,v_n)^\perp \otimes P[v_1/x_1,\ldots,v_n/x_n], x(v_1,\ldots,v_n), \Gamma} \otimes}{\vdash \exists x_1 \cdots \exists x_n.(x(x_1,\ldots,x_n)^\perp \otimes P), x(v_1,\ldots,v_n), \Gamma} \exists$$

**Fig. 1.** Inference corresponding to Message Reception

`(m(1) | m(x) => n(x+1))` makes transitions as follows:

$$(\texttt{m(1) | m(x) => n(x+1))} \longrightarrow \texttt{n(1+1)} \longrightarrow \texttt{n(2)}$$

Message predicates (like m and n above), which construct messages, are created by the $(\forall$, in linear logic notation) operator. `$x.P` creates a message predicate and binds $x$ to it in $P$. A choice `(m(x)=>P)&(n(x)=>Q)` either receives a message `m(v)` and becomes `P[v/x]`, or receives a message `n(v)` and becomes `Q[v/x]`. A **proc** statement defines a recursive process just as a **fun** statement defines a recursive function in ML. For example,

```
proc forwarder m n = m x => n x;
```

defines a process *forwarder* as a process which takes two message predicates m and n as arguments, and receives a value of x via a message m and sends it via a message n.

A process `counter[13]` is defined in HACL as follows:

```
proc counter n (inc, read, reset) =
     inc() => (counter (n+1) (inc, read, reset))
  & read(reply) => (reply n | counter n (inc, read, reset))
  & reset() => (counter 0 (inc, read, reset));
```

The process **counter** is parameterized by message predicates **inc**, **read**, and **reset**. If it receives a message `inc()`, then it increments a counter value n by 1. If it receives a message `read(reply)`, it sends a value of n to **reply**. If it receives a message `reset()`, it resets a counter value to 0. Higher-Order ACL can be viewed as an asynchronous counterpart of Milner's higher-order, polyadic $\pi$-calculus. For those who are familiar with $\pi$-calculus, we give a rough correspondence between higher-order ACL and polyadic $\pi$-calculus in Appendix B.

## 2.2 Syntax and Operational Semantics

Now, we formally define the syntax and operational semantics of HACL. First, we define *preterms* of HACL.

| Textual Notation | Linear Logic Formula | Description |
|---|---|---|
| - | $\perp$ | inaction |
| T | $\top$ | terminator |
| $x(e_1,\ldots,e_n) \mid P$ | $x(e_1,\ldots,e_n) \,\rotatebox[origin=c]{180}{\&}\, P$ | *1 |
| $x(x_1,\ldots x_n) \Rightarrow P$ | $\exists x_1 \cdots \exists x_n.(x(x_1,\ldots,x_n)^{\perp} \otimes P)$ | *2 |
| $R_1 \& R_2$ | $R_1 \oplus R_2$ | behaves like $R_1$ or $R_2$ |
| $P_1 \mid P_2$ | $P_1 \,\rotatebox[origin=c]{180}{\&}\, P_2$ | parallel composition |
| $\$x.P$ | $\forall x.P$ | name creation |
| $?P$ | $?P$ | unbounded replication |
| let proc $Ax_1\ldots x_n = P$ in $Ae_1\ldots e_n$ end | let $A=\mathbf{fix}(\lambda A.\lambda x_1.\cdots\lambda x_n.P)$ in $Ae_1\cdots e_n$ | process definition |

*1 $\cdots$ sends a message $x(e_1,\ldots,e_n)$, and then behaves like $P$
*2 $\cdots$ receives a message $x(e_1,\ldots,e_n)$, and then behaves like $P[e_1/x_1,\ldots,e_n/x_n]$

**Fig. 2.** Syntax of $HACL$ process expressions

**Definition 2.1 (preterms)** A set of *preterms*, ranged over by $e$, is defined by the following syntax:

$$e ::= x \mid c \mid e_1 e_2 \mid \lambda x.e \mid (e_1,e_2) \mid fst(e_1) \mid snd(e_2) \mid \text{let } x = e_1 \text{ in } e_2 \text{ end}$$
$$\mid \mathbf{fix}(\lambda x.e) \mid e_1 \,\rotatebox[origin=c]{180}{\&}\, e_2 \mid r \mid \forall x.e \mid ?e$$
$$r ::= \exists x_1 \cdots \exists x_n.(x(x_1,\ldots,x_n)^{\perp} \otimes e) \mid r_1 \oplus r_2$$

where $x$ stands for variables and $c$ for constants including logical connectives $\top, \perp$ and basic values such as integers.

Not all preterms are valid terms in HACL. For example, a term

    m(true) | m(x) => n(x+1)

(in the textual notation) transits to n(true+1), which results in type error. In order to exclude such terms, we introduce a notion of types. Since each process in Higher-Order ACL corresponds to a formula of higher-order linear logic, the notion of *well-typed processes* corresponds to *well-formed formulas* of higher-order linear logic. In order to allow polymorphism, we introduce type schemes as follows.

**Definition 2.2 (monotypes, type schemes)** A set of *monotypes*, ranged over by $\tau$, and a set of *type schemes*, ranged over by $\sigma$, are given by the following syntax:

$$\tau ::= \alpha \mid b \mid o \mid \tau \to \tau \mid \tau \times \tau$$
$$\sigma ::= \tau \mid \forall \alpha.\sigma$$

where $\alpha$ stands for type variables and $b$ for base types. $o$ is the distinguished type for propositions (i.e., processes or messages).

For example, $int \rightarrow o$ is a type of predicates on integer, that is, a type of processes or messages which take an integer as an argument. $\forall \alpha. \alpha \times \alpha \rightarrow o$ represents a set of all monotypes of the form $\tau \times \tau \rightarrow o$.

Typing rules for preterms are given in Figure 3. In the figure, $T$, called a *type*

<br>

(const) $T \vdash c : \tau$ if $\langle c, \sigma \rangle \in$ **Const** and $\tau$ is a generic instance of $\sigma$

(var) $T \vdash x : \tau$ if $x \in dom(T), T(x) = \tau$.    (abs) $\dfrac{T\{x \mapsto \tau_1\} \vdash e : \tau_2}{T \vdash \lambda x.e : \tau_1 \rightarrow \tau_2}$

(app) $\dfrac{T \vdash e_1 : \tau_1 \rightarrow \tau_2 \quad T \vdash e_2 : \tau_1}{T \vdash e_1 e_2 : \tau_2}$    (let) $\dfrac{T \vdash e_1 : \tau_1 \quad T \vdash e_2[e_1/x] : \tau_2}{T \vdash \text{let } x = e_1 \text{ in } e_2 \text{ end} : \tau_2}$

**Fig. 3.** Typing Rules

<br>

*assignment*, is a map from a finite set of variables to monotypes. **Const** is a set of pairs $(c, \sigma)$, where $c$ is a constant and $\sigma$ is its type scheme. A monotype $\tau$ is called a generic instance of $\forall \alpha_1 \cdots \forall \alpha_n . \tau'$, if $\tau \equiv \tau'[\tau_1/\alpha_1, \ldots, \tau_n/\alpha_n]$ for some $\tau_1, \ldots, \tau_n$. We assume **Const** contains at least the following constants:

$(\bullet, \bullet) : \forall \alpha. \forall \beta. \alpha \rightarrow \beta \rightarrow \alpha \times \beta$
$fst : \forall \alpha. \forall \beta. \alpha \times \beta \rightarrow \alpha, \; snd : \forall \alpha. \forall \beta. \alpha \times \beta \rightarrow \beta$
$\otimes, \otimes, \oplus : o \rightarrow o \rightarrow o$
$\top, \bot : o$
$(\bullet)^{\bot}, ? : o \rightarrow o$
$\Sigma : \forall \alpha. (\alpha \rightarrow o) \rightarrow o$
$\Pi : \forall \alpha. ((\alpha \rightarrow o) \rightarrow o) \rightarrow o$

Binary logical connectives $\otimes, \otimes, \oplus$ has a type $o \rightarrow o \rightarrow o$, because they take two propositions and produce a proposition. Computationally, they take two processes and make a process. $\exists x.e$ and $\forall x.e$ is respectively regarded as an abbreviated form of $\Sigma(\lambda x.e)$ and $\Pi(\lambda x.e)$.[2] The resulting typing rules for $\exists$ and $\forall$ are given in Figure 4.

<br>

(exists) $\dfrac{T\{x \mapsto \tau\} \vdash e : o}{T \vdash \exists x.e : o}$    (forall) $\dfrac{T\{x \mapsto \tau \rightarrow o\} \vdash e : o}{T \vdash \forall x.e : o}$

**Fig. 4.** Derived Typing Rules

<br>

Please note that the typing rules are the same as Damas-Milner type system for ML. *Principal typing* can be defined in the usual manner as follows:

---

[2] The reason we assign different types to $\Sigma$ and $\Pi$ is that we restrict that $x$ in $\forall x.e$ must be a message predicate, hence must be of type $\tau \rightarrow o$ for some $\tau$.

**Definition 2.3 (principal typing)** *A pair consisting of a type assignment $T$ and a monotype $\tau$ is a principal typing of $e$, if it satisfies the following conditions.*

1. $T \vdash e : \tau$
2. *If $T' \vdash e : \tau'$, then there exists a substitution $S$ on type variables such that $ST \subseteq T'$ and $S\tau = \tau'$.*

From the definition, principal typing is unique up to renaming on type variables. The followings are the well-known theorems on Damas-Milner type system.

**Proposition 2.1** *If $T \vdash e : \tau$ for some $T$ and $\tau$, then there is the principal typing of $e$.*

**Proposition 2.2** *There is an algorithm which, given a preterm $e$, computes the principal typing for $e$ if it exists, or reports failure otherwise.*

Now, we consider only the well-typed subset of preterms.

**Definition 2.4 (terms)** A preterm $e$ is called a *term* (or expression) of type $\tau$, if there is a derivation of $T \vdash e : \tau$ for some $T$. A term of type $o$ is called a *process expression*.

We often write $g$ for a process expression.

We have implemented a type inference system for Higher-Order ACL. The followings are sample sessions of the HACL type inference system.

```
proc forwarder m n = m x => n x;
(* This type writer style is user's input *)
val forwarder = proc: ('a->o)->('a->o)->o
(* This slanted style is system's output. *)

proc buffer(in, out) =
  in(x, ack) =>
    (ack() | $ack2.(out(x, ack2)
                     | ack2() => buffer(in, out)));
```

*val buffer = proc: ('a\*(unit->o)->o)\*('a\*(unit->o)->o)->o*

The inferred type for **forwarder** implies that it takes two message predicates (i.e., communication channels) as arguments, and that m and n take an argument of the same type. A process **buffer(in, out)** receives a message **in(x, ack)**, and then sends an acknowledgement message **ack()** and a message **out(x, ack2)**. Then, the process waits for an acknowledgement message from a receiver of the **out** message, and then becomes the original process **buffer(in, out)**. The inferred type implies that in and out has the same type $\tau \times (unit \rightarrow o) \rightarrow o$ for some $\tau$, where $\tau$ is a type of **x** and $unit \rightarrow o$ is a type of ack, ack2.

Now, we give an operational semantics of HACL in the style of structural operational semantics. The following *structural congruence* simplifies the presentation of transition rules.

**Definition 2.5 (structural congruence: $\cong$)** *Structural congruence* $\cong$ over expressions is the smallest reflexive and transitive congruence relation including the following relations. (The last relation corresponds to $\alpha$-conversion rule in $\lambda$-calculus.)

1. $g_1 \otimes g_2 \cong g_2 \otimes g_1$
2. $(g_1 \otimes g_2) \otimes g_3 \cong g_1 \otimes (g_2 \otimes g_3)$
3. $g_1 \oplus g_2 \cong g_2 \oplus g_1$
4. $(g_1 \oplus g_2) \oplus g_3 \cong g_1 \oplus (g_2 \oplus g_3)$
5. $\forall x.(g_1 \otimes g_2) \cong g_1 \otimes \forall x.g_2$ if $x$ is not free in $g_1$.
6. $\forall x.g \cong \forall y.g[y/x]$ where $y$ does not appear free in $g$.

Please notice that the above structural congruence is based on logical equivalence of formulas in linear logic.

   Reduction relation $\longrightarrow_\lambda$ on $\lambda$-terms, and transition relation $\longrightarrow$ over expressions is respectively defined in Figure 5 and Figure 6. In the figures, $v$ ranges over a set of *values*, which is a subset of terms and defined by the following syntax:

$$v ::= x \mid c \mid \lambda x.e \mid \forall x.e$$

where $e$ ranges over terms.

$\lambda$: $(\lambda x.e)v \longrightarrow_\lambda e[v/x]$

**App1:** $\dfrac{e_1 \longrightarrow_\lambda e_1'}{e_1 e_2 \longrightarrow_\lambda e_1' e_2}$
   **App2:** $\dfrac{e \longrightarrow_\lambda e'}{ve \longrightarrow_\lambda ve'}$

**Pair1:** $\dfrac{e_1 \longrightarrow_\lambda e_1'}{(e_1, e_2) \longrightarrow_\lambda (e_1', e_2)}$
   **Pair2:** $\dfrac{e \longrightarrow_\lambda e'}{(v, e) \longrightarrow_\lambda (v, e')}$

**Let1:** $\dfrac{e_1 \longrightarrow_\lambda e_1'}{\text{let } x = e_1 \text{ in } e_2 \text{ end} \longrightarrow_\lambda \text{let } x = e_1' \text{ in } e_2 \text{ end}}$
**Let2:** $\text{let } x = v \text{ in } e \text{ end} \longrightarrow_\lambda e[v/x]$

**Fix:** $\text{fix}\lambda x.e \longrightarrow_\lambda e[(\text{fix}\lambda x.e)/x]$

**Fig. 5.** Definition of $\longrightarrow_\lambda$

   The following theorem indicates that no type mismatch error occurs in the evaluation of well-typed terms.

**Proposition 2.3** *If $T \vdash e : \tau$ and $e \longrightarrow e'$, then $T \vdash e : \tau$.*

A proof sketch of this proposition is given in Appendix .

   We write $\longrightarrow^*$ for a reflexive and transitive closure of $\longrightarrow$. Then, the following theorem can be proved in the same manner as in the first-order ACL[11].

**Proposition 2.4** *Let $g$ be a process expression. Then, $g \longrightarrow^* \top$ only if $\vdash g$ is provable in $HLL_{\lambda\text{let}}$.*

$$\cong: \frac{g_1 \cong g_2 \quad g_1 \longrightarrow g_1' \quad g_1' \cong g_2'}{g_2 \longrightarrow g_2'} \quad \lambda: \frac{g_1 \longrightarrow_\lambda g_2}{g_2 \longrightarrow g_2'}$$

**Com:** $(\exists x_1 \cdots \exists x_n.(x(x_1,\ldots,x_n)^\perp \otimes g) \wp x(v_1,\ldots,v_n) \longrightarrow g[v_1/x_1,\ldots,v_n/x_n]$

$$\wp: \frac{g_1 \longrightarrow g_1'}{g_1 \wp g_2 \longrightarrow g_1' \wp g_2} \qquad\qquad \oplus: \frac{g_1 \wp g_3 \longrightarrow g'}{(g_1 \oplus g_2) \wp g_3 \longrightarrow g'}$$

$$\forall 1: \frac{g \longrightarrow g'}{\forall x.g \longrightarrow \forall x.g'} \qquad\qquad \forall 2: \forall x.g \longrightarrow g \text{ if } x \text{ is not free in } g$$

$$?: \frac{g_1 \wp g_2 \longrightarrow g'}{?g_1 \wp g_2 \longrightarrow ?g_1 \wp g'}$$

$$\top: \top \wp g \longrightarrow \top \qquad\qquad\qquad \bot: \bot \wp g \longrightarrow g$$

**Fig. 6.** Transition rules for expressions

Inference rules of higher-order linear logic $HLL_{\lambda,let}$ are given in Appendix C. The above proposition says that every process that can reach the terminal state ($\top$) is a valid formula of higher-order linear logic.

The converse of Proposition 2.4 does not hold. For example,

    m(fn x=>(p=>q)) | m(y)=>(y()=>T) | p=>q

transits to:

    (p=>q)=>T | p=>q

This is not a preterm, hence there is no transition sequence:

    m(fn x=>(p=>q)) | m(y)=>(y()=>T) | p=>q   ⟶   T

On the other hand, the corresponding formula has a proof in linear logic shown in Figure 7. The problem is that the set of terms are not closed with respect to transition relation. It will be resolved in Section 4.1 by refining the basic type system.

$$\frac{\vdash m(\lambda x.(p^\perp \otimes q)), m(\lambda x.(p^\perp \otimes q))^\perp \quad \dfrac{\dfrac{\vdash (p^\perp \otimes q)^\perp, p^\perp \otimes q \quad \vdash \top}{\vdash (p^\perp \otimes q)^\perp \otimes \top), p^\perp \otimes q}}{\vdash m(\lambda x.(p^\perp \otimes q)), (m(\lambda x.(p^\perp \otimes q))^\perp \otimes (p^\perp \otimes q)^\perp \otimes \top), p^\perp \otimes q}}{\vdash m(\lambda x.(p^\perp \otimes q)), \exists y.(m(y)^\perp \otimes y()^\perp \otimes \top), p^\perp \otimes q}$$

**Fig. 7.** Proof in Linear Logic

## 3 Higher-Order Concurrent Programming in HACL

This section demonstrates the power of higher-order concurrent programming in HACL. In Higher-Order ACL, processes can be parameterized by other processes and interfaces (message predicates), just as functions can be parameterized by other functions in functional programming. This dramatically improves the modularity and code reuse of concurrent programs. We also show that HACL extended with records naturally allows concurrent object-oriented style programming.

## 3.1 Hierarchical Construction of Processes

By using higher-order processes, we can construct a large process by composing smaller subprocesses. Although it might look possible with only first-order processes (as is shown in [13]), higher-order processes are very important in the sense that it makes a process independent of a particular implementation of its subcomponent processes, by which enhancing modularity.

For example, consider the following **point** process:

```
proc point (x, y) move =
    move (dx, dy, ack) =>
            (ack() | point (x+dx+0.0, y+dy+0.0) move);
val point = proc: real*real->(real*real*(unit->o)->o)->o
```

For the simplicity, we assume that the **point** process handles only one message **move**. After receiving a message **move**, it sends an acknowledgement **ack** and updates values of **x** and **y**. We can define a **rectangle** process by composing two **point** processes as follows.

```
local proc rectangle' move1 move2 move =
        move(dx, dy, ack) =>
            $ack1.(move1(dx, dy, ack1)
                | ack1() => (move2(dx, dy, ack)
                            | rectangle' move1 move2 move)
    in proc rectangle(p1, p2) move =
            $m1.$m2.(p1 m1 | p2 m2 | rectangle' m1 m2 move);
val rectangle = proc: (('a*'b*(unit->o)->o)->o) ->(('a*'b*(unit->o)-
>o)->o)->('a*'b->o)->o
```

A particular instance of **rectangle** process is created by instantiating **p1** and **p2** to **point** processes as follows:

```
proc new_rectangle (x1, y1, x2, y2) move =
        rectangle(point(x1, y1), (point(x2, y2)) move;
val new_rectangle = proc: real*real*real*real->(real*real*(unit->o)->o)-
>o
```

```
$move.(new_rectangle(0.0, 0.0, 1.0, 2.0) move | ...);
```

A **new_rectangle** process makes a new rectangle, which is internally composed of two **point** processes and a new component **rectangle'** (see Figure 8). When a **move** message is sent to the **rectangle** process, the **rectangle'** process receives it, and forwards it to the two **point** processes. Important point about the **rectangle** process is that it is independent of a particular implementation of **point** processes. For example, let us define another point process:

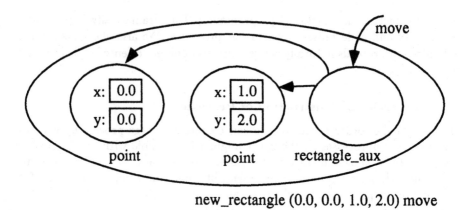

new_rectangle (0.0, 0.0, 1.0, 2.0) move

**Fig. 8.** Rectangle Process

```
proc point2 (r, theta) move =
    move(dx, dy,ack) =>
         let x=r*cos(theta) and y=r*sin(theta) in
             (ack() | point2 (radius(x+dx, y+dy),
                               angle(x+dx, y+dy)) move)
         end;
```
*val point2 = proc: real\*real->(real\*real\*(unit->o)->o)->o*

Then, `rectangle` can take `point2` as an argument in place of `point`.

```
proc new_rectangle2 (x1, y1, x2, y2) move =
    rectangle (point2(radius(x1, y1), angle(x1, y1)),
               point(x2, y2)) move;
```
*val new_rectangle = proc: real\*real\*real\*real->(real\*real\*(unit->o)->o)->o*

A `new_rectangle2` process is composed of two point processes where one of them is `point2` and the other is `point`. Such independence of a particular implementation is very important in providing abstractions for concurrent programs. In the example of the rectangle process, we need not know how point processes are actually implemented; the point processes might be composed of multiple sub-processes or of a single process. This provides a separation between abstraction and granularity of processes. In the above example, if we require more parallelism, we can divide point processes into multiple processes. Such change of the component is transparent to the rectangle process. In contrast, in the first-order concurrent language, the implementation of rectangle process must be also modified, which violates the principle of *structured programming*.

## 3.2 Higher-Order Processes for Making Communication Topologies between Processes

Higher-order processes are also useful for making various communication topologies between processes. For example, consider the following higher-order process linear:

```
proc linear procs (left, right) =
    case procs of
        nil => _
      | pr::nil => pr(left, right)
      | pr::procs' =>
            $link.(pr(left, link) | linear procs' (link, right));
val linear = proc: (('a->o)*('a->o)->o) list->('a->o)*('a->o)->o
```

We use the notation of ML for the case statement and list expressions. The higher-order process linear takes a list of processes procs as the first argument, and connects them in a linear topology. We can easily construct $n$-place buffer by applying a list of $n$ buffer processes as an argument of linear process.

```
fun nlist(n, x) = if n=0 then nil else x::nlist(n-1, x);
val nlist = fn: int*'a->'a list

proc nbuffer n (in, out) = linear (nlist(n, buffer)) (in, out);

val nbuffer = proc: int->('a*(unit->o)->o)*('a*(unit->o)->o)->o
```

We can also construct a higher-order process for making a ring structure:

```
proc ring procs = $link.(linear procs (link, link));
val ring = proc: (('a->o)*('a->o)->o) list->o
```

The higher-order process ring can be constructed by instantiating left and right to the same message predicate (i.e. communication channel). The dining philosopher problem can be described by defining a behavior of each philosopher, and then connecting them by ring: (Note that the program presented here is the simplest one and does not prevent deadlock.)

```
local
  proc philosopher n (lfork, rfork) =
    (* get left and right forks *)
    lfork()=>rfork()=>
    (* start eating *)
      seq(soutput(makestring(n)^": I am eating\n"),
    (* finish eating *)
          fn ()=>seq(soutput(makestring(n)^": finished\n"),
    (* release forks, and *)
          fn ()=> (lfork() | rfork()
    (* repeat the same behavior *)
```

```
                        | philosopher n (lfork, rfork)))));
  in
    (* philosopher who has a fork in his left hand *)
    proc philosopher_and_fork n (lfork, rfork) =
                        lfork() | philospher n (lfork, rfork)
  end;
  fun nlist n f = if n=0 then nil else f(n)::(nlist (n-1) f);
  (* connects 5 philosophers by ring *)
  proc philosophers () = ring (nlist 5 philosopher_and_fork);

  philosophers();
  5: I am eating
  5: finished
  3: I am eating
  1: I am eating
  3: finished
  ....
```

In the above program, **seq** is a process for sequencing the execution, defined by:

```
proc seq(e1, e2) = $token.(e1(token) | token()=>e2());
val seq = proc: ((unit->o)->o)*(unit->o)->o
```

**seq(e1, e2)** creates a new message predicate **token** and executes **e1(token)**, and after a message **token()** is sent, **e2()** is invoked. **ring** can be also used for constructing a ring scheduler, a ring buffer, etc.

In the same manner, we can also define higher-order processes for making any communication topologies between processes, such as mesh topology and torus topology.

### 3.3   Concurrent Object-Oriented Style Programming

Sequential object-oriented programming has been often discussed based on $\lambda$-calculus extended with *records*.[7] In an analogous manner, we can support concurrent object-oriented style programming by extending HACL with record calculus. Let us consider the following **point** process:

```
proc point (x, y) (getx, gety, set) =
    getx(reply) =>
            (reply(x) | point(x, y)(getx,gety,set))
  & gety(reply) =>
            (reply(y) | point(x, y) self)
  & set(newx,newy, ack)=>
            (ack() | point(newx, newy) self);
```

The **point** process receives three kinds of messages **getx**, **gety** and **set**. If we put three message predicates **getx**, **gety** and **set** together into a record, we obtain the following refined process definition:

```
proc point (x, y) self =
   #getx self (reply) =>
           (reply(x) | point(x, y) self)
 & #gety self (reply) =>
           (reply(y) | point(x, y) self)
 & #set self (newx, newy, ack) =>
           (ack() | point(newx, newy) self);
```
val point = proc: 'a∗'b-> 'c::{getx:('a->o)->o, gety:('b->o)->o, set:'a∗'b∗(unit->o)->o}->o

#⟨field-name⟩ is an operator for field extraction. The resulting process definition just looks like the definition of concurrent objects[27]. A field name corresponds to a method name. self, which is a record consisting of at least three fields getx, gety, and set, can be considered as an *identifier* of a concurrent object point. self can be used for sending a message to itself, as in ordinary object-oriented languages. The above type infered for point is based on Ohori's type inference algorithm for polymorphic record calculus[18]. 'c::{getx:('a->o)->o, gety:('b->o)->o, set:'a∗'b∗(unit->o)->o} represents a type variable which ranges over a set of the following types:

$$\{getx:('a->o)->o, gety:('b->o)->o, set:'a∗'b∗(unit->o)->o, ...\}$$

The following is an expression for creating a new point object and sends to it a message getx.

```
$id.(point (1.0, 2.0) id  (* create a point object *)
    | $reply.(#getx id reply (* send getx message *)
            | reply(x)=> ...) (* get a value of x *)
```

Thus, message sending in concurrent object-oriented programming languages is encoding as (i)extracting the corresponding field from the identifier of the receiver (which is implemented as a record of message predicates) and (ii)sending an HACL message via the extracted message predicate.

If a programmer wants to ensure that messages except for getx, gety, and set are never sent to the point object, he can explicitly attach the following type constraints on self:

```
proc point (x, y) (self:{getx:'a, gety:'b, set:'c}) =
   #getx self (reply) => (reply(x) | point(x,y) self)
 & #gety self (reply) => (reply(y) | point(x,y) self)
 & #set self (newx,newy)=> (point(newx,newy) self);
```
val point = proc: 'a∗'b->{getx:('a->o)->o, gety:('b->o)->o, set:'a∗'b->o}->o

Then, self is ensured to be a record consisting of *just* three fields getx, gety and set. Sending a message other than getx, gety and set is statically detected as an invalid field extraction from the record self.

```
$id.(point (1.0, 2.0) id | #move id (1.0, 1.0))
(* create a point object and send to it a move message *)
```
*Type Mismatch on Variable id*

In [14][12], we describe more extensively how statically-typed concurrent object-oriented programming languages which support various mechanisms such as inheritance, method overriding, and method access control, can be realized on top of HACL.

# 4 Refinement of The Basic Type System

Since the basic type system of Higher-Order ACL presented in Section 2 is Damas-Milner's one, we can easily extend the basic type system with subtyping, recursive types, record types, etc., by which obtaining the more expressive power of Higher-Order ACL. In fact, we have briefly shown in the previous section that HACL can support concurrent object-oriented style programming by introducing record types. This section introduces somewhat different extensions of the basic type system. We refine the type system in two ways, not for making the language more expressive, but for extracting computationally more useful information from programs.

## 4.1 Distinction between Messages and Processes

The first refinement is introduced for distinguishing between messages and processes. Since both messages and processes are represented by formulas, they are both assigned a type $o$ in the basic type system. However, from the computational point of view, it is valuable to distinguish between them. For example, consider the expression x(y) => y(z) => P (=> is right associative), which receives a value of y via a message predicate x, then receives a value of z via y. Clearly, y should be a message predicate. However, the basic type system requires only that y be of type $\tau \rightarrow o$ for some $\tau$. Therefore, the example given in Section 3 is well-typed:

```
m(fn x=>(p=>q)) | m(y)=>(y()=>T) | p=>q
```

although it transits to

```
(p=>q)=>T | p=>q
```

hence goes wrong! Although we can derive a type $o$ for (p=>q)=>T in the basic typing rules, it is not a preterm any more.

Another problem arises when we want to *efficiently* implement the Higher-Order ACL. Transition relation $g_1 \longrightarrow g_2$ is intended to correspond to $g_1 \circ\!\!-\, g_2$. Therefore, it is incorrect to deduce $fg_1 \longrightarrow fg_2$ from $g_1 \longrightarrow g_2$. For example, let $f$ be a formula $\lambda x.(x^\perp \otimes g)$ (we assume $g$ does not contain $x$ in free). Then, even if $g_1 \circ\!\!-\, g_2$ hods, we cannot deduce $fg_1 \circ\!\!-\, fg_2 (\equiv g_1^\perp \otimes g \circ\!\!-\, g_2^\perp \otimes g)$. Therefore, whether the evaluation of a process expresion proceeds or not depends on the context of the expression. $g$ can be evaluated in a context $C[g] = g \, ⅋ \, g'$, while it cannot be evaluated in a context $C[g] = eg$. The operational semantics presented in Section 3 reflects this by distinguishing evaluations of $\lambda$-terms and transitions of process expressions. However, as for the implementation, it is costly to check the context at each evaluation step.

In order to overcome these problems, we divide a type $o$ into $m$, a type of messages, and $p$, a type of processes. $m$ and $p$ can be considered a kind of subtypes of $o$. To keep type inference simple, instead of introducing a general form of subtyping, we consider the following refined type scheme.

$$\tau \ (\text{monotypes}) ::= \alpha \mid b \mid m \mid p \mid \tau \times \tau \mid \tau \to \tau$$
$$k \ (\text{kinds}) ::= U \mid O \mid NonM \mid NonO$$
$$\sigma \ (\text{type schemes}) ::= \tau \mid \forall \alpha :: k.\sigma$$

A kind $U$ stands for a set of all monotypes, $O$ for a set $\{m, p\}$, $NonM$ for a set of all monotypes except for $m$, and $NonO$ for a set of all monotypes except for $m$, $p$. "$\forall \alpha :: k.\sigma$" means that $\alpha$ in $\sigma$ can be instantiated to an element of $k$. We often write $\forall \alpha.\tau$ for $\forall \alpha :: U.\tau$. Types of constants are accordingly refined as follows:

$$⅋, \otimes, \oplus : \forall \alpha :: O.\forall \beta :: O.\alpha \to \beta \to p$$
$$\top, \bot : p$$
$$(\bullet)^\perp : m \to p$$
$$? : \forall \alpha :: O.\alpha \to p$$
$$\Sigma : \forall \alpha.(\alpha \to p) \to p$$
$$\Pi : \forall \alpha.((\alpha \to m) \to p) \to p$$

The type of $⅋, \otimes, \oplus$ ensures that concurrent composition, message receiver, and choice are not a message but a process. The type of $(\bullet)^\perp$ ensures that $m$ in $m(x)^\perp \otimes g$ must not be a process. Refined typing rules are shown in Figure 9. $\mathcal{K}$, called a *kind assignment*, is a map from a finite set of variables to kinds. A kinding judgement $\mathcal{K} \vdash \tau :: k$ should be read, "A type $\tau$ has a kind $k$ under a kind assignment $\mathcal{K}$." A typing judgement $\mathcal{K}, \mathcal{T} \vdash e : \tau$ should be read, "An expression $e$ has a type $\tau$ under $\mathcal{K}, \mathcal{T}$. $\mathcal{K} \vdash \tau_1 :: NonO$ in the assumptions of the rules **abs** and **let** forbids a process expression $g$ to appear in the context $C[g] = eg$ or $C[g] = \textbf{let } x = g \textbf{ in } e \textbf{ end}$, by which overcoming the second problem stated above.

The definition of the principal typing is modified as follows.

**Definition 4.1** A pair $(\mathcal{K}, S)$ consisting of a kind assignment and a type substitution *respects* a kind assignment $\mathcal{K}'$ if, for any $\alpha \in dom(\mathcal{K}')$, $\mathcal{K} \vdash S\alpha :: \mathcal{K}'(\alpha)$.

**Definition 4.2** A pair consisting of a kind assignment $\mathcal{K}$ and a monotype $\tau$ is called an *instance* of a type scheme $\forall \alpha_1 :: k_1 \cdots \forall \alpha_n :: k_n.\sigma$ if there exists a substitution $S$ that satisfies the following conditions:

1. $(\mathcal{K}, S)$ respects a kind assignment $\{\alpha_1 \mapsto k_1, \ldots, \alpha_n \mapsto k_n\}$
2. $\tau = S\sigma$

**Kinding Rules**

$\mathcal{K} \vdash \tau :: U$ for any $\tau$

$\mathcal{K} \vdash m :: O$

$\mathcal{K} \vdash p :: O$

$\mathcal{K} \vdash \alpha :: O$ if $\mathcal{K}(\alpha) = O$

$\mathcal{K} \vdash \tau :: NonM$ if $\tau \neq m$ and $\tau$ is not a type variable

$\mathcal{K} \vdash \alpha :: NonM$ if $\mathcal{K}(\alpha) = NonM$ or $NonO$

$\mathcal{K} \vdash \tau :: NonO$ if $\tau \neq m, p$ and $\tau$ is not a type variable

$\mathcal{K} \vdash \alpha :: NonO$ if $\mathcal{K}(\alpha) = NonO$

**Typing Rules**

(const) $\mathcal{K}, T \vdash c : \tau$ if $(c, \sigma) \in \mathbf{Const}$ and $(\mathcal{K}, \tau)$ is an instance of $\sigma$

(var) $\mathcal{K}, T \vdash x : \tau$ if $x \in dom(T), T(x) = \tau$.

(abs) $\dfrac{\mathcal{K}, T\{x \mapsto \tau_1\} \vdash e : \tau_2 \quad \mathcal{K} \vdash \tau_1 :: NonO \quad \mathcal{K} \vdash \tau_2 :: NonM}{T \vdash \lambda x.e : \tau_1 \to \tau_2}$

(app) $\dfrac{\mathcal{K}, T \vdash e_1 : \tau_1 \to \tau_2 \quad \mathcal{K}, T \vdash e_2 : \tau_1}{\mathcal{K}, T \vdash e_1 e_2 : \tau_2}$

(let) $\dfrac{\mathcal{K}, T \vdash e_1 : \tau_1 \quad \mathcal{K} \vdash \tau_1 :: NonO \quad \mathcal{K}, T \vdash e_2[e_1/x] : \tau_2}{\mathcal{K}, T \vdash \text{let } x = e_1 \text{ in } e_2 \text{ end} : \tau_2}$

**Fig. 9.** Refined Typing Rules

**Definition 4.3 (principal typing)** A triple $(\mathcal{K}, T, \tau)$ is a *principal typing* of $e$ if the following conditions hold:

1. $\mathcal{K}, T \vdash e : \tau$
2. If $\mathcal{K}', T' \vdash e : \tau'$, then there exists a substitution $S$ on type variables such that
   (a) $(\mathcal{K}', S)$ respects $\mathcal{K}$
   (b) $ST \subseteq T'$
   (c) $S\tau = \tau'$

It is trivial that the principal typing is unique up to renaming. The existence of principal typing and type reconstruction algorithm is preserved.

**Proposition 4.1** *If $\mathcal{K}, T \vdash e : \tau$ for some $\mathcal{K}, T$ and $\tau$, then there is the principal typing of $e$.*

**Proposition 4.2** *There is an algorithm which, given a preterm $e$, computes the principal typing for $e$ if it exists, or reports failure otherwise.*

The following subject reduction theorem for the refined type system is proven in the same manner as that for the basic type system.

**Proposition 4.3 (subject reduction)**

1. *If $\mathcal{K}, T \vdash e : \tau$ and $e \longrightarrow_\lambda e'$, then $\mathcal{K}, T \vdash e' : \tau$ holds.*
2. *If $\mathcal{K}, T \vdash e : \tau$ and $e \cong e'$, then $\mathcal{K}, T \vdash e' : \tau$ holds.*

3. If $\mathcal{K}, T \vdash e : p$ and $e \longrightarrow e'$, then $\mathcal{K}, T \vdash e' : p$ or $\mathcal{K}, T \vdash e' : m$ holds.

**Lemma 4.4** Let $e$ be a (well-typed) closed term of HACL. If $e \longrightarrow e'$, then $e'$ is also a (well-typed) closed term of HACL.

**Proposition 4.5** Let $e$ be a (well-typed) closed term of HACL. If $e$ is provable in $HLL_{\lambda let}$, then there is a transition sequence $e \longrightarrow'^* \top$, where $\longrightarrow'$ is a transition relation obtained by replacing the **Com** rule of $\longrightarrow$ by:

$$(\exists x_1 \cdots \exists x_n.(x(x_1, \ldots, x_n)^{\perp} \otimes g) \mathbf{?} x(e_1, \ldots, e_n) \longrightarrow g[e_1/x_1, \ldots, e_n/x_n]$$

The following is a sample session in the refined type inference system.

```
proc forwarder m n = m x => n x;
val forwarder = proc: ('a->m)->('a->'b::O)->p
```

The above output of the refined type inference system means that **forwarder** has the following type:

$$\forall \alpha. \forall \beta :: O.((\alpha \rightarrow m) \rightarrow (\alpha \rightarrow \beta) \rightarrow p)$$

It indicates that the first argument (**m**) of a process **forwarder** must be a message predicate. The second argument (**n**) can be either a message predicate or a process. The type of process **buffer** is refined as follows.

```
proc buffer(in, out) = ...;
val buffer = proc: ('a*(unit->'b::O)->m)* ('a*(unit->m)->'c::O)->p
```

## 4.2   I/O modes of messages

The basic type system does not convey any information on how message predicates are used in a particular process. For example, **m** and **n** in a process **forwarder m n** are assigned the same type, although **m** and **n** are used in a different way (i.e., **m** for input, and **n** for output). Such input/output information is useful for efficient implementation and also for statically detecting errors such as orphan messages (i.e., messages that have no receiver processes) and processes that wait for a never-returned message. For example, consider the following **worker** process:

```
proc worker job? =
        $reply.(job?(reply) | reply(job) => work(job));
```

Process **worker** asks for a job by sending a message **job?**, and receives a job via a channel **reply**. (We assume **work** is a previously defined process.) Obviously, **worker** process assumes that a receiver of the **job?** message should send a message **reply**. However, consider the following process **master**:

```
proc master job? = job?(reply) => _;
```

The **master** process receives a **job?** message, but just ignores it and produces no message. If we combine a **master** process and a **worker** process as follows:

```
$job?.(master job? | worker job?);
```

no type error is statically reported by the basic type system (and also by the extended type system in the previous subsection). However, it does go wrong in some sense at runtime, because the **worker** process never receives a **reply** message. It is better for a type system to statically detect such cases and produce some warning message. Although complete detection of such errors is difficult,[3] we can statically detect many of them by refining types for messages. We divide $m$, a type of messages, into the four types: $m$, $m^-$, $m^+$, $m^\pm$. Type $m$ represents a type of messages that are used for neither input nor output. $m^-$ ($m^+$, resp.) stands for a type of messages that are used only for input (output), and $m^\pm$ for both input and output. We accordingly refine the monotype and type scheme as follows:

$$\tau ::= \alpha \mid b \mid m \mid m^- \mid m^+ \mid m^\pm \mid p \mid \tau \times \tau \mid \tau \to \tau$$
$$k ::= U \mid NonM \mid NonO \mid M \mid M^- \mid M^+ \mid O \mid O^+$$
$$\sigma ::= \tau \mid \forall \alpha :: k.\sigma$$

$M, M^-, M^+, O, O^+$ represents the following sets of monotypes.

$$M = \{m, m^-, m^+, m^\pm\}, M^- = \{m^-, m^\pm\}, M^+ = \{m^+, m^\pm\}$$
$$O = \{p, m, m^-, m^+, m^\pm\}, O^+ = \{p, m^+, m^\pm\}$$

The types of constants are refined as follows:

$$\otimes, \otimes, \oplus : \forall \alpha :: O^+.\forall \beta :: O^+.\alpha \to \beta \to p$$
$$\top, \bot : p$$
$$(\bullet)^\perp : \forall \alpha :: M^-.\alpha \to p$$
$$? : \forall \alpha :: O^+.\alpha \to p$$
$$\Sigma : \forall \alpha.(\alpha \to p) \to p$$
$$\Pi : \forall \alpha.\forall \beta :: M.((\alpha \to \beta) \to p) \to p$$

Kinding rules are modified as is shown in Figure 10. The existence of principle typing and type reconstruction algorithm is again preserved. Subject reduction theorem is given as follows.

**Proposition 4.6 (subject reduction)**  *1. If $K, T \vdash e : \tau$ and $e \longrightarrow_\lambda e'$, then $K, T \vdash e' : \tau$.*

*2. If $K, T \vdash e : p$ and $e \longrightarrow e'$, then $K, T \vdash e' : \tau$ for some $\tau \in O$.*

As a corollary of the subject reduction theorem, we obtain the following theorem.

**Corollary 4.7**  *If there is a derivation $x : \tau \to m^+ \vdash e : p$ for some $\tau$, then $x$ is never used for input in the evaluation of $e$.*

---

[3] Because flow of messages often depends not only on types but on values, type information is not enough for the complete detection.

**Kinding Rules**

$\mathcal{K} \vdash \tau :: U$ for any $\tau$

$\mathcal{K} \vdash \tau :: NonM$ if $\tau \neq m$ and $\tau$ is not a type variable

$\mathcal{K} \vdash \alpha :: NonM$ if $\mathcal{K}(\alpha) = NonM$ or $NonO$

$\mathcal{K} \vdash \tau :: NonO$ if $\tau \neq m, p$ and $\tau$ is not a type variable

$\mathcal{K} \vdash \alpha :: NonO$ if $\mathcal{K}(\alpha) = NonO$

$\mathcal{K} \vdash \tau :: O$ if $\tau \in O$

$\mathcal{K} \vdash \alpha :: O$ if $\mathcal{K}(\tau) = M, M^+, M^-, O^+,$ or $O$

$\mathcal{K} \vdash \tau :: O^+$ if $\tau \in O^+$

$\mathcal{K} \vdash \alpha :: O^+$ if $\mathcal{K}(\tau) = M^+$ or $O^+$

$\mathcal{K} \vdash \tau :: M^+$ if $\tau \in M^+$

$\mathcal{K} \vdash \alpha :: M^+$ if $\mathcal{K}(\tau) = M^+$

$\mathcal{K} \vdash \tau :: M^-$ if $\tau \in M^-$

$\mathcal{K} \vdash \alpha :: M^-$ if $\mathcal{K}(\tau) = M^-$

$\mathcal{K} \vdash \tau :: M$ if $\tau \in M$

$\mathcal{K} \vdash \alpha :: M$ if $\mathcal{K}(\tau) = M^-, M^+,$ or $M$

**Fig. 10.** Refined Kinding Rules

**proof** Suppose that $x$ is used for input. Then,

$$e \longrightarrow^* (\$y_1 \cdots \$y_m.\exists x_1 \cdots \exists x_n.(x(x_1,\ldots,x_n)^\perp \otimes e_1)\b8 e_2)$$

for some $e_1, e_2$. However, from the type of $(\bullet)^\perp$, there is no derivation for

$$x : \tau \to m^+ \vdash \$y_1 \cdots \$y_m.\exists x_1 \cdots \exists x_n.(x(x_1,\ldots,x_n)^\perp \otimes e_1)\b8 e_2) : p,$$

which contradicts the subject reduction theorem. □

Similarly, we obtain the following theorems.

**Corollary 4.8** *If there is a derivation* $x : \tau \to m^- \vdash e : p$ *for some* $\tau$, *then* $x$ *is not used for output in the evaluation of* $e$.

**Corollary 4.9** *If there is a derivation* $x : \tau \to m \vdash e : p$ *for some* $\tau$, *then* $x$ *is used for neither input nor output in the evaluation of* $e$.

Processes **worker** and **master** now have the following types:

worker : $\forall \alpha_1.\forall \alpha_2 :: M^-.\forall \alpha_3 :: O^+.((\alpha_1 \to \alpha_2) \to \alpha_3) \to p$
master : $\forall \alpha_1.\forall \alpha_2 :: M^-.(\alpha_1 \to \alpha_2) \to p$

Therefore, there is a derivation for

$$reply : \tau \to m^- \vdash e : p$$

where

```
e ≡$job?.(master job? | worker'(job?)),
worker'(job?)≡(job?(reply) | reply(job) => work(job)).
```

By Corolloary 4.8, $e$ does not send a message `reply`. Because `$reply`.$e \cong$ `$job?.(master job? | worker job?)`, it also implies that no `reply` message is sent in the evaluation of `$job?.(master job? | worker job?)`. The current type inference system incorporates this technique and produces warnings for orphan messages.


# 5 Discussion

*Concurrent Logic Programming* Although both concurrent logic programming[22] and HACL are both based on *computation as controlled deduction*, they are quite different, because of the difference in the underlying logics and representations of messages. Both paradigms have their advantages and disadvantages; concurrent logic programming better models stream-based communication, while HACL better models asynchronous message passing. However, type systems and inference for I/O modes on communication channels seem to be simpler and clearer in the context of HACL; because messages in HACL are represented at logic level, I/O modes of messages are distinguishable as negative/positive occurence of formulas. On the other hand, in traditional concurrent logic programming, I/O modes seem to be found only by analyzing how unification on terms proceeds.

*Type Inference v.s. Abstract Interpretation* Andreoli and Pareschi[3] proposed an abstract interpretation technique for linear logic programming languages. Although the abstract interpretation technique has a potential power for obtaining much more information than our type inference, their abstract interpretation technique for a large program is likely to become intractable. On the other hand, our type inference can be compositionally performed, hence it would be tractable in most cases. The refined type system in Section 4 allows static detections of orphan messages, dead-code eliminations, etc. Moreover, type information is also useful for the abstract interpretation, because it gives information to decide which arguments can be dropped during abstract interpretation.

*Typed Concurrent Calculi* Recently, type systems for concurrent calculi such as polyadic $\pi$-calculus and object calculus, were proposed by several people[5][9][19] [24][25]. Gay's sorting algorithm[5] can be considered a specific instance of the basic type system of HACL, where base types are restricted to only $o$, and let-polymorphism and higher-order processes are dropped. Pierce and Sangiorgi[19] introduced I/O modes to $\pi$-calculus in a different manner from ours. They consider explicitly-typed programs without let-polymorphism, and did not address the problem of type reconstruction.[4] Thus, by viewing a process as a formula of linear logic, HACL clarifies the essence of those type systems. Since the basic type system is just the same as Damas-Milner type system for ML, we can naturally integrate other extensions of typed $\lambda$-calculus, such as subtyping, recursive

---

[4] The simple I/O mode analysis in this paper is weaker than subtyping on I/O modes[19]. More powerful analysis is presented in a separate paper[10].

types, polymorphic recursion, and polymorphic record calculus. Another advantage is that types of processes, functions and basic values are uniformly typed in our type system. Most of the previous type systems for concurrent calculi only deal with types of names. Function definitions `let fun f(x)=e in ...` can be *simulated* by: `$f.(!(f(x, rep)=>e') | ...)` where `e'` is an encoding of `e` and `rep` is a channel for returning the result. However, this encoding does not allow polymorphic use of `f`, because channels have imperative natures. As a result, we need a more sophisticated type system than let-polymorphism. Moreover, from a pragmatic point of view, this encoding loses some information for efficient implementation of functions. That is, channels introduced for encoding functions are used in a very restictive manner (for example, `rep` is used only once for output inside the function), while naive type systems[5][24] for concurrent calculi fail to capture these properties. I/O modes on channels as in this paper and in [19] recover some of the lost properties, but it still seems necessary to step further, in order to claim that functions can be encoded in name passing calculi in a pragmatic sense.

$\lambda Prolog$ Our approach to introducing type system is similar to that taken in $\lambda$Prolog[16]. The major difference is that in $\lambda$Prolog, types take an important role at runtime as well as at the type checking phase, while they do not in HACL. It is because the purpose of computation in HACL is not to find answer substutions, and HACL is designed so that higher-order unification is not required.

*Higher-order linear* cc Saraswat and Lincoln[21] proposed higher-order linear cc, a kind of higher-order concurrent linear logic programming. In the untyped setting, the expressive power of their system and our system are almost the same; a message $x(v_1, \ldots, v_n)$ in higher-order ACL corresponds to $x : [v_1, \ldots, v_n]$ in higher-order linear cc. Their system, however, uses only a single binary predicate ":" to represent messages. Therefore, the difference between his system and our system is like that between $\pi$-calculus and polyadic $\pi$-calculus; in order to introduce a type system, our setting would be better. Moreover, in order to safely use the power of higher-order concurrent programming, type refinements as shown in Section 4 are indispensable, which they have not addressed.

*Concurrent ML* Concurrent ML[20] also allows higher-order concurrent programming. However, patterns of communication and process evolutions are more naturally expressed in HACL. Although effect analysis has recently been proposed to extract such patterns from Concurrent ML programs[17], it would be better for programmers to directly write such patterns.

## 6  Conclusion

We proposed a higher-order concurrent linear logic programming called Higher-Order ACL (HACL). HACL naturally integrates typed functional programming and concurrent programming in terms of a proof search in higher-order linear logic. HACL is equipped with an elegant ML-style type system, which allows static detection of type errors and also polymorphic use of processes. We have also refined the basic type system to infer more useful information such as I/O modes of messages, which allows detection of errors such as orphan messages. Such type information is also useful for efficient implementation of message passing. As demonstrated in Section 3, higher-order processes in HACL provide high modularity of concurrent programs.

We have already implemented an interpreter of Higher-Order ACL with the refined type system in Section 4.[5] We are now developing static analysis techniques for HACL[10], and constructing an efficient compiler system on multi-computers, based on this work.

# References

1. Andreoli, J.-M., and R. Pareschi, "Linear Objects: Logical processes with built-in inheritance," *New Generation Computing*, vol. 9, pp. 445–473, 1991.
2. Andreoli, J.-M., and R. Pareschi, "Communication as Fair Distribution of Knowledge," in *Proceedings of OOPSLA '91*, pp. 212–229, 1991.
3. Andreoli, J.-M., R. Pareschi, and T. Castagnetti, "Abstract Interpretation of Linear Logic Programming," in *Proceedings of International Logic Programming Symposium*, pp. 315–334, 1993.
4. Damas, L., and R. Milner, "Principal type-schemes for functional programs," in *Proceedings of ACM SIGACT/SIGPLAN Symposium on Principles of Programming Language*, pp. 207–212, 1982.
5. Gay, S. J., "A Sort Inference Algorithm for the Polyadic $\pi$-calculus," in *Proceedings of ACM SIGACT/SIGPLAN Symposium on Principles of Programming Language*, pp. 429–438, 1993.
6. Girard, J.-Y., "Linear Logic," *Theoretical Computer Science*, vol. 50, pp. 1–102, 1987.
7. Gunter, C. A., and J. C. M. (ed.), *Theoretical Aspects of Object-Oriented Programming*. The MIT Press, 1994.
8. Hodas, J., and D. Miller, "Logic programming in a fragment of intuitionistic linear logic," in *Proceedings of Sixth Annual Symposium on Logic in Computer Science*, pp. 32–42, 1991.
9. Honda, K., "Types for Dydadic Interaction," in *Proceedings of CONCUR '93*, 1993.
10. Kobayashi, N., "Static Analysis on Communication for Asynchrnous Concurrent Programming Languages." draft, 1994.
11. Kobayashi, N., and A. Yonezawa, "Asynchronous Communication Model Based on Linear Logic." to appear in Journal of Formal Aspects of Computing, Springer-Verlag.
12. Kobayashi, N., and A. Yonezawa, "Towards Foundations for Concurrent Object-Oriented Programming – Types and Language Design." submitted.

---

[5] A prototype interpreter of HACL is available via anonymous ftp from `camille.is.s.u-tokyo.ac.jp`: `pub/hacl`

13. Kobayashi, N., and A. Yonezawa, "ACL – A Concurrent Linear Logic Programming Paradigm," in *Logic Programming: Proceedings of the 1993 International Symposium*, pp. 279–294, MIT Press, 1993.

14. Kobayashi, N., and A. Yonezawa, "Type-Theoretic Foundations for Concurrent Object-Oriented Programming," in *Proceedings of ACM SIGPLAN Conference on Object-Oriented Programming Systems, Languages, and Applications (OOPSLA '94)*, pp. 31–45, 1994.

15. Milner, R., "The polyadic π-calculus: a tutorial," Tech. Rep. ECS-LFCS-91-180, University of Edinburgh, 1991.

16. Nadathur, G., and F. Pfenning, "The Type System of a Higher-Order Logic Programming Language," in *Types in Logic Programming*, pp. 245–283, The MIT Press, 1992.

17. Nielson, H. R., and F. Nielson, "Higher-Order Concurrent Programs with Finite Communicationn Topology," in *Proceedings of ACM SIGACT/SIGPLAN Symposium on Principles of Programming Language*, pp. 84–97, 1994.

18. Ohori, A., "A Compilation Method for ML-Style Polymorphic Record Calculi," in *Proceedings of ACM SIGACT/SIGPLAN Symposium on Principles of Programming Language*, pp. 154–165, 1992.

19. Pierce, B., and D. Sangiorgi, "Typing and Subtyping for Mobile Processes," in *Proceedings of IEEE Symposium on Logic in Computer Science*, pp. 376–385, 1993.

20. Reppy, J. H., "CML: A Higher-order Concurrent Language," in *Proceedings of the ACM SIGPLAN'91 Conference on Programming Language Design and Implementation*, pp. 293–305, 1991.

21. Saraswat, V., and P. Lincoln, "Higher-order, linear, concurrent constraint programming," July 1992. draft.

22. Shapiro, E., "The Family of Concurrent Logic Programming Languages," *ACM Computing Surveys*, vol. 21, no. 3, pp. 413–510, September 1989.

23. Troelstra, A. S., "Tutorial on Linear Logic," 1992. Tutorial notes in JICSLP'92.

24. Vasconcelos, V. T., and K. Honda, "Principal typing schemes in a polyadic π-calculus," in *Proceedings of CONCUR'93*, Lecture Notes in Computer Science, pp. 524–538, Springer Verlag, 1993.

25. Vasconcelos, V. T., and M. Tokoro, "A Typing System for a Calculus of Objects," in *Proceedings of the International Symposium on Object Technologies for Advanced Software*, vol. 742 of *Lecture Notes in Computer Science*, pp. 460–474, Springer Verlag, 1993.

26. Yonezawa, A., *ABCL: An Object-Oriented Concurrent System*. MIT Press, 1990.

27. Yonezawa, A., and M. Tokoro, *Object-Oriented Concurrent Programming*. The MIT Press, 1987.

# A   Informal Review of Concurrent Linear Logic Programming

This section informally reviews a basic idea of concurrent linear logic programming, independently developed by Saraswat and Lincoln[21], Kobayashi and Yonezawa[13][11].[6]

---

[6] The first concurrent linear logic language has been proposed by Andreoli and Pareschi[1][2]. However, we do not review it here because it uses a different approach for formalizing communication.

## A.1  Brief Guide to Linear Logic

In this subsection, we give an intuitive idea for understanding Girard's linear logic[6] using the well-known examples[23]. Let us consider the following three formulas $A$, $B$ and $C$:

  $A$ : You have one dollar.
  $B$ : You can buy a chocolate.
  $C$ : You can buy a candy.

We assume here that each of a chocolate and a candy costs \$1. Then, it is trivial that $A$ *implies* $B$, and $A$ *implies* $C$. But what's the meaning of "*implies*"? Let's consider it as an implication in classical logic, that is, interpret "$A$ implies $B$" as "$A \supset B$" and "$A$ implies $C$" as "$A \supset C$." Then, we can deduce $A \supset (B \wedge C)$ from $A \supset B$ and $A \supset C$. Therefore, we are led to the strange conclusion that "if you have one dollar, then you can buy both a chocolate and a candy."

What was wrong with the above reasoning? It was the interpretation of "*implies*." If you have one dollar, then you can buy a chocolate, but at the same time, *you lose one dollar*, that is, you can deduce $B$ from $A$, but you do not have $A$ any more. In order to express the above "*implies*," we need to introduce a new implication '—o' of linear logic, which is called *linear implication*. $A$ —o $B$ means that if we have $A$, we can obtain $B$ by *consuming* $A$. Therefore, each formula of linear logic should be considered as a kind of consumable resource.

Going back to the above example, we also need to reconsider the interpretation of "*and*." If you have one dollar, it is both true that you can buy a chocolate and that you can buy a candy. But they cannot be true at the same time. In order to express it, we need to use '&', one of linear logic conjunctions. $A$ —o $B \& C$ means that "we can obtain any one of $B$ and $C$ from $A$, but *not both at the same time*". In contrast, the other linear logic conjunction '$A \otimes B$' means that we have both $A \otimes B$ at the same time. Therefore, $A \otimes A$ —o $B \otimes C$ means that "If you have one dollar and one dollar (that is, two dollars), you can buy *both* a chocolate *and* a candy *at the same time* (and you lose two dollars!)."

Linear logic disjunction $\oplus$ and $\otimes$ is respectively de Morgan dual of $\&$ and $\otimes$:

$$(A \& B)^{\perp} \equiv A^{\perp} \oplus B^{\perp}$$
$$(A \otimes B)^{\perp} \equiv A^{\perp} \otimes B^{\perp}$$

where $(\bullet)^{\perp}$ is a linear negation. $A \oplus B$ means that "at least one of $A$ and $B$ holds." (Compare with $A \& B$.) $A \otimes B$ can be also defined as $A^{\perp}$ —o $B \equiv B^{\perp}$ —o $A$. $1$ and $\perp$ is respectively a unit of $\otimes$ and $\&$. The above Girard's choice of symbols for connectives seems to be motivated by the following distributive laws:

$$A \otimes (B \oplus C) \equiv (A \otimes B) \oplus (A \otimes C)$$
$$A \& (B \otimes C) \equiv (A \& B) \otimes (A \& C)$$

Girard also introduced exponential '!' for expressing unbounded resource. If we have '!$A$', we can use $A$ any number of times. '?' is de Morgan dual of '!'.

## A.2   Connection between Linear Logic and Concurrent Computation

What is the connection between linear logic and concurrent computation?[7]

Consider the computational model where multiple processes perform computation while communication with each other via asynchronous message passing. The basic observation is that each message disappears after read by a process, that is, a message is a consumable resource. Therefore, it is natural to interpret a message as a formula of linear logic. From now on, we represent a message by an atomic formula of linear logic. How about processes? Consider a process $A$, which waits for a message $m$ and behaves like $B$ after reception. $A$ consumes $m$ and produces $B$, hence $A$ is interpreted by a linear logic implication $m \multimap B$. Therefore, a process is also represented by a formula of linear logic. Consumption of a message $m$ by a process $m \multimap B$ is represented by the following deduction:

$$m \otimes (m \multimap B) \otimes C \multimap B \otimes C$$

where $C$ can be considered as other processes and messages, or an environment. Note that we cannot interpret it by connectives of classical logic. With classical logic, we can deduce

$$m \wedge (m \supset B) \supset B$$

but we can also deduce

$$m \wedge (m \supset B) \supset m \wedge (m \supset B) \wedge B$$

which implies that the original message $m$ and process $m \supset B$ may still remain after message reception!

Let us try to interpret other connectives. $A \otimes B$ means that we have both a process $A$ and a process $B$ at the same time, i.e., we have two concurrent processes $A$ and $B$. Therefore, $\otimes$ represents a concurrent composition. If $A$ is a message, we can also interpret $A \otimes B$ as a process which throws a message $A$ and behaves like $B$.

$(m_1 \multimap A_1)\&(m_2 \multimap A_2)$ means that we have any one of $m_1 \multimap A_1$ and $m_2 \multimap A_2$, but not both at the same time. So, if there is a message $m_1$, we can obtain a process $A_1$, and if there is $m_2$, we can obtain $A_2$. But even if we have both $m_1$ and $m_2$, we can only obtain either $A_1$ or $A_2$ (compare with $(m_1 \multimap A_1) \otimes (m_2 \multimap A_2)$):

$$m_1 \otimes ((m_1 \multimap A_1)\&(m_2 \multimap A_2)) \otimes C \multimap A_1 \otimes C$$
$$m_2 \otimes ((m_1 \multimap A_1)\&(m_2 \multimap A_2)) \otimes C \multimap A_2 \otimes C$$

Therefore, $(m_1 \multimap A_1)\&(m_2 \multimap A_2)$ can be interpreted as a process which waits for any one of $m_1$ and $m_2$, and becomes $A_1$ or $A_2$ depending on the received message.

Let us consider predicate logic. An atomic formula $m(a)$ can be interpreted as a message carrying a value $a$. A predicate $m$ can now be considered a communication channel, or a port name. Then, what does $\forall x.(m(x) \multimap A(x))$ mean? It

---

[7] This subsection gives a connection based on *proof search paradigm*. Regarding the alternative approach, *proof reduction paradigm*, please refer to other materials.

implies that for any $x$, if $m(x)$ holds, we can deduce $A(x)$. Computationally, it can be interpreted as "for any $x$, if there is a message $m$ carrying $x$, we obtain a process $A(x)$." Therefore, $\forall x.(m(x) \multimap A(x))$ represents a process which receives a value of $x$ via a message $m$, and becomes $A(x)$:

$$m(a) \otimes \forall x.(m(x) \multimap A(x)) \otimes C \multimap A(a) \otimes C$$

How about existential quantification? $\exists x.A$ hides $x$ from externals. Therefore, $x$ can be used as a private name, which is used for identifying a message receiver.

There are several minor variants for expressing communication. For example, if we allow a formula of the form: $\forall x.(m(a, x) \multimap A(x))$, it receives only a message $m$ whose first argument matches to $a$, hence we can realize Linda-like generative communication. $\forall x.(m(x, x) \multimap A(x))$ receives only a message $m$ whose first and second arguments match. A formula $\forall x.\forall y.(m(x) \otimes n(y) \multimap A(x, y))$ receives a value $x$ via $m$, and $y$ via $n$, and behaves like $A(x, y)$. Since the formula is equivalent to:

$$\forall x.(m(x) \multimap \forall y.(n(y) \multimap A(x, y))) \equiv \forall y.(n(y) \multimap \forall x.(m(x) \multimap A(x, y))),$$

it can receives a message $m(a)$ and $n(b)$ in any order. Whether or not to delay the message reception until both $m(a)$ and $n(b)$ are ready is up to the choice of language designer.

Figure 11 summarizes the connection between linear logic formula and process. Some of concurrent linear logic programming languages, including ACL and Higher-Order ACL, are formalized using dual connectives. We show this dual representation in the second column (In the second column, positive and negative atoms are also exchanged).

| Linear Logic Formula | Dual Representation | Process Interpretation |
|---|---|---|
| $1$ | $\perp$ | inaction |
| $m$ (atomic formula) | $m$ | message |
| $A \otimes B$ | $A \parr B$ | concurrent composition |
| $\forall x.(m(x) \multimap A(x))$ | $\exists x.(m(x)^{\perp} \otimes A(x))$ | message reception |
| $R_1 \,\&\, R_2$ | $R_1 \oplus R_2$ | selective message reception |
| $\exists x.A$ | $\forall x.A$ | name creation |
| $!P$ | $?P$ | unbounded replication |

Fig. 11. Connection between formula and process

## A.3 Higher-Order ACL

Higher-Order ACL is based on Girard's second-order linear logic[6] with $\lambda$-abstraction. Note that with higher-order linear logic, a predicate can take predicates as arguments, hence we can express processes which take processes as arguments. Quantifications can be also over predicates, hence processes can communicate processes and communication channels via a message.

Higher-Order ACL is equipped with an ML-style type system. Note that types in Higher-Order ACL have nothing to do with Curry-Howard isomorphism, because we regard formulas as processes, not as types. Higher-Order ACL took the similar approach to $\lambda$Prolog in introducing types. We have a special type '$o$' for propositions. Computationally, it corresponds to the type of processes and messages. $int \rightarrow o$ is a type of predicate on integers. Computatinally, it is a type of processes or messages which take an integer as an argument. $(int \rightarrow o) \rightarrow o$ is a type of processes or messages which take a process or a message that takes an integer as an argument. $(int \rightarrow o) \rightarrow int$ is a type of functions which take a process that takes an integer as an argument, and returns an integer. Processes can be defined and used polymorphically, by using `let proc p(x) = e1 in e2 end` statement, which is analogous to `fun` statement in ML. Process definitions could be expressed by a formula $!(p(x) \negthinspace-\negthinspace o\, e1)$, (or $!(p(x) o\negthinspace-\, e1)$ by the dual encoding), which corresponds to clause in traditional logic programming. However, we preferred to interpret it as `let` $p = \mathbf{fix}(\lambda p.\lambda x.e1)$ `in` $e2$ `end` where **fix** is a fixpoint operator, for the introduction of ML-style polymorphic type system. It makes sense because unlike traditional logic programming, we can restrict so that each predicate has only one definition clause.

# B Correspondence between Higher-Order ACL and Polyadic $\pi$-calculus

For those who are familiar with $\pi$-calculus, the following table summarizes a rough correspondence between higher-order ACL (in short, HACL) and Milner's polyadic $\pi$-calculus[15].

| Polyadic $\pi$-calculus | HACL(Textual Representation) |
|---|---|
| $0$ | - |
| $P_1 + P_2$ | $P_1$ & $P_2$ |
| $\overline{y}\langle x_1, \ldots, x_n \rangle.P$[8] | y($x_1$,...,$x_n$) \| P |
| $y(x_1, \ldots, x_n).P$ | y($x_1$,...,$x_n$) => P |
| $P_1 \| P_2$ | $P_1$ \| $P_2$ |
| $(\nu x)P$ | \$x.P |
| $!P$ | ?P |
| $A(v_1, \ldots, v_n)$ where $A(x_1, ..., x_n) \overset{\text{def}}{=} P$ | let proc A $x_1$ ... $x_n$ = P in A $v_1$ ... $v_n$ end |

---

[8] Strictly speaking, this should be $\overline{y}\langle x_1, \ldots, x_n \rangle.0 | P$, since communication in $\pi$-calculus is synchronous.

# C  Higher-Order Linear Logic

We give the inference rules of higher-order linear logic $HLL_{\lambda\mathbf{let}}$, following [21]. $\longrightarrow_\lambda$ represents the relation defined in Section 2.

- Logical axioms

$$\vdash A, A^\perp$$

- $\longrightarrow_\lambda$

$$\frac{\vdash A, \Gamma \qquad B \longrightarrow_\lambda A}{\vdash B, \Gamma}$$

- Cut rule

$$\frac{\vdash A, \Gamma \qquad \vdash A^\perp, \Delta}{\vdash \Gamma, \Delta}$$

- Exchange rule

$$\frac{\vdash \Gamma}{\vdash \Delta}$$

where $\Gamma$ is a permutation of $\Delta$.

- Additive rules

$$\vdash \top, A$$

$$\frac{\vdash A, \Gamma \qquad \vdash B, \Gamma}{\vdash A \& B, \Gamma}$$

$$\frac{\vdash A, \Gamma}{\vdash A \oplus B, \Gamma} \qquad \frac{\vdash B, \Gamma}{\vdash A \oplus B, \Gamma}$$

- Multiplicative rules

$$\vdash \mathbf{1} \qquad\qquad \frac{\vdash A}{\vdash \perp, A}$$

$$\frac{\vdash A, \Gamma \qquad \vdash B, \Delta}{\vdash A \otimes B, \Gamma, \Delta} \qquad \frac{\vdash A, B, \Gamma}{\vdash A \otimes B, \Gamma}$$

- Exponential rules

$$\frac{\vdash A, \Gamma}{\vdash ?A, \Gamma} \text{ dereliction}$$

$$\frac{\vdash \Gamma}{\vdash ?A, \Gamma} \text{ weakening}$$

$$\frac{\vdash ?A, ?A, \Gamma}{\vdash ?A, \Gamma} \text{ contraction}$$

$$\frac{\vdash A, ?\Gamma}{\vdash !A, ?\Gamma}$$

- Quantifier rules

$$\frac{\vdash A, \Gamma}{\vdash \forall x.A, \Gamma} x \text{ not free in } \Gamma$$

$$\frac{\vdash A[B/x], \Gamma}{\vdash \exists x.A, \Gamma}$$

# D  Proof Sketch of Proposition 2.3

This section gives a brief sketch of proof of Proposition 2.3. We skip the most part of the proof, because the proof is almost the same as that for the subject reduction on ML.

The following lemma is proven by structural induction on $e$.

**Lemma D.1 (term substitution)** *If $T\{x \mapsto \tau'\} \vdash e : \tau$ and $T \vdash v : \tau'$ then $T \vdash e[v/x] : \tau$.*

The following lemma is proven in the same manner as that for ML.

**Lemma D.2 (subject reduction on $\lambda$-terms)** *If $T \vdash e : \tau$ and $e \longrightarrow_\lambda e'$, then $T \vdash e' : \tau$.*

The following lemma is trivial from the definition of $\cong$ and types of connectives.

**Lemma D.3** *If $T \vdash e : \tau$ and $e \cong e'$, then $T \vdash e' : \tau$.*

Now, proposition 2.3 is proven by case analysis on the last rule of deduction of $T \vdash e : \tau$. We show several main cases.

**case $\cong$:** Immediate from the lemma D.3 and induction hypothesis.

**case $\lambda$** Immediate from the lemma D.2 and induction hypothesis.

**case Com:** In this case, $e \equiv (\exists x_1 \cdots \exists x_n.(x(x_1,\ldots,x_n)^\perp \otimes e_1) \,\mathbf{?}\, x(v_1,\ldots,v_n)$
and $e' \equiv e_1[v_1/x_1,\ldots,v_n/x_n]$. From the typing rules, $T \vdash x(v_1,\ldots,v_n) : o$, hence $T \vdash x : \tau_1 \times \cdots \times \tau_n \to o$ and $T \vdash v_i : \tau_i$ for each $i(1 \leq i \leq n)$. Again from the typing rules, $T\{x_1 \mapsto \tau_1,\ldots,x_n \mapsto \tau_n\} \vdash e_1 : \tau$. By lemma D.1 we have $T \vdash e_1[v_1/x_1,\ldots,v_n/x_n] : \tau$.

**case $\mathbf{?}$:** $e$ must be $e_1 \,\mathbf{?}\, e_2$, $e'$ be $e_1' \,\mathbf{?}\, e_2$ and $e_1 \longrightarrow e_1'$. From the typing rules and type of $\mathbf{?}$, $T \vdash e_1 : o$ and $T \vdash e_2 : o$. From induction hypothesis, $T \vdash e_1' : o$, which implies $T \vdash e' : o$.

□

# A Parallel Object-Oriented Language OCore

Hiroki Konaka, Takashi Tomokiyo,
Munenori Maeda, Yutaka Ishikawa, Atsushi Hori

Real World Computing Partnership,
1-6-1 Takezono, Tsukuba-shi, Ibaraki 305, JAPAN

**Abstract.** We propose a parallel object-oriented language, called OCore. OCore is designed to generate efficient code especially for multi-computers. As a research vehicle for massively parallel computation models, advanced communication models, and optimization techniques, OCore supports the notion of *community*, *meta-level architecture*, and a *distributed garbage collection mechanism* on top of a fundamental concurrent object-oriented layer. OCore supports both control- and data-parallel programming. A prototype language processing system for the Intel Paragon XP/S and Sun SPARC stations is currently available.

In this paper we describe an overview of OCore, especially emphasizing community. Some OCore programming examples and the performance of the prototype system are also presented.

## 1 Introduction

As a result of recent advances in VLSI technology, a variety of multi computers have become available. Although they have the potential to offer high computing power, it is often difficult to use them to their full advantage because of the insufficient descriptive power of existing parallel programming languages. Even a massively parallel machine has limited resources. Increasing parallelism and communication latency make it more complex to write efficient parallel programs to be executed on such a machine.

We propose a parallel programming language OCore especially for multi computers[10]. OCore introduces the notion of *community*, *meta-level architecture*, and a *distributed garbage collection mechanism* to reduce the above complexity and provide programmers with a research vehicle for massively parallel computation models, advanced communication models, and optimization techniques. A prototype language processing system for the Intel Paragon XP/S[8] and Sun SPARC stations is currently available[11].

The rest of this paper describes a parallel object-oriented language OCore, putting emphasis on community. Sect. 2 describes the background of this research. In Sect. 3, after overviewing OCore, we introduce a fundamental concurrent object-oriented layer of OCore. Then we describe other enhanced features such as community. Sect. 4 shows an outline of the prototype system and its performance. Sect. 5 describes programming with community. We take an artificial life simulation program as an example.

# 2 Background

As we approach the limit of single-CPU architectures, various parallel architectures have been proposed. Above all, multi computers having distributed memory are attracting considerable attention because of their scalability of implementation and flexibility of processing. Some exhibit not only good cost-performance ratio but also high absolute performance. Our language is targeted at workstations to multi computers, but especially at massively parallel machines such as the RWC-1[19], being developed by the Real World Computing Partnership.

The applications to be executed on such multi computers are also more diverse than ever before. Some scientific computations exhibit regular parallelism, while other applications such as knowledge processing, self-organization, and social simulation exhibit irregular parallelism or both regular and irregular parallelism. Therefore, the programming languages used to describe these applications should support a combination of both regular and irregular parallelism.

Numerous programming languages have been applied to the writing of parallel applications. Even sequential languages, such as Fortran, are used with some automatic parallelization techniques. However, many languages have introduced explicit parallelism. Some are based on existing sequential languages extended with some parallel concepts, while others feature inherent parallelism. In terms of parallelism, they are also divided into data parallel languages and control parallel languages.

Data parallel languages are suitable for regular scientific computation. They have good programmability, since they are rather deterministic and exhibit some continuity with sequential languages in terms of control. However, they have difficulty in making irregular processing efficient. C*[25], HPF[7], pC++[5] fall under this category.

On the other hand, control parallel languages are suitable for irregular computation. They include functional languages such as Id[2], procedural languages such as EM-C[20], committed-choice languages such as GHC[27], and concurrent object-oriented languages such as Actor[1], ABCL/1[30], CA[3], and pSather[14]. Above all, concurrent object-oriented languages are attractive because of their good programmability and attempts have been made to introduce the notion of abstract parallelism to some of them.

For example, CA (Concurrent Aggregates) introduces the notion of *aggregate*, a set of the same kind of objects, called *representatives*. An object may send a message to an aggregate in the same way as it would to an ordinary object. A message sent to an aggregate is actually sent to one of the representatives. The runtime system arbitrarily chooses the receiving representative. Then, if necessary, the receiver forwards the message to an appropriate representative. This feature enables a programming style where we can make a program more efficient by replacing bottleneck objects with aggregates. However, message forwarding overhead is incurred even if the receiver is known to the sender. CA supports neither broadcast nor global operations in its language specification.

pSather, based on sequential object-oriented language Sather[18], introduces monitors and distributed collections for parallelization. It enables the data parallel processing of objects in a distributed collection, although it is written not in an object-oriented way, but in a procedural way. And besides, each object in a distributed collection can not be treated as an independent object.

Thus, we need a more flexible means of abstraction that can reduce the complexity of writing regular and irregular computations.

## 3   OCore

### 3.1   Overview of OCore

OCore adopts concurrent object-orientation that makes it easy to map applications directly to programs and to exploit data locality. OCore provides the notion of *community*, *meta-level architecture*, and a *distributed garbage collection mechanism*, on top of a concurrent object-oriented layer, to improve the programmability of efficient parallel applications to be executed on multi computers.

In the concurrent object-oriented layer, objects perform a range of operations including message passing. A class defines the behavior of an object. A class is used merely as a template. No class objects exist. Classes can be defined parametrically to improve reusability. While an inheritance mechanism is being introduced, however, we do not cover the details about inheritance in this paper.

OCore provides a simple message passing mechanism. Message passing is either synchronous or asynchronous. Messages are handled sequentially in a single object. No intra-object concurrency is extracted to avoid extra concurrency control within an object. Synchronizing structures[17][21] are supported to enable flexible communication and synchronization.

OCore adopts static typing to improve the debuggability and efficiency of programs.

Community has been introduced to reduce complexity due to the increase of parallelism in various applications. Community supports multi-access data abstractions as well as data parallel computations with the following properties.

1. A community can structure a set of objects (called member objects) in a logical space.
2. The member objects of a community can be distributed to realize parallel message handling in the community.
3. Even a non-member object can broadcast a message to all member objects in a community, thus supporting data parallel computations.
4. Even a non-member object can send a message to or obtain the name of any member object in a community, without significant overhead, thus supporting multi-access data abstractions.

Corresponding to these properties, the behavior of a community should be defined in an appropriate manner. In OCore, the class of member objects and what we call a *community template* define the behavior. A community template, which can also be defined parametrically, defines the logical space of a community and its mapping to real processors. The class of member objects defines the behavior corresponding to sent or broadcast messages. Separating the definition of community behavior improves reusability.

Meta-level architecture has been introduced to separate algorithmic descriptions from the descriptions for optimization, resource management, exception handling, profiling, and so on. From an application programmer's point of view, OCore meta-level architecture is carefully designed not to degrade performance or the soundness of statically typed semantics.

OCore will also provide a garbage collection mechanism to assist modular and reliable programming. For multi computers, we propose a distributed garbage collection algorithm, called RBGC[15, 16], that is designed to be efficient, scalable, and incremental.

## 3.2 Types

OCore is a statically typed language. All slots, arguments, and variables are typed. As built-in data types, OCore provides structured data types such as tuples ({ }), vectors (Vector-of), lists (List-of), and synchronizing structures (Bstr-of, Qstr-of), as well as atomic data types such as integers (Int), floating-points (Float), booleans (Boolean), and atoms (Atom). Synchronizing structures are explained in Sect. 3.4.

The name of a user-defined class or a community template is used as the type name for their instances. Type names must begin with an uppercase letter.

## 3.3 Objects

An object in OCore is a computing entity that performs operations such as message passing. The processing of an object is done either at the base-level or at the meta-level. The OCore meta-level architecture is explained in Sect. 3.6. Messages sent to an object are handled at the base-level.

**Classes.** The behavior of an object is described in a class. Slots, methods, broadcast handlers, local functions, meta-level variables, meta-level handlers, and others, are defined in a class. Meta-level variables and meta-level handlers are explained in Sect. 3.6, and broadcast handlers in Sect. 3.5.

Fig. 1 shows simple examples of classes.

The syntax of OCore is based upon S-expression. Some of the control structures are borrowed from Common Lisp (if, cond, let).

Class Counter has one slot and two methods. The slot count is of integer type and initialized with 0. Each method definition consists of a message pattern enclosed in [ ], reply type declaration (replies) if applicable, and a body expression. A method is synchronous if it has the replies declaration, otherwise it is asynchronous. Lines 4 to 7 define a synchronous method that replies with an integer. Operator reply performs reply and completes the method processing. Line 8 defines an asynchronous method that does not perform reply.

```
 1 (class Counter
 2   (vars (Int count :init 0))
 3   (methods
 4     ([:add (Int x)] (replies Int)
 5       (let ()
 6         (set count (+ count x))
 7         (reply count)))
 8     ([:show] (printf "%d\n" count))
 9     ))
10
11 (class Foo
12   (vars (Counter counter :init (new Counter)))
13   (methods
14     ([:add10] (replies Int)
15     (let ((Int val))
16       (set val (send counter [:add 5]))
17       (send counter [:show])))
18     (send-with-cont counter [:add 5])))
19     ))
```

**Fig. 1.** Simple class examples

Classes can be defined using inheritance and/or parametric types. These improve the reusability of definitions.

**Creation of Object.** Operator new is used to create an object:

(new *Class*)

Class Foo in Fig. 1 has a slot counter initialized with an instance of class Counter, created using operator new. Objects can be created remotely with an optional meta-level argument, as follows:

(new Counter :on 7)

**Message Passing.** Operator send sends a message, enclosed in [ ], to a given object:

(send *object* [*selector argument...*])

Message passing is done either synchronously or asynchronously according to the corresponding method. In line 16, a message is sent synchronously and execution is suspended until a reply is received, which will then be the value of the send expression. That is, the invocation of a synchronous method is associated with a continuation. In line 17, however, a message is sent asynchronously, and the method processing is continued.

Operator send-with-cont, which can be used only in a synchronous method as in line 18, sends a message with the current continuation of the method to complete the method processing. The reply to the message goes directly to the continuation.

## 3.4 Synchronizing Structures

In addition to its simple message passing mechanism, OCore provides synchronizing structures such as the B-structures[23][17] and Q-structures[21], as built-in structured data types.

A B-structure (Bstr-of) realizes synchronization between one writer and multiple readers. bread operations on a B-structure that has not received a bwrite operation will be suspended until bwrite is received. From then on, bread returns the value written by bwrite. Double bwrite to a B-structure causes an error.

A Q-structure (Qstr-of) realizes synchronization between multiple readers and writers. For a Q-structure, qread requests correspond to qwrite requests on a one-to-one basis. When many qread requests are received but while no qwrite requests come, or vice versa, one-sided requests are enqueued in FIFO order. The thread of the caller of qwrite continues its execution, while that of qread is suspended until a corresponding qwrite request is received. qread returns the value of the corresponding qwrite request.

Similar to send-with-cont, OCore provides the operators bread-with-cont and qread-with-cont that operate with the current continuation of a synchronous method to complete the method processing.

These synchronizing structures enable flexible communication and synchronization. By passing a message containing synchronizing structures, data can be sent or returned through them at any time. Streams, often used in concurrent logic programming, are realized by a synchronizing structure consisting of a tuple of data and a subsequent synchronizing structure.

Fig. 2 shows an example where B-structures are used effectively. In this example, several clients independently request a server to solve one of DOMAINSIZE problems. To avoid the same calculation being performed repeatedly, the server uses a memo of B-structures solving-memo each element of which indicates whether solving of the corresponding problem has been started, and where the result can be obtained.

Operators get-at and put-at access an element in a vector. Line 1 defines a type alias.

When a server receives a request, it checks whether the corresponding B-structure exists. If not, it creates and memorizes a new B-structure in lines 10 and 11, and spawns an instance of class Solver to solve the problem. Whether or not the B-structure initially existed, solving of the problem has now been started and the result may be obtained from B-structure solving. bread-with-cont in line 14 forwards the result, that the solver will bwrite in line 21, directly to the client. If bread were used instead of bread-with-cont, the method processing would not finish, instead continuing with the following request message not being served until the solver wrote the result.

```
 1 (typedef B-Int (Bstr-of Int))              ;; type definition
 2
 3 (class Server
 4   (vars ((Vector-of B-Int DOMAINSIZE) solving-memo))
 5   (methods
 6     ([:solve (Int n)] (replies Int)       ;; synchronous
 7       (let ((B-Int solving))
 8         (set solving (get-at solving-memo n))
 9         (cond ((undefined solving)         ;; not yet started solving
10               (set solving (new B-Int))
11               (put-at solving-memo n solving)
12               (send (new Solver) [:solve n solving])))
13                        ;; spawn a solver (better to distribute)
14        (bread-with-cont solving)))))
15
16 (class Solver
17   (methods
18     ([:solve (Int n) (B-Int bstr)]        ;; asynchronous
19       (let ((Int result))
20        ;; ... solve the problem ...
21        (bwrite bstr result)))))
```

**Fig. 2.** Example of using synchronizing structures

## 3.5  Community

Community structures a set of objects in a multi-dimensional space. Each member object can handle messages independently. Community supports the description of multi-access data as well as data parallel computations and their efficient execution on multi computers. The behavior of a community is specified by the class of member objects (*member class*, for short), and a *community template*.

Community is designed to be implemented efficiently on multi-computers. The implementation of community depends heavily on whether member objects vary dynamically. Therefore we have two kinds of community: *static community* and *dynamic community*.

Fig. 3 shows the images and descriptions of some operations related to community. They are explained in the following sections.

**Community Templates.**  A community template defines the logical space of a community and the mapping from the logical space to real processors. The base-level descriptions of a community template include a member class, whether the community is static (by default) or dynamic, the dimension of the logical space where member objects are structured, and what we call *community procedures*. Community procedures are used mainly to describe the logical space of the community.

Mapping from the logical space to the processor space is specified at the

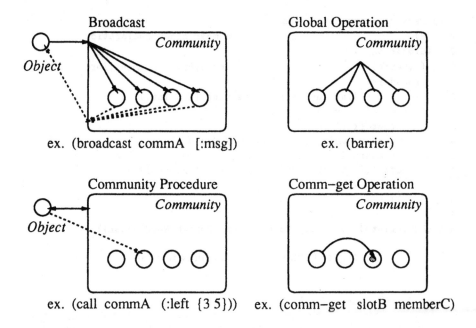

**Fig. 3.** Operation images related to communities

meta-level, but cannot be changed in the current version, since the design of the meta-level descriptions of community has not yet been completed.

Community templates can also be defined parametrically. Therefore, programmers often need not program templates themselves, instead drawing on templates in a library. Fig. 4 shows a parametric definition of static community template Comm2D together with its use. The first (P) in line 1 declares that P is used as a type parameter in the definition, and the second declares P as the member class. The template structures member objects into a two dimensional space. It also defines some community procedures that calculate indices according to the logical structure of the community. { } forms a tuple of types or data.

Parametric definitions must be substantiated to be practical. A community template CounterComm with NewCounter as the member class is obtained from Comm2D in line 15.

**Creation of Community.** Operator new is also used for creating a community instance:

(new *community-template  tuple-of-sizes*)

The following expression creates a community instance, using a community template CounterComm with a logical space of 50 × 70:

```
1 (parametric-community Comm2D (P)
2   (P)                                ;; member class declaration
3   (dimension 2)
4 ;; (dynamic)                         ;; for dynamic communities
5   (procedures
6     (:right (({Int Int} idxs)) (returns {Int Int})
7       (let ((Int x y))
8         (set {x y} idxs)
9         (set x (mod (+ x 1) (size-of-dim 0)))
10        (return {x y})))
11    (:left (({Int Int} idxs))  (returns {Int Int})
12          ...)
13    ...))
14
15 (substantiated-community CounterComm (Comm2D NewCounter))
```

**Fig. 4.** Definition of a community template

(new CounterComm {50 70})

In the case of a dynamic community, only the logical space is created first, then members may be added to or removed from the community.

On the other hand, in the case of a static community, member objects are also created, aligned to the logical space, to improve efficiency. Member objects cannot be added to or removed from the community.

**Reorganization of Dynamic Community.** To add an object to a dynamic community, the following operators are supported:

(add-member *community object*)
(put-member *community tuple-of-indices object*)

add-member adds an existing object to a community. The object is given unoccupied indices, mapped to the current processor, if possible. An object can be put in a logical subspace, which is mapped remotely, with an optional meta-level argument:

(add-member commA objB :on 7)

put-member puts an existing object in a community with given indices, if those indices are unoccupied.

Note that add-member and put-member do not involve object migration.

For removing member objects from a dynamic community, the following operators are supported:

(remove-member *community tuple-of-indices*)
(remove-any-member *community*)
(remove-all-members *community*)

Member objects are not actually added to or removed from a community until the following operation is invoked:

(reorganize *community*)

**Operations to Community.** Any object that knows a community, whether it is a member of the community or not, can:

1. broadcast a message to all members in the community,
   (broadcast *community message*)
2. send a message to a member object having given indices in the community,
   (send-at *community tuple-of-indices message*)
3. and call a community procedure of the community.
   (call *community* (*procedure argument...*))

broadcast operation supports data parallel computation, while send-at operation supports multi-access data. During the reorganization of a dynamic community, however, these operations cause runtime errors. Community procedures make it easy to describe communication according to the logical structure of the community.

**Operations in Member Objects.** Each member object may use the pseudo variables comm, indices and dimension to obtain the name of the community instance to which it belongs, the tuple of its indices, and the community dimension, respectively. The size of a community of a given dimension and the name of some other member object with given indices are obtained from the following operators:

(size-of-dim *dimension*)
(member *tuple-of-indices*)

These operators are also available in the definition of community templates.

The following operators perform barrier synchronization or reduction for all members in a community:

(barrier)
(reduce-*op expression*)        (*e.g.* reduce-add)

Fuzzy global operations are also available. These operations support data parallel computations. Reorganization during a global operation causes a runtime error in the case of a dynamic community, however.

(comm-get *slot-name member-object*)
(comm-update)

The comm-get operation obtains the value of the slot of another member object in the same community at the last comm-update. comm-update is another global operation that makes it possible to cache the slot values to improve efficiency on multi computers.

**Broadcast Handlers.** A broadcast message is handled by a *broadcast handler* rather than a method. Broadcasting a message is also either synchronous or asynchronous according to whether the corresponding broadcast handler has the `replies` declaration.

The main difference between a broadcast handler and a method appears in synchronous communication. In synchronous message broadcasting, after synchronizing at the `reply` operation for all members, one arbitrary member replies to the broadcast message on behalf of all members. Members can also perform reduction and return the result by the following operator:

(reply-*op expression*)        (*e.g.* reply-add)

**Example of Community.** Fig. 5 shows an example of a member class together with its use. Class `NewCounter` is an extension of class `Counter`, shown in Fig. 1, where a `belongs-to` declaration and two broadcast handlers are added[1]. Line 2 declares that the instances of this class use community template `CounterComm`, shown in Fig. 4.

```
1 (class NewCounter
2   (belongs-to CounterComm)
3   (vars (Int count :init 0))
4   (methods
5     ([:add (Int x)] (replies Int)
6       (let ()
7         (set count (+ count x))
8         (reply count)))
9     ([:show] (printf "%d\n" count)))
10  (broadcast-handlers
11    ([:sum] (replies Int)
12      (reply-add count))
13    ([:shift] (replies Void)
14      (let ((NewCounter neighbor))
15        (comm-update)
16        (set neighbor (member (call comm (:right indices))))
17        (set count (comm-get count neighbor))))))
18
19 (class Bar
20   (methods
21     ([:start]
22       (let ((CounterComm cc :init (new CounterComm {7 5})))
23             (Int sum))
24         (send-at cc {1 2} [:add 5])
25         (set sum (broadcast cc [:sum]))))))
```

**Fig. 5.** Code for a member class and a class using a community

---

[1] Actually class `NewCounter` can be derived from class `Counter` using inheritance.

Both broadcast handlers are synchronous. :sum performs reduction and then returns the result. In :shift, the global operation comm-update guarantees the following comm-get operations to read the slot values at this time until the next comm-update. In line 16, the name of the neighboring member is obtained from the indices returned from community procedure :right. Then, comm-get reads the slot of the neighboring member in line 17. After all, the slot values are shifted right to left among community members. Note that reading a slot of another member through synchronous message passing may cause a deadlock, since the message might arrive at a member that has already been suspended due to some global operation, and so on.

In line 22, a community instance of size $7 \times 5$ is created. Line 24 sends a message to a member object. Line 25 broadcasts a message to all community members to obtain the sum of all counters.

## 3.6 Meta-level Architecture

Class definition may include meta-level descriptions such as meta-level variables and meta-level handlers. Meta-level handlers are classified into *event handlers*, *operation handlers*, and *exception handlers*. Meta-level operations are performed in these handlers.

*Event handlers* are associated with *state transition events*. Each object is always in one of four states of activity: *dormant*, *running*, *waiting*, or *defunct*. Each state transition event invokes a corresponding event handler, if defined.

*Operation handlers* are associated with operations such as new, send, and broadcast. When one of these operations is applied, the corresponding operation handler is invoked, if it is defined with type parameters matching with the arguments. The default semantics of the operator can be altered using an operation handler. In [26], operation handlers are used in two examples: the caching of access to remote objects and the realization of object creation/deletion by a free-list.

An *exception handler* is invoked when an exception occurs. It is executed in a different thread of control from that for the normal processing of an object. In an exception handler, an object may raise another exception and/or make a state transition.

The meta-level architecture in OCore will be detailed in another paper.

## 3.7 Distributed Garbage Collection

OCore will also provide a garbage collection mechanism. For efficient, scalable, and incremental garbage collection on multi computers, we propose a distributed garbage collection algorithm, called RBGC[15, 16]. RBGC identifies candidate objects that may be obsolete in inter-space cycles. Then, it incrementally performs (i) red-marking on their transitive subgraph to investigate whether the subgraph contains some objects that are currently in use, (ii) red-bleaching on the reddened subgraph to release the objects in use, and (iii) collection of the remaining red objects. The RBGC algorithm is based on [9] and is essentially different from existing global tracing algorithms in that it aggressively traces objects suspected of being obsolete, while existing algorithms trace entire accessible objects.

RBGC may satisfy both efficiency and scalability, with respect to the number of messages, by adopting the local GC policy[22] and moderated red-marking and -bleaching on any subgraph. The local collector reclaims each local memory without communication for tracing remote references. When global and cyclic garbages are scattered in localized spaces, red-marking and -bleaching incurs fewer messages than existing global tracing algorithms, which trace whole accessible objects in the universe.

The incremental processing of RBGC may not only contribute to improving the throughput of a user's application, but also suggest the possibility of real-time storage management in multi computers.

## 4 Prototype System

### 4.1 Outline of Implementation

We have developed a prototype language processing system. Its execution environments include the Intel Paragon XP/S[8], the Sun SPARC station, and a cluster of SPARC stations. However, inheritance, dynamic communities, part of the meta-level architecture, and garbage collection have not yet been implemented.

The prototype system consists of an OCore translator, C++ compiler, and OCore runtime systems for the above targets. The OCore translator takes OCore source programs and generates C++ codes with OCore runtime system calls.

OCore runtime systems are written in C++ on top of our multi-thread libraries that support the creation and scheduling of threads, remote memory access, lock, synchronizing structures, global operations both between processors (one thread per processor) and between threads (arbitrary number of threads per processor).

Inter-processor system messages are sent and received using the NX message passing library on Paragon, or the PVM message passing library[6] on a cluster of SPARC stations. Messages are received asynchronously on Paragon, then handled as in the Active Messages[28].

An object obtains its activation frame when it becomes *running*, and releases the frame when it becomes *dormant*. Activation frames are managed in a free-list. When calling a function or community procedure, another activation frame is allocated dynamically.

A community instance is created as follows. At first, what we call local community managers are created on all processors for managing the logical space of the community and supporting global operations. In case of a static community, each manager also creates and initializes member objects to be mapped on the same processor, and inform the members of the local manager and their indices. Finally the managers perform initialization for global operations.

To enable the efficient implementation of global operations, local managers in a community instance are allocated at the same local address on each processor. It goes for the member objects of a static community with the same indices in order to implement member without remote message passing.

A global operation in a community is realized using a global operation between threads provided by the multi-thread library. After the completion of the local processing on each processor, it performs an inter-processor global operation, then returns the result to all members or to the current continuation of a broadcast handler.

comm-get is realized by local/remote memory access, however, caching may improve efficiency by sharing remote data on multi computers such as the Paragon. To preserve the semantics of comm-get regardless of whether caching is operational, the space for the slots that can be accessed by comm-get is doubled. One space is used in normal method processing, while the other is used for comm-get and never changed between comm-update's. A comm-update operation copies the former space to the latter, invalidating the local cache in the case of caching. A meta-level description would be able to determine whether caching is on/off. Currently, however, a runtime parameter is used to specify it.

## 4.2 Performance on the Paragon XP/S

The performance of the prototype system was measured on the Paragon XP/S, a multi-computer where each node has two i860XP chips running at 50 MHz: one for computation and the other for communication. The operating system was OSF/1 R1.2.

Table 1 lists some basic operation times. Context switch includes the saving and restoring of registers, and the checking of arrived messages and other ready threads. Created objects had one integer slot while sent messages had no arguments. With respect to global operations, synchronous broadcasting with a reduction of the integer sum, as well as barrier synchronization in a broadcast handler, was timed in a community of 1024 objects on 64 nodes. comm-get operations were timed without caching.

# 5 Community Programming

## 5.1 Data Parallel Programming

Data parallel programming is straightforward; a programmer can distribute data to member objects, then start the computation by broadcasting a message.

Member objects perform global operations if and when necessary. Exchanging data between member objects can be realized by message passing or comm-get operation.

A molecular dynamics simulation program Water, originally in the SPLASH benchmark[24], has been written using community, as an example of data parallel computations. In this program, a system of water molecules is represented

**Table 1.** Basic operation times

| Operation | Time ($\mu s$) |
|---|---|
| Switch Context | 4.2 |
| Create Local Object | 11.5 |
| Create Remote Object | 154.7 |
| Asynchronous Send to Local *dormant* Object | 5.2 |
| Asynchronous Send to Local *running* Object | 2.1 |
| Asynchronous Send to Remote Object | 49.0 |
| Synchronous Send to Local Object | 12.7 |
| Synchronous Send to Remote Object | 156.3 |
| Community Procedure Call | 1.3 |
| Local comm-get | 0.2 |
| Remote comm-get | 142.0 |
| Synchronous Broadcast to Community | 1223.4 |
| Barrier Synchronization in Community | 1114.5 |

naturally by a community of water molecule objects. The class of molecule objects has some broadcast handlers to calculate potentials of each molecule, using reductions, barrier synchronizations and comm-get operations. See [12] for more details.

OCore enables data parallel computations to be encapsulated in a community. Multiple data parallel computations can run in parallel using multiple community instances. A dynamic community allows the size of data to vary at runtime. These features support data parallel programming in a more structured and flexible manner.

## 5.2 Communication using Community

Flexible and global communication models may also be described by using a community; a programmer uses a community as a communication medium where each member object is used to pool data. Objects may access member objects according to their status and other conditions; some objects put data into a member object while others take data out of it. Data are exchanged between objects that access the same member, thus realizing a kind of group communication where the grouping may be changed dynamically.

More interesting communication models are realized when each member object propagates data according to the logical structure of the community, or pre-processes data using the results obtained from global/local operations. For example, when a community models a physical field, data propagation may simulate physical transmission. For a search problem a community can be used to pool sub-problems. Each member may prune some of sub-problems according to the globally best value acquired so far, that may be propagated through a global operation, and convey others to assure load balancing. See [13] for details about abstract, distributed, and hierarchical communication models built on communities.

## 5.3 Example of Community Programming

As an example of community programming, we take a simple artificial life simulation program where ants sort eggs into common clusters[4].

There are ants and several kinds of eggs on a 2-D plane consisting of small squares. Different kinds of eggs have different odors that diffuse to adjacent squares. Only one egg and/or one ant are allowed on a square at the same time.

The simulation consists of given time steps. At each time step, each ant behaves as follows.

1. (a) If he has no egg but finds an egg at the square, the weaker the odor of its kind there is, the more probably he will pick it up.
   (b) If he has an egg and finds no egg at the square, the stronger the odor of its kind there is, the more probably he will put it down.
2. Then he randomly moves to an adjacent square, if he can within limited trials.

After a while eggs of the same kind are clustered. Such a collective behavior can be applied to clustering texts[29], and so on.

In parallel processing of this simulation, it is critical how to realize dynamic communication necessary between ants. We show how it is described in OCore.

Squares and ants are represented by the objects of classes Square and Ant, respectively. Eggs are represented by integer data exchanged between a square and an ant.

A 2-D plane is represented naturally by a static community of Square member objects. The template for the community is obtained from the parametric community template Comm2D in Fig. 4 as follows:

```
(substantiated-community Plane (Comm2D Square))
```

For the distribution and synchronization of ants, 1-D community AntGroup is also defined similarly.

Fig. 6 shows the definition of class Ant. Slots x, y, egg represent the position and the kind of carrying egg (0, 1, 2... or -1 with no egg), respectively. :step is a synchronous broadcast handler for the above processing at each time step. send-at operations are used in lines 11 and 12 to communicate with the square where the ant is.

Fig. 7 shows the definition of class Square. The odor of eggs are represented by the slot odor of integer vector type. The methods for putting and getting an egg are defined from line 6. The diffusion of odors are simulated in a synchronous broadcast handler :step, where comm-get-at, a variant of comm-get for slots of vector type, is used after comm-update to collect odors from adjacent squares.

It is noteworthy that the community Plane is used both for data parallel computation such as the diffusion of odors and for dynamic communication such as the exchange of eggs between ants and plane.

```
1 (class Ant
2   (belongs-to AntGroup)
3   (vars (Int x y egg)
4         (Plane plane) ...)
5   (broadcast-handlers
6     ([:start (Plane p)] (replies Void)
7       (let () (set plane p) ...))
8     ([:step] (replies Void)
9       (let ()
10        (if (< egg 0)              ;; has no egg
11            (set egg (send-at plane {x y} [:get-egg]))
12          (set egg (send-at plane {x y} [:put-egg egg]))))
13        ;; moves, communicating with the plane (omitted)
14        (reply))))               ;; waits for others then replies
15  (functions ...))               ;; class-local functions
```

Fig. 6. Definition of class Ant

```
1 (class Square
2   (belongs-to Plane)
3   (vars (Int egg :init -1)           ;; the kind of egg here
4         ((Vector-of Int EGG-KINDS) odor) ...)
5   (methods
6     ([:put-egg (Int e)] (replies Int)
7       (if (>= egg 0) (reply e)        ;; an egg already exists
8         (cond ((eggs-are-dense e)     ;; else if similar eggs are dense
9                (set egg e)            ;;   put the egg here
10               (reply -1))            ;;   reply no egg to the ant
11              (else (reply e)))))     ;; else don't put the egg
12    ...)
13  (broadcast-handlers
14    ([:step] (replies Void)
15      (let ((Int incoming-odor i)
16            (Square neighbor))
17        ...
18        (comm-update)
19        (dotimes (i EGG-KIND)
20          ...
21          (set neighbor (member (call comm [:right indices])))
22          (set incoming-odor
23                (+ incoming-odor (comm-get-at odor i neighbor)))
24          ...
25          (set odor (+ odor (/ incoming-odor DIFFUSION-RATIO))))
26        (reply))))
27  (functions (eggs-are-dense ((Int e)) (replies Boolean) ...) ...))
```

Fig. 7. Definition of class Square

Fig. 8 shows the main loop of this program. After initializing plane and ants, the loop iterates the processing of plane and ants step by step. The encapsulation of data parallel computations in communities results in this simple loop.

```
1 (let ((Plane plane :init (new Plane {WIDTH HEIGHT}))
2        (AntGroup antgroup :init (new AntGroup {ANT-NUM})) ...)
3   ;; set eggs (omitted)
4   (broadcast antgroup [:start plane])
5   (loop
6     (broadcast plane [:step])
7     (broadcast antgroup [:step]))))
```

**Fig. 8.** Main loop of artificial life simulation

This program can be improved by overlapping the processing of two communities. This is realized by making a broadcast handler :step of Square asynchronous and reporting its completion using a synchronizing structure and another community of the same size that just performs barrier instead of Plane. However, we do not go into details here.

## 6  Conclusions

We have overviewed the parallel object-oriented language OCore. OCore provides the notion of *community, meta-level architecture*, and a *distributed garbage collection mechanism* on top of a fundamental concurrent object-oriented layer. These will be helpful in writing efficient parallel programs. A prototype language processing system of OCore for the Intel Paragon XP/S and Sun SPARC stations is currently available, and we have shown the implementation and performance of the prototype system. We have also described community programming together with an example of an artificial life simulation program.

Further research includes the refinement of OCore language specification, the improvement of the system, and the implementation on RWC-1 and other multi-computers.

## References

1. G. Agha. *Actors: A Model of Concurrent Computation in Distributed Systems.* MIT Press, 1986.
2. Arvind, R. Nikhil, and K. Pingali. *Id Nouveau Reference Manual.* MIT Laboratory for Computer Science, 1987.
3. A. A. Chien. *Concurrent Aggregates.* The MIT Press, 1993.
4. J. Denenbourg, S. Goss, N. Franks, A. Sendova-Franks, C. Detrain, and L. Chretién. The Dynamics of Collective Sorting Robot-like Ants and Ant-like Robots. In J. Meyer and S. Wilson, editors, *From Animals to Animats*, pages 356–363. The MIT Press, 1991.

5. D. Gannon. Libraries and Tools for Object Parallel Programming. In *Proc. CNRS-NSF Workshop on Environments and Tools For Parallel Scientific Computing*, 1992.

6. G. Geist, A. L. Beguelin, J. Dongarra, W. Jiang, R. Manchek, and V. Sunderam. PVM 3 User's Guide and Reference Manual. Tech. Report TM-12187, Oak Ridge National Laboratory, 1993.

7. High Performance Fortran Forum. *High Performance Fortran Language Specification, Version 1.0 DRAFT*, 1993.

8. Intel Supercomputer Systems Division. *Paragon OSF/1 C System Calls Reference Manual*, 1993.

9. R. Jones and R. Lins. Cyclic Weighted Reference Counting without Delay. *Lecture Notes in Computer Science*, 694:712–715, 1993. 5th Int. PARLE Conf. Proc.

10. H. Konaka, Y. Ishikawa, M. Maeda, T. Tomokiyo, and A. Hori. An Overview of OCore : A Massively Parallel Object-based Language. In *IPSJ SIG Notes*, 93-PRG-13, pages 89–96. IPS Japan, 1993. (In Japanese).

11. H. Konaka, Y. Ishikawa, M. Maeda, T. Tomokiyo, and A. Hori. A Prototype Implementation of Massively Parallel Object-based Language OCore. In *JSPP'94*, pages 113–120, 1994. (in Japanese).

12. H. Konaka, Y. Ishikawa, M. Maeda, T. Tomokiyo, and A. Hori. Data Parallel Programming in Massively Parallel Object-based Language OCore. *Proc. of the 49th Annual Convention IPS Japan*, 5(2U–6):31–32, 1994. (in Japanese).

13. H. Konaka, T. Yokota, and K. Seo. Indirect Communication between Objects on a Parallel Machine. *Proc. of SIGPRG, IPS Japan*, 9(3):17–24, 1992. (in Japanese).

14. C.-C. Lim, J. A. Feldman, and S. Murer. Unifying Control- and Data-parallelism in an Object-Oriented Language. In *Joint Symp. on Parallel Processing 1993*, pages 261–268, 1993.

15. M. Maeda, H. Konaka, Y. Ishikawa, T. Tomokiyo, and A. Hori. An incremental global garbage collection to reclaim inter-space cycles of garbage. Technical Report TR–94016, RWCP, Aug. 1994.

16. M. Maeda, H. Konaka, Y. Ishikawa, T. Tomokiyo, and A. Hori. On-the-fly global garbage collection in a distributed environment. In *Proc. JSSST 11th Annual Conf.* Japan Society for Software Science and Technology, Oct. 1994.

17. R. Nikhil and K. Pingali. I–Structure: Data Structures for Parallel Computing. *ACM Trans. on Prog. Lang. and Syst.*, 11(4):598–639, 1989.

18. S. M. Omohundro. The Sather Language. Technical report, International Computer Science Institute, Berkeley, Ca., 1991.

19. S. Sakai, K. Okamoto, H. Matsuoka, H. Hirono, Y. Kodama, M. Sato, and T. Yokota. Basic Features of a massively Parallel Computer RWC-1. *Proc. of Joint Symp. on Parallel Processing*, pages 87–94, 1993. (in Japanese).

20. M. Sato, Y. Kodama, S. Sakai, and Y. Yamaguchi. EM-C: A Parallel Programming Language for the EM-4 Multiprocessor. *Trans.IPS.Japan*, 35(4):551–560, 1994. (in Japanese).

21. M. Sato, Y. Kodama, S. Sakai, Y. Yamaguchi, and S. Sekiguchi. Distributed Data Structure in Thread-based Programming for a Highly Parallel Dataflow Machine EM–4. *Proc. of ISCA 92 Dataflow Workshop*, 1992.

22. M. Shapiro, D. Plainfossé, and O. Gruber. A Garbage Detection Protocol for a Realistic Distributed Object-support System. Rapport de Recherche 1320, INRIA, 1990.

23. T. Shimada, S. Sekiguchi, and K. Hiraki. Data Flow Language DFC: Design and Implementation. *IEICE Trans.*, J71-D(3):501–508, 1988.

24. J. P. Singh, W.-D. Weber, and A. Gupta. SPLASH: Stanford parallel applications for shared-memory. Technical Report CSL-TR-92-526, Computer Systems Laboratory, Stanford Univ., 1992.

25. Thinking Machines Corporation. *C\* Reference Manual.*

26. T. Tomokiyo, H. Konaka, Y. Ishikawa, M. Maeda, and A. Hori. Meta-Level Programming in the Massively-Parallel Object-Based Language OCore. In *Proc. of JSST 11th Annual Conf.*, 1994. (in Japanese).

27. K. Ueda. Parallelism in Logic Programming. In *IFIPS*, pages 957–964, 1989.

28. T. von Eicken, D. Culler, S. Goldstein, and K. Schauser. Active Messages: A Mechanism for Integrated Communication and Computation. In *Proc. of the 19th Intl. Symp. on Computer Architecture*, 1992.

29. T. Yasui. A Document Clustering Method with Ant-like Agents. *Proc. of the 46th Annual Convention IPS Japan*, 3(4L–4):247–248, 1993. (in Japanese).

30. A. Yonezawa. *ABCL – An Object-Oriented Concurrent System –*. The MIT Press, 1990.

# Concurrent Objects
# in a Process Calculus

**Benjamin C. Pierce**
Department of Computer Science
University of Edinburgh
bcp@dcs.ed.ac.uk

**David N. Turner**
Department of Computer Science
University of Glasgow
dnt@dcs.gla.ac.uk

### Abstract

A programming style based on concurrent objects arises almost inevitably in languages where processes communicate by exchanging data on channels. Using the PICT language as an experimental testbed, we introduce a simple object-based programming style and compare three techniques for controlling concurrency between methods in this setting: explicit locking, a standard *choice* operator, and a more refined *replicated choice* operator.

## 1   Introduction

Process calculi have become a popular vehicle for research on the foundations of concurrent object-oriented programming languages [Pap92, Nie92, VT93, Jon93, Wal94, Smo94, KY94, Vas94, etc.]. Their usual role is as a notation for the rigorous explanation of existing high-level language features. We propose that process calculi may also be viewed as design tools for high-level structures. approach. Beginning from the observation that objects arise naturally from the requirements of programming in a standard process calculus, we consider the suitability of various idioms for defining the behavior of objects in this setting. For this investigation we use a fragment of PICT, a programming language based on Milner, Parrow, and Walker's $\pi$-calculus [MPW92, Mil91].

### 1.1   Processes as Objects

The $\pi$-calculus is the best-known member of a family of "mobile" process calculi [MT91, Bou92, HT91, etc.], in which communication topologies can evolve dynamically during evaluation. The primitive constructs in these systems include sending data along a channel, receiving data from a channel, creating channels, and running processes in parallel. Communication along channels is the primary means by which computations progress. Channels are created dynamically and may be passed as data along other channels. Nondeterminism arises from multiple senders or receivers trying to use the same channel simultaneously.

In such calculi, a concurrent system may be thought of as a kind of "process community" (or "process soup"): an unstructured collection of autonomous agents communicating in arbitrary patterns over channels (c.f. left-hand side of Figure 1.1). In practice, however, programs contain significantly more structure

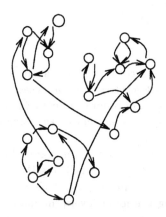 

than this picture would suggest. In particular, their correct behavior usually depends on the maintainence of numerous *invariants*. To control the complexity of the task of programming, these invariants tend to be maintained *locally* by small groups of processes that cooperate in presenting to the rest of the world some abstraction of a shared internal state. Given the existence of such groupings, it is tempting to speak of them as distinct units, and of communications across group boundaries as messages from one *group* to another (right-hand side of Figure 1.1).

## 1.2 Objects as Records

In a pure process calculus, these groups of processes exist nowhere but in the programmer's mind. But adding only a little more structure — the ability for a program to refer explicitly to groups of processes — suffices to give them the status of rudimentary *objects*.

In the $\pi$-calculus, there is no way for one process to directly affect or even refer to another process; it can only send messages on some channel where, by convention, the other process listens. By analogy, referring to a group of processes consists exactly in referring to a collection of channels where these processes are listening. The standard notion of *records* is attractive for this purpose, since it allows members of a group of channels to be selected by name.

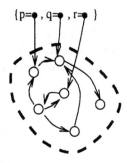

$\{p=\bullet, q=\bullet, r=\bullet\}$

Packaging a set of "service ports" together in a record provides a simple, well-defined interface through which a set of related services may be accessed. Moreover, this packaging promotes a *higher-order* style of programming with objects, since the complete interface to an object may be manipulated as a single value.

Some variants of the $\pi$-calculus have included basic facilities for manipulating collections of channels. For example, Milner's *polyadic* $\pi$-calculus [Mil91] includes simple syntax for constructing and transmitting tuples of channels. Operations on tuples may easily be encoded using the lower-level ("monadic") communication facilities, so the polyadic $\pi$-calculus can be regarded as a simple syntactic sugaring of a monadic calculus. Similarly, we may add special syntax for records of channels without fundamentally changing the nature of the calculus.

## 1.3   Derived Forms and Typing

We can go on to provide many more layers of derived forms to ease the programmer's task. For example, the $\pi$-calculus can be used to encode algebraic datatypes [Mil91], higher-order processes [San92], and even $\lambda$-expressions [Mil90].

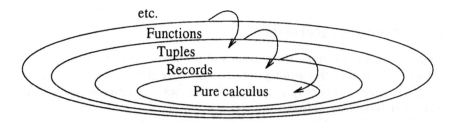

If we only consider the abstract behaviour of programs there is no difference in expressive power between these layers. For simplicity, we might therefore choose the smallest calculus as our theoretical core. However, we are interested in strongly typed programming languages, and this brings other concerns into play. Ideally, the types of higher-level forms should be derived from the translations: to typecheck a high-level program, one should simply translate it and then typecheck according to the rules of the lower-level system. From this perspective, the smallest $\pi$-calculus is too homogeneous: the translations of records and tuples into the pure ("monadic") $\pi$-calculus do not preserve enough structure to give rise to the expected typing rules.

Another concern that may influence our choice of core calculus is efficiency. In the design of the PICT core language, we have retained both tuples and records, even though tuples and their typing rules *can* be satisfactorily encoded in a core calculus with just records. Tuples are used very frequently in our programs and cannot be implemented in terms of records with acceptable efficiency using current compilation technology, since we allow single-field extension of records and hence the relative positions of fields are not necessarily known at compile time.

## 1.4 Synchrony vs. Asynchrony

The fundamental communication primitive in most process calculi is *synchronous rendez-vous*, in which both sender and receiver are blocked until the communication occurs. For example, in the process expression

$$(c!v > d!w > P) \quad | \quad (c?x > d?y > Q)$$

the output expression d!w > P cannot proceed until the preceding output on c has completed; similarly, the input expression d?y > Q cannot proceed until the value x has been received from c. Thus, the whole parallel composition has only one possible communciation sequence:

$$
\begin{aligned}
&(c!v > d!w > P) \quad | \quad (c?x > d?y > Q) \\
\longrightarrow \quad &d!w > P \quad | \quad \{x \mapsto v\}Q \\
\longrightarrow \quad &P \quad | \quad \{y \mapsto w\}\{x \mapsto v\}Q
\end{aligned}
$$

In principle, the fact that output is synchronous enables a client object to tell when a request has been received by some other object that is acting as a server.

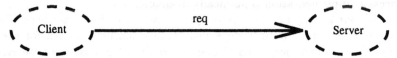

For example, if the request involves some update of the server's state, then the fact that it has been accepted may be used by the client as a signal that it is safe to make further requests of the same server, if it knows that the server will actually perform the update before accepting any more communications.

However, such reasoning is prone to error, since it is invalidated by the simple act of interposing a buffer between client and server. For example, if the client and server are sometimes run on separate machines, we may need to add a *surrogate* object on the client's machine, which forwards requests to the server's machine.

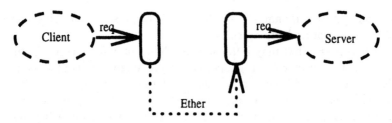

Now any assumptions that the client makes about the state of the server may be incorrect, since a synchronization on the client-side "req" channel indicates only that the surrogate, not the server, has received the request.

To guard against such errors, we allow only asynchronous output in PICT, essentially restricting the "continuation" of each output expression to the null process. This forces the programmer to use an explicit acknowledgement signal from server to client, eliminating any possible sensitivity to buffering of requests.

Even in a language with synchronous communication, explicit acknowledgements are necessary in most client-server interactions, either because some time may elapse between the receipt of a request and the completion of its processing, or because some result value must be sent back to the client. In the common case where the client must wait for the server's response before proceeding, the synchrony or asynchrony of communication of the request is irrelevant.

## 1.5 The Pict Language

The foregoing considerations have strongly influenced the design of PICT, a high-level concurrent language in the tradition of ML. Like ML, PICT is constructed from a tiny core calculus — an asynchronous, choice-free $\pi$-calculus with tuples and extensible records (we discuss the omission of choice in Section 6.2) — plus a variety of higher-level features defined by simple encodings into the core. Also like ML, the core calculus, and hence the derived forms, are statically typed. A uniprocessor implementation is publically available.

The full PICT language and type system are described elsewhere [Pie94, PT94a]. In this paper, we introduce just those constructs needed for the development of the examples; in particular, we shall not discuss the type system further. Most of the examples shown here do actually typecheck in the current version of PICT; in a few places, however, typing annotations must be added to help the partial type inference algorithm.

## 1.6 Outline of the Remainder

Section 2 defines the core language of PICT and its operational semantics. Section 3 shows how rudimentary objects may be implemented directly in this low-level calculus, using explicit locking to protect internal invariants. Section 4 introduces some higher-level derived forms to improve readability; these are used in Section 5 to develop additional examples of objects based on explicit locking. Section 6 introduces a higher-level programming idiom in which objects may have many internal states, each accepting a different set of messages; the basis of this construction is a library module implementating the familiar external *choice* operator. Section 7 proposes a more appropriate abstraction, called *replicated choice*, and shows how to use it to express earlier examples. Section 8 considers some abstraction mechanisms that allow synchronization code to be reused.

# 2 Core Language

We now proceed to a rigorous definition of the syntax and semantics of the core of PICT.

## 2.1 Syntax

The entities that can be communicated on channels are called *values*. They include channels (this is what makdes PICT and the $\pi$-calculus *mobile* calculi) as well as tuples and records.

```
Val = Id                         variable
      [Val,...,Val]              tuple
      record end                 empty record
      Val with Id=Val end        record extension
```

As in the $\pi$-calculus, there are no channel constants in the concrete syntax, only variables ranging over channels. Record values are constructed by incrementally extending the empty record with single fields. We allow the usual multi-field form record $l_1=v_1,\dots,l_n=v_n$ end as an abbreviation for record end with $l_1=v_1$ end ... with $l_n=v_n$ end.

If v is a record that already contains a field with the label 1, the record extension operator v with 1=v' end creates a copy of v where the field labelled 1 is modified to contain the value v'. If 1 is not present in v, it creates a copy of v extended with a new field. For example,

```
record x=3, y=4 end with z=5 end
    = record x=3, y=4, z=5 end
record x=3, y=4 end with x=0 end
    = record x=0, y=4 end
```

Values are decomposed by means of *patterns* in input prefixes.

```
Pat = Id                              variable pattern
      [Pat,...,Pat]                   tuple pattern
      record Id=Pat,...,Id=Pat end    record pattern
      -                               wildcard pattern
```

For example, the process expression

```
x?[y,z] > e
```

reads a pair from the channel x, matches it against the pattern [y,z], and continues with e, where y is bound to the left-hand side of the pair and z is bound to the right-hand side. Placing this expression in parallel with a corresponding output yields the reduction

$$(x?[y,z] > e) \mid x![a,[]]$$
$$\longrightarrow \quad \{y \mapsto a\}\{z \mapsto []\}e$$

Wildcard patterns are convenient when we wish to ignore some part of a value that we are matching against. For example, matching the value [3,[]] against the pattern [_,y] results in y being bound to [].

A process prefixed by a pattern is called an *abstraction*.

```
Abs = Pat > Proc                          abstraction
```

Introducing abstractions as a separate syntactic class, even though they are quite simple, gives some "growing room" to the syntax. We make use of this in the full language to allow higher-order functions to appear wherever process abstractions are allowed.

The basic forms of processes are input prefixes, output atoms, parallel compositions, and processes prefixed by declarations.

```
Proc = Val?Abs                    input prefix
       Val?*Abs                   replicated input
       Val!Val                    output atom
       Proc|Proc                  parallel composition
       let Dec in Proc end        declaration
```

The replicated input prefix is a combination of ordinary input with the *replication* operator (usually written !Proc) of the $\pi$-calculus. We restrict replication to this form for reasons of efficiency; the unrestricted replication operator can be encoded using only replicated input. In the concrete syntax, the scope of an abstraction extends as far to the right as possible, so that, for example, c?x > x![] | a!b is parsed as c?x > (x![] | a!b).

A new declaration introduces a fresh channel:

```
Dec = new Id                           channel creation
```

Again, Dec is provided as a separate syntactic category so that other kinds of declarations can be added as derived forms. For convenience the compiler translates

$$\text{let new } x_1, \ldots, x_n \text{ in e end}$$

into:

$$\text{let new } x_1 \text{ in } \ldots \text{ let new } x_n \text{ in e end } \ldots \text{ end}$$

## 2.2 Semantics

The operation semantics of PICT programs is presented in two steps. First, we define a *structural congruence* relation $e_1 \equiv e_2$ on process expressions; this relation captures the fact that, for example, the order of the branches in a parallel composition has no effect on its behavior. Next, we define a *reduction relation* $e_1 \rightarrow e_2$ on process expressions, specifying how processes evolve by means of communication.

Structural congruence plays an important technical role as a device for simplifying the statement of the reduction relation. For example, the processes x!v | (x?y > e) and (x?y > e) | x!v both reduce to [v/x]e. Since these two are structurally congruent, it suffices to write the reduction rule just for the first case and stipulate, in general, that if a process expression e contains some possibility of communication, then any expression structurally congruent to e has the same possible behavior.

The first two structural congruence rules state that parallel composition is commutative and associative:

$$e_1 \mid e_2 \equiv e_2 \mid e_1 \qquad \text{(STR-COMM)}$$

$$(e_1 \mid e_2) \mid e_3 \equiv e_1 \mid (e_2 \mid e_3) \qquad \text{(STR-ASSOC)}$$

The third rule, often called the rule of *scope extrusion* in the $\pi$-calculus literature, plays a crucial role in the treatment of channels:

$$\frac{x \notin FV(e_2)}{\texttt{let new x in } e_1 \texttt{ end} \mid e_2 \equiv \texttt{let new x in } e_1 \mid e_2 \texttt{ end}} \text{(STR-EXTRUDE)}$$

Informally, this rule says that a declaration can always be moved toward the root of the abstract syntax tree ("always," because the preconditions are always satisfied when the rule is read from left to right). For example, the process expression

    let new y in x!y end | (x?z > z![])

may be transformed to:

    let new y in x!y | (x?z > z![]) end

It is precisely this rule that allows the new channel y to be communicated outside of its original scope.

A *substitution* is a finite map from variables to values. The empty substitution is written { }. A substitution mapping the variable x to the value v is written $\{x \mapsto v\}$. If $\sigma_1$ and $\sigma_2$ are substitutions with disjoint domains, then $\sigma_1 \cup \sigma_2$ is a substitution that combines the effects of $\sigma_1$ and $\sigma_2$. A substitution $\sigma$ can be extended to a function from values to values by applying $\sigma$ to variables that fall in its domain and leaving the rest of the value unchanged. For example, applying the substitution $\sigma = \{x \mapsto a\} \cup \{y \mapsto []\}$ to the value $[b,[x],x,y]$, written $\sigma([b,[x],x,y])$, yields the value $[b,[a],a,[]]$.

When a value $v$ is successfully matched by a pattern $p$, the result is a substitution $match(p, v)$, defined formally as follows:

$$
\begin{aligned}
match(x, v) &= \{x \mapsto v\} \\
match([p_1,\ldots,p_n],[v_1,\ldots,v_n]) &= match(p_1, v_1) \cup \cdots \cup match(p_n, v_n) \\
match(\_, v) &= \{\} \\
match(\texttt{record end}, \texttt{record end}) &= \{\} \\
match(\texttt{record } j_1{=}p_1,\ldots,j_n{=}p_n,l{=}p \texttt{ end}, v_0 &\texttt{ with } l{=}v \texttt{ end}) \\
= \quad match(p, v) \cup match(\texttt{record } j_1{=}p_1,&\ldots,j_n{=}p_n \texttt{ end}, v_0) \\
match(\texttt{record } j_1{=}p_1,\ldots,j_n{=}p_n \texttt{ end}, v_0 &\texttt{ with } l{=}v \texttt{ end}) \\
= \quad match(\texttt{record } j_1{=}p_1,\ldots,j_n{=}p_n \texttt{ end}, v_0), &\quad \text{if } l \notin \{j_1,\ldots,j_n\}
\end{aligned}
$$

The last three clauses specify how record values are matched against record patterns: if the final field in the record appears in the pattern, it is added to the results of the match; if not, it is discarded. Either way, the matching process continues with the rest of the fields until the pattern becomes empty, at which point it succeeds. If $v$ and $p$ do not have the same structure (or if both are records but $v$ is missing a field), then $match(p, v)$ is undefined.

The reduction relation $e \rightarrow e'$ may be read as "The process $e$ can evolve to the process $e'$." That is, the semantics is nondeterministic, specifying only what *can* happen as the evaluation of a program proceeds, not what *must* happen. Any particular execution of a PICT program will follow just one of the possible paths.

The most basic rule of reduction is the one specifying what happens when an input prefix meets an output atom:

$$
\frac{match(p, v) \text{ defined}}{\texttt{x!v} \mid (\texttt{x?p > e}) \rightarrow match(p, v)(e)} \qquad \text{(RED-COMM)}
$$

Similarly, when a replicated input prefix meets an output atom, the result is a running instance of the input's body *plus* a fresh copy of the replicated input itself:

$$
\frac{match(p, v) \text{ defined}}{\texttt{x!v} \mid (\texttt{x?*p > e}) \rightarrow match(p, v)(e) \mid (\texttt{x?*p > e})} \qquad \text{(RED-RCOMM)}
$$

The next two rules allow reduction to proceed under declarations and parallel composition:

$$
\frac{e \rightarrow e'}{\texttt{let d in e end} \rightarrow \texttt{let d in e' end}} \qquad \text{(RED-DEC)}
$$

$$
\frac{e_1 \rightarrow e_1'}{e_1 \mid e_2 \rightarrow e_1' \mid e_2} \qquad \text{(RED-PAR)}
$$

The body of an input expression, on the other hand, *cannot* participate in reductions until after the input has been discharged.

The structural congruence relation captures the distributed nature of reduction. Any two subprocesses at the "top level" of a process expression may be brought into proximity by structural manipulations and allowed to interact.

$$\frac{e_1 \equiv e'_1 \; \rightarrow \; e'_2 \equiv e_2}{e_1 \; \rightarrow \; e_2} \qquad \text{(RED-STR)}$$

# 3  Objects with Locks

The following program fragment, implementing integer reference cell objects, illustrates most of the features of the core language:

```
ref?*[init, res] >
  let
    new contents, s, g
  in
    contents!init
  | res!record set=s, get=g end
  | (s?*[v, c] > contents?_ > contents!v | c![])
  | (g?*[r]    > contents?x > contents!x | r!x)
  end
```

This process defines a "function" ref — a process that repeatedly listens on the channel ref for a pair of parameters: init, the initial value to be stored in the cell, and res, a "result channel" on which the newly constructed reference cell object is to be returned. When it is invoked by another process sending a pair of values on ref, it creates three new channels: contents, s, and d. The channel contents acts as a container for the current value of the reference cell. Sending a value on contents represents the action of placing a value in the container. Receiving a value from contents empties the container; it is then the receiver's responsibility to refill the container by transmitting a new value along contents. The container is initialized by sending init along contents. In parallel with initializing contents, ref returns on res a record containing s and d. The channels s and d are the set and get service ports for the new object. Finally, ref starts two server processes, one handling requests on s and one handling requests on d. Each server waits for a request on its service port, reads contents to obtain the current value of the cell, refills contents as appropriate, and sends a result or acknowledgement to the client.

Here is a process that interacts with ref. It creates a fresh channel r, upon which it will receive the new object, and sends to ref the initial value, 3, paired with r. In parallel, it waits for ref's reply along r:

```
let
  new r
in
  ref![3,r]
| (r?myRef > ...)
end
```

Similarly, to get the current value of a reference cell, we create a fresh reply channel r, send r along the object's **get** channel, and wait in parallel for the result.

# 4   Derived Forms

In Section 2, we mentioned that the compiler actually accepts a richer syntax than the pure core language, desugaring higher-level forms (like **new** declarations with multiple identifiers) into expressions of the core. The full PICT language uses several layers of desugarings to provide a high-level syntax reminiscent of the core language of Standard ML [MTH90]. The complete set of derived forms is listed in Appendix A; here, we explain just those used in the examples.

First, PICT allows conditional process expressions like **if** v **then** e **else** f, where v must evaluate to a boolean value.

More interestingly, a variety of *complex values* are supported, including **let** and **if** expressions whose bodies are values, and record selection v.l (which extracts the field labelled l from v). When a complex value appears in a position where a simple (core language) value is expected, the compiler generates a process that evaluates the complex value and sends the result over a channel. For example, if v is a complex value, then x!v is transformed to:

```
let
  new t
  run <compute v and send the result on t>
in
  t?r > x!y
end
```

Special syntax for standard primitive types like numbers and strings is also provided.

We allow a number of additional forms of declaration clause besides **new**. The sequence of declarations **let** $d_1$ $d_2$ **in** e **end** is equivalent to the nested declaration **let** $d_1$ **in** **let** $d_2$ **in** e **end** **end**. A **run** declaration introduces a process expression that is executed in parallel with the body of the declaration: **let** **run** e **in** f **end** is equivalent to e | f.

Recursive definitions of processes are extremely common in PICT. The declaration **def** x a introduces a process definition, where a is a process abstraction (a pattern and process expression, separated by a > symbol). The abstraction a can refer to x recursively. The declaration **def** d x > e is translated as follows:

```
new d
run d?*x > e
```

More generally, a set of mutually recursive declarations (where both e and f may refer to c and d) can be written

```
def c x > e
and d y > f
```

and is equivalent to:

```
new c,d
run c?*x > e
run d?*y > f
```

Using these forms, the ref example can be rewritten as:

```
def ref [init, res] >
  let
    new contents
    run contents!init
    def s [v, c] > contents?_ > contents!v | c![]
    def g [r]    > contents?x > contents!x | r!x
  in
    res!record set=s, get=g end
  end
```

We can even avoid having to make up names for the definitions s and g by substituting the definitions themselves for the channels s and g in the record record set=s, get=g end. This makes set and get look more like method definitions.

```
record
  set = abs [v, c] > contents?_ > contents!v | c![] end,
  get = abs [r]    > contents?x > contents!x | r!x end
end
```

A value expression of the form abs [x,y,z] > e end is called an *anonymous abstraction*; it is equivalent to let def t [x,y,z] > e in t end.

Lambda-calculus-style function definition and application are also supported, using the special form of abstraction $[p_1, \ldots, p_n] = v$ with the left-hand side a tuple of patterns and the right-hand side a value instead of a process; the two are separated by = instead of >. This is translated into $[p_1, \ldots, p_n, r] > r!v$, which uses the implicit parameter r to return the value on the right-hand side. So, for example, the definition

```
def d[x] = [x,x,x]
```

becomes:

```
def d[x,r] > r![x,x,x]
```

The dual operation of function application is supported by translating value expressions of the form $f[a_1, \ldots, a_n]$ into expressions that explicitly construct a new result channel $r$, pass it to $f$ along with the arguments $a_1, \ldots, a_n$, and wait for the result on $r$. The result of the overall expression is whatever is received on $r$.

The declaration val $p$ = $v$ matches the value $v$ against the pattern $p$. Thus, pattern matching the result of applying d to 7 binds x, y and z to 7:

```
let
  val [x,y,z] = d[7]
in ... end
```

This program is translated as:

```
let
  new r
  run d![7,r]
in
  r?[x,y,z] > ...
end
```

We often execute "functions" which perform some operation and then return the trivial value [] to indicate that they have finished. The expression $f[x]$ ; e is equivalent to let val [] = $f[x]$ in e end. It waits for the function application $f[x]$ to signal completion and then executes e.

Infix operators are provided by a simple extension of the parser: if the name of a channel is symbolic rather than alphanumeric, then it can be applied to a pair of arguments by placing it between them. For example, a+b means the same as (+) [a,b] (placing + in parentheses takes away its infix status).

As a function, the ref constructor looks like this:

```
def ref [init] = let
  new current
  run current!init
in
  record
    set = abs [v, c] > current?_ > current!v | c![] end,
    get = abs [r]    > current?x > current!x | r!x end
  end
end
```

To use a reference cell in a program, we create it by applying ref to an initial value, 0, and then send it set and get messages by projecting the appropriate fields:

```
val r = ref[0]
val v1 = r.get[]
val _ = r.set[5]
val v2 = r.get[]
```

The PICT runtime system provides a special channel `printi` that prints integer values on the standard output stream:

```
run printi!v2
```

Running all these clauses together produces the expected output:

```
5
```

Of course, this version of `ref` is still fairly low-level. We could continue the process of adding higher-level syntactic forms, but we have already reached the point where the behavior of the program is not greatly obscured by low-level details, and this is enough for our purposes. Our goal in this paper is to experiment with different styles of behavior for objects; if we find one that we like, we may later consider "canonizing" it as an official, recommended idiom by providing special syntax.

# 5   More Objects With Locks

Other kinds of reference cells may be implemented almost as easily as `ref`. For example, here is a "null reference cell" that starts out in an uninitialized state instead of being given a starting value at creation time:

```
def nullRef [] = let
  new contents, set
  run set?[v,c] > contents!v | c![] |
    (set?*[c,v] > contents?_ > contents!v | c![])
in
  record
    set = set,
    get = abs [r] > contents?x > r!x | contents!x end
  end
end
```

The `get` method is implemented exactly as before: it receives a request, reads a value from the internal channel `contents` (thus blocking out any other instances of `set` or `get` that are also trying to read the current contents), returns a result to the process that invoked `get`, and restores `contents` by writing the same value. The `set` method, on the other hand, is prefixed with a new clause that reads a single request from `set`, sends the given value along `contents` *without* first reading a value from `contents`, and then enters a state where it behaves like the `set` of ordinary `ref` cells. Notice that `nullRef` returns an object with the same interface as `ref`; the only difference that can be detected by clients is that all `get` requests to a `nullRef` will block until the first `set` request has been processed.

Another variation on reference cells adds a `quit` method that grabs the current contents and fails to restore it, rendering the object unable to process any further requests.

```
def quitRef[init] = let
  new contents
  run contents![]
in
  record
    set = abs [v,c] > contents?_ > contents!v | c![] end,
    get = abs [r] > contents?x > r!x | contents!x end,
    quit = abs [c] > contents?_ > c![] end
  end
end
```

Finally, here is a more sophisticated refinement of reference cells, supporting an extra pair of messages, init and clear. Like the instances of nullRef, a clearRef cell starts life in an uninitialized state. But instead of waiting for a first set message, it delays both set and get messages until it receives an init. It then accepts set and get messages until it receives a clear, which sends it back to the initial state, listening only for init.

```
def clearRef [] = let
  new contents, clear, init
  def server[] >
    init?[x,c] > c![] | contents!x |
    (clear?[c] > contents?_ > c![] | server![])
  run server![]
in
  record
    set = abs [v,c] > contents?_ > contents!v | c![] end,
    get = abs [r] > contents?x > r!x | contents!x end,
    clear = clear,
    init = init
  end
end
```

The alternation between init and clear is handled by a single process. The auxiliary definition server implements a tail-recursive loop whose body first accepts init, then accepts clear, and then restarts server. The set and get methods are identical to the ones in our original ref cells.

Notice that this implementation of clearRef is somewhat unsatisfying: it describes an object with two distinct internal states, but this fact is not apparent from the organization of the code. The server loop must be examined carefully in order to decide when set and get messages will be accepted. We shall return to this point in Section 6.3.

# 6 Choice

The examples from Sections 3 and 5 illustrate how channels can be used as repositories for shared state, yielding a simple mechanism for ensuring mutual exclusion between method bodies. Another obvious means of selectively processing messages is a *choice* (or *summation*) operator. Indeed, such operators are often assumed as basic in foundational models of concurrency.

In PICT, choice is not part of the core language, but is available as a library module. Instead of writing (c?x > e) + (d?y > f), we write:

```
sync!(
  c => abs x > e end
$
  d => abs y > f end
)
```

This expression may perform an input on either c or d, but not both: if the first input succeeds, the second clause is thrown away, and vice versa. Informally, c=>abs x > e end is like the ordinary input clause c?x > e, except that, when it is composed with other such clauses using the choice operator $, only the first one to become ready will actually proceed. The sync operator takes a list of clauses built in this way (i.e. a description of a choice to be performed) and yields a process (the running choice itself).

## 6.1  Objects with Choice

Using choice, all the service ports of an object may be handled by a single server process of the form, yielding a style of object definition similar to Actors [Hew77, Agh86]:

```
def server[] >
  sync!(
    c=>abs x > ... <handle request c> ... server![] end
  $
    d=>abs y > ... <handle request d> ... server![] end
  )
```

For example, we can use choice to implement reference cell objects as follows:

```
def ref[init] = let
  new set,get
  def server x >
    sync!(
      get=>abs [r] > r!x | server!x end
    $
      set=>abs [v,c] > c![] | server!v end
    )
  run server!init
in
  record set = set, get = get end
end
```

The current contents of the cell are held in the server parameter x. The set method restarts the server with the new value v, while the get method passes on the old contents.

## 6.2 Implementing Choice

One of the reasons that we avoided building the choice operator into PICT since it is actually possible to implement it as a library module (see Section 6 for more details). This has the useful effect of simplifying the representation of channels in our runtime system. In PICT it is very important that communication is as cheap as possible, since communication is our only means of computation. Many channels, such as those involved in encoding functions as processes, are never used with the choice operator, so it is important that we do not pay the cost of using choice on every channel that we create. This section presents a simple implementation of choice.

The basic abstraction used in the implementation is a *lock*. A lock is queried by sending it a boolean result channel. The first time this happens, it sends back the value **true** over the result channel; for all future requests, it returns the value **false**. In other words, a process that tries to "obtain" a lock by querying its value receives **true**, indicating that it has succeeded; all subsequent tries fail.

```
def newLock [] = let
  new lock
  run lock?[r] > r!true | (lock?*[r] > r!false)
in
  lock
end
```

In essence, there is a race going on between all of the receivers in a choice. The first one that is ready to proceed is allowed to do so; the rest become garbage. This race is mediated by a single lock, which is created by the sync operation and distributed to all the individual receiver clauses.

It is important to distinguish the description of a choice from the running choice process that is created when sync is applied to this description. Following Reppy [Rep92, Rep88, Rep91], we call the description of a choice an *event*. The $ operation takes two events and creates a new event that, when it receives its lock, transmits it to both component events.

```
def ($)[e1, e2] =
  abs lock >
    e1!lock | e2!lock
  end
```

The sync operation takes an event and triggers it with a freshly created lock.

```
def sync e > e!(newLock[])
```

Finally, the => operation takes a channel c and a continuation **receiver** that is waiting to accept a data value over c, and returns an event.

```
def (=>) [c, receiver] =
  abs lock >
    c?v >
    if lock[] then
```

```
        receiver!v
    else
        c!v
    end
end
```

It first waits for a lock; then it waits for a value to arrive on c. Once a value **v** arrives, it checks to see whether the lock has already been taken — i.e., whether it has won or lost the race. If it wins (gets the value **true** from the lock), it sends **v** along to the receiver. If it loses, it re-sends **v** along c, so that another receiver has the chance to pick it up.

Note, in passing, that the correctness of this simple implementation of events depends crucially on the fact that output in this setting is asynchronous: since the original sender on c cannot observe when the value it sent is recieved, we may safely perform a receive, check whether we actually want the value, and resend it if not.

The identifiers **sync**, **=>**, and **$** form part of an events library, which provides selective communication in the style of CML [Rep92, Rep88, Rep91].

## 6.3  Multi-State Objects

For most of the examples we have considered so far, locks and choice can be used to build implementations of comparable clarity. The explicit locking idiom, being closer to the base language, is more efficient for these examples. However, the more powerful choice operator has its advantages: in particular, it allows us to conveniently express objects whose methods are not always available.

Here is an alternative implementation of the **clearRef** example from Section 5. Like the earlier one, it has two internal states: an **empty** state where it can only receive an **init** message, and a **full** state where get, set, and clear are allowed.

```
def clearRef [] = let
  new set,get,clear,init

  def empty [] >
    sync!(
      init => abs [v,c] > full!v | c![] end
    )
  and full x >
    sync!(
      set=>abs [v,c] > full!v | c![] end
      $
      get=>abs [r] > r!x | full!x end
      $
      clear=>abs [c] > c![] | empty![] end
    )
  run empty![]
in
```

```
      record set = set, get = get, clear = clear, init = init end
   end
```

In effect, the alternation between states in the **server** loop of Section 5 has been expanded to include the receivers of all messages.

## 6.4 Efficiency

The simple implementation of events described in Section 6.2 has a fairly serious shortcoming: most programs that use these events to build objects will eventually run out of memory! To see why, consider what happens if a program creates a **clearRef** and repeatedly sends it **set** and **get** messages without ever sending a **clear**. Each time the server loop **full** is executed, a fresh lock is created and passed to the three receivers. But the receiver for **create**, like the other two, does not actually read the lock until it has first read a data value from the channel **create**; only at this point does it read pair of a lock and a receiver and checking to see whether it has won the race for the lock. So, each time **full** is executed, a new lock/receiver pair is added to a queue in the runtime system. If no data is ever sent on **clear**, this queue will grow until it exhausts the available virtual memory.

The implementation of events in the PICT distribution uses a more complex algorithm to patch this space leak. Each channel on which events are being performed is associated with a *channel manager* process that periodically scans the receiver queue and throws away any potential receivers whose locks have already been grabbed. This reduces the space overhead for a choice-style object to a constant depending on the number of channels involved in each choice.

However, even with this improved implementation, choice remains somewhat expensive. Even if it were pushed down into the core language for maximum efficiency, it is hard to see how it could be implemented without at least one memory allocation each time a choice is evaluated.

Our conclusion is that the choice operator is not well-suited to the communication patterns in object-style programs. It is wasteful to create a possibly large set of potential communications, allow one to proceed, discard the others, execute a short critical section, and then create from scratch another very similar set of potential communications. It would be better to recognize explictly that the *very same* set of potential communications is invoked again and again, only changing the value of the current state that is passed from one instance to the next.

# 7 Replicated Choice

It is not hard to implement a more refined variant of the choice primitives by extending the simple implementation from Section 6.2. We call this variant *replicated choice*, since each potential communication that is created may be triggered repeatedly. We replace the receiver constructor => by a replicated receiver constructor ==> and the choice-instantiation operation **sync** by an initialization operation **start**.

Each replicated event is associated with an *event manager* that coordinates the actions of receivers. It is the job of the **start** operation to create this manager.

```
def start [trigger, e] > let
  new state, ready, count, suspended
  run ready!false | count!0

  def manager [restart,nack,ack] >
    ready?b >
    if b then
      state?s > ready!false | ack!s | restart![]
    else
      count?n > ready!false | nack![] | suspended!restart | count!(n+1)
    end

  def unblock n >
    if n == 0 then
      ready!true | count!0
    else
      suspended?restart > restart![] | unblock!(n-1)
    end

  run trigger?*s >
    ready?b > count?n >
    if b then
      fatalError!"Received a trigger on an already triggered event"
    else
      state!s | unblock!n
    end
in
  e!manager
end
```

When **start** is invoked, it is passed a trigger channel **trigger** and a replicated event **e**. It creates an event manager (the definition **manager**) and sends it to **e**; also, it starts a server process listening to the channel **trigger**. Four internal channels are used to coordinate these processes:

**ready** carries a boolean value: **true** if the event has been triggered since the last time one of its receivers was allowed to proceed, or **false** if it is waiting for a trigger;

when **ready** is **true**, **state** carries the current-state value that was provided when the event was last triggered (**state** carries no value when **ready** is false);

**suspended** is an internal queue of receivers that have received data values and tried unsucessfully to proceed since the last trigger;

**count** contains the number of receivers in **suspended** (so that we know how many times we can read from **suspended** without blocking).

The **suspended** queue prevents the inactive states of multi-state objects from consuming too much energy attempting to fire: when a replicated receiver obtains a data value, asks the event manager whether it may proceed, and is told "No," it is suspended until the event is triggered again. At this point, all of the receivers blocked on the **suspended** queue are released (by the process defined by **unblock**).

The definition of the replicated receiver constructor is comparatively simple:

```
def (==>) [chan, receiver] =
  abs manager > let
    def loop [] >
      chan?v > manager![
        loop,
        abs [] > chan!v end,
        abs s > receiver![v,s] end
      ]
    in
      loop![]
    end
  end
```

After being told what channel to use to communicate with its event manager, a replicated receiver waits (as before) for a data value to arrive along the channel **chan**. When one does, it sends off a packet of three values to the manager: 1) its own continuation (the server process **loop**), so that the manager can suspend it if necessary; 2) an abstraction to be invoked if the event is not currently triggered; and 3) another abstraction to be invoked if the event is current triggered. The "not-triggered" (**nack**) abstraction simply resends the data value on **chan** so that another receiver can pick it up. The "triggered" (**ack**) abstraction receives the current state (the one that was used to trigger the event manager) and sends both this and the data value to the body of the receiver.

The choice constructor is exactly the same as before:

```
def ($) [e1, e2] =
  abs manager > e1!manager | e2!manager end
```

Using these primitives, we can build a **clearRef** cell that looks nearly the same as before. The main difference is that **empty** and **full** are now names of channels rather than definitions.

```
def clearRef [] = let
  new get,set,clear,init,empty,full

  run start![empty,
      init ==> abs [[v,c],[]] > c![] | full!v end
  ]
```

```
run start![full,
   get ==> abs [[r],x] > r!x | full!x end
$
   set ==> abs [[v,c],x] > c![] | full!v end
$
   clear ==> abs [[c],x] > c![] | empty![] end
]

run empty![]
in
   record set = set, get = get, clear = clear, init = init end
end
```

# 8 Abstraction and Code Reuse

Code reuse is a common theme in discussions of object-based programming idioms. In this section, we briefly discuss some simple techniques for reusing the code of object definitions.

We do not discuss more powerful techniques for *inheritance* of method bodies and synchronization code here. Based on previous experience with foundational models of sequential objects [PT94b], we believe that any reasonable high-level scheme for concurrent objects with inheritance can be expressed in the setting we have described. However, inheritance in the presence of concurrency seems necessarily to involve separating the interfaces of objects into external and internal parts (depending on whether messages are being sent by external clients or "through self"), and both typing and behavioral issues quickly become complex. See [Vas94] for a recent proposal along these lines and further citations.

## 8.1 Simple Delegation

Probably the simplest way of reusing object definitions is writing new object constructors that act as "front ends" for other, perhaps more complex, objects. For example, suppose we have already implemented clearRef cells. Then quitRef can be implemented very easily by creating a clearRef cell, invoking its init method, and renaming its clear method to quit:

```
def quitRef [init] = let
  val cr = clearRef[]
  val _ = cr.init[init]
in
  cr with quit = cr.clear end
end
```

Similarly, we can define nullRef by creating a clearRef, creating a fresh set channel, and returning an object with the fresh set and a copy of the clearRef's get. A small process listens to the new set, accepts a single request, performs an init of the clearRef, and then forwards all further requests to the set channel of the clearRef itself.

```
def nullRef [] = let
  new set
  val cr = clearRef[]
  run set?[v,c] > cr.init![v,c] | forward![set,cr.set]
in
  record set = set, get = cr.get end
end
```

The definition of the forwarder is:

```
def forward [inChan, outChan] > inChan?*x > outChan!x
```

## 8.2 Synchronization Skeletons

In PICT's standard libraries, heavy use is made of another abstraction mechanism called *synchronization skeletons*. For example, here is a skeleton for a simple printer object:

```
def printerSkel [doPrint,doQuit] = let
  new lock
  run lock![]
in
  record
    print = abs [c] > lock?[] > doPrint[]; lock![] end,
    quit = abs [c] > lock?[] > doQuit[]; c![] end
  end
end
```

Given a pair of abstractions, doPrint and doQuit, printerSkel creates an object with print and quit methods. An internal lock is used to prevent simultaneous execution of two methods. Each time a method is invoked, the lock is grabbed and held while the appropriate abstraction is invoked; when it returns, the lock is released. Note that, although we have chosen a simple lock-style synchronization mechanism for this example, we could equally well have used a multi-state replicated event. In general, synchronization skeletons can be used to set up arbitrarily complicated patterns of synchronization. The essential point is to write this code only once.

This skeleton can be refined by adding a "front end" that supplies null behavior for the quit operation:

```
def simplePrinterSkel [doPrint] =
  printerSkel[doPrint,abs [] = [] end]
```

Now an object constructor can easily be built by calling the specialized skeleton:

```
def stringPrinter [string] =
  simplePrinterSkel[abs [c] > print!string | c![] end]
```

This constructor can be used to build

```
val printHello = stringPrinter["Hello"]
```

and use

```
val _ = printHello.print []
val _ = printHello.quit []
val _ = printHello.print []
```

objects in the usual way.

Continuing the example, we might further extend `simplePrinterSkel` with a counter that keeps track of the number of times that the `print` method is invoked.

```
def countPrint [doPrint] = let
  new count
  run count!0
in
  simplePrinterSkel[abs [c] > count?x > doPrint []; count!(x+1) | c![] end]
end
```

In some cases, we can even create an object from a skeleton and extend it with additional methods. For example, instances of `zeroCount` provide a `zero` method that resets the internal counter.

```
def zeroCount [doPrint] = let
  new count
  run count!0
in
  simplePrinterSkel[abs [c] > count?x > doPrint []; count!(x+1) | c![] end]
  with
    zero = abs [c] > count?_ > count!0 | c![] end
  end
end
```

The synchronization skeleton method works very well in a limited range of cases. It performs best when used to define a large number of similar object constructors, all creating objects with the same methods and the same synchronization behavior, but with differing responses to some messages.

# Acknowledgements

The ideas presented here have been refined by enjoyable conversations with Robert Halstead, Martin Müller, John Reppy, and Aki Yonezawa.

This research was carried out at the Laboratory for Foundations of Computer Science, University of Edinburgh, and the Department of Computer Science, University of Glasgow. Pierce was supported by a fellowship from the British Science and Engineering Research Council and by the ESPRIT Basic Research Actions TYPES and CONFER. Turner was jointly supported by Harlequin Limited and the U.K. Science and Engineering Research Council.

# References

[Agh86]  Gul A. Agha. *Actors: a Model of Concurrent Computation in Distributed Systems*. MIT Press, Cambridge, MA, 1986.

[Bou92]  Gérard Boudol. Asynchrony and the $\pi$-calculus (note). Rapporte de Recherche 1702, INRIA Sofia-Antipolis, May 1992.

[Hew77]  C. Hewitt. Viewing control structures as patterns of passing messages. *Artificial Intelligence*, 8:323–364, 1977.
*Influential description of a method for implementing distributed control structures: the ACTOR paradigm.*

[HT91]  Kohei Honda and Mario Tokoro. An object calculus for asynchronous communication. In Pierre America, editor, *Proceedings of the European Conference on Object-Oriented Programming (ECOOP)*, volume 512 of *Lecture Notes in Computer Science*, Geneva CH, 1991. Springer-Verlag , Berlin, Heidelberg, New York, Tokyo.

[Jon93]  Cliff B. Jones. A pi-calculus semantics for an object-based design notation. In E. Best, editor, *Proceedings of CONCUR'93*, LNCS 715, pages 158–172. Springer-Verlag, 1993.

[KY94]  Naoki Kobayashi and Aki Yonezawa. Towards foundations for concurrent object-oriented programming — Types and language design. Submitted for publication, 1994.

[Mil90]  Robin Milner. Functions as processes. Research Report 1154, INRIA, Sofia Antipolis, 1990. Final version in *Journal of Mathematical Structures in Computer Science* 2(2):119–141, 1992.

[Mil91]  Robin Milner. The polyadic $\pi$-calculus: a tutorial. Technical Report ECS–LFCS-91-180, Laboratory for Foundations of Computer Science, University of Edinburgh, October 1991. *Proceedings of the International Summer School on Logic and Algebra of Specification*, Marktoberdorf, August 1991.

[MPW92]  R. Milner, J. Parrow, and D. Walker. A calculus of mobile processes (Parts I and II). *Information and Computation*, 100:1–77, 1992.

[MT91]  Robin Milner and Mads Tofte. *Commentary on Standard ML*. The MIT Press, Cambridge, Massachusetts, 1991.

[MTH90]  Robin Milner, Mads Tofte, and Robert Harper. *The Definition of Standard ML*. The MIT Press, 1990.

[Nie92]  Oscar Nierstrasz. Towards an object calculus. In M. Tokoro, O. Nierstrasz, and P. Wegner, editors, *Proceedings of the ECOOP '91 Workshop on Object-Based Concurrent Computing*, Lecture Notes in Computer Science number 612, pages 1–20. Springer-Verlag, 1992.

[Pap92]  Michael Papathomas. A unifying framework for process calculus semantics of concurrent object-oriented languages. In M. Tokoro, O. Nierstrasz, and P. Wegner, editors, *Proceedings of the ECOOP '91 Workshop on Object-Based Concurrent Computing*, LNCS 612, pages 53–79. Springer-Verlag, 1992.

[Pie94]  Benjamin C. Pierce. Programming in the pi-calculus: An experiment in programming language design. Tutorial notes on the PICT language. Available electronically, 1994.

[PT94a]  Benjamin C. Pierce and David N. Turner. PICT user manual. Available electronically, 1994.

[PT94b]  Benjamin C. Pierce and David N. Turner. Simple type-theoretic foundations for object-oriented programming. *Journal of Functional Programming*, 4(2):207–247, April 1994. A preliminary version appeared in Principles of Programming Languages, 1993, and as University of Edinburgh technical report ECS-LFCS-92-225, under the title "Object-Oriented Programming Without Recursive Types".

[Rep88]  John Reppy. Synchronous operations as first-class values. In *Programming Language Design and Implementation*, pages 250–259. SIGPLAN, ACM, 1988.

[Rep91]  John Reppy. CML: A higher-order concurrent language. In *Programming Language Design and Implementation*, pages 293–259. SIGPLAN, ACM, June 1991.

[Rep92]  John Reppy. *Higher-Order Concurrency*. PhD thesis, Cornell University, June 1992. Technical Report TR 92-1285.

[San92]  Davide Sangiorgi. *Expressing Mobility in Process Algebras: First-Order and Higher-Order Paradigms*. PhD thesis, Department of Computer Science, University of Edinburgh, 1992.

[Smo94]  Gert Smolka. A Foundation for Concurrent Constraint Programming. In *Constraints in Computational Logics*, volume 845 of *Lecture Notes in Computer Science*, Munich, Germany, September 1994. Invited Talk.

[Vas94]  Vasco T. Vasconcelos. Typed concurrent objects. In *Proceedings of the Eighth European Conference on Object-Oriented Programming (ECOOP)*, volume 821 of *Lecture Notes in Computer Science*, pages 100–117. Springer-Verlag, July 1994.

[VT93]  Vasco T. Vasconcelos and Mario Tokoro. A Typing System for a Calculus of Objects. In *First International Symposium on Object Technologies for Advanced Software*, volume 742 of *Lecture Notes in Computer Science*, pages 460–474, November 1993.

[Wal94]  David Walker. Algebraic proofs of properties of objects. In *Proceedings of European Symposium on Programming*. Springer-Verlag, 1994.

# A  Operational Semantics and Derived Forms

## A.1  Core Language

### A.1.1  Matching

$$match(x, v) = \{x \mapsto v\}$$
$$match([p_1, \ldots, p_n], [v_1, \ldots, v_n]) = match(p_1, v_1) \cup \cdots \cup match(p_n, v_n)$$
$$match(\_, v) = \{\}$$
$$match(\texttt{record end}, \texttt{record end}) = \{\}$$
$$match(\texttt{record } j_1\texttt{=}p_1, \ldots, j_n\texttt{=}p_n, \texttt{l=}p \texttt{ end}, v_0 \texttt{ with l=}v \texttt{ end})$$
$$= match(p, v) \cup match(\texttt{record } j_1\texttt{=}p_1, \ldots, j_n\texttt{=}p_n \texttt{ end}, v_0)$$
$$match(\texttt{record } j_1\texttt{=}p_1, \ldots, j_n\texttt{=}p_n \texttt{ end}, v_0 \texttt{ with l=}v \texttt{ end})$$
$$= match(\texttt{record } j_1\texttt{=}p_1, \ldots, j_n\texttt{=}p_n \texttt{ end}, v_0), \quad \text{if } l \notin \{j_1, \ldots, j_n\}$$

## A.1.2 Structural Congruence

$$e_1 \mid e_2 \equiv e_2 \mid e_1 \qquad\qquad \text{(STR-COMM)}$$

$$(e_1 \mid e_2) \mid e_3 \equiv e_1 \mid (e_2 \mid e_3) \qquad\qquad \text{(STR-ASSOC)}$$

$$\frac{x \notin FV(e_2)}{\texttt{let new x in } e_1 \texttt{ end} \mid e_2 \equiv \texttt{let new x in } e_1 \mid e_2 \texttt{ end}} \qquad \text{(STR-EXTRUDE)}$$

## A.1.3 Reduction

$$\frac{e_1 \equiv e'_1 \rightarrow e'_2 \equiv e_2}{e_1 \rightarrow e_2} \qquad\qquad \text{(RED-STR)}$$

$$\frac{e_1 \rightarrow e'_1}{e_1 \mid e_2 \rightarrow e'_1 \mid e_2} \qquad\qquad \text{(RED-PAR)}$$

$$\frac{e \rightarrow e'}{\texttt{let d in e end} \rightarrow \texttt{let d in e' end}} \qquad\qquad \text{(RED-DEC)}$$

$$\frac{match(\texttt{p, v}) \text{ defined}}{\texttt{x!v} \mid (\texttt{x?p > e}) \rightarrow match(\texttt{p, v})(\texttt{e})} \qquad\qquad \text{(RED-COMM)}$$

$$\frac{match(\texttt{p, v}) \text{ defined}}{\texttt{x!v} \mid (\texttt{x?*p > e}) \rightarrow match(\texttt{p, v})(\texttt{e}) \mid (\texttt{x?*p > e})} \qquad \text{(RED-RCOMM)}$$

# A.2 Derived Forms

**A.2.1 Definition:** A PICT abstract syntax tree that is generated by the core grammar is called *simple*. We write, for example, *simple*(v) iff v ∈ Val according to the core grammar. By convention, the metavariable sv ranges only over simple values.

## A.2.1 Complex Outputs

$$\frac{\text{not } simple(\texttt{v}_i)}{\texttt{sv![sv}_1\texttt{,}\ldots\texttt{,sv}_{i-1}\texttt{,v}_i\texttt{,}\ldots\texttt{,v}_n\texttt{]} \Rightarrow} \qquad \text{(TR-TUPLE)}$$
$$\texttt{let new r in r!v}_i \mid \texttt{r?x}_i \texttt{ > sv![sv}_1\texttt{,}\ldots\texttt{,sv}_{i-1}\texttt{,x}_i\texttt{,}\ldots\texttt{,v}_n\texttt{] end}$$

$$\frac{\text{not } simple(\texttt{v}_2)}{\texttt{sv}_1\texttt{!(v}_2 \texttt{ with l=v}_3 \texttt{ end)} \Rightarrow} \qquad \text{(TR-RCDL)}$$
$$\texttt{let new r in r!v}_2 \mid \texttt{r?x > sv}_1\texttt{!(x with l=v}_3 \texttt{ end) end}$$

$$\frac{\text{not } simple(\texttt{v}_3)}{\texttt{sv}_1\texttt{!(sv}_2 \texttt{ with l=v}_3 \texttt{ end)} \Rightarrow} \qquad \text{(TR-RCDR)}$$
$$\texttt{let new r in r!v}_3 \mid \texttt{r?x > sv}_1\texttt{!(sv}_2 \texttt{ with l=x end) end}$$

$$sv!(\texttt{let d in v end}) \Rightarrow \texttt{let d in sv!v end} \qquad (\text{TR-LETV})$$

$$\frac{\text{not } simple(v)}{sv!(v[v_1,\ldots,v_n]) \Rightarrow \texttt{let new r in r!v | r?x > x![}v_1,\ldots,v_n,sv\texttt{] end}} \qquad (\text{TR-APP})$$

$$sv!(\texttt{if b then } v_1 \texttt{ else } v_2 \texttt{ end}) \Rightarrow$$
$$\texttt{let new t in let new f in} \qquad (\text{TR-IFV})$$
$$\texttt{primif![b,t,f] | (t?} \square \texttt{ > } sv!v_1 \texttt{) | (f?} \square \texttt{ > } sv!v_2\texttt{) end end}$$

## A.2.2  Declarations

$$\texttt{let run } e_1 \texttt{ in } e_2 \texttt{ end} \Rightarrow e_1 \texttt{ | } e_2 \qquad (\text{TR-RUN})$$

$$\texttt{local } d_1 \texttt{ in } d_2 \texttt{ end} \Rightarrow d_1 \ d_2 \qquad (\text{TR-LOCAL})$$

$$\texttt{let in e end} \Rightarrow e \qquad (\text{TR-NULLDEC})$$

$$\texttt{let d end} \Rightarrow \texttt{let d in skip end} \qquad (\text{TR-NULLIN})$$

$$\texttt{new } x_1,\ldots,x_n \Rightarrow \texttt{new } x_1 \ \ldots \ \texttt{new } x_n \qquad (n \neq 1) \qquad (\text{TR-NEWS})$$

$$\texttt{let def } x_1 \ p_1 \texttt{ > } e_1 \texttt{ and } \ldots \texttt{ and } x_n \ p_n \texttt{ > } e_n \texttt{ in e end}$$
$$\Rightarrow$$
$$\texttt{let new } x_1,\ldots,x_n \texttt{ in } (x_1 \texttt{ ?* } p_1 \texttt{ > } e_1) \texttt{ | } \ldots \texttt{ | } (x_n \texttt{ ?* } p_n \texttt{ > } e_n) \texttt{ | e end}$$
$$(\text{TR-DEF})$$

$$\texttt{let } d_1 \ d_2 \texttt{ in e end} \Rightarrow \texttt{let } d_1 \texttt{ in let } d_2 \texttt{ in e end end} \qquad (\text{TR-DECSEQ})$$

$$\texttt{let val p = v in e end} \Rightarrow \texttt{let new r in r!v | r?p > e end} \qquad (\text{TR-VAL})$$

## A.2.3  Abstractions

$$[p_1,\ldots,p_n] = v \Rightarrow [p_1,\ldots,p_n,r] \texttt{ > r!v} \qquad (\text{TR-VABS})$$

## A.2.4  Values

$$v_1 \texttt{ InfixId } v_2 \Rightarrow (\texttt{InfixId})[v_1,v_2] \qquad (\text{TR-INF})$$

$$v_1 \texttt{ `v` } v_2 \Rightarrow v[v_1,v_2] \qquad (\text{TR-INFQ})$$

$$\texttt{abs a end} \Rightarrow \texttt{let def x a in x end} \qquad (\text{TR-ANONABS})$$

$$v_1;v_2 \Rightarrow \texttt{let val [] = } v_1 \texttt{ in } v_2 \texttt{ end} \qquad (\text{TR-SEMIV})$$

$$\frac{n \geq 1}{\texttt{record } l_1=v_1, \ \ldots, \ l_n=v_n \texttt{ end} \Rightarrow} \qquad (\text{TR-NONEMPTYRCD})$$
$$\texttt{record end with } l_1=v_1, \ \ldots, \ l_n=v_n \texttt{ end}$$

$$\frac{n \neq 1}{\text{v with } l_1 = v_1, \ \ldots, \ l_n = v_n \ \text{end} \ \Rightarrow}$$
v with $l_1 = v_1$ end with ... end with $l_n = v_n$ end

(TR-BIGRCD)

v with l a end $\Rightarrow$ v with l = let def l a in l end end   (TR-ABSFIELD)

## A.2.5  Processes

$$\frac{\text{not } simple(v)}{\text{v?p > e} \ \Rightarrow \ \text{let val x = v in x?p > e end}}$$

(TR-IN)

$$\frac{\text{not } simple(v_1)}{v_1 ! v_2 \ \Rightarrow \ \text{let val x = } v_1 \text{ in x!}v_2 \text{ end}}$$

(TR-OUT)

skip $\Rightarrow$ let new x in x![] end   (TR-SKIP)

v;e $\Rightarrow$ let val [] = v in e end   (TR-SEMI)

v; $\Rightarrow$ let val [] = v in skip end   (TR-SEMISKIP)

if b then $e_1$ else $e_2$ end $\Rightarrow$
let new t in let new f in
primif![b,t,f] | (t?[] > $e_1$) | (f?[] > $e_2$) end end

(TR-IF)

## A.2.6  Conditionals

$$\frac{n \geq 2}{\text{if } b_1 \text{ then } e_1 \text{ elif } \ldots \text{ elif } b_n \text{ then } e_n \text{ else e end} \ \Rightarrow}$$
if $b_1$ then $e_1$ else if ... else if $b_n$ then $e_n$ else e end ... end end

(TR-ELIF)

$$\frac{n \geq 2}{\text{if } b_1 \text{ then } v_1 \text{ elif } \ldots \text{ elif } b_n \text{ then } v_n \text{ else v end} \ \Rightarrow}$$
if $b_1$ then $v_1$ else if ... else if $b_n$ then $v_n$ else v end ... end end

(TR-ELIFV)

if $b_1$ then $e_1$ elif ... elif $b_n$ then $e_n$ end $\Rightarrow$
if $b_1$ then $e_1$ elif ... elif $b_n$ then $e_n$ else skip end

(TR-NULLELSE)

if $b_1$ then $v_1$ elif ... elif $b_n$ then $v_n$ end $\Rightarrow$
if $b_1$ then $v_1$ elif ... elif $b_n$ then $v_n$ else [] end

(TR-NULLELSEV)

# A Formalism for
# Remotely Interacting Processes
—— *Working Paper* ——

Ichiro Satoh* and Mario Tokoro**

Department of Computer Science, Keio University
3-14-1, Hiyoshi, Kohoku-ku, Yokohama, 223, Japan

**Abstract.** An earlier paper [21] introduced process calculi with notions of time suited to express concurrent and distributed real-time computations. However, they cannot sufficiently model asynchronous communication in distributed systems. In this paper we present a process calculus with the ability to express asynchronous message passing with location-dependent transmission delay. It allows us to describe temporal and behavioral properties of asynchronous interactions among remotely located processes. Based on the process calculus, we also develop a "speed-sensitive" order relation for distributed real-time processes. It is formulated based on the notion of bisimulation and can distinguish between behaviorally equivalent processes performing at different speeds.

## 1 Introduction

Distributed systems consist of multiple processors cooperating by sending messages over communication networks. These communication networks often have transmission delay: a physical and logical function of geographic distance, communication bandwidth, and communication protocol overhead. The delay makes it to be difficult to develop correct distributed systems. This is because it affects the arrival timings of messages and thus often leads these systems to failure. Also, a sender process in distributed systems must be blocked for at least the length of communication delay in synchronous communication settings. For the sake of efficiency, communication among remotely located processes is often realized in an asynchronous form. However, asynchronous communication often creates unpleasant non-determinism. Therefore, in order to construct correct programs for distributed real-time systems, we must take communication delay and its influences into consideration. The objective of this paper is to propose a framework to describe communication delay and to analyze the behavioral and temporal properties of asynchronous interactions among distributed real-time processes.

* Email: *satoh@mt.cs.keio.ac.jp*, Partially supported by JSPS Fellowships for Japanese Junior Scientists.
** Email: *mario@mt.cs.keio.ac.jp*, Also with Sony Computer Science Laboratory Inc. 3-14-13 Higashi-Gotanda, Shinagawa-ku, Tokyo, 141, Japan.

The framework is formulated by extending a timed process calculus [16, 21] with the ability to express communication delay and asynchronous message passing. We also develop a performance analysis for distributed real-time systems by means of a "speed-sensitive" order relation on processes. It is formulated on the basis of the bisimulation technique[11, 15] and can can relate two distributed processes with respect to their speeds. If two processes are behaviorally equivalent and if the first process can execute faster than the second one, it asserts that the first process is *faster* than the second one.

There have indeed been several process calculi for distributed systems. They are extensions of existing process calculi with some features of distributed computing: causality between events (e.g., [6]), location information (e.g., [4]), port passing mechanism (e.g., [8, 11]), and local time (e.g., [17]), but none addresses the issue of communication delay. Also, there have been several temporal extensions of process calculi for synchronous communication, for example [7, 13, 14, 16, 20, 22]. Among these, Moller and Tofts in [13] studied a preorder relating timed processes with respect to speed. However, the order relation is inherently dependent on synchronous communication and thus cannot compare the performances of asynchronously communicating processes. On the other hand, there are many process calculi with the ability to express asynchronous communication (e.g., [1, 3, 5, 8, 9, 10]). However, there are only a few that deal with both delay and asynchrony in communication. Among them, in [2] Baeten and Bergstra proposed a process calculus with the ability to express asynchronous communication with delay and failure, based on a timed extended calculus of ACP [1]. It represents asynchronous message transmission as the creation of a process corresponding to the message like the methods developed in [8, 10] and like our approach it can represent communication delay by suspending the created process for the amount of the delay. However, it provides just a language to describe systems with asynchronous communication with delay and failure and it does not provide any kind of analysis for these systems.

The organization of this paper is as follows: In the next section we briefly present our basic ideas concerning the process calculus and then define its syntax and semantics. In Section 3 we define a timed pre-bisimulation that can relate two processes according to their speeds. In Section 4 we show some examples. The final section contains some concluding remarks.

## 2  Timed Calculus

Our framework is an extension of an existing process calculus, CCS [11], with the ability to express communication delay, delayed processing, and non-blocking message sending. Its syntax and semantics are essentially those of CCS, except for these extensions. Before formally defining the framework, we summarize our basic assumptions.

## Basic Framework

We assume that time is dense and that the passage of time in every processor elapses at the same rate.[3] The passage of time is represented as a special transition that proceeds synchronously in all processes. Also, several real distributed systems have some behaviors depending on the passage of time. We introduce an operation that explicitly suspends its execution for a specified period.

Distributed systems are often based on asynchronous message passing instead of a synchronous form. In the formalism, we assume that processes communicate with each other through reliable one-way asynchronous message passing. However, since most of process calculi are essentially based on synchronous communication, we need extensions of a process calculus with the ability to express *asynchronous message* and *non-block message send*. In these extensions, an asynchronous message is modeled as a process, and a non-blocking message sending as a creation of a process representing the message.

Communication delay is strongly dependent on distance between the locations of the sender process and the receiver one. We therefore introduce the concept of process location in order to specify communication delay between processes appropriately.[4] Each process has its location name and can receive only the messages that arrive at the location. Communication delay for a message is given as the temporal length from when a process is ready to send the message to when the message reaches its destination location. Communication delay is known and the order of message arrival is indeterminate.

**Remark** In this paper, for focusing temporal aspects in distributed real-time systems, we avoid to introduce the expressive capability for a distributed system where topological connections between processes can change dynamically; but our calculus can easily model such a system by incorporating with the port-passing mechanism developed in [12].

## Definition

The syntax of our formalism is an extension of Milner's CCS [11] by introducing communication delay, non-blocking message send, and delaying. We first define the notation that we will follow hereafter.

### Definition 2.1

- Let $M$ be a non-empty infinite set of message names, ranged over by $a, b, \ldots$.
- Let $Loc$ be an infinite set of location name, ranged over by $\ell, \ell_1, \ell_2, \ldots$.
- Let $T$ denote the set of the positive reals including 0.

---

[3] By using the method developed in [17], we can express multiple and inaccurate clocks.

[4] The notion of process location in this paper is introduced only to express temporal distance between locations; we do not intend to investigate the notion itself.

- Let $\mathcal{D} \subseteq \mathcal{L}oc \times \mathcal{L}oc \to \mathcal{T}$ be the set of communication delay functions, ranged over by $d, d_1, d_2, \ldots$.[5] $\qquad$ ☐

In our formalism, we describe distributed processes by means of the language defined below.

**Definition 2.2** The set $\mathcal{P}$ of process expressions, ranged over by $P, P_1, P_2, \ldots$, is the smallest set containing the following expressions:

$$
\begin{array}{lll}
P ::= P|P & & (\textit{Parallel Execution}) \\
\quad | \ P \setminus N & & (\textit{Restriction}) \\
\quad | \ Q : \ell & & (\textit{Located Process}) \\
\\
Q ::= \sum_{i \in I} \downarrow a_i . Q_i & & (\textit{Selective Receive}) \\
\quad | \ \ell \uparrow a . Q & & (\textit{Non-blocking Send}) \\
\quad | \ \langle t \rangle . Q & & (\textit{Suspension}) \\
\quad | \ A \overset{\text{def}}{=} Q & & (\textit{Definition})
\end{array}
$$

where $N$ is a subset of $\mathcal{M}$ and $I$ is a finite index set $\{1, 2, \ldots, n\}$. $t$ is an element of $\mathcal{T}$, and $A$ is an element of a process constant set, ranged over by $A, B, \ldots$. We sometimes write $0$ for an empty summation (i.e. $\sum_{i \in \emptyset} \downarrow a_i . Q_i$) and abbreviate $\epsilon \uparrow a.0$ to $\uparrow a.0$ (where $\epsilon$ is an empty location name), and $\ell \uparrow a.0$ to $\ell \uparrow a$. We often use the simpler notation $(\downarrow a_1 . Q_1 + \cdots + \downarrow a_n . Q_n) : \ell$ instead of $\sum_{i \in \{1, \ldots, n\}} \downarrow a_i . Q_i : \ell$. We often write $A : \ell \overset{\text{def}}{=} Q : \ell$ if $A \overset{\text{def}}{=} Q$, and $(Q|Q) : \ell$ if $Q : \ell | Q : \ell$. $\qquad$ ☐

We show the intuitive meaning of constructors in $\mathcal{P}$ in below:

- $P_1 | P_2$ presents that $P_1$ and $P_2$ may execute in parallel.
- $P \setminus N$ encapsulates all messages in set $L$.
- $Q : \ell$ presents a process located at $\ell$.
- $\sum_{i \in I} \downarrow a_i . Q_i$ presents a selectively blocking message receive. If it receives a message named $a_i$, then it behaves as $Q_i$. $0$ presents a terminated process.
- $\ell' \uparrow a . Q$ sends a message to an input port $a$ of a process at location $\ell'$ and continues to execute $Q$ without any blocking.
- $\langle t \rangle . Q$ presents a process which is idle for $t$ time and then behaving as $Q$.
- $A \overset{\text{def}}{=} Q$ shows that $A$ is (recursively) defined as $Q$.

The operational semantics of our language is given by two kinds of state transition relations: $\longrightarrow \subseteq \mathcal{P} \times \mathcal{P}$ (called *behavioral transition*) and $\longmapsto \subseteq \mathcal{P} \times \mathcal{T} \times \mathcal{P}$ (called *temporal transition*). In this paper we will use a structural congruence $\equiv$ over processes. This is the method followed by Milner in [12] to deal with the $\pi$-calculus. The use of the structural congruence technique provides an equivalence between processes which allows us to concentrate on the investigation of inequalities between processes with respect to their speeds.

---

[5] In order to express non-deterministic communication delay, we should define $\mathcal{D} \subseteq \mathcal{L}oc \times \mathcal{L}oc \to 2^{\mathcal{T}}$ as a multivalued function; but in this paper we do not investigate the details of this extension.

**Definition 2.3** $\equiv$ is the least syntactic congruence defined by the following equations:

$$P_1 \mid P_2 \equiv P_2 \mid P_1 \qquad P_1 \mid (P_2 \mid P_3) \equiv (P_1 \mid P_2) \mid P_3 \qquad P \mid 0:\ell \equiv P$$
$$(0).Q:\ell \equiv Q:\ell \qquad Q \setminus N:\ell \equiv Q:\ell \setminus N \qquad P \setminus N_1 \setminus N_2 \equiv P \setminus N_2 \setminus N_1$$
$$(\ell'{\uparrow}a.Q:\ell \mid P) \setminus N \equiv \ell'{\uparrow}a.Q:\ell \mid P \setminus N \text{ where } a \notin N$$

We now present the operational semantics of our language.

**Definition 2.4** *Behavioral transition* $\longrightarrow \subseteq \mathcal{P} \times \mathcal{P}$ is the least binary relation given by the following rules.

$$\ell'{\uparrow}a.Q:\ell \longrightarrow (d(\ell, \ell')).\epsilon{\uparrow}a.0:\ell' \mid Q:\ell \quad (\ell' \text{ is not } \epsilon)$$
$$\textstyle\sum_{i \in I} {\downarrow}a_i.Q_i:\ell \mid \epsilon{\uparrow}a_i.Q:\ell \longrightarrow Q_i:\ell \mid Q:\ell$$
$$P_1 \longrightarrow P_1' \quad \text{implies} \quad P_1 \mid P_2 \longrightarrow P_1' \mid P_2$$
$$P \longrightarrow P' \quad \text{implies} \quad P \setminus N \longrightarrow P' \setminus N$$
$$Q:\ell \longrightarrow Q':\ell \quad \text{implies} \quad A:\ell \longrightarrow Q':\ell \quad (A \stackrel{\text{def}}{=} Q)$$
$$P_1 \equiv P_2, \quad P_1 \longrightarrow P_1' \quad \text{implies} \quad P_2 \longrightarrow P_1'$$

where $d \in \mathcal{D}$. We often write $(\equiv)^* \longrightarrow (\equiv)^*$ as $\longrightarrow$. □

**Definition 2.5** *Temporal transition* $\longmapsto \subseteq \mathcal{P} \times \mathcal{T} \times \mathcal{P}$ is the least binary relation defined by the following rules.

$$(d).Q:\ell \stackrel{t}{\longmapsto} (d\dot{-}t).Q:\ell$$
$$\epsilon{\uparrow}a.Q:\ell \stackrel{t}{\longmapsto} \epsilon{\uparrow}a.Q:\ell$$
$$\textstyle\sum_{i \in I} {\downarrow}a_i.Q_i:\ell \stackrel{t}{\longmapsto} \sum_{i \in I} {\downarrow}a_i.Q_i:\ell$$
$$P_1 \stackrel{t}{\longmapsto} P_1', \quad P_2 \stackrel{t}{\longmapsto} P_2' \quad \text{implies} \quad P_1 \mid P_2 \stackrel{t}{\longmapsto} P_1' \mid P_2'$$
$$P \stackrel{t}{\longmapsto} P' \quad \text{implies} \quad P \setminus N \stackrel{t}{\longmapsto} P' \setminus N$$
$$Q:\ell \stackrel{t}{\longmapsto} Q':\ell \quad \text{implies} \quad A:\ell \stackrel{t}{\longmapsto} Q':\ell \quad (A \stackrel{\text{def}}{=} Q)$$
$$P_1 \equiv P_2, \quad P_1 \stackrel{t}{\longmapsto} P_1' \quad \text{implies} \quad P_2 \stackrel{t}{\longmapsto} P_1'$$

where $t_1 \dot{-} t_2 = t_1 - t_2$ if $t_1 \geq t_2$ and otherwise 0. We often write $(\equiv)^* \stackrel{t}{\longmapsto} (\equiv)^*$ as $\stackrel{t}{\longmapsto}$. □

**Example 2.6** Consider the following interaction between two processes:

$$A_1:\ell_1 \stackrel{\text{def}}{=} (2.0)({\downarrow}a.P_1 + {\downarrow}b.P_2):\ell_1 \qquad \text{and} \qquad A_2:\ell_2 \stackrel{\text{def}}{=} (1.0)\ell_1{\uparrow}a.P_3:\ell_2$$

$A_1$ is allocated at location $\ell_1$. It is idle for 2.0 time and then waits for message $a$ and message $b$. $A_2$ is allocated at location $\ell_2$. It is idle for 1.0 time and then sends message $a$ to a process at location $\ell_1$. We assume that the communication delay from location $\ell_1$ to $\ell_2$ is 2.0 time. That is, $d(\ell_2, \ell_1) = 2.0$ where $d \in \mathcal{D}$. An interaction between these processes is described by the following transitions:

$$A_1:\ell_1 | A_2:\ell_2 \xrightarrow{1.0} \langle 1.0 \rangle (\downarrow a.P_1 + \downarrow b.P_2):\ell_1 \mid \ell_1 \uparrow a.P_3:\ell_2$$
$$\longrightarrow \langle 1.0 \rangle (\downarrow a.P_1 + \downarrow b.P_2):\ell_1 \mid \langle 2.0 \rangle \epsilon \uparrow a.0:\ell_1 \mid P_3:\ell_2$$
$$\xrightarrow{2.0} (\downarrow a.P_1 + \downarrow b.P_2):\ell_1 \mid \epsilon \uparrow a.0:\ell_1 \mid P_3:\ell_2$$
$$\longrightarrow P_1:\ell_1 \mid P_3:\ell_2$$

**Remark** The calculus has a restriction in its expressive capability. It cannot model *timeout* contexts, which allow a certain computation to be performed within a specified amount of time, but proceeds an alternative computation if the amount of the time passes without the desired computation being performed and restricts the executionability of the desired computation. This problem arises due to the non-preemptive nature of executable behavioral transitions in the operational semantics of the calculus. Therefore, executable behavioral transitions do not have to be performed as soon as they are executable and may be suspended for an arbitrary period of time. This non-preemptiveness is *needed* in defining a speed-sensitive order relation which can be preserved in a parallel composition. Also, we would insist that this problem is not an unreasonable restriction in the expressive capability of the calculus. This is because we never lose the expressive capability for time-dependent operations which make some other event executable due to the passing of time, in particular this restriction never affects any required expressiveness of the language in describing hard real-time systems.

## 3 Ordering Processes with Respect to Speed

This section proposes an order relation on distributed real-time processes with respect to speed. Several timed equivalence relations have already been explored in for example [7, 14, 16, 22]. These relations equate two processes only when their temporal and behavioral properties completely match. However, such equivalence relations are often too strict to analyze distributed systems. This is because these systems have a lot of non-determinacy in their temporal properties. Also, in developing and improving distributed systems, we often need to compare the performances of two processes having the same functions. Based on the notion of bisimulation [11, 15], we develop a "speed-sensitive" order relation that decides whether two processes are behaviorally equivalent and that one of them has a capability to execute its behaviors *faster* than the another.

We first illustrate the basic idea of the relation. For example, suppose two processes: $A_1 : \ell_A \stackrel{\text{def}}{=} \langle 1 \rangle \ell \uparrow a.Q : \ell_A$ and $A_2 : \ell_A \stackrel{\text{def}}{=} \langle 3 \rangle \ell \uparrow a.Q : \ell_A$, where $\ell$ is the process location of an observer. Since $A_1$ can send message $a$ to the observer *sooner* than $A_2$, we would consider process $A_1$ to be *faster* than process $A_2$.

**Definition 3.1** The transitive translations are denoted as follows:

$$P \overset{t}{\Longrightarrow} P' \overset{\text{def}}{=} P \,(\longrightarrow)^* \overset{t_1}{\longmapsto} (\longrightarrow)^* \cdots (\longrightarrow)^* \overset{t_n}{\longmapsto} (\longrightarrow)^* P'$$

where $t_1 + \cdots + t_n = t$. □

**Definition 3.2** The function $\mathcal{PL}(\cdot) : \mathcal{P} \to \mathcal{Loc}$ which presents the location names of processes is defined as follows:

$$\mathcal{PL}(P_1|P_2) = \mathcal{PL}(P_2) \cup \mathcal{PL}(P_2) \quad \mathcal{PL}(P \setminus L) = \mathcal{PL}(P) \quad \mathcal{PL}(S:\ell) = \{\ell\} \quad □$$

**Definition 3.3** A binary relation $\mathcal{R} \subseteq (\mathcal{P} \times \mathcal{P}) \times \mathcal{T} \times \mathcal{Loc}$ is a *t-speed sensitive pre-bisimulation* on $L$ if $(P_1, P_2) \in \mathcal{R}_t^L$ $(\mathcal{PL}(P_1) = \mathcal{PL}(P_2))$ implies, for all $a, b \in \mathcal{M} \cup \{\epsilon\}, \ell, \ell' \in L, \ell_P \in \mathcal{PL}(P_1)(= \mathcal{PL}(P_2))$, and $d_1, d_2 \in \mathcal{T}$ such that $d_1 \leq d_2 + t$;

(i) $\forall m_1, \forall P_1' : (d_1).\ell_P \uparrow a.0{:}\ell \,|\, P_1 \overset{m_1}{\Longrightarrow} \epsilon \uparrow b.0{:}\ell' \,|\, P_1'$ then
$\exists m_2, \exists P_2' : (d_2).\ell_P \uparrow a.0{:}\ell \,|\, P_2 \overset{m_2}{\Longrightarrow} \epsilon \uparrow b.0{:}\ell' \,|\, P_2'$ and $(P_1', P_2') \in \mathcal{R}_{t-m_1+m_2}^L$

(ii) $\forall m_2, \forall P_2' : (d_2).\ell_P \uparrow a.0{:}\ell \,|\, P_2 \overset{m_2}{\Longrightarrow} \epsilon \uparrow b.0{:}\ell' \,|\, P_2'$ then
$\exists m_1, \exists P_1 : (d_1).\ell_P \uparrow a.0{:}\ell \,|\, P_1 \overset{m_1}{\Longrightarrow} \epsilon \uparrow b.0{:}\ell' \,|\, P_1'$ and $(P_1', P_2') \in \mathcal{R}_{t-m_1+m_2}^L$

For $P_1, P_2 \in \mathcal{P}$, we let $P_1 \trianglelefteq_t^L P_2$ if there exists a speed sensitive pre-bisimulation such that $(P_1, P_2) \in \mathcal{R}_t^L$. We call $\trianglelefteq_t^L$ *t-speed sensitive order* on $L$. We shall often abbreviate $\trianglelefteq_0^L$ as $\trianglelefteq^L$. □

We explain the meaning of $P_1 \trianglelefteq_t^L P_2$. $\trianglelefteq_t^L$ is given as the largest set of $\mathcal{R}_t^L$. $\mathcal{R}_t^L$ is a family of relations indexed by a non-negative time value $t$. The value is the relative difference between the time of $P_1$ and that of $P_2$; that is, it means that $P_1$ precedes $P_2$ by $t$ time.[6] $\trianglelefteq_t^L$ starts with a pre-bisimulation indexed by $t$ (i.e., $(P_1, P_2) \in \mathcal{R}_t^L$) and then can change $t$ as the bisimulation proceeds if $t \geq 0$. $L$ corresponds to the set of the locations of conceptual observers. The bisimulation makes two processes interact with the observers (or arbitrary processes) at locations in $L$ and the observers relates the processes according to the temporal and behavioral results of the interactions. In the definition of $\mathcal{R}_t^L$, an observer at location $\ell$ ($\ell \in L$) sends a message to $P_1$ at $d_1$ time (written as $(d_1).\ell_P \uparrow a.0{:}\ell$ in (i)). The observer also sends the same message to $P_2$ at arbitrarily later timing (written as $(d_2).\ell_P \uparrow a.0{:}\ell$ in (ii)). And then an observer at location $\ell'$ ($\ell' \in L$) receives a return message from $P_1$ and the same message from $P_2$ (written as $\epsilon \uparrow b.0{:}\ell'$ in (i) and (ii)). If the arrival timing of the return message from $P_1$ is earlier than that from $P_2$,[7] and if $P_1'$ and $P_2'$ can be successfully observed in $(P_1', P_2') \in \mathcal{R}_{t-m_1+m_2}^L$ in the same way, the observers judge that $P_1$ and $P_2$ are behaviorally equivalent and that $P_1$ can perform its behaviors *faster* than $P_2$.

---

[6] This means that the performance of $P_1$ is at most $t$ time faster than that of $P_2$.

[7] Note that $P_1$ already precedes $P_1$ by $t$ time units. Hence, the relative difference between the arrival time of the message from $P_2$ and that from $P_1$ is $t - m_1 + m_2$ time units.

**Proposition 3.4**    For all $P, P_1, P_2, P_3 \in \mathcal{P}$ then,

(1) $P \unlhd_t^L P$    (2) If $P_1 \unlhd_{t_1}^L P_2$ and $P_2 \unlhd_{t_2}^L P_3$ then $P_1 \unlhd_{t_1+t_2}^L P_3$    □

From the above result, we directly have that $P \unlhd^L P$ and that if $P_1 \unlhd^L P_2$ and $P_2 \unlhd^L P_3$ then $P_1 \unlhd^L P_3$. Hence, $\unlhd^L$ is a preorder relation.

**Proposition 3.5**    For all $P_1, P_2 \in \mathcal{P}$ such that $P_1 \unlhd_t^L P_2$ then,

(1) If $L' \subseteq L$    then    $P_1 \unlhd_t^{L'} P_2$    (2) If $t \leq t'$    then    $P_1 \unlhd_{t'}^L P_2$    □

**Proposition 3.6**    For all $Q_1:\ell, Q_2:\ell, P_1, P_2 \in \mathcal{P}$ such that $Q_1:\ell \unlhd^L Q_2:\ell$ and $P_1 \unlhd_t^L P_2$, and $t_1 \leq t_2$ then,

(1) $\downarrow a.Q_1:\ell \unlhd^L \downarrow a.Q_2:\ell$    (2) If $\ell'\uparrow a.Q_1:\ell \unlhd_t^L \ell'\uparrow a.Q_2:\ell$

(3) $(t_1)Q_1:\ell \unlhd_t^L (t_2)Q_2:\ell$    (4) $P_1 \setminus N \unlhd_t^L P_2 \setminus N$    □

The following proposition shows an important relationship between the order and communication delay.

**Proposition 3.7**    For all $P_1, P_2 \in \mathcal{P}$, $d_1, d_2 \in \mathcal{D}$ such that $\forall \ell \in L, \forall \ell_2 \in \mathcal{PL}(P_2):$ $d_1(\ell, \ell_2) \leq d_2(\ell, \ell_2)$ and $d_1(\ell_2, \ell) \leq d_2(\ell_2, \ell)$,

If $P_1 \unlhd_t^L P_2$ assuming $d_1$    then    $P_1 \unlhd_t^L P_2$ assuming $d_2$    □

This proposition shows that a slower process is still slower even from the further observer. However, we cannot hope the similar proposition about the first expression, that is, a faster process is not usually faster from the nearer observer. We show a counterexample.

**Example 3.8**    Suppose two processes: $A_1:\ell_A \overset{\text{def}}{=} (1). \downarrow a.\ell'\uparrow b.0 : \ell_A$ and $A_2:\ell_A \overset{\text{def}}{=} (3). \downarrow a.\ell'\uparrow b.0 : \ell_A$, where $\ell' \in L$.

$A_1:\ell_A \unlhd^L A_2:\ell_A$ and $A_2:\ell_A \unlhd^L A_1:\ell_A$ where $\forall \ell \in L: d(\ell, \ell_A) \geq 3$

$A_1:\ell_A \unlhd^L A_2:\ell_A$ and $A_2:\ell_A \ntrianglelefteq^L A_1:\ell_A$ where $\forall \ell \in L: d(\ell, \ell_A) < 3$

This example tells a notable fact that $\unlhd_t^L$ cannot notice any temporal and behavioral difference between its ordered processes before their first messages can arrive at it.

**Proposition 3.9**    For all $P_1, P_2, Q_1, Q_2 \in \mathcal{P}$, $L \subseteq \mathcal{L}$ such that $\mathcal{PL}(P_1) = \mathcal{PL}(P_2) \subseteq L$, $\mathcal{PL}(Q_1) = \mathcal{PL}(Q_2) \subseteq L$,

If $P_1 \unlhd_t^L P_2$ and $Q_1 \unlhd_t^L Q_2$ then $P_1|Q_1 \unlhd_t^L P_2|Q_2$    □

*Proof.* (Outline) It is enough to show that $\mathcal{R}_t^L \overset{\text{def}}{=} \{(P_1|Q_1, P_2|Q_2) : P_1 \unlhd_t^L P_2, Q_1 \unlhd_t^L Q_2, \mathcal{PL}(P_1) = \mathcal{PL}(P_2) \subseteq L$, and $\mathcal{PL}(Q_1) = \mathcal{PL}(Q_2) \subseteq L\}$ is a speed sensitive pre-bisimulation. We here assume that $(d_1)\ell\uparrow a.0 : \ell|P_1|Q_1 \overset{m}{\Longrightarrow} \uparrow b.0 : \ell'|R_1$. There are some cases but we show the outline proof of the most difficult

case: Let $\langle d_1 \rangle \dot{\ell} \restriction a.0 : \ell | P_1 \overset{m_1}{\Longrightarrow} \uparrow c.0 : \hat{\ell} | \hat{P}_1$, $\hat{\ell} \in \mathcal{PL}(Q_1)$, $\langle m_1 \rangle \uparrow c.0 : \ell | Q_1 \overset{m_1 + m_2}{\Longrightarrow} \uparrow b.0 :$ $\ell' | Q_1'$, $\hat{P}_1 \overset{m_2}{\Longrightarrow} P_1'$, $m = m_1 + m_2$, and $R_1$ is $P_1' | Q_1'$. Then, since $P_1 \trianglelefteq_t^L P_2$, we have $d_1 \leq d_2 + t$ and $\langle d_2 \rangle \dot{\ell} \restriction a.0 : \ell | P_2 \overset{n_1}{\Longrightarrow} \uparrow c.0 : \hat{\ell} | \hat{P}_2$ and $\hat{P}_1 \trianglelefteq_{t-m_1+n_1}^L \hat{P}_2$. Since $Q_1 \trianglelefteq_t^L Q_2$, $m_1 \leq n_1 + t$, we have $\langle n_1 \rangle \uparrow c.0 : \ell | Q_2 \overset{n_1 + n_2}{\Longrightarrow} \uparrow b.0 : \ell' | Q_2'$, and $Q_1' \trianglelefteq_{t-m+n_1+n_2}^L Q_2'$. Also, $\hat{P}_1 \overset{n_2}{\Longrightarrow} P_1'$ and $P_1' \trianglelefteq_{t-m+n_1+n_2}^L P_2'$. We write $n = n_1 + n_2$, then we have that $(P_1' | Q_1', P_2' | Q_2) \in \mathcal{R}_{t-m+n}^L$. This prove (i) of Definition 3.9 and (ii) is similar.
$\square$

This proposition shows that the speed-sensitive order relation is preserved by the parallel construction. We directly have that if $P_1 \trianglelefteq^L P_2$ and $Q_1 \trianglelefteq^L Q_2$ then $P_1 | Q_1 \trianglelefteq^L P_2 | Q_2$. Also, if two processes are behaviorally equivalent and one of them can execute faster than the another, we can guarantee that the faster process can be substituted for the slower one in parallel composition without altering the behavioral properties nor lowering the performance characteristics of the whole system. We have many occasions to replace a slower process (e.g., an old fashioned computer) of a system by a faster process (e.g., its latest fashioned computer). Therefore, the proposition provides a practical method in reconstructing distributed real-time systems.

**Remark** The speed-sensitive order relation indeed analyzes the performances of two processes in a optimistic way. That is, the relation shows only that a process may *possibly* execute faster than another. Thus, for example, the order relation cannot be available in verifying whether a process can *always* perform its behaviors at *earlier* timings than the timings given in its temporal specification. This problem is very related with the non-preemptive nature of behavioral transitions stated in the previous section. We can define another order relation tells that a process will *necessarily* execute than another, if we exclude the non-preemptiveness. However, this alternation creates another undesirable problem in defining an order relation with respect to speed which is preserved in a parallel composition. For example, suppose three processes: $A_1 : \ell_A \overset{\text{def}}{=} \langle 1 \rangle . \ell_B \uparrow a.0 : \ell_A$, $A_2 :$ $\ell_A \overset{\text{def}}{=} \langle 3 \rangle . \ell_B \uparrow a.0 : \ell_A$, and $B : \ell_B \overset{\text{def}}{=} ((\downarrow a.B' + \downarrow b.B'') : \ell_B | \langle 2 \rangle . \dot{\epsilon} \uparrow b.0 : \ell_B) \setminus \{b\}$ where $d(\ell_A, \ell_B) = 0$. We clearly have $A_1 \trianglelefteq^L A_2$ but cannot expect that $A_1 | B \trianglelefteq^L A_2 | B$.
[8]

# 4 Example

In this section we present some examples in order to demonstrate how we describe and analyze distributed real-time systems by using the calculus and the order relation.

---

[8] By reconstructing the whole semantics of the calculus, we can have a possibility to define another speed-sensitive order relation which can be preserved in a parallel composition and which shows a process can *always* execute faster than another; but we leave the details of the semantics and the relation to [19].

**Example 4.1** Suppose an airline reservation system in a distributed system. The system consists of two distributed processes: an air-company process at location $\ell_c$, written as $Company_1$, and a passenger process at location $\ell_p$, written as $Passenger_1$. We denote the location of their environment as $\ell$.

After receiving a $\downarrow seat$ message from the environment, the passenger process sends $ask$ to the company process in order to query whether the company has a seat or not. If it receives a $yes$ message, it sends a $reserve$ message to reserve the ticket and then waits a $ticket$ message. After receiving the notice, it sends a $ok$ message to the environment.

The company process waits for a $ask$ message and then returns a $yes$ message after 2.0 time and waits for a $reserve$ message. After an internal execution for 8.0 time, it returns a $ticket$ message. These processes are described as follows:

$$Passenger_1 \stackrel{\text{def}}{=} \downarrow seat . \ell_c \uparrow ask . \downarrow yes . \ell_c \uparrow reserve . \downarrow ticket . \ell \uparrow ok . 0$$

$$Company_1 \stackrel{\text{def}}{=} \downarrow ask . (2.0) . \ell_p \uparrow yes . \downarrow reserve . (8.0) . \ell_p \uparrow ticket . Company_1$$

The whole system is described as follow:

$$(Company_1 : \ell_c \mid Passenger_1 : \ell_p) \setminus N_1 \quad \text{where } N_1 \stackrel{\text{def}}{=} \{ask, reserve, ticket yes\}$$

where we assume that the communication delay between $\ell_p$ and $\ell_c$ is 5.0 time, that is, $d(\ell_c, \ell_p) = d(\ell_p, \ell_c) = 5.0$ where $d \in \mathcal{D}$.

**Example 4.2** Consider another reservation system. The system consists of three distributed processes: an air-company process, at location $\ell_c$, written as $Company_2 : \ell_c$, a travel agent process at location $\ell_a$, written as $Agent : \ell_a$, and a passenger process at location $\ell_p$, written as $Passenger_2 : \ell_p$. The agent process interacts with the company process and the passenger one. The company process is identical to that of Example 4.1 except for its message destinations.

After receiving a $seat$ message, the passenger process sends the agent process a request message, $req$, and then knows that it can get a seat through a $started$ message. After receiving the message, it sends a $ok$ message to the environment.

On the other hand, the agent process receives a $req$ message and then after an internal execution of 1.0 time, it sends a $ask$ message. If it receives message $yes$, it asks the company to reserve a ticket through message $reserve$ after an internal execution of 4.0 time. After that, it sends a $started$ message to the passenger. It receives a $ticket$ message and then waits for next ticket request, $req$. These processes are described as follows:

$$Passenger_2 \stackrel{\text{def}}{=} \downarrow seat . \ell_a \uparrow req . \downarrow started . \ell \uparrow ok . 0$$

$$Agent \stackrel{\text{def}}{=} \downarrow req . (1) . \ell_c \uparrow ask . \downarrow yes . (4.0) . \ell_c \uparrow reserve . \ell_p \uparrow started .$$
$$\downarrow ticket . Agent$$

$$Company_2 \stackrel{\text{def}}{=} \downarrow ask . (2.0) . \ell_a \uparrow yes . \downarrow reserve . (8.0) . \ell_a \uparrow ticket . Company_2$$

The whole system is described as a parallel composition of the three process as follows:

$$(Company_2 : \ell_c \mid Agent : \ell_a \mid Passenger_2 : \ell_p) \setminus N_2$$
$$\text{where } N_2 \stackrel{\text{def}}{=} \{ask, req, reserve, started, ticket, yes\}$$

where we assume that the communication delay between $\ell_a$ and $\ell_c$ is 3.0 time and that between $\ell_p$ and $\ell_a$ is 3.0 time, that is, $d(\ell_a, \ell_c) = d(\ell_c, \ell_a) = 3.0$ and $d(\ell_p, \ell_a) = d(\ell_p, \ell_a) = 3.0$, where $d \in \mathcal{D}$.

**Example 4.3**
By using the speed-sensitive order relation, we can compare the performances of the reservation systems as follows:

$$(Company_1 : \ell_c \mid Passenger_1 : \ell_p) \setminus N_1$$
$$\preceq^L (Company_2 : \ell_c \mid Agent : \ell_a \mid Passenger_2 : \ell_p) \setminus N_2$$
$$\text{where } L \subseteq \mathcal{L}oc \text{ such that } \ell \in L$$

The above result shows that they are behaviorally equivalent but that the reservation system of Example 4.1 can perform faster than that of Example 4.2.

**Example 4.4**  We improve the reservation system presented in Example 4.4. Suppose another agent process (a new implementation) described as the following $Agent'$:

$$Agent' : \ell_a \preceq^{L'} Agent : \ell_a \text{ where}$$
$$Agent' \stackrel{\text{def}}{=} {\downarrow}req \,. (1) \,. \ell_c {\uparrow}ask \,. {\downarrow}yes \,. (2) \,. \ell_c {\uparrow}reserve \,. \ell_p {\uparrow}started \,. {\downarrow}ticket \,. Agent'$$
$$\ell_a, \ell_c, \ell_p \in L' \text{ and } L \subseteq L'$$

This inequality shows that $Agent$ and $Agent'$ are behaviorally equivalent and $Agent$ can perform faster than $Agent'$. Also, from Proposition 3.9, we know the following desired fact:

$$Company_2 : \ell_c \mid Agent' : \ell_a \mid Passenger_2 : \ell_p$$
$$\preceq^{L'} Company_2 : \ell_c \mid Agent : \ell_a \mid Passenger_2 : \ell_p$$

This shows that $Agent'$ can be behaviorally substituted for $Agent$ in the system of Example 4.4 and that the system with $Agent'$ can still perform faster than that with $Agent$ From Proposition 3.5, we have that the system with $Agent'$ can perform faster than the system given in Example 4.1.

$$(Company_2 : \ell_c \mid Agent' : \ell_a \mid Passenger_2 : \ell_p) \setminus N_2$$
$$\preceq^L (Company_1 : \ell_c \mid Passenger_1 : \ell_p) \setminus N_1$$

# 5 Conclusion

In this paper we proposed a formalism to specify and analyze distributed real-time processes, linked by communication networks with transmission delay. It is an extension of Milner's CCS, and is able to express features of distributed real-time systems: location-dependent communication delay, and non-blocking message sending. Through its expressive capabilities, we can strictly describe and analyze the influences of the delay upon behavioral and temporal properties of interactions among distributed real-time processes. Based on the formalism, we developed an order relation for distributed processes with respect to speed. It can distinguish between behaviorally equivalent processes performing at different speeds.

Finally, we would like to point out some further issues. The order relation can show that a faster process has a possibility to perform their same behaviors faster than the slower process, but cannot guarantee that the faster process is *always* faster then the slower one. We are interested in defining a more pessimistic speed-sensitive relation on processes.[9] We have already developed a framework to define semantics for concurrent real-time programming languages through a timed extended process calculus in [18]. We plan to investigate semantics definition for distributed real-time programming languages by using the calculus presented in this paper.

**Acknowledgements** We would like to thank Professor C. Queinnec and Professor A. Yonezawa for giving the beneficial suggestions in the Sendai workshop. We thank Dr. V. Vasconcelos who read the first version of the paper.

# References

1. Baeten, J. C. M., and Bergstra, J. A., *Process Algebra*, Cambridge University Press, 1990.
2. Baeten, J. C. M., and Bergstra, J. A., *Asynchronous Communication in Real Space Process Algebra*, Proceedings of Formal Techniques in Real-Time and Fault-Tolerant System, LNCS 591, p473-491, Springer-Verlag, May, 1991.
3. Bergstra, J. A., and Klop, J. W., *Process Algebra with Asynchronous Communication Mechanisms*, Seminar on Concurrency, LNCS 197, p76-95, Springer-Verlag, 1985.
4. Boudol, G., Castellani, I., Hennessy, M., and Kiehn, A., *A Theory of Processes with Localities*, Proceedings of CONCUR'92, LNCS 630, p108-122, August, 1992.
5. de Bore, F.S., Klop, J.W., and Palamidessi, *Asynchronous Communication in Process Algebra*, Proceedings of LICS'92, p137-147, June, 1992.
6. Degano, P, deNicola, R. D., and Montanari, U., *A Distributed Operational Semantics for CCS Based on Condition / Event Systems*, Acta Informatica, Vol.26, p59-91, 1988.

---

[9] To define this, we need to extend the semantics of the calculus; but we leave the details of the extensions to [19].

7. Hennessy, M., *On Timed Process Algebra: a Tutorial*, Technical Report 2/93, University of Sussex, 1993

8. Honda, K., and Tokoro, M., *An Object Calculus for Asynchronous Communication*, Proceedings of ECOOP'91, LNCS 512, p133-147, June, 1991.

9. Jifeng, M. B, and Hoare, C. A. R., *A Theory of Synchrony and Asynchrony*, Proceedings of IFIP WG2.2/2.3 Programming Concepts and Methods, p459-478, 1990

10. Krishnan, P., *Distributed CCS*, Proceedings of CONCUR'91, LNCS 527, p393-407, Springer-Verlag, August, 1991.

11. Milner, R., *Communication and Concurrency*, Prentice Hall, 1989.

12. Milner, R., Parrow. J., Walker, D., *A Calculus of Mobile Processes*, Information and Computation, Vol.100, p1-77, 1992.

13. Moller, F., and Tofts, C., *Relating Processes with Respect to Speed*, Proceedings of CONCUR'91, LNCS 527, Springer-Verlag, August, 1991.

14. Nicollin. X., and Sifakis, J., *An Overview and Synthesis on Timed Process Algebras*, Proceedings of Computer Aided Verification, LNCS 575, p376-398, Springer-Verlag, June, 1991.

15. Park, D., *Concurrency and Automata on Infinite Sequences*, Proceedings of Theoretical Computer Science, LNCS 104, p167-187, Springer-Verlag, 1981.

16. Satoh, I., and Tokoro, M., *A Formalism for Real-Time Concurrent Object-Oriented Computing*, Proceedings of 7th ACM Object Oriented Programming Systems and Languages, and Applications, p315-326, October, 1992.

17. Satoh, I., and Tokoro, M., *A Timed Calculus for Distributed Objects with Clocks*, Proceedings of 8th European Conference on Object Oriented Programming, LNCS 707, p326-345, Springer-Verlag, July, 1993.

18. Satoh, I., and Tokoro, M., *Semantics for a Real-Time Object-Oriented Programming Language*, Proceedings of IEEE Conference on Computer Languages'94, p159-170, May, 1994.

19. Satoh, I., and Tokoro, M., *Time and Asynchrony in Interactions among Distributed Real-Time Objects*, Keio CS Technical Report, 1994.

20. Schneider, S., Davies, J., Jackson, D.M., Reed, G.M., Reed, J.N., and Roscoe, A.W., *Timed CSP: Theory and Practice*, Proceedings of REX Workshop on Real-Time: Theory and Practice, LNCS 600, p640-675, Springer-Verlag, 1991.

21. Tokoro, M., and Satoh, I., *Asynchrony and Real-Time in Distributed Systems*, Proceedings of Parallel Symbolic Computing: Languages, Systems, and Application, LNCS 748. p318-330, Springer-Verlag, 1993.

22. Yi, W., *CCS + Time = an Interleaving Model for Real Time Systems*, In proceedings of Automata, Languages and Programming'91, LNCS 510, Springer-Verlag, 1991.

# ProCSuS: A Meta System for Concurrent Process Calculi based on SOS *

Atsushi Togashi, Sen Yoshida, Shigetomo Kimura, Norio Shiratori

Research Institute of Electrical Communication, Tohoku University
2-1-1, Katahira, Aoba-ku, Sendai, 980, Japan
E-mail: {togashi,yoshida, kimura, norio}@shiratori.riec.tohoku.ac.jp

## 1  Introduction

The studies of process calculi started from the latter half of 1970's to deal with formally the behavior of concurrent processes, or multi agents. In the literature, a variety of process calculi have been proposed. The typical systems are CSP by Hoare[8], CCS by Milner[11], $\pi$-calculusby Milner, Parrow, Walker [10], $\gamma$ calculus by Boudol[4], CHOCS by Thomsen[13] and ACP by Bergstra, Klop[2]. In Feb. 1990, ISO adopted LOTOS[5] as the international standard for OSI specification description language. Algebraic formalization techniques are utilized as the descriptive languages for communicating processes and concurrent programs. They are also applied to the verification problem, by virtue of the mathematical formality.

In general, implementation of such calculi may take much efforts, and this has disturbed developing new process calculi. So, it is promising to propose a meta system for process calculi, a general designing environment of process calculi.

The advantages of the meta system can be stated as follows:

- It works as a general interpreter of existing process calculi.
- It works as a support system in developing a new calculus.
- It gives a formal method to deal with various calculi uniformly.

In this paper, we propose a Language of Concurrent process Calculi, LCC, as a underlying meta language to describe process calculi uniformly based on structural operational semantics (SOS) by Plotkin [12]. We also describe the outline of a meta system for concurrent process calculi **ProCSuS**, a Process Calculus Support System consisting of the LCC interpreter and several attractive tools. Finally we conclude with a discussion about on going works.

## 2  Many Sorted SOS Format

In this section, we propose a *many sorted SOS format*, a general framework for process calculi, which is a proper extension of TSS by Groote, Vaandrager [7]

---

* A part of this study is supported by Grants from the Asahi Glass Foundation and Science Grant from Min. of Education

GSOS by Bloom, Istrail, Meyer[3] based on the paradigm of SOS by Plotkin [12]. We begin with the definition of a language in which processes, actions, and transitions are represented as terms of specific sorts.

Let $\langle S, \Sigma \rangle$ be a *signature*. $S$ is a (finite) set of *sorts* and $\Sigma = \langle \Sigma_{w,s} \rangle$ is a family of sets $\Sigma_{w,s}$ of symbols, where $w \in S^*, s \in S$. An element of $\sigma \in \Sigma_{w,s}$ is called an *operator symbol* of sort $s$ with *rank w*, denoted by $\sigma : w \to s$. It is assumed that we have a family of denumerable sets $X = \langle X_s \rangle_{s \in S}$ such that $X_s \cap X_{s'} = \emptyset$ if $s \neq s'$. An element $x$ in $X_s$ is called a *variable* of sort $s$. A *transition language* is specified as a tuple $\langle S, \Sigma, X, \rightsquigarrow \rangle$, where $\langle S, \Sigma \rangle$ is a signature, $X$ is a family of variable sets, and $\rightsquigarrow$ is the special symbol used for transition rules. Let $\langle S, \Sigma, X, \rightsquigarrow \rangle$ be a transition language. A *term* of sort $s \in S$ is defined inductively in the usual way. Let $T(\Sigma, X)_s$ denote the set of all terms of sort $s \in S$ and set $T(\Sigma, X) = \langle T(\Sigma, X)_s \rangle_{s \in S}$. $T(\Sigma)_s$ denotes the set of all *ground* (*closed*) terms of sort $s$ and set $T(\Sigma) = \langle T(\Sigma)_s \rangle_{s \in S}$. A *substitution* is a mapping $\theta : X \to T(\Sigma, X)$ such that $\theta(x) \in T(\Sigma, X)_s$ for all $x \in X_s$ $(s \in S)$. A substitution can be easily extended from variables to terms.

A *transition assertion* is an expression of the form $\xi \xrightarrow{\alpha} \eta$, where $\xi$ and $\eta$ are terms of the same sort. A *transition rule* is an expression of the form $\varphi / \varphi_1 \cdots \varphi_n$ where $\varphi_1, \ldots, \varphi_n$ and $\varphi$ are transition assertions. $\varphi_1, \ldots, \varphi_n$ are called the *assumptions* and $\varphi$ is called the *conclusion* of the rule. An *abstract transition system* is a pair $\langle \mathcal{L}, \Gamma \rangle$, where $\mathcal{L} = \langle S, \Sigma, X, \rightsquigarrow \rangle$ is a transition language and $\Gamma$ is a set of transition rules. In the usual manner, we can define the notion of *provability* of an transition assertion $\varphi$ from a set $\Gamma$ of transition rules. Let $\Gamma \vdash \varphi$ denote that a transition assertion $\varphi$ is provable from a set of transition rules $\Gamma$.

In the literature, labeled transition systems have been used to give operational semantics for concurrent systems based on the idea of SOS. Its definition and its related notations are given formally as follows:

A *labeled transition system*(LTS) is a triple $\langle S, \mathcal{A}, \to \rangle$, where $S$ is a set of *states* and $\to$ is a *transition relation* defined as $\to \subset S \times \mathcal{A} \times S$. The transition relation defines the dynamical change of states as actions may be performed. For $(s, a, s') \in \to$, we normally write $s \xrightarrow{a} s'$. Thus, the transition relation can be written as $\to = \{ \xrightarrow{a} | a \in \mathcal{A} \}$. $s \xrightarrow{a} s'$ may be interpreted as "in the state $s$ an action $a$ can be performed and after the action the state moves to $s'$".

## 3 Language for Concurrent process Calculi: LCC

LCC (Language of Concurrent process Calculi) is a meta language designed to formally describe concurrent processes based on structural operational semantics, represented as transition rules, of various process calculi. Usually a process calculus is provided by the operators used in the calculus and the transition rules which characterize the nature of it. In LCC, an operator is represented in the style of Abstract Data Type, and a transition rule in the formal logic which regards transition relations as formulae.

For example, we give the simplest calculus, named EXAMPLE. It has only one transition rule which provides the behavior of the action prefix operator, expressed by '*'.

```
calculus EXAMPLE is
sorts action expression.
ops a b c : -> action.
op 0 : -> expression.
op * : action expression -> expression.
var A : action.
vars E : expression.
rule => *(A,E) - A -> E.
endcalc
```

As a more complicated example, we will show the description of CCS by Milner as below. In the description, we use the operator symbols for representing the original CCS operators indicated by Table 1.

| Operator | CCS | LCC |
|---:|:---:|:---:|
| silent action | $\tau$ | tau |
| label complement | $\bar{l}$ | ~ |
| prefix | $a.E$ | *(a,E) |
| composition | $E \mid F$ | &(E,F) |
| summation | $E + F$ | +(E,F) |
| restriction | $E \backslash L$ | \ (E,L) |

Table 1. The operator symbols for CCS

```
calculus CCS is
sorts name co-name label action expression.
subsorts name < label < action.
subsorts co-name < label.
subsorts internal < action.

ops a b c d e f : -> name.
op tau : -> internal.
ops 0 x : -> expression.
op ~ : name -> co-name.
op * : action expression -> expression.
ops & + : expression expression -> expression.
op \ : expression set -> expression.
op rec : expression -> expression.

set restricted : d e f.
var N : name.
var A : action.
vars E E1 E2 El El1 El2 Er Er1 Er2 Ex : expression.
```

```
var L : set.

rule => *(A,E) - A -> E.
rule El1 - A -> El2 => +(El1,Er) - A -> El2.
rule Er1 - A -> Er2 => +(El,Er1) - A -> Er2.
rule El1 - A -> El2 => &(El1,Er) - A -> &(El2,Er).
rule Er1 - A -> Er2 => &(El,Er1) - A -> &(El,Er2).
rule El1 - A -> El2 Er1 - ~(A) -> Er2
     => &(El1,Er1) - tau -> &(El2,Er2).
rule E1 - N -> E2 => \(E1,L) - N -> \(E2,L)
     where N not contained L.
rule E1 - ~(N) -> E2 => \(E1,L) - ~(N) -> \(E2,L)
     where N not contained L.
rule E1 - tau -> E2 => \(E1,L) - tau -> \(E2,L).
rule repl(Ex,x,rec(Ex)) - A -> E => rec(Ex) - A -> E.
endcalc
```

## 4  Support System: ProCSuS

In this section we describe the outline of the process calculus support system
**ProCSuS** designed as an interpreter for LCC. **ProCSuS** interprets a designed
process calculus as follows: given a LCC description of the calculus and its behavior expression, **ProCSuS** interprets it in terms of the operational semantics
by deriving transition relations in the calculus. **ProCSuS** has two tools: LTS
Viewer and Equivalence Checker. We can use these tools as a support environment for designing process calculi.

The components of **ProCSuS** is illustrated in fig. 1. It has five modules:
Compiler, Database, Calculator, Tools and Interface. Compiler reads a LCC
file and compiles it to the format in which Database accumulates. Calculator
is an engine to infer transition relations of given processes referring informations about transition rules accumulated in Database. Tools consists of LTS
Viewer and Equivalence Checker. Interface accepts commands from users and
draws graphs on the display. LTS Viewer draws the Labeled Transition System
of given LCC terms. Given a LCC term, the tool enumerates all accessible terms
by performing some actions using Calculator. Then the tool explores and checks
those terms recursively and finally makes the entire LTS. LTS is displayed on the
window as a labeled directed graph. There are two major notions of equivalence
between processes: bisimulation equivalence and observation equivalence. Equivalence Checker can decide automatically equivalence of finite processes where
two equivalences on processes are concerned. Given two terms, the checker in-
vestigates equivalences according to their definitions, and returns equivalences
satisfied between them.

Now we show an example. The following terms are in the form of CCS.

$$P_1 = *(a,+(*(b,0),*(tau,*(c,0))))$$
$$P_2 = +(*(a,*(c,0)),*(a,+(*(b,0),*(tau,*(c,0)))))$$

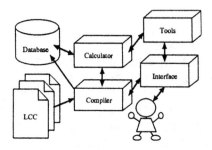

**Fig. 1.** The components of **ProCSuS**

The LTSs derived from the above terms are shown in fig. 2. The result of equivalence checking is illustrated in fig. 3. The output **"weak"** says that $P_1$ and $P_2$ are observation equivalent but not bisimulation equivalent.

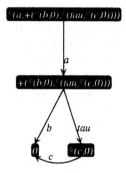

**Fig. 2.** LTSs of $P_1$ and $P_2$

## 5 Conclusion

Finally we discuss on going works. We are now updating a graphical tool for labeled transition systems and more intelligent equivalence checker for infinite processes. Where equivalence between two processes in different calculi are uniformly treated.

A process verifier and a process synthesizer are now implementing as well. The verifier verifies process w.r.t. formulae in Hennessy-Milner logic or $\mu$-calculus, kinds of modal logic. The synthesizer generates the intended processes from their concrete properties expressed as formulae in the logic.

```
| ?- equivalence('*(a,+(*(b,0),*(tau,*(c,0)))))',
       '+(*(a,*(c,0)),*(a,+(*(b,0),*(tau,*(c,0))))))',
       Equiv).

Equiv = weak ?

yes
| ?-
```

**Fig. 3.** The results of equivalence checking

# References

1. Aceto, L., Bloom, B., Vaandrager, F., Turing SOS Rules in to Equations, *Information and Computation*, vol.111, pp.1–52, 1994.
2. Bergstra, J.A., Klop, J.W.: *Algebra of communicating process*, CWI Monographs, North-Holland (1986).
3. Bloon, B., Istrail, S., Meyer, A.R., Bisimulation can't be traced: Preliminary Report, in /POPL, pp.229–239, 1988
4. Boudol, G., Towards a lambda-calculus for concurrent and communicating systems, *Lecture Notes in Computer Science*, Vol.351, pp.149–161, 1989.
5. Brinksma, E.: A Tutorial on LOTOS, *Proc. IFIP Workshop on Protocol Specification, Testing and Verification V*, North-Holland (1986) pp.73–84.
6. Fokkink, W. J.: The Tyft/Tyxt Format Reduces to Tree Rules, *Proc. of the 2nd International Symposium on Theoretical Aspects of Computer Software*, Lecture Notes in Computer Science **789**, Springer-Verlag (1994) pp.440–453.
7. Groote, J.F., Vaandrager, F.: Structured Operational Semantics and Bisimulation as a Congruence, *Information and Computation* **100** 2 (1992) pp.202–260.
8. Hoare, C.A.R.: *Communicating Sequential Process*, Prentice Hall (1985).
9. Meseguer, J., Rewriting as a Unified Model of Concurrency, in Concur'90, 1990.
10. Milner, R., Parrow, J., Walker, D., *A calculus of mobile processes*, Part I and II, Reports ECS-LFCS-89-85 and -86, Laboratory for Foundations of Computer Science, University of Edinburgh, 1989.
11. Milner, R.: *Communication and Concurrency*, Prentice-Hall (1989).
12. Plotkin, G.D.: *A Structural Approach to Operational Semantics*, Computer Science Department, Aarhus University, DAIMI FN-19 (1981).
13. Thomsen, B., A calculus of higher order communicating systems, *Principle of Programming Language* pp.143–154, 1989.
14. Sen Yoshida, Atushi Togashi and Norio Shiratori: "Integrated Support Environment for Concurrent Process Calculi", Proceeding of the ACM 13th Ann. Symposium on Principles of Distributed Computing, pp.395–395, 1994.

# First-class Synchronous Operations

John H. Reppy

AT&T Bell Laboratories

**Abstract.** The idea of making synchronous operations into first-class values is an important one for supporting abstraction and modularity in concurrent programs. This design principle has been used with great success in the concurrent language **CML**, but what are the limitations of this approach? This paper explains the rationale for first-class synchronous operations, and discusses their use in **CML**. It also presents some recent and fundamental results about the expressiveness of rendezvous primitives, which define the limitations of synchronous abstractions.

## 1  Introduction

Abstraction is a key tool for managing complexity. The design of programming languages is one area where application of this idea has paid significant dividends. Languages have evolved from providing a fixed set of abstractions of the underlying hardware, such as arithmetic expressions and arrays, to providing support for programmer-defined abstractions, such as abstract data-types and higher-order procedures. By providing mechanisms for the programmer to define her own abstractions, the language aids the management of application-specific complexity.

This paper looks one recent application of the principle that languages should support programmer-defined abstraction: *first-class synchronous operations*. First-class synchronous operations were developed originally as part of the **PML** language design [Rep88], and were further refined in the language *Concurrent ML* (**CML**) [Rep91, Rep95]. They provide a mechanism for programmers to define new synchronization and communication abstractions on top of a simple collection of primitives.

### 1.1  Concurrent programming

Concurrent programming is the task of writing programs consisting of multiple independent threads of control, called processes. Conceptually, we view these processes as executing in parallel, but in practice their execution may be interleaved on a single processor. For this reason, we distinguish between concurrency in a programming language, and parallelism in hardware. We say that operations in a program are *concurrent* if they could be executed in parallel, and we say that operations in hardware are *parallel* if they overlap in time.

One important motivation for concurrent programming is that processes are a useful abstraction mechanism: they provide encapsulation of state and control with well-defined interfaces. This paper focuses on the use of concurrent programming for applications with naturally concurrent structure. These applications share the property that flexibility in the scheduling of computation is required. Whereas sequential languages force a total order on computation, concurrent languages permit a partial order, which provides the needed flexibility.

The area of *interactive* systems is probably the richest source of examples of naturally concurrent systems. Interactive applications must deal with multiple asynchronous input streams and support multiple contexts, while maintaining responsiveness. Sequential implementations of interactive systems typically rely on the *faux* concurrency of event-loops and call-backs. A number of authors, ourselves included, have argued that programming interactive systems in a concurrent language results in cleaner and more flexible program structures [CP85, RG86, Pik89b, Pik89a, Haa90, GR92, GR93].

While interactive systems have been the main motivation for the author's work, concurrent program structures also appear in other application domains. Discrete event simulations, for example, can be structured as a collection of processes representing the objects being simulated. Distributed programs are, by their very nature, concurrent; each processor, or node, in a distributed system has its own state and control flow. In addition to the obvious concurrency that results from executing on multiple processors, there are natural uses of concurrency in the individual node programs.

## 1.2 Background

The ideas presented in this paper have been developed in the context of the **ML** family of languages, and we use the notation of *Standard ML* (**SML**) [MTH90] throughout. **SML** is a statically-typed higher-order language, which is used for a tasks ranging from theorem provers [Sli90] to low-level systems programming [BHLM94]. The interested reader is directed to either [Pau91] or [Ull94] for an introduction to the **SML** programming language.

Concurrent ML extends **SML** with support for dynamic thread creation and synchronous message passing. It is implemented as a library on top of the *Standard ML of New Jersey* system [AM91]; a discussion of **CML**'s implementation can be found in [Rep92]. The most significant use of **CML** is the multithreaded user interface toolkit **eXene** [GR93], and the applications built using **eXene** [Lin91, GM92, KSI94]. **CML** has also been used as the basis for research into distributed programming language design [Kru93].

## 1.3 Overview

In the next section, we motivate and introduce the concept of first-class synchronous operations in detail. Following this, we discuss **CML**, which is probably the most widely used language that provides first-class synchronous operations. To illustrate the usefulness of first-class synchronous operations, we describe a library for **CML** that supports distributed programming in the style of **Linda** [CG90]. We then examine the expressiveness of this approach, and show that there are inherent limitations on the amount of synchronization that one can implement as an abstraction, when starting from a particular set of primitives. Lastly, we discuss some other languages that provide mechanisms similar in nature to first-class synchronous operations, although they differ in purpose.

## 2 First-class synchronous operations

For the purposes of this discussion, we assume a traditional synchronous message-passing model with a *blocking* send operation. In an **SML** framework, this might have the following interface:

```
type 'a chan
val channel : unit -> '_a chan
val accept  : 'a chan -> 'a
val send    : ('a chan * 'a) -> unit
```

where the channel operation dynamically creates a new channel, and the accept and send operations implement the two halves of synchronous communication.

Most **CSP**-style languages (e.g., **occam** [Bur88] and **amber** [Car86]) provide similar rendezvous-style communication. In addition, they provide a mechanism for *selective communication*, which is necessary for threads to communicate with multiple partners. It is possible to use polling to implement selective communication, but to do so is awkward and requires busy waiting. Usually selective communication is provided as a multiplexed I/O operation. This can be a multiplexed input operation, such as **occam**'s ALT construct [Bur88]; or a generalized (or symmetric) select operation that multiplexes both input and output communications, such as **Pascal-m**'s select construct [AB86]. Implementing generalized select on a multi-processor can be difficult [Bor86], but as we discuss in Section 5, it is provably more expressive.

Unfortunately, there is a fundamental conflict between the desire for abstraction and the need for selective communication. For example, consider a server thread that provides a service via a *request-reply* (or *remote procedure call* (RPC) style) protocol. The server side of this protocol is something like:

```
fun serverLoop () = if serviceAvailable()
     then let
       val request = accept reqCh
     in
       send (replyCh, doit request);
       serverLoop ()
     end
     else doSomethingElse()
```

where the function doit actually implements the service. Note that the service is not always available. This protocol requires that clients obey the following two rules:

1. A client must send a request before trying to read a reply.
2. Following a request the client must read exactly one reply before issuing another request.

If all clients obey these rules, then we can guarantee that each request is answered with the correct reply, but if a client breaks one of these rules, then the requests and replies will be out of sync. An obvious way to improve the reliability of programs that use this service is to bundle the client-side protocol into a function that hides the details, thus ensuring that the rules are followed. The following code implements this abstraction:

```
fun clientCall x = (send(reqCh, x); accept replyCh)
```

While this insures that clients obey the protocol, it hides too much. If a client blocks on a call to clientCall (e.g., if the server is not available), then it cannot respond to other communications. Avoiding this situation requires using selective communication, but the client cannot do this because the function abstraction hides the synchronous aspect of the protocol. This is the fundamental conflict between selective communication and the existing forms of abstraction. If we make the operation abstract, we lose the flexibility of selective communication; but if we expose the protocol to allow selective communication, we lose the safety and ease of maintenance provided by abstraction.

To resolve the conflict between abstraction and selective communication requires introducing a new abstraction mechanism that preserves the synchronous nature of the abstraction. First-class synchronous operations provide this abstraction mechanism [Rep88, Rep91]. The basic idea is to introduce a new type constructor, event, for typing synchronous operations, much the same way that we introduce the -> type constructor to type functional values. This allows us to represent synchronous operations as first-class values, instead of merely as functions, which, in turn, allows us to define a collection of combinators for defining new event values from some small collection of primitives. In this scheme, selective communication is expressed as a choice among event values, which means that user-defined abstractions can be used in a selective communication without breaking the abstraction.

The choice of combinators is motivated by analyzing the traditional select construct, which has four facets: the individual I/O operations, the actions associated with each operation, the nondeterministic choice, and the synchronization. To make this concrete, consider the following loop (using an **Amber** style select construct [Car86]), which implements the body of an accumulator that accepts either addition or subtraction input commands and offers its contents:

```
fun accum sum = (
        select addCh?x => accum(sum+x)
          or subCh?x => accum(sum-x)
          or readCh!sum => accum sum)
```

The select construct consists of three I/O operations: addCh?x, subCh?x, and readCh!sum. For each of these operations there is an associated action on the right hand side of the =>. Taken together, each I/O operation and associated action define a clause in a nondeterministic synchronous choice. It is also worth noting that the input clauses define a scope: the input operation binds an identifier to the incoming message, which has the action as its scope.

In the framework of first-class synchronous operations, each of these facets is supported independently. We start with *base-event* values to represent the communication operations, and provide combinators to associate actions with events and to build nondeterministic choices of events. Lastly, an operation is provided to synchronize on an event value. This decomposition of the select construct results in a flexible mechanism for building new synchronization and communication abstractions. We postpone discussion of the details of these until the next section.

One of the benefits of this framework is that other synchronous operations can be added uniformly by introducing new primitive event constructors. These can include timeout events, blocking input/output operations, and even other synchronization mechanisms, such as synchronizing memory operations [ANP89, BNA91]. Because these additional primitives are just event-value constructors, they can be combined freely. For example, adding a timeout to a message-passing operation or to a blocking I/O operation is easily done using the choice combinator and the timeout constructor. This should be contrasted with **Ada**, for example, where there are two different syntactic forms provided to support timeouts [DoD83].

# 3 Concurrent ML

*Concurrent ML* is *higher-order* concurrent language. By this we mean that it supports sequential higher-order programming in the form of first-class function values, and concurrent higher-order programming in the form of first-class synchronous operations. In this section, we give a brief description of the core **CML** features, and some examples of their use.

Figure 1 gives the signature of the most commonly used **CML** primitives. The first four of these operations are fairly standard:

spawn *f* creates a new thread to evaluate the function *f*, and returns the ID of the newly created thread.

channel () creates a new channel. The "_" in its return type denotes an *imperative* type variable, which is a technical restriction necessary to ensure type soundness [Tof90, Rep92].

accept *ch* accepts a message from the channel *ch*. This operation blocks the calling thread until there is another thread sending a message on *ch*.

send (*ch*, *msg*) sends the message *msg* on the channel *ch*. This operation blocks the calling thread until there is another thread accepting a message from *ch*.

The remaining functions support the mechanism of first-class synchronous operations (or events):

```
type thread_id
type 'a chan
type 'a event

val spawn : (unit -> unit) -> thread_id

val channel  : unit -> '_a chan
val accept   : 'a chan -> 'a
val send     : ('a chan * 'a) -> unit

val receive  : 'a chan -> 'a event
val transmit : ('a chan * 'a) -> unit event

val guard    : (unit -> 'a event) -> 'a event
val wrap     : ('a event * ('a -> 'b) -> 'b event
val choose   : 'a event list -> 'a event

val sync     : 'a event -> 'a
val select   : 'a event list -> 'a
```

**Fig. 1.** The common CML operations

receive *ch* constructs an event value that represents the operation of accepting
a message from the channel *ch*. When this event is synchronized on, it accepts
a message from the channel and returns it as the synchronization result.

transmit (*ch, msg*) constructs an event value that represents the operation of
sending the message *msg* on the channel *ch*. When this event is synchronized
on, it sends the message on the channel and returns unit as the synchronization result.

guard *f* creates an event out of the pre-synchronization action *f*, which is called
a *guard function*. When this value is synchronized on, the guard function is
evaluated and its result is used in the synchronization.

wrap (*ev, f*) wraps the event value *ev* with the post-synchronization action *f*,
which is called a *wrapper function*. When this event is synchronized on, the
function *f* is applied to the synchronization result of *ev*.

choose [$ev_1, \ldots, ev_n$] forms the nondeterministic choice of the event values
$ev_1, \ldots, ev_n$. When this event is synchronized on, one of the events $ev_i$ will
be selected, and its result will be the synchronization result.

sync *ev* forces synchronization of the event value *ev*, returning the synchronization result.

select [$ev_1, \ldots, ev_n$] synchronizes on the nondeterministic choice of the event
values $ev_1, \ldots, ev_n$. This is the composition of sync and choose, and is provided for notational convenience.

We illustrate these operations with some examples, a formal semantics can be
found in either [Rep92] or [Rep95].

The simplest example is the definition of the synchronous message passing operations:

```
fun accept ch = sync (receive ch)
fun send (ch, msg) = sync (transmit (ch, msg))
```

Another example is the example of selective communication given in the previous section. In **CML**, this would be written as:

```
fun accum sum = select [
        wrap (receive addCh, fn x => accum(sum+x)),
        wrap (receive subCh, fn x => accum(sum-x),
        wrap (transmit(readCh, sum), fn () => accum sum)
    ]
```

Here we are using receive instead of ?, transmit instead of !, and wrap for associating actions with the communications.

## 3.1  A new abstraction — swap channels

The purpose of first-class synchronous operations is to provide a mechanism for defining new synchronization and communication abstractions. In this section, we present a simple example of a communication abstraction called a *swap channel*. This is a new type of channel that allows two processes to swap values when they rendezvous (one might call this *symmetric rendezvous*, since there is no sender or receiver distinction). The interface consists of an abstract type:

```
type 'a swap_chan
```

and functions for creating channels and "*swap*" events:

```
val swapChannel : unit -> '_a swap_chan
val swap        : ('_a swap_chan * '_a) -> '_a CML.event
```

When two processes communicate on a swap channel, each sends a value and each receives a value. Implementing this correctly requires some care.

Our implementation is based on the asymmetric message passing operations, so to insure the symmetry of the operation, each thread in a swap must both offer to send a message and to accept a message on the same channel. We can use the choose combinator for this purpose. Once one thread completes a send (which means that the other has completed an accept), we need to complete the swap, which means sending a value in the other direction. A first solution might be to use another channel for completing the swap, but unfortunately, this results in a race condition when two separate pairs of threads attempt swap operations on the same swap channel at the same time. For example, Figure 2 shows what might happen if threads $P_1$, $P_2$, $Q_1$ and $Q_2$ all attempt a swap operation on the same swap channel at roughly the same time (where the swap channel is represented by the channels ch and ch'). In this scenario, $P_1$ and $P_2$ are initially paired, as are $Q_1$ and $Q_2$. But there is a race in the second phase of the swaps, and $P_1$ ends up being paired with $Q_2$, and $P_2$ ends up with $Q_1$

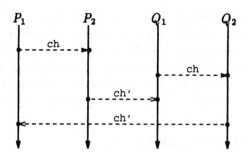

**Fig. 2.** A swap mismatch

```
datatype 'a swap_chan = SC of ('a * 'a chan) chan

fun swapChannel () = SC(channel ())

fun swap (SC ch, msgOut) = guard (fn () => let
        val inCh = channel ()
    in
      choose [
          wrap (receive ch,
            fn (msgIn, outCh) => (send(outCh, msgOut); msgIn)),
          wrap (transmit (ch, (msgOut, inCh)),
            fn () => accept inCh)
      ]
    end)
```

**Fig. 3.** The swap channel implementation

(because $Q_1$ beats $P_1$ to reading a value from ch', and $P_2$ beats $Q_2$ to sending a value on ch').

To avoid this problem, we need to allocate a fresh channel for completing the second phase of the swap operation each time the swap operation is executed. Figure 3 gives the implementation of the swap channel abstraction. The representation of a swap channel is a single channel that carries both value communicated in the first phase, and a channel for communicating the other value in the second phase. The channel for the second phase must be allocated before the synchronization on the first message, which is the kind of situation for which guard was designed. The guard function first allocates the channel for the second phase, and then constructs the swap event using the choose combinator. Because of the symmetry of the operation, each side of the swap must allocate a channel, even though only one of them will be used. Fortunately, allocating a channel is very cheap, and the garbage collector takes care of reclaiming it after we are done.

The swap channel example illustrates several important CML techniques. The use of dynamically allocating a new channel to serve as a unique identifier for a transaction comes up quite often in client-server protocols. It is also an example where the nondeterministic choice is used inside an abstraction, which is why we have both choose and sync, instead of just the select operator. And, lastly, this example illustrates the use of the guard combinator.

## 3.2 Negative acknowledgements

One place where CML extends the traditional synchronous message-passing operations is in the support for *negative acknowledgements*. When implementing client-server protocols, it is sometimes necessary for the server to know whether to *commit* or *abort* the transaction. The synchronization involved in sending the reply allows the server to know when the client has committed to the transaction, but there is no way to know when the client has aborted the transaction by selecting some other event. While a timeout on the reply might work in some situations, the absence of a reply does not guarantee that the client has selected some other event; the client just might be slow. To insure the correct semantics, we need a mechanism for *negative acknowledgements*. Furthermore, we would like this mechanism to be compatible with the abstraction provided by event values. To achieve this, CML provides the event combinator:

```
val withNack : (unit event -> 'a event) -> 'a event
```

which is a variation of the guard combinator.[1] As does guard, withNack takes a function whose evaluation is delayed until synchronization time, and returns an event value. The main difference is that at synchronization time, the guard function is applied to an *abort event*, which is enabled only if some other event is selected in the synchronization.

To make the workings of negative acknowledgements more concrete, consider the following simple use of withNack:

```
fun mkEvent (ev, ackMsg, nackMsg) = withNack (fn nack => (
    spawn (fn () => (sync nack; CIO.print nackMsg));
    wrap(ev, fn _ => CIO.print ackMsg))
```

This function takes an event, and returns one that will print the message ackMsg, if it is chosen, and the message nackMsg if another event is chosen.[2] Printing the acknowledgement is easy — mkEvent wraps the event with a wrapper function that prints ackMsg. To print the negative acknowledgement message, mkEvent spawns a thread that waits for the negative acknowledgement event nack and then prints nackMsg. If the event is chosen, then the nack event will never be

---

[1] Earlier versions of CML used a different combinator for supporting abort actions, called wrapAbort [Rep91, Rep92]. The two combinators have the same expressive power, but the withNack combinator is more natural to use. See [Rep95] for a discussion of this.

[2] The function CIO.print prints a string to the standard output.

enabled, and thus the `nackMsg` will not be printed (instead, the thread will be garbage collected). For example, consider what happens ch2 is chosen when executing the following synchronization:

```
select [
    mkEvent (receive ch1, "ch1\n", "not ch1\n"),
    mkEvent (receive ch2, "ch2\n", "not ch2\n")
]
```

This will cause the messages "ch2" and "not ch1" to be printed (the actual order of the messages is nondeterministic).

As a more realistic example, consider the implementation of a *lock service*. This service provides a collection of locks that can be acquired or released (much like mutex locks). The interface is:

```
type lock

val acquireLock : lock -> unit event
val releaseLock : lock -> unit
```

where the type lock is an abstract lock identifier. For purposes of this example, we ignore the question of how lock names are created.

If a client attempts to acquire a lock that is held, then it must wait until the holder of the lock releases it. Since a client may not want to wait indefinitely, the `acquireLock` operation is event-valued so that it can be used in selective communication (with a timeout, for example). This is clearly a case where we want to synchronize on the acquiring of the lock, rather than on the sending of the request. Thus, we need to use a guard function to send the request, and return an event that represents the acquisition of the lock.

The server maintains a set of locks that are currently held; for each lock in the set, it keeps a queue of pending requests for the lock. When a lock is released, the next requesting thread on the queue gets the lock. There is a subtlety to the servicing of pending requests. Consider the case where a client $A$ requests a lock $l$ that is held by some other thread $B$. By the time $B$ releases $l$, $A$ may no longer be interested in it (e.g., its attempt to synchronize on acquiring the lock may have timed out). In this case, if the server still thinks that $A$ wants the lock $l$, it will assign $l$ to $A$, resulting in starvation for any future attempt to acquire the lock. Clearly, this is a problem — we need to structure the protocol so that the server gets the *negative* information that requesting client is no longer interested in the lock.

While the details of the implementation are beyond the scope of this paper, the basic idea is simple. To do this, we implement the client side of the `acquireLock` protocol using the `withNack` combinator wrapped around a guard function that constructs and sends the acquire request to the server. The request consists of a freshly allocated channel for the server to use to notify the client that the lock is acquired, and the abort event that was passed to the guard function. The client synchronizes on receiving the notification message from the server, while the server synchronizes on the choice of sending the notification and the abort event. The interested reader is directed to [Rep95] for the complete story.

# 4 Extending CML for distributed programming

One of the principle uses of concurrency is for distributed programming. A distributed program consists of processes running in different address spaces on logically different processors. Because the processes are physically disjoint, there are a number of issues that come up in distributed systems that are not present in concurrent programming:

- communication latency is significantly higher over a network (e.g., on the order of several milliseconds on a high-performance workstation, versus less than $50\mu S$ for a **CML** send/accept on a SPARCstation-2).
- processors and network links can go down, and come back up, during the execution of a distributed program.
- because programs running on different nodes may be compiled independently, type security cannot be guaranteed statically.

For these reasons, the synchronous model used in **CML** does not map well to the distributed setting. One needs to provide a different programming model for dealing with remote communication.

Although they may not be directly usable for distributed programming, concurrent programming languages, such as **CML**, do have a role in the distributed setting. Since the individual programs running on the different processors must manage communication with each other, it is convenient to structure these programs as concurrent programs. For this reason, most distributed programming languages and toolkits provide concurrent programming features as well.

In this section, we examine an implementation of one possible model for distributed programming, called *tuple spaces*. This model has been popularized by the **Linda** family of programming languages. The implementation discussed in this section illustrates both how **CML** can be used to implement low-level systems services, and it shows how the **CML** primitives can provide a useful interface to asynchronous distributed programming primitives.[3]

## 4.1 Tuple spaces

*Tuple spaces* are a model of communication for parallel distributed-memory programming [GB82, Gel85]. A tuple space is basically an associative memory that is shared by the processes of a system. Unlike hardware memory, the values in a tuple space are tuples of typed fields, which are similar to **SML** tuples. Processes communicate by reading and writing tuple values. Reading a tuple is done by *pattern matching* on a subset of the tuple's fields.

Tuple spaces have been popularized by **Linda**, which is a family of programming languages. The **Linda** languages are traditional sequential languages, such as **C**, extended with a small collection of tuple-space operations. There are four basic operations in the **Linda** model:

---

[3] This example was inspired by Cooper and Siegel's **SML** implementation of **Linda** [SC91].

**out** is used to add a tuple to the tuple space.

**in** takes a tuple *template* (or *pattern*) as an argument, and removes a tuple that matches the template from the tuple space, binding the values in the tuple to the formal parameters in the template. If there is no tuple that matches the template, then the process suspends until the **in** can complete.

**rd** is like **in**, but does not remove the tuple from the tuple space.

**eval** is used to add an *active* tuple to the tuple space. This is the mechanism for creating new processes. A new process is created that computes the tuple value; when it finishes, the tuple becomes *passive*, and may be read by other processes.

There are also non-blocking variants of **in** and **rd**, called **inp** and **rdp**.

Communication in **Linda** differs from most other distributed-memory communication models, in that the messages (i.e., tuples) are not directed at any particular destination. Instead, once inserted into tuple space, a tuple can be read by any process that executes a matching **rd** operation. This flexibility of communication is further aided by the fact that both the templates used in **rd** operations, and the tuples used in **out** operations can have undefined fields, called *formals*. A formal matches any field of the right type, no matter what its value. When used in a template, a formal also provides a mechanism to bind the values in the tuple being read to local variables in the process.

## 4.2 CML-Linda

In this section, we describe the **CML** interface to **Linda**-style primitives. In their full generality, tuple-spaces are quite hard to implement with any sort of efficiency. For this reason, most implementations of tuple spaces constrain the model in various ways to make the implementation more tractable. The most common restriction is the requirement that the first element of every tuple be a defined string-valued field, which serves as the primary key for tuple matching. Another common restriction is only allowing formals in patterns, and not in the tuples in tuple-space. We make both of these restrictions in **CML-Linda**; furthermore, we do not implement the **eval** operation.

Figure 4 gives the signature of the **CML-Linda** interface. We use **SML** datatypes to represent the fields of tuples and templates. A tuple consists of an initial string-valued field followed by a list of zero or more values, while a template is an initial string-valued field followed by a list of pattern fields, where a pattern field is either a typed formal, an untyped wildcard, a tuple of patterns, or a constant value. The two blocking input operations (input and read) are provided as event-valued constructors to allow clients to use them in selective communications (e.g., in conjunction with timeouts). This illustrates how first-class synchronous operations can play a role in managing asynchronous distributed communication.

```
datatype value
  = INT of int
  | STR of string
  | BOOL of bool
  | TUPLE of value list

datatype pat
  = INT_FORMAL
  | STR_FORMAL
  | BOOL_FORMAL
  | WILDCARD
  | CONST of value
  | TUPLEPAT of pat list


type tuple_space

val output : tuple_space -> (string * value list) -> unit
val input  : tuple_space -> (string * pat list) -> value list event
val read   : tuple_space -> (string * pat list) -> value list event
```

**Fig. 4. CML**-Linda interface


## 4.3  Implementation issues

While space does not permit a detailed description of the implementation, we give an overview with some details (a full description can be found in [Rep95]).

The main design issue is how to distribute the tuples of a tuple space over the processors in a system. There are two basic ways to implement a distributed tuple space [BCGL87]:

- *Read-all, write-one:* where the tuples are distributed over the processors. A write operation adds a tuple to some processor, while a read operation must query all processors for a match.
- *Read-one, Write-all:* where each processor has a copy of every tuple. A write operation must add the tuple to all processors, while a read operation need only query the local processor's copy of tuple space.

For our implementation, we use the first technique.

With a read-all, write-one distribution, the implementation of the write operation is straightforward. When a tuple is written, some decision must be made as to where the tuple should be placed, and then a message is sent to the appropriate processor. Simple policies for tuple placement include always placing tuples locally, and round-robin placement. More sophisticated schemes might use static analysis or dynamic information for better placement.

The input operations (input and read) require more complicated protocols. The basic protocol for input, which is adopted from [SC91], is as follows:

1. The reading processor, call it $P$, broadcasts the template to all the tuple-space servers in the system.

2. Each tuple-space server checks for a match; if it finds one, then it places a *hold* on the tuple and sends the tuple to $P$, otherwise, it remembers the read request. If some subsequent write matches the read request, then it will then send the tuple to $P$.

3. The processor $P$ waits for a matching tuple. Once $P$ receives a matching tuple, say from $Q$, it sends $Q$ a message acknowledging the tuple, and sends a *cancellation* message to the other processors.

4. When $Q$ receives the acknowledgement, it removes the tuple from its space. When a processor that has a matching tuple receives a cancellation message, it cancels the hold it placed on the tuple, which allows the tuple to be used to match other requests. When a processor that does not have a matching tuple receives a cancellation message, it removes the record of the original request.

The protocol for read is similar; the main difference is that the tuple is not removed in step 4.

For each input (or read) request, we spawn a new thread to manage the operation. This thread broadcasts the template to be matched to the tuple servers, and coordinates the replies. Once a matching tuple has been found, it is communicated to the reading thread, and the cancellation messages are sent out to the other processors. Since the input and read operations are event valued, there is the added complication that these operations can be used in a selection context, where they must be aborted. We use negative acknowledgements to handle this situation. The basic implementation of the input operation has the form:

```
fun input ts req = withNack (fn nackEvt => let
    val replyCh = channel()
  in
    spawn (inputManager (ts, replyCh, nackEvt, req));
    receive replyCh
  end)
```

Of course, most of the details are hidden in the implementation of the manager thread. In addition to waiting for a matching tuple, the manager thread also waits for the nackEvt to be enabled. If the manager thread receives a negative acknowledgement, then it sends cancellation messages to all of the tuple-space servers. We also take care not to send the acknowledgement message until we are sure that the tuple has been accepted. We do this by synchronizing on the choice of sending the matching tuple on the replyCh and receiving the negative acknowledgement. The semantics of **CML** guarantee that only one of these can occur.

The input and read operations are good examples of how complex protocols can be abstracted as simple synchronous operations.

# 5   Limitations of CML events

When proposing a new abstraction mechanism, it is fair to ask "what are the limitations?" What things can be expressed in a non-abstract way that cannot be expressed abstractly. For **CML**events, this question can be stated as:

> For a given set of base-event constructors, and combinators, what kinds of synchronization abstractions can we build?

By *abstract*, we mean independent of context, which in this case means can be placed in a selective communication. Recent work by Prakash Panangaden and the author have explored this question using a knowledge-theoretic framework [PR94]. The main result of this work is the following theorem:

**Theorem.** *Given the standard* **CML** *event combinators and an n-way rendezvous base-event constructor, one* cannot *implement an* $(n+1)$*-way rendezvous operation abstractly (i.e., as an event value).*

For **CML**, which provides 2-way rendezvous primitives, this means that it is impossible to construct an event-valued implementation of 3-way rendezvous.

While the technical arguments are beyond the scope of this paper, the intuition behind them is fairly straightforward. An $n$-way rendezvous mechanism is a way for $n$ processes to simultaneously agree. For example, in a synchronous message transmission, both the sender and acceptor agree to the transmission. Another way of viewing this is that the processes involved in a $n$-way rendezvous achieve some form of *common knowledge*.[4] The intuition behind the theorem is that if a language provides a primitive mechanism for $n$-way agreement (or $n$-way common knowledge), there is no way get $(n+1)$ processes to agree (attain common knowledge) in an abstract fashion; i.e., in a way that is independent of context. The problem is that while one can get $n$ of the processes in agreement, the $(n+1)$th process is not constrained to make the same choice.

One of the immediate conclusions from these results is that there is a real difference in the expressiveness of synchronous and asynchronous message passing. A language based on asynchronous message passing, even if it supports first-class synchronous operations, cannot support abstract implementations of synchronous message passing. For the programmer, this means that situations that require both synchronous message passing and selective communication will have to be programmed on a case-by-case basis. It is interesting to note, however, that if the language does not have generalized selective communication, then one can abstractly implement synchronous communication using a simple acknowledgement-based protocol. This is because the non-blocking send operation is not a synchronous operation, and thus cannot be placed in a selective

---

[4] The strength of the common knowledge achieved depends on the form of the rendezvous mechanism. For example, a primitive notion of atomic rendezvous achieves common knowledge in the sense of Halpern and Moses [HM90], while a rendezvous protocol achieves the weaker *concurrent common knowledge* [PT92].

communication context. From this, we conclude that generalized selective communication is strictly more expressive than the input-only form found in many languages. Furthermore, given a language with 2-way rendezvous, but selective communication limited to input guards only, one cannot implement a communication abstraction that would allow output guards.

## 6 Related work

The concurrent languages **Facile** [GMP89] and **LCS** [Ber93] support communication and synchronization is way that also allows abstraction. These language make *behaviors* (a concept taken from the process calculus world) into first-class values. In many respects these behaviors are like **CML**'s event values; they can encode basic communication, choice, and actions. Behaviors are also used to implement multiple threads of control, which is their main difference from **CML**'s events. The implementations of these languages are both based on extending **ML**, and in practice, programming in these languages is likely to be quite similar to **CML** programming.

## 7 Conclusion

This paper has given an overview of first-class synchronous operations, along with some illustrative examples using the higher-order concurrent language **CML**. In addition to illustrating how first-class synchronous operations can be used to implement synchronization abstractions, we have also discussed their limitations, which are a result of fundamental properties of rendezvous and selective communication.

## References

[AB86]    Abramsky, S. and R. Bornat. Pascal-m: A language for loosely coupled distributed systems. In Y. Paker and J.-P. Verjus (eds.), *Distributed Computing Systems*, pp. 163–189. Academic Press, New York, N.Y., 1986.

[AM91]    Appel, A. W. and D. B. MacQueen. Standard ML of New Jersey. In *Programming Language Implementation and Logic Programming*, vol. 528 of *Lecture Notes in Computer Science*, New York, N.Y., August 1991. Springer-Verlag, pp. 1–26.

[ANP89]   Arvind, R. S. Nikhil, and K. K. Pingali. I-structures: Data structures for parallel computing. *ACM Transactions on Programming Languages and Systems*, 11(4), October 1989, pp. 598–632.

[BCGL87]  Bjornson, R., N. Carriero, D. Gelernter, and J. Leichter. Linda, the portable parallel. *Technical Report YALEU/DCS/TR-520*, Department of Computer Science, Yale University, February 1987.

[Ber93]   Berthomieu, B. Programming with behaviors in an ML framework — the syntax and semantics of LCS. *Technical Report 93133*, LASS/CNRS, April 1993.

[BHLM94] Biagiono, E., R. Harper, P. Lee, and B. G. Milnes. Signatures for a network protocol stack: A systems application of Standard ML. In *Conference record of the 1994 ACM Conference on Lisp and Functional Programming*, June 1994, pp. 55–64.

[BNA91] Barth, P., R. S. Nikhil, and Arvind. M-structures: Extending a parallel, non-strict, functional language with state. In *Functional Programming Languages and Computer Architecture*, vol. 523 of *Lecture Notes in Computer Science*, New York, N.Y., August 1991. Springer-Verlag, pp. 538–568.

[Bor86] Bornat, R. A protocol for generalized occam. *Software – Practice and Experience*, 16(9), September 1986, pp. 783–799.

[Bur88] Burns, A. *Programming in occam 2*. Addison-Wesley, Reading, Mass., 1988.

[Car86] Cardelli, L. Amber. In *Combinators and Functional Programming Languages*, vol. 242 of *Lecture Notes in Computer Science*, New York, N.Y., July 1986. Springer-Verlag, pp. 21–47.

[CG90] Carriero, N. and D. Gelernter. *How to Write Parallel Programs: A First Course*. The MIT Press, Cambridge, Mass., 1990.

[CP85] Cardelli, L. and R. Pike. Squeak: A language for communicating with mice. In *SIGGRAPH '85*, July 1985, pp. 199–204.

[DoD83] *Reference Manual for the Ada Programming Language*, January 1983.

[GB82] Gelernter, D. and A. J. Bernstein. Distributed communication via global buffer. In *ACM SIGACT-SIGOPS Symposium on Principles of Distributed Computing*, August 1982, pp. 10–18.

[Gel85] Gelernter, D. Generative communication in Linda. *ACM Transactions on Programming Languages and Systems*, 7(1), January 1985, pp. 80–112.

[GM92] Griffin, T. and R. Moten. Tactic trees in eXene. Included in the eXene distribution, 1992.

[GMP89] Giacalone, A., P. Mishra, and S. Prasad. Facile: A symemetric integration of concurrent and functional programming. In *TAPSOFT'89 (vol. 2)*, vol. 352 of *Lecture Notes in Computer Science*, New York, N.Y., March 1989. Springer-Verlag, pp. 184–209.

[GR92] Gansner, E. R. and J. H. Reppy. A foundation for user interface construction. In B. A. Myers (ed.), *Languages for Developing User Interfaces*, pp. 239–260. Jones & Bartlett, Boston, Mass., 1992.

[GR93] Gansner, E. R. and J. H. Reppy. *A Multi-threaded Higher-order User Interface Toolkit*, vol. 1 of *Software Trends*, pp. 61–80. John Wiley & Sons, 1993.

[Haa90] Haahr, D. Montage: Breaking windows into small pieces. In *USENIX Summer Conference*, June 1990, pp. 289–297.

[HM90] Halpern, J. Y. and Y. Moses. Knowledge and common knowledge in a distributed environment. *Journal of the ACM*, 37(3), July 1990, pp. 549–587. An earlier version appeared in the *Proceedings of the 3rd ACM Conference on Principles of Distributed Computing*.

[Kru93] Krumvieda, C. D. *Distributed ML: Abstractions for Efficient and Fault-Tolerant Programming*. Ph.D. dissertation, Department of Computer Science, Cornell University, Ithaca, NY, August 1993. Available as Technical Report TR 93-1376.

[KSI94] Kawaguchi, N., T. Sakabe, and Y. Inagaki. TERSE: Term rewriting support environment. In *Proceedings of the 1994 ACM SIGPLAN Workshop on ML and its Applications*, June 1994, pp. 91–100.

[Lin91]    Lin, H. PAM: A process algebra manipulator. In *Proceedings of the Third Workshop on Computer Aided Verification*, July 1991.

[MTH90]    Milner, R., M. Tofte, and R. Harper. *The Definition of Standard ML*. The MIT Press, Cambridge, Mass, 1990.

[Pau91]    Paulson, L. C. *ML for the Working Programmer*. Cambridge University Press, New York, N.Y., 1991.

[Pik89a]   Pike, R. A concurrent window system. *Computing Systems*, **2**(2), 1989, pp. 133–153.

[Pik89b]   Pike, R. Newsqueak: A language for communicating with mice. *Technical Report 143*, AT&T Bell Laboratories, April 1989.

[PR94]     Panangaden, P. and J. H. Reppy. On the relative expressiveness of rendezvous primitives. unpublished draft, 1994.

[PT92]     Panangaden, P. and K. Taylor. Concurrent common knowledge: Defining agreement for asynchronous systems. *Distributed Computing*, 1992, pp. 73–93.

[Rep88]    Reppy, J. H. Synchronous operations as first-class values. In *Proceedings of the SIGPLAN'88 Conference on Programming Language Design and Implementation*, June 1988, pp. 250–259.

[Rep91]    Reppy, J. H. CML: A higher-order concurrent language. In *Proceedings of the SIGPLAN'91 Conference on Programming Language Design and Implementation*, June 1991, pp. 293–305.

[Rep92]    Reppy, J. H. *Higher-order concurrency*. Ph.D. dissertation, Department of Computer Science, Cornell University, Ithaca, NY, January 1992. Available as Technical Report TR 92-1285.

[Rep95]    Reppy, J. H. *Concurrent Programming in ML*. Cambridge University Press, 1995. (forthcoming).

[RG86]     Reppy, J. H. and E. R. Gansner. A foundation for programming environments. In *Proceedings of the ACM SIGSOFT/SIGPLAN Software Engineering Symposium on Practical Software Development Environments*, December 1986, pp. 218–227.

[SC91]     Siegel, E. H. and E. C. Cooper. Implementing distributed Linda in Standard ML. *Technical Report CMU-CS-91-151*, cmu-cs, October 1991.

[Sli90]    Slind, K. An implementation of higher order logic. Master's dissertation, University of Calgary, Department of Computer Science, December 1990.

[Tof90]    Tofte, M. Type inference for polymorphic references. *Information and Computation*, **89**, 1990, pp. 1–34.

[Ull94]    Ullman, J. D. *Elements of ML Programming*. Prentice Hall, Englewood Cliffs, NJ, 1994.

# Self-Describing Files + Smart Modules = Parallel Program Visualization

Robert H. Halstead, Jr.*

**Abstract.** Many tools have been built for gathering and visualizing parallel program performance data, but all too often these tools are (1) tied closely to a specific programming system or computing model and (2) monolithic and hard to customize. We attack problem (1) by using SDF, a self-describing file format that allows a flexible representation of performance information. An SDF file can be processed as a sequence of named records containing named fields without sacrificing the efficiency normally associated with custom-designed binary data representations. Descriptive annotations can be included to further document the contents of an SDF file.

To attack problem (2), we are implementing a system in which reusable performance analysis and visualization modules can be combined in a wide range of configurations. These modules use SDF for their inputs and outputs and are "smart" in that they automatically use the annotations and mnemonic names present in their input data sets to pick appropriate default behaviors, which can be modified interactively if desired. Key to this design is the classification of performance information into general categories such as "event history" and "histogram," along with the definition of suitable conventions for annotating SDF files containing information of each type.

## 1 Introduction

It is widely agreed that a serious obstacle faced by developers of parallel programs is the difficulty of understanding the execution behavior of these programs. Even the behavior of sequential programs can be hard to understand, but various generic profiling and tracing tools have come into general use and are adequate to diagnose many causes of poor performance in sequential programs. The execution of a parallel program, however, is characterized by the interaction of many asynchronous, autonomous agents. Much more complicated interactions need to be understood before program performance can be improved. Parallel programming also offers the programmer many more "degrees of freedom" for improving performance. This increases the difficulty of identifying the right "knob" to turn to solve a particular performance problem.

The need for understanding parallel program execution has spawned many visualization and analysis tools, but all too often these tools are tightly integrated into a particular parallel programming system and have detailed "wired-in" knowledge of the particular data formats (and their semantics) that are used

---

* DEC Cambridge Research Lab, Cambridge, MA 02139, U.S.A.,
  halstead@crl.dec.com

by that system. Such an architecture serves the immediate needs of the tool developers but impedes the application of these tools on other parallel programming systems.

Some projects [1, 2, 5, 6, 8] have stepped past these limitations to offer parallel program visualization and analysis tools in a package that is fairly platform-independent; however, of these projects only Pablo[2] [8, 9] offers a truly flexible data format and extensible processing framework that can accommodate the needs of widely divergent systems.

Another frequently mentioned problem is that tools can be complicated to use and difficult to learn. Often, programmers do not get interested in using a tool until they have a difficult problem to solve, and due to past experiences they may be skeptical that a tool will really be able to help. In such a situation, programmers will not make a major time investment in learning how to use a tool until they see evidence that their effort will be well repaid. Therefore, it is desirable that a tool should have good default behavior: when the tool is initially applied, it should immediately do something useful. Ideally, if the tool's default behavior is not quite what is desired, the user will be able to customize the tool's behavior by a "hill-climbing" process of incremental steps without ever needing to stop for a lengthy period of learning how to operate the tool.

The conclusions from the above discussion can be summarized as follows:

- The way to bring better tools to the great masses of parallel programmers is to develop generic tools that can be applied to many different parallel programming systems. Such tools must be based on flexible data formats and must be extensible so that capabilities specific to particular systems can be implemented in modules that can be "plugged in" and work together with the more generic parts of the tool suite.
- To gain wide acceptance, tools must be approachable: they must have good default behaviors and customization capabilities that do not demand extensive user sophistication.

These are challenging goals that require clever design at many architectural levels; however, an important initial building block is a framework that defines standard but flexible representations for the major types of performance data, including standard ways to annotate the data to indicate default behaviors and appropriate customizations. This paper reports on the design of *Vista*, a framework that provides this capability and enables the interconnection of analysis and visualization modules to process performance data.

Vista's modular approach is similar to that of Pablo, AVS[3] [10], and other visualization systems that use a two-pronged attack:

1. Define a set of supported data types.
2. Provide a set of useful, generic modules that operate on those data types.

---

[2] Pablo is a registered trademark of the Board of Trustees of the University of Illinois.
[3] AVS is a trademark of Advanced Visual Systems, Inc.

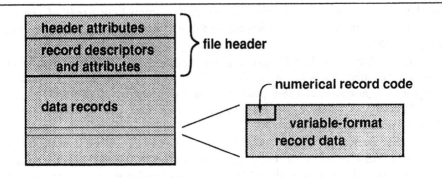

**Fig. 1.** Overall structure of an SDF file.

In both Pablo and AVS, a user builds a data visualization or analysis application by connecting modules together into data-flow graphs; both systems provide a "visual programming" interface for building these graphs. Vista uses the same data-flow metaphor for interconnecting modules but does not yet include a graphical tool for building the graphs.

To accommodate flexibly the great variety of performance data that may be of interest, Vista follows the lead of Pablo and uses a self-describing format for data files. Vista's self-describing file format is called SDF and is described in Section 2. However, simply using a self-describing format is not enough. To enable independently designed modules to communicate with each other, it is important to take the further step of identifying the major types of performance data sets and designing a standard SDF convention for representing each type. This is where Vista goes beyond Pablo and other systems for visualizing performance data. Sections 3–7 describe the data set types recognized by Vista and outline the representation of each type using SDF. Section 8 discusses how to use Vista's data types to make modules "smart." Section 9 outlines directions for future work and offers some concluding thoughts.

## 2 The SDF Self-Describing File Format

An SDF file consists of a descriptive header followed by a series of data records, as shown in Fig. 1. The header describes the structure and meaning of the data records. It describes the format of data records and specifies mnemonic (ASCII) names for data-record types and data-record fields. This information is analogous to struct definitions in C programs, which give a mnemonic name to each structure type and to each field within a structure, as well as specifying the sequence of fields in each structure and the type and representation for the data in each field.

Fields in SDF files may be scalar fields or array fields. A selection of basic types is available for scalar fields, including both signed and unsigned integers, floating-point numbers, and enumeration types, in several sizes ranging from 8 to 64 bits. Array fields contain arrays of elements of any of the available scalar types. Arrays may have any number of dimensions and may be fixed or variable in size. ASCII character strings and arrays of character strings are also available as field types.

In addition to describing the format of data records and giving names to data fields, the SDF file header provides a capability to specify arbitrary information in the form of *attributes*, which may be attached to the file as a whole (*header attributes*), to an individual record descriptor (*record attributes*), or to a field within a record descriptor (*field attributes*). Attributes are specified as (key, value) pairs of ASCII character strings. Attributes can be used to supply meta-information such as the source of data or the meaning of a record or field:

```
"creation date"  "May 12 1994 18:01"
"units" "1.0e-6 seconds"
"format" "%7.3f"
"pretty name" "Block on semaphore"
```

Except for a few reserved attribute keys, the SDF definition assigns no particular semantics to any attribute keys or values; the attributes are for communication between programs that produce and consume SDF files and may follow any conventions established by those programs.

An SDF file's data records follow the descriptive header information described above. Data records are represented in a compact binary form that can be transferred efficiently between SDF files and memory-resident data structures, yet the presence of the header information allows the data to be presented and used as though it were stored in a much more human-oriented file format, with named record types and record fields.

## 2.1 An Example: Representing an Event History Using SDF

As an example, let us consider the use of the SDF format for one type of performance data—event histories. Each event is represented as one SDF record. Header, record, and field attributes give information about the events to help applications process and display the event history in a meaningful way. The discussion below is illustrated with excerpts from a human-readable "dump" of an SDF file.

Fig. 2 shows the file's header attributes. The first three attributes give an example of using header attributes for identification information. The last three attributes communicate meta-information that can help a viewer or analyzer module process the file in a more reasonable way. The "time base" attribute tells us that "timestamp" is the name of a field that appears in each event record and can be used to order events in time. Similarly, each "threading field" attribute gives a field name that can be used to organize events into threads of related events. In this case, computation occurs in tasks that can move from processor to processor, and the header attributes tell us that it can be meaningful

```
"expression"   "(TREE-POLY-TEST 10)"
"software system"   "Mul-T"
"number of processors"   "12"
"time base"   "timestamp"
"threading field"   "task"
"threading field"   "cpu"
```

**Fig. 2.** Header attributes for an example SDF file.

to group events into threads either based on the "task" field (giving a view close to the programming model) or the "cpu" field (giving a view that emphasizes the activities of the physical processors). Using the information in these attributes, an event-log viewer can, for example, ask the user which of the two threading fields should be used.

Fig. 3 gives a partial dump of a representative record descriptor. The record and field attributes in this record descriptor serve several purposes established by the conventions for representing event histories. The "pretty name" record attribute gives a name for the record that is "prettier" than the actual record name and therefore is useful in user-interface components such as menus. The remaining record attributes provide other information about the create-with-task event type; see Section 4.2 for details. Each field also has a "pretty name" field attribute, along with a "format" field attribute whose value is a printf-style format string suggesting an appropriate way to format the contents of that field when producing a textual representation of the event. The "causee thread(task creation)" field attribute is discussed in Section 4.2.

A collection of records from a typical event log, rendered into a human-readable format based on the descriptions in the file header, is given in Fig. 4. Only the data shown in typewriter font is actually stored in the data records; all the information shown in italics is derived from the record descriptions in the file header. Note that the suggested formats encoded in "format" field attributes have been used to make the dump more readable.

## 2.2 Discussion

SDF files offer several advantages for storing performance data:

- SDF can handle large data sets efficiently by storing data using a binary representation that is either identical to the "ideal" binary representation that would otherwise be chosen, or is nearly as compact as that representation.
- Extra information included in SDF files can easily be ignored by applications that do not need it. SDF supports a view of a file as a sequence of data records described using record and field names rather than rigid binary formats, so applications can ask by name for the data they need and can

```
#11 "create-with-task":
  Record attributes:
    "pretty name"  "Create with task"
    "transient?"  "yes"
    "color"  "green"
    "arrow thickness(task creation)"  "2"
    "arrow color(task creation)"  "black"
  End of record attributes.
  Field descriptors:
    "timestamp" (64-bit IEEE float)
      Field attributes:
        "format"  "%.6f"
        "pretty name"  "Timestamp"
      End of field attributes.
    "cpu" (unsigned 8-bit)
      Field attributes:
        "format"  "%d"
        "pretty name"  "CPU"
      End of field attributes.
    "created task" (unsigned 32-bit)
      Field attributes:
        "format"  "0x%x"
        "pretty name"  "Created task"
      End of field attributes.
    "task" (unsigned 32-bit)
      Field attributes:
        "format"  "0x%x"
        "causee thread(task creation)"  "created task"
        "pretty name"  "Task"
      End of field attributes.
    "instruction count" (unsigned 32-bit)
              .
              .
              .

    "task name" (16-bit enumeration)
              .
              .
              .
  End of field descriptors.
```

**Fig. 3.** A dump of a typical SDF record descriptor.

#3 *"run"* *("timestamp"* = 0.009633, *"cpu"* = 12, *"task"* = 0x28000008*)*
#11 *"create-with-task"* *("timestamp"* = 0.009760, *"cpu"* = 12,
    *"created task"* = 0x0C00000C, *"task"* = 0x28000008, *"instruction count"* = 8,
    *"task name"* = *"(P* (CDR X) Y)")*
#11 *"create-with-task"* *("timestamp"* = 0.009826, *"cpu"* = 12,
    *"created task"* = 0x0C000010, *"task"* = 0x28000008, *"instruction count"* = 12,
    *"task name"* = *"(PC* (CAR X) Y)")*
#9 *"await"* *("timestamp"* = 0.009871, *"cpu"* = 12, *"task"* = 0x28000008,
    *"awaited task"* = 0x0C000010*)*
#3 *"run"* *("timestamp"* = 0.009893, *"cpu"* = 12, *"task"* = 0x0C000010*)*
#4 *"terminate"* *("timestamp"* = 0.010767, *"cpu"* = 12, *"task"* = 0x0C000010*)*
#8 *"resume-runnable"* *("timestamp"* = 0.010797, *"cpu"* = 12, *"task"* = 0x28000008,
    *"resumer task"* = 0x0C000010*)*
#3 *"run"* *("timestamp"* = 0.012265, *"cpu"* = 12, *"task"* = 0x10000004*)*

**Fig. 4.** A dump of a set of typical SDF records.

easily ignore other information that may also be present. One consequence of this flexibility is that data-set types defined in terms of SDF have great potential for upward-compatible extension: new fields or record types can be added in a way that allows old programs to accept the new data files without even needing to be recompiled.

- The SDF representation helps cooperating application programs define information-passing conventions. Attributes can be used to include arbitrary information in an SDF file, and a program reading an SDF file can look for attributes with particular keys that are associated by convention with useful values. Other attributes, used for communication between other programs that may also use the same data set, can be present without causing confusion (as long as they use different keys). This flexibility supports the construction of generic programs that use the attribute and record definition information in SDF files to determine what processing steps are appropriate. Such programs, with standard SDF interfaces, can be connected together into a wide variety of useful configurations.

One capability that SDF does not offer is the capability to represent data in a compressed form. Some performance-data representations that are not self-describing offer this capability, which can be a significant benefit when dealing with large event logs. Finding an elegant way to marry SDF and compression technology is one project that should get some attention in the future.

Self-describing file formats are not a new idea. They have been proposed before in Pablo [8, 9] and by standards committees such as CCITT X.409. SDF is quite similar to Pablo's SDDF self-describing format. Compared to the very general self-describing approach specified by X.409, both SDF and SDDF are much more focused on describing only particular data formats that are likely to be of interest when dealing with performance data.

There are three main differences between SDF and SDDF. First, SDF defines a binary format only, while SDDF defines both a binary and an ASCII format. Second, SDF offers a wider selection of binary representations—SDDF defines only one size of integer and floating-point number, while SDF defines many integer and floating-point sizes, along with an enumeration type similar to an enum type in C. Third, record descriptors all appear at the beginning of an SDF file, while they can appear anywhere in an SDDF file. An application can thus plan its attack on an SDF file before reading any data records, but the need to decide all record formats before writing the first data record is a constraint on producers of SDF files that is not imposed on producers of SDDF files.

In the long run, however, the bit-level details of SDF matter less than how it can be used to represent performance data. We now turn to that subject.

## 3   Data Types for Performance Information

### 3.1   The Basic Data Types

Although a great variety of performance information can be collected or derived from program executions, this information can be classified into three broad categories:

- *Event histories* record events that happened during a program execution. Each event is labeled with information about the time at which it occurred, along with information about the context (e.g., task ID or processor ID) in which the event occurred, and arbitrary other parameters.
- *Static histograms* are collections of numerical data derived from an execution. A static histogram is like an array except that the array indices need not be numbers and need not have a natural sequential ordering such as numbers have. The output of the familiar UNIX[4] prof profiling command is an example of a static histogram whose indices are procedure names or source-code line numbers.
- *Dynamic histograms* contain sets of time-dependent variables. The number of busy processors in a multiprocessor is a simple example of a time-dependent variable, but time-dependent variables can also occur in indexed groups similar to static histograms. The heap size or stack depth on each processor in a multiprocessor, or the communication volume currently pending between each pair of processors, are examples of such indexed groups. These histogram-like examples motivate the term "dynamic histograms."

### 3.2   The Basic Module Types

In addition to considering the types of performance data, we should consider the three basic categories of modules that work with this data:

---

[4] UNIX is a registered trademark in the United States and other countries, licensed exclusively through X/Open Company, Ltd.

- *Data sources* are modules that "create" data and make it available to other modules. A typical data-source module reads data from a file and outputs it to one or more ports from which other modules can consume it, but other types of data-source modules are possible: for example, a module that runs an experiment (with specified parameters) and pipes the resulting data directly to its output port or ports.
- *Filters and transformers* consume data through one or more input ports, process it in some way, and output the result to their output port or ports.
- *Viewers and other data sinks* consume data through input ports but have no output ports. There are several possibilities for what a data sink could do with its input data. The data could just be written to a file for later use, but a particularly important kind of data-sink module is a *viewer*, which provides a graphical view of its input data set.

## 3.3 General Data-Representation Conventions

Vista's strategy for representing performance data as SDF files is to represent the actual data as SDF data records and use SDF attributes for annotations that (1) describe the meaning of the data and (2) give hints about how it should be processed or displayed. It is useful to distinguish these two kinds of attributes; we refer to the former as *semantic attributes* and to the latter as *customization attributes*. Normally, semantic attributes would be attached to an SDF data set at the time of its creation. Customization attributes, however, could be attached at the time of creation or they could be attached later by filter modules as a way of controlling the subsequent actions of modules farther "downstream" in the processing pipeline. These customization attributes include capabilities for representing interactive annotations such as cursor positions, which can be propagated to several modules to help users relate different views of the same data to each other. This part of the data-type design has taken much of its inspiration from Klinker's work on cursor linking[3, 4].

Some conventions for using SDF attributes are applicable to all three of the basic performance data types. Those conventions are discussed in the remainder of this section. Other conventions, which are specific to particular data types, are discussed in Sections 4–7. SDF offers a large number of design alternatives (such as whether to use header, record, or field attributes for a particular purpose), so the details of these conventions are necessarily somewhat arbitrary, but they have served Vista's needs until now. This paper is too brief to discuss all the relevant design options or serve as a reference manual, but we present this overview of the conventions that have been chosen for Vista to give a flavor of the issues that need to be addressed by the data representations and present one way to address them.

Another point about the data-representation conventions is that some modules will work with data "subtypes" derived by specializing the data types described in this paper. For example, a module might require an input to be an "event history with a tree hierarchy defined on threads" in order to do some specialized processing on it. Such subtypes would be defined by specifying additional conventions beyond those described in this paper.

Finally, this paper is a report on work in progress. Some of the conventions set out here are not yet implemented by the set of prototype Vista modules, and some details of how the representations are defined are still evolving as Vista matures.

**Header Attributes.** There should be some general conventions for encoding identification information such as the date and time when data was gathered, the experimental conditions, the sequence of processing steps that it has been through, etc., but these conventions still need to be specified.

## Record Attributes

"pretty name" is the key for a customization attribute whose value is a clear, human-readable name for the record. Modules that display menus of record types or otherwise present record-type names to the user are encouraged to use a record's pretty name, instead of the record's SDF name, whenever a "pretty name" attribute is present.

## Field Attributes

"pretty name" is the key for a customization attribute giving a clear, human-readable name for the field, analogous to the "pretty name" record attribute.

"format" is the key for a customization attribute whose value is a printf-style format specifying the preferred way to format the field's contents for textual display.

## 4  The Event History Data Type

An event history contains information about a collection of events that occurred during a program execution. We should not confuse the event-history data type itself with the various ways of viewing event histories, but in understanding the needs that the data type should satisfy, it is helpful to begin by considering how we might like to view event histories.

Fig. 5 shows one example each of the two major kinds of event-history views:

– *Strip charts* are views in which time is displayed explicitly as a spatial dimension, with the other spatial dimension being used for some other property, such as the execution thread or processor associated with each event. Fig. 5(a) shows a strip chart in which the horizontal axis is used as the time axis and the vertical axis is used to group events by thread.

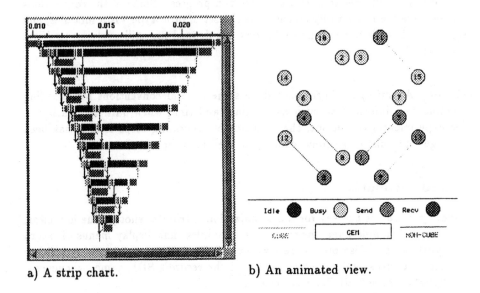

a) A strip chart.  b) An animated view.

**Fig. 5.** Some typical event-history views.

- *Animated views* and *snapshots* are views in which time is *not* displayed as an explicit spatial dimension. This choice frees both spatial dimensions for other uses, making it possible to display more information about the program state, at the cost of being able to show only the instantaneous state of the program rather than a perspective of the program state's evolution over time. If such a view is static, it furnishes a snapshot of the program state at a particular moment. Animated views are also possible: they are essentially sequences of snapshots. Fig. 5(b) shows a snapshot of an event history involving 16 communicating processors. Each processor is shown as a circle whose color indicates its state at the moment represented by this snapshot. Lines drawn between processors show communication operations that are in progress.

### 4.1 Semantics of Event Histories

From these two views we can abstract some general requirements for the kinds of information that an event history must be able to include. An event history must be able to record "time" and "place" information for each event. The "time" (or *time base*) indicates *when* the event occurred. An event may have more than one associated "time" if more than one time base can be used for measurement (e.g., "user time" vs. "wall-clock time," or "observed time" vs. "estimated time after compensation for measurement overhead"). An event's "place" (or *threading field*) indicates the context in which it occurred and helps to establish its relationship with other events. An event may have multiple "places" corresponding to different perspectives on program execution (e.g., "thread ID" vs. "processor ID").

In addition to these basic items of information, the event-history representation can contain several others:

- Miscellaneous other event parameters. An event stemming from a procedure call might include information about call arguments, and perhaps even the source-code file name and line number of the call operation. Similarly, an event resulting from sending a message might include the size of the message and identify the variable whose data was sent.

- Binary relationships between events. Fig. 5(a) includes several arrows that go from events in one thread to events in another. Fig. 5(b) includes lines drawn between pairs of processors. These arrows and lines indicate relationships between pairs of events in the event history: for example, between a "send" event in one thread and the matching "receive" event in another. The event-history representation should provide a way to indicate such relationships between events so that viewers can display them. Many of these relationships are asymmetric and are often shown as arrows. We shall use the term "causer" for the event or thread shown at the tail of an arrow and "causee" for the event or thread shown at the head, even when the relationship does not involve causation.

- Relationships between threads. Separate from the question of relationships between individual events is the question of relationships between entire threads: for example, "thread $X$ is the parent of thread $Y$." Such relationships are often induced by relationships between events (e.g., a "create" event in thread $X$ may match up with a "start" event in thread $Y$) but some interthread relationships may not arise that way (e.g., an "await" event in thread $X$ may name thread $Y$ as the thread waited for, even if there is no specific event in $Y$ to match $X$'s "await" event). Information about interthread relationships can be used to organize a view more logically and informatively by displaying related threads close to each other or even combining groups of related threads into single units for display. Event histories are frequently characterized by overwhelming detail, so information about relationships among threads is especially valuable when it can be used to simplify displays.

- Distinguish *state-changing* from *transient* events. The concept of *state* is often important in interpreting event histories (for example, it governs the choice of colors used to paint threads and processors in Fig. 5), and events often mark changes in the state of a processor or thread. For example, a "run" event might mark a state change from "blocked" to "running." Nevertheless, some events do not mark state changes. For example, a "create task" event would typically occur while in the "run" state and would not change that state. Event histories should provide a way to distinguish these two kinds of events.

The discussion above addresses the semantics of event-history data. In addition, many customizations should be expressible in an event history. These include specifying the color, arrangement, and viewpoint of event displays, along with the location of *cursors* in the display. Cursors provide a way to mark particular points along the time-base and threading-field dimensions and associate each marked point with a *cursor name*.

Certain cursor names are interpreted specially by viewers and other modules that process event histories. For example, a strip-chart viewer as in Fig. 5(a) should look for cursors named start and end in both its time-base and threading-field dimensions and use them, if found, to control the portion of the event history that is displayed. Other cursors that are present can be displayed as vertical or horizontal lines if they fall within the visible area. A snapshot event-history view, on the other hand, should look for a cursor named current in the time-base dimension and use it to determine the time of the snapshot that is displayed. Any cursors present in the threading-field dimension can be used to highlight the corresponding objects in the snapshot. Establishing conventions such as these, governing how cursors control modules, makes it easier for a data producer that is "upstream" from a set of modules to control all of those modules in a coordinated way by producing a data set containing suitable cursor specifications.

Another way to understand the semantics of a data type is to consider what operations can be performed on it. Here are some examples of filter and transformer modules that would operate on event histories:

- Select only those events within a given time range, set of threads, or set of event types.
- Add annotations to events (e.g., "this is the $n$th occurrence of event $E$").
- Adjust time bases measured on different processors to compensate for skew between their clocks.
- Add a new time base derived from an existing time base by compensating for measurement perturbations.
- Build a static histogram of the time spent by each thread in each state.
- Build a dynamic histogram of the number of threads in each state as a function of time.

## 4.2   Representation of Event Histories

Each event in an SDF event-history file is represented by one SDF record. Each different type of event can be represented by a different SDF record type, allowing great flexibility in the choice of information included in each event.

The "time" and "place" of events are specified using time-base and threading fields, as discussed above. A time-base field is a field that occurs with the same field name in every event record and contains a number (integer or floating-point) indicating each event's position on that time base's time scale. A threading field is also a field that should occur with the same field name in every event record where it appears. A threading field is used to organize events into "threads" that trace out the history of activities that occur in a particular place or have some other logical connection (such as belonging to the same distributed database transaction or operating on the same semaphore or synchronizing variable). Each event type may include arbitrary other fields in addition to its time-base and threading fields, containing any information that is considered useful.

An event history may also contain "global" events that belong to no particular thread but nevertheless do occur at a well-defined time. The beginning and end of a global garbage collection or log-flushing operation can be indicated in this way, as can changes in a global system parameter such as the network load. Such events can be represented as records with a time-base field but no threading field. An SDF event-history file can also include records with neither a time-base field nor a threading field; such records are not considered to be part of the event history, although they may carry other information that may be useful to some consumers.

### Header Attributes

"time base" is the key for a semantic attribute that may appear multiple times in the file header. Each value associated with this key gives the name of a field that can be used as a time base for the event history.

"threading field" is the key for a semantic attribute that may appear multiple times in the file header. Each associated value names a threading field that can be used to group related events into threads of activity.

"selected time base" and "selected threading field" are keys for customization attributes. Each should appear at most once, with a value naming the time base or threading field (respectively) that should be used by default.

"thread order(*threading-field*)" is the key for a customization attribute that specifies an order for displaying threads. When *threading-field* is the selected threading field, the value of the "thread order(*threading-field*)" attribute controls the display order. This value is a list of lists of thread ID's, where each thread ID is a character-string representation of a value that could appear in the threading field. (Since all attribute values must be character strings, we build lists using the string-based list syntax defined by Tcl [7].) Each list element at the top level corresponds to a thread "slot" in a view (such as Fig. 5(a)) that presents threads in a linear order. Each of these top-level list elements is in turn a list of the ID's of the one or more threads that should be displayed in this slot. This attribute provides a mechanism that a producer module can use to control the thread ordering used by a subsequent display module. Although this mechanism is particularly suited to views that display threads in a 1-dimensional array of slots, the information about which thread ID's to group together can be used even by other kinds of views.

For example, a header attribute with the key "thread order(cpu)" and the value "3 {5 7 9} {1 4}" indicates that when a viewer uses "cpu" as the threading field, the thread whose "cpu" value is 3 should be displayed in the first thread slot; the threads whose "cpu" values are 5, 7, and 9 should be combined (in some view-specific way) and displayed in the second thread slot; and the threads whose CPU ID's are 1 and 4 should be combined and displayed in the third thread slot. Threads with other CPU ID's should not be displayed at all.

"cursor(*field-name*)*cursor-name*" is the key for a customization attribute whose value indicates the position of a cursor associated with the event history. *field-name* should be the name of a time-base or threading field. If *field-name* is the name of a time-base field, then the associated attribute value is a string representing a number that could appear in that time-base field. If *field-name* is the name of a threading field, then there are two possibilities for the attribute value:

1. It can be a string that represents a single number. In this case it designates a position in the list of thread-slot contents that appears as the value of the "thread order(*threading-field*)" attribute. The fractional part of this number, if nonzero, specifies the positioning of the cursor within the designated slot, for displays where such fine positioning control is meaningful. Thus, a header attribute with the key "cursor(cpu) start" and the value "2.1" indicates that a cursor called start is located in the third thread slot (because the first is numbered 0) at a position 10% of the way from its beginning (e.g., its top) to its end.

2. It can be a pair "*offset thread-ID*" where $0 \leq offset < 1$ is a number and *thread-ID* is a thread ID associated with the threading field *field-name*. This cursor value specifies that the cursor is positioned at the thread whose ID is *thread-ID* (or in the thread slot where this thread is displayed). *offset* plays the same role as the fractional part in case (1) above and indicates, where appropriate, where in the designated thread's slot the cursor appears.

"cursor color(*field-name*)*cursor-name*" and "cursor display?(*field-name*) *cursor-name*" are customization attributes that apply to the cursor or cursors named with *cursor-name*, controlling their color and whether or not they should be visible in a display.

## Record Attributes

"transient?" is the key for a semantic attribute that is attached to an event type to indicate whether events of this type should be treated as transient events or as state-change events.

"causee(*relation-name*)" is the key for a semantic attribute that is attached to an event that can be a "causer" in a binary relationship. The attribute's value is the type name of the "causee" event in the relationship. *relation-name* is a different string for each different relationship. "causee match(*relation-name*)" field attributes (see below) explain how to determine which event of the causee type is the causee event associated with a particular causer event.

"color" and "display?" are customization attributes controlling the appearance of events to which they are attached.

"arrow color(*relation-name*)", "arrow thickness(*relation-name*)", and "arrow display?(*relation-name*)" are customization attributes controlling the appearance of arrows associated with the interevent or interthread relationship named *relation-name*.

## Field Attributes

"causee match(*relation-name*)" is a semantic attribute that complements the "causee(*relation-name*)" record attribute and indicates how the contents of two events must match in order for them to be considered as a causer-causee pair under *relation-name*. If a record type $R$ has a "causee(*relation-name*)" attribute whose value is $R'$ and field $F$ of $R$ has a "causee match(*relation-name*)" attribute whose value is $F'$, then an event $E$ of type $R$ will be considered as the causer under *relation-name* of an event $E'$ of type $R'$ only if the contents of the field $F$ of $E$ equal the contents of the field $F'$ of $E'$. If several fields in the same record each have a "causee match(*relation-name*)" attribute, all the indicated pairs of fields must match before a causer-causee relationship is recognized. Note that one causer event can have several causees and one causee can have several causers.

For example, suppose an event history contains "send" and "receive" events, where each "send" event contains a "sent ID" field and each "receive" event contains a "received ID" field (in addition to their time-base and threading fields). Suppose further that we want to define a binary relationship called message on "send" and "receive" events that declares each "send" event to be the causer of any "receive" event whose "received ID" field matches the "sent ID" field of the "send" event. To declare the existence of this relationship, the "send" record type would have a record attribute with the key "causee(message)" and the value "receive". The "sent ID" field of the "send" record would have a field attribute with the key "causee match(message)" and the value "received ID". If other fields (e.g., "message type") also had to match in order for a relationship to be recognized, then additional "causee match(message)" attributes would be attached to the other fields of the "send" event type that need to match with fields of the matching "receive" event.

"causee thread(*relation-name*)" is a semantic attribute that establishes an interthread, rather than interevent, relationship. When this attribute is attached to a field $F$ of a record type $R$ and the attribute value is $F'$, then every occurrence of an event $E$ of type $R$ establishes an interthread relationship in which the thread whose ID is found in the field $F$ of $E$ is the causer and the thread whose ID is found in the field $F'$ of $E$ is the causee. ($F$ should be one of the event history's threading fields.)

For example, suppose an "await" event has an "awaited task" field that contains the ID of a logical task whose completion is awaited, and suppose further that "task" is a threading field that contains the ID of the logical task in which an event occurs. To declare a waits for relationship from a task that executes an await operation to the task whose completion is awaited, we can attach a field attribute to the "task" field of the "await" record type. This attribute will have a key "causee thread(waits for)" and a value "awaited task".

"causer thread(*relation-name*)" is an attribute analogous to "causee thread (*relation-name*)", except that it indicates a causer-causee relationship in the opposite direction.

"thread name" is a customization attribute that can be attached to a threading field in an event record. Its value names a field that contains a human-oriented name for the thread whose ID is in the threading field.

# 5   The Static Histogram Data Type

A *static histogram*[5] is a sparse $N$-dimensional array of numbers. The indices of this array are *labels* that can be numbers or character strings and need not form a contiguous, ordered range. The usual interpretation of a static histogram is that each of its elements represents a "bucket" containing values associated with the bucket's index labels. It can be useful to bundle several static histograms together in one data set so that, for example, computation and communication statistics about a program execution can be packaged together. Thus, we would like to devise a representation for a static histogram *data set* that can include one or more static histograms.

Fig. 6 shows several ways to display static histograms. Aside from the familiar bar-graph presentation, we can see several other presentations, including a "heat map" that displays a 2-dimensional histogram as a matrix of cells whose colors show the value of the underlying histogram buckets, a Kiviat diagram that plots bucket values as distances radially outward from the center of a circle, and a normalized bar-graph presentation in which bucket contents have been scaled so they sum to 100 for each processor. Yet other presentations, such as "pie charts," come immediately to mind.

## 5.1   Semantics of Static Histograms

The principal characteristics of the static histogram set data type are as follows:

- One or more *histogram variables* are defined. Each histogram variable corresponds to one histogram in the set.
- Zero or more *dimensions* are defined, to serve as indices into the histogram.
- A set of *labels* is defined for each dimension. Labels can be numbers or character strings. There is no default assumption about the ordering of labels along a dimension, but a label ordering can be specified in the histogram data set, if desired.
- It would be useful to be able to specify hierarchical groupings for the labels along a dimension: for example, it would be useful if a histogram containing line-by-line profiling information could also include data about the grouping

---

[5] Static histograms contrast with dynamic histograms, which are discussed in Section 6.

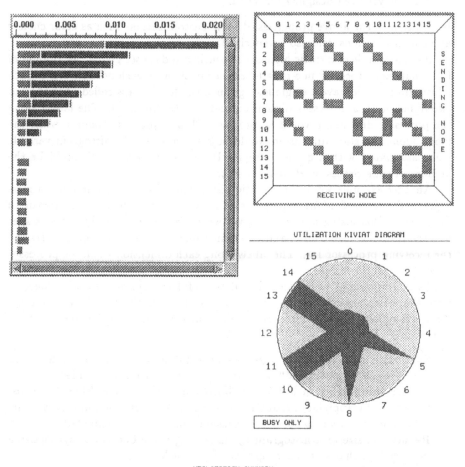

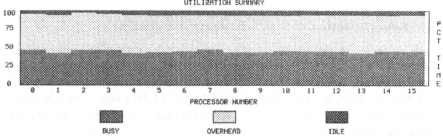

**Fig. 6.** Four typical histogram views. Clockwise from top left: a bar graph, a "heat map," a Kiviat diagram, and a normalized bar graph.

of lines into procedures. However, except for the "display order" field attribute discussed below, a standard mechanism for expressing such grouping has not yet been designed for Vista.

In addition to the above properties, display customizations such as color choices and cursor positions can also be specified.

As an example of a static histogram, consider a data set giving the amount of time that each processor in a parallel execution spent in each possible state. Such a histogram would have a single histogram variable (perhaps called "time") and two dimensions: a processor dimension and a state dimension. The labels along the processor dimension would be processor ID's or processor names, while the labels along the state dimension would be state names. The histogram-variable value associated with a given processor ID $P$ and state name $S$ would be the amount of time processor $P$ spent in state $S$.

Another example would be a static histogram recording the number of messages and the total number of bytes of message traffic between each pair of processors. This histogram would have two variables (the number of messages and the total message traffic) and two dimensions (the sending processor ID and the receiving processor ID). The labels along each dimension would be processor ID's.

As in the case of event histories, it is useful to consider static histograms from the viewpoint of the operations that can be performed on them. Here are some examples of useful filter and transformer modules to operate on static histograms:

- Synthesize new histogram variables by combining existing variables (e.g., "idle time"+"overhead" or "total time"/"number of calls").
- Reduce the number of histogram dimensions by taking a "slice" of a histogram or by applying a reduction operation (such as minimum, maximum, summing, or averaging) over a dimension that is to be eliminated.
- Reduce the size of a histogram by discarding some buckets or synthesizing new buckets that summarize groups of old buckets.

## 5.2   Representation of Static Histogram Data Sets

While records and record names play a major role in the SDF representation of event histories, the SDF representation of histograms focuses on fields. Each record in a static histogram data set has one or more $N$-dimensional array fields, each of which contains an $N$-dimensional "cube" of data values for a histogram variable. Each record also contains $N$ 1-dimensional array fields containing label values associated with each of the cube's dimensions. Each field that contains histogram data is marked with a "histogram data" field attribute, and each field that contains an array of label values is marked with a "histogram index" field attribute whose value indicates the dimension (among the histogram's $N$ dimensions) to which this array of labels pertains. Thus, a data record for the first static histogram example given above might contain a 2-dimensional histogram data field called "time" and two label arrays called "processor" (for the first histogram dimension) and "state" (for the second histogram dimension). The value found in the array element "time"$[i, j]$ would be associated with the processor ID found in "processor"$[i]$ and the state name found in "state"$[j]$.

If there is more than one record in a histogram data set, each record can cover a different region of the $N$-dimensional space by including different labels in its label arrays. Each record can thus specify a different subcube of the histogram data. The entire histogram is constructed as the union of these subcubes. This architecture permits a sparse representation in which data values for empty histogram buckets need not be included explicitly in the SDF file.

**Header and Record Attributes.** None are specified.

**Field Attributes.** In addition to "histogram data" and "histogram index", described above, we have the following:

"display order" is the key for a customization attribute that may be attached to any field that has the "histogram index" attribute. The associated attribute value is a list of lists of index labels, interpreted like the value of the "thread order(*threading-field*)" event-history header attribute.

"cursor()*cursor-name*" is the key for a customization attribute analogous to the "cursor(*field-name*)*cursor-name*" event-history header attribute. Here, the "cursor()*cursor-name*" field attribute can be attached to any histogram index field to specify a cursor position along the corresponding histogram dimension. The value for this attribute is similar in format and meaning to the value of the "cursor(*field-name*)*cursor-name*" event-history attribute for the case where *field-name* is the name of a threading field; in other words, the value can be either a string representing a single number or a string of the form "*offset thread-ID*" designating a particular histogram display slot and a position within that slot.

"color" is the key for a customization attribute that can be attached to a histogram-variable or index field. When attached to a histogram-variable field, the "color" attribute value is just a string specifying the color to use for displaying this histogram variable. When attached to an index field, the "color" attribute key may appear multiple times, associated with different values. Each value is a list (using the Tcl representation) of two elements: a label name that appears in this histogram dimension and the name of a color to use for that label name. In this case, the "color" attribute instructs display modules to use the specified color for displaying histogram elements associated with the given index label.

For example, a "state" field could have a "color" attribute with the value "run green", indicating that green should be used for the histogram bars, pie-chart wedges, etc., associated with the state label "run". Another "color" attribute with the value "blocked red" could be attached to the same field, specifying red as the color for displaying values associated with the "blocked" state.

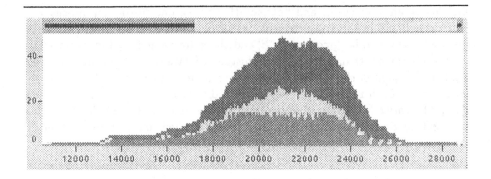

**Fig. 7.** A strip-chart view of a dynamic histogram.

# 6 The Dynamic Histogram Data Type

The third major performance data type is *dynamic histograms*. A dynamic histogram records the variation of a collection of time-dependent variables as a function of time. This data type shares some features with both event histories and static histograms. Dynamic histograms can be viewed as the result of generalizing static histograms to include time-dependent values. Accordingly, a dynamic histogram display can look like any of the static-histogram views shown in Fig. 6, except that the introduction of the time dimension means that the display should now be viewed either as a snapshot of the histogram at a particular instant in time or as an animated display showing how the variables change over time. Like event histories, dynamic histograms can also be displayed as strip charts with time as an explicit dimension; Fig. 7 gives an example.

## 6.1 Semantics of Dynamic Histograms

A dynamic histogram can be thought of as a static histogram that has been extended so that each of its variables can vary over time, or as an event history all of whose events have the form, "At time $T$, change the value of variable $V$ to be $X$." Like a static histogram, a dynamic histogram has variables, dimensions, and labels; like an event history, it has one or more time bases that are used to establish when changes in variable values occur.

All changes to variable values in a dynamic histogram occur abruptly, as steps. The dynamic-histogram data type does not accommodate variables that change continuously in time. Most performance data (such as the number of bytes in a buffer or the number of busy processors) also change discontinuously, so this seems like a good match, but it does rule out continuously changing variables such as might arise from applying a smoothing operation to a set of performance observations.

Examples of filter and transformer modules that would operate on dynamic histograms include the following:

- Create a static histogram by taking a snapshot in time or performing an average, maximum, or minimum operation over a specified time range.
- Restrict to a subrange along the time scale.
- Along the non-time dimensions of a dynamic histogram, perform any slicing, grouping, averaging, etc., operation that is valid on a static histogram.

## 6.2 Representation of Dynamic Histogram Data Sets

The representation of dynamic histograms closely resembles that of static histograms, except that in the dynamic case each data record includes one or more time-base fields in addition to the data fields that are present in the static histogram representation. The value of a histogram variable with a given set of index labels at a given point $T$ in time (using a given time base) is found by locating the data records that contain data "subcubes" for that variable including the given set of index labels and have timestamps (using the given time base) less than or equal to $T$. If there is more than one such record, the variable's value is taken from the record with the greatest timestamp.

The header attributes used in representing dynamic histograms are the attributes used in event histories for dealing with time bases ("time base", "selected time base", "cursor(*field-name*) *cursor-name*", "cursor color(*field-name*) *cursor-name*", and "cursor display?(*field-name*) *cursor-name*"). The field attributes used in dynamic histograms are the same as the the field attributes used in static histograms ("histogram data", "histogram index", "display order", "cursor() *cursor-name*", and "color").

## 7 Discussion of the Data-Type Representations

The event-history representation described in Section 4 can represent the basic information that one would want to include in an event trace, and has some nice extras such as the capability to describe binary relationships and cursor positions. The same can be said for the static and dynamic histogram representations described in Sections 5 and 6. There are, however, some useful capabilities whose representation has not yet been designed:

1. Although cursors can be positioned at points in time or at specific threads, the cursor mechanisms defined for event histories cannot express the positioning of a cursor at a specific event. (A viewer module might respond to the presence of such a cursor by highlighting the event.) If no thread ever has more than one event with the same timestamp (which is not a safe assumption, in general), then a cursor to designate a specific event could be synthesized using one time-base cursor and one threading-field cursor, but a more direct mechanism would be more elegant.
2. It would be useful to allow users to attach arbitrary (character-string) annotations to particular times, places, or events. Building such a capability as an extension of the cursor mechanisms might be one solution, but then

attaching annotations to events in event histories would require a solution to problem (1) above.

3. Opportunities for linkage with textual views of source code would be enhanced by defining a standard way to associate source-file names and line numbers with events and histogram labels.

4. Event histories can represent binary relationships, but none of Vista's datatype representations offers a standard way to describe hierarchical relationships among threads or histogram buckets. In the presence of large numbers of threads, event-history viewers could use such relationships to combine subtrees of threads into single units for display. Histogram viewers could often exploit similar information about hierarchical relationships among histogram labels: for example, we would like a histogram containing line-by-line profiling data to also explain how the lines can be combined into larger-scale units, such as loops and procedures, for a higher-level look at the data. The "thread order(*threading-field*)" and "display order" attributes can express the combination of threads or histogram buckets into single units but cannot capture, in all its richness, the hierarchical data that should be used to decide which threads to combine.

5. Binary relationships also seem inadequate to capture the relationships among the components of collective operations such as barrier synchronizations. For example, it would be nice to be able to declare that a specified set of send and receive operations can be viewed simply as the constituents of one higher-level operation.

In addition, there are certainly opportunities to optimize the data representations. Perhaps there should be an abbreviation for histogram label sets that are regularly spaced integers so they need not be stored explicitly as labels in histogram records. Perhaps the representation for dynamic histograms will generate too many small records and need to be redesigned to save space. These may be problems to solve eventually, but right now it is more important to continue investigating the semantics that the performance data types should have and the techniques for making "smart modules" to use them.

## 8  Making Modules Smart

Since the primary emphasis of the Vista project up to this point has been specifying the basic data types and designing the infrastructure for modules to plug into, only a few modules have been implemented yet, and the development of even these modules has been largely a project to exercise the framework so that its weaknesses can be exposed and corrected. Nevertheless, the current Vista prototype does include an event-history viewer, a static-histogram viewer, and an "event history⇒static histogram" module that processes an event history and produces a static histogram showing the amount of time each thread has spent in each state. (There are also several simpler modules.) These modules offer an initial illustration of how modules can be "smart" by using the semantic and customization information encoded in their input data sets.

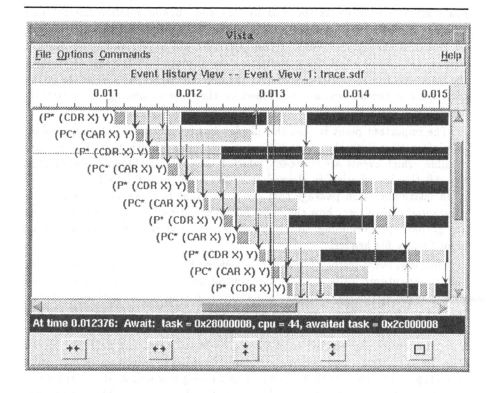

**Fig. 8.** An example Vista event-history view.

Fig. 8 shows a strip-chart display produced by Vista's event-history viewer. From the scrollbar positions we can tell that this display represents only a portion of the overall event history; the portion that is displayed has been controlled by the position of start and end cursors as discussed in Section 4. The scrollbars and the row of command buttons along the bottom of the display can be used to change the region of the event history that is displayed and the magnification that is used; these effects are achieved by repositioning the start and end cursors. Two more cursors that are defined in the data set are displayed as a horizontal line positioned in the third thread from the top and a vertical line positioned at a time value of about 0.013. The mouse pointer (not visible in this screen snapshot) has been positioned near the place where these two cursors intersect, causing the event-history viewer to display information about the event at this position as white text in the dark band below the display. This text shows the event name, the field names, and the field contents. The formatting of this text follows the instructions supplied as attributes in the event history.

The textual label to the left of each thread is extracted from the event history as dictated by the "thread name" field attribute. Arrows indicating interthread relationships are drawn as specified by "causee thread(*relation-name*)" and "causer thread(*relation-name*)" field attributes. Events marked as transient by means of the "transient?" record attribute are drawn as narrow vertical stripes that do not affect the underlying state displayed for the thread. Finally, the colors used in this display to depict the different states, as well as the colors and styles of the arrows, are controlled by their corresponding customization attributes.

The important point is that this display has been created without building any information into the event-history viewer about which thread states are possible, which events are transient, which binary relationships are meaningful, etc. All this information is gleaned from the event history itself. The author of an instrumentation package that produces event histories can thus exercise substantial control over how the event histories will be displayed without doing any graphics programming, simply by choosing the attributes to include in the event-history file header.

Similarly, event-history filters can be defined that consume an event history and, either automatically or under user control, produce a modified event history with changed attributes, adding information or altering customizations to change the way subsequent viewer modules display the events. Fig. 9 shows a dialog box that a Vista user can use to control such customizations. This dialog box allows a user to control the selected time base, the selected threading field, the thread order for the display, and the "color" and "display?" attributes of individual event types. The module that generated this dialog box first analyzed the event history to determine what choices should be offered to the user. Thus, the "Time Base" and "Threading Field" panes offer only valid time-base and threading field names as choices. Similarly, the "Event Attributes" pane displays the event names that exist in this event history and is initialized with the default display options extracted from the event history.

The "Sort Order" pane (which controls the value that will be produced for the "thread order(*threading-field*)" attribute that governs the ordering of threads in the event-history display) offers some standard sort keys for ordering the threads ("thread ID" through "thread start") but also offers three choices that are derived from binary relationships defined in the event history ("await" through "resume-runnable"). Threads can be organized into a tree based on any of these binary relationships and a thread ordering can be computed by performing a preorder walk of this tree. (If the relationship itself forms a DAG or contains directed cycles, the tree-building phase applies pruning rules to discard excess arcs until the result is a tree or a set of disconnected trees.)

Looking back at Fig. 8, we see that the arrangement of threads on the display is not ideal. The way the threads are arranged, there are many places where arrows are drawn on top of other information, giving the display a cluttered look. Using the dialog box of Fig. 9 we can specify a different thread order based on the "create-with-task" sort criterion. Fig. 10, which has been "zoomed out" so that more of the computation can be seen, shows the resulting thread order. For this data set, this display order reduces clutter and clarifies the relationships be-

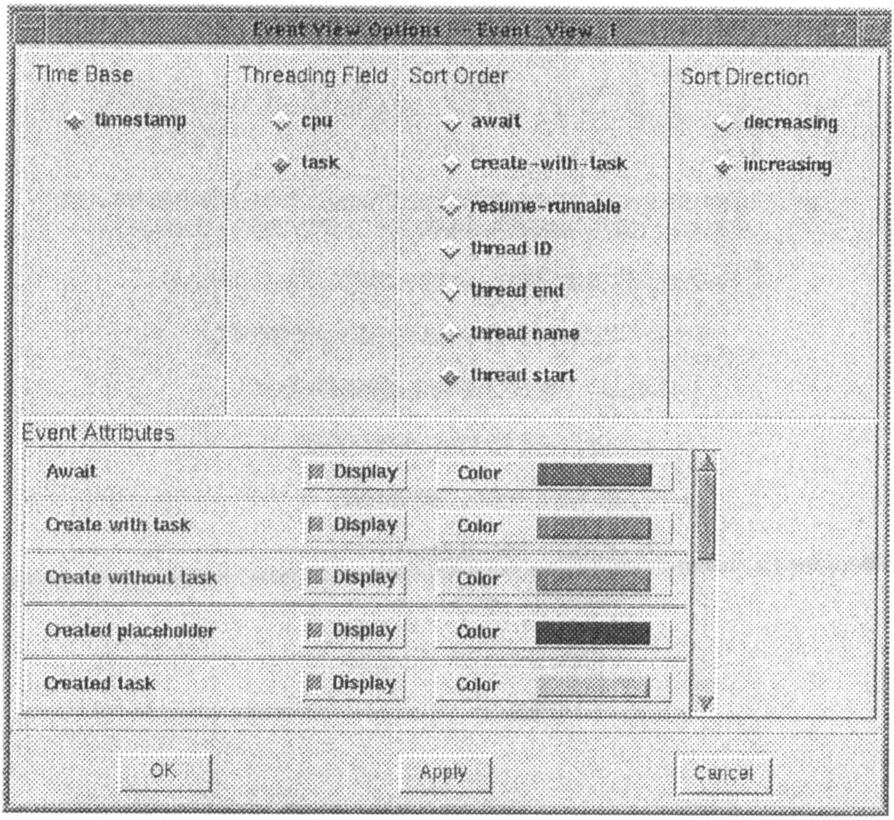

**Fig. 9.** An example Vista customization dialog box.

tween the threads. It is significant that, simply by extracting binary-relationship information from the event history in a generic way, Vista can give the user the capability to produce this thread order. No specialized knowledge about task-spawning trees needed to be "wired into" Vista or the event-history viewer, which increases the chances that Vista will be able to do useful things with a wide range of event histories.

Finally, the value of building a system based on "smart" modules that can interpret customization information that travels along with data sets becomes the most evident when there are multiple data views to be co-ordinated, as in Fig. 11. This display could be generated by the module network shown in Fig. 12, which includes four viewer modules—two event-history displays and two static histogram displays.[6] Each of the four viewer modules generates one of the panes

---

[6] In the actual Vista prototype, the three "customize" modules are replaced by a more complex mechanism for propagating customizations, but a discussion of this mechanism is beyond the scope of this paper.

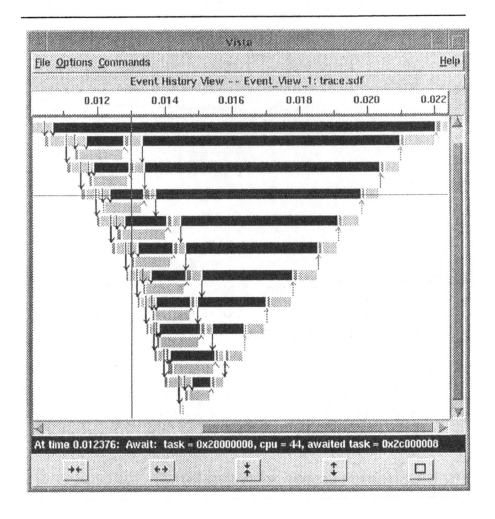

**Fig. 10.** A Vista event-history view with an improved thread ordering.

in the window shown in Fig. 11. The left-hand branch of the module network in Fig. 12 corresponds to the top two views in Fig. 11, while the right-hand branch of the module network corresponds to the bottom two views.

In the configuration used for this example, the top two views use "task" as the threading field (giving a logical view of the program execution) while the bottom two views use "cpu" as the threading field (giving a physical view). The two views on the left in Fig. 11 are event-history displays and each view on the right is a static-histogram display showing a histogram extracted (by an "event

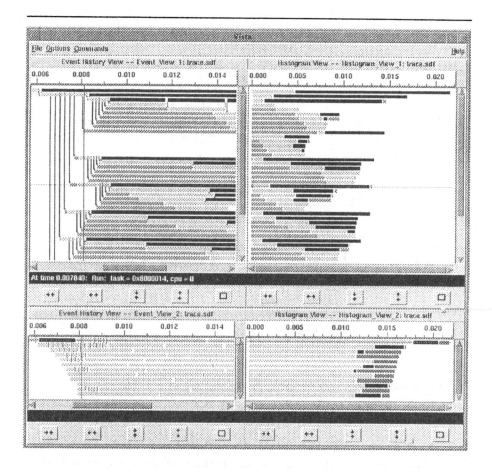

**Fig. 11.** A Vista window combining two event views and two histogram views.

history⇒histogram" module) from the event history that is displayed to its left. The "event history⇒histogram" module takes note of the selected threading field in its input event history and creates a static histogram giving the total time each thread spent in each state. It also notes the color, thread order, and cursor customizations specified in its input and translates them as appropriate into customizations in the static histogram that it produces. Thus, it is easy to create an arrangement such as the one in both the top and bottom half of Fig. 11, where a histogram view always shows the same threads (and in the same order) as an associated event-history view, no matter what customizations have been specified in the event history.

Linkage between the different views in Fig. 11 can be controlled by introducing customizations at the appropriate point in the module network. For example, the two event-history displays in Fig. 11 share a common time scale. This can

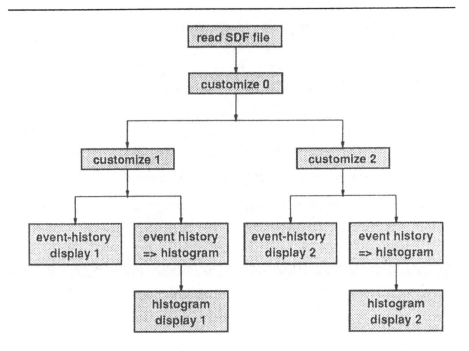

**Fig. 12.** A module network to generate the display in Fig. 11.

be achieved by inserting the **start** and **end** time cursors at "customize 0" in the module network. Any changes in the position of these cursors will automatically propagate to both event-history displays. On the other hand, the two event-history displays use different threading fields. This effect can be achieved by introducing different **"selected threading field"** attributes at "customize 1" and "customize 2." Finally, the views in Fig. 11 display one time cursor (at about time 0.008) and two thread cursors (one relative to the **"task"** threading field and one relative to the **"cpu"** threading field). All of these cursors can be introduced at "customize 0." Since a viewer module will only display threading-field cursors associated with its current threading field, each module automatically selects the right cursor to display. Note in Fig. 11 how the "event history⇒histogram" modules have propagated the threading-field cursors so that the histogram views can also display the thread cursors as lines across their own displays.

## 9    Conclusion

This paper has described an approach to parallel program performance visualization and analysis that is based on identifying the key types of performance data, designing flexible and expressive representations of these types using a self-describing file format, and implementing "smart" analysis and visualization modules that can use the self-describing nature of their input to provide good default behaviors and user-friendly customization facilities. While it is already possible to give some interesting demonstrations using the Vista prototype, it still needs more work before it becomes a serious performance-analysis tool. Moreover, until Vista can be used for serious work, the real value of its architecture will remain unproven. Therefore, the highest-priority action items involve

1. Building or obtaining enough modules to reach "critical mass" for performance visualization.
2. Optimizing the performance of the modules to the point where they can tackle "industrial strength" performance data sets.
3. Refining and augmenting user-interface components to make the underlying flexibility of the data representations accessible to users.
4. Recruiting users to test Vista and suggest improvements. (There is at least one in-house test user but we will need more than that.)

When these issues have been addressed, we will be able to evaluate the basic hypothesis that defining a rich enough data representation makes it possible to build generic, user-friendly modules that are actually useful for processing performance data. It would also be interesting to see whether a generic framework of this type attracts vendors and the research community to contribute additional plug-compatible modules, creating a richer set of performance tools over time. There is a large collection of user-contributed AVS modules, so there is some precedent to suggest that a phenomenon like this could occur.

Finally, the experience of using Vista for serious work will shed light on a whole spectrum of design questions, ranging from identifying needed optimizations to clarifying whether a graphical data-flow graph editor or some other technique will be the most effective way to help users assemble module graphs.

## 10   Acknowledgments

The prototype Vista implementation would not be what it is without the substantial contributions made by Manojith Padala during the summer of 1994.

## References

1. Heath, M., and J. Etheridge, "Visualizing the Performance of Parallel Programs," *IEEE Software 8:5*, Sept. 1991, pp. 29–39.
2. Herrarte, V., and E. Lusk, *Studying Parallel Program Behavior with* Upshot, Technical Report ANL-91/15, Argonne National Laboratory, Argonne, Illinois, U.S.A., 1991.
3. Klinker, G., "An Environment for Telecollaborative Data Exploration," *IEEE Visualization '93*, San Jose, California, Oct. 1993.

4. Klinker, G., et al., *Scientific Data Exploration Meets Telecollaboration*, Technical Report CRL 94/6, Cambridge Research Lab, Digital Equipment Corp., June 1994.

5. Malony, A., D. Hammerslag, and D. Jablonowski, "Traceview: A Trace Visualization Tool," *IEEE Software 8:5*, Sept. 1991, pp. 19–28.

6. Miller, B., M. Clark, J. Hollingsworth, S. Kierstead, S.-S. Lim, and T. Torzewski, "IPS-2: The Second Generation of a Parallel Program Measurement System," *IEEE Trans. on Parallel and Distributed Systems 1:2*, April 1990, pp. 206–217.

7. Ousterhout, J., *Tcl and the Tk Toolkit*, Addison-Wesley, 1994.

8. Reed, D., R. Olson, R. Aydt, T. Madhyastha, T. Birkett, D. Jensen, B. Nazief, and B. Totty, "Scalable Performance Environments for Parallel Systems," *Sixth Distributed Memory Computing Conference* (IEEE), April 1991.

9. Reed, D., R. Aydt, T. Madhyastha, R. Noe, K. Shields, and B. Schwartz, *The Pablo Performance Analysis Environment*, Technical Report, Dept. of Computer Science, University of Illinois, Urbana, Illinois, November 1992.

10. Upson, C., T. Faulhaber, D. Kamins, D. Laidlaw, D. Schlegel, J. Vroom, R. Gurwitz, and A. van Dam, "The Application Visualization System: A Computational Environment for Scientific Visualization," *IEEE Computer Graphics and Applications 9:4*, July 1989, pp. 30–42.

# A Performance Debugger for Parallel Logic Programming Language Fleng

Junichi Tatemura[t], Hanpei Koike[t], Hidehiko Tanaka[t]
{tatemura@sak.iis,{koike,tanaka@mtl.t}}.u-tokyo.ac.jp

[t]Institute of Industrial Science, University of Tokyo,
7-22-1 Roppongi, Minato-ku Tokyo, 106 JAPAN
Phone : +81-3-3402-6231, FAX: +81-3-3402-5078.
[t]Faculty of Engineering, University of Tokyo

## 1 Introduction

For practical parallel computers to come into wide use, it is important that they execute practical application programs efficiently. This is why we need programming techniques and environments to develop high-performance parallel programs.

We propose a method of performance debugging for a parallel logic program, and describe our performance debugger. Performance debugging a parallel program is very difficult because execution of the program is regarded as enormous and complicated information. Since performance data on a parallel machine results from many various factors, it is necessary to analyze performance into these factors.

Our approach has two stages: "performance debugging" to improve inherent parallelism of a program, and "performance tuning" to make partitioning / scheduling of the program suitable for a particular environment. Dealing with these stages separately makes the problem of performance clear, and improves portability of a program. The first stage is an essential task of a programmer using a parallel programming language, since the main purpose of parallel programming, instead of parallelizing a sequential program, is to describe parallelism. To support a programmer on the first stage, we developed a performance debugger for a parallel logic program.

Our performance debugger helps a programmer to find unexpected sequentiality. It consists of a performance profiler to comprehend performance of a program, and a dataflow tracer to analyze sequentiality of a program. They visualize execution history recorded on an ideal environment where inherent parallelism of a program is fully extracted.

In this paper, we describe the method and tools of performance debugging. Then we give an example and show the improvement of actual performance on a parallel machine PIE64.

# 2 Parallel Programming in a Committed-Choice Language

## 2.1 Committed-Choice Language Fleng

Committed-Choice Languages (CCLs) such as Guarded Horn Clauses (GHC) ,Concurrent Prolog and PARLOG are parallel logic programming languages which introduce a control primitive "guard" for synchronization. Fleng [1] is a CCL designed in our laboratory. We are developing the Parallel Inference Engine PIE64 [2] which executes Fleng programs. Fleng is a simpler language than other CCLs ; Fleng has no guard goal, and only the head realizes the guard mechanism.

A Fleng program is a set of horn clauses like:

$$H:-B_1,\cdots,B_n.\quad n \geq 0$$

The side to the left of :- is called the *head*, and the right side is called the *body* whose item $B_i$ is called a *body goal*.

Computation of a Fleng program is repetition of rewriting a set of goals in parallel. For each goal, one of the clauses whose head can match with the goal, is selected, and then the goal is rewritten into the body goals. The new goals are added to the set of goals. The execution begins when an initial goal is given and is completed when no goal remains. The rewriting operation is called *reduction*, and the matching operation is called *unification*.

Unification is an algorithm which attempts to substitute values for variables such that two logical terms are made equal. In order to realize communication and synchronization in concurrent logic programs, unification in CCL is divided into two classes : *guarded unification* and *active unification*. Guarded unification is applied in the head part of a clause, and prevents variables in a goal being substituted; such unification is *suspended* until these variables have values. Active unification is applied in the body part of a clause and is able to substitute values for variables of goals. Thus, a clause in a Fleng program defines control flows through *goal reduction* and data flows through *active / guarded unification*.

## 2.2 Optimization of CCL Programs

A CCL program only defines relationship among control flows (goal reduction) and data flows (read / write operations on a single-assignment variable) without declaring explicitly where or when these operations are executed. Therefore, "annotations"[3] or "pragmas"[7] can be added to the program in order to specify where processes and data are assigned to and priority or partial order of operations. Under this flexibility of execution of a CCL program, the following techniques on compilation and implementation have been researched.

- static load partitioning (assignment of processes and data) with inter-process communication restrained [3].
- extraction and execution of sequential threads with data-flow analysis [5][8].

- dynamic and static choice between parallel and sequential execution adapted to a state of a machine [6].
- optimization of sending and receiving data with mode-type analysis [9].
- scheduling with priority, and dynamic load distribution / balancing on a parallel management kernel [4].

If two goals are known to be executed in sequence, overhead due to parallel execution is reduced and optimization techniques for a sequential program can be appliedd.

Proper sequentialization with the optimization described above reduces the costs of surplus parallelism. On the other hand, no optimizing parallel compiler can speedup execution of a program which has little inherent parallelism. In such cases, a programmer should re-design the algorithm of the program.

### 2.3 Performance-conscious Parallel Programming

A CCL is designed to describe parallelism, and this parallelism can be fully extracted from the CCL program. However, whether original parallelism of a problem can be extracted depends on how a programmer describes the problem. Therefore, a programmer should design parallel programs taking account of their performance.

There are other ways to make use of parallel machines; parallelization of a sequential program and generating parallel programs from specifications. However, these methods also can improve performance only within the limit of the given sequential programs or specifications. Thus, it is an essential problem to describe a program taking account of the performance.

Programming a high-performance parallel program is a different technique from sequential programming. We need much more experience of parallel programming to establish programming techniques, algorithms, and libraries. A parallel programming environment is now necessary to support parallel programmers.

## 3 Past Performance Tuning Tools

To help a programmer to enhance performance of a parallel program, some tools have been developed ; profiling tools which summarize performance data grouped by places of a source code [10], and tracing tools which visualize events of each process in order of their timestamps [11][12].

However these performance tuning tools deal with performance data, which results from many various factors of performance, as it is. It becomes very difficult to find a cause of bad performance in such data, when we deal with enormous and complicated information on execution of a highly parallel program. Therefore, we consider it is necessary to analyze performance into various factors and to search a cause of bad performance with a clear policy.

# 4 Method of Performance Debugging

Our approach to develop high-performance parallel programs has two stages :

- description of parallelism
  to improve inherent parallelism of a program — sequentiality is reduced.
- mapping processes and data
  to make partitioning / scheduling of the program suitable for a particular
  environment — proper sequentialization is applied.

In this paper, we call the first task *"performance debugging"* and the second task
*"performance tuning"*. Although these stages influence each other, dealing with
them separately makes the problem of performance clear. On the first stage,
a performance debugger is used to modify an algorithm of a program. On the
second stage, partitioning / scheduling of the program is optimized with a performance tuner, an optimizing compiler, and a mechanism of optimum execution
on a run-time system as described in the section 2.2.

We have developed a performance debugger to be used on the first stage.
The performance debugger helps programmers to find unexpected sequentiality
and to improve parallelism of a program.

# 5 Performance Debugging Tools

## 5.1 Requirements of Functions

Since information on execution of a parallel program is enormous and complicated, it is necessary to comprehend performance of a program as the first task
of performance debugging. A performance debugger is required to show the information on the performance summary, and to help a programmer to extract
a part of the program which makes the performance worse.

After extracting the part of the program, the programmer analyzes the relation among control and data flows and finds unnecessary sequentiality which
causes the bad performance. A performance debugger needs to support the analysis of sequentiality.

Our performance debugger consists of a performance profiler to comprehend
performance of a program, and a dataflow tracer to analyze sequentiality of a
program.

## 5.2 Virtual Time Stamps

Our performance debugger deals with inherent parallelism of a program, before
tuning partitioning / scheduling of the program. Therefore, we introduce a virtual time stamp to the performance debugger : the time stamp is recorded on
an ideal environment where any executable goal is executed immediately (that
is, there are enough processors and bandwidth of the network).

# 6 Performance Profiler

The performance profiler shows the information on performance of a program summarily. It displays time - parallelism diagrams for any part of the execution of the program.

Figure 1 is a display of the performance profiler. The upper part of the window shows time - parallelism diagrams, and the lower part shows a computation tree diagram which represents control flow of the execution. The horizontal axis of each diagram represents virtual time. When a node of the tree diagram is clicked with a mouse, the corresponding goal is selected and displayed on the window. Then, if "select" button is pushed down, a time-parallelism diagram is displayed for the process with respect to this goal. If "dftrace" button is pushed down, a dataflow tracer for the process is opened.

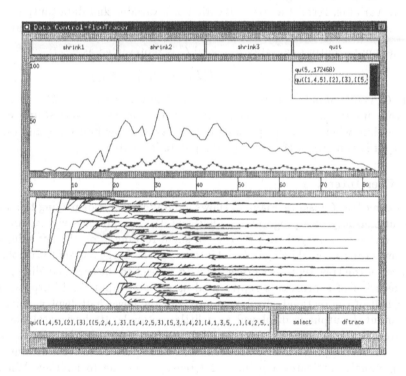

**Fig. 1.** Performance Profiler

Using the performance profiler, a programmer extracts a part of the program which makes the performance worse, and opens a dataflow tracer to analize this part.

# 7 Dataflow Tracer

A dataflow tracer shows graphs composed of control and data flows derived from an execution history of a program. A programmer examines them and removes unnecessary sequentiality by modifying the program.

## 7.1 Input / Output Causality

Execution of CCL program is represented as a history of inputs and outputs and their causality. Since this input / output causality is regarded as a declarative semantics of a CCL program [13], optimizing compilers can not modify this causality automatically without changing the meaning of the program. The dataflow tracer deals with this input / output causality.

Unifications are divided into the following categories to represent inputs and outputs:

- in(Variable, Term) : guarded unification (input)
- out(Variable, Term) : active unification of a variable and data (output)
- unify(Variable$_1$, Variable$_2$) : active unification of two variables (output)

The input / output causality of a goal $G$ is represented as a set:

$$IO(G) = \{io_i | io_i = (\{I_{i1}, \cdots, I_{in}\} \rightarrow O_i)\},$$

where $O_i$ is one of outputs and $I_{i1}, \cdots, I_{in}$ are inputs required by $O_i$.

Every inputs and outputs have virtual time stamps: a time stamp of an input is time when the corresponding data is read for the first time, and one of an output is time when the corresponding data is written.

## 7.2 User Interface

*Visualizing I/O Causality* Figure 2 shows a dataflow tracer displaying the input /output causality of a program. The horizontal axis represents virtual time. A tree diagram is displayed with its root (a small rectangle) on the left side, and represents the root goal being reduced into two goals. Large rectangles, displayed as leaves of the tree, represent processes with respect to the corresponding goals.

Execution of a process is represented as a set of inputs and outputs. The upper half of the rectangle displays inputs and the lower half displays outputs. Each input / output is displayed as a little rectangle. Its horizontal position indicates its virtual time (and its vertical position is picked arbitrarily to avoid too much overlapping of lines between the rectangles). A line connecting two little rectangles indicates a pointer (reference) from one to another. When a rectangle is pointed with a mouse cursor, the details of the input / output is displayed, and inputs and outputs which have relation to the input / output are highlighted.

A process with respect to a goal can be replaced with a sub-tree which root is the goal and which leaves are processes with respect to its sub-goals. This function enables a user to zoom in on the inside of the process, and to locate a performance bug.

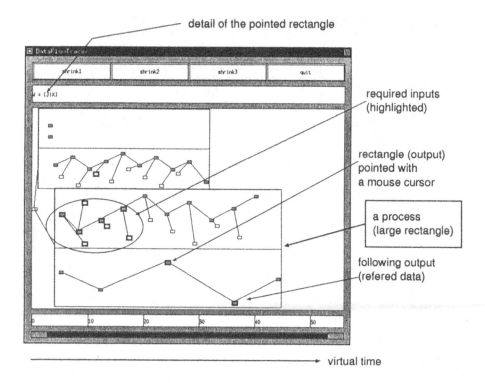

**Fig. 2.** Dataflow Tracer

*Tracing Dataflow* The dataflow tracer provides a tracing window which is opened when any input / output is clicked. This window is used to trace the following four types of dataflow relationship with an output (input):

- an input/output which has a pointer to the output (input),
- an input/output to which the output (input) has a pointer,
- an input which receives data from the output (an output which sends data to the input),
- an input required by the output (an output which requires the input).

Figure 3 shows the tracing window. The current data is displayed in the center of the window. Four sub-windows display inputs and outputs which have relation to the current data. When a mouse cursor points one of these data, the corresponding rectangle on the process is highlighted. Selecting one of the data, a programmer can traverse the dataflow relationship. The tracks of the traverse is represented as bold lines on the display of the dataflow tracer (Figure 4).

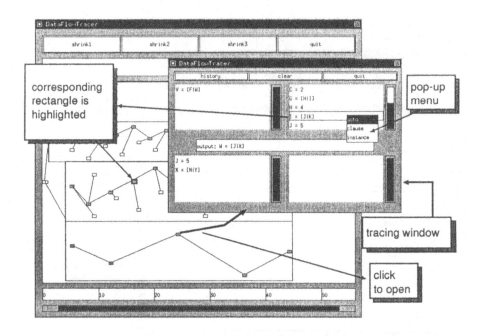

**Fig. 3.** Tracing Dataflow (1)

# 8 Example

## 8.1 Problem for Example

We take up a program to solve " best-path problem" as an example of performance debugging. This program searches the shortest paths from a node to the other nodes on the directed graph. The algorithm to solve this problem is as follows:

> A goal "searcher" traces the graph and searches a path from the node to the other nodes. A searcher on a node creates new searchers for the every next nodes. Each searcher calculates cost from the start to the current node, and reports it to a goal "evaluator". The goal "evaluator" manages a record of the shortest paths. When the evaluator receives a report from a searcher, it checks if the cost breaks a record.

A searcher sends a message to the evaluator with stream-based communication. Streams from searchers to the evaluator could be independent of each other. However, the example program has the following performance bug:

> Streams from searchers to the evaluator have sequential relation (see Figure 5).

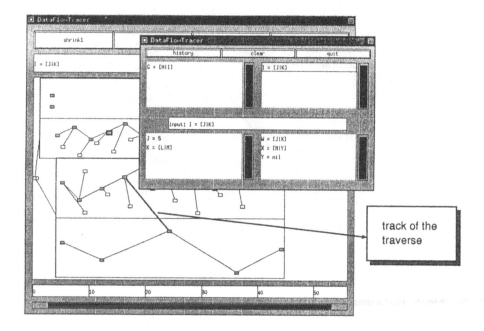

**Fig. 4.** Tracing Dataflow (2)

Although this program solves the problem correctly, this sequentiality makes the performance worse.

## 8.2 Scenario of Debugging

In figure 6, a performance profiler displays two time-parallelism diagrams: one is for the whole part of the program and the other is for the evaluator. The diagram for the evaluator is now highlighted (dotted with black points). The parallelism of the whole part is almost always 1. Since sometimes the evaluator is not working, searchers and the evaluator are considered to run by turns.

A dataflow tracer is opened to examine the dataflow relationship between the searcher and the evaluator (Figure 7). The upper and lower rectangles on the window indicate the evaluator and the searcher respectively. The relation about queries and answers between their processes is shown as bold lines. When the evaluator receives a message from a searcher, it checks the record of paths and replys to the searcher. Since the evaluator has an interval between tasks of answering queries, the searcher is considered as a bottleneck.

In Figure 8, the searcher process is replaced by its sub-processes. Two searchers communicate to the evaluator. The lower searcher sends a message on the left side of the rectangle and receive a message on the right side. The interval between them is much longer than the response time of the evaluator. This delay

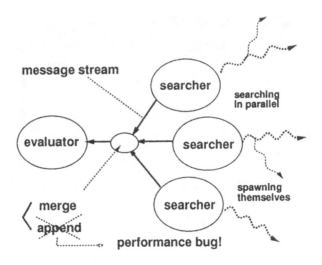

**Fig. 5.** Performance bug of the best-path program

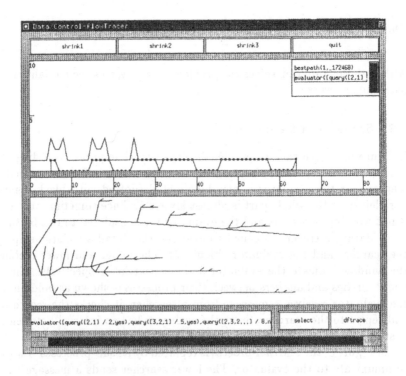

**Fig. 6.** Time-parallelism Diagram (1)

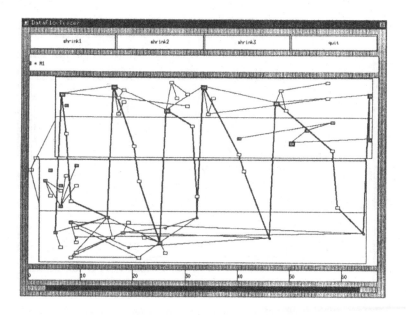

**Fig. 7.** Communication between evaluator and searcher (1)

occurs because the message from the searcher is not given to the evaluator before the other searcher completes its communication with the evaluator.

A new program is given by removing the performance bug found here. In the program, the streams of the searchers are joined together by "merge". The evaluator has no restriction on the order of receiving messages from two separate searchers.

Figure 9 shows the performance of the new program. The parallelism is enhanced, and the total time is reduced. Figure 10 is a dataflow tracer opened to display the communication between the evaluator and searchers. This indicates that tasks of responding queries are overlapped.

## 8.3 Results

The programs take the virtual time on the performance debugger and the actual time on PIE64 as follows.

| program | virtual [generation] | actual [msec] |
|---|---|---|
| original | 830 | 282 |
| improved | 106 | 40 |

The programs solve best paths for 8 nodes, and were executed by the interpreter on PIE64 (using 12 processors). The interpreter made use of the automatic load-balancing mechanism of PIE64, and no static optimization was applied.

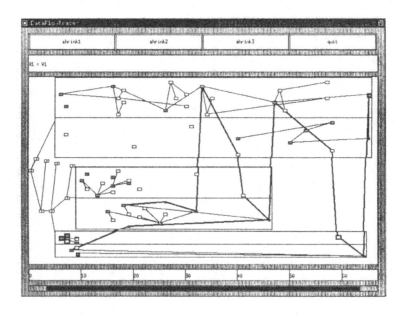

**Fig. 8.** Relation among messages from searchers

The speedups of the programs are measured as Figure 11. The speedup of the improved program exceeds the linear speedup when the number of processors is small, because the amount of queries from searchers depends on their scheduling. Since the searchers of the original program send queries sequentially and search paths in a depth-first fashion, many records are broken by following messages.

## 9 Related Work

Paragraph [14] is one of performance debugging / tuning tools for CCL programs. This tool gathers various performance data of each processor and provides three-dimensional statistics ( with "what", "where", and "when" axes) to a user graphically.

While our performance debugger deals with inherent parallelism and amount of computation of a program, Paragraph mainly helps to design algorithms on load distribution. These tools take charge of the two stages to improve performance of a parallel program: "description of parallelism" and "mapping processes and data", respectively.

## 10 Future Works

We have the following subjects as future works.

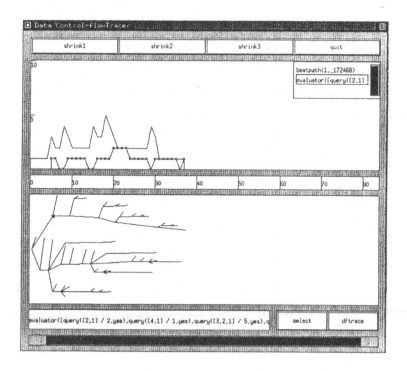

**Fig. 9.** Time-parallelism Disgram (2)

## 10.1 System Integration

- visualizing performance data in actual time
  Our performance debugger visualizes performance data in virtual time to show inherent parallelism of a program. Visualizing actual performance data, the debugger will able to show the effect of performance debugging, and to be applied to performance tuning to optimize partitioning and scheduling.
- integration with an optimizing compiler
  Our debugger only takes charge of the first stage of developing a high-performance parallel program. We must evaluate the effects of performance debugging in cooperation with an optimizing compiler as a total system.
- integration with a *"logical"* debugger
  We have developed a debugger HyperDEBU [15] for *logical* bugs. Although HyperDEBU and the performance debugger visualize execution history of control and data flow, their policies differ from each other: (1) HyperDEBU visualizes the execution dynamically (at runtime) to enable interactive examination of erroneous behavior, (2) HyperDEBU omits timestamps from the history to let a user concentrate logical relationships among read/write operations. However, since they could share some of their finctions and informations, cooperation of logial and performance debuggers is a considerable future work.

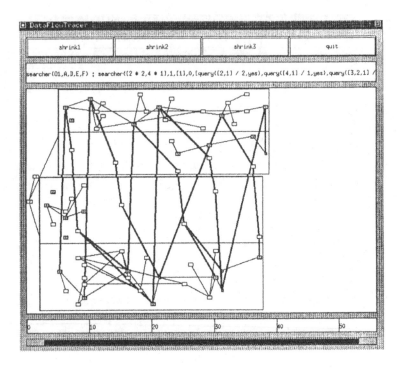

**Fig. 10.** Communication between evaluator and searcher (1)

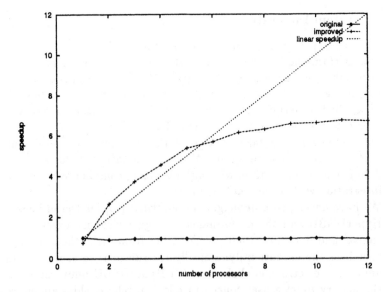

**Fig. 11.** Speedups of the programs

## 10.2 Scalability

The current version of the dataflow tracer is not applicable to realistically large applications (for example, the performance debugger itself) for the following reasons:

1. [space] The tracer requires the execution history that includes all the goals executed.
2. [time] The algorithm to analyze the dataflow relationship is naive : a bottom-up way which requires I/O causality of all subgoals.
3. [complexity] The dataflow relationship between processes which include large number of goals tends to be too complex.

These problem will be solved with the following future works respectively.

1. Deterministic replay and demand-driven reconstruction of the partial execution history.
2. Static analysis of the source code which provides useful information to calculate I/O causality efficiently.
3. Macroscopic view of dataflow to be provided by the performance profiler (After locating the erroneous core of the global dataflow with the profiler, we can make use of the dataflow tracer to examine it in detail).

## 10.3 Performance Debugging of Scheduling

Our method of performance debugging deals with inherent parallelism and scheduling separately. In execution of some programs, however, scheduling can vary the amount of the computation ("speculative computation" is an example). Performance debugging such programs requires different technique from our method.

# 11 Conclusion

We have developed a performance debugger for a parallel logic program to improve inherent parallelism of a program. This debugger helps programmers to find unexpected sequentiality visualizing execution history in a virtual environment. We demonstrated an example of performance debugging, and showed how the debugger helps to improve performance of a program on a parallel machine PIE64.

# References

1. M. Nilsson, and H. Tanaka : "Massively Parallel Implementation of Flat GHC on the Connection Machine", Proc. of the Int. Conf. on Fifth Generation Computer Systems, p1031-1040 (1988).

2. H. Koike, and H. Tanaka : "Parallel Inference Engine PIE64", Parallel Computer Architecture, bit, Vol.21,No.4,1989, pp.488-497 (in Japanese).

3. Y. Hidaka, H. Koike, J. Tatemura, and H. Tanaka : "A Static Load Partitioning Method Based on Execution Profile for Committed Choice Languages", Proceedings of International Logic Programming Symposium '91, MIT Press, pp. 470-484 (1991).

4. Y. Hidaka, H. Koike, and H. Tanaka : "Architecture of Parallel Management Kernel for PIE64", Proceedings of PARLE'92, LNCS 605, Springer-Verlag, pp.685-700 (1992).

5. H. Nakada, T. Araki, H. Koike, and H. Tanaka : "A Fleng Compiler for PIE64", Proceedings of PACT '94, (1994).

6. H. Nakada, H. Koike, and H. Tanaka : "Static analysis for dynamic granuality control of fleng", IPSJ SIG Notes 94-PRG-18, pp.1-8 (1994) (in Japanese).

7. T. Chikayama : "Operating Sysyem PIMOS and Kernel Language KL1", International Conference on Fifth Generation Computer Systems 1992, pp. 73-88 (1992).

8. K. Ueda, M. Morita : "Message-Oriented Parallel Implementation of Moded Flat GHC", International Conference on Fifth Generation Computer Systems 1992, pp. 799-808 (1992).

9. K. Ohno, H. Nakashima, and S. Tomita : "Optimization of Concurrent Logic Language with Static Analysis", IPSJ SIG Notes 94-PRG-18, pp. 17-24 (1994) (in Japanese).

10. T. E. Anderson and E. D. Lazowska : "Quartz : A Tool for Tuning Pararell Program Performance", ACM SIGMETRIC,1990.

11. R. H. Halstead, Jr. and D. A. Kranz, "A Replay Mechanism for Mostly Functional Parallel Programs", Proc. Int. Symposium on Shared Memory Multiprocessing, 1991.

12. T. Lehr, Z. Segall, D. F. Vrsalovic, E. Caplan, A. L. Chung and E. Fineman, "Visualizing Performance Debugging", IEEE Computer Octover 1989,pp.38-51.

13. M. Murakami : "A Declarative Semantics of Flat Guarded Horn Clause for Programs with Perpetual Processes", Theoret. Comp. Sci, Vol.75 No.1/2, pp. 67-83 (1990).

14. S. Aikawa, M. Kamiko, H. Kubo, F. Matsuzawa, and T. Chikayama : "Paragraph : A Graphical Tuning Tool for Multiprocessor Systems", International Conference on Fifth Generation Computer Systems 1992, pp. 286-293 (1992).

15. J. Tatemura, H. Koike, and H. Tanaka : Control and Data Flow Visualization for Parallel Logic Programs on a Multi-window Debugger HyperDEBU, PARLE '93, pp. 414-425 (1993).

# First Class Continuation Facilities in Concurrent Programming Language Harmony/2

Ken Wakita

Tokyo Institute of Technology, 2-12-1 Meguro-ku, Tokyo 152, Japan
e-mail: wakita@is.titech.ac.jp

**Abstract.** HARMONY/2 is an Actor based object-oriented concurrent programming language. Its novel features include two frameworks of first class continuations, namely method continuations and message continuations. The article addresses the technical difficulty in integration of first class continuation facilities and concurrency models (VST problem) and then proposes two frameworks of first class continuation. Both frameworks prevent VST problem and guarantee system's soundness. Method continuation framework is a variant of traditional first continuation facility with added delayed installation semantics. It allows the safe use of continuations beyond objects' boundary and thus enabling construction of arbitrary control structures in concurrent environment. Message continuation framework is based on the observation that a message represents the continuation after the message sending. History sensitive semantics (one-shot property) and dynamic extent property given to message continuations makes the system free of VST. Two-way characteristics and synchronization semantics enables construction of arbitrary communication structures with high degree of concurrency.

## 1 Introduction

Concurrent object-oriented programming languages provide powerful mechanisms for data abstraction and code reuse through encapsulation, inheritance, delegation and so on. This extensibility in the dimension of data abstraction is one of the reasons for the current popularity of object-oriented programming. They also provide various control structures and communication protocols. However, most of them provide limited (or no) support of control abstraction. This unbalance between extensible data abstraction mechanism and *unextensible* control structures sometimes reduce the programmer's productivity as they have to deal with compound data structures through (unextensible) primitive control structures. Also the resulting program code may not be very readable nor maintainable because the ad hoc implementation of control structures hide the logical structure of the algorithm.

Lack of extensible communication structure becomes a serious problem in concurrent/distributed programming as required communication structures (i.e., multicast, cache, concurrency control, rollback, etc.) differ from an application to another and there is no common set of communication primitives that suffices all the requirements. To program new communication protocol in terms of unextensible communication primitives, the programmer has to modify the interface of every object that participate in the communication at the sacrifice of readability, modularity, and maintainability of the program.

This article tackles the above problem by incorporation of *first-class continuations* in a concurrent object-oriented programming language. The concept of *continuations* is a sound basis in denotational style of semantics theory in understanding control structures of sequential programming languages[Sto77]. Informally, a continuation of an expression is a function that represents *"the rest of the computation that remains to be done after the evaluation of the expression."* With continuations, we can describe the semantics of arbitrary control structures, such as **goto** and **while** statements, exception handling, and so on. A few programming languages provide continuations as first class objects [CR91, AM91]. As a continuation is usable in its indefinite extent, it may be invoked in an arbitrary future time, possibly multiple times. With this flexibility it is possible to realize arbitrary sequential control structures including such dynamic behavior as exception handling, back-tracking and coroutines.

The proposed concurrent object-programming language HARMONY/2 provides two kinds of continuations, which we call *method continuations* and *message continuations*. The former is mainly used for abstraction of sequential control structures and the latter is mainly used for abstraction of communication structures. The key point in the design is *semantic safeness*. We designed the first class continuation facilities not to be too powerful to avoid semantic clash against the underling object-oriented concurrency model. A naive introduction of continuations will cause such flaws as violation of single threadness and possible multiple replies for single message passing (*violation of single threadness problem* or shortly *VST problem*).

Delayed invocation semantics added to method continuation safely eliminates the chance of VST problem. Method continuation framework retains traditional use of first class continuations, thus it allows construction of sophisticated control flow within method definition in a similar manner as traditional continuation programming in Scheme. Moreover, with the added synchronization semantics, the programmer may safely use first class continuations beyond the boundary of objects. Applying the coroutine technique [Wan80], we can control the degree of concurrency of the system [Wak93]. Together with interrupt message, method continuation framework constructs flexible interrupt mechanism of HARMONY/2 (5.1).

Message continuation framework is based on the observation that a message represents the continuation after the message sending. This framework treats messages as representing continuations. History sensitive semantics (*single-shot* property) and *dynamic extent* semantics given to invocation of a message continuation avoids VST problem. Unlike traditional continuations a message continuation represents two kinds of continuations: continuations before and after the evaluation of the message passing expression. This functionality allows the programmer to add pre- and post-action to the message passing. With embedded concurrency and synchronization semantics, the programmer can construct arbitrary communication structures and make the resulting communication structure highly concurrent. Based on this framework, the programmer can embed various communication structure in HARMONY/2 such as, multicast, message transmission monitor, future type message passing (5.2), encrypted messages, concurrent aggregates (5.3), and so on.

The structure of the rest of the article is as follows. Section 2 introduces an object-oriented concurrent programming language HARMONY/2 and identifies the problem of introducing first class continuations in object-oriented concurrent programming languages. Section 3 and section 4 present two continuation frameworks and section 5 shows example uses of them. Section 6 compares the framework with related work and Section 6 concludes the article.

# 2 An Object-Oriented Concurrency Model and Continuations

HARMONY/2 is an object-oriented concurrent programming language designed by the author[Wak93]. The computation model of HARMONY/2 is based on an extension of Actor model[Agh86]. Computation proceeds through message passing between autonomous objects. Serialized acceptance of messages by each object establishes object-wise synchronization. In addition to Actor-like asynchronous message passing, HARMONY/2 supports synchronous message passing as well.

This section explains the concurrent computation model of HARMONY/2 with its syntax and then describes technical difficulty in incorporation of first class continuations in the model.

## 2.1 Concurrency model

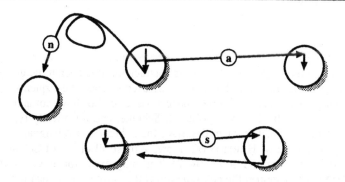

**Fig. 1.** Computation model of HARMONY/2

ⓐsynchronous message passing ⓢynchronous message passing
ⓤpdate of instance variables    ⓝew object

The concurrent environment in HARMONY/2 comprises autonomous *objects* and *messages*. An object has its local state called *instance variables* and local procedures called *methods*. The computation proceeds with message transmission and associated method execution as shown in fig. 1.

*Method Execution:*   In response to a message, an object executes the corresponding method. During the method execution it may perform some of the following actions:

1. Send messages to other actors (ⓐ and ⓢ).
2. Update the instance variables of the object.
3. Create new objects (ⓝ).

*Message Transmission:*   Messages sent to objects are eventually delivered in an indeterminate order (message transmission order is not preserved). Each object repeatedly accepts messages and processes one at a time (processing of messages may not overlap).

HARMONY/2 supports synchronous message passing as well as Actor-like asynchronous message passing. If an object σ sends a message asynchronously (ⓐ in

Fig. 1), method execution continues while the message is delivered to $\tau$. Asynchronous message passing increases the concurrency in the system. If an object ($\sigma'$) sends a message synchronously to another object ($\tau'$, ⓢ), method execution at the sender ($\sigma'$) blocks until $\tau'$ accepts the message and the method execution sends reply back to $\sigma'$. The functionalities of synchronous message passing are synchronization of the sender with the target and communication through reply message.

*Note:* In the concurrency model, each object is concurrency-free (i.e., no two methods execute in the same object) because message acceptance is serialized and no action creates concurrency inside the object. Concurrent languages based on a single thread model include ABCL/1[Yon90], ConcurrentSmalltalk[YT86], Concurrent Aggregates[Chi92], HACL[KY94], ACT1[Agh86], POOL[Ame87], Hybrid[Nie87], and so on. In this sense, Actor model (including HARMONY/2's computation model) is single thread model in contrast with multiple thread model. Examples of multiple thread model are Multilisp, Ada, Concurrent C, among many others. Single threadness imposed by the computation model significantly affected the design of first class continuation framework as will be shown in this section.

## 2.2 HARMONY/2

The computation model described above is abstract and it is open to language designer which sequential programming language to be used to code the sequential part of the model. So far we have designed three dialects based on the above computation model, which are based on Standard ML [Wak93], Scheme, and a statically typed Lisp-like language (Harmony/ST). The paper describes the Scheme based language.

The core language of HARMONY/2 allows almost all entity of Scheme language to appear within the method body (fig. 2). The only exception is call-with-current-continuation which captures the continuation at the point of its invocation.

The syntax and semantics of HARMONY/2 can be best understood through an example. The class definition shown in fig. 3 implements a class named Plus which represents mathematical addition operation. An instance of the class has two instance variables named l-exp and r-exp which correspond to the two operands of the plus operator. The class definition involves a definition of initialization method and two methods. Initialization method is automatically executed when an instance is created. Given two arguments, the initialization method initialize the two instance variables to them, respectively. The expression [ivar := exp] denotes assignment to the instance variable. Format method formats the representation in a prefix notation and calc method evaluates the represented expression. If the method execution originates in synchronous message passing, Reply expression takes an expression and sends its evaluation result to the sender of the message as reply. Reply expression may be executed multiple times in a method execution but only the first one takes effect and the rest are simply ignored. In case of asynchronous message passing Reply has no effect except for evaluation of its argument.

A new instance of the class is created with New expression. New expression requires class name and optionally more values. The supplied arguments are passed to the initialization method (if any). Evaluation of New expression, invokes the initialization method *asynchronously* and immediately results in a reference to the newly created object. The example creates an object tree that represents a mathematical expression "$3 \times 3 + 4 \times 4$" and returns the string value, "(+ (* 3 3) (* 4 4)) -> 25".

⟨expression⟩ ≡ ⟨Scheme expression⟩
| (Class ⟨class name⟩ ((ivar)*)  {Class definition}
      (Initial ((⟨arg⟩)*) ⟨expression⟩*)  {Initialization method definition}
      (Method ((⟨method name⟩ ⟨arg⟩*)  {Method definitions}
          ⟨expression⟩*)*)
| [⟨ivar⟩ := ⟨Hexp⟩]  {Assignment}
| [⟨target⟩ <= ⟨method⟩ ⟨Hexp⟩*]  {Asynchronous message passing}
| [⟨target⟩ <== ⟨method⟩ ⟨Hexp⟩*]  {Synchronous message passing}
| [reply ⟨Hexp⟩]  {Reply}

**Fig. 2.** Syntax of HARMONY/2

```
(Class Plus (l-exp r-exp)
  (Initial (e1 e2) [l-exp := e1] [r-exp := e2])
  (Method (format)
    [reply (string-append "(+ " [l-exp <== format]
                              [r-exp <== format] ")")])
  (Method (calc)
    [reply (+ [l-exp <== calc] [r-exp <== calc])])))

(let ((exp [New Plus [New Times 3 3] [New Times 4 4]]))
  (string-append [exp <== format]
                 " -> " [exp <== calc]))
```

**Fig. 3.** An implementation of addition expression and its use

## 2.3  Conflict between concurrency model and first class continuations

When enhancing a programming language with a new language construct, the designer must be careful so that the new language construct does not change the semantics of the original programming language or at least minimize such change.

In the context of parallel Lisp, semantic conflict between the future construct and the behavior of continuation invocation has already been pointed out in several literatures. R. H. Halstead, Jr. states in [RHH89] that:

> A major hurdle in defining a continuation mechanism for a language including future is the clash between the multiple-use potential of continuations and the "resolve once" character of futures.

Several researchers approach this problem by modifying the semantics of continuation and/or future construct [RHH89].

In the context of concurrent object-oriented model, the multiple-use potential of continuations conflicts with the single thread nature of the objects. We call this flaw *violation of single threadness* problem or shortly *VST problem*.

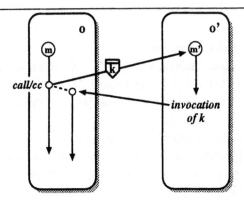

**Fig. 4.** An illustration of violation of single threadness

```
(define (continuation) (call/cc (lambda (k) k)))

(Class VST ()
  (method (foo)
    (let ((k (continuation)))
      [reply k])))    ;; Send the continuation as reply

(let* ((o (New VST))
       (k [o <== foo]))  ;; Foo returns the continuation.
  (k 'dummy))             ;; Invoke the continuation.
```

**Fig. 5.** A simple example that may exhibit VST problem

The essential source of the flaw is the fact that a continuation ($k$) created by a method execution ($m$) at an object ($o$) maybe exported to other object ($o'$) and the continuation may be invoked well after the method execution terminates (Fig. 4). It may be the case that invocation of the continuation takes place at $o'$ while another method ($m$) is running at $o$. In this case the invocation violates single threadness of $o$ because this results in two methods ($m'$ and the continuation, $k$) are running.

The code shown in fig. 5 would be the simplest example of VST problem. Suppose here that call/cc is given the standard semantics as defined in [CR91]: it packages the current continuation and passes it to the unary function given as the argument of call/cc. The method foo simply replies the continuation of the method execution of itself.

For safe incorporation of first class continuations in a concurrent programming model, modified version of first class continuations is required. Below we review three possible design schemes of continuations focusing on the restriction on the use of continuation that originates in a single thread part of the program. The three schemes are *don't-use scheme*, *don't-export scheme*, and *no-restriction scheme*. They are presented in restrictive to less restrictive order.

*Don't-use scheme:* A simple but too conservative scheme is to prohibit the creation of first class continuations inside single thread part of the program. This scheme does not make sense for single thread models. However it is useful for multiple thread models because invocation of continuations that originate in multiple threads part is allowed.

*Don't-export scheme:* We can relax the don't-use scheme scheme to allow creation of first class continuations inside the single thread part but restrict its use only inside the same single thread part. Though sending a continuation with message and replying a continuation are prohibited, this scheme is useful for single thread concurrency model because the programmer can use the continuations within method definitions to establish arbitrary control structures in a similar way as traditional continuation programming techniques. With object-oriented concurrent programming languages, where encapsulation prohibits information sharing between objects, we can statically detect export of continuation at compile time.

*No-restriction scheme:* This scheme allows export of a first class continuations. Consequently, a first class continuation that originates inside a single thread part may be invoked from outside. If the continuation is invoked when a thread is running in the single thread part where the continuation originates, invocation must synchronize with the thread execution.

Both method continuation and message continuation frameworks are categorized in this scheme. Method continuation framework achieves the required synchronization through delayed invocation semantics. Message continuation framework incorporates history sensitiveness in its invocation semantics and dynamically change the semantics of full continuation to dynamic extent one in order to eliminates the chance of VST.

## 3 Method Continuations

The section reviews the semantics of first class continuation facilities in Scheme and then proposes the method continuation which is a continuation mechanism with delayed installation semantics.

### 3.1 First class continuations in Scheme

With Scheme the continuation is obtained by a call to a function named call-with-current-continuation, which casually is abbreviated to call/cc. Call/cc is a function that accepts a unary function ($f$). Upon its invocation, call/cc packages the continuation of itself ($k$) and applies $f$ to $k$. The language specification of Scheme[CR91] defines a denotational definition of call/cc as follows (here we omit semantics related to type checking and memory allocation in favor of brevity):

$$cwcc = \lambda \varepsilon \kappa \sigma . \varepsilon (\lambda \varepsilon' \kappa' . \kappa \varepsilon') \kappa$$

where, $\varepsilon$ denotes the unary function ($f$) given as the argument to call/cc, $\kappa$ denotes the continuation of call/cc, and $\sigma$ denotes the environment where the application of call/cc takes place. The continuation is packaged up as a first class object in a form of a function ($\lambda \varepsilon' \kappa . \kappa \varepsilon'$) which upon the invocation replaces its continuation ($\kappa'$) with that of call/cc ($\kappa$).

The simplest use of call/cc would be an application to an identity function (i.e., (call/cc (lambda (k) k))) which evaluates to the continuation of call/cc.

As a more sophisticated example, we describe, in terms of Scheme primitives, the behavior of call/cc (fig. 6). Note that the code introduces intended redundancy to make the difference between the semantic object (k) and its representation cob explicit.[1] This definition is extended to define the behavior of method continuations in fig. 7.

---

[1] The code can be $\eta$-reduced to: (define (cwcc f) (f (call/cc (lambda (k) k))))

```
(define (cwcc f)
  (letrec ((k (call/cc (lambda (k) k)))
           (cob (lambda (v) (k v))))
    (f cob))))
```

**Fig. 6.** A description of the behavior of call/cc

## 3.2 Delayed installation of continuations

Traditional continuations have *immediate installation* semantics: a continuation installs itself and becomes active immediately after its invocation. Though it is safe to regard every part of *sequential* programming languages as single thread, VST problem does not occur due to system-wide single threadness of the sequentiality: invocation of a continuation gives life back to a saved continuation but there is no other thread running and thus the invocation conflicts with no other thread.

As mentioned in 2.3, this is not the case with a concurrent programming languages that provide single threadness. The source of VST problem is the possibility of a continuation being exported out of a single thread part and invoked from outside. To avoid concurrent execution of the invoked continuation and the possibly running thread in the single thread part, the two threads must synchronize.

Delayed installation is a mechanism that properly achieves this synchronization. When a continuation that originates in a single thread part is invoked from outside, the continuation waits until no other thread is running inside the single thread part. Note that continuation invocation performed from inside the single thread part does not need this synchronization from the same reason as invocation in sequential languages, which have immediate invocation semantics.

## 3.3 Implementation of delayed installation

The synchronization semantics of delayed invocation semantics can be efficiently implemented utilizing serialized message acceptance of HARMONY/2. Fig. 7 implements a variant of cwcc named call/mth-f with added delayed installation semantics. Its interface is the same as that of call/cc. Upon invocation, it saves the name of the object that is executing call/cc and then packages the continuation (k) as a continuation object named cob, which is passed to the unary function ($f$) given as the argument of call/mth-c.

If the method continuation is invoked from the same object as where it originates, the test of if expression evaluates to true and installation of the continuation takes place as in traditional semantics. If, on the other hand, the method continuation is invoked from another object, the continuation and the value ($k$ and $v$, respectively) are sent, via a message, to the object where the method continuation originates. We assume that a method Fire-cont is commonly defined for all the classes. It simply installs the continuation. Serialized message acceptance properly realizes required synchronization of delayed installation. An example use of method continuations are presented in section 5.

## 4  Message Continuations

A message continuation framework is another first class continuation framework incorporated in HARMONY/2. The design is based on the observation that a message takes the

```
(define (call/mth-c f)
  (let ((k (call/cc (lambda (k) k)))
        (obj (current-object)))
    (let ((cob (lambda (v)
                 (if (eq? (current-object) obj)
                     (k v)
                     [obj <== Fire-cont k v]))))
      (f cob))))

(Class AnyObject (...)
  ...
  (Method (Fire-cont k v) (k v))
  ...)
```

**Fig. 7.** An implementation of method continuation facilities.

role of continuation in object-oriented programming languages. Message continuations proved useful in extending the concurrent programming language in the dimension of communication structures in the similar manner as traditional first class continuations give extensibility in the dimension of control structures.

To avoid VST problem, a history sensitive semantics (*one-shot* property) is given for the invocation of message continuations. Unlike traditional continuation facilities, a message continuation models two kinds of continuation: the rest of computation starting from passing the message up to reply sending and the rest of computation after sending the reply for the message, which we call *before-* and *after-continuation*, respectively. To make message continuations useful in describing various communication structures, operations on a message continuation is given concurrency and synchronization semantics.

### 4.1 Design Considerations

| Entities in OOPL | Entities in Functional PL |
|---|---|
| Class | → Function definition |
| Instance variable | → Local variable of a function |
| Method | → Local variable of a function |
| Object | → Function |
| Message passing | → Function application |
| Message | → Function application + Continuation |

**Fig. 8.** Similarity between object-oriented and functional programming paradigm

It would be fruitful to start from the idea behind the message continuation framework: there is a good mapping between object-oriented programming paradigm and functional programming paradigm. We can map the essential entities in object-oriented programming to those in functional programming (fig. 8): an object to a function, an instance variable and a method to lexical variables (where the latter is bound to functional values), and message passing to function application.

Furthermore, we can regard a transmitted message as a continuation of a function application. In fact, a message contains all the information needed to construct the *rest of the computation* of message passing: which object the reply should be passed to and the sender's continuation. Moreover, a message carries the information to construct the *subcomputation performed through processing of the message*: which object the message is sent to and which method to be invoked.

Based on the above consideration, message continuation framework of HARMONY/2 was designed. HARMONY/2 provides facilities to treat messages as first class citizen and thus provides the way to handle continuations in terms of messages. Note through out the article the terms "message continuation" and "first class message" are used interchangeably.

There are many possible choices in the design of message continuation framework. However, naive introduction of first class messages will demonstrate VST problem. Suppose a method execution performs a synchronous message passing and the first class representation of the message (= the message continuation) is obtained. Reactivation of the first class message proceeds to message delivery, method invocation, and reply sending, which in turn result in invocation of the sender's continuation. Consequently, multiple reactivation of the same message continuation results in multiple invocation of the sender's continuation and thus may cause multiple threads to run at the sender object, which is against the single threadness (VST problem!).

There are two possible solutions for the VST problem shown above: incorporation of delayed invocation semantics or disallow multiple invocation of a message continuation. We took the latter approach (one-shot continuation) in favor of single-message-single-reply basis. Note that the first invocation of the message continuation never shows VST problem because the sender blocks until it receives reply from for (synchronous) message sending and also the serialized acceptance scheme does not allow processing of another message during blocking of the sender. The one-shot property of the continuation is provided via history sensitive semantics that changes the continuation to dynamic extent continuation.

## 4.2 Message continuation framework

The framework comprises two parts: (1) conversion of a message into its first class representation and (2) use of the message continuation. We call the former *message conversion*. The programmer has access to the first class message via three operations, namely *activation, forced reply*, and *copy*.

Fig. 9 depicts a rough sketch of the framework. When message conversion takes place, a message $(m)$ is converted to its first class representation $(\mu)$ and sent to an object $(\chi)$. The object accepts the first class message and accesses it via a special method called Cont.

Fire operation turns the first class message into a message $(m')$ and thus the rest of message sending resumes, reply operation given a reply value sends the reply to the original sender $(\sigma)$, and copy makes a copy of the first class message.

We call the object, $\chi$, the *communicator* of message conversion because Cont method can add arbitrary communication protocols to the message passing of $m$. For instance,

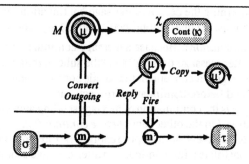

**Fig. 9.** Message continuation framework

the communicator can send first class messages to a priority queue to realize a priority based message acceptance scheme. Another example is multicast: the communicator makes copies of the message continuation and activates them retargetting them to the designated objects.

### 4.3 Message conversion

To incorporate message conversion, we extended message passing syntax to provide a way to specify message conversion on particular message sending:

⟨Hexp⟩ ≡ ⟨Sexp⟩ | ...
     | (⟨target⟩ ⟨communicator⟩ <= ⟨method⟩ ⟨Hexp⟩*)
     | (⟨target⟩ ⟨communicator⟩ <== ⟨method⟩ ⟨Hexp⟩*)

When either of these expressions are evaluated, a first class message ($\mu$) is created. The first class message contains all the information that a message carries, such as the destination of the message, the method selector, arguments to the method, the mode of the message sending (either asynchronous or synchronous). If the message conversion corresponds to synchronous message passing, the first class message contains the reference to the sender, which is used as the destination of the reply for the message. The first class message, is represented as an instance of Message class which is one of the built-in classes of HARMONY/2. The first class message is delivered by a newly created message ($M$) to the specified in ⟨communicator⟩ object ($\chi$).

Because the method selector of the message $M$ is assigned to Cont, $M$ invokes the unary method named Cont of $\chi^2$. Note that the first class message ($\mu$) is bound to the formal argument of Cont and thus can be manipulated upon its execution.

### 4.4 Primitive operations on message continuations

Semantics of message continuations are given through three operations defined for them. They are implemented as primitive methods defined for Message class. Three

---

[2] HARMONY/2 has more sophisticated naming mechanism and pattern matching features but we will only give an outline in this article. These features are discussed in another literature[Wak94]

important issues concerning the design of message continuation semantics are (1) after- and before-continuations, (2) one-shot property, and (3) asynchronous installation.

*After- and before-continuation:* Because a message continuation models both "the rest of the continuation after message passing" and "the subcomputation performed through processing of the message", it convenient to provide both as handles for the programmer. We call them after- and before-continuation, respectively.

*After-continuation* is the continuation of message sending and thus can be regarded as traditional continuation. On the other hand, *before continuation* is a partial continuation starting from message delivery up to reply sending. Before-continuation connected to after-continuation constructs a full continuation after message sending. Two operations, fire and reply, correspond to installation of before- and after-continuation, respectively.

*One-shot property:* To protect the system from VST problem, one-shot property is given to the semantics of message continuations. In terms of before- and after-continuations, one-shot property can be interpreted as *"an after-continuation is invoked at most once."* To achieve this property a *history sensitive semantics* is given to invocation of after-continuations. The idea is simply replacing after-continuation with the identity function when the after-continuation is invoked (either with fire or reply).

After this replacement takes place, after-continuation loses its full continuation character and thus protects the system from VST problem. The effect of reply operation (whose meaning is invocation of after-continuation, which became identity) is nullified. The behavior of fire operation whose meaning is to pass the result of invocation of the before-continuation to after-continuation (which became identity) becomes functional invocation of the before-continuation.

It is sometimes desirable to have an access to the before-continuation. Two typical cases are addition of post-action after the method execution and interception of the reply being passed to the after-continuation. The third primitive, copy, is for this purpose. It creates a copy of the message continuation whose after-continuation being replaced with the identity function.

*Asynchronous installation:* The last concern is concurrency and synchronization semantics given to three operations. In sequential programming languages, installation of continuations results in replacement of the current continuation with the specified continuation. This design is due to sequentiality. In a concurrent programming languages, we can install a continuation without replacing the current continuation but with creating a new thread of control that installs the continuation. This asynchronous feature can make more use of concurrency inherent in the continuation framework.

In HARMONY/2, we gave the above asynchronous semantics for installation via fire and reply operation if the after-method represents a full continuation. On the other hand, if the after-method is identical with the identity function, the behavior is synchronous as the after-continuation is connected with current continuation.

When we need synchronous behavior when after-continuation is not identity yet, we can have synchronous behavior through the copy of the it because the after-continuation of the copy is always the identity function which will result in synchronous behavior. This technique is found in the implementation of future type communication (5.2).

The behavior of the three primitives are summarized as follows:

**Fire** The fire operation takes no argument. It invokes the before-continuation after replacing the after-continuation with the identity function. Informally, it reactivates the message which the message continuation represents: reactivated message is delivered to the target, executes the method, and sends the reply of the method to the reply destination represented by the after-continuation. If the after-continuation the identity function the result is sent back to the current continuation.

**Reply** The reply invokes the after-continuation feeding its argument ($v$) after replacing the after-continuation with the identity function. Informally, it sends the reply value ($v$) to the reply destination represented by the after-continuation.

**Copy** The copy method takes no argument. It makes a copy of the message continuation with its after-continuation being the identity function. With an optional argument, the programmer can specify the target for the message that the message continuation represents. This functionality allows *retargetting* of the message.

## 5 Examples

### 5.1 Method continuations and interrupt mechanism of HARMONY/2

```
(Class test ()
  (method (Kill k))
  (method (Kill-object k)
    (let ((s (New Binary-Semaphor)))
      [s <== P] [s <== P]))
  (method (Suspend k) [reply k])
  (method (Resume k)
    (do-something) (k 'continue)))
```

**Fig. 10.** Four Interrupt scheme programmed with method continuations

The functional meaning of method continuations is consistent as traditional continuations. In this sense, any sequential structure built with traditional continuations works with method continuations without any change. As an example of method continuation facility, we show how various interrupt mechanism can be programmed using method continuation.

The original idea of the interrupt mechanism comes from express mode message sending of ABCL/1[Yon90]. In ABCL/1, an express message interrupts the method execution of the target object and immediately invokes its corresponding method. The programmer can chose either resume or abort behavior of execution of the interrupted method. HARMONY/2 combines express mode message passing with method continuation and thus provides flexible interrupt mechanism to the programmer.

When a message is sent in express mode, execution of the corresponding method *immediately* takes place. If a method is running at this time, it is paused and its continuation is supplied as one of the argument of the method of express message.

Fig. 10 demonstrates four interruption scheme: Kill kills current execution of the method by forgetting the continuation (k) of the method execution. Kill-object makes the object inactive by suspending itself on a binary semophor. Suspend replies the continuation to the sender of the express mode message so that the interrupter has control over the interrupted method. With Resume, the execution of the method is paused while the interrupt method executes and resumes back afterwards.

## 5.2 Future type message passing

Future type message passing is a well-known programming technique with Actor family of languages. Some object-oriented concurrent programming languages such as ABCL/1[YBS86, Yon90] and Concurrent Smalltalk[YT86, YT87] support it as a built-in communication primitive. Though HARMONY/2 provides only asynchronous and synchronous message passing, it is easy to realize future-type communication structure with message continuation facilities.

*Future type message passing:* Future type message passing can be considered as a mixture of asynchronous message passing and synchronous message passing. In asynchronous message passing the sender receives no reply and thus does not synchronize with the reply. In synchronous message passing, the sender synchronizes with the reply. In future type message passing, synchronization with the reply is postponed until when the reply value is needed. The sender sends a message in future mode and immediately receives an object called *future object* which is a place holder of the reply for the message. After receiving the future object, the sender may proceed its method execution and when the reply for the message is needed, the sender sends value message to the future object. If the reply is available, value immediately returns the value otherwise synchronization on the reply takes place.

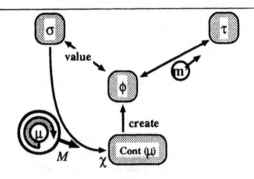

**Fig. 11.** Future type message passing

```
(Class Future-X ()
   (Method (Cont msg)
     [msg <== reply (New Future [msg <== copy])])))

(Class Future (result)
   (Initial (msg) [result := [msg <== fire]])
   (Method (value) [reply result])))
```

**Fig. 12.** An implementation of future type message passing

Fig. 11 illustrates the implementation scheme of future type message passing in HARMONY/2 and the HARMONY/2 code in fig. 12 implements it. The method Cont of the future communicator (Future-X) creates a future object ($\phi$) and replies it back to the sender ($\sigma$) of the message through invocation of the after-continuation with reply operation.

The future object initializes itself with its Initial method. It invokes the before-continuation. Consequently, the message that the message continuation represents is delivered to the target ($\tau$) and invokes the corresponding method. Because the message continuation is a copy of the original, whose after-continuation is nullified, the reply of the method execution is directed to the future object. The reply value is saved in the instance variable (value) of the future object.

The value method of the future object simply returns the content of result. Note that synchronization between the reply of the method execution and value method is implicitly realized by serialized message acceptance mechanism of the underlying concurrency model. The execution of value method is serialized after the initialization method which receives the reply and stores in result.

```
(Class Delay (msg value? result)
  (Initial (the-msg) [value? := #f]
                     [msg := the-msg])
  (Method (value)
    (if (not value?) [result := [msg <== fire]])
    [reply result])))
```

**Fig. 13.** An implementation of delay type message passing

Fig. 13 shows the implementation of *delay type communication*, which was inspired by delay primitive of Multilisp. In this communication scheme, message delivery is postponed until the first value message is processed. This communication scheme is especially useful in processing infinite data structure such as a stream of all the prime numbers.

## 5.3 Concurrent aggregates

Hierarchical modeling of applications has been effective in sequential programming. However, as A. Chen points out[Chi92], hierarchically modeled object structure suffers from excessive synchronization and thus result in poor concurrency. Concurrent aggregates is a hierarchical abstraction tool designed by A. Chen for his Actor-like concurrent programming language. To resolve excessive synchronization, A. Chen proposes for his Actor-like language a hierarchical abstraction tool called *concurrent aggregates*.

A concurrent aggregates comprises homogeneous collection of objects sharing the same name. Message passing in concurrent aggregates model establishes one-to-one-of-many communication. A message sent to a concurrent aggregate is received by one of the element of the concurrent aggregate. In this sense, the functionality of an aggregate can be considered as multiplexing the service. [Chi92] shows many interesting result of programming with concurrent aggregates.

Two of the key features of concurrent aggregates are one-to-one-of-many communication and message forwarding. Both features can be easily coded with HARMONY/2 as shown in fig. 14. One-to-one-of-many communication is established with a communicator which is an instance of Aggregate. Message forwarding can be realized with retargetting with copy operation.

We assume that the aggregate is accessed via following message conversion expression:

[any aggregate <== (some arg ...)]

One-to-one-of-many communication implemented by the aggregate delegates processing of the message continuation (msg) to one of the elements of the aggregate via do message. Do method calculates the appropriate element and forwards msg to it. This is done by a combination of copy and fire operations.

---

```
(Class Aggregate (n agg*)
  (Initial (size)
    [n := size] [agg* := (make-vector n)]
    (do ((i 0 (+ i 1))) ((= i n))
      (vector-set! agg* i [New Element self])))
  (Method (agg*) [reply agg*])
  (Method (Cont msg)
    [(vector-ref agg* (random n)) <= do msg]))

(Class Element (agg*)
  (Initial (X) [agg* := [X <== agg*]])
  (Method (do msg)
    (let* ((rep ...)
           (copy [msg <== copy rep])
           (result [copy <== fire]))
      [msg <== reply result]))
  (Method (some arg ...)
    ...))
```

**Fig. 14.** A template of concurrent aggregates

---

# 6 Discussion

## 6.1 Method continuations vs message continuations

The article introduced two frameworks of first class continuations into a single thread concurrency model. The semantics of method continuations are close to the semantics of traditional first class continuations. Message continuation framework incorporated concurrency and synchronization semantics.

An interesting discussion concerning a one-shot continuation and its expressiveness is found in [FH84]. They implement a version of call/cc called call/cc-one-shot which produces a continuation with one-shot property. The paper shows that call/cc can be implemented in terms of call/cc-one-shot. The primary difference between a message continuation and a continuation produced from call/cc-one-shot is that the former lives only in the dynamic extent of message conversion expression, while the latter lives in the indefinite extent of call/cc-one-shot. With this dynamic extent property we cannot implement full continuation such as method continuations in terms of message continuations. In this sense, method continuations are strictly more powerful than message continuations.

The powerful expressiveness of multi-shot property of method continuations, however, makes the framework difficult to incorporate in existing concurrent programming languages, especially when the base programming language does not provide first class continuation facilities.

In contrast, message continuations are much easier to incorporate in message-based concurrency model, whether it is based on single thread model or multiple thread model because message continuations are simply first class messages which is already there in the message passing computation model. We have already developed a message continuation framework for a multiple thread model [Wak93].

## 6.2 Asynchronous communication models

Because original Actor model is based on asynchronous communication, message sending does not have its continuation. However, it is possible to encode synchronous message passing by means of supplying the reply destination in the argument of the message. In this encoding the reply destination serves as the continuation a la message continuation.

As this encoding does not require any change of the computation model, single threadness is guaranteed in any use of the (encoded) continuation. However, it is the case that the reply destination is used multiple times, resulting in multiple invocation of the continuation. Though this does not violate Actor's semantics, it conflicts with the synchronous message passing semantics where single message sending results in at most one reply. With this observation, it is programmers responsibility to avoid this kind of VST-problem, which is automatically resolved with message continuation framework.

HACL (Higher-order ACL) is a concurrent programming language designed by Kobayashi. HACL is based on a theoretical foundation in linear logic and provides Actor-like asynchronous communication [KY94]. It was found that message continuation framework can be encoded as HACL functions through its use of first class communication ports [Kob]. As far as the encoded message continuation is used through these functions, the system becomes free of VST problem.

## 6.3 Continuation in Parallel Lisps

VST problem has less significance on concurrent programming languages based on multiple threads model. However, even with multiple threads model, the programmer may make use of synchronization primitives (e.g., semaphores) to make portions of the program single thread. If a continuation is exported out from such user-constructed single thread part, it is the case that invocation from outside the single thread part creates multiple threads in the user-constructed single thread part. In case of HARMONY/2 this should be system's crash and thus avoided with the frameworks. However, in the above case, the programmer takes all the responsibility to avoid such occasion.

In presence of structured language constructs of controlling concurrency issues related to VST problem appears: possible multiple termination of a threads group and multiple resolutions of future objects, for instance.

Queinnec gives dynamic extent semantics to the continuations produced in a threads group [QD93]. This approach is a possible solution of VST problem in don't-export scheme (see 2.3). This approach is partially taken in message continuation framework. The after-continuation of the message continuation is effective within the dynamic extent of the associated message passing. One-shot property gives less expressiveness to the message continuation than Queinnec's continuation because its after-continuation is effective only once. However, multiple invocation and invocation from outside the dynamic extent is permitted. In this sense, message continuations can be used in wider extent than dynamic extent continuations by Queinnec.

The problem of multiple resolutions of future objects in parallel Lisps can be compared with the problem of single message passing resulting in multiple replies in HARMONY/2. Katz and Weise approach by spawning multiple continuations for multiple future resolutions [KW89]. Method continuation framework takes a similar approach. Possible concurrency within an object is avoided with delayed installation of the continuation. Possible multiple reply problem is avoided because the basic computation model simply ignores multiple replies (see 2.2).

On the other hand, Multilisp [Hal85] ignores multiple resolutions of the future object. History sensitive semantics of message continuations takes a similar approach. Because message continuations replaces its after-continuation at the first use and further invocations of after-continuation are effectively ignored.

PaiLisp [IM89] proposes a very expressive framework called p-continuations, which effectively are used as interrupt mechanism in parallel environment and proved to be effective in systems programming. Though neither of the continuation facilities of HARMONY/2 provides interrupt mechanism, in combination with express mode messages, the programmer can program various interrupt mechanisms with method continuations.

# 7 Summary

The article identified the technical difficulty (VST problem) of introducing first class continuation facilities in object-based concurrency models and proposed two framework that do not suffer from VST problem.

The *method continuation framework* is a variant of call/cc which is the first class continuation primitive of Scheme. *Delayed installation* prevents VST problem to occur. Added synchronization semantics allows the safe use of continuations beyond objects' boundary and thus enabling construction of arbitrary sequential control structures in concurrent environment. Though expressive, this framework would be difficult to incorporate in a concurrent programming language whose base programming language does not provide first class continuation facilities.

Message continuation framework is based on the observation that a message represents the continuation after the message sending. History sensitive semantics (one-shot property) of message continuations avoids VST problem and provides a sound basis. With embedded concurrency and synchronization semantics, the programmer can construct arbitrary communication structures and make the resulting communication structure highly concurrent. Though this framework is less expressive than method continuation framework, it is easy to adopt in a message passing concurrent programming language, whether or not it provides first class continuation facilities. It is also possible to integrate with multiple thread concurrency models.

Ongoing research topics include:

- Producing highly efficient code from HARMONY/2 program. A compiler to C code is being developed. We designed a statically type checkable dialect of HARMONY/2. Thanks to the support of StackThreads[TMY93], the compiler produces highly efficient code.
- Optimizing programs utilizing message continuation facilities. A naive implementation of message continuation facilities is not too inefficient (each of fire, reply, and copy can be implemented at the same cost as single message passing). However, we would like to make the system more efficient not to make the communication structure developed with message continuations become the bottle neck of the system. For an instance, the future type communication presented in Section 4 requires nine message transmissions while three is enough for hand coded future type communication. We are interested in the object-fusion technique through program transformation [Shi88] in order to eliminate unnecessary synchronization.

**Acknowledgment:** Many thanks for the insightful comments by the readers of earlier drafts, especially to C. Queinnec, R. H. Halstead, Jr., T. Ito, and N. Kobayashi. The author would like to thank M. Aksit, L. Bergmans, J. Bosch, S. Inohara, H. Morizane, Y. Saito, M. Sassa, E .Shibayama, M .Tokoro, H. Tsuiki, A .Yonezawa, among others who discussed and supported this work. Hiroto Morizane and Yutaka Saito implemented a prototype HARMONY/2 system. Finally, I would like to address my thanks to colleagues at the Department of Mathematical and Computing Sciences, Tokyo Institute of Technology.

# References

[Agh86]  G. Agha. *Actors: A Model of Concurrent Computation in Distributed Systems*. MIT Press, Cambridge, 1986.

[AM91]  A. Appel and D. MacQueen. Standard ML of New Jersey. In M. Wirsing, editor, *Third International Symposium on Programming Language Implementation and Logic Programming*, Lecture Notes in Computer Science, New York, August 1991. Springer-Verlag.

[Ame87]  P. America. POOL-T: A parallel object-oriented language. In A. Yonezawa and M. Tokoro, editors, *Object-Oriented Concurrent Programming*, pages 199 – 220. MIT Press, Cambridge, Mass., 1987.

[Chi92]  A. Chien. *Concurrent Aggregates*. MIT Press, 1992.

[CR91]  W. Clinger and J. Rees. Revised[4] report on the algorithmic language scheme. *ACM LISP Pointers*, IV(3), July 1991.

[FH84]  D. P. Friedman and C. T. Haynes. Constraining control. In *Conference Record of the ACM Symposium on Principles of Programming Languages*, pages 245–254, 1984.

[Hal85]  R. Halstead. Multilisp: A language for concurrent symbolic computation. *ACM Trans. on Programming Languages and Systems*, pages 501–538, October 1985.

[IM89]  T. Ito and M. Matsui. A parallel lisp language pailisp and its kernel specification. In T. Ito and Jr. R. H. Halstead, editors, *Proceedings of US/Japan Workshop on Parallel Lisp*, volume 441 of *LNCS*, pages 58 – 100. Springer-Verlag, June 1989.

[Kob]  N. Kobayashi. Personal discussion.

[KW89]  M. Katz and D. Weise. Continuing into the future: On the interaction of futures. In T. Ito and Jr. R. H. Halstead, editors, *Proceedings of US/Japan Workshop on Parallel Lisp*, volume 441 of *LNCS*, pages 101–102, 1989.

[KY94]  N. Kobayashi and A. Yonezawa. Towards foundations for concurrent object-oriented programming. In *Proceedings of ACM Conference on Object-Oriented Systems, Languages, and Applications*, pages 31 – 45, 1994.

[Nie87] O. M. Nierstrasz. Active objects in Hybrid. In *Object-Oriented Programming Systems, Languages and Applications*, volume 22(12), pages 243 – 253. SIGPLAN Notices (ACM), December 1987.

[QD93] C. Queinnec and D. DeRoure. Design of a concurrent and distributed language. In Jr. R. H. Halstead and T. Ito, editors, *Proceedings of US/Japan Workshop on Parallel Symbolic Computing: Languages, Systems, and Applications*, volume 748 of *LNCS*, pages 234 – 259. Springer-Verlag, October 1993.

[RHH89] Jr. R. H. Halstead. New ideas in parallel lisp: Language design, implementation, and programming tools. In T. Ito and Jr. R. H. Halstead, editors, *Proceedings of US/Japan Workshop on Parallel Lisp*, volume 441 of *LNCS*, pages 2–57. Springer-Verlag, June 1989.

[Shi88] Etsuya Shibayama. How to invent distributed implementation schemes of an object-based concurrent language: A transformational approach. In *Proceedints of Object-Oriented Programming Systems, Languages and Applications (OOPSLA '88)*, pages 297–305, 1988.

[Sto77] J. Stoy. *Denotational Semantics: The Scott-Strachey Approach to Programming Language Theory*. MIT Press, Cambridge, MA, 1977.

[TMY93] K. Taura, S. Matsuoka, and A. Yonezawa. An efficient implementation scheme of concurrent object-oriented languages on stock multicomputers. In *Proceedings of the Symposium on Principles & Practices of Parallel Programming (PPoPP '93)*, pages 218–228, 1993.

[Wak93] K. Wakita. First class messages as first class continuations. In *proceedings of ISOTAS '93 (LNCS 742)*, pages 442–459, Kanazawa, November 1993.

[Wak94] K. Wakita. A concurrent language harmony/2 and its first class continuation mechanism (in Japanese). Technical Report COMP93-79, SS93-47, IEICE (The Institute of Electronics, Information and Communication Engineers), 1994.

[Wan80] M. Wand. Continuation-based multiprocessing. In *Conference Record of the 1980 Lisp Conference*, pages 19–28, 1980.

[YBS86] A. Yonezawa, J.-P. Briot, and E. Shibayama. Object-oriented concurrent programming in ABCL/1. In *Object-Oriented Programming Systems, Languages and Applications*, volume 21(11), pages 258 – 268. SIGPLAN Notices (ACM), November 1986.

[Yon90] A. Yonezawa. *ABCL: An Object-Oriented Concurrent System*. MIT Press, Cambridge, Mass., 1990.

[YT86] Y. Yokote and M. Tokoro. The design and implementation of ConcurrentSmalltalk. In *Object-Oriented Programming Systems, Languages and Applications*, volume 21(11), pages 331 – 340. SIGPLAN Notices (ACM), November 1986.

[YT87] Y. Yokote and M. Tokoro. Concurrent programming in ConcurrentSmalltalk. In A. Yonezawa and M. Tokoro, editors, *Object-Oriented Concurrent Programming*, pages 129 – 158. MIT Press, Cambridge, Mass., 1987.

# Locality Abstractions for Parallel and Distributed Computing

Suresh Jagannathan

Computer Science Research, NEC Research Institute, 4 Independence Way, Princeton, NJ 08540, *suresh@research.nj.nec.com*

**Abstract.** Temporal and spatial locality are significant concerns in the design and implementation of any realistic parallel or distributed computing system. Temporal locality is concerned with relations among objects that share similar lifetimes and birth dates; spatial locality is concerned with relations among objects that share information. Exploiting temporal locality can lead to improved memory behavior; exploiting spatial locality can lead to improved communication behavior. Linguistic, compiler, and runtime support for locality issues is especially important for unstructured symbolic computations in which lifetimes and sharing properties of objects are not readily apparent.

Language abstractions for spatial and temporal locality include mechanisms for grouping related threads of control, allowing programs flexibility to map computations onto *virtual processors*, reusing dynamic contexts efficiently, and permitting asynchronous garbage collection across multiple processors. These abstractions give users and implementations a large degree of mobility to exploit inherent locality properties found within many dynamic parallel applications.

We have investigated a number of these abstractions within a high-level language framework and within compilers targeted for such a framework. In this paper, we discuss several of these abstractions and justify their importance.

## 1 Introduction

Despite significant advances in hardware construction and parallel algorithm design, there remain a large class of algorithms which typically perform poorly on conventional stock multiprocessors. These problems (broadly classified under the name *symbolic programming*) include combinatorial optimization, simulation, symbolic algebra, database searches, graph algorithms, expert systems, etc.. Symbolic programming applications exhibit characteristics not found in more well-structured numerical algorithms: data is generated dynamically and often have irregular shape and density, data sets typically consist of objects of many different types and structure, the communication requirements of generated tasks is a rarely apparent from simple examination of the source program, and the natural unit of concurrency often is difficult to determine statically.

High-level symbolic programming languages such as Scheme[3] or ML[25] nonetheless offer the promise of being ideal vehicles within which to express a variety of issues related to concurrency, distribution and communication. Because these languages support the liberal use of abstract data types and structures, first-class procedures with well-defined encapsulation rules, and first-class continuations[13], many concerns in the design of parallel or distributed system can be elegantly defined. However, there has been little effort to investigate the role of these languages and their implementations within such contexts.

One obvious way of integrating concurrency into a high-level symbolic language is to use generic thread packages[4, 34] or operating system-defined library routines. At first glance, such an approach appears to offer greater extensibility and generality than available within a high-level language optimized for a particular paradigm. Efficiency and expressivity are compromised in several significant respects, however: (1) because there is no compile-time or runtime system sensitive to the semantics of the concurrency abstractions being implemented, there is little or no optimization performed on these abstractions; (2) relying on external libraries and operating system services for concurrency management and communication effectively prohibits utilizing features of the sequential language to implement concurrent and distributed extensions, and (3) because scheduling and migration policies, storage management decisions, etc., are managed exclusively by generic thread routines, building customized implementations of different paradigms is problematic. The latter shortcoming makes this approach especially ill-suited for implementing diverse parallel and distributed symbolic algorithms.

In this paper, we present design, compilation and implementation strategies that address the issue of implementing high-level parallel languages for symbolic computing. We focus predominantly on locality issues since most symbolic applications exercise communication seriously and in ways that are often difficult to analyze statically. We first describe a system geared towards high-performance tightly-coupled parallel applications. We then present a compile-time analysis framework for a higher-order language core capable of deriving information that can be used by optimizers sensitive to locality considerations.

We classify locality considerations into two categories: *temporal locality* is concerned with relations among objects that share similar lifetimes and birth dates; *spatial locality* is concerned with relations among objects that share information. Exploiting temporal locality requires mechanisms which allow objects that are created close to another in time to live close to another in space. Exploiting spatial locality requires mechanisms which allow objects that live close to another in space to be accessed close to another in time. Temporal locality is most directly influenced by memory organization – caches, for example, improve temporal locality since caches are organized to allow short access times for newly allocated objects. Spatial locality is most directly influenced by communication structure – a shared immutable data structure that is replicated, for example, does not require inter-processor communication in order to be referenced.

In the next section, we present an overview of Sting, a high-level operating system for parallel computing implemented in Scheme. In Section 3, we define Sting's storage organization model tuned for optimizing locality inherent in lightweight parallel computations. Section 4 describes *virtual topologies*, an abstraction that provides a mapping between a logical task structure and a physical interconnection. Section 5 presents some benchmark results, and Section 6 presents work related work to the Sting design. Section 7 discusses compile-time optimizations for shared locations in the context of a system such as Sting's.

# 2 Sting Overview

Sting is a parallel dialect of Scheme[3] designed to serve as a high-level operating system for modern symbolic parallel programming languages. A detailed description of its implementation is given in [19, 20, 28]; we concentrate here on features explicitly designed to exploit locality.

The abstract architecture of Sting (see Figure 1) is organized hierarchically as a layer of abstractions. The lowest level abstraction is a *physical machine*. A physical machine consists of a collection of *physical processors*. A physical processor is a faithful abstraction of an actual computing engine. A physical machine contains as many physical processors as there are nodes in a multiprocessor environment.

A *virtual machine* is an abstraction that is mapped onto a physical machine or a portion thereof. Virtual machines manage a single address space. They are also responsible for mapping global objects into their local address space. In addition, virtual machines contain the root of a live object graph (*i.e.,* root environment) that is used to trace the set of live objects in this address space. A virtual machine is closed over a set of *virtual processors* in the system. Virtual processors execute on physical processors.

Physical machines are responsible for defining new address spaces, managing global shared objects, handling hardware device interrupts and coordinating physical processors. Associated with each physical processor $P$ is a virtual processor policy manager that implements policy decisions for the virtual processors that execute on $P$.

Virtual processors (VPs) are responsible for managing user-created *threads*, an abstraction of a separate locus of control; threads are represented as a generalized form of one-shot continuations[13]. In addition, virtual processors also handle non-blocking I/O and software interrupts (page faults, thread quantum expiration, etc.). Each virtual processor $V$ is closed over a policy manager (TPM) that (a) schedules threads executing within $V$, (b) migrates threads to/from other

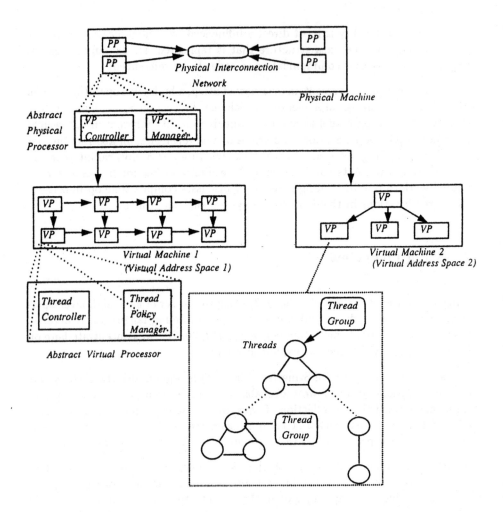

**Fig. 1.** The Sting software architecture.

VPs, and (c) performs initial thread placement on the VPs defined within a given virtual machine .

Just as VPs context switch threads, a physical processor will context switch virtual processors because of preemption, or because a VP specifically requests a context switch (*e.g.,* because of an I/O call initiated by its current thread). We discuss virtual processors in greater detail in the following sections. Thread functionality is implemented by a thread controller that implements the thread interface and thread state transitions.

Physical machines, physical processors, virtual machines, virtual processors and threads are all first-class objects in Sting. This implies that the policy decisions of a processor (both physical and virtual) can be customized; for example, different virtual processors (even in the same virtual machine) may be closed over different policy managers. No performance penalty is incurred as a result of this flexibility.

## 2.1  Locality

A major goal of the Sting design was to exploit inherent locality in parallel Scheme programs. Consequently, there are a number of optimizations and design features in the system that are sensitive to temporal locality:

1. Threads allocate private data on local heaps; thus, data with close birth dates are likely to be allocated close to one another within a thread.
2. Thread control blocks (TCBs) are recycled on a per processor basis. Thus, a thread that terminates on processor $P$ will have its TCB assigned to a new thread subsequently instantiated on $P$, thus improving cache and page locality.
3. TCBs can be shared by many threads simultaneously if data dependencies warrant. Thus, data allocated by a thread $T$ can use the same memory resource as data allocated by $T'$ if $T$ has a data dependency with $T'$.

Sting also provides mechanisms for exploiting spatial locality:

1. *Thread groups* are first-class objects that encapsulate a shared heap. Data shared among threads within a given group is allocated on the shared heap; in general, inter-thread communication is mediated via access and mutation of the shared heap.
2. *Virtual topologies* provide a means for a program's logical task structure to be mapped onto a physical topology. A virtual topology can be thought of as a scheduler and thread placement manager parameterized over logical and concrete algebraic structures whose elements are processors. For example, one can construct a virtual topology that maps logical trees to concrete meshes; the nodes in the tree and mesh correspond to virtual and physical processors, respectively. The role of a topology is to provide a mapping that optimizes communication among related threads in a program's logical task structure with respect to an underlying physical interconnect.

# 3 Sting Storage Management

Storage management decisions are undertaken at various points during the evaluation of a thread; these decisions relate directly to temporal locality:

## Local Storage Management

Threads are closed over their own local stack and heap. Thus, they are free to garbage collect inaccessible data without having to synchronize with other evaluating threads. Since a thread-local object $O$ may contain references to other objects on shared heaps, garbage collecting $O$ requires notifying the shared heaps into which $O$ has references that $O$ is no longer a live object. When these shared heaps garbage collect, they use such information to determine the root set used to trace all their live objects.

## 3.1 Thread Control Blocks

The Sting implementation defers the allocation of storage for a thread until necessary. In many thread packages, the act of creating a thread involves not merely setting up the environment for the process to be forked, but also allocating and initializing storage. This approach lowers efficiency in two important respects: first, in the presence of fine-grained parallelism, the thread controller may spend more time creating and initializing threads than actually running them. Second, since stacks and process control blocks are immediately allocated upon thread creation, context switches among threads often cannot take advantage of cache and page locality.

Page locality in thread create operations is obviously important. Consider a virtual processor $P$ executing thread $T_1$. Suppose $T_1$ spawns a new thread $T_2$. Under a fully eager thread creation strategy, storage for $T_2$ will be allocated from a new TCB. $T_2$'s heap and stack will be mapped to a new set of physical pages in $P$'s virtual machine. Thus, assume $T_2$ runs on $P$ only after $T_1$ completes (*e.g.*, because there is no other free processor available or because $T_1$ is strict in the value yielded by applying $T_2$'s thunk). Setting up $T_2$ now involves a fairly costly context switch. The working set valid when $T_1$ was executing is now possibly invalid; in particular, the contents of the data and instruction cache containing $T_1$'s physical pages will probably need to be flushed when $T_2$ starts executing.

Thread control blocks are recyclable resources that are managed by virtual processors. A dynamic context (*i.e.*, thread control block) is allocated for a thread *only* when the thread begins evaluation. A thread control block consists of stacks and heaps plus a small amount of bookkeeping information used to record the status of the evaluating thread.

Thread control blocks are allocated from a pool local to each VP. This pool is organized as a LIFO queue. When a thread terminates, its TCB is recycled on the TCB pool of the VP on which it was executing; the LIFO organization of this pool guarantees that this TCB will be allocated to the next thread chosen for execution on this VP. Since it is likely that the most recently used pieces of the TCB will be available in the physical processor's working set, temporal locality between newly terminated threads and newly created ones can be exploited. Sting incorporates one further optimization on this basic theme: if a thread $T$ terminates on VP $V$, and $V$ is next scheduled to begin evaluation of a new thread (*i.e.*, a thread that is not yet associated with a dynamic context), $T$'s TCB is immediately allocated to the new thread; no pool management costs are incurred in this case.

Besides local VP pools, VPs share access to a global TCB pool. Every local VP pool maintains an overflow and underflow threshold. When a pool overflows, its VP moves half the TCBs in the pool to the global pool; when the pool underflows, a certain number of TCBs are moved from the global pool to the VP-local one. Global pools serve two purpose: (1) they minimize the impact of program behavior on TCB allocation and reuse, and (2) they ensure a fair distribution of TCBs to all virtual processors. Since new new TCBs are created only if both the global and the VP local pool are empty, the number of TCBs actually created during the evaluation of a Sting program is determined collectively by all VPs.

## 3.2 Dynamic Storage Management

The distinction between threads that are scheduled and those that are evaluating is used in Sting to optimize the implementation of non-strict structures such as *futures*[12]; it is also used to throttle the unfolding of the process call tree in fine-grained parallel programs. In a naive implementation, a process that accesses a future (or which initiates a new process whose value it requires) blocks until the future becomes determined (or the newly instantiated process yields a value). This behavior is sub-optimal for the reasons described above -- temporal locality is compromised, bookkeeping information for context switching increases, and processor utilization is not increased since the original process must block until the new process completes.

Sting implements the following optimization: a thunk $t$ associated with a thread $T$ that is in a *scheduled* or *delayed* state is applied using the dynamic context of a thread $S$ if $S$ demands $T$'s value[1]. The semantics of future/touch (or any similar producer/consumer protocol) is not violated. The rationale is straightforward: since $T$ has not been allocated storage and has no dynamic state information associated with it, $t$ can be treated as an ordinary procedure and evaluated using the TCB already allocated for $S$. In effect, $S$ and $T$ share the same dynamic storage. $T$'s state is set to *absorbed* as a consequence. A thread is absorbed if its thunk executes using the TCB associated with another running thread.

---

[1] Scheduled and delayed threads do not have an associated TCB.

Thus, a thread can run the code associated with another unevaluated thread whose value it requires using its own dynamic context – no TCB is allocated in this case and the accessing thread does not block. A consumer blocks only when the producer has already started evaluating. The producer is already associated with a TCB in this case, and no opportunity for absorption presents itself.

## 3.3  Thread Groups

Sting allows threads to be organized in ways that improve spatial locality. In particular, threads that share information among one another can be organized logically into groups. There are two kinds of groups supported in the system. Thread groups define a locus that programmers can use to clump related threads; such groups permit efficient sharing of data, but have no implications for thread placement or migration. A more elaborate group structure can be constructed using virtual topologies. Topologies are implicitly associated with a thread placement and scheduling discipline.

Sting provides *thread groups* as a means of gaining control over a related collection of threads[23]. A thread group is created by a call to `fork-thread-group`; this operation creates a new group and a new thread that becomes the *root thread* of that group. A child thread shares the same group as its parent unless it explicitly creates a new group. A thread group is includes a *shared heap* accessible to all its members. When a thread group terminates via the call,

`(thread-group-terminate `*group*`),`

all live threads in the group are terminated and its shared heap is garbage collected.

A thread group also contains debugging and thread operations that may be applied *en masse* to all of its members. Thread groups provide operations analogous to ordinary thread operations (*e.g.,* termination, suspension, etc.) as well as operations for debugging and monitoring (*e.g.,* listing all threads in a given group, listing all groups, profiling, genealogy information, etc.) Thus, when thread $T$ is terminated, users can request all of $T$'s children (which are defined to be part of $T$'s group to be terminated) thus:

`(thread-group-terminate (thread.group `*T*`))`

Thread groups are an important tool for controlling sharing in a hierarchical memory architecture. Since objects shared by members in a group are contained in the group's shared heap, they are physically close to one another in virtual memory, and thus better spatial locality can be realized. Threads groups can also be used as a locus for scheduling. For example, a thread policy manager might implement a scheduling policy in which no thread in a group is allowed to run unless all threads in the group are allowed to run; this scheduling regime is similar to a "gang scheduling"[7] protocol.

# 4 Virtual Topologies

Sting programs can be parameterized over a virtual topology. A virtual topology defines a relation over a collection of Sting virtual processors; processor topologies configured as trees, graphs, hypercubes, and meshes are some well-known examples[31]. A virtual topology need not have any correlation with a physical one; it is intended to capture the interconnection structure best suited for a given algorithm. We consider a virtual processor to be an abstraction that defines scheduling, migration and load-balancing policies for the threads it executes. Thus, virtual topologies are intended to provide a simple and expressive high-level framework for defining complex thread/processor mappings that abstracts low-level details of a physical interconnection.

Efficient construction of virtual topologies and processor mappings lead to several important benefits; among the most important is improved communication and data locality:

1. *Improved Data Locality:* If a collection of threads share common data, we can construct a topology that maps the virtual processors on which these threads execute to the same physical processor. Virtual processors are multiplexed on physical processors in the same way threads are multiplexed on virtual processors.
2. *Improved Communication Locality:* If a collection of threads have significant communication requirements, we can construct a topology that maps threads which communicate with one another onto virtual processors close together in the virtual topology.

## 4.1 An Example

To help motivate the utility of virtual topologies, consider the program fragment shown in Figure 2.

D&C defines a parallel divide-and-conquer abstraction; when given a merge procedure $M$, and a list of data streams as its arguments, it constructs a binary tree that uses $M$ to merge pairs of streams. Each pair of leaves in the tree are streams connected to a merge node that combines their contents and outputs the results onto a separate output stream. The root of the tree and all internal nodes are implemented as separate threads.

There is significant spatial locality in this program since data generated by child streams are accessed exclusively by their parents. Load-balancing is also an important consideration. We would like to avoid mapping internal nodes at the same depth to the same processor whenever possible since these nodes operate over distinct portions of the tree and have no data dependencies with one another. For example, a merge node $N$ with children $C_1$ and $C_2$ ideally should be mapped onto a processor close to both $C_1$ and $C_2$, and should be mapped onto a processor distinct from any of its siblings.

```
(define (D&C merge streams)
  (let loop ((streams streams))          ;; iteration
    (future
      (let ((output-stream (make-stream)))
        (cond ((null? (cddr streams)) ;; even number of streams
               (merge (car streams) (cadr streams) output-stream))
              (else (let ((left  (left-half  streams))
                          (right (right-half streams))
                     merge results onto output stream
                     (merge (loop left)
                            (loop right)
                            output-stream)))))))))
```

**Fig. 2.** A divide-and-conquer parallel program parameterized over a merge procedure.


## 4.2 A Topology Abstraction

To address the issues highlighted in the previous section, we define a high-level abstraction that allows programmers to specify how threads should be mapped onto a virtual topology corresponding to a logical process graph. In general, we expect programmers to use a library of topologies that are provided as part of a thread system; each topology in this library defines procedures for constructing and accessing its elements. The cognitive cost of using topologies is thus minimal for those topologies present in the topology library.

However, because virtual processors are first-class objects, building new topologies is not cumbersome. Programmers requiring topologies not available in the library can construct their own using the abstractions described in the next section. For example, a tree is an obvious candidate for the desired thread/processor map in the example shown in Figure 2. A tree, however, may not correspond to the physical topology of the system; virtual topologies provide a mechanism for bridging the gap between the algorithmic structure of an application and the physical structure of the machine on which it is to run. Mapping a tree onto a physical topology such as a bus or hypercube is defined by a topology that relates virtual processors to physical ones.


## 4.3 Virtual Processors

In instances where a desired virtual topology is not available, programmers can build their own using operations over virtual and physical processors:

- (make-vp *pp*) returns a new virtual processor mapped onto physical processor *pp*.

- (current-vp) returns the virtual processor on which this operation is evaluated.
- (vp->address *vp*) returns the address of *vp* in the topology of which it is a part.
- (set-vp->address *vp addr*) sets *vp*'s address in a virtual topology to be *addr*.
- (vp->pp *vp*) returns the physical processor on which *vp* is currently executing.

Note that running a new VP is tantamount to shifting the locus of control to a new node in a virtual topology.

## 4.4 Physical Processors

The second abstraction necessary to construct topologies are *physical processors*. Operations analogous to those available on virtual processors exist for physical ones.

A set of physical processors along with a specific physical topology form a *physical machine*. Each physical machine provides a set of topology dependent primitive functions to access physical processors. For example, a machine with a ring topology may provide: (a) (current-pp) which returns the physical physical processor on which this operation executes; (b) (pp->address *pp*) that returns the address in the physical topology to which pp is associated; (c) (move-left *i*) which returns the pp *i* steps to the left of (current-pp) ; and, (d) (move-right *i*) which behaves analogously.

A topology object defines procedures for navigating on a particular topology, but we also require a mapping that translates addresses of virtual processors in a given virtual topology to addresses in the current physical topology. Given procedures for accessing virtual and physical processors, such mappings can be expressed using well-known techniques [11].

## 4.5 Example Revisited

We use topologies in parallel programs by allowing virtual processors to be provided as explicit arguments to thread creation operators. Consider the merge stream example shown in Figure 2. Using topologies, this program fragment could be rewritten as shown in Figure new-merge-streams.

The changes to the code from the original are slight, but lead to potentially significant gains in efficiency and expressivity. In fact, the only modification (outside of the structure of the outer loop which now binds a virtual processor to the root of a topology tree) is in the interface to future . Each application of future now takes a virtual processor as its argument that specifies where the thread

```
(define (D&C merge streams)
  (let loop ((streams streams)  ;; letrec
             (root (make-static-tree-topology (log (length streams)))))
    (future
      (let ((output-stream (make-stream)))
        (cond ((null? (cddr streams))
               (merge (car streams) (cadr streams) output-stream))
              (else (let ((left  (left-half streams))
                          (right (right-half streams)))
                      merge results onto output stream
                      (merge (loop left  (left-child))
                             (loop right (right-child))
                             output-stream)))))
        (tree-node-vp root)))))
```

**Fig. 3.** A divide-and-conquer procedure using virtual topologies.

created by the future should evaluate on the virtual topology; `tree-node-vp` returns the VP associated with the tree node passed as its argument. `Left-child` and `right-child` return the left and right child in the virtual topology created by `tree`.

### 4.6 Built-in Topologies And Their Interface Functions

We have constructed a number of topologies that reside as part of the Sting environment; some of these topologies along with their interfaces are enumerated in Fig. refbuilt-in.

## 5 Sting Benchmarks

The benchmarks shown in this section were implemented on an eight processor Silicon Graphics 75MHz MIPS-R3000 shared memory machine. The machine contains 256 MBytes of main memory and a one Mbyte unified secondary cache; each processor has a 64Kbyte data and a 64Kbyte instruction primary cache.

Fig. 5 gives baseline figures for various thread operations; these timings were derived using a single global FIFO queue.

Figure 6 gives some baseline costs for creating and managing virtual processors:

"Creating a VP" is the cost of creating, initializing, and adding a new virtual to a virtual machine; note that it is roughly the cost of creating a thread on a tree or vector processor topology. "Fork/Tree" is the cost of creating a thread on a static tree topology; "Fork/Vector" is the cost of creating a thread on a vector

| Topology | Interface Procedures |
|---|---|
| Array | `(make-array-topology` *dimensions*`)`<br>`(get-node` *dim₁ dim₂ ... dimₙ*`)`<br>`(move-up-in-nth-dimension)`<br>`(move-down-in-nth-dimension)` |
| Ring | `(make-ring-topology` *size*`)`<br>`(get-vp` *n*`)`<br>`(move-right` *n*`)`<br>`(move-left` *n*`)` |
| Static Tree<br>Dynamic Tree | `(make-static-tree-topology` *depth*`)`<br>`(make-dynamic-tree-topology` *depth*`)`<br>`(get-root)`<br>`(left-child)`<br>`(right-child)` |
| Butterfly | `(make-butterfly-topology` *levels*`)`<br>`(move-straight-left)`<br>`(move-straight-right)`<br>`(move-cross-left)`<br>`(move-cross-right)` |

**Fig. 4.** Some built-in topologies.

| Case | Timings(in μseconds) |
|---|---|
| Thread Creation | 40 |
| Thread Fork and Value | 86.9 |
| Thread Enqueue/Dequeue | 14.5 |
| Synchronous Context Switch | 12.8 |
| Thread Block and Resume | 27.9 |

**Fig. 5.** Baseline timings.

| Operation | Times (μ-seconds) |
|---|---|
| Creating a VP | 31 |
| Adding a VP to a VM | 5.4 |
| Fork/Tree | 25 |
| Fork/Vector | 20 |
| VP Context Switch | 68 |
| Dynamic Tree | 207 |

**Fig. 6.** Baseline times for managing virtual processors and threads.

topology. "Adding a VP to a VM" is the cost of updating a virtual machine's state with a new virtual processor. "VP Context Switch" is the cost of context-switching two virtual processors on the same physical processor; it also includes the cost of starting up a thread on the processor. "Dynamic Tree" is the cost of adding a new VP to a tree topology.

Fig. 7 shows benchmark times for four applications (solid lines indicate actual wallclock times; dashed lines indicate ideal performance relative to single processor times):

| Benchmark | Processors | | | |
|---|---|---|---|---|
| | 1 | 2 | 4 | 8 |
| Alpha-Beta | 108 | 57.6 | 31.9 | 16.7 |
| N-Body | 751 | 363 | 251 | 137 |
| MST | 81.8 | 43.5 | 24.3 | 13.7 |
| Primes | 219.5 | 112.6 | 58.1 | 34.1 |

**Fig. 7.** Wallclock times on benchmark suite.

1. **Primes:** This program computes the first million primes. It uses a master-slave algorithm; each slave computes all primes within a given range.
2. **Minimum Spanning Tree:** This program implements a geometric minimum spanning tree algorithm using a version of Prim's algorithm. The input data is a fully connected graph of 5000 points with edge lengths determined by Euclidean distance. The input space is divided among a fixed number of threads. To achieve better load balance, each node not in the tree does a parallel sort to find its minimum distance among all nodes in the tree. Although 46,766 threads are created with this input, only 16 TCBs are actually generated. This is again due to Sting's aggressive treatment of storage locality, reuse and context sharing.
3. **Alpha-Beta:** This program defines a parallel implementation of a game tree traversal algorithm. The program does $\alpha/\beta$ pruning[8, 14] on this tree to minimize the amount of search performed. The program creates a fixed number of threads; each of these threads communicate their $\alpha/\beta$ values via distributed data structures. The input used consisted of a tree of depth 10 with fanout 8; the depth cutoff for communicating $\alpha$ and $\beta$ values was 3. To make the program realistic, we introduced a 90% skew in the input that favored finding the best node along the leftmost branch in the tree.
4. **N-body:** This program simulates the evolution of a system of bodies under the influence of gravitational forces. Each body is modeled as a point mass and exerts forces on all other bodies in the system. The simulation proceeds over time-steps, each step computing the net force on every body and thereby updating that body's position and other attributes. This benchmark ran the simulation on 5000 bodies over six time-steps.

Speedup and efficiency ratios for these problems are shown in Fig. 8.

| Benchmark | Speedup | Efficiency |
|-----------|---------|------------|
| Primes | 6.4 | 81 |
| MST | 5.9 | 75 |
| N-Body | 5.5 | 69 |
| Alpha-Beta | 6.5 | 81 |

**Fig. 8.** Efficiency and speedup rations on 8 processors.

We consider two application points to highlight the potential impact of virtual topologies in exploiting spatial locality (see Figure 9); in one of the applications (quicksort), topology mapping also had a beneficial impact on temporal locality, illustrating that spatial and temporal locality are *not* mutually distinct attributes of an application.

1. **Quicksort** sorts a vector of $2^{18}$ integers using a parallel divide-and-conquer strategy. We use a tree topology that dynamically allocates virtual processors; the maximum depth of the topology tree in this problem was 6; calls to left-child and right-child result in the creation of new virtual processors if required. The virtual to physical topology mapping chooses one child at random to be mapped onto the same physical processor as its parent in the virtual topology. Internal threads in the process tree generated by this program yield as their value a sorted sub-list; because of the topology mapping used, more opportunities for thread absorption [19], or task stealing [26] present themselves relative to an implementation that performs round-robin or random allocation of threads to processors. This is because at least one child thread is allocated on the same virtual processor as its parent; since the child will not execute before the parent unless migrated to another VP, it will be a strong target for dynamic inlining or thread absorption. The impact of improved temporal locality is evident in the times – on eight processors, the mapped version was roughly 1.4 times faster than the unmapped one; roughly 14% more threads were absorbed in the topology mapped version than in the unmapped case (201 threads absorbed vs. 171 absorbed with a total number of 239 threads created).

2. **Hamming** computes the extended hamming numbers up to 100000 for the first 16 primes. The extended hamming problem is defined thus: given a finite sequence of primes $A, B, C, D, \ldots$ and an integer $n$ as input, output in increasing magnitude without duplication all integers less than or equal to $n$ of the form

$$(A^i) \times (B^j) \times (C^k) \times (D^l) \times \ldots$$

This problem is structured in terms of a tree of mutually recursive threads that communicate via streams. The program example shown in Figure 2 captures the basic structure of this problem. There is a significant amount of communication or spatial locality exhibited by this program. A useful virtual topology for this example would be a static tree of depth equivalent to the depth of the process tree. By mapping siblings in the tree to different virtual processors, and selected children to the same processor as their parent, we can effectively exploit communication patterns evident in the algorithm. On eight processors, the implementation using topologies outperformed an unmapped round-robin scheduling policy by over a factor of six.

Offhand, it might appear that the benefits of virtual topologies would be nominal on a physical shared-memory machine since the cost of inter-processor communication is effectively the cost of accessing shared memory. However, even in this environment, virtual topologies can be used profitably. Spatial and temporal locality effects easily observable on a distributed memory system are modeled on a shared-memory machine in terms of memory locality. For example, programs can exhibit better spatial locality if communicating threads (or threads with manifest data dependencies) are mapped onto the same processor when possible, provided that such mappings will not lead to poor processor utilization. A system that supports fast creation and efficient management of threads and virtual processors would thus benefit from using virtual topologies regardless of the underlying physical topology.

| Benchmark | Processors | | | |
|-----------|------|--------|-----|------|
|           | 1    | 2      | 4   | 8    |
| Hamming   | 143.5 | 108.3 | 46  | 15.3 |
|           | 140.4 | 118.24 | 100 | 96.5 |
| Quicksort | 8.57 | 4.51   | 2.45 | 1.7 |
|           | 8.49 | 4.95   | 3.16 | 2.51 |

**Fig. 9.** Wallclock times for two benchmarks. A static tree topology of depth 5 was used for Hamming; a dynamic tree of depth 6 was used for Quicksort. The first row for each benchmark indicates processor times when virtual topologies were used; the second row indicates times using a default round-robin scheduler with no topology information.

# 6 Related Work

Besides providing an efficient multi-threaded programming system similar to other lightweight thread systems[4, 5, 24], Sting's liberal use of procedural and control abstractions provide added flexibility and important efficiency gains through improved temporal locality. Advanced memory management techniques are facilitated as a consequence of this design; TCB reuse, thread absorption, per-thread garabage collection all contributed to increased locality benefits. Sting is built on an abstract machine intended to support long-lived applications, persistent objects, and multiple address spaces. Thread packages provide none of this functionality since (by definition) they do not define a complete program environment.

Concurrent dialects of high-level languages such as Scheme [17, 23], ML [27, 29], or Concurrent Prolog [2, 32] typically encapsulate all scheduling, load-balancing and thread management decisions as part of a runtime kernel implementation; programmers have little control in exploiting locality and communication properties manifest in their applications. Consequently, such properties must often be inferred by a runtime system, since they cannot be specified by the programmer even when readily apparent. In contrast, Sting's virtual topology abstraction give programmers greater flexibilty to optimize programs based on the application's logical task structure.

Concurrent computing environments such as PVM [33] permit the construction of a type of virtual machine; such machines, however, consist of heavyweight Unix tasks that communicate exclusively via message-passing. In general, it is expected that there will be as many tasks in a PVM virtual machine as available processors in the ensemble.

Our work on virtual topologies is closely related to *para-functional* programming [15]. Para-functional languages extend implicitly parallel, lazy languages such as Haskell [16] with two annotations: *scheduling expressions* that provide user-control on evaluation order of expressions that would otherwise be evaluated lazily, and *mapping expressions* that permit programmers to map expressions onto distinct virtual processors.

While the goals of para-functional programming share much in common with ours, there are numerous differences in the technical development. First, we subsume the need for *scheduling expressions* by allowing programmers to create lightweight threads wherever concurrency is desired; thus, our programming model assumes explicit parallelism. Second, because VPs are closed over their own scheduling policy manager and thread queues, threads with different scheduling requirements can be mapped onto VPs that satisfy these requirements; in contrast, virtual processors in the para-functional model are simply integers. Third, there is no distinction between virtual and physical processors in a para-functional language; thus virtual to physical processor mappings cannot be expressed. Finally, para-functional languages, to our knowledge, have not been the focus of any implementation effort; by itself, the abstract model provides no insight into the efficiency impact of a given virtual topology in terms of increased data and communication locality, etc..

Finally, there has been much work in realizing improved temporal and spatial locality by sophisticated compile-time analysis [30, 36] or by explicit data distribution annotations [1]; the focus of these efforts has been on developing compiler optimizations for implicitly parallel languages. Outside of the fact that we assume explicit parallelism, our work is distinguished from these efforts insofar as virtual topologies require annotations on threads, not on the data used by them.

# 7 Static Analysis of Locality Properties

Despite various runtime optimizations to support locality, it is clear that without sophisticated compile-time support, parallel symbolic computing systems will be too inefficient to work well on large, realistic problems. To address this issue, we have investigated compile-time analysis techniques for parallel languages well-suited to run in an environment of the kind provided by Sting.

In this section, we informally introduce an analysis of a parallel language in which tasks communicate via first-class mutable shared locations. Details on the implementation and underlying theory of the analysis can be found in [21, 35].

## 7.1 The Language

Consider a simple language that could form the basis of a Scheme or SML[25] core. The language has constants, variables, functions, primitive applications, call-by-value function applications, conditionals, recursive function definitions, and a process creation operation. The primitives include operations for creating and accessing pairs and *shared locations*. Constants include integers and Booleans. (See Fig. 10.)

Communication in this language takes place through shared locations. We think of shared locations as an implementation substrate on top of which higher-level abstractions (*e.g.*, futures[12], tuple-spaces[18], etc.) may be constructed. Shared locations are created using the **mk-loc**operator, and are initially unbound. If $x$ is a location, both **read**($x$) and **remove**($x$) return the value of $x$, blocking if $x$ is unbound. In addition, if $x$ is bound, **remove**($x$) marks $x$ as unbound. Blocked **remove** and **read** expresions may unblock when a **write** subsequently occurs on the location of interest. The value of a **write** expression is the location written. The act of writing or reading a location, or removing a location's contents is atomic.

To create a lightweight thread of control to evaluate $e$, we evaluate **spawn** $e$. **Spawn** returns immediately after creating a new thread; its value is TRUE. The environment in which a newly spawned thread evaluates is the same as its parent thread. Threads are completely asynchronous, and communicate exclusively via shared locations.

For example, the MultiLisp [12] expression, (**future** $e$), is equivalent to,

$$
\begin{aligned}
e &\ \in\ Exp \\
c &\ \in\ Const = Int + Bool \\
x &\ \in\ Var \\
f &\ \in\ Func \\
p &\ \in\ Prim = \{\text{cons}, \text{car}, \text{cdr}, \text{mk-loc}, \text{write}, \text{read}, \text{remove}, \ldots\}
\end{aligned}
$$

$$
\begin{aligned}
e ::=&\ c \\
 |&\ x \\
 |&\ f \\
 |&\ p(e_1 \ldots\ e_n)\ |\ (p) \\
 |&\ e_1\,(e_2\ e_3\ \ldots\ e_n)\ |\ (e) \\
 |&\ \textbf{if } e \textbf{ then } e_1 \textbf{ else } e_2 \\
 |&\ \textbf{letrec } x_1 = f_1\ \ldots\ x_n = f_n \textbf{ in } e \\
 |&\ \textbf{spawn } e
\end{aligned}
$$

$$
f ::= \lambda x_1\ x_2\ \ldots\ x_n.e
$$

**Fig. 10.** The kernel language.

```
let loc = (mk-loc)
in begin
      spawn write(loc, e)
      loc
   end
```

and (**touch** $v$) is equivalent to,

```
if location? (v)
   then read(v)
   else v
```

(Note that "let" and "**begin**" are syntactic sugar for simple and nested application, respectively.)

As another example, the following expression implements a simple *fetch-and-op* abstraction [10] using locations. The procedure representing this abstraction atomically returns the current contents of the cell, and stores a new value using the procedure argument provided.

```
λ init. let  cell  =  (mk-loc)
      in begin
          write(cell, init)
          λ op. let  val  =  remove(cell)
                in begin
                      write(cell, op (val))
                      val
                   end
      end
   end
```

## 7.2   The Analysis

With shared locations as the main synchronization vehicle, it is natural to focus on compile-time analyses targeted at tracking the movement of these locations through procedures, and across independently executing threads of control. Effective analysis of how and where shared locations are manipulated may lead to a number of interesting and important optimizations. We consider several in the next section.

Our approach to analyzing the behavior of shared locations is based on an abstract interpretation framework[6]. Operationally, abstract interpretation is concerned with the construction of an interpreter for a language that generates *abstract* or approximate values; this is in contrast to the behavior of an exact interpreter that generates exact values. We consider an interpretation framework that is based on a *labelled* transition system for an operational semantics. In this context, every expression is uniquely labelled.

Typically, an approximate value is a finite description of the set of (exact) values its generating expression may yield. Thus, one approximate value of the variable $x$ in the following expression would be the set of (syntactic) **mk-loc** program points to whose dynamic instances $x$ could be bound; the elements in this set correspond to the abstract values of the procedure's arguments:

$$\lambda\ x.\mathbf{read}(x)$$

Broadly speaking, we can regard an abstract interpreter as a constraint based evaluator. The abstract state is represented as a directed graph in which nodes correspond to expressions and edges represent the flow of data. Each node stores an abstract value which corresponds to the value of the expression at that node. Each edge can be viewed as a (subset) constraint on the abstract values stored at the nodes it connects. The evaluation of an expression can change the abstract value stored at a node, which in turn may violate a number of constraints (i.e., edges) emanating from that node. This may cause the evaluation of further expressions, the violation of further constraints, etc. as a further complication, because the input language contains data structures and higher-order procedures, edges may be added dynamically. The interpreter terminates when all constraints are satisfied.

In the presence of asynchronously executing threads, we have a variety of choices in choosing our approximations. For example, we might consider ignoring threads altogether in the abstract interpretation. In such a formulation, the value of an abstract location might be the label (*i.e.*, syntactic program point) from which its dynamic instances are created. Such an approximation chooses not to disambiguate different instances of a value based on the abstract threads which create them. Alternatively, we might choose to label an abstract location with both its syntactic program point, as well as the syntactic label of the **spawn** expression from which it was created. The latter analysis is clearly more accurate, but also incurs greater cost.

We have developed a framework[22] in which the accuracy and precision of such an analysis is parameterized along several dimensions:

1. *Contours:* A contour represents an abstraction of an activation frame or call string. The abstract value of an expression is determined in part by the contour within which it is evaluated. Thus, an interpretation that has only one contour effectively collapses all instances of a given (syntactic) expression. Alternatively, an interpretation that treats a contour as a call-string of length one effectively uses the current (syntactically apparent) application point to disambiguate the abstract values of expressions found in the procedure being applied from other calls made to the same procedure from different (syntactially apparent) call sites.

2. *Abstract binding environments:* The abstract values of free variables found in a procedure are determined via an abstract binding environment associated with the procedure. Abstract binding environments map variables to contours; given a contour, the abstract value of a variable is determined via an abstract store. As with contours, the choice of how binding environments are constructed influences the accuracy and cost of the analysis. Consider the expression,

$$\lambda x.\lambda y.x$$

The outer lambda may be instantiated at a number of different points in a program. However, the abstract value of $x$ in the inner procedure depends on the definition of environment extension and creation. A refined environment extension function will map $x$ in each instance of the inner procedure to its abstract value defined by the appropriate application of the outer procedure. A coarse environment extension function will join all abstract values of $x$ in all instances of the outer procedure.

3. *Spawn Contours:* Contours help to abstract intra-thread control-flow; spawn contours help abstract inter-thread control-flow. In the presence of asynchronously executing threads, an abstract value is associated with a $<contour, spawn contour>$ pair. A spawn contour, like a regular contour,

is represented as a sequence of labels, each element in the sequence corresponding to a spawn point.

For example, an interpretation that disregards spawn contours completely is not concerned with inter-thread control-flow. Values generated by a thread during its evaluation will be visible to other threads even if these values are used locally and are not accessible via shared data structures. A spawn contour of length one will disambiguate control-flow emanating from syntactially different occurrences of spawn expressions in a program, but will not disambiguate different instances generated from the same spawn point.

4. *Spawn Binding Environments:* The binding environment within which a thread begins execution is also a target for parameterization. One obvious choice for the environment in which a spawned thread evaluates is the environment of its parent. However, other possibilities also exist. For example, evaluating threads in an empty environment causes control-flow information to not cross thread boundaries; in this formulation, each thread effectively builds and maintains its own "copy" of relevant bindings.

## 7.3 An Example

To illustrate the utility of this analysis, consider the following program written in our kernel language. Both procedures and locations are used in higher-order contexts, thus making it non-trivial to understand the control-flow behavior of the program by mere textual examination of the source.

$$
\begin{aligned}
&\textbf{let } f = \lambda \langle q, r \rangle. \\
&\qquad\qquad \textbf{if null?}(q) \\
&\qquad\qquad \textbf{then } \lambda ().r \\
&\qquad\qquad \textbf{else spawn let } z = (\text{read}(q)) \\
&\qquad\qquad\qquad\qquad \textbf{in } \ldots z \ldots \\
&\textbf{in spawn let } x = (\text{mk-loc}) \\
&\qquad\qquad g = \text{write}(x, (\text{cons }(\textbf{let } v = (\text{mk-loc}) \\
&\qquad\qquad\qquad\qquad\qquad\qquad\qquad w = (\text{mk-loc}) \\
&\qquad\qquad\qquad\qquad\qquad \textbf{in write}(v, \lambda ().f(\textbf{ nil write}(w, 0))) \\
&\qquad\qquad\qquad\qquad \text{nil})) \\
&\qquad\qquad \textbf{in} f(\text{ car}(\text{read}(g)) (\text{mk-loc}))
\end{aligned}
$$

A simple (polynomial-time) instantiation of our interpretation framework can deduce several interesting properties of this program:

1. The argument $q$ in $f$ is always bound to either the constant **nil** or a location created by the **mk-loc** operation in the outer **spawn**.
2. The argument $r$ in $f$ is always bound to a location.
3. Location $x$ is written and read only by threads created by the outer **spawn**.
4. The contents of $x$ is a cons cell created by the **cons** operation in the outer **spawn**.

5. The contents of location $v$ is the procedure,

$$\lambda\,().f(\ \text{nil write}(y,0)\ )$$

6. The **car** of $g$ is always bound to an instance of a location created by the inner **mk-loc** in the outer spawn, *i.e.*, the **mk-loc** operation bound to $v$.
7. Location $v$ is written in the outer **spawn**, but only read in the inner one, *i.e.*, the **spawn** found in $f$.
8. The value of the **mk-loc** argument to the outer application of $f$ is unbound.
9. The result of $f$ is a procedure precisely when $x$ is **nil**.

Based on such information, we can apply a number of important optimizations and heuristics related to locking, synchronization, type checks, and locality management:

1. No locks need to to be allocated for the location bound to $f$'s second argument in $f$'s outermost call.
2. Since all instances of the location bound to $x$ are written and read by threads created by the outer **spawn**, a separate heap for $x$ accessed exclusively by these threads can be created.
3. Since locations are never removed once written, no locks need to be acquired by readers when accessing a non-empty location.
4. The types of the contents of all locations are known, thus obviating the need to introduce runtime type checks when applying a strict operation (such as **car**) on a location's contents.
5. Since threads created by the inner **spawn** (defined in $f$) read locations created by the outer **spawn**, instances of these threads can be allocated close to another in a topology since share an explicit data dependency via location $v$.

Applying such an analysis may lead to significantly improved performance especially for programs that use higher-order procedures, or in which inter-thread control flow is non-trivial. Many parallel symbolic algorithms would likely be significantly more efficient if they were the subject of such analyses.

Effective analysis of shared locations directly leads to improved locality. Both temporal and spatial locality are improved because tasks that never share locations need not be placed close to one another, or share common storage. Tasks that do are likely to exhibit improved performance if they reside close to another in a virtual topology, or if locations they share reside in a separate heap accessible only to these tasks.

Besides the optimizations listed above, one can imagine other optimizations more closely allied with a particular program methodology or abstraction. For example, touch elimination[9] is a potentially important optimization in programs that use *futures* exclusively for synchronization and task creation. In the absence of this optimization, strict operations must explicitly check their arguments to see if they are bound to a placeholder object of the kind yielded by *future* evaluation. Touch elimination, much like runtime type elimination, eliminates such checks when it can be determined that the arguments are not placeholders. It is easy to show that an abstract interpretation technique of the kind described here can be used to implement touch elimination operations.

## Acknowledgments

Sting was designed jointly with James Philbin, who is responsible for its shared-memory implementation. Work on compile-time analysis techniques for higher-order parallel languages is joint with Stephen Weeks.

## References

1. Marina Chen, Young-il Choo, and Jingke Li. Compiling Parallel Programs by Optimizing Performance. *Journal of Supercomputing*, 1(2):171–207, 1988.
2. K.L Clark and S. Gregory. PARLOG: Parallel Programming in Logic. *ACM Transactions on Programming Languages and Systems*, 8(1):1–49, 1986.
3. William Clinger and Jonathan Rees, editors. Revised[4] Report on the Algorithmic Language Scheme. *ACM Lisp Pointers*, 4(3), July 1991.
4. Eric Cooper and Richard Draves. C Threads. Technical Report CMU-CS-88-154, Carnegie-Mellon University, June.
5. Eric Cooper and J.Gregory Morrisett. Adding Threads to Standard ML. Technical Report CMU-CS-90-186, Carnegie-Mellon University, 1990.
6. Patrick Cousot. Semantic Foundations of Program Analysis. In *Program Flow Analysis: Theory and Foundation*, pages 303–342. Prentice-Hall, 1981.
7. J. Dongarra, D. Sorenson, and P. Brewer. Tools and Methodology for Programming Parallel Processors. In *Aspects of Computation on Asynchronous Processors*, pages 125–138. North-Holland, 1988.
8. Raphael Finkel and John Fishburn. Parallelism in Alpha-Beta Search. *Artificial Intelligence*, 19(1):89–106, 1982.
9. Cormac Flanagan and Matthias Felleisen. The Semantics of Future and Its Use in Program Optimization. In *ACM 22$^{nd}$ Annual Symposium on Principles of Programming Languages*, January 1995.
10. Allan Gottlieb, B. Lubachevsky, and Larry Rudolph. Basic Techniques for the Efficient Coordination of Very Large Numbers of Cooperating Sequential Processors. *ACM Transactions on Programming Languages and Systems*, 5(2):164–189, April 1983.
11. David Saks Greenberg. *Full Utilization of Communication Resources*. PhD thesis, Yale University, June 1991.
12. Robert Halstead. Multilisp: A Language for Concurrent Symbolic Computation. *Transactions on Programming Languages and Systems*, 7(4):501–538, October 1985.

13. Christopher Haynes and Daniel Friedman. Embedding Continuations in Procedural Objects. *ACM Transactions on Programming Languages and Systems*, 9(4):582–598, 1987.

14. Feng hsiung Hsu. *Large Scale Parallelization of Alpha-Beta Search: An Algorithmic and Architectural Study with Computer Chess*. PhD thesis, Carnegie-Mellon University, 1990. Published as Technical Report CMU-CS-90-108.

15. Paul Hudak. Para-functional Programming in Haskell. In Boleslaw K. Szymanski, editor, *Parallel Functional Languages and Compilers*. ACM Press, 1991.

16. Paul Hudak *et.al.* Report on the Functional Programming Language Haskell, Version 1.2. *ACM SIGPLAN Notices*, May 1992.

17. Takayasu Ito and Robert Halstead, Jr., editors. *Parallel Lisp: Languages and Systems*. Springer-Verlag, 1989. LNCS number 41.

18. Suresh Jagannathan. TS/Scheme: Distributed Data Structures in Lisp. *Lisp and Symbolic Computation*, 7(2):283–305, 1994.

19. Suresh Jagannathan and James Philbin. A Customizable Substrate for Concurrent Languages. In *ACM SIGPLAN '91 Conference on Programming Language Design and Implementation*, June 1992.

20. Suresh Jagannathan and James Philbin. A Foundation for an Efficient Multi-Threaded Scheme System. In *Proceedings of the 1992 Conf. on Lisp and Functional Programming*, June 1992.

21. Suresh Jagannathan and Stephen Weeks. Analyzing Stores and References in a Parallel Symbolic Language. In *Proceedings of the ACM Symposium on Lisp and Functional Programming*, pages 294–306, 1994.

22. Suresh Jagannathan and Stephen Weeks. A Unified Treatment of Flow Analysis in Higher-Order Languages. In *ACM 22nd Annual Symposium on Principles of Programming Languages*, January 1995.

23. David Kranz, Robert Halstead, and Eric Mohr. Mul-T: A High Performance Parallel Lisp. In *Proceedings of the ACM Symposium on Programming Language Design and Implementation*, pages 81–91, June 1989.

24. Sun Microsystems. *Lightweight Processes*, 1990. In SunOS Programming Utilities and Libraries.

25. Robin Milner, Mads Tofte, and Robert Harper. *The Definition of Standard ML*. MIT Press, 1990.

26. Rick Mohr, David Kranz, and Robert Halstead. Lazy Task Creation: A Technique for Increasing the Granularity of Parallel Programs. In *Proceedings of the 1990 ACM Conference on Lisp and Functional Programming*, June 1990.

27. J. Gregory Morrisett and Andrew Tolmach. Procs and Locks: A Portable Multiprocessing Platform for Standard ML of New Jersey. In *Fourth ACM Symposium on Principles and Practice of Parallel Programming*, pages 198–207, 1993.

28. James Philbin. *An Operating System for Modern Languages*. PhD thesis, Dept. of Computer Science, Yale University, 1993.

29. John Reppy. CML: A Higher-Order Concurrent Language. In *Proceedings of the SIGPLAN'91 Conference on Programming Language Design and Implementation*, pages 293–306, June 1991.

30. Anne Rogers and Keshave Pingali. Process Decomposition Through Locality of Reference. In *SIGPLAN'89 Conference on Programming Language Design and Implementation*, pages 69–80, 1989.

31. Karsten Schwan and Win Bo. "Topologies" – Distributed Objects on Multicomputers. *ACM Transactions on Computer Systems*, 8(2):111–157, 1990.

32. Ehud Shapiro, editor. *Concurrent Prolog Collected Papers*. MIT Press, Cambridge, Mass., 1987.

33. V.S. Sunderam. PVM: A Framework for Parallel Distributed Computing. *Concurrency: Practice & Experience*, 2(4), 1990.

34. A. Tevanian, R. Rashid, D. Golub, D. Black, E. Cooper, and M. Young. Mach Treads and the UNIX Kernel: The Battle for Control. In *1987 USENIX Summer Conference*, pages 185–197, 1987.

35. Stephen Weeks, Suresh Jagannathan, and James Philbin. A Concurrent Abstract Interpreter. *Lisp and Symbolic Computation*, 7(2):171–191, 1994.

36. Michael Wolfe. *Optimizing Supercompilers for SuperComputers*. MIT Press, 1989.

# An Algorithm for Efficient Global Garbage Collection on Massively Parallel Computers (Extend Abstract *)

Tomio Kamada, Satoshi Matsuoka, and Akinori Yonezawa
{kamada,matsu,yonezawa}@is.s.u-tokyo.ac.jp

Dept. of Information Science, The University of Tokyo
7-3-1, Hongo, Bunkyo-Ku, Tokyo 113 JAPAN

## 1   Introduction

Several distributed GC algorithms have been proposed in the past. But, realistic applications to commercially-available, large-scale MPPs have not been entirely successful. This is because algorithms (1) incurred excessive message traffic, (2) involved prohibitive runtime overhead, (3) did not properly scale to larger numbers of processors, and/or (4) have not been implemented to test their validity/efficiency.

In general, GC algorithms for distributed-memory architectures can be roughly classified into two types:

- Using reference counts: This type of GC algorithm mainly performs local GC on each node and uses reference counting to decide which objects are referenced to from other nodes [3, 14, 8, 11]. However, no algorithms we know to date can collect cyclic garbage ranging over nodes with low runtime overhead required for parallel computation.
- Distributed marking over nodes: This type of GC algorithm is an extension of the standard mark-and-sweep algorithm, and traverses/marks both local and inter-node references[1, 5, 6, 12]. They can collect cyclic garbages, but many involve long pause time and/or excessive message traffic. Messages by the garbage collector not only marks objects in other nodes, but also used to detect termination of marking traversal. Some algorithms allow independent local GC on each node to exploit reference locality[5, 6, 12].

We present an efficient real-life distributed GC algorithm based on an asynchronous message passing model and distributed marking. It assumes distributed-memory high-performance MPPs where processors are interconnected by a high-speed (asynchronous) network.

Our GC algorithm has the following favorable properties:

- Our global GC traverses inter-node references, and can collect distributed cyclic garbages quickly and efficiently.

---

* The contents of this extend abstract was also presented at Supercomputing '94[7]

- GC algorithms that use distributed marking tend to involve excessive message traffic, incurring high runtime overhead and also disturb ongoing computation. Our global GC reduces message traffic by over 50% compared to straightforward algorithms, featuring efficient handling of outstanding references within messages and low-communication termination cost for detection of marking.
- Our global GC admits minimum pause time for user applications (mutators), and allows concurrent mutator/collector operations. As we will discuss later, this property is essential for performance reasons because it allows effective latency hiding of the communications.
- Our GC algorithm allows local generational GC on each node to operate independently of other nodes (without invoking global GC), facilitating efficient collection of local garbage, taking advantage of reference locality.
- Experimental results show that our algorithm is scalable to 1024 processors on Fujitsu AP1000, in that global GC time remains nearly constant even as the number of nodes increases.

Where object references may change in real-time by message passing, it is necessary for global GC to consider pending messages on asynchronous networks. We use two different methods for confirming the arrival of pending messages, *bulldozing method* [12] and *message counting method*. We evaluate their respective performances and compare their advantages/disadvantages.

Marking Termination must also be detected with low message traffic. We uses *Weighted Throw Counting (WTC) scheme*[10, 9] to reduce message traffic.

We have implemented a prototype version of our algorithm on Fujitsu AP1000, a multicomputer with 32–1024 nodes, and validated its correct operation and did several performance benchmarks, including the measurement of reduction in message traffic of global GC.

## 2   Our GC System

Our global GC system consists of *local collectors* on each node and a *GC host*. Each local collector traverses references in its node. If an inter-node reference is found, the local collector sends a mark message to the collector on the owner node of the referenced object to mark the referenced objects and traverse the references from there.

The GC host is a special node that decides the initiation of global GC, and also detects termination of marking. The GC host determines termination of marking based on information from each local collector. Existence of such a central management node may seem that the node might become a scalability bottleneck, but as we shall show in Section 5, performance benchmarks have so far shown that this is not a problem.

To allow local GC to operate independently of other nodes without invoking global GC, each node has an *export set*, that consists of pointers to objects possibly referenced from other nodes, and are treated as a part of the root set during local GC.

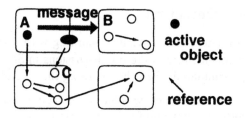

**Fig. 1.** Old Messages

## 3 Which Objects to Mark in Global GC?

Global GC in a distributed environment poses difficulties in determining (1) which objects to mark and (2) how to detect termination of marking. This section discusses the issue (1), and the issue (2) is discussed in Section 4.

First, we define live objects and garbage in our global GC:

1. Objects that are executing methods, or (potentially) have unprocessed messages, are live (called *active objects*).
2. Objects referenced from (lexically) top-level variables are live.
3. The transitive closure of references from live objects are live.
4. All other objects are garbage.

The global GC algorithm marks objects by globally traversing references from top-level variables, logically active objects, and their unprocessed messages. Pending messages in the network, however, complicate the treatment of reference relationships among objects. In Fig.1, a mutator message with a sole global reference to object C is sent from object A and has not arrived at its destination object B, whose sole global reference held at A is lost immediately after the message has been sent. If global GC starts at this point, B and C are live because B will become active when the message arrives, and C will be referenced by B. However, if the global GC would fail to recognize the message, both B and C would be mistakenly collected as garbage.

Unprocessed messages that are sent just prior to the start of global GC and have not yet arrived at their destination are called *old messages*, and their destination objects are logically active. When a node receives an old message, the local collector on the node marks from the destination object and the objects that are referenced by the message. Confirming the arrival of all the old messages must be done before determination of marking termination. Algorithms for arrival confirmation are discussed in Section 4.1, and marking termination algorithm is presented in Section 4.2.

Finally, in our global GC, as marking and mutators are concurrently processed, mutators may write into untraversed objects. We use the standard technique of *(local) write barrier* to detect such a overwrite, and local collectors mark from the references. But if write barrier cost is high, we can further omit the write barrier by reducing the concurrency between marking and ordinary computations as described in Section 4.3.

# 4  Termination Detection

It is also difficult to detect termination of marking with low message traffic in a distributed environment. Reviewing the discussions in Section 3, marking can be judged as being terminated when the following three conditions are satisfied:

1. The arrivals of all the old messages have been confirmed.
2. All the local collectors have no further objects to mark.
3. No mark messages are in transit within the network.

We refer to the set of global states that satisfy conditions 2 and 3 as *quiescent states*. Section 4.1 presents two methods for the arrival confirming of all the old messages that work concurrently with mutators and marking, and Section 4.2 describes an algorithm to detect the quiescent state with low message traffic.

## 4.1  Arrival Confirmation of Old Messages

Our global GC confirms the arrival of all the old messages to assure marking from all the references contained therein. We have two alternative methods for arrival confirmation, *message counting method* and *bulldozing method*. Both algorithms work concurrently with marking, and do not block sending of new messages.

**Message Counting Method.** ACKs are messages that are sent to the sender node to confirm the arrival of mutator messages\*\*. However, naive employment of ACKs would double the number of messages sent by mutators during the entire computation.

The message counting method eliminates the need of ACKs. All the nodes count the number of outgoing and incoming mutator messages. During global GC, the GC host watches the sum of the number of sent and received old messages in the system. To distinguish the old messages from mutator messages sent after the start of global GC (called *new messages*), we assign a color to each mutator message. Each node sends the number of sent old messages to the GC host at the initiation of global GC. The GC host will know the number of all the sent messages in the system when it receives the information from all the nodes. Each node sends the number of received old message to the GC host when it has no objects to mark for a certain time period. If an old message arrives afterwards, the local collector resumes marking from it, and sends the number of newly received old messages to the GC host again when it has no more objects to mark. The GC host will have confirmed the arrival of all the old messages when the sum of the number of all the received messages and the total number of all the sent messages are equal.

In comparison, even if ACK information were to be stored/combined, and exchanged only during global GC, ACK information would have to be exchanged between all the node pairs leading to a $O(n^2)$ algorithm where $n$ is the number of nodes. In contrast, the message counting method sends messages for arrival confirmation only during global GC, and more importantly, the number of messages required for global arrival confirmation is reduced to $O(n)$.

---

\*\* Note that this is different from acknowledgement of *mark messages*

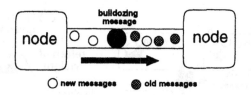

**Fig. 2.** Bulldozing

**Bulldozing Method.** The bulldozing method uses hardware-assisted network clearing operation that can be used in networks that guarantee message FIFOness [12]. Bulldozing does not block sending of new messages; instead *Bulldozing messages* are sent through all the network paths of the system, and arrivals of bulldozing messages through a given path guarantee the arrival of old messages through that path.

No actual global GC implementations on MPPs have used bulldozing to our knowledge, however. In our implementation on AP1000, we reduce message traffic and latency by taking advantage of the physical network topology. Nodes store and forward bulldozing messages 6 times for each particular path for an arbitrary $n$, and $8 \times n$ bulldozing messages are in the system in total.

We do not need to color mutator messages, as the arrival of the bulldozing message guarantee that the old message have been processed. As a result, we totally eliminate the runtime overhead in mutator message passing (no counting/coloring is required), although we might recognize a small fraction of new messages as old and mark from them (Fig.2).

## 4.2 Detection of Quiescent State

Another problem of distributed marking is the termination detection of marking with low message traffic. Many global GC algorithms return an acknowledgement message *** per every mark message to indicate the arrival of the message, or the termination of marking from it. Thus, the number of messages required for termination detection would be more than twice the number of mark messages.

In order to reduce this cost, we use *WTC scheme*[10, 9] to detect quiescent state of marking. Mark messages and marking local collectors are given positive weights by the GC host. The GC host finds the quiescent state of marking when all weights are returned to the GC host. Local collectors send mark messages with positive weight dividends. A local collector that receives a mark message adds the weight of the message to its own current weight(Fig.3(a)). The invariant is that the sum of the weights of mark messages and local collectors are equal to the weight that the GC host gives out.

Each local collector returns its weight to the GC host if it has no objects to mark for a certain period(Fig.3(b)). If all the weights are returned to the GC

---

*** Again, not to be confused with ACKs, which are acknowledgements to *mutator* messages.

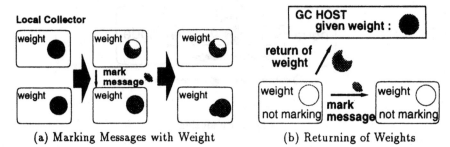

(a) Marking Messages with Weight    (b) Returning of Weights

**Fig. 3.** Detection of Quiescent States

host, the GC host can judge that the system is in the quiescent state. The GC host judges the termination of marking when it confirms the arrival of all the old messages and the marking state is quiescent.

Comparing with methods that return acknowledgement for each mark message, our method only needs to communicate infrequently with the GC host to return/request weight that is managed by each local collector as a unit, and it requires substantially less message traffic. On the other hand, our method could result in concentration of weight messages to the GC host, but experimental results so far show that this is not a problem because weight message traffic is very infrequent compared to other types of messages.

## 4.3 Optimizations

We can further optimize our algorithm to reduce messages traffic to the GC host. Our implementation on AP1000 currently incorporates the following optimizations. Firstly, for the message counting method, we can combine the messages that send the number of received old message and that return weight into one message. Secondly, each local collector could delay the returning of weight for a certain time period after local marking terminates, letting the mutator execute in the node. In our global GC, it is sometime the case that, immediately after returning the weight, an old messages or a mark message would arrive and marking must be resumed. By incorporating such a delay, we can reduce such cases and reduce messages to the GC host.

In addition, we can omit write barriers by reducing concurrency between marking and ordinary computations, if write barrier cost is high. We can avoid assignment on unmarked objects by using a scheme that is based on the idea proposed in [4]. At the start of the marking phase, each node traverses/marks local references transitively from all the root objects of each node, and then ordinary computations are allowed to execute. For messages from other nodes, each node traverses/marks references transitively from local objects referenced directly by the message on the node, and then execution of the activity associated with the message is allowed. In this case, ordinary computations are executed in the node without accessing unmarked objects. Fortunately, this scheme does not invalidate our termination detection algorithm.

| application | 12-Queens | | 13-Queens | | 20000 Body | |
|---|---|---|---|---|---|---|
| # of nodes | 64 | | 1024 | | 512 | |
| method for arrival confirmation | msg count | bulldozing | msg count | bulldozing | msg count | bulldozing |
| # of gc messages excluding mark messages: A | 410 | 640 | 3700 | 9200 | 1360 | 4100 |
| # of mark messages: B | 13700 | 15700 | 24000 | 23000 | 45500 | 49000 |
| A / B | 3.0 % | 4.1 % | 15 % | 40% | 3.0 % | 8.3 % |
| marking time(msec) | 190 | 190 | 170 | 190 | 210 | 220 |
| # of gc messages to host | 410 | 210 | 3700 | 2100 | 1360 | 1540 |
| # of marked objects ($\times 10^5$) | 6.7 | 6.6 | 1.5 | 1.3 | 6.5 | 6.5 |
| # of ordinary messages during global GC: C (old messages) | | | | | 9100 (5) | 10500 (3) |

**Table 1.** Performance Evaluation of Global GC

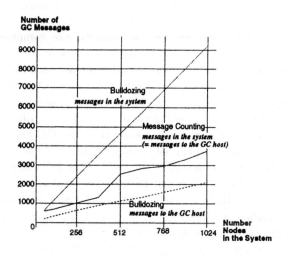

**Fig. 4.** The Number of GC Messages Excluding Mark Messages (13-Queens)

## 5    Performance Evaluation

We have implemented a prototype of our global GC algorithm on a 32–1024 nodes Fujitsu AP1000 MPP (each node consists of 25MHz SPARC and 16MB memory). In order to evaluate the performance, we employed a fine-grain, naive combinatorial N-Queen search problem (Table1,Fig.4), and a fine-grain, one-dimension Newtonian N-body problem solution based on algorithm presented in [15], that is a parallel extension of [2] (Table1).

The number of messages for global GC excluding mark messages, i.e. weight return/request or bulldozing messages (row A), is 3–15 % of the number of mark messages (row B), when the number of remote references are substantially larger than the number of the nodes in the system by orders of magnitude(Table1). In other words, the total number of messages for global GC is a small fraction greater than the number of remote references. In the case of acknowledging every mark message, the number of message for global GC would be more than twice the number of remote references. Our method reduces message traffic of global GC by about half.

Both the message counting method and the bulldozing method terminates marking in about 200–300 msec irrespective of the number of nodes. Furthermore, since mutators are concurrently executed during that time, the latency involved in remote marking is effectively hidden. The only case the mutator becomes blocked is when the node physically runs out of memory during this period. For N-body (Table1), the number of ordinary messages (row C) is almost equal to 20 % of the number of GC messages during global GC (row A + B), and most of ordinary messages are colored new. This implies ordinary computations proceeded substantially during the global GC phases.

Comparing the message counting method with the bulldozing method, the bulldozing method involves more message traffic than message counting method (Table1). This is because the latter uses bulldozing messages exclusively for arrival confirmation, while message counting method can combine messages for arrival confirmation and for detection of quiescent state. In addition, whether or not effective bulldozing algorithm would be possible depends on the network architecture of the underlying hardware. On the other hand, the bulldozing method has the advantage that it would involve little mutator overhead as it does not have to deal with runtime color information or message counting.

In this benchmark, the number of messages to the GC host are small, and thus message concentration on the GC host does not become a problem. More specifically, the number of messages to the GC host is 3–5 times as many as the number of nodes (Table1,Fig.4). In our performance evaluation with 1024 nodes AP1000, the number of the GC messages to the GC host does not exceed 5000, and that did not become a bottleneck in our benchmark. However, concentration of messages to the GC host would become higher and could potentially cause problems if the number of nodes increases by orders of magnitude. In such a case, improvements will be needed such as creating a hierarchy of GC hosts.

## 6 Discussions

### 6.1 Concurrent GC and Latency Hiding

In centralized memory architectures, concurrent GC, which allow concurrent mutator and collector activities, is usually employed for reducing the interactive response time of the system, and do not result in performance benefits. For parallel GC in a distributed memory parallel architectures, however, the observation is that concurrent GC is *a requirement for BETTER performance*. This is primarily due to the following reasons. First, multithreading of the mutator and the collector allows *latency hiding*. This simple fact is nevertheless more important then it seems for distributed-memory GC on MPPs. Detailed logging of global GC shows that the bulk of the marking phase completes relatively quickly, and most nodes will remain idle for the rest of the GC phase. By multithreading with the mutator, such latency is effectively hidden, allowing full utilization of the processors. In addition, even for stop-and-go collection, the algorithm has to guarantee the global consistency in the state mutator state. This means that the network has to be cleared of in-transit messages in the same manner as our current algorithm. This will further lengthen the pause time, in which most of computational resources are wasted.

## 6.2 Coexisting with Active Messages

Up until now, we have not discussed what kind of message passing mechanism one would use. The recent proposal of Active Messages[13] greatly reduced the latency involved in message passing. Active Messages involve compiling a customized preamble procedure for each specific message type, and passing only the pointer to the procedure at the head of the message. Upon reception of this pointer, the receiver node immediately jumps to the customized preamble. Active Messages are being used in various high-performance programming language implementations. However, it is not possible to employ Active Messages *naively* in our GC algorithm, because our algorithm requires generic/dynamic checking.

Fortunately, our GC algorithm and Active Messages can coexist in the following way: The idea is to customize *both* the preamble procedure and the initial message handler. For each message type, alternative preamble procedures are compiled for global GC. The standard behavior of the initial message handler is to make a dispatch to the preamble procedure. When global GC starts, the original initial message handler is replaced with the one which makes a dispatch to the corresponding alternative preamble procedure. Although such a mechanism is a small penalty, since majority of the computation is done during which GC is not active, it is better to optimize for normal computation by retaining the full efficient characteristics of Active Messages, which this technique does.

# 7 Conclusion and Future Work

Our parallel global GC algorithm reduces the runtime overhead and message traffic for global GC significantly. The number of messages for termination detection of marking is about 3–15% of the number of mark messages. This implies our global GC needs less than half the message traffic compared to previous algorithms. Comparing the two alternatives of old message arrival detection — the bulldozing method and the message counting method —, the bulldozing method has the advantage that it does not require coloring or counting of messages, but its viability depends on the underlying hardware, and latency of bulldozing could be longer as a result.

Since our implementation is still a prototype version, we plan to evaluate realistic performances in various parallel program benchmarks. Although the current algorithm has shown to scale to 1024 nodes on a relatively standard MPP, we also plan to extend the system to have better scalability for MPPs with over thousands of nodes, by making the GC host and the arrival/termination detection algorithms to be hierarchical.

## Acknowledgements

We would like to express our thanks to Fujitsu Laboratory for allowing us to use the AP1000(1024 nodes version). We would also like to thank Prof. Queinnec for his insightful comments and suggestions. We also thank all the members of the ABCL project group for their discussions.

## References

1. L. Augusteijn. Garbage Collection in a Distributed Environment. In *Proc. of PARLE*, volume 259 of *LNCS*, 1987.
2. J. Barnes and P. Hut. A Hierarchical $O(N \log N)$ Force-Calculation Algorithm. *Nature*, 324:446–449, 1986.
3. D. I. Bevan. Distributed Garbage Collection Using Reference Counting. In *Proc. of PARLE*, volume 259 of *LNCS*, 1987.
4. H. C. and B. H. Actors and continuous functionals. In *Proc. of IFIP Woking Conference on Formal Description of Programming Concepts*, pages 1–21, 1988.
5. E. Jul, H. Levy, N. Hutchinson, and A. Black. Fine-grained Mobility in the Emerald System. In *ACM Transactions on Computer Systems*, 1988.
6. N. C. Juul and E. Jul. Comprehensive and Robust Garbage Collection in a Distributed System. In *Memory Management*, volume 637 of *LNCS*, 1992.
7. T. Kamada, S. Matsuoka, and A. Yonezawa. Efficient Parallel Global Garbage Collection on Massively Parallel Computers. In *Proc. of Supercomputing*, 1994.
8. B. Lang, C. Queinnec, and J. Piquer. Garbage Collecting the World. In *Proc. of POPL*, 1992.
9. F. Mattern. Global quiescence detection based on credit distribution and recovery. *Inf. Proc. Lett.*, 30(4):195–200, 1989.
10. K. Rokusawa, N. Ichiyoshi, T. Chikayama, and H. Nakashima. An Efficient Termination Detection and Abortion Algorithm for Distributed Processing Systems. In *Proc. of ICPP*, volume 1, pages 18–22, 1988.
11. M. Schelvis. Incremental Distribution of Timestamp Packets: A New Approach To Distributed Garbage Collection. In *Proc. of OOPSLA*, 1989.
12. N. Venkatasubramanian, G. Agha, and C. Talcott. Scalable Distributed Garbage Collection for System of Active Objects. In *LNCS637*, 1992.
13. T. von Eicken, D. E. Culler, S. C. Goldstein, and K. E. Schauser. Active Messages: a Mechanism for Integrated Communication and Computation. In *Proc. of ISCA*, pages 256–266, 1992.
14. P. Watson and I. Watson. An Efficient Garbage Collection Scheme For Parallel Computer Architectures. In *Proc. of PARLE*, volume 259 of *LNCS*, 1987.
15. M. Yasugi. A Councurrent Object-Oriented Programming Language System for Highly Parallel Data-Driven Computers and its Applications. Technical Report 94-7e, Dept. of Info. Sci., Univ. of Tokyo, 1994. (Doctoral Thesis, Mar. 1994).

# I/O Mode Analysis in Concurrent Logic Programming

Kazunori Ueda

Department of Information and Computer Science
Waseda University
4-1, Okubo 3-chome, Shinjuku-ku, Tokyo 169, Japan
ueda@ueda.info.waseda.ac.jp

**Abstract.** This paper briefly reviews concurrent logic programming and the I/O mode system designed for the concurrent logic language Flat GHC. The mode system plays fundamental rôles both in programming and implementation in almost the same way as type systems do but in different respects. It provides us with the information on how data are generated and consumed and thus the view of "data as resources". It statically detects bugs resulting from ill-formed dataflow and advocates the "programming as wiring" paradigm. Well-modedness guarantees the safety of unification, the basic operation in concurrent logic programming. Information on the numbers of access paths to data can be obtained by slightly extending the framework, which can be used for compile-time garbage collection and the destructive update of structures.

## 1   Concurrent Logic Programming

Concurrent logic programming was born around 1980 from the study of the parallel execution of logic programs, and became an important paradigm for concurrent programming in its own right. Relational language [3] was the first to appear in the form of a complete programming language. Guarded Horn Clauses (GHC) was designed in the Fifth Generation Computer Project in 1984 [11], after thorough examination of its predecessors Concurrent Prolog [9] and an early version of PARLOG [4]. Because of its simplicity, GHC was soon accepted in the Project as the base of KL1, the full-fledged kernel language for the Parallel Inference Machine. GHC was soon subsetted to Flat GHC with a simpler guard construct, and the design of KL1 started based on Flat GHC. While GHC was designed as a concurrent language that did not address *how* programs should be executed, KL1 was designed as a parallel language in which programmers could specify what processor should execute what processes and at what priorities [13]. For the detailed history of the kernel language design in the Fifth Generation Computer Project, the readers are referred to [14].[1]

Several more concurrent logic programming languages were proposed in the past decade, but the difference between all those languages is rather small as

---

[1] An efficient KL1-to-C compiler system for Unix-based general-purpose computers, named KLIC, can be obtained via anonymous ftp from ftp.icot.or.jp.

far as the constructs for reactive concurrent programming are concerned—it's definitely smaller than the difference between CSP, CCS and ACP. All those languages feature asynchronous communication using single-assignment variables which people call *logical* variables. All the languages after (and including) Concurrent Prolog supported *incomplete messages*, a bidirectional communication technique using a single stream, and dynamic process creation and reconfiguration. Although they do not support processes as first-class objects, they support dynamic creation of processes and dynamic creation of streams connected to the processes. Since streams are first-class in concurrent logic programming and can freely passed from one process to another, those languages have effectively supported "mobile" processes since early 1980's.

## 2  How Processes Communicate

In concurrent logic programming, processes communicate by observing and generating substitutions, namely bindings between variables and their values. Consider an I/O process, say io(S), which models a CRT display terminal and receives a stream S of I/O commands such as get(C) and put(63). The stream S can be represented as a list of get and put commands, so S may be instantiated to a list [put(63),get(C),get(C'), ...], which means that the I/O process should display "?" and then read two characters. The same list may be constructed incrementally as S = [put(63)|S'], S' = [get(C)|S''], S'' = [get(C')|S'''], and so on. The I/O process will interpret these commands in the order they appear in the stream. If you key in "A" (65 in ASCII) and then "B" (66), it will generate the bindings C = 65 and C' = 66.

The observation of bindings is done by matching (one-way unification) and the generation is done by (two-way) unification. Interestingly, this algebraic account can be restated logically: Bindings can be viewed as equality constraints on the values of variables, matching can be viewed as the checking (*asking*) of whether one constraint implies another, and unification can be viewed as the publication (*telling*) of a constraint. This view was first given by Maher [6] and studied extensively by Saraswat [7] in a generalized setting of *concurrent constraint programming* (CCP).

## 3  GHC as a Model of Concurrency

Although the family of concurrent logic languages [10] was initially proposed as a tool for programming rather than a model of concurrency, its essence is simple enough to be viewed as a model of concurrency. The somewhat simplified syntax of GHC, which ignores guard goals, is given in Figure 1. The syntax is rule-based rather than expression-based simply for historical and practical reasons.

Rule (1) in concerned with indeterminate choice. Rule (2) is concerned with information receiving (at A, called the *head*) and subsequent reduction to B (the *body*). It implicitly expresses the hiding of variables occurring only in B as well. Information receiving is done by matching $A$ with a goal (say $G$) to be reduced, where only the variables in $A$ can be instantiated. If $A$ and $G$ are not unifiable, $G$ cannot be reduced using the program clause $A$ :- $B$. If they are unifiable but only by instantiating $G$, the matching is suspended until $G$ is sufficiently instantiated by the execution of other unification goals. Thus the matching between $A$ and $G$ may involve equality checking and synchronization as well as information receiving.

Rule (3) is concerned with parallel composition. Rule (4) says that each goal is either a unification goal to publish information or a non-unification goal to be reduced using program clauses. The initial multiset of goals to be reduced is given by a goal clause (Rule (7)).

The CCP framework considered a lot more combinators, but we have made sure that the above (small) set of constructs, which corresponds to indeterminate CCP with *ask* and (eventual) *tell*, is usually enough.

$$
\begin{array}{rll}
\text{(program)} \ P & ::= \text{set of } C\text{'s} & (1) \\
\text{(program clause)} \ C & ::= A \ \text{:-} \ B & (2) \\
\text{(body)} \ B & ::= \text{multiset of } G\text{'s} & (3) \\
\text{(goal)} \ G & ::= T_1 = T_2 \quad | \quad A & (4) \\
\text{(non-unification atom)} \ A & ::= p(T_1, \ldots, T_n), \quad p \neq \text{'='} & (5) \\
\text{(term)} \ T & ::= \text{(as in first-order logic)} & (6) \\
\text{(goal clause)} \ Q & ::= \text{:-} \ B & (7)
\end{array}
$$

**Fig. 1.** The (simplified) syntax of GHC

## 4 Channels as First-Class Objects

What makes concurrent logic/constraint programming unique is that communication channels (streams) are first-class data structures (lists). Ordinary list operations are used for sending and receiving messages, while in other models of concurrency, channels and operations on channels are usually provided as *built-in* language constructs. This uniformity in the language constructs was achieved by the ability of (concurrent) logic languages to deal with partial information such as lists with uninstantiated tails. The uniformity contributes much to the simplicity of the semantical framework and program analysis.

Channels as data structures turned out to be quite flexible. Various communication protocols have been used in actual programming, including streams of streams (of streams ...), demand-driven communication, and incomplete messages with reply boxes. In addition, difference lists invented in logic programming turned out to be extremely useful also in concurrent logic programming. Difference lists allow us to form fragments of a message sequence independently—in an arbitrary order or in parallel—, connect them later on, and feed the result to the receiver process.

# 5 Experiences with GHC/KL1 Programming

Hundreds of thousands of lines of GHC/KL1 programs have been written inside and outside the Fifth Generation Project. The applications include an operating system for the Parallel Inference Machine (PIMOS), a parallel theorem prover (MGTP) that discovered a new fact in finite algebra, genetic information processing, and so on.

People found the communication and synchronization mechanisms of GHC/KL1 quite natural. They were seldom bothered by synchronization bugs[2] and gradually learned to model their problems in an object-oriented manner using concurrent processes and streams. Although writing correct *concurrent* programs was not so hard, writing efficient *parallel* programs turned to be a quite separate issue. A visual performance debugger played an important rôle.

We have found that logical variables are normally used for cooperative rather than competitive communication. Most variables in a run-time configuration have exactly two occurrences each, in which case they are used as *cables* for one-to-one communication. This is closely related to the fact that (surprisingly) many program clauses in Prolog and concurrent logic programs are *linear* in the sense that each variable in a clause occurs exactly twice. Consider append in Prolog:

```
append([],    Y,Y).
append([A|X],Y,[A|Z]) :- append(X,Y,Z).
```

The two clauses are linear in our sense, though they are not *left-linear* in that some variables occur more than once in the heads. On the other hand, the GHC counterpart of append is both linear and left-linear:

```
append([],    Y,Z ) :- Z=Y.
append([A|X],Y,Z0) :- Z0=[A|Z], append(X,Y,Z).
```

Some GHC variables occur three or more times, most of which are used to distribute ground terms such as numbers or shared global data. Clauses containing such variables will generate variables with three or more occurrences in a run-time configuration, which will be used as *hubs* for one-to-many communication.

Whether communication is one-to-one or one-to-many, unification goals will always succeed as long as they are used for cooperative communication. Nevertheless, programmers have often got an error message "unification failure", which indicates that variables are inadvertently used for non-cooperative communication. For instance, goals X = [] and X = [H|T] will noncooperatively attempt to

---

[2] Bugs regarding the causality of information flow are a higher-level problem that often arises in, for example, programs dealing with circular process structures.

bind X to different values. A static means to ensure the security of unification was strongly desired.

Note that unification failure is very similar to division-by-zero; for instance, a Pascal statement X := 5 div 0 can be viewed as insisting that different values, X * 0 (= 0) and 5, should become identical.

# 6 Mode System for Flat GHC

To guarantee the security of unification statically, a mode system for Flat GHC was designed in 1990 [12]. This and subsequent sections will introduce it rather informally but from various aspects. We refer the readers to [15] for the precise and detailed description.

As a metaphor, consider two electric devices connected by a cable for conveying signals. The cable may have a structure such as an array of wires. As the nature of a cable, its both ends, viewed from outside the cable, should have opposite polarity structures. That is, a signal given to one end of a wire will go out from the other end, though different wires may have different directionalities. The plug at an end of a cable will be inserted into the socket on a device. For the plug and the socket to be compatible, they should again have opposite polarity structures when viewed from outside. These constraints together imply that the two sockets on the two devices should have opposite polarity structures.

Our mode system infers such polarity structures of goal arguments in essentially the same manner. (To be exact, it infers the polarity structures of the arguments of *predicates* defining the behavior of goals, rather than dealing with individual goals themselves.) A mode represents the polarity structure of goal arguments. While an electric cable has an array structure, a logical variable may be instantiated to a nested structure with a complicated communication protocol. To deal with such protocols, a mode is a function from the set of paths specifying positions in data structures occurring in goals, denoted $P_{Atom}$, to the set $\{in, out\}$. Paths here are not strings of argument positions; instead they are strings of $\langle symbol, argument\text{-}position \rangle$ pairs in order to be able to specify positions in data structures that *can* be formed as the result of computation. For instance, when the argument S of an I/O server io(S) is instantiated to [put(63),get(C),get(C'), ...], the variable C' is said to occur at

$$\langle \text{io}, 1 \rangle \langle ., 2 \rangle \langle ., 2 \rangle \langle ., 1 \rangle \langle \text{get}, 1 \rangle \ ,$$

where '.' is a list constructor. Formally, the sets of paths for specifying positions in terms and atoms are defined, respectively, using disjoint union as:

$$P_{Term} = \left( \sum_{f \in Fun} N_f \right)^* , \quad P_{Atom} = \left( \sum_{p \in Pred} N_p \right) \times P_{Term} \ ,$$

where *Fun* and *Atom* are the sets of function and predicate symbols, respectively, and $N_p$ and $N_f$ are the sets of positive integers up to and including the arities of $p$ and $f$, respectively.

Mode analysis tries to find a mode (i.e., polarity structure) under which every piece of communication will be performed cooperatively. Such a mode is called a *well-moding*.

A well-moding is computed by constraint solving. Function and variable symbols in a program/goal clause will impose constraints on the possible polarities of the path at which they occur. For example, a variable occurring exactly twice, both in the body of a clause, imposes a constraint that the two occurrences should have opposite polarity structures—as an electric cable does. A variable occurring exactly once in the head and exactly once in the body imposes a constraint that the two occurrences should have the same polarity structure, because the head can be compared to a device viewed from *inside*, not from outside. The two arguments of a unification goal should have opposite polarity structures, because a unification goal can be viewed as an adaptor that simply connects its two arguments and transmits information from one side to another. A function symbol occurring in a body goal represents a signal to be input to the goal, while a function symbol in a head represent a signal to be received. In either case, the path where a function symbol occurs is constrained to *in*. All these constraints are merged to find a well-moding of the arguments of user-defined goals.

As an example, consider the program for indeterminate stream merging:

```
merge([],    Y,     Z ) :- Z=Y.
merge(X,     [],    Z ) :- Z=X.
merge([A|X],Y,      Z0) :- Z0=[A|Z] , merge(X,Y,Z).
merge(X,     [A|Y],Z0) :- Z0=[A|Z] , merge(X,Y,Z).
```

The first clause has two occurrences of Y, one in the head and one in the body, so they should have the same mode. The two occurrences of Z should have the same mode as well. On the other hand, the occurrences of Z and Y in the body should have opposite modes because they occur in the opposite sides of a unification goal. So we obtain the constraint

$$\forall q \in P_{Term}\big(m(\langle \texttt{merge}, 2\rangle q) \neq m(\langle \texttt{merge}, 3\rangle q)\big) \ . \tag{1}$$

Also, because the function symbol [] occurs in the first argument, we have

$$m(\langle \texttt{merge}, 1\rangle) = in \ . \tag{2}$$

Similarly, from the second clause we have

$$\forall q \in P_{Term}\big(m(\langle \texttt{merge}, 1\rangle q) \neq m(\langle \texttt{merge}, 3\rangle q)\big) \ . \tag{3}$$

We have $m(\langle \texttt{merge}, 2\rangle) = in$ as well, but this is implied by (1), (2), and (3).

The third clause contains a unification goal between Z0 and [A|Z]. Let this goal be the $k$th unification goal. (We suffix unification goals here because we allow different unification goals to have different modes.) Then we have $m(\langle =_k, 2\rangle) = in$ and hence $m(\langle =_k, 1\rangle) = out$. The latter constraint is conveyed by Z0 and we have $m(\langle \texttt{merge}, 3\rangle) = out$, but this is again implied by the constraints we already have. The constraint imposed by the list constructor in the head is exactly the same as (2).

Because A occurs twice, once in the head and once in the body, we have

$$\forall q \in P_{Term}(\quad m(\langle \mathtt{merge}, 1 \rangle \langle ., 1 \rangle q) = m(\langle =_k, 2 \rangle \langle ., 1 \rangle q)$$
$$\neq m(\langle =_k, 1 \rangle \langle ., 1 \rangle q) = m(\langle \mathtt{merge}, 3 \rangle \langle ., 1 \rangle q)) \ ,$$

namely

$$\forall q \in P_{Term}(m(\langle \mathtt{merge}, 1 \rangle \langle ., 1 \rangle q) \neq m(\langle \mathtt{merge}, 3 \rangle \langle ., 1 \rangle q)) \ .$$

This happens to be implied by (3). The variable X occurs at $\langle \mathtt{merge}, 1 \rangle \langle ., 2 \rangle$ in the head and at $\langle \mathtt{merge}, 1 \rangle$ in the body, so we have

$$\forall q \in P_{Term}(m(\langle \mathtt{merge}, 1 \rangle \langle ., 2 \rangle q) = m(\langle \mathtt{merge}, 1 \rangle q)) \ . \tag{4}$$

The variable Z occurs twice as well, and we have

$$\forall q \in P_{Term}(\quad m(\langle \mathtt{merge}, 3 \rangle q) \neq m(\langle =_k, 2 \rangle \langle ., 2 \rangle q)$$
$$\neq m(\langle =_k, 1 \rangle \langle ., 2 \rangle q) = m(\langle \mathtt{merge}, 3 \rangle \langle ., 2 \rangle q)) \ ,$$

namely

$$\forall q \in P_{Term}(m(\langle \mathtt{merge}, 3 \rangle q) = m(\langle \mathtt{merge}, 3 \rangle \langle ., 2 \rangle q)) \ ,$$

which is, again, implied by the constraints we already have.

We can obtain constraints from the fourth clause a similar way, but all the constraints turn out to be implied by the constraints obtained from other clauses. To summarize, the four constraints (1), (2), (3), and (4) are all what are imposed by the merge program.

There are many good reasons to use a constraint-based framework. First of all, because it is inherently incremental, program modules making up a large program can be analyzed separately so that the results may be merged later. Secondly, the system provides a unified framework for mode inference, mode declaration and mode checking, where mode declaration is simply a mode constraint given by a programmer. Thirdly, it can deal with generic modes quite naturally. A predicate of a generic nature may have many possible well-modings, in which case the analysis will return the principal (i.e., most-general) mode. In these respects, our mode system has much in common with the type system of ML, though their purposes are quite different. A generic mode is represented as a finite set of (satisfiable) mode constraints that all well-modings must satisfy.

Mode analysis as constraint solving is decidable and efficient. As mentioned above, a variable occurring in a linear and left-linear clause imposes a binary constraint; a unification goal imposes a binary constraint; and each occurrence of a function symbol imposes a unary constraint. A set of binary and unary mode constraints can be represented as a feature graph (feature structures with cycles) in which

1. paths represent paths in $P_{Atom}$,

2. nodes may have mode values determined by unary constraints,
3. arcs may have "negative signs" that invert the interpretation of the mode values beyond those arcs, and
4. binary constraints are represented by the sharing of nodes.

The union (i.e., conjunction) of two sets of constraints can be computed efficiently as unification over feature graphs. The cost of the unification is almost proportional to the size of the program and the complexity of the data structures used (in terms of the size of the grammar to generate them). The *size* of the data structures that can be generated does not matter. A variable with more than two occurrences imposes a non-binary constraint, but in most cases they can be reduced to unary or binary constraints using other constraints. There are non-binary constraints that may require generate-and-test search. However, they are rather exceptional and our solution is *not* to implement generate-and-test search but let programmers declare the modes of predicate arguments involving such variables.

Concurrent languages Doc [5], $A'UM$ [16] and Janus [8] attempt to ensure well-modedness by allowing each variable to occur only twice and letting programmers distinguish between input and output occurrences using annotations. These annotations can be regarded as mode declarations and contribute to readability and/or ease of compilation, but they are optional because they can be inferred in principle. In addition, our mode system can naturally deal with variables with three or more occurrences.

Another good news with our mode system is that, with slight extension, it can statically distinguish between paths that are used only for one-to-one communication and paths that may be used for one-to-many communication. In other words, we can analyze whether a datum occurring at some path has exactly one reader or possibly many. This information is fundamental for memory management, as we will see later.

# 7 Fundamental Properties of the Mode System

The mode system guarantees the following basic properties. Let $P$ be a program, $Q$ a goal clause containing the multiset of goals to be reduced, and $m$ be a mode. Let $P : m$ and $Q : m$ mean that $m$ is a well-moding of $P$ and $Q$, respectively.

**Lemma 1.** *If $Q : m$ and $Q$ contains a unification goal $t_1 = t_2$, then at least one of $t_1$ and $t_2$ is a variable.*

The lemma says that a unification goal in a well-moded goal clause will not fail unless the occur check does not fail.

**Theorem 2 (Subject reduction theorem).** *Suppose $P : m$, $Q : m$, and $Q$ is reduced in one step to $Q'$ using $P$. Then $Q' : m$ holds unless the extended occur check fails in that reduction.*

The theorem is not obvious because of its *unless* condition. The extended occur check is occur check that additionally excludes the unification between identical variables. In an electric device metaphor, unifying identical variables corresponds to connecting the two ends of a cable together and forming a self-loop not connected to anywhere else. This is certainly an operation which is not likely to be performed in meaningful programs.

From Lemma 1 and Theorem 1, the following important corollary follows:

**Corollary 3.** *Suppose $P : m$ and $Q : m$. Then the execution of $Q$ under $P$ does not cause unification failure (failure of unification goals) unless the extended occur check does not fail.*

Another basic property is:

**Theorem 4 (Groundness theorem).** *Suppose $P : m$, $Q : m$, and $Q$ has been reduced (in one or more steps) to an empty clause, using $P$, without causing the failure of the extended occur check. Then all the variables in $Q$ are instantiated to ground (i.e., variable-free) terms.*

This theorem says that if the termination of $Q$ can be proved, the groundness property comes for free. The proofs of all the above results can be found in [15].

# 8 Implication of the Mode System

The mode system of Flat GHC has been exhibiting a vast influence on programming, implementation, and language design.

## 8.1 Programming

Introducing a mode system means to subset a language, but we have felt almost no loss of expressive power. The mode system can deal with (i) complex data structures such as streams of incomplete messages and streams of streams, (ii) difference lists, and (iii) mutual recursion, all with no difficulty. A difference list is considered a fragment of a longer list whose tail will eventually be connected to another difference list or a (complete) list. Hence its head and tail will have exactly opposite modes.

The mode system provides us with useful debugging information and programming guidelines. Firstly, it is useful for the detection of careless mistakes like the misspelling of variable names. A variable occurring only once can be compared to a cable not connected to anywhere else and very often indicates a program error. Such a variable imposes a strong mode constraint in our mode system. Let $p$ be the path where the variable occurs. Then for any $q \in P_{Term}$, $m(pq)$ will be constrained to *in* or *out*, depending on whether the occurrence is in the head or the body. This strong constraint is highly likely to be incompatible with the other mode constraints and cause a mode error. We have found that even without a mode system, many careless mistakes can be detected by simply counting the number of occurrences of each variable; it is as useful as checking whether there are unplugged sockets or dangling cables before using an electric device.

Secondly, the mode system advocates the "programming as wiring" paradigm, or equivalently, programming with linear clauses. (A variable in a linear clause can be regarded as a cable that wires two atoms.) This programming style leads to more generic well-modings and also encourages "structured programming" in terms of dataflow. We found that this style is less error-prone than allowing unrestrictive use of variables with more occurrences. For instance, we have programmed operations on self-adjusting binary trees and unification over feature graphs using processes and streams (rather than records and pointers). The reconfiguration of processes they involve is rather complicated, but debugging was not so hard.

Thirdly, the mode system encourages the graceful termination of processes; that is, a process cannot discard its arguments upon termination if it contains variables to be instantiated by that process. Thanks to graceful termination, we can prove that a well-moded terminating program instantiates all the variables to ground terms (Theorem 2). In stream programming, this means that all streams will be closed upon termination.

## 8.2 Implementation

While unification is bidirectional by nature, mode analysis determines the direction of dataflow at compile time. This information is particularly useful in the distributed implementation of unification goals. Another important aspect is that mode analysis will make the use of native code more realistic. Without it, the compiled code must prepare for exceptional situations that will not happen in normal programs.

Compile-time distinction between one-to-one and possibly one-to-many communication provides fundamental information for memory management. Since a compiler can now pinpoint when each datum used in one-to-one communication becomes unnecessary, it can be reclaimed (compile-time garbage collection) or destructively updated to create a new datum. Update-in-place is extremely important for the efficient support of arrays. Previous implementations of KL1 featured a one-bit reference counting scheme [2]. The reference counting worked quite efficiently on Parallel Inference Machines, but a static scheme is clearly more desirable on stock microprocessors.

Analysis of the mode and the number of receivers enables a sophisticated implementation technique that we call *message-oriented implementation* [12] [15]. Message-oriented implementation compiles unification for stream communication into low-latency message passing, which is particularly beneficial to programs in which processes suspend frequently and incur much process switching overhead.

## 8.3 Language Design

We are currently exploring the possibility of using concurrent logic languages for (massively) parallel array processing. KL1 supports data structures called vectors (one-dimensional arrays) and provides several vector operations. However, the mode analysis tells us some of them have more generic modes than others. An operation with a more generic mode is considered more fundamental. For element access, for instance, the most basic operation turns out to be

```
set_vector_element(V, I, E, NewE, NewV) .
```

This operation receives an array V and the index value I, and returns through E the Ith value of V. In addition, it returns through NewV an array which is identical to V except that the Ith element is replaced by NewE.

Interestingly, this seemingly "combined" operation is more generic than just either reading or setting an array element. The reason is that it keeps unchanged the number of references to the whole original array and its elements. For instance, the above set_vector_element consumes one reference V to the whole array and one reference NewE to the new element, and generates a reference E to the old Ith element and a reference NewE to the updated array. Thus the operation preserves the number of access paths to any of the elements in the original or updated array. In contrast, an access operation that simply returns a reference to the Ith element, such as Prolog's arg, will impose stronger mode constraints because it loses access paths to the other elements.

The moral of the above result is that in a moded framework, data have an aspect of *resources* whose access paths should not be copied or discarded freely. An array element should, by default, be *removed* from the array once accessed, and the resulting blank should be filled with another value. When performing some operation on an array element and storing the result back to the array, the blank can be tentatively filled with a variable which will be instantiated to the result value. Another typical example of data as resources is a bidirectional communication stream, which could be passed to another process but should not be copied.

An exception to the above principle is that *read-only* arrays, namely arrays whose elements are (or are to be instantiated to) ground terms, can be accessed without removing their elements. Because ground terms are read-only, the principle of cooperative communication allows them to be freely copied or pointed to by a new read-only reference.

Other generic array operations include splitting an array, concatenating two arrays, changing the dimensionality or the shape of an array, and exchanging two elements in an array. Note that they all preserve the number of access paths to elements. All those operations except concatenation are constant-time operations as long as the original arrays are single-reference arrays. Concatenation can be done in constant time as well, provided the two arrays to be concatenated happens to lie next to each other.

The "data as resources" paradigm clearly has some connection with the "propositions-as-resources" view of Linear Logic and also with Linear Lisp [1], though the precise connection is yet to be studied.

# 9 Conclusions

The static mode system for concurrent logic programming has been described informally but from various aspects. The mode system plays fundamental rôles both in programming and implementation in almost the same way as type systems do but in different respects. It also brings two paradigms, data as resources and programming as wiring, into the language. Mode analysis is quite efficient and can be done incrementally.

In previous implementations, I/O modes and the number of access paths were checked either at runtime or analyzed by abstract interpretation. The mode system we propose is much simpler and more systematic. We do not claim that the mode system can completely replace abstract interpretation. For instance, the time-of-call/exit properties of goals such as the instantiation states of their arguments, which in general depend on the scheduling of goals, can be obtained only by abstract interpretation. However, sophisticated program analysis should benefit from the basic information provided by the mode system.

Programmers may find the rigid handling of "data as resources" enforced by the mode system rather awkward, but we believe that the benefit of the mode system in programming and implementation will more than make up the rigidness in most applications of concurrent logic programming.

# References

1. Baker, H. G., Lively Linear Lisp—'Look Ma, No Garbage!' *Sigplan Notices*, Vol. 27, No. 8 (1992), pp. 89–98.
2. Chikayama, T. and Kimura, Y., Multiple Reference Management in Flat GHC. In *Proc. 4th Int. Conf. on Logic Programming*, MIT Press, Cambridge, MA, 1987, pp. 276–293.
3. Clark, K. L. and Gregory, S., A Relational Language for Parallel Programming. In *Proc. ACM Conf. on Functional Programming Languages and Computer Architecture*, ACM, 1981, pp. 171–178.
4. Clark, K. L. and Gregory, S., PARLOG: Parallel Programming in Logic. *ACM. Trans. Prog. Lang. Syst.*, Vol. 8, No. 1 (1986), pp. 1–49.
5. Hirata, M., Programming Language Doc and Its Self-Description or, $X = X$ is Considered Harmful. In *Proc. 3rd Conf. of Japan Society of Software Science and Technology*, 1986, pp. 69–72.
6. Maher, M. J., Logic Semantics for a Class of Committed-Choice Programs. In *Proc. Fourth Int. Conf. on Logic Programming*, MIT Press, Cambridge, MA, 1987, pp. 858–876.
7. Saraswat, V. A. and Rinard M., Concurrent Constraint Programming (Extended Abstract). In *Conf. Record of the Seventeenth Annual ACM Symp. on Principles of Programming Languages*, ACM, 1990, pp. 232–245.

8. Saraswat, V. A., Kahn, K. and Levy, J., Janus: A Step Towards Distributed Constraint Programming. In *Proc. 1990 North American Conference on Logic Programming*, Debray, S. and Hermenegildo, M. (eds.), MIT Press, 1990, pp. 431–446.

9. Shapiro, E. Y., A Subset of Concurrent Prolog and Its Interpreter. ICOT Tech. Report TR-003, Institute for New Generation Computer Technology, Tokyo, 1983.

10. Shapiro, E., The Family of Concurrent Logic Programming Languages. *Computing Surveys*, Vol. 21, No. 3 (1989), pp. 413–510.

11. Ueda, K., Guarded Horn Clauses. ICOT Tech. Report TR-103, ICOT, Tokyo, 1985. Also in *Logic Programming '85*, Wada, E. (ed.), Lecture Notes in Computer Science 221, Springer-Verlag, Berlin Heidelberg, 1986, pp. 168–179.

12. Ueda, K. and Morita, M., A New Implementation Technique for Flat GHC. In *Proc. Seventh Int. Conf. on Logic Programming*, The MIT Press, Cambridge, MA, 1990, pp. 3–17.

13. Ueda, K. and Chikayama, T., Design of the Kernel Language for the Parallel Inference Machine. *The Computer Journal*, Vol. 33, No. 6 (1990), pp. 494–500.

14. Ueda, K., The Fifth Generation Project: Personal Perspectives, *Commun. ACM*, Vol. 36, No. 3 (1993), pp. 65–76.

15. Ueda, K. and Morita, M., Moded Flat GHC and Its Message-Oriented Implementation Technique. *New Generation Computing*, Vol. 13, No. 1 (1994), pp. 3–43.

16. Yoshida, K. and Chikayama, T., *A'UM* — A Stream-Based Concurrent Object-Oriented Language, in *Proc. Int. Conf. on Fifth Generation Computer Systems 1988*, ICOT, Tokyo, 1988, pp. 638–649. Also in *New Generation Computing*, Vol. 7, No. 2–3 (1990), pp. 127–157.

# Advanced Component Interface Specification[1]

Manfred Broy
Institut für Informatik
Technische Universität München
80290 München, Germany

## Abstract

We introduce a method for the specification of reactive asynchronous components with a concurrent access interface and outline its mathematical foundation. The method supports the specification of components that show a complex reactive behavior including timing aspects. Examples are the nonstrict fair merge or the arbiter. The method supports the specification of reactive systems and their modular composition into data flow networks. The specification approach is compositional. It supports the integrated specification and verification of both safety and liveness conditions in modular system descriptions. We outline particular specification styles that may be useful for the better readability of such specifications.

# 1. Introduction

A descriptive functional semantic model of distributed systems of interacting components is of major interest in many research areas and applications of computing science and systems engineering. For the modular systematic development of systems we need precise and readable interface descriptions of system components. We require that such interface descriptions contain all informations about its syntactic and semantic properties needed in order to use it properly. In the interface specification we also describe the time dependency of a component.

Although ignored in theoretical computer science for a while, the incorporation of time and its formal representation is of essential interest for system models. In time dependent systems, the timing and the data values of the output depend upon the timing and the data values of the input. However, for certain components the timing of the input does not influence the data values of the output, but only their timing. Then we can describe the input/output behavior of a component without explicit reference to time.

---

[1] This work was partially sponsored by the Sonderforschungsbereich 342 "Werkzeuge und Methoden für die Nutzung paralleler Rechnerarchitekturen" and the industrial research project SysLab.

We are interested in the description of components that react by output to input. Both input and output takes place within a frame of time. When dealing with the time properties of systems we distinguish three basic classes of components characterized by their time dependencies:

- *time independence:* the data output values of a component do not dependent on the timing of the input data but only on their values,

- *weak time dependency:* some of the nondeterministic decisions in the behavior of a nondeterministic component is controlled by the timing of the input such as the relative order of messages on different input channels or the relative order of messages on input and output channels. But this is done in a superficial way that does not allow control of the nondeterministic decisions in the behavior (the output) by the quantitative timing of the input,

- *strong time dependency:* the behavior (the timing as well as the data output) depends on the quantitative timing of the input data.

The class of weak time dependent components brings specific problems for their functional specification. Examples are fair nonstrict merge or the arbiter (see section 4.2 and 6.3 for a detailed treatment). This has already been observed in [Park 83].

The modular specification of the observable behavior of interactive systems is an important technique in system and software development. We speak of *black box specification* or *interface specification*. An adequate concept of interface specification does not only depend on a simple notion of observability, but also on the operators that we apply to compose components into systems.

In the following we introduce a semantic model of interface behavior and study composition operators. On the basis of this semantic model we introduce more pragmatic specification techniques for the description of reactive components.

The paper is divided into a more theoretical and a more practical part. In the theoretical part we introduce and discuss the mathematical foundations. In the more practical part we give examples of component specifications and specification styles.

In a first chapter we introduce our mathematical basis. Then we show how to describe the syntactic interfaces and the dynamic behaviors of interactive systems. We treat composition operators. Finally, we briefly demonstrate different specification styles by some examples.

# 2. Streams

In this section we introduce the basic mathematical concepts for the description of systems by functional techniques. We define the set of streams over a given set of messages. We introduce a number of functions on this set. Finally we define the notation of stream processing function.

In the following we concentrate on interactive systems that communicate asynchronously through channels. We use streams to denote histories of communications on channels. Given a set M of messages a stream over the set M is a finite or infinite sequence of elements from M. By $M^*$ we denote the finite sequences over the set M. The set $M^*$ includes the empty sequence that we denote by $\langle\rangle$.

By the set $M^\infty$ we denote the infinite sequences over the set M. The set $M^\infty$ can be understood to be represented by the total mappings from the natural numbers $\mathbb{N}$ into M. We denote the set of all streams over the set M by $M^\omega$. Formally we have

$$M^\omega =_{def} M^* \cup M^\infty.$$

We introduce a number of functions on streams that are useful in system descriptions.

A classical operation on streams is the *concatenation* of two streams that we denote by the infix operator $\hat{\ }$. The concatenation is a function that takes two streams (say s and t) and produces a stream $s\hat{\ }t$ as result starting with the elements in s and continuing with those in the stream t. Formally the concatenation has the following functionality:

$$\hat{\ } : M^\omega \times M^\omega \to M^\omega$$

If a stream s is infinite, then concatenating s with a stream t yields the stream s again:

$$s \in M^\infty \Rightarrow s\hat{\ }t = s$$

Concatenation is associative and has the empty stream $\langle\rangle$ as its neutral element:

$$r\hat{\ }(s\hat{\ }t) = (r\hat{\ }s)\hat{\ }t, \qquad\qquad \langle\rangle\hat{\ }s = s = s\hat{\ }\langle\rangle,$$

For a message $m \in M$ we denote by $\langle m \rangle$ the one element stream. For keeping our notation simple we extend concatenation also to elements from the set M (treating them like one element sequences) and to tuples of streams (by concatenating the streams in the tuples elementwise).

On the set $M^\omega$ of streams we define a *prefix ordering* $\sqsubseteq$. We write $s \sqsubseteq t$ for streams s and t to express that the stream s is a *prefix* of the stream t. Formally we have for streams s and t:

$$s \sqsubseteq t \ \text{ iff } \ \exists r \in M^\omega: s\hat{\ }r = t.$$

The prefix ordering defines a partial ordering on the set $M^\omega$ of streams. If $s \sqsubseteq t$ holds, then we also say that the stream s is an *approximation* of the stream t. The set of streams ordered by $\sqsubseteq$ is complete in the sense that every directed set $S \subseteq M^\omega$ of streams has a *least upper bound* denoted by $\sqcup S$. A nonempty subset S of a partially ordered set is called *directed*, if

$$\forall x, y \in S: \exists z \in S: x \sqsubseteq z \wedge y \sqsubseteq z.$$

By least upper bounds of directed sets of finite streams we may describe infinite streams. A *stream processing function* is a function

$$f: M^\omega \to M^\omega$$

that is *prefix monotonic* and *continuous*. The function f is called prefix *monotonic*, if for all streams s and t we have:

$s \sqsubseteq t \Rightarrow f.s \sqsubseteq f.t$ .

For better readability we often write f.x instead of the more common notation f(x) for function application. Infinite streams are also of interest as (and can also be described by) fixpoints of prefix monotonic functions. The streams associated with feedback loops in interactive systems correspond to such fixpoints.

The function f on streams is called *continuous*, if for all directed sets $S \subseteq M^\omega$ of streams we have

$$\sqcup \{f.s: s \in S\} = f. \sqcup S .$$

By $\sqcup$ S we denote the least upper bound of a set. If a function is continuous, then we can already predict its results for infinite input from its results on all finite approximations of the input.

By $\bot$ we denote the pseudo element that represents the result of diverging computations. We write $M^\bot$ for $M \cup \{\bot\}$. Here we assume that $\bot$ is not an element of the set M. On the set $M^\bot$ we define also a simple partial ordering by:

$$x \sqsubseteq y \qquad\qquad \text{iff} \qquad\qquad x = y \vee x = \bot$$

We use the following functions on streams

$$\text{ft}: M^\omega \to M^\bot,$$

$$\text{rt}: M^\omega \to M^\omega.$$

We define their properties as follows: the function ft selects the first element of a stream, if the stream is not empty. The function rt deletes the first element of a stream, if the stream is not empty. We can express the properties of the functions by the following equations (let $m \in M, s \in M^\omega$):

$$\text{ft.} \diamond = \bot, \qquad \text{rt.} \diamond = \diamond, \qquad \text{ft}(m\hat{\ }s) = m, \qquad \text{rt}(m\hat{\ }s) = s.$$

All the introduced concepts and functions for streams such as the prefix ordering and the concatenation carry over to tuples of streams and functions on streams or tuples of streams by applying them pointwise.

By #x we denote the length of a stream. This is a natural number for finite streams. Infinite streams have infinite length.

Given a set $S \subseteq M$ and a stream $x \in M^\omega$ we denote by S©x the substream of x consisting of the elements in S.

We denote the function space of (n,m)-ary stream processing functions by:

$$[(M^\omega)^n \to (M^\omega)^m]$$

The operations ft and rt are prefix monotonic and continuous, whereas concatenation $\hat{\ }$ as defined above is prefix monotonic and continuous only in its second argument.

# 3. Asynchronous Interactive Components

In this section we outline a domain theoretic approach to the modeling of the black box behavior of nondeterministic reactive systems. We use the fundamental observation that the concept of approximation chains as it appears in fixpoint computations is a central mean for modeling computations.

## 3.1 Parallel and Sequential Interfaces

In theoretical computer science there is a long dispute whether explicit concurrency (sometimes even called "true" concurrency) is necessary or at least helpful when treating interactive, distributed systems. This issue is mainly discussed on the grounds of an operational semantics of a closed system. The discussion has led to a controversy between the proponents of the so-called interleaving semantics and the so-called "true" concurrency semantics. However, there was not much discussion, so far, how these issues are reflected in modular system descriptions. In this section we briefly discuss sequential interfaces in contrast to parallel (or concurrent) interfaces. Let us start with a basic informal definition.

An interactive (or reactive) system is an information processing object that interacts with its environment by sending or receiving messages. Its *syntactic interface* is defined by its set of input and output channels and by the sort of the messages it may send or receive on its channels. Its semantic interface that we also call its *black box behavior* is defined by the causal relationship between the messages that it receives or sends. We call every instance of the sending or receiving of a message an *event*.

For a reactive component we call its interface *sequential*, if it can only process one event at a time. As a consequence, in every behavior of a sequential component there is a linear order for the execution of its events. Moreover, its output events may of course depend on the specific linear order of its input events.

A typical example of a component with a sequential interface is a deterministic state machine with the set of input messages I, the set of output messages O and a set of states S. The dynamic behavior of the state machine can be described by a transition function:

$$\delta: S \times I \to S \times O$$

With such a state machine we can associate traces with a straightforward linear order of events. Here we assume that every element in the trace taken from the set I or the set O stands for one event of sending and receiving messages. The behavior of a state machine can be easily represented by stream processing functions associated with its states

$$f: S \to (I^{\omega} \to O^{\omega})$$

The function f is specified by the following equation (for input messages $i \in I$, input streams $x \in I^{\omega}$, states $\sigma \in S$, output messages $o \in O$):

$$(f.\sigma).\langle\rangle = \langle\rangle$$

$(f.\sigma)\,(i\ \&\ x) = o\ \&\ (f.\sigma').x$ where $(\sigma', o) = \delta(\sigma, i)$

Since our state machine has such a simple "ping pong" behavior we immediately obtain the following equation (for every state $\sigma$ and every input stream x):

$\#x = \#(f.\sigma).x$

The equation expresses the obvious fact that for every input message exactly one output message is generated.

A state machine nevertheless shows a kind of "parallel" behavior since input and output are processed in one step although we may assume that the output occurs only after the input has been received. A strictly sequential view is obtained by state transition systems defined by transition relations (cf [Lynch, Stark 89])

$R \subseteq S \times (I \cup O) \times S$

where for simplicity we assume that the sets of input messages I and output messages O are disjoint.

A transition step represented by $(\sigma, a, \sigma') \in R$ may either be an input or an output step. We obtain a strictly sequential order for each of the steps (each event) in a computation. We maintain the character of input steps and assume that input events are completely determined by the environment of the system. Therefore we assume that all input transitions can be executed in every state without any restrictions. We call this the principle of *input enabledness*. It is formally expressed by the following proposition:

$\forall\ \sigma \in S, a \in I:\ \exists\ \sigma' \in S:\ (\sigma, a, \sigma') \in R$

Stream processing functions with one input stream and one output stream model reactive systems with sequential interfaces such as given by state machines with input, output and an initial state.

For a component with a concurrent interface several input and output events may take place concurrently. We can model a component with n input channels and m output channels by a stream processing function

$f:\ (M^{\omega})^n \rightarrow (M^{\omega})^m$

A graphical representation of f is given in Fig. 1.

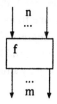

**Fig. 1** Graphical representation of a component with n input and m output channels

This model of component behavior works well for a large variety of specifications. However, for certain components we run into difficulties that are caused by the following fact: according to the monotonicity assumption the relative order of the messages on different input channels cannot be used to determine the result of the function. We demonstrate this by the following basic example.

**Example** (Independence of the output of the relative order of input on different channels): Let

$$n = 2$$

hold and assume that $x$, $x_1$, $x_2$ are pairs of streams where

$$x_1 \sqsubseteq x \wedge x_2 \sqsubseteq x$$

holds and where the pair $x_1$ contains an additional message in its first component while $x_2$ contains an additional message in its second component. Monotonicity implies the validity of the following formula:

$$f(x_1) \sqsubseteq f(x) \wedge f(x_2) \sqsubseteq f(x)$$

So the result of the function $f$ on input history $x$ cannot depend on the fact that the message on channel 1 comes first or that the message on channel 2 comes first. Such differences in the timing of messages cannot even be expressed for pairs of streams $x$. In other words, messages on the different channels may be received in parallel.

Allowing that messages arrive in parallel on different channels has the consequence that we cannot observe a relative order between these messages. Thus the behavior of a component cannot depend on this relative ordering. The function $f$ models a nonsequential interface for components with a number of input channels $n > 1$. ☐

Recall that monotonicity models the causality between input and output histories.

Unfortunately, the interface modeled by prefix monotonic stream processing functions is so highly parallel that we cannot represent any relative order of messages on different input channels and therefore cannot use it to determine the result.

For specific components we need to have information about the relative order of input messages on its different input channels. A simple solution to this problem reads as follows: we consider streams

$$z \in (M^*)^\omega$$

instead of streams $x \in M^\omega$. We understand the stream $z$ as a representation of a communication history of a channel in a time frame formed by an infinite sequence of time intervals. The $k$th entry in the stream represents the sequence of messages that are communicated along the channel in the time interval $k$.

If we model the behavior of a component by a function

$$g: ((M^n)^*)^\omega \rightarrow ((M^m)^*)^\omega$$

mapping streams of tuples of finite sequences onto streams of tuples of finite sequences then we obtain a function representing the behavior of a parallel interface which allows nevertheless to speak about the relative order of messages on different input or output channels. A stream

$$x \in ((M^*)^n)^\omega \qquad \text{where} \qquad x = x_1 \mathbin{\&} x_2 \mathbin{\&} x_3 \ldots$$

with $x_i \in (M^*)^n$ can be understood as the representation of an input history given in some discrete time frame. The tuple $x_i$ of sequences of messages represents the sequences of messages received on the channels in parallel in the time interval i.

# 3.2 Theoretical Foundation: Approximation Chains

A complete communication history for n channels is given by an infinite stream which is an element of the set

$$((M^*)^n)^\infty.$$

We can understand every stream in this set as an infinite sequence of tuples of sequences of messages. The tuple represents the sequences of messages received on the individual channels during the time interval i.

Note that the sets $((M^*)^n)^\infty$ and $((M^*)^\infty)^n$ are isomorphic. This allows us to construct an input history for the n channels from the input histories for each of the n channels a.

In the following we give a theoretical foundation for stream processing functions operating on streams from $(M^*)^\infty$. However, to keep the theory as abstract as possible we represent $(M^*)^\infty$ by chains of streams from $M^\omega$.

In domain and fixpoint theory we model the stepwise progress in computations of the output of a component by the concept of approximation. The basic idea is that during a computation step by step more information about the output of the component is generated. A partial order $\sqsubseteq$ is used to express for the partial (information about the) output x and y by $x \sqsubseteq y$ that the output y gives more (or at least as much) information about the output of the computation as x does and that the information of x is consistent with the perhaps more specific information of y.

We call the partially ordered set $(D, \sqsubseteq)$ an *algebraic domain*, if there is a subset $D_{fin} \subseteq D$ containing the "finite" elements of D such that every element $x \in D$ is the least upper bound of a directed set $S \subseteq D_{fin}$.

An element $e \in D$ is called *finite* if for every directed set $S \subseteq D$ we have

$$e \sqsubseteq \sqcup S \Rightarrow \exists d \in S: e \sqsubseteq d$$

In the case of the streams the finite elements are exactly the finite sequences.

Let $(D, \sqsubseteq)$ be an algebraic domain with approximation ordering $\sqsubseteq$ and the set $D_{fin} \subseteq D$ its set of finite elements. Any mapping

$$x: N \to D_{fin}$$

with

$$x_i \sqsubseteq x_{i+1}$$

is called an *approximating chain* for the possibly infinite element $\sqcup x \in D$, where

$$\sqcup \; x = \sqcup \; \{x_i \in D_{fin} : i \in \mathbb{N}\}$$

Such a chain represents an *infinite stepwise approximation* of the element $\sqcup \; x \in D$ by finite elements. Such approximation chains clearly are closely related to computations and in particular to the timing of a computation.

By a chain we represent a computation of the element $\sqcup \; x$ that has computed the partial output represented by $x_i$ until time point i.

We denote the set of chains of finite elements from the set D by

$$\mathbf{C}(D)$$

Of course there exists a surjective mapping from the set $\mathbf{C}(D)$ of chains over the domain D to the set D that maps every chain $x \in \mathbf{C}(D)$ to its least upper bound $\sqcup \; x$.

For streams $M^\omega$ and tuples of streams $(M^\omega)^n$ the set of finite elements is given by $M^*$ and $(M^*)^n$ respectively. Every chain

$$x \in \mathbf{C}((M^\omega)^n)$$

represents also a stream

$$y \in ((M^*)^n)^\infty$$

by the following definition which defines for given finite stream $x_i$ the stream $y_i$ uniquely.

$$x_0 = y_1$$

$$x_{i+1} = x_i \hat{\;} y_i$$

Obviously we can also always represent a chain in $\mathbf{C}((M^\omega)^n)$ by a stream $((M^*)^n)^\infty$.

This shows that the sets $\mathbf{C}((M^\omega)^n)$ and $((M^*)^n)^\infty$ are isomorphic. We prefer to work with $\mathbf{C}((M^\omega)^n)$ instead of $((M^*)^n)^\infty$ in this section, since the concept of a chain is more general and therefore we can apply our construction for arbitrary domains.

We can understand a chain x of tuples of finite streams as a collection of observations about a system at time points $t_0 < t_1 < t_2 < \dots$ . We do not use a specific concrete physical time such as seconds or microseconds, but quite abstractly just assume that the elements of the tuple $x_k$ represent the streams of observed messages up to time point $t_k$. In analogy, we interpret chains of input or output elements as observations about communication histories up to certain time points $t_k$.

Given a chain $x \in \mathbf{C}(D)$ we write $x|_i$ to denote the sequence of the first i elements of the chain x.

A function

$$F: \mathbf{C}(D_1) \to \wp(\mathbf{C}(D_2))$$

mapping chains onto sets of chains is called a *behavior*, if the first i elements (more precisely the messages received till timepoint i) of the input chain determine the first i elements in the output chain. In mathematical terms, for all $i \in \mathbb{N}$ we require:

$$x|_i = z|_i \Rightarrow \{y|_i : y \in F(x)\} = \{y|_i : y \in F(z)\}$$

The definition expresses that for a behavior the output history till time point i is determined exclusively by the input history till time point i.

A behaviour is called *time guarded*, if the first i elements in the input chain determine the first i+1 elements in the output chain. Time guardedness is equivalent to a delay property of a component.

We call a set-valued function

$$F: C(D_1) \rightarrow \wp(C(D_2))$$

*limit closed*, if for every chain $x \in C(D_1)$ and every chain $y \in C(D_2)$ we have

$$(\forall k \in N: \exists z \in F(x): y|_k = z|_k) \Rightarrow y \in F(x)$$

We assume that every behavior function F is the union of a set of limit closed behaviors.

We call a component with the behavior F *timing independent*, if

$$\sqcup x = \sqcup z \Rightarrow \{\sqcup y: y \in F(x)\} = \{\sqcup y: y \in F(z)\}$$

We call a behavior F *consistent*, if it has at least one possible output history for every input history. Mathematically expressed, if for all input histories $x \in C(D_1)$

$$F.x \neq \emptyset$$

We use the set $C(D)$ to model the behavior of system components by set-valued functions

$$F: C(D_1) \rightarrow \wp(C(D_2))$$

that are behaviors and associate with every approximation of an input element in $D_1$ a set of approximations for the possible output histories of the component.

**Example** (The arbiter): An arbiter is a component that receives elements form a message set M. It reproduces all its input elements as output, but adds to its output stream an infinite number of clock signals that we can interpret as time out signals. Given a set of data elements M and the element $\sqrt{}$ called a *clock signal* we specify the function

$$arb: C(M^\omega) \rightarrow \wp(C((M \cup \{\sqrt{}\})^\omega))\backslash\{\emptyset\}$$

by the following formulas

$$y \in arb(x) \Rightarrow \sqcup x = M©(\sqcup y) \wedge \#\{\sqrt{}\}©(\sqcup y) = \infty$$

The specification is consistent, since there exists a behavior function that fulfills this specification. For instance, we may define for a chain $x = \{x_i \in D_{fin}: i \in N\}$ the function arb by

$$arb(x) = \{y \in C((M \cup \{\sqrt{}\})^\omega): \quad y_0 = \diamond \wedge$$
$$\forall i \in N: M©y_{i+1} = x_i \wedge$$
$$M©(\sqcup x) = M©(\sqcup y) \wedge \#\{\sqrt{}\}©(\sqcup y) = \infty \}$$

There is an essential difference between time and clock signals in our approach. We consider the timing as a physical frame modeled by the intervals of the streams while clock signals are technical means to synchronize behaviors. □

The output of functions on approximation chains x may depend, such as the output of I/O-machines, on the particular information *how* the input streams ⊔ x are approximated by the chain x (which can be used to model its "timing") and thus on the approximation granularity of the input and not only on the least upper bound ⊔ x. Under certain conditions we can, however, obtain a more abstract view of such functions that work on elements of D rather than on elements of $C(D)$ when we abstract away the information given by the approximation.

## 3.3 Abstractions from Functions on Approximations

In this section we describe properties of functions on approximations that allow to abstract from set-valued functions on approximation chains to functions on the approximated elements. We start by introducing a number of notions and definitions that are useful for reaching our goal.

The construction of appropriate abstractions is an important requisite for the treatment of complex systems. Here abstraction means the elimination of (unimportant) details. We begin with the introduction of a number of definitions that define a relationship between behaviors and stream processing functions.

A function

$$f: C(D_1) \rightarrow C(D_2)$$

is called a *descendant* of a function

$$F: C(D_1) \rightarrow \wp(C(D_2))$$

if for all chains $x \in C(D_1)$ we have

$$f(x) \in F(x).$$

For a timing independent function

$$F: C(D_1) \rightarrow \wp(C(D_2))$$

which by definition has the property

$$⊔ x = ⊔ z \Rightarrow \{⊔ y: y \in F(x)\} = \{⊔ y: y \in F(z)\}$$

we may construct an abstraction of the timing aspects contained in the behavior F by functions on $D_1$ as follows. Given a set valued F function

$$F: C(D_1) \rightarrow \wp(C(D_2))$$

we call a continuous function

$$f: D_1 \rightarrow D_2$$

a *weak abstraction* of the behavior F and we write

**f abs F**

if for all input elements $x \in D_1$ we have:

$$\exists\, z \in C(D_1): x = \sqcup\, z \wedge \exists\, y \in F(z): \forall\, i \in \mathbb{N}: f(z_i) \sqsubseteq y_i$$

A weak abstraction f is partially correct for the behavior F. In other words, f is correct with respect to the safety properties of F, but not necessarily with respect to the liveness properties of F.

   We call the function f a weak abstraction, since it guarantees only output consistent with output contained in F, but it might not produce any output at all. If in addition $f(z_i) = y_i$ holds in the formula above, we call the function f a *strong abstraction*. We then write

**f abs+ F.**

Weak abstractions always exist. Strong abstractions do not always exist according to the monotonicity requirement for the function f.

**Example** (Behavior without strong abstractions): The arbiter of the example above does not have strong abstractions. According to the specification of the arbiter for a weak abstraction f of the arbiter specification we assume

$$M©f.x \sqsubseteq x$$

For a strong abstraction we, in addition we require

$$\#\{\sqrt{}\}©f.x = \infty$$

So we may conclude

$$f.\diamond = \sqrt{}^{\infty}$$

$$\exists\, k: f.\langle m \rangle = \sqrt{}^{k}\,{}^{\wedge}\,\langle m \rangle\,{}^{\wedge}\,\sqrt{}^{\infty}$$

There does not exist a monotonic function that fulfills these equations, since

$$\diamond \sqsubseteq \langle m \rangle$$

and therefore

$$f.\diamond \sqsubseteq f.\langle m \rangle$$

is required which does not hold for the function specified above.   □

We call a behavior function a *strongly time independent*, if its behavior can be described by its set of strong abstractions. In mathematical terms, then we have

$$F(x) = \{y \in C(D_2): \exists\, f: \sqcup\, y = f(\sqcup\, x) \wedge f\ \text{abs+}\ F\}$$

As we have seen already, not all behaviors have strong abstractions. This is not surprising, since we cannot expect strong abstractions for strongly time dependent specifications. However, for a subclass of the time dependent specifications we can find abstractions by so-called *input choice specifications* (for a detailed description see [Broy 93]).

An *input choice specification* for a component with input domain $D_1$ and an output domain $D_2$ is a relation

$$R: [D_1 \rightarrow D_2] \times D_1 \rightarrow \mathbb{B}$$

R is called *abstract specification* of a behavior F, if the following formula is valid

$$R(f, x) \equiv f \text{ abs } F \wedge \exists z \in C(D_1): x = \sqcup z \wedge \exists y \in F(z): \forall i \in N: f(z_i) = y_i$$

The proposition $R(f, x)$ expresses that f fulfills the safety properties required by F and for input x also the liveness properties of F. In general, the predicate R cannot characterize the behavior of F. But for time independent behavior R characterizes F. So R can be seen as a description of F in a model without time.

**Theorem:** Every time independent behavior can be defined by an input choice specification.

**Proof:** Given a time independent behavior

$$F: C(D_1) \rightarrow \wp(C(D_2))$$

We define an input choice specification

$$R: [D_1 \rightarrow D_2] \times D_1 \rightarrow \mathbb{B}$$

by the definition

$$R(f, x) \equiv f \text{ abs } F \wedge \forall z \in C(D_1): x = \sqcup z \Rightarrow f.x \in \{\sqcup y: y \in F.z\}$$

We define a behavior F' based on R by

$$F'(z) = \{y \in C(D_2): \exists f: R(f, \sqcup z) \wedge \sqcup y = f(\sqcup z)\}$$

By the definition of R and the time independence of F we obtain $F = F'$. $\qquad\qquad\square$

We can use the input choice specification R of F as a representation or a specification of F at a more abstract level.


# 4. Composition Operators

When modeling systems and system components the composition of larger systems from smaller ones is a basic structuring technique. We consider only three basic composition operators, namely *sequential* composition, *parallel* composition and *feedback*.

As well known these three composition operators suffice to formulate all kinds of networks of reactive information processing components, provided we have simple components available for permuting and copying input and output lines.

## 4.1 Parallel Composition

To define parallel composition we first introduce an operation that allows to form a chain of tuples (of streams) out of two chains of tuples (of streams). Let $D_1$ and $D_2$ be domains. Given two chains of streams

$$x \in C(D_1), y \in C(D_2)$$

we construct a chain

$$x \oplus y \in C(D_1 \times D_2)$$

by elementwise composition as follows:

$$(x \oplus y).i = x.i \oplus y.i$$

where $x.i \oplus y.i$ is the tuple obtained by concatenating the tuples $x.i$ and $y.i$.

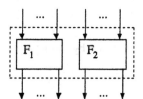

**Fig. 2** Parallel composition

Given two behaviors

$$F_1 : C(D_{1,1}) \to \wp(C(D_{2,1}))$$

$$F_2 : C(D_{1,2}) \to \wp(C(D_{2,2}))$$

we define the parallel composition

$$F_1 \| F_2 : C(D_{1,1} \times D_{1,2}) \to \wp(C(D_{2,1} \times D_{2,2}))$$

by the behavior defined by the following formula (let $x_1 \in C(D_{1,1})$, $x_2 \in C(D_{1,2})$):

$$(F_1 \| F_2) (x_1 \oplus x_2) = \{y_1 \oplus y_2 : y_1 \in F_1(x_1) \wedge y_2 \in F_2(x_2)\}$$

It is a straightforward proof to show that the parallel composition $F_1 \| F_2$ leads to a behavior provided $F_1$ and $F_2$ are behaviors.

## 4.2 Sequential Composition

Sequential composition is simple to define by functional composition. Give two behaviors

$$F_1: C(D_0) \to \wp(C(D_1))$$

$$F_2: \mathbf{C}(D_1) \to \wp(\mathbf{C}(D_2))$$

we define the sequential composition

$$(F_1 ; F_2) : \mathbf{C}(D_0) \to \wp(\mathbf{C}(D_2))$$

by

$$(F_1 ; F_2).x = \{y : \exists z : z \in F_1(x) \wedge y \in F_2(z)\}$$

Again it is a straightforward proof to show that the sequential composition $(F_1 ; F_2)$ is a behavior provided $F_1$ and $F_2$ are behaviors.

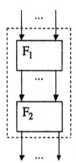

**Fig. 3** Sequential composition

## 4.3 Feedback Operator

Given a behavior

$$F: \mathbf{C}(D_1 \times D_0) \to \wp(\mathbf{C}(D_2 \times D_0))$$

we define the behavior

$$\mu F: \mathbf{C}(D_1) \to \wp(\mathbf{C}(D_2))$$

by the equation

$$(\mu F).x = \{(z, y) \in D_2 \times D_0 : (z, y) \in F(x, y)\}.$$

Again it is a straightforward proof to show that the feedback $\mu F$ is a time guarded behavior provided $F$ is a time guarded behavior.

**Theorem**: A time guarded consistent behavior

$$F: \mathbf{C}(D) \to \wp(\mathbf{C}(D))$$

has a (least) fixpoint $c \in F(c)$.

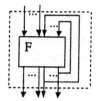

**Fig. 4** Feedback operator

**Proof:** Define the elements $z_i \in D$ by

$$z_0 = \bot$$

and

$$z_{i+1} \in \{y_{i+1}: \exists\, x \in C(D): y \in F.x \wedge \forall\, j: j \leq i \Rightarrow x_j = z_j\}$$

The elements $z_i$ form a chain $z$. Furthermore for this chain $z$ we have

$$z \in F(z)$$

since F is limit closed. So $z$ is a fixed point. $\qquad\qquad\qquad\qquad\square$

If a behaviour F is time independent, then $\mu F$ is time independent. If F is strongly time independent, then $\mu F$ is strongly time independent.

# 5. Specifications

The model introduced above is very powerful. It supports the specification of reactive systems with and without timing aspects. Many small case studies have shown the power and flexibility of the specification, development and verification methods based on this model. However, writing such specifications is a difficult task. From the mathematical and logical basis it is a long way to a applicable specification method that can be used by an engineer. In the following section we demonstrate how a more practical specification method can be based on the model introduced so far.

We introduce a number of specification techniques for the description of reactive components. As we have demonstrated above we can specify systems with a parallel interface and a possibly time dependent behavior by mathematical formulas describing functions on chains of tuples of streams that yield sets of chains of tuples of streams. However, for many applications it is more appropriate to use more specific and better readable specification techniques. We demonstrate such specification techniques in the following by a number of simple examples.

# 5.1 Relations Between Input and Output Histories

For practical purposes one might be interested in a more formalized syntax. It is not difficult to provide a logic based syntax for our formalism. A simple form of such a syntax could be predicate logic to specify the relation between the input and output histories.

We have already seen a simple relational specifications (the arbiter). We give an additional example that illustrates the important concept of an interrupt.

Many concepts in systems programming, in process control, and in telecommunication show a behavior of the following type: do something until a certain event happens. For message passing components we can express this often as: send (or receive) messages until a particular message is received. Such a behavior corresponds to what we call an interrupt. A typical example is the sender in a protocol of the type of the alternating bit protocol or many other similar communication protocols.

**Example** (Sender protocol): We consider a component with the behavior

$$SP: \mathbb{C}(M^{\omega} \times A^{\omega}) \to \wp(M^{\omega})$$

where M is a set of messages and A = {ack}. We define the sender protocol SP by the following formula

$$y \in SP(x, z) \equiv \exists r \in \mathbb{N}^{\omega}: \#r = \#\sqcup z \wedge \sqcup y = do(\sqcup x, r^\frown\langle\infty\rangle)$$

where

$$do: M^{\omega} \times (\mathbb{N} \cup \{\infty\})^{\omega} \to M^{\omega}$$

with (let $m \in M, n \in \mathbb{N}, x \in M^{\omega}, r \in (\mathbb{N} \cup \{\infty\})^{\omega}$):

$$do(\langle m \rangle^\frown x, n^\frown r) = m^{n\frown}do(x, r). \qquad\qquad \square$$

We can understand many of our example problems given so far as instances of such an interrupt behavior:

(1) Fair nonstrict merge: process messages from the left input line until a message arrives on the right input line.

(2) Arbiter: Send signals $\sqrt{}$ until a message arrives on the input line.

Interrupt behavior is a very typical and important behavior when dealing with reactive systems. Of course, we have given very abstract specifications of interrupts. More specific interrupt specifications may take the timing into consideration, too, and model behaviors that react "immediately" (more precisely, within a certain amount of time) for any interrupt.

## 5.2 State Transition Specifications

In a state transition specification we specify the behavior of a component by a state transition system with input and output. In a state transition specification we use a set of states as an auxiliary structure.

For a state transition specification we introduce a set of states. In the example of the arbiter we may choose as states the messages received but not sent so far.

We can choose any appropriate set as the set of states. Let State be the set of states. We define a relation:

$$R: State \times D_1{}^* \to \wp(State \times D_2{}^*)$$

and an initial state set $State_0$. We can define this relation in many ways using logic, tables or just plain mathematics. We then define a behavior

$$F: \mathbb{C}(D_1{}^\omega) \to \wp(\mathbb{C}(D_2{}^\omega))$$

as follows: we define that a history y is a possible result of the behavior F applied to the input history x, in mathematical terms

$$y \in F(x),$$

if and only if there exists a sequence of states $\sigma_i$ that form a computation for the relation R. The sequence of states $\sigma_i$ that forms a computation if for every $i \in N$ there exists a state transition from state $\sigma_i$ to $\sigma_{i+1}$ such that the input and output of this transition define the messages that have to be added to $x_i$ and $y_i$ to obtain $x_{i+1}$ and $y_{i+1}$. Formally we have

$$\exists\, a, b: x_{i+1} = x_i{}^\frown\langle a\rangle \wedge y_{i+1} = y_i{}^\frown\langle b\rangle \wedge (\sigma_{i+1}, b) \in R(\sigma_i, a)$$

and $\sigma_0$ is in the set of initial states $State_0$:

$$\sigma_0 \in State_0.$$

This way a state machine defines a function on chains (of tuples) of streams.

**Example** (Locked Access to Data): A component that guarantees locked access to a number of memory cells can be specified as follows. We use the following sets:

Data        data values to be read or written,

Key        identifier for the memory cells,

Id        identifier for the processes that access the memory cells.

We define the state set as follows

State: $Key \to Data \times (Id \cup \{nil\})$

For a state $\sigma$ and a key k the value $(\sigma.k).2 \in Id$ indicates for which process the key k is locked. The special value nil (where we assume $nil \notin Id$) expresses that the key is not locked for a process. We use the following set In of input messages.

In =   {Lock(k, i): $k \in$ Key $\wedge i \in$ Id} $\cup$

     {Read(k, i): $k \in$ Key $\wedge i \in$ Id} $\cup$

     {Write(k, i, d): $k \in$ Key $\wedge i \in$ Id $\wedge d \in$ Data} $\cup$

     {Unlock(k, i): $k \in$ Key $\wedge i \in$ Id}

and the following set Out of output messages.

Out =   {Ack(x): $x \in$ In\Re} $\cup$

     {Fail(x): $x \in$ In} $\cup$

     {Ack(x, v): $x \in$ Re $\wedge v \in$ Data}

Where Re is the set of messages in the set of input messages In labeled with a read.
 Now we define the transition relation R by the following proposition:

$(\sigma', o) \in R(\sigma, x) \equiv$

  (x = Lock(k, i) $\wedge$  $((o = Ack(x) \wedge \sigma(k).2 = nil \wedge \sigma' = \sigma[i/k.2]) \vee$

         $(o = Fail(x) \wedge \sigma(k).2 \neq nil \wedge \sigma' = \sigma)) \vee$

  (x = Write(k, i, d) $\wedge$ $((o = Ack(x) \wedge \sigma(k).2 = i \wedge \sigma' = \sigma[d/k.1]) \vee$

         $(o = Fail(x) \wedge \sigma(k).2 \neq i \wedge \sigma' = \sigma)) \vee$

  (x = Read(k, i) $\wedge$  $((o = Ack(x, \sigma(k).1) \wedge \sigma(k).2 = k \wedge \sigma' = \sigma) \vee$

         $(o = Fail(x) \wedge \sigma(k).2 \neq i \wedge \sigma' = \sigma)) \vee$

  (x = Unlock(k, i) $\wedge$ $((o = Ack(x) \wedge \sigma(k).2 = i \wedge \sigma' = \sigma[nil/k.2]) \vee$

         $(o = Fail(x) \wedge \sigma(k).2 \neq i \wedge \sigma' = \sigma))$

Here we write

 $\sigma[i/k.2]$

and

 $\sigma[d/k.1]$

to denote the update of the second or first respective component of $\sigma(k)$ by the vakue d.
 For such a problem a state-oriented description seems much more appropriate than one in terms of pure history relations. By the relation R we describe the behavior of a locked access component we call LAC.             $\square$

State based specifications often are helpful to express the data dependencies between messages in a more suggestive if the state space is chosen carefully.

## 5.3 Relational Specifications

In a relational specification we specify a component by a formula referring to the input and output streams written in first order predicate logic.

A relational specification of a weakly time dependent specification can also be given by a relation

$$R \subseteq D_1 \times D_2$$

The relation R defines a function

$$F: C(D_1) \to \wp(C(D_2))$$

by the following formula

$$F(x) = \{y : (\sqcup\, x, \sqcup\, y) \in R\}$$

In addition we can indicate that the relation is time independent.

**Example** (Fair Merge): We define the relation R by the formula

$$((x_1, x_2), y) \in R \Leftrightarrow \exists\, b \in \mathbb{B}^\infty: x_1 = \text{sched}(y, b) \wedge x_2 = \text{sched}(y, \neg *b)$$

where the function sched is defined by the following formula

$$\text{sched}(x, b) = \quad \textbf{if } \text{ft.b} \quad \textbf{then } \text{ft.x \& sched(rt.x, rt.b)}$$
$$\textbf{else } \text{sched(rt.x, rt.b)}$$
$$\textbf{fi}$$

$$\neg *b = \neg\text{ft.b \& } \neg *\text{rt.b} \qquad\qquad\qquad \square$$

We give a second example of a time independent component.

**Example** (Delayed Permutation Component): A behavior that we can observe in many examples of the type of remote procedure control mechanisms are delayed permutation function. Given a set M a behavior

$$DPC: C(M^\omega) \to \wp(C(M^\omega))$$

is called a delayed permutation component provided DPC fulfills the following specification:

$$y \in DPC(x) \equiv \forall\, m \in M: \{m\}\copyright\sqcup\, y = \{m\}\copyright\sqcup\, x$$

A delayed permutation accepts messages from the set M as input and reproduces them as output after a while. DPC produces only messages as output that have been received as input (safety). All messages are delayed only for a finite amount of time and then produced as output (liveness). It is one of the advantages of the presented specification method that an artificial separation of properties into safety and liveness properties is not required, but possible, if wanted. We can combine the component LAC with the delayed permutation component by

$$DPC\,;\,LAC\,;\,DPC$$

This component may rearrange the order of its input messages and the order of its output messages.  □

All the specification techniques we have available for defining relational specifications can this way be used for defining behavior functions.

# 5.4 Pragmatic Specification Techniques

In principle we can write specifications by predicates that characterize set valued functions that we call behaviors. However, such specifications are hardly readable by software engineers that are not familiar with predicate logic and the foundations of fixpoint theory. For them it is certainly helpful if more pragmatic specification techniques are available.

Useful pragmatic specification techniques, that are familiar to engineers, may be graphics, tables and diagrams.

**Example** (Table of a relation): For the example given in section 5.2 a table is more readable than the rather lenghty logical formula. In the following tabele every line corresponds to a formula.

| $(\sigma', o) \in R(\sigma, x) \equiv (x = ... \wedge \sigma(k).2 ... \Rightarrow o = ... \wedge \sigma' = ... ) \wedge ...$ | | | |
|---|---|---|---|
| x = | $\sigma(k).2$ | o = | $\sigma'$ |
| Lock(k, i) | = nil | Ack(x) | $\sigma[i/k.2]$ |
|  | $\neq$ nil | Fail(x) | $\sigma$ |
| Write(k, i, d) | = i | Ack(x) | $\sigma[d/k.1]$ |
|  | $\neq$ i | Fail(x) | $\sigma$ |
| Read(k, i) | = i | Ack(x, $\sigma(k).1$) | $\sigma$ |
|  | $\neq$ i | Fail(x) | $\sigma$ |
| Unlock(k, i) | = i | Ack(x) | $\sigma[nil/k.2]$ |
|  | $\neq$ i | Fail(x) | $\sigma$ |

□

Of course we can use tables both for describing relations and for describing state machines. This way we obtain more practical techniques both for relational and for state oriented specifications.

The semantic model of a reactive system may be difficult to handle for a systems engineer, since it is tuned too much towards mathematics. Nevertheless, we may give rather intuitive explanations for our model. Furthermore we can give more syntactic sugar for the specification of a component. We shortly outline (without going into a concrete syntax) how such a specification technique might look like.

We describe a component by introducing identifiers for each of its input or output channels and a sort for the messages of its identifiers. The sorts of the messages can be defined by any appropriate specification mechanism for describing data types.

Then the relation between the input and the output streams is described. For doing so for an input or output stream x we can refer by x.t (where $t \in N$) to the input or output produced up to time point t. By $x[t_1 : t_2]$ we refer to the input or output in the time interval $[t_1 : t_2]$. We write $x[t]$ instead of $x[t : t]$. Both x.t and $x[t_1 : t_2]$ are always finite sequences.

If appropriate we may introduce a local state in a component to write a state-based specification.

# 6. Conclusions

The specification of interactive system has to be done in a time/space frame. A specification should indicate which events (communication actions) can take place where, when and how they are causally related. Such specification techniques are an important prerequisite for the development of safety critical systems.

Modeling information processing systems appropriately is basically a matter of choosing the adequate abstractions in terms of the corresponding mathematical models. Giving operational models that contain all the technical computational details of interactive nondeterministic computations is relatively simple. However, for system engineering purposes operational models are not very helpful. Only, if we manage to find good abstractions is it possible reach a tractable basis for system specifications.

Abstraction means forgetting information. Of course, we may forget only information that is not needed. Which information is needed does not only depend upon the explicit concept of observation, but also upon the considered forms of the composition of systems.

Finding appropriate abstractions for operational models of distributed systems is a difficult but nevertheless important task. Good abstract nonoperational models are the basis of a discipline of system development.

# Acknowledgment

I am grateful to Ketil Stølen for a number of discussions that were helpful to clarify the basic concepts.

# References

[Broy 83]
M. Broy: Applicative real time programming. In: Information Processing 83, IFIP World Congress, Paris 1983, North Holland Publ. Company 1983, 259-264

[Broy 85]
M. Broy: Specification and top down design of distributed systems. In: H. Ehrig et al. (eds.): Formal Methods and Software Development. Lecture Notes in Computer Science 186, Springer 1985, 4-28, Revised version in JCSS 34:2/3, 1987, 236-264

[Broy 86]
M. Broy: A theory for nondeterminism, parallelism, communication and concurrency. Habilitation, Fakultät für Mathematik und Informatik der Technischen Universität München, 1982, Revised version in: Theoretical Computer Science 45 (1986) 1-61

[Broy 87a]
M. Broy: Semantics of finite or infinite networks of communicating agents. Distributed Computing 2 (1987), 13-31

[Broy 87b]
M. Broy: Predicative specification for functional programs describing communicating networks. Information Processing Letters 25 (1987) 93-101

[Broy 93]
M. Broy: Functional Specification of Time Sensitive Communicating Systems. REX Workshop. ACM Transactions on Software Engineering and Methodology 2:1, Januar 1993, 1-46

[Broy, Stølen 94]
M. Broy, K. Stølen: Specification and Refinement of Finite Dataflow Networks – a Relational Approach. In: Langmaack, H. and de Roever, W.-P. and Vytopil, J. (eds): Proc. FTRTFT'94, Lecture Notes in Computer Science 863, 1994, 247-267

[Kahn, MacQueen 77]
G. Kahn, D. MacQueen: Coroutines and networks of processes, Proc. IFIP World Congress 1977, 993-998

[Lynch, Stark 89]
N. Lynch, E. Stark: A proof of the Kahn principle for input/output automata. Information and Computation 82, 1989, 81-92

[Lynch, Tuttle 87]
N. A. Lynch, M. R. Tuttle: Hierarchical correctness proofs for distributed algorithms. In: Proceedings of the Sixth ACM Symposium on Principles of Distributed Computing, 1987

[Park 80]
D. Park: On the semantics of fair parallelism. In: D. Björner (ed.): Abstract Software

Specification. Lecture Notes in Computer Science 86, Berlin-Heidelberg-New York: Springer 1980, 504-526

[Park 83]
D. Park: The ``Fairness" Problem and Nondeterministic Computing Networks. Proc. 4th Foundations of Computer Science, Mathematical Centre Tracts 159, Mathematisch Centrum Amsterdam, (1983) 133-161

[Pannangaden, Shanbhogue91]
P. Pannangaden, V. Shanbhogue: The expressive power of indeterminate dataflow primitives. Information and Computation 98, 1992, 99-131

# GRAPH NOTATION FOR CONCURRENT COMBINATORS

NOBUKO YOSHIDA

yoshida@mt.cs.keio.ac.jp

Department of Computer Science, Keio University

3-14-1 Hiyoshi, Kohoku-ku, Yokohama, 223, Japan

ABSTRACT. We introduce graph notation for concurrent processes which does not use the notion of port names for its formulation. The operators in the algebra of graphs proposed in this paper are quite different from those in the original term representation, making such notions as connection and correspondence of communication ports explicit. We show how basic elements of process calculi such as agents, reduction, and behavioural equivalences are soundly formulated in the new setting. The work is based on the authors' study on concurrent combinators [9, 10], and can be considered as offering another mathematical representation of the formal notion studied therein.

## 1. INTRODUCTION

The aim of the present paper is to introduce process graphs and their algebra, a formalism of concurrent processes which does not use the notion of port names for its formulation. The intention is to gain a deeper understanding about the basic elements of theory of processes by formulating them with a quite different orientation from the usual term-based one. The resulting construction may also serve as a theory of processes in its own right, where explicit manipulation of ports connection and correspondence is a fundamental element. We show how basic elements of process calculi such as agents, reduction, and behavioural equality are formulated in the new setting, shedding a fresh light on those familiar notions. Some applications of the theory to other graphical formalisms are also given along the way. The work is based on the authors' study on concurrent combinators [9, 10], offering another presentation of the formal notion studied therein.

Systems of concurrent combinators introduced in [9, 10] were born as a "combinatory" decomposition of calculi of mobile processes, where finite atoms and their combination give the same expressive power as e.g. $\pi$-calculus in [17] and $\nu$-calculus in [8, 9]. That is, without using inductively defined constructs for prefix and replication, a system with finite atoms and fixed interaction rules among them is nevertheless capable of representing the same functionalities. Just with the same motivation, now we try to "analyse away" port names from the name-based process formalism.

We will begin by considering how we represent concurrent combinators in the nameless world of graphs. Let us suppose parallel composition of two messages $\mathcal{M}(ab)$, $\mathcal{M}(ac)$ and a duplicator $\mathcal{D}(ade)$[1] in the original term-based concurrent combinators [9, 10]. As

---

[1]In $\pi$-calculus [17], $\mathcal{M}(ab)$ and $\mathcal{D}(abc)$ mean $\bar{a}b.0$ and $a(x).(\bar{b}x.0 \mid \bar{c}x.0)$, respectively.

the fundamental elements of concurrent computation, the name "$a$" functions as an interaction point for multiple processes, so we can naturally represent this as a vertex • which is shared by three agents as seen in Figure 1 (a).

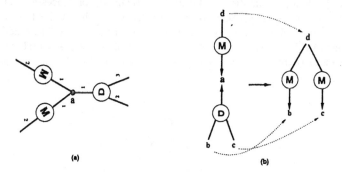

FIGURE 1. Atoms and Reduction with Names

In the next step, we consider how to formalise the process dynamics without using names. Let us turn to the notion of reduction relation in the world of processes which have names. In Figure 1 (b), an example of reduction: $\mathcal{D}(abc), \mathcal{M}(ad) \longrightarrow \mathcal{M}(bd), \mathcal{M}(cd)^2$ is shown. Thus the common interaction port invokes reduction, but what we notice is that the correspondence of free communication ports between two configurations is implicitly maintained by free names. Note also (1) no two distinct names in the left hand side (l.h.s for short) are collapsed into the same name in the right hand side (r.h.s for short), (2) it is possible that names (here $a$) will be lost after the reduction, and (3) all free names in r.h.s come from l.h.s. Now take off names from the processes: then clearly this correspondence can only be maintained in the nameless graphs by introducing *surjective partial injection between free handles of two graphs*, say $\delta$. Thus one-step reduction from a graph $G$ to a graph $G'$ is defined by a triple $\langle G, \delta, G' \rangle$. The idea (possibly without surjectivity) is pertinent to defining any binary relations over processes such as behavioural semantics, as we shall see.

This paper presents the basic constructs of algebra of graphs and their elementary properties with illustrative examples. Section 2 defines the basic entities called *process graphs* together with operators for their algebra. Section 3 formulates several technical ideas needed to deal with graphs and operations over them with precision. Then they are immediately used in isomorphism laws (which may correspond to some equality laws in process algebra). Section 4 defines reduction with the above ideas and gives some examples. Section 5 presents the construction of behavioural equalities over process graphs with examples and studies their elementary properties. Section 6 summarises other results on process graphs and discusses related work and further issues.

## 2. PROCESS GRAPHS (1): BASIC DEFINITION

Process graphs (cf. [12]) are nameless representation of processes, using the notion of graphs and their composition. Any graph is composed from a finite number of atomic agents and their connection. The results in [9, 10] already showed that the full expressive power of interacting processes can be obtained using a finite number of atoms and their interaction. Our process graphs are developed on this simplest possible basis, though its adaptation to other (possibly more complex) formalisms is possible (cf. 6.2).

---

[2]In [17], this reduction means: $a(x).(\bar{b}x.0 \mid \bar{c}x.0) \mid \bar{a}d.0 \longrightarrow \bar{b}d.0 \mid \bar{c}d.0$.

**2.1. Atomic Graphs.** Let A be a finite set of *atoms*, ranged over by $C, C', ...$, with two associating functions $ar : A \to N^+$ and $pol : A \to \{+, -\}$. $ar(C)$ and $pol(C)$ are called the *arity* and the *polarity* of $C$, respectively. $\theta, \theta', ..$ range over the set $\{+, -\}$. Essentially speaking, atoms denote the *units of behaviour* of processes: arities are the number of connections they can have with the outside, while polarities are the basic "type" of such behaviour (a positive atom and a negative atom will interact). Then the *atomic graph* of $C^{(n)}$, written $g(C)$, is a graph with only one *agent vertex* labeled with $C$, $n$ *free vertices* represented by •, and $n$ *edges* numbered by $\{1, 2, ..., n\}$ such as:

FIGURE 2. Atomic Graph

The handles are nameless representation of communication ports. A free handle corresponds to a free port name in usual process calculi, where "free" means "connectable to other handles". We call an edge numbered by 1 a *principal edge*, and a handle connected with such an edge a *principal handle*. A principal handle is a place where interaction takes place, like the initial prefix in CCS [16].[3] We also say the second, (third, ...) handle of an agent, if it is connected to the edges numbered accordingly.

**2.2. Example.** We take cc in [9], which was born in the course of analysis of prefix. With base $A_{cc} \overset{def}{=} \{M^{(2)+}, D^{(3)-}, FW^{(2)-}, K^{(1)-}, B_l^{(2)-}, B_r^{(2)-}, S^{(3)-}\}$, seven atomic graphs are given in Figure 3. Each agent vertex is labeled by the name of the corresponding atom. As shown, we sometimes write polarities of atoms in their principal edges.

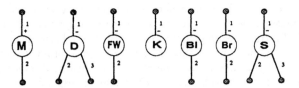

FIGURE 3. Atomic Graphs from $A_{cc}$

**2.3. Process Graphs.** Hereafter we fix A as given. Let E be a set of *edges*, ranged over by $e, e_1, e_2, ..$, $V_A$ be a set of *agent vertices*, ranged over by $a, a_1, a_2, ..$ and $V_F$ be a set of *free handles*, ranged over by $h, h_1, h_2, ...$ Then the set of *process graphs* with base A, ranged over by $G, G', ...$, is defined inductively in the following.

- **(empty graph)** The empty graph, denoted by 1, is a process graph.
- **(atomic graph)** An atomic graph is a process graph.

---

[3] A process which has more than one interaction point can be represented by some combination of the original atomic graphs with dyadic interaction rules defined later: accordingly we treat this type of a simple graph as an atom.

- **(juxtaposition)** If two graphs, say $G_1$ and $G_2$, are process graphs, then their *juxtaposition*, which is the (graph) union of $G_1$ and $G_2$, written $G_1 \parallel G_2$, is a process graph (Figure 4 (a)).
- **(connection)** Suppose that $\Sigma$ is a partition on a set of free handles of a process graph $G$. Then the *connection of $G$ by $\Sigma$*, written $G\langle\Sigma\rangle$, which is a graph $G'$ such that handles grouped together by $\Sigma$ are adjoined in $G$, is a process graph (Figure 4 (b)).
- **(hiding)** Suppose that $H$ is a subset of free handles in a process graph $G$. Then the *hiding of $H$ on $G$*, denoted by $H \blacktriangleright G$, which is a graph replacing each $h_i \in H$ of $G$ with a new (distinct) hidden handle denoted by $\circ$, is a process graph (Figure 4 (c)).

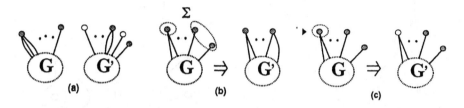

FIGURE 4. Process Graphs

In *juxtaposition*, two processes are composed to run on parallel but without any interaction between them (this corresponds to "$P|Q$" in CCS where the sets of free names in $P$ and $Q$ are disjoint). Interactivity between subsystems increases by *connection* of hitherto unconnected handles (roughly this is like making $(a.0\,|\,\bar{b}.0)$ to $(a.0\,|\,\bar{a}.0)$ by name substitution). Finally the *hiding* makes some handles unconnectable to other handles ($P\backslash L$ in CCS).

**2.4. Notations.** We let $\mathbf{V_R}$ denote a set of *hidden handles*, ranged by $r, r_1, r_2, \dots$. Note that $\mathbf{V_A}$, $\mathbf{V_F}$ and $\mathbf{V_R}$ are disjoint. Then $\mathbf{V_A}(G)$, $\mathbf{V_F}(G)$, $\mathbf{V_R}(G)$ and $\mathrm{E}(G)$ denote agent vertices, free handles, hidden handles and edges, in a process graph $G$, respectively. An *isomorphism* between two process graphs, written as $G_1 \simeq G_2$, is a usual one for graphs except that it should respect two labeling functions as well as distinction between free and hidden handles. We regard two isomorphic graphs as denoting the same object, as in the usual practice in the graph theory. A *pre-atomic graph* of $\mathcal{C}$ is a graph $G$ with one agent vertex labeled with $\mathcal{C}$, such that $ar(\mathcal{C}) \supseteq |\mathbf{V_F}(G)|$ and $\mathbf{V_R}(G) = \emptyset$. If a graph is not pre-atomic, then it is *composite*.

**2.5. Example.** Assume the base $\mathbf{A_{CC}}$ again. Figure 5 (a) gives a simple example of juxtaposition. The hiding replaces $\bullet$ with $\circ$, as in (b). The connection is also simple in diagram. Suppose, in $G$ of Figure 5 (c)-1, that $\Sigma_1 = \{\{h_1\}, \{h_2, h_3\}\}$ and $\Sigma_2 = \{\{h_1, h_2, h_3\}\}$. Then $G\langle\Sigma_1\rangle$ becomes like (c)-2 and $G\langle\Sigma_2\rangle$ becomes like (c)-3. Figure 5 (d) is an example of a composite graph. (e) shows all the pre-atomic graphs for $\mathcal{D}$ except the atomic graph itself (already given in Figure 3). So we have 5 pre-atomic graphs of $\mathcal{D}$ up to isomorphism.

**2.6. Parallel Composition.** The operation of *connection* we have introduced has no analogue in the operators in the usual process calculi, while being quite natural from a graph-theoretic point of view. However there is yet another fairly natural — but less general — way of "connecting agents," which is directly related to parallel composition in the term based process algebra.

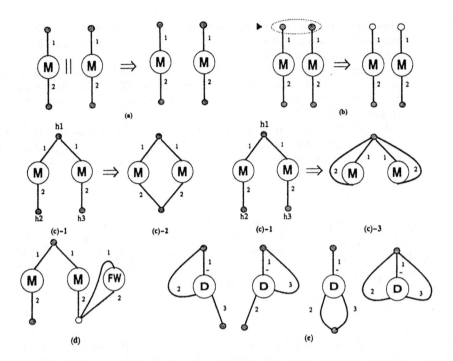

FIGURE 5. Operations and Pre-atomic Graphs

Think of a CCS term "$a.b.0|\bar{a}.0$." This simple example already makes it clear that the usual idea of parallel composition includes *both* juxtaposition *and* connection. But the involved connection has a specific feature, in that a single port of l.h.s agent is connected to a single port of r.h.s agent, and vice versa.

Let $\delta$ be a partial injection from $\mathbf{V}_F(G_1)$ to $\mathbf{V}_F(G_2)$. Then *a parallel composition of* $G_1$ *and* $G_2$ *by* $\delta$, written $G_1 \|_\delta G_2$, is the union of $G_1$ and $G_2$ where if $\delta : h \mapsto h'$ we adjoin $h$ into $h'$.

Note that $G_1 \| G_2$ corresponds to the case when the above $\delta$ is empty.

**2.7. Example.** Given two $\mathbf{g}(\mathcal{M})$'s and their correspondence $\delta$ as in Figure 6 (a)-1, $\mathbf{g}(\mathcal{M}) \|_\delta \mathbf{g}(\mathcal{M})$ is as (a)-2. Note that any two distinct free handles in the source graph must not be connected to the same handle in the target graph; so (b)-2 is not obtained from (b)-1 because the function $f$ is not injection, but from (b)-3. We find that this is precisely what is happening in parallel composition in the usual process algebra.

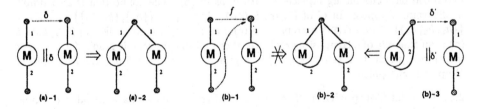

FIGURE 6. Concurrent Composition

More technical discussions on these operators will be developed in the next section.

## 3. Process Graphs (2): the Basic Algebra

This section continues the study of the graph-based theory of processes. By definition of our process graphs, we know any process graph is constructed by three basic operators. To begin with, we define textual notations which have been used somewhat informally so far but will be used as a rigorous basis for formulating various ideas in the algebra of process graphs. Then the equality laws for isomorphic graphs are developed as an example of such an algebra. Finally we establish that parallel composition which has been regarded as a "primitive" operation in the usual process calculi can be translated in our three basic operations which are more in the spirit of graph theory.

**3.1. Textual Notation.** We introduce the following formal textual notations which can express any process graph, fixing a base. Assuming the set of atoms and handles as given, the *textual notations*, again ranged over by $G_1, G_2, ...$, are given by:

- **1**,
- $C^{(n)}[h_1..h_n]$ ($h_i \neq h_j$ if $i \neq j$) for each atom $C^{(n)}$. Then $V_F(C^{(n)}[h_1..h_n]) = \{h_1, .., h_n\}$, which *occur free* in this notation.
- $G_1 \parallel G_2$, where we assume no common free handles occur in both $G_1$ and $G_2$.
- $G\langle \Sigma \rangle^f$, where $\Sigma$ is a partition on $V_F(G)$ and $f$ is a total map from $V_F(G)$ to distinct fresh handles, its kernel inducing the partition $\Sigma$. Then the fresh handles become the free handles in the new notation. A notation like $G\langle \{h_1, h_2\}_{h_1'}, \{h_3\}_{h_2'} \rangle$ is also used (assuming $V_F(G) = \{h_1, h_2, h_3\}$): then this notation denotes a new graph with the new set of free handles $\{h_1', h_2'\}$.
- $H \blacktriangleright G$, when $H$ is a subset of free handles in a notation $G$. Then the complement of $H$ becomes the free handles of the new notation.
- $G_1 \parallel_\delta G_2$, where no free handles occur common between two $G_1$ and $G_2$ and $\delta$ is a partial injection between $V_F(G_1)$ and $V_F(G_2)$. The free handles in $G_1$ are assumed to be rewritten by $\delta$.

Also, when writing down composed operations, we assume both of $\parallel$ and $\parallel_\delta$ are the weakest in association and associate to the left, and $\blacktriangleright$ is weaker than $\langle \Sigma \rangle$ in association. Note that, as in graph theory, e.g. $h_1 \blacktriangleright \mathcal{M}[h_1 h_2]$ denotes the same process graph as $h_3 \blacktriangleright \mathcal{M}[h_3 h_4]$: accordingly we introduce the global injective relabeling of handles from $G_1$ to $G_2$, denoted by $G_1 \triangleright G_2$.

**3.2. Normal Form.** Assume a composite graph in Figure 5 (d) again. Then we find a lot of ways to construct this graph by applying the operations to atomic graphs. However we immediately know that we can generate the same (isomorphic) process graphs with the fixed order of operations.

**Proposition.** *Any process graph can be generated from atomic graphs by applying firstly juxtapositions, secondly connections, and finally hiding.*

**Proof:** First observe that, for any graph $G$, there exists $G'$ with $V_R(G') = \emptyset$, for which $G = H \blacktriangleright G'$ for some $H \subset V_F(G')$. Now it is easy to observe that $(G_1\langle \Sigma_1 \rangle \parallel G_2\langle \Sigma_2 \rangle)$ can be also composed as $(G_1 \parallel G_2)\langle \Sigma' \rangle$, and that composition of a sequence of connections is again a connection. Applying this fact to $G'$ repeatedly, we know any $G'$ can be written: $(\mathbf{g}(C_1)\|\mathbf{g}(C_2)\|...\|\mathbf{g}(C_n))\langle \Sigma \rangle$. Hence the result. $\square$

Now let us define a *normal form* of a textual notation: we say a textual notation is a normal form if it is formed as: $H \blacktriangleright ((\mathbf{g}(C_1)\|...\|\mathbf{g}(C_n))\langle \Sigma \rangle)$. Then in the scheme of Chemical Abstract Machine [1] we present the graph in Figure 5 (d) as a triple of a multi-set of atomic graphs, a partition, and an indication of a set of hidden handles like: $\langle \{|\mathcal{M}[h_1 h_2], \mathcal{M}[h_3 h_4], \mathcal{FW}[h_5 h_6]|\}, \{\{h_1, h_3\}, \{h_2\}, \{h_4, h_5, h_6\}_{h_7}\}, \{h_7\}\rangle$. Considering this representation, we say that two textual notations are the same normal form if firstly all atomic graphs are represented as the same multi-set, and secondly partitions and indications of hiding coincide, after using $\triangleright$.

**3.3. Isomorphism Laws.** We now develop the isomorphism laws for textual notations. Some of them resemble what we find as equality laws in the process algebra [1, 17]. The following proposition says that if and only if $G$ and $G'$ denote the same (isomorphic) graph, we can rewrite $G$ to $G'$ applying the following laws plus global relabeling. We use a notation: $\{H_i\}_{i \leq n}$ stands for $\{H_1, H_2, ..., H_n\}$.

**Proposition.** (soundness and completeness of the isomorphism laws) $G \simeq G'$ iff $G \overset{iso}{=} G''$ and $G'' \triangleright G'$ where $\overset{iso}{=}$ is the smallest congruent relation over textual notations derived by the following rules.

    I. $G_1 \| G_2 \overset{iso}{=} G_2 \| G_1$     $G \| 1 \overset{iso}{=} G$    $(G_1 \| G_2) \| G_3 \overset{iso}{=} G_1 \| (G_2 \| G_3)$

    II. $(G \langle \Sigma_1 \rangle^{f_1}) \langle \Sigma_2 \rangle^{f_2} \overset{iso}{=} G \langle \Sigma \rangle^f$ with $f = f_2 \circ f_1$.

    III. $(G_1 \| G_2 \langle \Sigma \rangle^f) \overset{iso}{=} (G_1 \| G_2) \langle \Sigma' \rangle^{f'}$ where $f' = f \cup \{h_i \mapsto h'_i\}_{i \leq n}$ with $V_F(G_1) = \{h_1, ..., h_n\}$ and $h'_i$ fresh.

    IV. $H_2 \triangleright (H_1 \triangleright G) \overset{iso}{=} (H_1 \cup H_2) \triangleright G$.

    V. $(H \triangleright G_1) \| G_2 \overset{iso}{=} H \triangleright (G_1 \| G_2)$ with $H \cap V_F(G_2) = \emptyset$.

    VI. $(H \triangleright G) \langle \Sigma \rangle^f \overset{iso}{=} H' \triangleright (G \langle \Sigma' \rangle^{f'})$ where $f' = f \cup \{h_i \mapsto h'_i\}_{i \leq n}$ with $H = \{h_1, ..., h_n\}$, $H' = \{h'_1, ..., h'_n\}$ and $h'_i$ fresh.

PROOF: First we show soundness, i.e. l.h.s. is isomorphic to r.h.s. in each rule. I, II and V are obvious. For III, we can easily check $H_1 \cap H_2 = \emptyset$ and $H_1 \cup H_2 \subset V_F(G)$ iff $H_1 \subset V_F(G)$, $H_2 \subset (V_F(G) \setminus H_1)$. For VI, with $f_1 \overset{def}{=} \{h_i \mapsto h'_i\}_{i \leq n}$, we know $(G_1 \| G_2) \langle \Sigma' \rangle^{f'} \simeq (G_1 \langle \Sigma_1 \rangle^{f_1} \| G_2 \langle \Sigma \rangle^f) \simeq (G_1 \| G_2 \langle \Sigma \rangle)$. IV is proved similarly.

For completeness, by Proposition 3.2 and I, we can claim that $G \simeq G'$, then $G$ and $G'$ can be written as the same normal form [since: we can show that two graphs which can not have the same normal form are not isomorphic by induction on the size of a textual notation]. Therefore if we can rewrite any $G$ to some normal form by $\overset{iso}{=}$ (and $\triangleright$), then the result is obtained. But this is mechanically proved by induction on the size of a textual notation applying $\overset{iso}{=}$ from l.h.s. to r.h.s. □

Now we can check mechanically whether two notations denote the same graph or not.

**3.4. Parallel Composition (2).** As we already noted, a graph given by $G_1 \|_\delta G_2$ can also be composed as $(G_1 \| G_2) \langle \Sigma \rangle$. From this, we know that adding this operation into our repertoire cannot increase the number of constructible graphs. A more interesting point however is whether it can make the substitute for the connection operation or not. Before answering this question, we show a small lemma.

**Lemma.** For all $G_1, G_2, \langle \Sigma \rangle$, $(G_1 \| G_2) \langle \Sigma \rangle$ is also written $G_1 \langle \Sigma_1 \rangle \|_\delta G_2 \langle \Sigma_2 \rangle$ for some $\delta$, $\langle \Sigma_1 \rangle$ and $\langle \Sigma_2 \rangle$.

PROOF: We use the argument with colored handles. Given $G_1 \| G_2$, put a (distinct) color to each set of free handles to be adjoined by $\langle \Sigma \rangle$. Since the graph is still disconnected, we can think of its $G_1$ element and $G_2$ element separately. Now, in each subgraph, connect free handles with the common colors until each color appears exactly in one free handle. Call these graphs by $G_1\langle \Sigma_1 \rangle$ and $G_2\langle \Sigma_2 \rangle$. Finally define $\delta$ as partial injection which maps a free handle of $G_1\langle \Sigma_1 \rangle$ to a free handle of $G_2\langle \Sigma_2 \rangle$ with the same color. Clearly the resulting graph is the same as that which l.h.s. denotes. $\square$

Now we give the answer in the following.

**Proposition.** *Any process graph can be generated from pre-atomic graphs only using operations* $\langle \, \|_\delta \, , \, \blacktriangleright \, \rangle$.

PROOF: By Proposition 3.2, we know any graph can be represented in some normal form such that: $H \blacktriangleright ((\mathbf{g}(C_1)\| \cdots \|\mathbf{g}(C_n))\langle \Sigma \rangle)$. Next note that composition of a sequence of connections is again a connection. Then applying the preceding lemma and the isomorphism laws starting from a graph in a normal form repeatedly, we get: $H \blacktriangleright (\mathbf{g}(C_1)\langle \Sigma_1 \rangle\|_{\delta_1} \cdots \|_{\delta_{n-1}} \mathbf{g}(C_n)\langle \Sigma_n \rangle)$. Hence the result since $\mathbf{g}(C_i)\langle \Sigma_i \rangle$ is pre-atomic. $\square$

However if we start from *atomic* graphs, parallel composition and restriction are not enough to generate all the graphs: just take a pre-atomic agent which is not an atomic agent (such an agent can always be constructed if the base has an atom with more than one arity). This is because the connection *within* an atomic graph cannot be done by parallel composition. For instance, if we use parallel composition, 19 bases are needed to represent any process graphs based on $\mathbf{A_{CC}}$, while only 7 are enough in the original operations: we still keep parallel composition due to its usefulness and its correspondence with the term-based counterpart (cf. 6.1).

## 4. Graph Relation (1): Reduction over Process Graphs

As mentioned in Section 1, one-step reduction from $G$ to $G'$ can be defined by a triple $\langle G, \delta, G' \rangle$ where $\delta$ is a partial injection from $\mathbf{V_F}(G)$ to $\mathbf{V_F}(G')$. Let us now attempt to extend the observation into the idea of general graph relations in the nameless format. Some related notations: $\mathrm{dom}(\delta)$ and $\mathrm{cod}(\delta)$ denote the set of handles in the domain and the codomain of $\delta$. $\delta^{-1}$ denotes the inverse of $\delta$. With $\mathrm{dom}(\delta_2) = \mathrm{cod}(\delta_1)$, $\delta_2 \circ \delta_1$ denotes the composition of $\delta_1$ and $\delta_2$. Note that both are correspondences again. $\mathrm{id}(G)$ denotes the correspondence induced from identity isomorphism on $G$.

### 4.1. Correspondence and Standard Operations.

A *correspondence* is any triple $\langle G_1, \delta, G_2 \rangle$ where $\delta$ is a partial injection from $\mathbf{V_F}(G_1)$ to $\mathbf{V_F}(G_2)$. By abuse of notation, we let $\delta, \delta', \delta'', \ldots$ range over the set of correspondences. A *g-relation* is any set of correspondences where if $\delta$ is in the set then so is $\rho \circ \delta \circ \rho'$ where $\rho$ and $\rho'$ are correspondences induced by isomorphisms at the domain and co-domain. g-relations will be denoted by $\mathfrak{R}, \mathfrak{R}', \ldots$. If $G_1$ and $G_2$ are related by $\delta$ in a g-relation $\mathfrak{R}$, we write this $G_1 \, \mathfrak{R}_\delta \, G_2$ (so $\mathfrak{R} \stackrel{\mathrm{def}}{=} \{\mathfrak{R}_{\delta_i}\}_{i \in I}$).

A *sub g-relation* of a g-relation $\mathfrak{R}$ is a subset of $\mathfrak{R}$ which is again a g-relation. Also note that the set of all g-relations is closed under union, intersection, difference, as well as having the top (called the *universal g-relation*) and the bottom (called the *empty g-relation*). The *identity g-relation* denoted by $\mathbf{ID}$ is the set of correspondences induced by all isomorphisms.

We define two operations on g-relations, reminiscent of those on usual relations. *Composition* of $\mathfrak{R}$ and $\mathfrak{R}'$, written $\mathfrak{R}' \circ \mathfrak{R}$, is defined: $\{\delta' \circ \delta \mid \delta \in \mathfrak{R} \, \wedge \, \delta' \in \mathfrak{R}' \wedge \mathrm{cod}(\delta) =$

$\text{dom}(\delta')\}$. Similarly the *inverse* of $\mathfrak{R}$, written $\mathfrak{R}^{-1}$, is defined as $\{\delta^{-1} \mid \delta \in \mathfrak{R}\}$. Note that **ID** is a (unique) unit for $\circ$.

Some g-relations have closure properties just as in usual relations. We say $\mathfrak{R}$ is *reflexive* if $\mathfrak{R} \supset$ **ID**, *transitive* if $\mathfrak{R} \circ \mathfrak{R} \subset \mathfrak{R}$, *symmetric* if $\mathfrak{R}^{-1} = \mathfrak{R}$, and *equivalence* if it is reflexive, transitive, and symmetric. Associated closure operations are called, as usual, the *reflexive* (resp. *symmetric, transitive, equivalence*) closure.

**4.2. Compatibility.** The notion of compatibility is defined with some side conditions concerning correspondences. We say a g-relation $\mathfrak{R}$ is *compatible* if $G_1 \, \mathfrak{R}_\delta \, G_2$ implies:

(JUX)    $(G_1 \| G) \, \mathfrak{R}_{\delta'} \, (G_2 \| G)$   with  $\delta' = \delta \cup \text{id}(G)$

(CON)   $G_1 \langle \Sigma_1 \rangle^{f_1} \, \mathfrak{R}_{\delta'} \, G_2 \langle \Sigma_2 \rangle^{f_2}$   with  $\delta' \circ f_1 \supset f_2 \circ \delta$

(RES)   $H_1 \blacktriangleright G_1 \, \mathfrak{R}_{\delta'} \, H_2 \blacktriangleright G_2$   with  (1) $\delta(H_1) \subset H_2$ and $\delta^{-1}(H_2) \subset H_1$

                                                           (2) $\delta' \circ (\text{id}(G_1) \backslash H_1) = (\text{id}(G_2) \backslash H_2) \circ \delta$

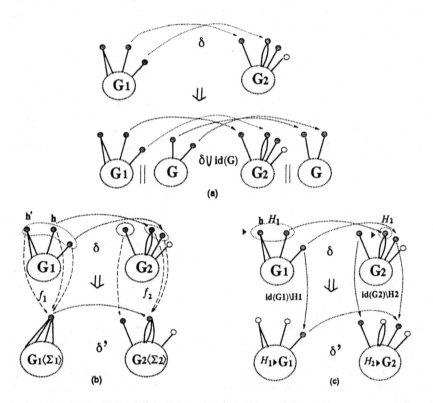

FIGURE 7. Compatibility over g-Relations

We show the idea of this definition in Figure 7. (JUX) illustrated in (a) is easy to understand, while (CON) and (RES) are somewhat cumbersome. (CON) described in (b) says that as far as the part related by $\delta$ is concerned, the connections $\langle \Sigma_1 \rangle$ and $\langle \Sigma_2 \rangle$, and the resulting correspondence $\delta'$ should work in a complete accordance with each other, i.e. $\delta'(f_1(h)) = f_2(\delta(h))$ for any $h \in V_F(G_1)$ s.t. $\delta(h) \in V_F(G_2)$. The inclusion comes from the observation that we may freely connect the free handles not related by $\delta$, e.g. $h'$ in (b). In (RES) whose picture is in (c), the first condition says that two hiding operations should function on the part related by $\delta$ in the correct way, but unrelated handles (here $h$) are not considered.[4] The second condition means that the new correspondence $\delta'$ is obtained by decreasing hidden handles from the domain of $\delta$.

We say that a g-relation is a *congruence* if it is an equivalence and compatible. Compatible and congruent closures are respective closure operations. Then we can easily check the set of all g-relations is closed under all the operations in this and the previous subsections.

**4.3. Reduction.** As one of the most significant g-relations in the present formalism, we introduce the process dynamics over graphs, following the original idea as given in [9, 10]: if a pair of atomic graphs with different polarities are connected through their principal handles, the graph is transformed into another graph via a certain correspondence. Each such pair, written by $\mathbf{g}(C_1^+) \bullet \mathbf{g}(C_2^-)$, is called *a reduction pair of $C_1$ and $C_2$*. Then the set of interaction rules with a base **A**, which is denoted by $\Re$, takes a form, with $C_1^+, C_2^-$ from **A**:

$$\mathbf{g}(C_1^+) \bullet \mathbf{g}(C_2^-) \; \Re_\delta \; G'$$

where $\delta$ should be surjective and, moreover, for each combination of a positive atomic graph and a negative atomic graph, there should be one and only one such rule in $\Re$. As an example, the set of interaction rules for atoms in 2.2 is given in Figure 8.

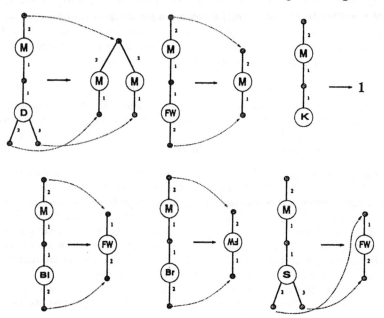

FIGURE 8. Reduction in Concurrent Combinators

Given a certain basis and the interaction rules, say $\Re$, the *one-step reduction* is the compatible closure of $\Re$, denoted by $\longrightarrow$ and the *multi-step reduction*, denoted by $\longrightarrow\!\!\!\!\rightarrow$, is the transitive and reflexive closure of $\longrightarrow$.

---

[4]This is related with the property that the usual binary relations of process calculi are closed under structure rules [1, 17]; especially note $e \blacktriangleright P \equiv P$ with $e \notin \mathcal{FN}(P)$ concerning restriction. Consider the reduction $a \blacktriangleright (\mathcal{M}(ab), \mathcal{D}(acd)) \longrightarrow (\mathcal{M}(cb), \mathcal{M}(db))$ for instance; the unrelated name in r.h.s (here $a$) can freely be restricted in l.h.s.

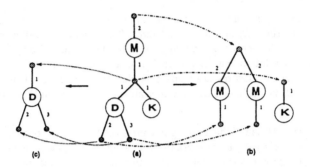

FIGURE 9. Nondeterminism in Process Graphs

Thus we write e.g. $G \to_\delta G'$ which we read: $G$ one-step reduces to $G'$ via the correspondence $\delta$. Similarly for multi-step reduction. We note that a correspondence in $\longrightarrow$ and $\longrightarrow\!\!\!\!\rightarrow$ is always surjective, as is inferred from the definition of compatibility.

**4.4. Semi-compatibility.** In addition to compatibility, we add the notion of *semi-compatibility*, and, consequently, *semi-congruence*, where connection is replaced by parallel composition. We need some preliminary notations: we call $\{\delta(t) \mid t \in \text{dom}(\delta)\}$ an *image* of $\delta$, written $\text{im}(\delta)$, and $\{t \mid \delta(t) \in \text{cod}(\delta)\}$ a *pre-image* of $\delta$, written $\text{preim}(\delta)$. We write $\delta \asymp \delta'$ when $\delta(h) = \delta'(h)$ for any $h \in \text{preim}(\delta) \cap \text{preim}(\delta')$, and $\delta^{-1}(h) = \delta'^{-1}(h)$ for any $h \in \text{im}(\delta) \cap \text{im}(\delta')$. Note $\asymp$ is equivalence and closed under inverse and composition. Then a g-relation is *semi-compatible* if $G_1 \, \mathfrak{R}_\delta \, G_2$ implies:

(PAR) $\quad (G_1 \,\|_{\delta_1} G) \, \mathfrak{R}_{\delta'} \, (G_2 \,\|_{\delta_2} G) \quad$ where $\delta_2 \circ \delta \asymp \delta_1$ and $\delta' = \text{id}(G) \cup (\delta \backslash \text{preim}(\delta_1))$

together with (RES) in 4.2. We say that it is *semi-congruence* if it is semi-compatible and equivalent. The set of g-relations is also closed under associated closure operations. This is used when we study the correspondence with the arbitrary congruence (possibly without name-substitutivity) in the term-based theory, cf. 6.1.

**4.5. Important Remark.** The reduction in process graphs has essential features of concurrent processes: (1) computation with sharing (or, equivalently, interference [13]), and, as a consequence, (2) non-determinism. They come from arbitrary connection of free handles using (CON) rule. Figure 9 (a) depicts the situation where the principal handle of a message is connected with those of two negative atomic graphs. The reduction inevitably becomes non-deterministic. (b) is the case when a message and a duplicator interact, while (c) shows a case when a message and a killer interact, resulting in distinct (and semantically different) configurations accordingly.

Now we proceed to some examples comparing our graph representation with Lafont's Interaction Nets [14], which can be regarded as a special form of process graphs without multiple connection of principal handles.

**4.6. SK-combinators (1): Interaction Nets.** We shall show the "interactive" version of Curry's classical combinators, where an interaction between atoms is always done via a hidden handle, to which only one negative atom and one positive atom are connected. Thus this system is exactly one of Lafont's Interaction Nets.[5] In this system, the original combinators **S** and **K** are decomposed into three or two atoms, respectively. Moreover we need to explicitly represent "Copy" and "Kill" of terms. Following this, all

---

[5]This encoding is the exactly same one as Simon Gay gave in [2], though it was independently defined and has been published in [6].

nine atomic graphs are defined in Figure 10 (a), and the interaction rules are specified in (b). In this encoding we use a generation of a linkage called a (generalised) forwarder: this is because a direct identification of two ports is prohibited in the present scheme (cf. 6.2). In this system **K** is regarded as an agent which just makes a link to the first argument.

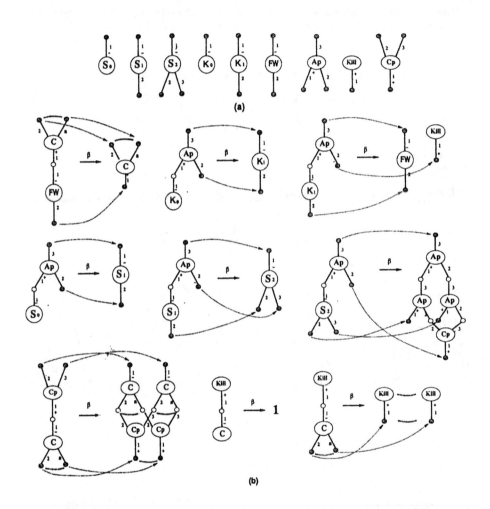

FIGURE 10. Interaction Net (SK-combinators)

Now let us map a sequential combinator $M$ to a process graph inductively; S and K are mapped to "$S_0$" and "$K_0$" respectively, and the application $MN$ to a graph in which the principal handles of two graphs representing $M$ and $N$ are connected with the first handle and the second one of "Ap" respectively, and they are finally hidden.

**4.7. SK-combinators (2): Shared Version.** In the above example, "$S_0$" and "$K_0$" cannot be shared. But by allowing overlapped free handles, we easily define a shared version of SK-combinators in Figure 11. Interestingly we do not need explicit "Copy" and "Kill" agents (so the numbers of atomic graphs and reduction rules decrease), the persistent behaviour of the shared negative atomic graphs is required. In (b), "$!\mathcal{FW}$" is a persistent (generalised) forwarder which links two handles and still remains after interaction.

The mapping of a sequential combinator to a process graph is given in the same way as in 4.6, though, in the new version, we can share "$S_0$" and "$K_0$" arbitrarily.[6]

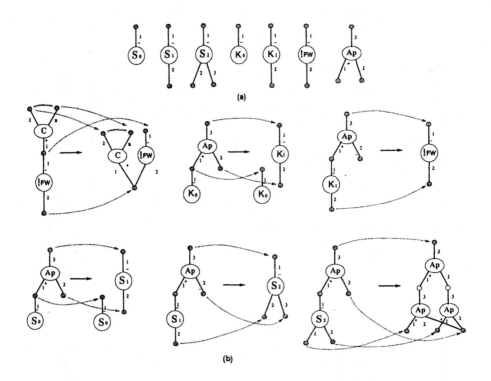

FIGURE 11. Shared SK-combinators

**4.8. Boolean Expression.** We show an encoding of Parallel Or which may not be represented as Lafont's Interaction Nets, but can be naturally described as our process graphs. First we introduce the following boolean atomic graphs in Figure 12 (a) and their interaction rules in Figure 12 (b). Note that we again use the persistent forwarder. Then Parallel Or is encoded as in Figure 12 (c) by simply connecting two free handles of two "OR" atomic graphs (this is not allowed in Interaction Nets). Thus "false or true" is reduced like (d); intuitively this is equated by "true" because two persistent forwarders

---

[6]We can easily extend this encoding to share any application (e.g. (SK) in ((SK)(SK))) by defining that $S_1$, $S_2$ and $K_1$ are persistent.

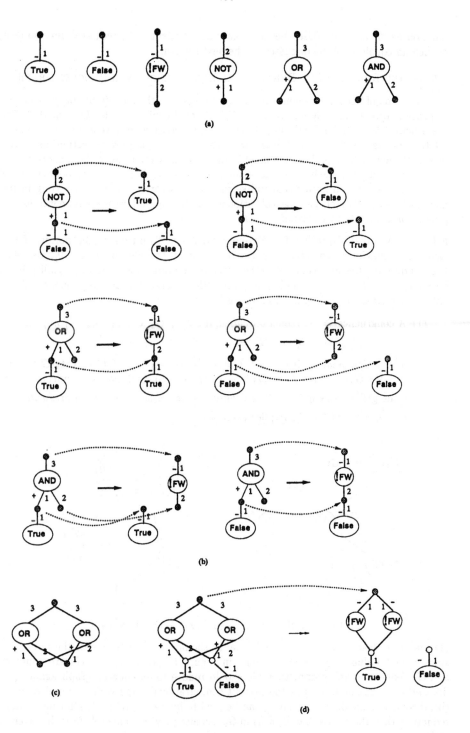

FIGURE 12. Boolean Agents

function as linkers and "false" becomes an inactive agent. The technical development of such an equality will be discussed in the next section.

## 5. GRAPH RELATION (2): BEHAVIOURAL EQUIVALENCE OVER PROCESS GRAPHS

The notion of behavioural equivalence over processes is the most fundamental element in process formalisms, originating from observational equivalence for CCS in [16]. For the process graphs to be a meaningful formalism for concurrency, we need some ways of relating agents based on their behaviour. This is done in the present section, using the notion of congruential g-relation defined in the previous section. Just like some relations over terms in a term algebra such as bisimulations, some g-relations are behaviourally significant. We should notice that unlike reduction, a correspondence in a congruence may *not* be surjective (cf. garbage collection in 5.2). At the end, we present an interesting general property of any congruence class.

**5.1. Behavioural Equality for Process Graphs.** To introduce the notion of the canonical behavioural equality over graphs based on the idea in [8, 9, 10], we need two conditions: the first condition, the *reduction-closure*, says that the equality is in harmony with the notion of reduction, while the second, the *action predicate*, filters only behaviourally meaningful congruences (cf. [19]).

(1) A congruence $\overset{s}{\cong}$ is *reduction-closed*, if $G_1 \overset{s}{\cong}_\delta G_2$ and $G_1 \twoheadrightarrow_{\delta_1} G_1'$ implies, for some $G_2'$, $G_2 \twoheadrightarrow_{\delta_2} G_2'$ and $G_1' \overset{s}{\cong}_{\delta'} G_2'$ with $\delta' = \delta_2 \circ \delta \circ \delta_1^{-1}$.

(2) The *action predicate* is give as: $G \Downarrow_{h^\bullet} \overset{\text{def}}{\Leftrightarrow} G \twoheadrightarrow_\delta G' \wedge \delta(h) \in \text{Act}_\theta(G')$ (note $h \in V_F(G)$) where $\text{Act}_\theta(G)$ is a set of free principal handles connected with some $g(C^\theta)$. Now let us call a congruence $\overset{s}{\cong}$ *respects the action predicates*, if $G_1 \overset{s}{\cong}_\delta G_2$ and $G_1 \Downarrow_{h^\bullet}$ implies $G_2 \Downarrow_{\delta(h)^\bullet}$.

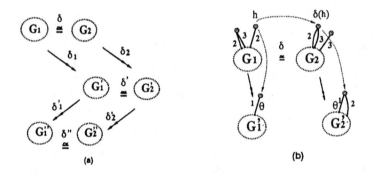

(a)  (b)

FIGURE 13. Reduction-closure and Action Predicate

(1) makes it clear that the notion of equality should be consistent with the notion of state change induced by reduction: e.g. in Figure 13 (a), if $G_1$ and $G_2$ are equated and $G_1$ reduces to any graph, then $G_2$ should reduce to an equated graph again. (2) fits the basic idea of actions in the present computational framework. As indicated in (b), if some free handle in $G_1$, say $h$, can be used to interact with $g(C^\theta)$ after multi-step reduction, then the related handle $\delta(h)$ in $G_2$ can also play the same role ($\bar{\theta}$ is the inverse of $\theta$).

The basic result of the equality defined with the above notions follows.

**Proposition.** *We say that a congruence is $\Downarrow_{h\bullet}$-sound, or simply sound, if it is re-duction closed and respects the action predicate. Then there is the maximum $\Downarrow_{h\bullet}$-sound congruence.*

PROOF: Note that, in the congruent closure of any family of congruences, a correspon-dence there can always be factored out by a chain of correspondences in the original congruences (this is essentially *Chain Lemma* in [8]). Using this, an easy reasoning based on commutativity of maps proves that the congruent closure of any family of reduction-closed congruences is again reduction-closed. Similarly for the condition on the action predicate. □

Some concrete sound congruences might be interesting.

**5.2. Example.** Let us see what is done in Interaction Net using the notion of congru-ence over g-relations. Suppose we are given two atomic graphs with different polarities, and construct the graph by connecting them only by their principal handles and then hide only that handle only. Now we have a reduction from such a graph, and take the congruent closure of such correspondences in any system of process graphs. We call this congruence a *simple β-equality* denoted by $\overset{\imath\beta}{=}$. Figure 14 (a) depicts one example of an equation by $\overset{\imath\beta}{=}$ (cf. Example 4.6). With the reasoning in the same way as that of Proposition 3.7 in [9], we get:

**Proposition I** *In any system of process graphs, $\overset{\imath\beta}{=}$ is sound.*

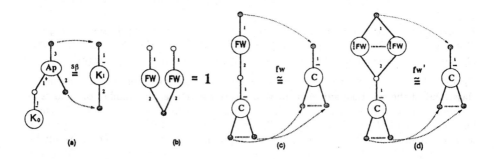

FIGURE 14. Behavioural Equalities

As another example, an idea frequently found in graph-based formalisms is *garbage collection*. To offer a process theoretic foundation to "garbages" in these examples, the following will give a tentative but useful answer.

**Proposition II** *Given a process graph $G$, if $G$ satisfies one of the following conditions, then the congruent closure of the equation $G =_0 1$ is always sound.*

(1) *$G$ does not one-step reduce, and $G$ has no free active handles, or*

(2) *$G$ has no free handles.*

Figure 14 (b) shows an example of garbage collection (1). More refined treatment will allow garbage collecting divergent configuration with free handles, which however would let us lose effective judgment of garbages.

Finally due to the existence of forwarders, the full justification of the examples needs the equalities from the two laws in Figure 14 (c) and (d) where $\mathbf{g}(C^-)$ in (c) is erased after interacting with any positive agent, while $\mathbf{g}(C^-)$ in (d) is persistent. Then we have:

**Proposition III** *The congruent closure of the equations given by Figure 14 (c) and (d) is sound.*

Now we recall Examples 4.6, 4.7 and 4.8. The easy inductive reasoning gives us if classical combinators $M$ and $N$ are weak-$\beta$ equated, then the encodings of $M$ and $N$ defined in 4.6 are also equated by the maximum sound equality using Proposition I and III-(c). Similarly for the encodings of 4.7 by Proposition II and III-(d). Finally in Example 4.8, we can check "false or true", "true or false", or even "true or $\Omega$" is "true" up to the maximum sound equality over boolean agents by Propositions II and III-(d).

We hope that the present construction over g-relations offers a rigorous basis for reasoning about various (static and dynamic) structures of concurrent computation in the graphical framework.

**5.3. The Minimum Graph in a Congruence Class.** Finally we show one important result in the general congruences: there is the minimum representation in some sense in any congruence class (e.g. l.h.s is simpler than r.h.s in each congruence in Figure 14). Let $\cong$ be a congruence. *A congruence class* from $\cong$ is a set of process graphs which is closed under $\cong$ and in which any two graphs are mutually equated by $\cong$.

**Proposition.** *Given any $\cong$ and any congruence class from $\cong$, say $\Phi$, there is a graph $G \in \Phi$ such that $G' \in \Phi \Rightarrow |V_F(G)| \lesssim |V_F(G')|$. Moreover, if we have $G_1 \cong_{\delta_1} G \cong_{\delta_2} G_2$ for such $G$, then $\delta_1$ and $\delta_2^{-1}$ are always surjective and $\mathrm{im}(\delta_1) = \mathrm{preim}(\delta_2)$.*

PROOF: Take the set of correspondences in $\cong$ which equate the graphs in the congruence class. Out of the set, take any element whose cardinality (i.e. the number of handles in its pre-image) is the minimum among them (any such element is fine). Call it $\delta$. Then, for some $G_1$ and $G_2$, we have $G_1 \cong_\delta G_2$. If $|\delta| \neq 0$, using (CON) rule of congruence, we can adjoin all free handles to those in the pre-image of $\delta$ in $G_1$. Let the result be $G$. Then we have $G \cong_{\delta'} G_2$ with $|\delta'| = |\delta|$. Now suppose there is some $G'$ in the congruence class, for which we have $|V_F(G')| \lesssim |V_F(G)|$. Then $G' \cong_{\delta''} G$ for some $\delta''$ but then $|\delta''| \lesssim |V_F(G')| \lesssim |V_F(G)| = |\delta|$ which contradicts the way of selecting $\delta$. Thus $|V_F(G)| \lesssim |V_F(G')|$ for any $G'$ in the congruence class. Moreover, by the above discussions, if we have $G_1 \cong_{\delta_1} G \cong_{\delta_2} G_2$, the conditions clearly hold. If $|\delta| = 0$, using (RES) rule of congruence, we hide all the free handles of $G_1$ and call the result $G$, for which we still have $G \cong_\delta G_2$. Take this $G$ and it clearly satisfies the conditions. $\square$

Note the proof uses connection and hiding in our graph-based formalism essentially. The result says that if the number of free handles in $G$ is the minimum in a congruence class, all free handles in $G$ are always connected by correspondences in the congruence class. Hence one may define some group of the process graphs as the minimum representation by checking firstly the number of *free handles*, secondly *atomic vertices* and finally *hidden handles*.

## 6. Discussions

In this section, we first summarise our result on the correspondence between the graph representation and term-based processes, as developed in [11]. Then we give comparisons with some related work and discuss further issues.

### 6.1. Correspondence with Term-Based Theory.

In view of our intention to study the nameless representation, it should be interesting to see how the concurrent computation in this graphical framework commutes with the one in the world which uses names, and also differs from it, so that both enrich our understanding about concurrency.

As the first step, to forget names from the terms, one can observe that there are not any essential "structural" difference between $P$ and $P\sigma$ where $\sigma$ is *a name permutation*, a one-one map over names. But the essential idea is not only processes and their composition, but *relationship* between (or predicate on) processes. Since the notion of operations in the graph-based theory itself does not conform to the framework of the $\Sigma$-algebra (it does not even induce so-called clones of operations), such mappings can *not* be a homomorphism in the usual sense. But what matters is, as in $\mathcal{M}(ab) \approx c \blacktriangleright (\mathcal{FW}(ca), \mathcal{M}(ab))$, *correspondence of names* between two terms. Thus we introduce the idea of the *name-coherent* relations over terms (i.e. relations for which $P \mathrel{\mathcal{R}} Q$ implies $P\sigma \mathrel{\mathcal{R}} Q\sigma$ for any name-permutation $\sigma$, and which are also closed under $\equiv$). Notice that the most of standard congruences in process calculi (e.g. bisimilarities in CCS) are name-coherent.

The set of name-coherent relations forms a boolean lattice which is closed under the boolean and relational operations. We note that the set of g-relations also forms a boolean lattice equipped with all the operations in 4.1, 4.2 and 4.4. Let A be fixed and call the two lattices NCoh and gRel respectively. Then the main result in [11] says: *With the common bases, there are mutually inverse bijections between NCoh and gRel such that:*

- *There are isomorphisms between two algebras w.r.t. the respective operations with the same names defined in 4.1.*
- *The compatible closure operation in NCoh is mapped to the semi-compatible closure in gRel and the compatible, name-substitution closure in NCoh to the compatible closure in gRel. Similarly for the inverse. The similar result is established by replacing (semi-)compatible with (semi-)congruent.*

The isomorphism at the level of the standard operations gives us the correspondence on such important notions as reduction, behavioural equivalences etc. between two domains. Note also that congruence notions in two domains are related, where congruence in graphs corresponds to congruence in terms which is also closed under general name substitution. Note that some "good" process equivalences indeed require that they are name substitutive (e.g. [20, 25]), so that this notion deserves further study. One of the most important remarks is the maximum sound equality in the system of concurrent combinators called $cc_\varphi$ in [10] is name-substitutive. This result says there is a leaner mathematical representation in which truly finite (at most 27) atoms and fixed interaction rules can operationally encode mobile processes (embedding of related calculi, e.g. Polyadic $\pi$-calculus [18] and CHOCS [26] as well as $\lambda$-calculus naturally follow) up to the sound equality proposed in 5.1.

### 6.2. Related Work and Further Issues.

From the original exposition on concurrent processes [16], Milner developed his formalism both in the usual syntax and in the corresponding graph-based formalism called flow graphs [15]. The flow graphs use port names and thus their algebra is homomorphic to the term-based one. Flow graphs are used in recent literature as an aid to grasp configuration of processes intuitively, e.g. [20]. Milner's recent $\pi$-*net* [21, 22] is another graphical representation of processes where the algebra and dynamics of the several versions of the $\pi$-calculus are graphically represented, which correspond to their formulations in action structure [21], using port names essentially. Parrow's Interaction Diagram [23] also presents the algebra and computation of $\pi$-calculus in a graphical format. In both cases analysis of computational structures is done making use of graphical ideas. An apparent difference between the present work and these graphical representations is, while theirs basically aim at faithful representation of the original term-based theory in a graphical format (though with additional insights), the present work tries to establish a formal theory of nameless processes where the graphical objects are formalised in an undiluted form, avoiding maybe sometimes unnecessary proliferation of entities (e.g. the number of atoms). Technically speaking, we can regard graphical representation with names as standing between terms and nameless graph representation, corresponding to terms modulo structural rules introduced by Berry and Boudol [1].

We already gave some discussions on Lafont's Interaction Net [14] in 4.6 and 5.2. In Lafont's work, the idea of named ports is not explicitly present, not because it has been abstracted away but because arbitrary connection among agents is not used. Furthermore Lafont does not develop algebraic structures underlying his construction, so the direct comparison is difficult. Nevertheless it suggests one of the restricted but disciplined ways of connecting agents. We hope that the formal study of various modes of connection in concurrent systems would be encouraged by the conscious formalisation of the notion in the present theory, possibly leading to effective engineering principles (cf. Sections 4 and 5). The work by Cliff Jones [13] (where the notion called *object graphs* is studied) may be suggestive in this respect.

One may also note that, while not oriented towards modeling graphical processes, the basic idea of Chemical Abstract Machine [1] naturally emerges in our graphical representation. In fact, a process graph is formulated as a multi-set of atomic graphs (see 3.2) and the scheme of dyadic interaction fits the idea of *reaction* without using the (somewhat unnatural) rule called *heavy ion* which forces to transfer a prefix. As seen in the isomorphism laws in 3.3, our graphs can successfully represent terms modulo structural rules *and* any name-permutations, though we need to introduce g-relations to reveal the role of names in the nameless word.

For another but related point, there are properties of a graph-based theory which *cannot* be easily translated into a term-based theory. For example, collapsing two *free* handles during reduction seems difficult to treat in the term-based framework (this relates to the use of *forwarder* in 4.6). Also we easily extend the definition of reduction so that correspondence is not surjective. Besides [5] suggests not only the untyped version (where atoms which have the same polarity may interact) but also an infinite number of atoms for Interaction Nets. The theoretical investigation of the generalisation to such graphs is one of interesting topics.

Finally our work can be regarded, in one aspect, as an investigation to find the analogue of SK-combinators in the concurrency setting, possibly sharing intention with several recent work including Raja and Shymasundar [24] and Simon Gay [3]. From this perspective, the semantic basis of the present graph-based theory would be of particular interest. One may refer to [7] for some work in this direction.

**Acknowledgments.** The author gratefully acknowledges helpful discussion with Kohei Honda on a lot of points on this paper. She is partially supported by JSPS Fellowship for Japanese Junior Scientists.

## REFERENCES

1. Berry, G. and Boudol, G., The Chemical Abstract Machine. *Theoretical Computer Science*, vol 96, pp. 217–248, 1992.
2. Gay, S., Interaction Nets, Diploma in Computer Science in Queens', 1991.
3. Gay, S., Combinators for Interaction Nets, draft, July 29, 1994.
4. Girard, J.-Y., Linear Logic, *Theoretical Computer Science*, Vol. 50, pp.1–102, 1987.
5. Gonthier, G., Abadi, M. and Levy, J.-J., The Geometry of Optimal Lambda Reduction, *POPL'92*, pp.15–26, ACM press, 1992.
6. Honda, K., *A Study of ν-calculus and its Combinatory Representation*, Phd Thesis in the Department of Computer Science, October, 1994.
7. Honda, K., *Notes on P-Algebra 1: Process Structure*, in this volume.
8. Honda, K. and Yoshida, N., On Reduction-Based Process Semantics, *13th. FST/TCS*, LNCS 761, pp.371–387, Springer-Verlag, 1993.
9. Honda, K. and Yoshida, N., Combinatory Representation of Mobile Processes, *POPL'94*, pp.348–360, ACM press, 1994.
10. Honda, K. and Yoshida, N., Replication in Concurrent Combinators, *TACS'94*, LNCS 789, pp.786–805, Springer-Verlag, 1994.
11. Honda, K. and Yoshida, N., *Graphs for Connection and Interaction*, the early version of this paper, May 1994.
12. Honda, K. and Yoshida, N., *Nameless Concurrent Combinators*, under preparation, December 1994, to appear as a Keio-CS-report.
13. Jones, C.B., Process-Algebraic Foundations for an Object-Based Design Notation, *Technical Report UMCS-93-10-1*, Manchester University, 1993.
14. Lafont, Y., Interaction Nets, *POPL'90*, pp. 95–108, ACM press, 1990.
15. Milner, R., Flowgraphs and Flow Algebras, *Journal of ACM*, 26(4), pp.794 – 818, 1979.
16. Milner, R., *A Calculus of Communicating Systems*, LNCS 76, Springer-Verlag, 1980.
17. Milner, R., Functions as Processes. *Mathematical Structure in Computer Science*, 2(2), pp.119–146, 1992.
18. Milner, R., Polyadic π-Calculus. *Logic and Algebra of Specification*, Springer-Verlag, 1992.
19. Milner, R. and Sangiorgi, D., Barbed Bisimulation. *ICALP'92*, LNCS 623, pp.685–695, Springer-Verlag, 1992.
20. Milner, R., Parrow, J.G. and Walker, D.J., A Calculus of Mobile Processes, *Information and Computation* 100(1), pp.1–77, 1992.
21. Milner, R., Action structure for the π-calculus. Research Report ECS-LFCS-93-264, Department of Computer Science, University of Edinburgh 1993.
22. Milner, R., Notes on actions I: π-nets with boxes and replication. Edinburgh, June 1993.
23. Parrow, J.G., Interaction Diagrams, *REX'93.*, LNCS, Springer-Verlag, 1993.
24. Raja, N. and Shymasundar, R.K., *The Next 700 Combinatory Representations of Mobile Processes*, a manuscript, 1994.
25. Sangiorgi, D., A Theory of Bisimulation for the π-calculus. *CONCUR'93*, LNCS 715, pp.127–142, Springer-Verlag, 1992.
26. Thomsen, B., A calculus of higher order communicating systems. *POPL'89*, 1989.

# A Calculus for Exploiting Data Parallelism on Recursively Defined Data
## (Preliminary Report)

Susumu Nishimura and Atsushi Ohori

Research Institute for Mathematical Sciences
Kyoto University, Kyoto 606-01, Japan
{nisimura,ohori}@kurims.kyoto-u.ac.jp

**Abstract.** Array based data parallel programming can be generalized in two ways to make it an appropriate paradigm for parallel processing of general recursively defined data. The first is the introduction of a parallel evaluation mechanism for dynamically allocated recursively defined data. It achieves the effect of applying the same function to all the subterms of a given datum in parallel. The second is a new notion of recursion, which we call parallel recursion, for parallel evaluation of recursively defined data. In contrast with ordinary recursion, which only uses the final results of the recursive calls of its immediate subterms, the new recursion repeatedly transforms a recursive datum represented by a system of equations to another recursive datum by applying the same function to each of the equation simultaneously, until the final result is obtained. This mechanism exploits more parallelism and achieves significant speedup compared to the conventional parallel evaluation of recursive functions. Based on these observations, we propose a typed lambda calculus for data parallel programming and give an operational semantics that integrates the parallel evaluation mechanism and the new form of recursion in the semantic core of a typed lambda calculus. We also describe an implementation method for massively parallel multi-computers, which makes it possible to execute parallel recursion in the expected performance.

## 1 Introduction

*Data Parallelism* is recently attracting much attention as a practical basis for massively parallel computing. The central idea underlying this paradigm is to evaluate a uniform collection of data, typically arrays, in parallel by simultaneously applying the same function to each data element in the collection. The practical importance of this paradigm is twofold. Firstly, it provides the programmer an easily understandable view of a single execution stream of a program, often called SPMD programming [Kar87], by coupling parallelism with a small set of elimination primitives for collection data types. Due to this property, development of an efficient parallel program is relatively easier than other forms of parallel programing. Secondly, this paradigm scales up to recently emerging massively parallel distributed memory multicomputers. By allocating a processor to each data element in a collection and restricting global synchronization to the end of iteration, data parallelism can achieve reasonable performance in a massively parallel multicomputer.

Despite these promising features, the applicability of current data parallel languages is limited to those applications whose main data structures are arrays or similar structures. Most of data parallel languages have been developed by embedding a set of parallel evaluation primitives for these structures in a conventional programming language. Examples include C* [RS87], Dataparallel C [HQ91], *Lisp [Las86], and High Performance Fortran [For93]. There are several recent proposals that integrate data parallelism in a functional calculus, including Connection Machine Lisp [WS87], Paralation Lisp [Sab88], TUPLE [Yua92], DPML [HF93] and Nesl [Ble93]. However, parallelism in these proposals is still limited to simple collection data types. From this current situation, one may think that data parallelism would be inherently restricted to applications manipulating arrays. The authors believe otherwise. By generalizing the idea of data parallelism to more general data structures and integrating it into a semantic core of a typed higher-order functional calculus, it should be possible to design a general purpose parallel programming language where the programmer can enjoy the obvious benefits of parallel evaluation in writing wider range of applications. The motivation of this work is to provide a formal account for designing such a language.

There are a few proposals to generalize array based parallelism to more general data structures. Gupta [Gup92] has considered the problem of processing dynamic data structures distributed over processors in SPMD mode and proposed a mechanism to allocate and access each cell in a given dynamic data structure by generating global names of the cells. Rogers, Reppy and Hendren [RRH92] have proposed an implementation mechanism for accessing subterms residing in different processors using process migration. Main focuses of these works are, however, parallelization of existing language mechanisms; these proposal do not provide any general language construct for writing data parallel programs with recursive data.

In this paper, we attempt to develop a computational model for data parallel evaluation of dynamically allocated recursively defined data, and integrate it in the typed lambda calculus with recursive types. Different from existing proposals of high level parallel languages, which embed a particular data structure with a set of parallel primitives, the approach taken here is to extend the lambda calculus with mechanisms to *define* parallel operations for recursively defined data structures. The calculus therefore supports far more general data parallel programming in a uniform manner. In particular, it allows data parallel programming with various common data structures in functional languages such as lists and trees, which are represented as dynamically allocated recursively defined data.

The crucial problem in achieving this goal is to find a proper mechanism for parallel application of a function to all the subterms of a given recursively defined data. In the case of an imperative language with arrays, it is sufficient to provide a simple primitive such as FORALL (k=1:N) ... END FORALL in High Performance Fortran to map an operation over the elements of an array. In the case of recursively defined data structures, however, finding a suitable set of parallel primitives requires more careful consideration. Since recursively defined data structures are manipulated by general recursive functions, a parallel evaluation mechanism for those data should be integrated with a form of recursive definition. In [RRH92], it was suggested that ordinary recursively defined functions can be used as units of parallel execution using speculative evaluation primitives such as future and touch of Multilisp [Hal85]. However, this strategy only exploits limited amount of parallelism, and is inadequate for data parallel programming. The problem is that a standard recursive function definition forces a series of recursive calls to be processed sequentially. For example, under this strategy, computing the sum of an integer list still requires the time proportional to the number of the elements. To achieve a proper integration of data parallelism in a functional calculus with recursive types, we should develop a new notion of recursion suitable for data parallel processing of those data.

In this paper we provide a solution to this problem and develop a typed calculus suitable for data parallel programming. We represent a recursively defined datum as a term consisting of a node constructor and a sequence of subterms, and define a mechanism to distribute each node of a recursive datum to a separate processor. A distributed recursive datum corresponds to the set of all the subterms of the datum represented by a system of equations of the form

$$\langle \alpha_1 = T_1(\alpha_2, \ldots, \alpha_n), \ldots, \alpha_i = T_i(\alpha_{i+1}, \ldots, \alpha_n), \ldots, \alpha_n = T_n \rangle$$

where $\alpha_i$ is a variable denoting a subterm that has the node constructor $T_i$ and possibly contains the subterms denoted by $\alpha_{i+1}, \ldots, \alpha_n$, and $\alpha_1$ denotes the root node. The usage of variables $\{\alpha_1, \ldots, \alpha_n\}$ was inspired by Gupta's global names for the cells in a dynamic data structure. We then develop a general mechanism for defining a data parallel recursive function that manipulates such a distributed datum by transforming the underlying system of equations recursively. In contrast with an ordinary recursive function, which only uses the final results of the recursive calls of its immediate subterms, the new recursion repeatedly transforms a recursive datum represented by a system of equations to another recursive datum by applying the same function to each of the equation simultaneously, until the final result is obtained. This mechanism exploits more parallelism than the speculative approach and achieves significant speedup compared to the sequential evaluation of recursive functions. We develop a calculus embodying these mechanisms, and describe an implementation method for distributed memory multicomputer.

We carry out this development in a formal framework of the typed lambda calculus with recursive types. The proposed calculus has a rigorous semantics that accounts for parallel evaluation of recursively defined data. There are a few formal accounts for semantics of a language with data parallel construct. Data Parallel Categorical Abstract Machine [HF93] describes an execution model of data parallel programming with arrays. However, this model relies on special primitives such as **get** which exchanges data between independently executing categorical abstract machines, and these special primitives are not part of the formal framework. Suciu and Tannen [ST94] have provided a clean formal semantics for their data parallel language which contains sequences and simple parallel primitives to map functions over sequences. Our language is far more powerful than theirs, and therefore providing a formal operational semantics is more challenging. A formal semantics we have worked out for our calculus will shed some light on better understanding of general nature of data parallel programming.

This paper is a preliminary report on the development of the calculus and its implementation method. The authors intend to present more complete description of the calculus with its formal properties and the experimentation result of a prototype implementation being developed at Kyoto University. The rest of the paper is organized as follows. In Section 2, we explain the basic idea of parallel recursive function definition for recursively defined data. Section 3 defines the calculus and gives some programming examples. In Section 4, we first describe the intended execution model of the calculus in a multicomputer. We then give a parallel operational semantics in the style of natural semantics [Kah87]. Section 5 describes implementation strategies. Finally, in Section 6, we discuss some future work and conclude the paper.

## 2 Parallel Recursion for Recursively Defined Data

To analyze the desirable properties of data parallel function for recursively defined data, let us consider the following simple function which computes the sum of a given integer list:

```
(defun sum(L) (if (null L) 0 (+ (car L) (sum (cdr L)))))
```

The semantics of this recursive definition implies that the application of sum to an $n$ element list results in a sequence of $n$ recursive calls of sum, and therefore straightforward parallel evaluation requires a series of $n$ communications that must be processed sequentially. However, Hillis and Steele [HS86] have shown that there is a data parallel algorithm to compute the sum of an $n$ element integer list in $O(\log n)$ parallel steps. The main idea in the algorithm is to use an extra chum pointer to maintain information about the necessary value to complete a partially computed recursive call. The following program describes such an algorithm that computes the suffix sum of an integer list with extra chum pointer, where value and next pointer represent car and cdr in Lisp respectively.

```
for all k parallel do
  chum[k] := next[k]
  while chum[k] ≠ nil
    value[k]:= value[k] + value[chum[k]]
    chum[k]:=chum[chum[k]] od
```

The following figure illustrates how the suffix sum of a list is computed by the algorithm.

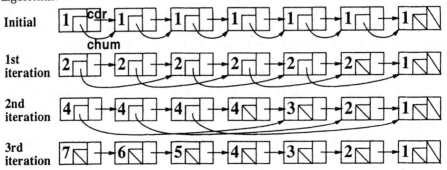

The above analysis suggests that there should be a new form of recursion that is to be formalized for parallel evaluation of recursively defined data other than ordinary recursion, which appears to contain inherently sequential nature. The new recursive construct proposed in the present paper is based on the observation that the techniques of Hillis and Steele can be regarded as a special case of more general form of recursion suitable for data parallel evaluation of recursively defined data. We present below the main idea using lists as an example.

The type of integer list is represented by the recursive type $\mu t.unit + int \times t$ where $unit$ is a trivial type whose only element is $*$ (which in this case is used to represent the empty list or $Nil$), and $+$ and $\times$ are disjoint union and product constructor, respectively. A recursive function $f$ of type $(\mu t.unit + int \times t) \to \sigma$ in general has the following structure:

$$\text{fix } f.\lambda x.\text{case } x \text{ of } inl(*) \Rightarrow c, \; inr((h,t)) \Rightarrow S \; h \; (f \; t)$$

where $c$ is some constant and $S$ is some function of type $int \to \sigma \to \sigma$. In the case of sum, $c = 0$ and $S = \lambda x.\lambda y.x + y$. Let $L$ be an $n$ element list. Also let $L_k$ be the $k$th sublist of $L$ with $L_1 = L$, and $x_k$ be the first element in the list $L_k$. Then the application of $f$ to $L$ results in the following sequence of applications:

$$f \; L_1 = S \; x_1 \; (f \; L_2), \; f \; L_2 = S \; x_2 \; (f \; L_3), \; \cdots, \; f \; L_n = S \; x_n \; (f \; L_{n+1}), \; f \; L_{n+1} = c$$

Let $S_i$ be the partially applied function $S \; x_i$, and for any $i \leq j$ let $S_{i,j}$ be the composition $S_i \circ S_{i+1} \circ \cdots \circ S_{j-1} \circ S_j$. By considering each application $f \; L_i$ as an unknown value $\alpha_i$, the above calling sequence can be considered as a system of equations over the set of unknowns $\alpha_1, \cdots, \alpha_{n+1}$. We can then compute the result $f \; L = \alpha_1$ by repeatedly transforming the system of equations itself in the following way:

$$
\begin{array}{lllll}
(initial) & \alpha_1 = S_{1,1}(\alpha_2) & \alpha_2 = S_{2,2}(\alpha_3) & \cdots \; \alpha_n = S_{n,n}(\alpha_{n+1}) & \alpha_{n+1} = c \\
(1st) & \alpha_1 = S_{1,2}(\alpha_3) & \alpha_2 = S_{2,3}(\alpha_4) & \cdots \; \alpha_n = S_{n,n}(c) & \alpha_{n+1} = c \\
(2nd) & \alpha_1 = S_{1,4}(\alpha_5) & \alpha_2 = S_{2,5}(\alpha_6) & \cdots \; \alpha_n = S_{n,n}(c) & \alpha_{n+1} = c \\
& \vdots & \vdots & \quad\;\; \vdots & \quad\;\; \vdots \\
(\log n \, th) & \alpha_1 = S_{1,n}(c) & \alpha_2 = S_{2,n}(c) & \cdots \; \alpha_n = S_{n,n}(c) & \alpha_{n+1} = c
\end{array}
$$

Furthermore, if the composition $S_{i,j} \circ S_{j+1,k}$ is computed in constant time resulting in a function $S_{i,k}$ whose application is computed in constant time, then the above method is expected to compute the application $f L$ in $O(\log n)$ time. Special pointers used in Hillis and Steele's algorithms, chum in the above example, can be regarded as a representation of unknown variables $\alpha_i$.

We call the parallel computation strategy explained above *parallel recursion*. Due to its uniformity, parallel recursion can be applied to various recursively defined data types, contributing to significant speedup in parallel programming. Furthermore, it has the conceptual generality that will serve as a basic tool for designing a parallel algorithm for recursively defined data.

To integrate parallel recursion in the typed lambda calculus, we introduce a recursive type $\mu t.\tau(t)$ as a data type whose value is represented by a system of equations of the form $\alpha_i = T(\alpha_{i+1}, \ldots, \alpha_k)$ we have explained, and a parallel function definition mechanism for these distributed recursively defined data. The basic idea is to apply a function that transforms a data constructor ($T(\_, \ldots, \_)$ above) to each equation and obtain a new system of equations. This mechanism is introduced as a term constructor that lifts a constructor transformer function of type $\tau(r) \to \sigma(s)$ to a function of type $\mu t.\tau(t) \to \mu t.\sigma(t)$. In the following sections, we will formally define the calculus where these constructs are available and give its parallel operational semantics that accounts for data parallel evaluation of recursive types.

## 3 Data Parallel λ-Calculus

We first define the calculus by giving its syntax and the type system. We then explain the intended meaning of the data parallel constructs introduced in this calculus and gives some programming examples. The detailed description of their semantics will be given later in section 4.

### 3.1 Definition of the Calculus

The set of types of the calculus is given by the following grammar:

$$\tau ::= b \mid unit \mid t \mid \tau \to \tau \mid \tau \times \tau \mid \tau + \tau \mid \mu t.\tau$$

$b$ stands for base types. $t$ stands for type variables, and $\mu t.\tau(t)$ for recursive types. We write $\tau(t)$ to represent a type which possibly includes a free type variable $t$, and $\tau(\sigma)$ for the type obtained from $\tau(t)$ by substituting all the free occurrences of $t$ with $\sigma$. As will become clear later, type variables are also used to denote identifiers of the nodes in a recursively defined datum.

The set of expressions of the calculus is given by the following syntax:

$$
\begin{aligned}
M ::= &\; * \mid c \mid x \mid \lambda x.M \mid MM \mid \text{fix } f(x).M \mid (M, M) \mid fst(M) \mid snd(M) \\
&\mid inl(M) \mid inr(M) \mid \text{case } M \text{ of } inl(x) \Rightarrow M, inr(x) \Rightarrow M \\
&\mid up\ M \text{ with } x_1 = M_1, \ldots, x_k = M_k \text{ end} \mid dn(M) \\
&\mid \mu(f, d)(x).M .
\end{aligned}
$$

**constant**

$$\Gamma \vdash c : b$$

**unit**

$$\Gamma \vdash * : unit$$

**identifier**

$$\frac{x : \tau \in \Gamma}{\Gamma \vdash x : \tau}$$

**λ-abstraction**

$$\frac{\Gamma, x : \tau_1 \vdash M : \tau_2}{\Gamma \vdash \lambda x.M : \tau_1 \to \tau_2}$$

**application**

$$\frac{\Gamma \vdash M : \tau_1 \to \tau_2 \quad \Gamma \vdash N : \tau_1}{\Gamma \vdash MN : \tau_2}$$

**fix**

$$\frac{\Gamma, f : \tau_1 \to \tau_2, x : \tau_1 \vdash M : \tau_2}{\Gamma \vdash \text{fix } f(x).M : \tau_1 \to \tau_2}$$

**product**

$$\frac{\Gamma \vdash M : \tau_1 \quad \Gamma \vdash N : \tau_2}{\Gamma \vdash (M, N) : \tau_1 \times \tau_2}$$

**fst**

$$\frac{\Gamma \vdash M : \tau_1 \times \tau_2}{\Gamma \vdash fst(M) : \tau_1}$$

**snd**

$$\frac{\Gamma \vdash M : \tau_1 \times \tau_2}{\Gamma \vdash snd(M) : \tau_2}$$

**inl**

$$\frac{\Gamma \vdash M : \tau_1}{\Gamma \vdash inl(M) : \tau_1 + \tau_2}$$

**inr**

$$\frac{\Gamma \vdash M : \tau_2}{\Gamma \vdash inr(M) : \tau_1 + \tau_2}$$

**case**

$$\frac{\Gamma \vdash M : \tau_1 + \tau_2 \quad \Gamma, x : \tau_1 \vdash N_1 : \tau \quad \Gamma, y : \tau_2 \vdash N_2 : \tau}{\Gamma \vdash \text{case } M \text{ of } inl(x) \Rightarrow N_1, inr(y) \Rightarrow N_2 : \tau}$$

**up**

$$\frac{\Gamma, x_1 : s, \cdots, x_k : s \vdash M : \tau(s) \quad \Gamma \vdash N_i : \mu t.\tau(t) \text{ for } 1 \le i \le k}{\Gamma \vdash \text{up } M \text{ with } x_1 = N_1, \cdots, x_k = N_k \text{ end} : \mu t.\tau(t)}$$

(s is a new type variable.)

**dn**

$$\frac{\Gamma \vdash M : \mu t.\tau(t)}{\Gamma \vdash dn(M) : \tau(\mu t.\tau(t))}$$

**μ-expression**

$$\frac{\Gamma, f : r \to s, d : r \to \tau(r), x : \tau(r) \vdash M : \sigma(s)}{\Gamma \vdash \mu(f, d)(x).M : \mu t.\tau(t) \to \mu t.\sigma(t)}$$

(r and s are new type variables, and $\sigma(s)$ does not contain r.)

**Table 1.** Typing rules

The type system for these expressions is defined by a set of rules to derive a typing of the form:

$$\Gamma \vdash M : \tau,$$

where $\Gamma$ is a type assignment, which is a mapping from a finite set of variables to types. We write $\Gamma, x : \tau$ for the type assignment $\Gamma'$ such that $domain(\Gamma') = domain(\Gamma) \cup \{x\}$, $\Gamma'(x) = \tau$, and $\Gamma'(y) = \Gamma(y)$ for any $y \in domain(\Gamma), y \ne x$.

The set of typing rules of the calculus is given in Table 1.

Expression constructors other than the last three are standard ones in the typed lambda calculus with unit, product and sum types. The expression constructors $up\ M\ with\ \ldots\ end$, $dn(M)$ and $\mu(f,d)(x).M$ are for manipulating recursively defined data distributed over processors, whose intended meaning will be explained below.

## 3.2 Constructors for Manipulating Recursive Data

A common method for introducing recursive types of the form $\mu t.\tau(t)$ in a typed lambda calculus is to treat them as types satisfying the isomorphism $\mu t.\tau(t) \cong \tau(\mu t.\tau(t))$ and to introduce the term constructors realizing the isomorphism. In an ordinary lambda calculus, this can be done by simply introducing mappings $Up$ of type $\tau(\mu t.\tau(t)) \to \mu t.\tau(t)$ and $Down$ of type $\mu t.\tau(t) \to \tau(\mu t.\tau(t))$.

In order to support parallel recursion explained in the previous section, we need to refine this strategy. First, we represent a recursively defined datum as a system of equations by a sequence of equations $<\alpha_1 \to V_1, \cdots, \alpha_k \to V_k>$ to model a datum distributed over processors. In each equation, $\alpha_i$ is an identifier, called a *communication variable*, representing an individual subterm of a given recursively defined datum, and $V_i$ is a value containing communication variables and corresponds to the constructor of the subterm identified by $\alpha_i$. We further assume that an association sequence is ordered so that $\alpha_1$ denotes the root node and that if $\alpha_i$ appears in $V_j$ then $i > j$. We call such a sequence of equation an *association sequence*. The intention is that a separate processor is allocated for each node $V_i$ and communication variables are used to link the nodes together.

The constructor $up\ M\ with\ x_1 = M_1, \ldots, x_k = M_k\ end$ creates an association sequence. This is an expression of type $\mu t.\tau(t)$ if $M_1, \ldots, M_k$ are expressions of type $\mu t.\tau(t)$, and $M$ is an expression of type $\tau(t)$ under the assumption that $x_1, \ldots, x_k$ are variables of type $t$, where $t$ represents immediate subterms of the recursive datum. This expression is equivalent to $Up(M[M_1/x_1, \ldots, M_k/x_k])$ in a standard representation explained above. In order to construct a proper association sequence for data parallel manipulation, however, it is essential to name the subterms $M_1, \ldots, M_k$ of type $\mu t.\tau(t)$ in $M$ explicitly. Suppose that each $M_i$ is evaluated to an association sequence of the form $<\alpha_1^i \to V_1^i, \cdots, \alpha_k^i \to V_k^i>$. The environment is augmented so that each $x_i$ is bound to $\alpha_1^i$, which is a "pointer" to the corresponding subterm, and then $M$ is evaluated to $V$, the content of the root node of the recursive datum. $V$ and subterms are linked together by merging all the association sequences obtained from the subterms $M_1, \ldots, M_k$ and then to add a top node $\alpha \mapsto V'$ to the merged sequence, where $\alpha$ is a new communication variable. The constructor $up\ M\ with\ x_1 = M_1, \ldots, x_k = M_k\ end$ denotes this operation. If $k = 0$, i.e. $M$ is a constant not containing any subterm of type $\mu t.\tau(t)$, then we simply write $up(M)$ instead of $up\ M\ with\ end$.

As a simple example, the two element list $L = [1,2]$ can be constructed as:

$$L = up\ inr((1, x_1))\ with\ x_1 = (up\ inr((2, x_2))\ with\ x_2 = up(inl(*))\ end)\ end$$

From this, the evaluator shall be able to construct an association sequence of the form:

$$<\alpha_1 \rightarrow inr((1, \alpha_2)), \alpha_2 \rightarrow inr((2, \alpha_3)), \alpha_3 \rightarrow inl(*)>.$$

$dn$ converts a value of type $\mu t.\tau(t)$ to a value of type $\tau(\mu t.\tau(t))$. Its operational semantics is to convert an association sequence $<\alpha_1 \rightarrow V_1, \cdots, \alpha_k \rightarrow V_k>$ to a value $V_1'$ obtained from $V_1$ by "dereferencing pointers", i.e. by substituting each communication variable $\alpha_i$ in $V_1$ with the association sequence corresponding to $\alpha_i$. For example, $dn(L)$, where $L$ is the list defined above, is equal to $inr((1, (up\ inr((2, x_2))\ with\ x_2 = up(inl(*))\ end)))$, and is evaluated to the value: $inr((1, <\alpha_2 \rightarrow inr((2, \alpha_3)), \alpha_3 \rightarrow inl(*)>))$.

$\mu(f, d)(x).M$ is the data parallel function constructor in the calculus. This transforms a value of type $\mu t.\tau(t)$ to a value of type $\mu t.\sigma(t)$ by simultaneously applying the function specified by $(x).M$, a synonym for $\lambda x.M$, to each node in the value. $(x).M$ must be a function of type $\tau(r) \rightarrow \sigma(s)$ under the assumption that $d$ and $f$ are variables of type $r \rightarrow \tau(r)$ and $r \rightarrow s$ respectively. Here, $r$ and $s$ are fresh type variables denoting communication variables, and $\tau(r)$ and $\sigma(s)$ are types of the nodes in the recursively defined data of type $\mu t.\tau(t)$ and $\mu t.\sigma(t)$ respectively. When $\mu(f, d)(x).M$ is applied to a recursively defined datum represented as an association sequence of the form $<\alpha_1 \rightarrow V_1, \cdots, \alpha_k \rightarrow V_k>$, it binds $d$ to the function that converts each communication variable $\alpha_i$ to the corresponding value $V_i$, and binds $f$ to the function that returns a fresh communication variable $\beta_i$ for each $\alpha_i$. It then applies the function $(x).M$ simultaneously to each element $V_i$ of the datum to obtain a new value $V_i'$. The result is a new association sequence of the form $<\beta_1 \rightarrow V_1', \cdots, \beta_k \rightarrow V_k'>$.

By this construct, the user can write a function that transforms a recursively defined datum in parallel by simply writing a function that transforms each node in the datum. Moreover, this construct is not limited to any particular presupposed data types such as lists or sequences; it enables us to write a parallel function that transforms a value of type $\mu t.\tau(t)$ to a value of type $\mu t.\sigma(t)$ for any $\tau(\_)$ and $\sigma(\_)$. The combination of this construct and the ordinary recursion achieves the parallel recursion explained in the previous section for general recursive types.

## 3.3   Programming Examples

Let us show some examples for data parallel programming in this calculus. As a simple example, a data parallel version of Lisp `mapcar` function of type $(t \rightarrow s) \rightarrow list(t) \rightarrow list(s)$ is implemented as:

$$\lambda F.\lambda L.((\mu(f, d)(x).(case\ x\ of\ inl(y) \Rightarrow inl(*), inr(y) \Rightarrow (F\ fst(y), f\ snd(y))))\ L)$$

Writing a function in the bare syntax of our extended lambda calculus is rather tedious, but we can supply several useful syntactic shorthands. First, ML style data type declaration and pattern matching for recursively defined data can be safely combined. A data type declaration of the form

```
datatype int_list = Nil | int :: int_list
```

can be regarded as a recursive type of the form $\mu t.int + int \times t$ together with the bindings: $\texttt{Nil} = inl(*)$ and $:: = \lambda(x,y).inr((x,y))$. After this, Nil and $x::y$ can also be used as patterns for $inl(*)$ and $inr((x,y))$. Other data structures can be similarly treated. In examples below, we use ML style syntax of the form case $e$ of $pat$ => $e$ | ... | $pat$ => $e$ for case statement with the above shorthand, where $pat$ denotes a pattern. Next, in spirit of High Performance Fortran and other data parallel languages, we allow the following syntactic shorthand

$$\texttt{foreach } x \texttt{ in } M \texttt{ with } (f,d) \texttt{ do } N \qquad \text{for} \qquad ((\mu(f,d)(x).N)\ M)$$

We also use ML style (possibly recursive) function definition $\texttt{fun } f\ x = \ldots$.

Using these shorthands, mapcar example can be written in the following more intuitive syntax:

```
fun mapcar F L =
    foreach x in L with (f,d) do
        case x of Nil => Nil | hd::tl => (F hd)::(f tl)
```

The data parallel algorithm to compute suffix sum of an integer list given in Section 2 can be expressed as in Figure 1.

```
fun suffix_sum L =
let fun mk_chum X =
        foreach x in X with (f,d) do
            case x of Nil => Nil | hd::tl => (hd,f tl)::(f tl)
    fun square X =
        foreach x in X with (f,d) do
            case x of Nil => Nil
                | (n,y)::z =>
                    (case (d y) of Nil => (n,f y)::(f z)
                        | (m,v)::w => (n+m,f v)::(f z))
    fun strip X = foreach x in X with (f,d) do
                    case x of Nil => Nil | (n,y)::z => n::(f z)
    fun scan x =
        case dn(x) of Nil => Nil
                | (n,y)::z => (case y of Nil => x
                                | (m,v)::w => scan (square x))
in
    strip (scan (mk_chum L))
end
```

**Fig. 1.** Data Parallel Suffix Sum Program

Data parallel programs for the other recursive data structures can be plainly expressed in the calculus. For example, Rytter [Ryt85] has given an algorithm "parallel pebble game" that computes the suffix sum of an $n$ node integer binary tree in $O(\log n)$ parallel steps. Such an algorithm can easily be written in our calculus. As seen from the SPMD execution model and the semantics of the calculus we shall give in the next section, the time required to execute a $\mu$-application is roughly equivalent to one parallel step in conventional data parallel languages such as Dataparallel C [HQ91]. The calculus therefore achieves the desired goal of extending data parallelism to general recursive data.

## 4 Semantics of the Calculus

We first give an SPMD execution model of the calculus by describing how parallel primitives are evaluated in multicomputers. This will serve as a basic strategy to implement the calculus. We then give a formal operational semantics of the entire calculus that accounts for data parallel computation on recursive types.

### 4.1 An SPMD Execution Model

For the purpose of describing the execution model, we assume that the underlying hardware system is a distributed memory multicomputer consisting of unbounded number of processors, each of which is uniquely identified by its processor id, and the system provides mechanisms for broadcasting and for interprocessor communication between any pair of processors.

The intended execution model of the calculus is a data parallel computation. Each processor executes the same program on its own copy of the data and yields the same memory state, *except for* recursively defined data created by special *up* primitive. As explained in the previous section, a recursively defined datum is modeled by an association sequence whose elements are distributed over processors, and is treated specially with the parallel constructs of the calculus.

In the multicomputer, we represent an association sequence in each processor $P$ as a *global pointer* $G_P$, which is a pair of a processor id and a pointer to a local datum. For an association sequence $< \alpha_1 \rightarrow V_1, \cdots, \alpha_k \rightarrow V_k >$, every processor $P$ in the system allocates a global pointer $G_P = (P_r, p_P)$. The global pointer in every processor has, as its first element, the same processor id $P_r$ where the root node $V_1$ is allocated. If a node $V_i$ is allocated to processor $P$ then $p_P$ is set to the local address of $V_i$. If no node is allocated to $P$ then $p_P$ is set to a special value *Undefined*. For example, a list $[1, 2]$ is represented as shown in Figure 2, where the special value *Undefined* is represented by the box with backslash. By this representation, we achieve simple and efficient execution of the parallel primitives for general recursive types. In what follows, we use lists to explain the parallel primitives. In Section 5 we describe a technique to implement them for general recursive data structure.

To execute *up* $inr((M, x))$ *with* $x = N$ *end*, i.e. a cons expression, every processor first evaluates $N$ to a global pointer $G_P = (P_r, p_P)$ and then evaluates $inr((M, x))$ under the environment in which $x$ is bound to the global pointer to obtain a cons cell. Then every processor selects the same processor $Q$ to which

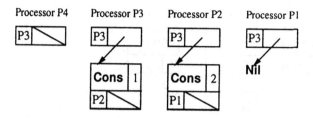

**Fig. 2.** Representation of a List by global pointers

any elements of recursive data have not been allocated. Then the processor $Q$ yields a global pointer $(Q, q)$ where $q$ is the pointer to the new cons cell. Every processor $P$ other than $Q$ yields a global pointer $(Q, p_P)$. Figure 3 illustrates how $0 :: [1, 2]$ is executed and yields a global pointer in each processor.

1. Evaluating $\lambda x. inr((M, x))N$ in each processor.

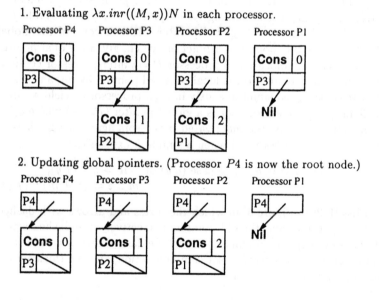

2. Updating global pointers. (Processor $P4$ is now the root node.)

**Fig. 3.** Execution of *cons* on a List

$dn(M)$, where $M$ is a distributed list, is executed as below. First, every processor $P$ evaluates $M$ to obtain a global pointer $G_P = (P_r, p_P)$. The processor $P_r$ broadcasts the cons cell pointed by $p_{P_r}$ to all the processors. Then each processor $P$ other than $P_r$ yields a cons cell which is obtained from the broadcasted cell by replacing the second element of the global pointer contained in its cdr part by $p_P$. The processor $P_r$ yields the cons cell pointed by $p_{P_r}$. Figure 4 shows the state just after $dn([1, 2])$ is executed.

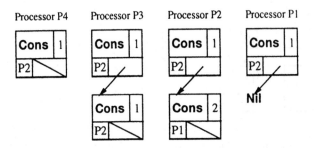

**Fig. 4.** Result of Applying $dn$ to a List

Execution of an application of a $\mu$-expression $\mu(f,d)(x).M$ is a little more complicated than the other two parallel constructs, since it includes execution of the renaming function denoted by $f$ and the down function denoted by $d$. Suppose $\mu(f,d)(x).M$ is applied to a list, which is represented by a set of global pointers $G_P = (P_r, p_P)$. Every processor $P$ in which $p_P$ is set to *Undefined* become inactive. Then, in each remaining active processor $P$, the variable $f$ is bound to a function which, given a global pointer, yields a copy of the global pointer, and the variable $d$ is bound to a function which, given a global pointer $(P,p)$, fetches the cons cell allocated to processor $P$ via inter-processor communication. The variable $x$ is bound to the local cons cell pointed by $p_P$, and under these bindings $M$ is evaluated simultaneously in each processor to yield a value. The final result in each active processor is a global pointer $(P_r, q_P)$ where $q_P$ is a pointer to the value. Finally, the inactivated processors again become active. We show how evaluation is performed when a simple $\mu$-expression:

$$\mu(f,d)(x).\text{case } x \text{ of } Nil \Rightarrow Nil, n :: y \Rightarrow \text{case } (d\,y) \text{ of } Nil \Rightarrow n :: (f\,y),$$
$$m :: z \Rightarrow (n+m) :: (f\,y)$$

is applied to a list $[1,2]$ in Figure 5, in which the boxes and arrows with dashed lines represent the old data and the old pointers respectively, the dashed arrow with letter $f$ represent copying of global pointer, the dashed arrow with letter $d$ represents data transfer by inter-processor communication, and the thick arrows represent data flow inside a processor.

## 4.2 Operational Semantics of the Calculus

An operational semantics is presented in natural semantics [Kah87].

**Semantic Values and Environments** We define the set of values (ranged over by $V$) for the calculus as follows:

$$V ::= * \mid c \mid \texttt{fcl}(\rho, \lambda x.M) \mid \texttt{fxcl}(\rho, \text{fix } f(x).M) \mid \texttt{mucl}(\rho, \mu(f,d)(x).M)$$
$$\mid (V,V) \mid inl(V) \mid inr(V) \mid \alpha \mid <\alpha_1 \to V_1, \cdots, \alpha_k \to V_k >$$
$$\mid ren(\beta_1/\alpha_1, \cdots, \beta_k/\alpha_k) \mid down(<\alpha_1 \to V_1, \cdots, \alpha_k \to V_k >) \mid wrong$$

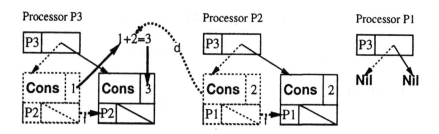

**Fig. 5.** $\mu$-application on a List

$\rho$ stands for an environment, which is a mapping from variables to values. $\mathtt{fcl}(\rho, \lambda x.M)$, $\mathtt{fxcl}(\rho, \mathrm{fix}\ f(x).M)$, and $\mathtt{mucl}(\rho, \mu(f,d)(x).M)$ represent the closures for function, fix, and $\mu$-expression, respectively. $(V,V)$, $inl(V)$, and $inr(V)$ are a pair, a left injected value, and a right injected value, respectively.

We say the occurrence of a communication variable $\alpha$ in $V$ is *free*, if it is neither in an association sequence containing an association $\alpha \to V'$ for some $V'$ nor in a renaming function of the form $ren(\cdots)$. We write $V[\alpha\backslash V']$ for the value obtained from $V$ by replacing all free occurrences of $\alpha$ in $V$ by $V'$.

$<\alpha_1 \to V_1, \cdots, \alpha_k \to V_k>$ is an association sequence representing a recursively defined datum. It satisfies the conditions: $\alpha_1, \cdots, \alpha_k$ are all distinct, if free $\alpha_j$ occurs in $V_i$ then $i < j$, and $\alpha_1$ corresponds to the root node of the datum. Association sequences are often denoted by $\chi, \chi', \cdots$. The concatenation of two sequences are represented as $\chi@\chi'$, and $@_{i=1}^k \chi_i$ is used to abbreviate $\chi_1@\cdots@\chi_k$.

$ren(\beta_1/\alpha_1, \cdots, \beta_k/\alpha_k)$ and $down(<\alpha_1 \to V_1, \cdots, \alpha_k \to V_k>)$, which are called renaming function and down function respectively, are generated and used respectively through variables $f$ and $d$ respectively, when an application of $\mu(f,d)(x).M$ to a distributed recursive value is evaluated.

Finally, *wrong* represents runtime error.

**Semantic Rules** We define the semantics by giving a set of rules to derive a formula of the form $\rho \vdash M \Downarrow V$, representing the fact that a term $M$ evaluates to a value $V$ under an environment $\rho$. The set of rules for the calculus is given in Table 2-a and 2-b, where we omit the rules yielding *wrong*; for each rule with conditions (specified as the shape of the values), it should be understood that the complementary rule yielding *wrong* is implicitly given.

The rules other than those for *up*, *dn*, and $\mu$-expression are standard.

The rule for *up $M$ with $x_1 = N_1, \cdots, x_k = N_k$ end* first evaluates each subterm $N_i$, and if each of them yields an association sequence $<\alpha_i \to V_i> @\chi_i$, then extracts the communication variable $\alpha_i$ of the first element from each of the sequences to obtain a sequence $\alpha_1, \ldots, \alpha_k$, and then it passes the extracted sequence to the constructor function to obtain a value $V$. The final result is the association sequence $<\alpha \to V> @(@_{i=1}^k(<\alpha_i \to V_1> @\chi_i))$ where $\alpha$ is a new communication variable. Introduction of a new communication variable

**unit**  **constant**  **identifier**

$$\rho \vdash * \Downarrow *$$

$$\rho \vdash c \Downarrow c$$

$$\frac{\rho(x) = V}{\rho \vdash x \Downarrow V}$$

**$\lambda$-abstraction**

$$\rho \vdash \lambda x.M \Downarrow \mathtt{fcl}(\rho, \lambda x.M)$$

**$\lambda$-application**

$$\frac{\rho \vdash M \Downarrow \mathtt{fcl}(\rho', \lambda x.M') \quad \rho \vdash N \Downarrow V' \quad \rho', x \mapsto V' \vdash M' \Downarrow V}{\rho \vdash MN \Downarrow V}$$

**fix**

$$\rho \vdash \mathrm{fix}\ f(x).M \Downarrow \mathtt{fxcl}(\rho, \mathrm{fix}\ f(x).M)$$

**fix-application**

$$\frac{\rho \vdash M \Downarrow \mathtt{fxcl}(\rho', \mathrm{fix}\ f(x).M') \quad \rho \vdash N \Downarrow V'}{\rho \vdash MN \Downarrow V}$$
$$\frac{\rho', f \mapsto \mathtt{fxcl}(\rho', \mathrm{fix}\ f(x).M'), x \mapsto V' \vdash M' \Downarrow V}{}$$

**up**

$$\rho \vdash N_i \Downarrow <\alpha_i \to V_i> @\chi_i \quad \text{for each } 1 \leq i \leq k$$
$$\rho, x_1 \mapsto \alpha_1, \cdots, x_k \mapsto \alpha_k \vdash M \Downarrow V$$
$$\overline{\rho \vdash up(\lambda x_1 \cdots x_k.M, N_1, \cdots, N_k) \Downarrow <\alpha \to V> @ (@_{i=1}^{k}(<\alpha_i \to V_i> @\chi_i))}$$
$$(\alpha \text{ is a new communication variable.})$$

**dn**

$$\frac{\rho \vdash M \Downarrow <\alpha_1 \to V_1, \cdots, \alpha_k \to V_k>}{\rho \vdash dn(M) \Downarrow V_1[\alpha_2 \backslash <\alpha_2 \to V_2, \cdots, \alpha_k \to V_k>] \cdots [\alpha_k \backslash <\alpha_k \to V_k>]}$$

**Table 2.-a** Parallel Operational Semantics (to be continued)

corresponds to allocation of a new processor. The rule for $dn(M)$ first evaluates $M$, resulting an association sequence $<\alpha_1 \to V_1, \cdots, \alpha_k \to V_k>$. Then, as the global pointer contained in the cdr part of the distributed cell is updated in the SPMD execution model, it returns the value obtained by instantiating its immediate subterms, i.e. by replacing each free occurrence of $\alpha_i (2 \leq i \leq k)$ in $V_1$ with association sequence $<\alpha_i \to V_i, \cdots, \alpha_k \to V_k>$.

The rule for a $\mu$-expression is simply to create a $\mu$-closure. The rule for an application of $\mu$-closure to an association sequence $<\alpha_1 \to V_1', \cdots, \alpha_k \to V_k'>$ first allocates a new communication variable $\beta_i$ for each $\alpha_i$, which corresponds to a node of the recursive datum to be created. Then it binds the variable $f$ to a renaming function and $d$ to a down function embedding the association sequence. The renaming function renames each old variable ($\alpha_i$) to new one ($\beta_i$), and the down function receives a communication variable and returns the

**pair**

$$\frac{\rho \vdash M \Downarrow V \quad \rho \vdash N \Downarrow V'}{\rho \vdash (M,N) \Downarrow (V,V')}$$

**fst**

$$\frac{\rho \vdash M \Downarrow (V,V')}{\rho \vdash fst(M) \Downarrow V}$$

**snd**

$$\frac{\rho \vdash M \Downarrow (V,V')}{\rho \vdash snd(M) \Downarrow V'}$$

**inl**

$$\frac{\rho \vdash M \Downarrow V}{\rho \vdash inl(M) \Downarrow inl(V)}$$

**inr**

$$\frac{\rho \vdash M \Downarrow V}{\rho \vdash inr(M) \Downarrow inr(V)}$$

**case**

$$\frac{\rho \vdash M \Downarrow inl(V') \quad \rho, x \mapsto V' \vdash N_1 \Downarrow V}{\rho \vdash case\ M\ of\ inl(x) \Rightarrow N_1,\ inr(y) \Rightarrow N_2 \Downarrow V}$$

$$\frac{\rho \vdash M \Downarrow inr(V') \quad \rho, y \mapsto V' \vdash N_2 \Downarrow V}{\rho \vdash case\ M\ of\ inl(x) \Rightarrow N_1,\ inr(y) \Rightarrow N_2 \Downarrow V}$$

**$\mu$-expression**

$$\rho \vdash \mu(f,d)(x).M \Downarrow \mathtt{mucl}(\rho, \mu(f,d)(x).M)$$

**$\mu$-application**

$$\frac{\begin{array}{c} \rho \vdash M \Downarrow \mathtt{mucl}(\rho', \mu(f,d)(x).M') \quad \rho \vdash N \Downarrow <\alpha_1 \rightarrow V_1', \cdots, \alpha_k \rightarrow V_k'> \\ \rho', f \mapsto ren(\beta_1/\alpha_1, \cdots, \beta_k/\alpha_k), \\ d \mapsto down(<\alpha_1 \rightarrow V_1', \cdots, \alpha_k \rightarrow V_k'>), x \mapsto V_i' \vdash M' \Downarrow V_i \quad for\ 1 \le i \le k \end{array}}{\rho \vdash MN \Downarrow <\beta_1 \rightarrow V_1, \cdots, \beta_k \rightarrow V_k>}$$

$$(\beta_1, ..., \beta_k\ are\ new\ communication\ variables.)$$

**renaming**

$$\frac{\rho \vdash M \Downarrow ren(\beta_1/\alpha_1, \cdots, \beta_k/\alpha_k) \quad \rho \vdash N \Downarrow \alpha \quad \alpha = \alpha_i}{\rho \vdash MN \Downarrow \beta_i}$$

**down**

$$\frac{\rho \vdash M \Downarrow down(<\alpha_1 \rightarrow V_1, \cdots, \alpha_k \rightarrow V_k>) \quad \rho \vdash N \Downarrow \alpha \quad \alpha = \alpha_i}{\rho \vdash MN \Downarrow V_i}$$

**Table 2.-b** Parallel Operational Semantics (continuing)

value associated with the variable, which corresponds to data transfer via inter-processor communication. Finally, the $\mu$-expression is applied to each value $V_i'$ to obtain a new value $V_i$ simultaneously. The result of the $\mu$-application is the new recursive datum whose nodes are replaced by the new ones on which the corresponding newly computed values are placed, i.e. $<\beta_1 \rightarrow V_1, \cdots, \beta_k \rightarrow V_k>$.

This operational semantics is apparently unsafe — there are some terms that evaluate to *wrong*. However, we believe that the type system is sound with respect to this operational semantics, and therefore the operational semantics is safe for any type correct terms. We intend to present a more complete account for the calculus including type soundness and other formal properties elsewhere.

# 5 Implementation Strategies

We have proposed in Section 4.1 to represent distributed recursive data by global pointers and shown how the parallel constructs are executed when they applied to a distributed list. A naïve integration of the proposed method in an implementation of a functional language, however, does not necessarily respect the formal operational semantics, and some programs may yield incorrect result.

One way to overcome the difficulty is to restrict the calculus and introduce the notion of *virtual processor*. We describe this strategy in some detail below. The method works well for the restricted calculus, and execution obeys the formal operational semantics. We also discuss, assuming a specific network configuration, an implementation method for less restricted calculus.

## 5.1 A Restricted Calculus and Its Compilation

We impose the following restriction on the calculus.

- *Nested parallelism is prohibited.*
  $\mu$-expression can not be applied in $\mu$-expression's body.
- *Nested recursive data is not allowed.*
  Types of the form $\mu t.(\cdots \mu s. \cdots)$ are disallowed. This prohibits the use of the data types such as list of list.
- *Executing up and dn inside $\mu$-expression is prohibited.*

These constraints considerably weaken the expressive power of the calculus. However, the restricted calculus is still worth considering, since it seems to preserve the enough power to express most of typical data parallel algorithms so far considered such as those described in Section 3.3. Furthermore, the restricted calculus can be implemented on a wide range of massively parallel machines without much difficulty.

Even with above restriction, there are some cases that a distributed recursive datum can not be expressed by global pointers, since more than two elements of the recursive datum may be allocated to a single processor. (Such a situation does not frequently arises. Indeed, the examples described so far does not create such a recursive datum.) To overcome this difficulty, we assume that computational power of each physical processor is shared by a non-empty set of *virtual processors* and that the number of virtual processors residing on a physical processor can be increased at run time. Computational power of a physical processor is shared by letting each virtual processor execute the same set of instructions in a loop.

A program is now compiled as below. The program starts in the state that each physical processor's computational power is shared by a single virtual processor. A global pointer is now a pair of a virtual processor id and the pointer to the heap area. The execution method for *up* described in Section 4.1 has to be changed slightly as follows. To execute *up M with* $x_1 = N_1, \cdots, x_k = N_k$ *end*, every virtual processor $Q_1$ first evaluates $(\lambda x_1 \cdots x_k.M)N_1 \cdots N_k$ to a value $V_{Q_1}$, and then selects the same virtual processor $P$, where no elements of recursive data have not been allocated to the physical processor on which processor $Q_1$ is residing. Suppose that, in each processor $Q_1$ other than the selected processor $P$, $V_{Q_1}$ contains $n$ global pointers $(P_1, p_1), \cdots, (P_n, p_n)$ as its immediate subterm and that each $p_i$ is either $q_1$, $q_2$, or $q_m$ where $q_i$'s are distinct and $m \leq n$. If $m \geq 2$, processor $Q_1$ creates $m - 1$ new virtual processors $Q_2, \cdots, Q_m$ sharing computational power of the physical processor on which the virtual processor $Q_1$ itself is residing. Then each processor $Q_i(1 \leq i \leq m)$ yields a global pointer $(P, q_i)$. The execution method for $dn$ also needs a slight extension. To execute $dn(M)$, all the second elements of the global pointers contained in the broadcasted datum as subterms of the recursive datum must be updated to the second element of the global pointer obtained by evaluating $M$. As for $\mu$-application, the body of a $\mu$-expression is compiled straight forwardly, since executing any parallel operations are not allowed by the restriction. However, there are some cases that an application of $d$ is left unevaluated in a function closure and its evaluation is delayed. To correctly retrieve a remote datum when such a delayed application is evaluated, each global pointer $(P, p)$ must be augmented with a local pointer, which points to the global pointer $(Q, q)$ from which the global pointer $(P, p)$ was obtained by applying a $\mu$-expression.

Let us roughly estimate how efficiently the code compiled by the above method is executed. $up$ can be executed in a constant time, since allocation of a new processor can be done by maintaining the same counter on every processor and increasing it. $dn$ requires broadcasting a datum all over the processors, which seems to cause slow-down. For example, a hypercube connected multicomputer with $p$ processors costs $O(\log p)$ time to execute a broadcast. However, broadcast by $dn$ does not cause much slow down, since the calculus is designed to process recursive data by applying a parallel function to them iteratively, which eliminates a number of $dn$ executed to unfold recursive data. In a typical program such as the suffix sum program, $dn$ is used only once for each iteration applying a parallel function to a recursive datum, as a program written in a conventional array-based language is compiled to the code which globally synchronizes and computes global-or for each time executing a loop. $dn$ therefore slows down execution at most by a constant factor compared to conventional array-based languages. $\mu$-application can also be executed as efficiently as mapping a set of instructions over the elements of an array in a conventional data parallel language.

## 5.2 Toward Full Implementation

Implementing the full calculus constitutes a challenge. One of major difficulties is parallel resource allocation, which significantly complicates the data distribution strategy and consequently causes the machine slow down. Finding a general solution to this problem appears to be difficult. Here we offer a solution specific to hypercube connected multicomputers. This solution allows a restricted form of nested parallelism and nested distributed recursive data so that the calculus is still implemented reasonably efficiently while maintaining its power to express some parallel version of typical functions for nested recursive data such as map-functions.

Let $d$ be the maximum nesting depth of the recursive types in a given program, which is determined by type checking. ($\mu t.unit + t \times (\mu s.unit + s)$) is, for example, a recursive type of depth 2.) Then the cube is divided into $sub^{d-1}$-cubes, where $sub^0$-cube is the whole cube, and $sub^{n+1}$-cube is obtained by dividing each $sub^n$-cube. The size of $sub^i$-cube for each $i$ is determined so that the data may be distributed well. Nested recursive data are implemented in the following way. The scalar values are loaded on every processor; the recursive data of first depth are distributed over every processors so that each element of the data is loaded on every processor of a subcube; the recursive data of $i$th depth are, inductively, distributed over every processors of a $sub^{i-1}$-cube so that each element of the data is loaded on every processor of a $sub^i$-cube of the $sub^{i-1}$-cube. The nested parallelism is then allowed if the following condition is satisfied: each $\mu$-expression of nesting level $i$ (with regarding nesting level 0 as outermost $\mu$-expression) is applied to the recursive datum distributed on a $sub^i$-cube.

## 6 Conclusion, Ongoing Work, and Further Investigation

We have proposed a typed functional calculus suitable for data parallel programming on massively parallel multicomputer systems. The calculus supports distributed recursive data and a parallel function application mechanism for those data. In this calculus, a new form of recursion, called *parallel recursion* is expressed, which overcomes inherent sequentiality of ordinary recursion, and exploits more parallelism in manipulating recursively defined data. We have developed a type system and parallel operational semantics for the calculus. We have described an SPMD execution model for the calculus, and proposed two implementation strategies based on it.

We believe that the calculus and its SPMD execution model provide a basis to design and implement a high level data parallel language. Such a claim needs to be substantiated by an actual implementation. We plan to develop a prototype language based on the proposed calculus. Our current strategy is to implement a restricted calculus by the method described in Section 5.1 by writing a translator that converts the restricted calculus to an existing data parallel language. We are designing a translator that converts ML like programming language extended with data parallel constructs into TUPLE [Yua92], a data parallel extension of Lisp.

The calculus presented here offers a number of interesting challenges. One of them is to find an efficient way of creating distributed recursive data. The calculus has not overcome the difficulty of the inherent sequentiality of the recursive data creation, since *up* must be called sequentially. One approach is compile time distribution of recursive data using a syntax for direct representation of recursive data. A more interesting approach would be to develop a form of parallel I/O interface to an external world.

## Acknowledgment

We would like to thank Kazuhiko Kato for insightful discussion about data parallel programming.

# References

[Ble93]   G.E. Blelloch. NESL: A nested data parallel language. Technical Report Tech. Report, CMU-CS-93-129, Carnegie Mellon University, 1993.

[For93]   High Performance Fortran Forum. *High Performance Fortran language specification*, May 1993.

[Gup92]   R. Gupta. SPMD execution of programs with pointer-based data structures on distributed-memory machines. *Journal of Parallel and Distributed Computing*, Vol. 16, pp. 92–107, 1992.

[Hal85]   R.H. Halstead. Multilisp: A language for concurrent symbolic computation. *ACM Transactions on Programming Languages and Systems*, Vol. 7, No. 4, pp. 501–538, 1985.

[HF93]    G. Hains and C. Foisy. The data-parallel categorical abstract machine. In *Proc. PARLE93: Parallel Architectures and Languages Europe (LNCS 694)*, 1993.

[HQ91]    P.J. Hatcher and M.J. Quinn. *Data-Parallel Programming on MIMD Computers*. The MIT Press, 1991.

[HS86]    W.D. Hillis and Guy L. Steele Jr. Data parallel algorithms. *Communications of ACM*, Vol. 29, No. 12, pp. 1170–1183, 1986.

[Kah87]   G. Kahn. Natural semantics. In *Proc. Symposium on Theoretical Aspects of Computer Science(LNCS 247)*, pp. 22–39. Springer Verlag, 1987.

[Kar87]   A. Karp. Programming for parallelism. *IEEE Computer*, pp. 43–57, May 1987.

[Las86]   C. Lasser. *The Essential *Lisp Manual*. Thinking Machine Corporation, Cambridge, MA, July 1986.

[RRH92]   A. Rogers, J. Reppy, and L. Hendren. Supporting SPMD execution for dynamic data structurs. In *Proc. 5th International Workshop on Languages and Compilers for Parallel Computing (LNCS 757)*, 1992.

[RS87]    J. Rose and Guy L. Steele Jr. C*: An extended C language for data parallel programming. Technical Report PL87-5, Thinking Machine Corporation, Cambridge, MA, 1987.

[Ryt85]   W. Rytter. The complexity of twoway push down automata and recursive programs. In A. Apostolica and Z. Galil, editors, *Combinatorial Algorithms on Words*. Springer-Verlag, NATO ASI Series F:12 1985.

[Sab88]   G. Sabot. *Paralation Lisp Manual*, May 1988.

[ST94]    D. Suciu and T. Tannen. Efficient compilation of high-level data prrallel algorithm. In *Proc. ACM Symposium on Parallel Algorithms and Architectures*, June 1994.

[WS87]    S. Wholey and Guy L. Steele Jr. Connection machine lisp: A dialect of common lisp for data parallel programming. In *Proc. International Conference on Supercomputing*, May 1987.

[Yua92]   T. Yuasa. A SIMD environment TUPLE for parallel list processing. In *Parallel Symbolic Computing: Languages, Systems, and Applications (LNCS 748)*, pp. 268–286. Springer Verlag, 1992.

# The Data-parallel C Language NCX and its Implementation Strategies

Taiichi Yuasa[1], Toshiro Kijima[1], and Yutaka Konishi[2]

[1] Toyohashi University of Technology, Toyohashi 441, Japan
[2] Aichi College of Technology, Gamagori, 443, Japan

**Abstract.** NCX is an extended C language for data-parallelism, which is one of the most important computation models to support realistic applications of massively parallel computers. The design criteria of the language include easy shifting from the C language, low-cost implementation of efficient compilers, and high integrity as a programming language. The language is based on the concept of *virtual processors*, each being powerful enough to execute the full-set C language. Several features for data-parallel computation, such as inter-processor communication, are added to the language so that they obey the design principles of the base language C. The language is intended to be used on various architectures, and is now being implemented for some machines with different architectures. In order to support low-cost but efficient implementation of NCX, a preprocessor, called NICS, has been developed, which performs common, machine-independent analysis and generates intermediate code. This paper overviews the major extended features of NCX, together with some programming examples, and shows that NCX provides sufficient expressive power for data-parallel computation while it is based on the simple and clear notion of virtual processors. This paper also introduces NICS and shows how it can be used in compiler construction.

## 1 Introduction

Several computation models have been proposed to support programming on massively-parallel computers with a huge number of processors. Among them, data-parallelism is one of the most promising models. In fact, many application programs of massively-parallel computers are known to be expressed with data-parallelism. As more computation power is required in these days, we expect more applications in data-parallelism in the future.

So far, some extended C languages have been proposed for data-parallel programming [1, 2, 8, 6]. Most of them have originally been designed for relatively low-level programming on specific SIMD (Single-Instruction, Multiple-Data) machines. Thus these languages tend to have restrictions that reflect the architecture of the target machine. As non-SIMD massively-parallel machines are getting more popular, these languages are sometimes used on machines other than the original target machines [2, 7, 10]. Even then, the language restrictions usually remain, to maintain the language-level compatibility. This results in low integrity as a modern programming language (see [11] for concrete examples of this discussion).

This paper introduces a new extended C language, called NCX [12], for data-parallel programming. NCX was designed as a common programming language that can be used on a wide class of parallel machines, including SIMD, SPMD (Single-Program, Multiple-Data), and MIMD (Multiple-Instruction, Multiple-Data) machines. It is also intended to be used on ordinary sequential machines, i.e., SISD (Single-Instruction, Single-Data) machines. With the current compiler technology, automatic parallelization of sequential programs is still in the experimentation stage, and thus explicit description of parallelism is inevitable to make use of the full power of parallel machines. This is, however, an expensive work, and it is not realistic to prepare separate parallel code for each machine. Rather, we would like to write a single code in a common language, that can be executed efficiently on various parallel machines. One of the design objectives of NCX is to serve as such a common language.

NCX has the following features to make it easy to write data-parallel programs.

1. The language assumes an infinite number of *virtual processors* (VPs for short), each having the power of executing the full-set C language [5] efficiently. By dynamically selecting a finite set of VPs at any time during the computation, the programmer explicitly expresses parallelism.
2. No extensions are made for data types. The concept of "parallel data types", which can be found in many data-parallel languages, does not exist in NCX.
3. Inter-VP communications are expressed in terms of remote accessing of variables from one VP to another VP.
4. The sequential part of a program is executed by a distinguished VP, called *root*. That is, by selecting the VP set that consists only of the root, the program code can be executed sequentially. No special concepts or notations for sequential execution are necessary.

With these features, expert C programmers are expected to shift to NCX without difficulties.

For implementation efficiency, NCX has the following features among others.

1. The programmer can explicitly specify data allocation for parallel computation. The allocation is specified in terms of VPs, to make it machine-independent. The mapping from a VP set to physical processors is determined by each language processor.
2. For each function, the programmer can specify those VP sets that the function is intended for. This gives the language processor the chance to generate efficient code dedicated for the specified VP sets.
3. In general, a function call in data-parallel languages requires processor synchronization. However, some functions do not actually require synchronization on their calls. By analyzing the entire program, the compiler could detect such functions and remove redundant synchronizations. This is, however, impossible when the program files are compiled separately as with almost all C compilers. Therefore, NCX provides a mechanism to declare such functions in the program file of the caller. For this purpose, we adopt the const declarations for functions that is found in some C compilers such as GCC [9].

In order to make NCX widely available on many machines with different architectures, a preprocessor, called NICS (NCX Intermediate Code Synthesizer), has been developed. NICS performs most program analysis that is independent of the target machine. The most important role of NICS is to determine synchronization points, which are necessary to implement data-parallel semantics. Finding an optimal set of synchronization points is the most difficult part of implementing a data-parallel language. By using NICS, the compiler writer of NCX can concentrate on optimization and code generation specific to the target machine. Thus NICS reduces the cost of developing an efficient language processor.

In the rest of this paper, we first introduce VP sets, called *fields*, in Section 2. Fields are the most fundamental concept for data-parallel computation in NCX. All extended features of NCX are defined in terms fields. In Sections 3 and 4, we describe variable allocation to fields and constructs for data-parallel computation, respectively. The assignment and reduction operations, described in Section 5, are similar to those in other data-parallel C languages, but are more flexible, because they are defined in terms of fields. In Sections 6 and 7, we present two unique features of NCX, the mechanism to dynamically extend parallelism and the indirect remote accessing via pointers. Then in Section 8, we introduce the extended mechanism of NCX to define functions, which is suitable to program in terms of fields. Finally in Section 9, we introduce NICS and show how it can be used in compiler construction.

## 2 Virtual Processors

As mentioned already, NCX programs are supposed to be executed by virtual processors (VPs). Although the language assumes an infinite number of VPs, only a finite number of VPs are *active* (i.e., executing) at any time during the computation, while the other VPs are *inactive*.

There are two ways to change the activity of VPs.

1. Select those VPs that satisfy a certain condition, among the currently active VPs. The selected VPs keep executing and the other VPs become inactive. NCX constructs such as the if statement, described later, are used for this purpose.
2. Select only VPs in a VP set, called *field*, that is defined in advance (statically or dynamically). It is possible to define multiple fields for a single program, but only one field is selected at any moment during the program execution. That field is called the *current field*.

### 2.1 Base-fields

Each field is defined as a finite subset of a predefined *base-field*. A base-field is an infinite set of VPs that are connected by a certain network. There are three base-fields: mesh, hypercube, and binarytree. The network of each base-field corresponds to a communication pattern that is frequently used in actual data-parallel computation.

The base-field mesh is a set of VPs that are arranged in a mesh structure with infinite number of dimensions and with infinite length in each dimension. More precisely, mesh is defined as follows. Each VP in mesh is uniquely identified by an index $(i_0, i_1, i_2, \ldots)$, which is an infinite sequence of integers. The VP with the index $(i_0, i_1, i_2, \ldots)$ is directly connected to the VPs with the following indexes.

$$(i_0 \pm 1, i_1, i_2, \ldots)$$
$$(i_0, i_1 \pm 1, i_2, \ldots)$$
$$(i_0, i_1, i_2 \pm 1, \ldots)$$
$$\ldots$$

By

$$P(i_0, i_1, i_2, \ldots),$$

we denote the VP in mesh with the index $(i_0, i_1, i_2, \ldots)$. If all $i_k(k \geq n)$ are 0 for some $n(> 0)$, then we abbreviate $P(i_0, i_1, i_2, \ldots)$ as

$$P(i_0, i_1, \ldots, i_{n-1}).$$

The base-field hypercube is a set of VPs that are arranged in a hypercube structure with infinite number of dimensions. The base-field binarytree is a set of VPs that are arranged in a binary tree structure with infinite depth. Since mesh will be used much more frequently than the other two base-fields in real applications, we will focus on mesh in the rest of the paper.

The VP $P(0)$ in mesh is called the *root processor*, and is denoted $P_{root}$. This VP is identical to the VP in hypercube at the origin and to the VP in binarytree at the root. Two base-fields do not share VPs except $P_{root}$, and no VP other than $P_{root}$ in a base-field is not connected to any VPs other than $P_{root}$ in another base-field. Although any VP can communicate with any other VP (even in a different base-field), communication between two connected VPs can be assumed faster.

## 2.2 Fields

Each *field* is declared as a finite subset of a base-field. The followings are the declarations of three fields a1, v1, and h1, which we will use throughout this paper.

```
field a1(10,10) on mesh;
field v1(10)    on mesh;
field h1(i:10)  on mesh(0,i);
```

These fields are subsets of mesh, and are called *mesh fields*. The field a1 is a set of VPs

$$\{P(i,j) \mid 0 \leq i < 10, 0 \leq j < 10\}$$

that are arranged in a $10 \times 10$ matrix. The field v1 is a one-dimensional set of VPs:

$$\{P(i) \mid 0 \leq i < 10\}$$

Figure 1 illustrates these fields. In the figure, the circle at the upper-left corner stands for the root processor $P_{root}$ $(= P(0,0))$, the circle at the lower-left corner for $P(9)$ $(= P(9,0))$, and the circle at the upper-right corner for $P(0,9)$.

The i in the declaration of h1 is called *index variable* and is used to specify the location of mesh where each one of the ten VPs of h1 resides. This correspondence is called a *field mapping*. In this example, the $i$-th VP of h1 is specified to be at $P(0,i)$, and thus h1 represents the VP set:

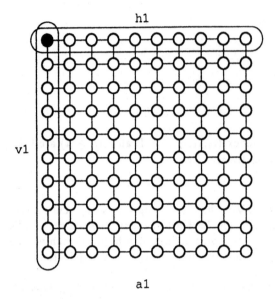

**Fig. 1.** Field examples

$$\{P(0, i) \mid 0 \leq i < 10\}.$$

The field mappings for the previous fields a1 and v1 are abbreviated in the declarations, because they use the default mappings. With explicit mapping specifications, their declarations would look:

```
field a1(i:10,j:10) on mesh(i,j);
field v1(i:10)      on mesh(i);
```

As will be explained later, each NCX variable is allocated to a specified field. By using field mappings, the programmer can easily specify data allocation for efficient communication.

Each expression used for a mapping specification in a mesh field declaration is either an integer constant or a polynomial $ax + b$ of an index variable $x$ with some integer constants $a$ and $b$. Therefore, the VP set in an arbitrary rectangular region can be declared as a mesh field. If a field mapping is explicitly specified in a **mesh** field declaration, then every dimension must be associated with an index variable, and each index variable must appear at least once in the mapping specification. With this condition, field mappings are guaranteed one-to-one.

## 2.3 The Built-in Field mono

A special field, called mono, is predefined in the language, which consists only of the root processor $P_{root}$. When the current field is mono, only one processor $P_{root}$ is active. Therefore, the program is executed sequentially. An NCX program begins to run with mono as the initial current field. That is, only the root processor $P_{root}$ is active when a program begins to run.

NCX is designed so that any C language program runs as an NCX program in exactly the same way, if all functions are declared to be mono-specific (see Section 8). The only VP that becomes active during the execution of such a program is the root processor $P_{root}$.

# 3 Variables

## 3.1 Variable Declarations

Variable declarations in NCX are associated with fields to which the variables are allocated. For example:

```
int a on a1;
int h on h1;
int v on v1;
int x on mono;
```

The first declaration declares an int variable a that is allocated to (all VPs in) the field a1. Similarly, h, v, and x are allocated to the fields h1, v1, and mono, respectively (see Figure 2). The keyword "on" and the rest of a variable declaration are optional. When abbreviated, variables are allocated to mono for top-level declarations, and to the current field for declarations inside function definitions.

NCX makes no extensions for data types. Structures and unions are declared in the same way as in C. Arrays, pointer variables, structure variables, and union variables are declared by adding the optional field specification to C language declarations. For instance, the following declaration allocates an int array m with 12 elements and an int pointer p, both to the field a1.

```
int m[12], *p on a1;
```

## 3.2 Variable References

Since a variable declaration allocates variables of the same name to all VPs in the specified field, the variable name is not enough to identify a variable. We need to specify the VP to which the intended variable is allocated. To do this, NCX uses the following syntax for variable reference.

$identifier@(expr_1, \ldots, expr_n)$

The value of each $expr$ is used as a field index to identify the VP. The VP is determined by the field mapping of the field to which the variable is allocated. For instance,

```
a@(2,3), v@(1), h@(1)
```

denotes a at $P(2,3)$, v at $P(1,0)$, and h at $P(0,1)$, respectively.

The VP specification can be abbreviated in the following cases.

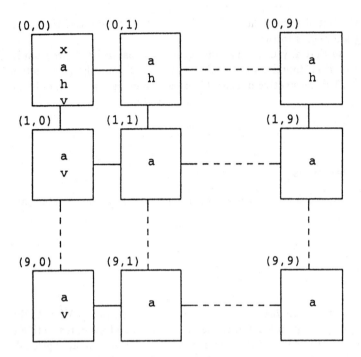

**Fig. 2.** Variable allocations to fields

- When a mono variable, i.e., a variable that is allocated to mono, is referenced. VP specification is unnecessary for mono variables, since they are allocated only to the root processor.
- When a variable that is allocated to the current field is referenced and each currently active VP references the variable that is allocated to the VP itself. This abbreviation allows concise coding and, more importantly, makes it clear that the reference is local to each VP.

## 4   Parallel Constructs

### 4.1   The in Statement

The in statement is introduced to NCX to switch the current field. An in statement

>   in *field stat*

makes *field* the current field. Only VPs in *field* become active and execute the body *stat*. After all VPs have finished the execution, the field that was the current field right before the in statement will become the current field again, and the VP activities before the in statement will be resumed.

Suppose a and b are variables in the field a1. With the following in statement, VPs in a1 will assign the value of b to a in parallel.

```
in a1
    a = b;
```

Since VPs in a1 are arranged in a 10 × 10 matrix, this statement can be interpreted as a parallel assignment from a two-dimensional square matrix b to another square matrix a.

An in statement may contain declarations for index variables that are used to specify individual VPs within the body. For example:

```
in a1(i,j)
    ...
```

This in statement declares two index variables i and j. For each VP $P(i,j)$ in a1, these variables are initialized to $i$ and $j$, respectively. Index variables can be used in exactly the same way as ordinary variables. For example, if we regard the variable a in a1 as a two-dimensional square matrix, the following statement is to assign to each element of a the sum of the row number and the column number of the element.

```
in a1(i,j)
    a = i + j;
```

Here are more assignment examples in an in statement.

```
in a1(i,j) {
    a = x;
    b = b@(i,0);
    a = a@(j,i);
}
```

By the first assignment, each VP in a1 assigns the value of the mono variable x to its own a. This is a broadcast operation from $P_{root}$ to the VPs in a1. With the next assignment statement, each $P(i,j)$ assigns the value of b at $P(i,0)$, to its own b. This can be regarded as a multicast operation from the left-most column to each row. The last assignment transposes the matrix a.

When a VP accesses a variable in another VP, it is called *remote access*. A remote access of a variable is performed by specifying another VP as the field index that follows the variable name. Any value is allowed as the field index as long as the value specifies a VP correctly. This implies that VPs can perform remote accesses of a random pattern. However, random remote accesses are expensive on most machines. It is recommended to use the network of each field for better performance. For this purpose, NCX provides several macros with which the programmer can specify VPs that are connected directly with each VP.

There are some constraints on the use of NCX statements as will be mentioned later, but any valid statement can be used in the body of an in statement. In particular, an in statement can be nested within another in statement. Incidentally, an in statement does not block the scope of a variable that is declared outside the in statement. Such a variable can be referenced from inside the in statement.

## 4.2  Statements

Statements in NCX are

labeled statement,
expression statement,
compound statement,

and statements that begin with the following keywords.

| | | | |
|---|---|---|---|
| if | while | for | do |
| switch | break | continue | return |
| goto | in | all | spawn |

Among these, statements that begin with `in`, `all`, and `spawn` are extensions of NCX. The other statements are defined also in C. They behave in exactly the same way as in C, when the current field is mono. In this sense, these NCX statements are upper compatible with those in the C language.

When the current field is other than mono, these statements have almost the same meaning as in other data-parallel C languages. For example, an `if` statement

if ( *expr* ) *stat*₁ else *stat*₂

is used to select some of the currently active VPs. All active VPs evaluate *expr* first. Then only those VPs whose values are true remain active and execute $stat_1$. After the execution of $stat_1$, only those VPs whose values were false become active and execute $stat_2$. After the execution of $stat_2$, the activity before the `if` statement will be resumed. For example, the following `if` statement doubles the values of a if they are larger than 100, and sets 100 to a otherwise.

```
in a1
    if (a > 100)
        a *= 2;
    else
        a = 100;
```

With a `while` statement,

while ( *expr* ) *stat*

each active VP executes the body *stat* repeatedly, while it satisfies the condition *expr*. All active VPs evaluate *expr* first. Those VPs whose values are false become inactive until the other VPs finish execution of the `while` statement. Those VPs whose values are true execute the body *stat* and then evaluate the condition *expr* again. This process repeats as long as there remain VPs whose values of *expr* are true. The execution of the entire `while` statement ends when all VPs that evaluate *expr* get false values. After that, the activity before the `while` statement will be resumed. The other iteration statements are defined similarly.

`goto` statements are allowed only when the current field is mono. This constraint comes from the nature of the data-parallel model. Similarly, some of the other statements have constraints on their use. One of such constraints is that a `break` statement cannot break from within an `in` statement to the outside.

An all statement

    all *stat*

activates all VPs in the current field to execute *stat*. After all VPs have finished the execution of *stat*, the activity before the all statement will be resumed. The third extended statement spawn will be explained in a later section.

## 5   Assignments and Reductions

Each assignment expression is executed in two steps. First, all active VPs evaluate the right-hand side. After all VPs have finished the evaluation, each VP assigns its value to the destination. If no two VPs assign to a same destination, then the assignment is a parallel version of the ordinary C assignment. If, however, more than one VPs are going to assign to a same destination, then the assignments are performed one after another, in an unspecified order. As the result, one of the values become the value of the destination, after the assignment expression.

For the assignment statements below, the destinations are shared by more than one VPs.

```
in a1(i,j) {
    x = a@(i,j);
    x = 1;
    v@(i) = a@(i,j);
}
```

By the first assignment statement, all active VPs assign to the same mono variable x. Since the assignments to x are performed one after another, the value of a in one of the active VPs will become the value of x after the assignment. Thus assignment expressions in NCX can be used for data selection among VPs. This feature is useful for some applications to select one of the solutions that the VPs have found independently. Since assignments to mono variables can be detected at compile time, the programmer may assume that only one assignment will actually be performed.

The destination of the second assignment statement is also a mono variable. Since all VPs are going to assign 1, the value of x always becomes 1. Thus this assignment statement is equivalent to

```
in mono
    x = 1;
```

If we regard a as a matrix and v as a column vector, then the last assignment statement assigns one of the values in each row $i$ of a to the $i$-th element of v. That is, this assignment statement performs row-wise selections in parallel.

Some assignment operators, such as +=, perform an arithmetic operation (an addition in the case of +=) before assignment. Such an operator is "atomic" in the sense that, if two VPs share a same destination, then either VP performs the operation first while the other VP is waiting. Thus, if a destination of += is shared by multiple VPs, then all values of the VPs are added to the destination.

```
in a1(i,j) {
```

```
        x += a;
        x += 1;
        v@(i) += a;
}
```

The first assignment statement adds the sum of the values of a to the mono variable x. The second assignment statement adds the number of actives VPs to x. The last assignment statement adds the values in each row to the corresponding element in v.

In NCX, some of the assignment operators can be used as prefix operators. When used as prefix operators, they perform the so-called *reduction* operations, i.e., combine values from all active VPs to produce a single value. For example, by

```
in a1(i,j) {
        x = (+= a)/(+= 1);
}
```

the average of a's in all active VPs will be assigned to x.

# 6  The spawn Statement

spawn is a construct to expand the rank of the current field temporarily. By expanding the rank, more VPs become active and thus more parallelism is obtained.

As an example of spawn, we will show the code to multiply $10 \times 10$ square matrices a and b. The result is stored in the third matrix c.

```
in a1(i,j) {
        c = 0;
        spawn(k:10)
            c@(i,j) += a@(i,k) * b@(k,j);
}
```

In this example, spawn expands the rank of the current field from a two-dimensional field a1 to a three-dimensional field. k is the index variable for the third dimension. For each active $P(i, j)$ in a1, VPs

$$\{P(i, j, k) \mid 0 \leq k < 10\}$$

become active during the spawn statement. As the result, the computation is performed by a three-dimensional field.

# 7  Pointers and Arrays

When a variable is allocated to a field, the address of the variable in each VP is not specified in the language. The variables may be allocated at the same location for all VPs. Or, they may be allocated at different locations of every VPs. Therefore, in order to obtain the address of a variable by the address operator &, the intended VP, to which the variable is allocated, must be specified in addition to the name of the variable. The same notation as for variable references is used for this purpose. That is, the address of an NCX variable can be obtained by the following expression.

   **&** *identifier*@(*expr*₁,..., *expr*ₙ)

As in C, the expression to access an array element

   *pointer-expr* [ *expr* ]

is equivalent to

   * (( *pointer-expr* ) + ( *expr* ))

in NCX. This equivalence relation is maintained even when the expression is used as an lvalue.

An NCX pointer may or may not contain the information to determine the VP to which the pointer points. Therefore, NCX determines the VP from the program text, by a certain rule. The determined VP is called the *home processor* of the pointer expression. Roughly speaking, the home processor is determined by the field index in the pointer expression. For references and assignments via a pointer variable, the home processor is the VP to which the pointer variable is allocated. For example, suppose the pointer variable p is declared as:

   `int *p on a1;`

Then the home processor of the right-hand side of

   `x = *p@(5);`

is $P(5)$. Therefore, this assignment statement first obtains the value of the pointer variable p in $P(5)$, and then assigns the value at the location of $P(5)$ to which the pointer points. The statement

   `*p@(1) = 3;`

first obtains the value of the pointer variable p in $P(1)$ and then assigns 3 to the location of $P(1)$ to which the pointer points.

# 8 Functions

A function call is performed by all active VPs in parallel. The invoked function and the number of arguments must be the same for all VPs, but the argument values may be different among VPs. The syntax of function calls is the same as in C, and a function call may appear wherever a function call is allowed in C.

When a function is invoked while the current field is $F$, the function is said to be "called from $F$". NCX functions are classified into three categories according to the fields that are allowed to call the function.

1. functions that can be called from any field
2. functions that can be called only from a certain field
3. functions that can be called from fields of a certain base-field

The header of the function definition determines the category to which the function belongs.

## Functions that can be called from any field

A function that is defined with a function header with the syntax of C can be called from any field. The function max below is such a function.

```
int max(x,y)
int x, y;
{
    if (x >= y)
        return(x);
    else
        return(y);
}
```

All standard library functions in C are also defined in NCX. Some of them, namely arithmetic functions, are defined so that they can be called from any field. For instance, sin is defined as follows (in the same manner as in C), and thus can be called from any field.

```
double sin(x)
double x;
{
    ...
}
```

## Functions that can be called only from a specific field

If a field name is specified in the function header, then the function can be called only from that field.

```
int matmul10(a,b) in a1(i,j)
int a, b;
{
    int c = 0;

    spawn(k:10)
        c@(i,j) += a@(i,k) * b@(k,j);
    return(c);
}
```

This function performs the matrix multiplication we have shown already as an example of spawn. This function is intended only for a1, and cannot be called from any other field. i and j are index variables that are similar to those declared in in statements, and are used to identify VPs in the body of the function.

Some of the standard library functions of NCX, namely I/O functions, are intended only for mono. For instance, getc is defined as follows, and can be called only from the field mono.

```
int getc(stream) in mono
FILE *stream;
{
    ...
}
```

### Functions that can be called from fields of a certain base-field

The above function matmul10 can be called only from a1. By modifying the function header, we can obtain a similar function which can be called from any field that is arranged in a two-dimensional square matrix.

```
int matmul(a,b) in field f(i:?n, j:n) on mesh
int a, b;
{
    int c = 0;

    spawn(k:n)
        c@(i,j) += a@(i,k) * b@(k,j);
    return(c);
}
```

The code after in in the first line is a *field pattern*. Only those fields that match this pattern can invoke this function. f is the name that can used to denote the field that actually invokes the function. f is not used in this example, but it could be used in the same way as ordinary field names, in such places as in statements (to specify the new current field) and variable declarations (to specify the field to which the variables are allocated). The part of the first line after f specifies only those mesh fields that are arranged in a two-dimensional square matrix match the pattern. "?n" means that the size of the first dimension is arbitrary and declares a variable n which is used to refer to the actual size of the first dimension. The size of the second dimension is specified to be n, i.e., the same as the size of the first dimension. The variable n is also used in the spawn statement to specify the size of the extended dimension.

## 9　An Overview of NICS

NICS (NCX Intermediate Code Synthesizer) is a preprocessor for NCX that receives an NCX source program and generates a machine-independent intermediate code. The main objective of NICS is to take care of common, machine-independent tasks of NCX compilation, and to provide the environment in which each compiler writer can concentrate on machine-dependent optimization and code generation. The program analysis of NICS includes:

- detection of syntax errors
- checking on all constraints of the extended features of NCX
- checking on some constraints of the base language C

– detection of synchronization points (see below)
– collection of useful information for code generation

NICS assumes that the generated intermediate code be translated into a C code of the target machine. Those constraints of the C language that NICS does not check will be automatically checked by the C compiler.

Detection of synchronization points is the most important task of NICS. For MIMD machines, a synchronization point means a point in the program text where the processors have to be synchronized. The notion of synchronization points is necessary also for SIMD and SISD machines. The number of VPs used in an NCX program is usually larger than the number of physical processors of the target machine. VPs are implemented by "emulation loops" that are executed by each physical processor to emulate some of the VPs. For SIMD and SISD machines, a synchronization point separates two such emulation loops. In other words, no emulation loop may contain a synchronization point in it. This is true also for MIMD machines.

In order to detect synchronization points independently of the target machine, NICS uses an NCX execution model that does not depend on machine architectures. This execution model also defines the data-parallel semantics of NCX.

## 9.1 The Execution Model

NICS assumes two kinds of processors to execute NCX programs.

– an infinite number of virtual processors running asynchronously
– a simple processor, called *supervising processor* (SP for short), which controls the execution of VPs

SP has a set of simple control mechanisms, including the followings.

**Operations on VP sets.** For example,

$$A \text{ <- } B \cup C$$

assigns the union of $B$ and $C$ to $A$.

$$A \text{ <- } \texttt{trueset}(B, V)$$

assigns to $A$ the set of those VPs in $B$ whose values of the variable $V$ are true.

**Code blocks to control VP execution.** Each code block is given in the following format.

$$A \text{ [ } statement_1 \cdots statement_n \text{ ]}$$

The statement sequence $statement_1, \ldots, statement_n$ are executed asynchronously by all VPs in the VP set $A$. During the execution, SP itself is suspended. Each VP executes $statement_1, \ldots, statement_n$ in this order. After all VPs have finished the execution, control returns to SP. If $A$ is an empty set $\emptyset$, then execution of the code block terminates immediately.

**Loops.** A loop

```
loop {
    ⋮
    break-if-empty(A)
    ⋮
}
```

executes the body repeatedly, until the set $A$ becomes empty.

**Shuffles.** A shuffle

```
shuffle
    S₁ ··· Sₙ
and
    T₁ ··· Tₘ
```
$$S_1 \cdots S_n$$
$$T_1 \cdots T_m$$

executes $S_1, \ldots, S_n, T_1, \ldots, T_n$ in arbitrary order that maintains the order of $S_1, \ldots, S_n$ and the order of $T_1, \ldots, T_n$.

**Function calls.** A function call

```
call(A, V, F, V₁, ···, Vₙ)
```

makes all VPs in $A$ invoke the function $F$. The arguments for each VP are stored in the variables $V_1, \cdots, V_n$ of the VP, and the return value of the function, if any, will be stored in the variable $V$ of the VP.

## 9.2 Program Transformation

Transformation of an NCX program to the NICS execution model is essentially performed by the statement transformation

$$S(A, C, R, statement)$$

and by the expression transformation

$$E(A, V, expression)$$

where $V$ is a VP variable to store the value of *expression*. $A$, $C$, and $R$ are set variables in SP. They respectively represent the set of active VPs, the set of VPs that have executed a continue statement, and the set of VPs that have executed a return statement. Therefore, continue statements, break statements, and return statements are transformed as follows.

$$S(A, C, R, \texttt{continue};)$$
$$\Rightarrow \quad C \texttt{ <- } C \cup A$$
$$\qquad A \texttt{ <- } \emptyset$$

$S(A, C, R, \texttt{break};)$
$\Rightarrow \quad A \texttt{ <- } \emptyset$

$S(A, C, R, \texttt{return};)$
$\Rightarrow \quad R \texttt{ <- } R \cup A$
$\qquad A \texttt{ <- } \emptyset$

If the `return` statement returns some value, then it is transformed as follows. Here, *result* is the VP variable to store the return value (see the above `call` construct of SP), and *temp* is a new temporary VP variable.

$S(A, C, R, \texttt{return}(expression);)$
$\Rightarrow \quad E(A, temp, expression)$
$\qquad A \texttt{ [ } result = temp; \texttt{ ]}$
$\qquad R \texttt{ <- } R \cup A$
$\qquad A \texttt{ <- } \emptyset$

if statements and do statements are transformed as follows. Here, $A_1$, $A_2$, $C_1$, and $R_1$ are new set variables.

$S(A, C, R, \texttt{if}(expression) \; statement_1 \; \texttt{else} \; statement_2)$
$\Rightarrow \quad E(A, temp, expression)$
$\qquad A_1 \texttt{ <- } \texttt{trueset}(A, \; temp)$
$\qquad A_2 \texttt{ <- } A - A_1$
$\qquad \texttt{shuffle}$
$\qquad\qquad S(A_1, C, R, statement_1)$
$\qquad \texttt{and}$
$\qquad\qquad S(A_2, C, R, statement_2)$
$\qquad A \texttt{ <- } A_1 \cup A_2$

$S(A, C, R, \texttt{do} \; statement \; \texttt{while}(expression);)$
$\Rightarrow \quad A_1 \texttt{ <- } A$
$\qquad R_1 \texttt{ <- } \emptyset$
$\qquad \texttt{loop } \{$
$\qquad\qquad C_1 \texttt{ <- } \emptyset$
$\qquad\qquad S(A_1, C_1, R_1, statement)$
$\qquad\qquad A_1 \texttt{ <- } A_1 \cup C_1$
$\qquad\qquad E(A_1, temp, expression)$
$\qquad\qquad A_1 \texttt{ <- } \texttt{trueset}(A_1, \; temp)$
$\qquad\qquad \texttt{break-if-empty}(A_1)$
$\qquad \}$
$\qquad A \texttt{ <- } A - R_1$
$\qquad R \texttt{ <- } R \cup R_1$

For the if statement, a break statement may be executed in *statement_1* and/or in *statement_2*. Therefore, the set $A$ must be adjusted ($A \texttt{ <- } A_1 \cup A_2$) at the end of the if statement. A similar adjustment must be made for the do statement. In addition, after each iteration, those VPs that have executed a continue statement must be added ($A_1 \texttt{ <- } A_1 \cup C_1$) before the evaluation of the condition expression.

Some other statements are transformed as follows.

$S(A, C, R, \{statement_1 \cdots statement_n\})$
$\Rightarrow \quad S(A, C, R, statement_1)$
$$\vdots$$
$\qquad S(A, C, R, statement_n)$

$S(A, C, R, expression;)$
$\Rightarrow \quad E(A, temp, expression)$

$E(A, temp, f(expression_1, \ldots, expression_n))$
$\Rightarrow \quad$ shuffle
$\qquad\qquad E(A, temp_1, expression_1)$
$\qquad$ and
$$\vdots$$
$\qquad$ and
$\qquad\qquad E(A, temp_n, expression_n)$
$\qquad$ call$(A, temp, f, temp_1, \ldots, temp_n)$

$E(A, temp, expression_1 \; binary\text{-}operator \; expression_2)$
$\Rightarrow \quad$ shuffle
$\qquad\qquad E(A, temp_1, expression_1)$
$\qquad$ and
$\qquad\qquad E(A, temp_2, expression_2)$
$\qquad A$ [ $temp = temp_1 \; binary\text{-}operator \; temp_2;$ ]

$E(A, temp, variable \; assignment\text{-}operator \; expression)$
$\Rightarrow \quad E(A, temp_1, expression)$
$\qquad A$ [ $variable \; assignment\text{-}operator \; temp_1;$ ]
$\qquad A$ [ $temp = variable;$ ]

$E(A, temp, variable)$
$\Rightarrow \quad A$ [ $temp = variable;$ ]

Figure 3 shows the transformation result for the following do statement.

```
do {
    prev = x;
    x = ( x@(i-1) + x@(i+1) ) / 2;
} while (endtest(x,prev));
```

In this example, i is an index variable of the current field. We will use this example throughout the rest of this section.

## 9.3 Detecting Synchronization Points

The program transformation explained above guarantees that a VP variable appears at most once in a code block. This implies that VPs can execute each code block asynchronously. If we put a synchronization point between adjacent code blocks,

```
A <- A0
R <- empty
loop {
    C <- empty
    A[ t1 = x; ]
    A[ prev = t1; ]
    shuffle
        A[ t2 = i; ]
        A[ t3 = t2 - 1; ]
        A[ t4 = x@(t3); ]
    and
        A[ t5 = i; ]
        A[ t6 = t5 + 1; ]
        A[ t7 = x@(t4); ]
    A[ t8 = t4 + t7; ]
    A[ t9 = t8 / 2; ]
    A[ x = t9; ]
    A <- A + C
    A[ t10 = x; ]
    A[ t11 = prev; ]
    call(A, t12, endtest, t10, t11)
    A <- trueset(A, t12)
    break-if-empty(A)
}
A0 <- A0 - R
R0 <- R0 + R
```

**Fig. 3.** An example of NICS transformation

the entire program runs correctly. However, the number of synchronization points directly affects the performance of the program. Therefore, NICS further transforms the SP code to combine some adjacent code blocks into one and thus to reduce the number of synchronization points. For example, for the previous do statement, the three adjacent code blocks

```
A[ t8 = t4 + t7; ]
A[ t9 = t8 / 2; ]
A[ x = t9; ]
```

can obviously be combined into the following single code block (though this is not optimal as will be shown later).

```
A[ x = ( t4 + t7 ) / 2; ]
```

Adjacent code blocks can be combined only if there is no "dependency" of program variables between the two blocks. For instance, the following code blocks

```
A[ t = x@(i+1); ]
A[ x = t; ]
```

cannot be combined into a single code block:

```
A[ x = x@(i+1); ]
```

This is because there is a so-called control dependency between the two code blocks. Also, the following code blocks cannot be combined, because there is a so-called anti-dependency.

```
A[ x@(i+1) = t; ]
A[ t1 = x; ]
```

Figure 4 illustrates the dependency table that is used to determine whether there is a dependency with respect to a program variable $x$. Each circle in the table indicates the existence of a dependency. Adjacent code blocks can be combined if and only if there is no dependency with respect to all variables that appear in both code blocks. For instance,

```
A[ t = x@(i+1); ]
A[ t1 = x; ]
```

can be combined into:

```
A[ t = x@(i+1);
   t1 = x;        ]
```

| | local reference $x$ | local assignment $x=e$ | remote reference $x@(i)$ | remote assignment $x@(i)=e$ |
|---|---|---|---|---|
| local reference $x$ | | | | O |
| local assignment $x=e$ | | | O | O |
| remote reference $x@(i)$ | | O | | O |
| remote assignment $x@(i)=e$ | O | O | O | O |

**Fig. 4.** The dependency table

The order of combining code blocks is significant, because the resulting set of code blocks often depends on the order and the number of code blocks may differ. Even if the number is the same, program performance may differ. For the previous example, if code blocks are combined upwards from the assignment to x, then we obtain:

```
A[ prev = x; ]
shuffle
    A[ t4 = x@(i-1); ]
and
    A[ t7 = x@(i+1); ]
A[ x = ( t4 + t7 ) / 2; ]
```

By removing shuffle, we obtain:

```
A[ prev = x;
   t4 = x@(i-1);
   t7 = x@(i+1); ]
A[ x = ( t4 + t7 ) / 2; ]
```

On the other hand, if code blocks are combined downwards, then we obtain:

```
A[ prev = x;
   t9 = ( x@(i-1) + x@(i+1) ) / 2; ]
A[ x = t9; ]
```

The latter contains less assignments to temporary variables, and thus is expected to be more efficient than the former.

With these considerations, NICS generates the following final code.

```
A <- A0
loop {
    A[ prev = x;
       t9 = ( x@(i-1) + x@(i+1) ) / 2; ]
    A[ x = t9; ]
    call(A, t12, endtest, x, prev)
    A <- trueset(A, t12)
    break-if-empty(A)
}
```

Then NICS outputs an intermediate code that represents this SP code. The actual intermediate code looks more like the source code. For the above example, NICS generates the intermediate code that represents the following pseudo NCX code.

```
do {
    prev = x;
    t9 = ( x@(i-1) + x@(i+1) ) / 2;
    sync;
    x = t9;
    sync;
    t12 = endtest(x,prev);
} while (t12);
```

The detected synchronization points are indicated by sync.

## 9.4 Code Generation

In this section, we will give a brief guideline to generate the C code for individual target machine. We will use the same example as before, and consider SISD, SIMD, and MIMD machines in this order.

On SISD machines, each VP variable is represented by an array.

```
do {
    for (each VP i in A) {
        prev[i] = x[i];
        t1[i] = ( x[i-1] + x[i+1] ) / 2;
    }
    for (each VP i in A) {
        x[i] = t1[i];
    }
    endtest(t2, x, prev);
    for (each VP i in A) {
        if (!t2[i])
            remove i from A;
    }
} while (not_empty(A));
```

Here, each

```
for (each VP i in A) { ··· }
```

is an emulation loop. A represents the set of currently active VPs. The concrete representation of A depends on the language processor.

Since SIMD machines have a single control flow, the code for them are similar to those for SISD machines.

```
do {
    for (each VP i in A) {
        prev[i] = x[i];
        t1[i] = ((mine(i-1) ? x[i-1] : receive(x, i-1))
                + (mine(i+1) ? x[i+1] : receive(x, i+1))) / 2;
    }
    for (each VP i in A) {
        x[i] = t1[i];
    }
    endtest(t2, x, prev);
    for (each VP i in A) {
        if (!t2[i])
            remove i from A;
    }
} while (not_empty(A));
```

The only difference from the SISD code is that the arrays to represent VP variables are distributed among the physical processing elements (PEs). On a remote reference, each PE has to determine which PE is taking care of the VP variable. If the PE itself is taking care of the variable, then the remote reference in NCX is actually a local reference within the PE. Otherwise, some kind of inter-PE communication will take place to receive the value of the variable. Since inter-PE communication is expensive in general, finding an optimal VP allocation is the most important task of the compiler. By using NICS, the compiler writer can concentrate on this task.

For MIMD machines, the actual synchronization points must be specified in the code. If barrier synchronization is available on the target machine, the generated code would look like:

```
do {
    for (each VP i in A) {
        prev[i] = x[i];
        t1[i] = ((mine(i-1) ? x[i-1] : receive(x, i-1))
                 + (mine(i+1) ? x[i+1] : receive(x, i+1))) / 2;
    }
    barrier;
    for (each VP i in A) {
        x[i] = t1[i];
    }
    barrier;
    endtest(t2, x, prev);
    for (each VP i in A) {
        if (!t2[i])
            remove i from A;
    }
} while (reduce-or(not_empty(A)));
```

The barrier synchronization points are indicated by barrier. The control of each PE will be suspended at each synchronization point until all other PEs transfer control to that point. Note that the above code uses an *OR*-reduction to determine when to exit from the do loop. Since NICS detects the necessary barrier synchronization points, again the compiler writer can concentrate on finding the optimal VP allocation.

## 10 Concluding Remarks

We have presented a new extended C language for data-parallel programming, called NCX. The basic idea of NCX is quite simple. It assumes an infinite set of VPs, each having the power of executing the full-set C language. Based on this simple model, several extensions for data-parallel programming are made so that they follow the design principles of the base language C. In spite of the simple base idea, NCX provides sufficient mechanisms for data-parallel programming. Our experiences show that expert C programmers can easily shift to NCX, after reading the reference manual [12].

Currently, several language processors of NCX are being developed for many machines with different architectures, including SIMD machines [13], distributed-memory MIMD machines [4], vector processors, shared-memory parallel machines, and engineering workstations. Some of the projects started independently before the idea of the common preprocessor NICS was found. After a while, we noticed that the most time-consuming part of language processor construction can be shared by all projects. Hence the idea of NICS. NICS is now used by all projects.

# References

1. Bagrodia, R., Chandy, K. M., and Kwan, E.: "UC: A Language for the Connection Machine", Proceedings Supercomputing '90, pp.525–534 (1990).
2. Hatcher, P. J. and Quinn, M. J.: "Data-Parallel Programming on MIMD Computers", MIT Press (1991).
3. High Performance Fortran Forum: "High Performance Fortran Language Specification (Version 1.0 DRAFT)", Rice University (1992).
4. Ishihata, H., Horie, T., Inano, S., Shimizu, T., and Kato, S.: "An Architecture of Highly Parallel Computer AP1000", IEEE Pacific Rim Conf. on Communications, Computers and Signal processing, pp.13–16 (1991).
5. Kernighan, B. W. and Ritchie, D. M.: "The C programming language second edition", Prentice Hall (1988).
6. MasPar Computer Corporation: "MasPar Parallel Application Language (MPL) User Guide", Document Part Number 9302-0100 (1991).
7. Prakash, S., Dhagat, M., and Bagrodia, R.: "Synchronization Issues in Data-Parallel Languages", Languages and Compilers for Parallel Computing, Springer Lecture Notes in Computer Science, pp.76–95 (1993).
8. Rose, J. R. and Steele Jr., G. L.: "C*: An Extended C Language for Data Parallel Programming", Proceedings of the 2nd International Conference on Supercomputing (1987).
9. Stallman, R. M.: "Using and Porting GNU CC", Free Software Foundation, Inc. (1990).
10. Thinking Machines Corporation: "C* Programming Guide" (1993).
11. Tichy, W. F., Philippsen, M, and Hatcher, P.: "A critique of the programming language C*", Comm. ACM, 35(6), pp. 21–24 (1992).
12. Yuasa, T. et.al. : "The Data-parallel C Language NCX Language Specification (Version 3)" (in Japanese), Toyohashi University of Technology, (1993).
13. Yuasa, T.: "SM–1 and Its Language Systems", in Parallel Language and Compiler Research in Japan edited by Nicolau, A., Sato, M., and Bic, L., Kluwer Academic Press (to appear).

# A Dataflow-Based Massively Parallel Programming Language "V" and Its Implementation on a Stock Parallel Machine

Shigeru Kusakabe and Makoto Amamiya

Dept. of Information Systems, Kyushu University, Kasuga Fukuoka 816, Japan
e-mail: {amamiya,kusakabe}@is.kyushu-u.ac.jp

We propose a dataflow-based massively parallel programming language, called "V," which would minimize the difficulties in writing massively parallel programs. The language V has both merits of functional programming and object-based programming.

Our starting point is a dataflow-based functional programming language, called "Valid," which we have developed so far, because functional programming paradigm is able to abstract away the timing problem, that is the problem of execution sequence and synchronization control, in writing massively parallel programs. The language V provides an object-based (or multi-agent) abstraction, called "agent," to write parallel entities which have their own states in them and communicate with each other. In addition, we can connect agents explicitly and abstract an ensemble of agents on a predefined topology description, called "field," in order to write a massively parallel program which naturally reflects the structure of the problem.

As the language V has its basis on a dataflow-based functional programming language originally designed for dataflow architecture, it is easy to extract parallelism of various level. In our implementation, the compiler extracts fine-grain parallel threads in the first stage, and then schedules the fine grain parallel threads and constructs coarser grain threads to exploit as much effective parallelism as target machines can provide. In this paper, implementation issues for a distributed-memory parallel machine, Fujitsu AP1000, are discussed. We also show and discuss a preliminary evaluation of our compiler and runtime system developed for AP1000.

## 1 Introduction

Despite the development of massively parallel computer architectures in recent years, writing programs on such parallel machines is still a difficult problem. We propose a dataflow-based massively parallel programming language, called "V," which has implicit parallelism of fine grain. The language V has both merits of functional programming language and object-based programming language to minimize the difficulties in writing massively parallel programs.

Our starting point is a dataflow-based functional programming language, called "Valid[3]," which we have developed so far, since dataflow-based functional language has the following features suitable for the basis of massively parallel programming language.

- Functional programming paradigm is able to abstract away the timing problem, that is the problem of execution sequence and synchronization control, in writing massively parallel programs.
- Merely extending a sequential computation model with some explicit parallel constructs is not appropriate for massively parallel language. Data-flow based language has various levels of implicit parallelism easy to exploit.
- Functional programming paradigm helps to write comprehensive and reusable program, and abstract away architectural peculiarity in order to promote portability of programs.

However, pure functional programming languages seem to be too restrictive for widespread general purpose use. In the functional programming, communications between function instances are limited to their input arguments and result values, and history sensitive computations are prohibited by pure functional semantics. Some problems are naturally expressed by using stateful object, each of which has its own local state, changes its behavior depending on the local state, and has a powerful communication facility to exchange information[1].

The language V provides an object-based (or multi-agent) abstraction, called "agent," to write parallel entities which have their own states in them and communicate with each other. An agent is a collection of functions which share local states. It has recursive structure in which state information is passed to itself. The explicit transmission of local state information among intra-agent functions is encapsulated. The agent may have input and output stream ports, and communicates with each other via such streams. Intra-agent functions are invoked by message arrivals in a data-flow synchronization scheme, like subexpressions in functions triggered by argument data. History sensitive intra-agent function is applied to pairs of message data and state. History sensitive behavior of an agent is treated by a sequence of function activations which are applied to a stream of message data and state pairs.

If producer/consumer relationship is clear in the problem, we can connect partner agent explicitly to reflect the relationship. Not only programmer can expect high readability of programs, but also implementation can do optimal mapping and efficient communication by the aid of this kind of information. In addition, we can abstract an ensemble of agents and its topology description with "field," to write massively parallel programs, with a number of parallel entities, naturally reflecting their structures.

As the language V has its basis on a dataflow-based functional programming language which is originally designed for dataflow architecture, it is easy to extract parallelism of various levels. Commercially available stock parallel machines, as well as special fine grain parallel machines like Datarol[10], are also our implementation targets. In our implementation, the compiler extracts fine-grain parallel threads in the first stage, and then schedules the fine grain parallel threads and constructs coarser grain threads to exploit as much effective parallelism as target machines can provide.

We present the language features of $V$ in section 2. We discuss some implementation issues of our compiler and runtime system developed for Fujitsu

AP1000, a distributed-memory parallel machine with conventional processors, in section 3 and 4, respectively. We also present a preliminary evaluation of the implementation on AP1000 in section 5.

## 2   Language V

We present language features of V in this section. Components of expressions are designated by syntactic variables, which are written using angle brackets, for example, ⟨expression⟩, ⟨variable⟩. Syntactic variables denote segments of program text; for example, ⟨expression⟩ stands for any string of characters which is a syntactically valid expression. The notation

⟨thing₁⟩ ...

indicates zero or more occurrences of a ⟨thing⟩, and

⟨thing₁⟩ ⟨thing₂⟩ ...

indicates one or more occurrences of a ⟨thing⟩. The notation [⟨thing⟩] means thing is a option.

In our programming paradigm, a program is basically described as a set of functions. In order to express concurrent processes with local states and flexible communications between them in a natural way, we introduce *agent*. Both agent instance and function instance are dynamically created from its definition with given arguments. An agent instance is a first class object containing local states.

The execution order is determined by data dependency. All of the computations are parallel by default. Synchronization is automatically performed along data dependency. If agents have data dependency, they are synchronized by data arrival (through streams) in a data-flow manner[1] . Message passings between agents are realized by data flow computation scheme like parameter passing in functional programming.

### 2.1   Agent

**Agent definition**  An agent instance is created from a template as a concurrent process, which can communicate with other processes. Following is an agent definition:

```
agent ⟨agent-definition-name⟩(⟨parameters-for-creation⟩)
⟨stream-interface⟩
= ⟨body-expression⟩ ;
```

The ⟨agent-definition-name⟩ is an identifier. The ⟨parameters-for-creation⟩ specifies the number of parameters and names of formal parameters, whose actual parameters are given in agent instance creation.

---

[1] If nondeterminism caused by history sensitive agents is not preferable, we can specify the execution order explicitly. Additional sequencing is allowed for coherent access.

Agent instances can have input and output stream ports specified in the
⟨stream-interface⟩ in addition to the ports of ⟨parameters-for-creation⟩, and they
can communicate with each other through the streams. The ⟨stream-interface⟩
consists of ⟨channels⟩ for input streams and ⟨exports⟩ for output streams as:

> { **channel** ⟨input-stream-name₁⟩; ⟨input-stream-name₂⟩;...}
> [ { **export** ⟨output-stream-name₁⟩; ⟨output-stream-name₂⟩;...} ]

The pseudo variable **ch**$_i$ stands for the i-th(from left) stream in the ⟨channels⟩
and the pseudo variable **ex**$_i$ stands for the i-th(from left) stream in the ⟨exports⟩.

When an agent has recursive computation structure which encapsulates local
states and successively handles data of its input stream, the agent instance can be
regarded as a history sensitive object instance. (As V employs single assignment
rule, explicit feedback is necessary to hold local states within agent.) Next local
states are calculated and passed to the next phase, by evaluating intra-agent
function contained in ⟨body-expression⟩ with current local states and stream
data in the current local context.

**Agent instance creation** Following expression creates a new agent instance.
As an agent instance is a first-class-object, an identifier can bind to it.

> **create**(⟨agent-definition-name⟩[,⟨expression₁⟩ ...])

The number and types of ⟨expression⟩s must correspond to those of ⟨parameters-for-creation⟩
in the agent definition(similar to a function definition and its applications)

## 2.2  Communication

It is possible to send data to input streams of the agent instances already created. We provide two types of communication though, in receiver agent instances,
uniform access to the input streams is ensured for both type of communication.

**Message passing communication** Data can be sent by specifying the target
instance name (and the input stream). Multiple data sent to an input stream
are merged and enqueued in the arrival order and processed in the FIFO order.
This style is similar to message passing of OOP.

> ⟨identifier⟩=**send**([**ch**$_k$**@**]⟨agent-instance⟩,⟨expression⟩)

This expression sends the value of the ⟨expression⟩ to the stream of the $k$-th
input stream in the agent instance. (**ch**$_k$**@** is option. If omitted, the default is
the first input stream.) In a message passing, the left_hand_side ⟨identifier⟩ is
implicitly specified in the message as continuation point.

The reply for the message is returned to the continuation point directly(not
via stream port) in a similar way to the return value of function application, by
reply(⟨expression⟩) in the receiver agent instance. Sub-expressions depending on
the left_hand_side ⟨identifier⟩ variable are triggered by the arrival of the result
value in a data-flow computation scheme. If no reply is necessary in a message
passing, !, which means sink value, is specified at the left_hand_side and this !
can be omitted.

**Connected stream communication** If agent instances have clear and fixed producer/consumer relationships, we can connect streams of the partner agents in order to express explicitly the structure of the problem and let agent instances perform regular communication. Not only programmer can expect high readability of programs, but also implementation can do optimal mapping and efficient communication by the aid of this kind of information.

>    link(⟨output-stream⟩,⟨input-stream⟩,⟨input-stream⟩,...)

This connects an ⟨output-stream⟩ of the producer agent instance to ⟨input-stream⟩s of the consumer agent instances. The type of ⟨input-stream⟩s must correspond to the type of ⟨output-stream⟩. Specifying multiple input-streams in link makes possible multi-cast.

In this connected type communication, data pushed into the output stream in the producer instance by put can be read as an input stream date in the consumer agent instance.

>    put(⟨expression⟩,⟨output-stream-name⟩)

**Example of connected stream** The selectmax agent receives an integer stream, and returns the maximum value in the stream and the rest of the input stream. By connecting two selectmax instances, the second maximum value is selected. The form is provided to express creations of agent instances and connections of their streams at the same time, while link is used to connect streams of agent instances already created. In this example, "eos" means the end of the stream, and "!" sinks the corresponding output stream.

**Stream handling** Intra-agent functions can refer the stream data by accessing variables assigned to input and output streams. Multiple data sent to a input stream are buffered in the arrival order and handled as a stream data. Sender can send data asynchronously to the target port. Our input and output stream ports are different from the port of CSP[9], where communication is synchronous and the port size is limited to one.

Primitive functions for stream handling are as follows:

>    head(⟨input-stream⟩)
>    tail(⟨input-stream⟩)
>    empty(⟨input-stream⟩)

The head returns the first element of the ⟨input-stream⟩. and the tail returns the rest of the ⟨input-stream⟩, similar to car and cons for list processing. As stream is lenient list structure, references to the empty input stream cause suspension (not error). Suspended accesses automatically resume when the stream data arrive. Thus, synchronization between agent is performed in a data-driven fashion. The empty primitive is provided in order to express some kind of synchronizing condition. This returns true if ⟨input-stream⟩ is empty, otherwise returns false.

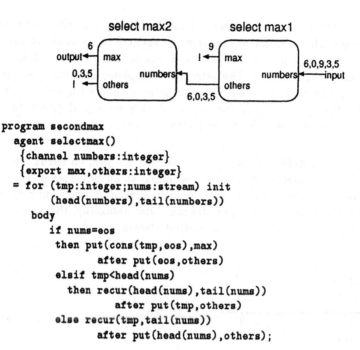

```
program secondmax
   agent selectmax()
   {channel numbers:integer}
   {export max,others:integer}
 = for (tmp:integer;nums:stream) init
        (head(numbers),tail(numbers))
     body
        if nums=eos
          then put(cons(tmp,eos),max)
                  after put(eos,others)
          elsif tmp<head(nums)
            then recur(head(nums),tail(nums))
                    after put(tmp,others)
          else recur(tmp,tail(nums))
                  after put(head(nums),others);

={form
  max1=create(selectmax){std_in}{!,strm1},
  max2=create(selectmax){strm1},{std_out,!}};
```

**Fig. 1.** An example of selecting the second maximum value from an integer stream.

## 2.3  Agent field

**Field** We can expect high performance with the programming of concurrent object-oriented style on parallel machine particularly if topology and communication of objects have some kind of regularity and compiler and runtime system can utilize the regularity. Logical structure and physical mapping of distributed data and concurrent objects, and communication topology are crucial in parallel processing. We can abstract an ensemble of agents and its topology description with "field," to write massively parallel programs, with a number of parallel entities, naturally reflecting their structures.

Followings are field definition and field instance creation:

```
field ⟨field-definition-name⟩(⟨agent-definition-parameters⟩)
      (⟨parameters-for-creation⟩) [ ⟨stream-interface⟩ ]
      [on ⟨structure-template⟩] [do ⟨specification⟩]
    = ⟨body-expression⟩

organize(⟨field-definition-name⟩,⟨agent-definition-name⟩[,⟨expression₁⟩ ...])
```

The ⟨agent-definition-name⟩ specifies a formal parameter to receive an agent definition name, whose instances organize the agent field. A field instance can have input and output streams and we can handle them like input and output stream of agent instance. The ⟨structure-template⟩ specifies basic topology of agent instances. Each agent instance in an agent field is indexed. When ⟨structure-template⟩ is omitted, field elements have no logical structure. Such an agent field is a set of merely indexed agent instances.

**Example of agent field** Following is an example of a field on torus template, consisting of agent comm4 with 4 input stream and an output stream. The agent comm4 repeats update of the own state by evaluating a function func with the current state and data from 4 input streams. Simultaneously, the agent comm4 repeatedly passes the new state to the output stream.

```
agent comm4(val:real)
{channel in1,in2,in3,in4: real}
{export out: real}
=for (v:real;count:integer;i1,i2,i3,i4:stream)
   init (val,0,in1,in2,in3,in4) body
   if count>=M then v
   else
   { slet put(v,out),
          next=func(head(i1),head(i2),
                   head(i3),head(i4))
     in recur(next,count+1,tail(i1),tail(i2),
                          tail(i3),tail(i4))};


field F(com4)(val:array of real; n:integer)
 on torus do connect4(n,n) ;
= foreach (i:integer) in ([1..n]) body
    foreach (j:integer) in ([1..n]) body
      create(com4,val[i][j]) ;
```

The connect4 in the ⟨specification⟩ means that the elements of this field communicate with their 4 neighbors. In this case of torus template, by specifying communications with 4 neighbors with up, down, right, left, connection pattern written as following program fragment can be specified in a brief description. This explicit description of communication pattern will also help the implementation to execute this program efficiently.

```
function connect4(m,n:integer;f:field)
 foreach (i:integer) in ([1..m]) body
  foreach (j:integer) in ([1..n]) body
   link(exOf[i,j],ch[1]Oup,ch[2]Oright,
           ch[3]Odown,ch[4]Oleft) ;
```

# 3    Compilation

Our compiler consists of a machine independent phase and a machine dependent phase. The machine independent phase generates a dataflow-based virtual machine code as an intermediate code. Then the machine dependent phase optimizes the intermediate code for each real target machine.

## 3.1    Intermediate Code

The intermediate code consists of Datarol[4] graph code and SST(Source level Structure Tree). Datarol reflects dataflows inherent in a source program. Datarol is an optimized data-flow code designed to remove redundant dataflows and to make code scheduling easy by introducing a concept of by-reference data access. Datarol instructions are similar to conventional three-address instructions, except that each instruction specifies its succeeding instructions explicitly. SST represents the source program structure and helps to determine the optimal grain size and code scheduling which can utilize the locality.

**Table 1.** Extracts from Datarol instructions

| instruction | semantics |
|---|---|
| op $r_{S1}$ $r_{S2}$ $r_D$ -> $D$ | conventional 3-address arithmetic and logical instructions |
| sw $r_{S1}$ -> $D_t$, $D_f$ | branch |
| call $r_{S1}$ $r_D$ -> $D$ | activate new instance |
| link $r_{S1}$ $r_{S2}$ slot | link $r_{S2}$ value to $r_{S1}$ |
| rlink $r_{S1}$ $r_D$ slot->$D$ | link $r_D$ address to $r_{S1}$ |
| receive $r_{S1}$ slot-> $D$ | receive parameter, $r_{S1}$ |
| return $r_{S1}$ $r_{S2}$ | return $r_{S2}$ value to $r_{S1}$ |
| rins | release current instance |

Table 1 shows the extracts from Datarol instruction set. Details of SST and synchronized memory access operations are omitted in this paper. A general Datarol instruction is expressed as

$l$: [*] op $r_{S1}$ $r_{S2}$ $r_D$ -> $D$

where $l$ is a label of this instruction and $D$, or continuation point, is a set of labels of instructions which should be executed successively. This instruction means that op operates on two operands $r_{S1}$ and $r_{S2}$, and stores the result in $r_D$ , which generally denotes a register name. The optional tag '*' ([] means the enclosed is optional.) indicates that a partner check is required for the instruction. The branch instruction SW transfers a control to continuation points $D_t$

or $D_f$ according to its boolean operand. Function application instructions are executed as split-phase transactions. In addition, to realize lenient execution, a process invocation request and the corresponding parameters are passed individually. A call instruction activates an instance of function specified by $r_{S1}$, and sets its instance name to $r_D$. A link instruction sends the value of $r_{S2}$ as the slot-th parameter to the instance specified by $r_{S1}$. An rlink instruction sends the current instance name and $r_D$ address as a continuation point. A receive instruction receives the slot-th value, stores it in $r_{S1}$, and triggers $D$. A return instruction returns the value of $r_{S2}$ to the continuation point $r_{S1}$ specified by the corresponding rlink in the parent instance. An rins instruction releases the instance.

## 3.2   Run-time Model for Conventional Multi-Processor

As conventional multi-processors have stock CPUs that exploit locality of computation to achieve high performance, direct mapping of fine grain DVMC to such machines is inefficient. We assume following run-time model that can utilize computational locality as well as fine grain parallelism.

Instance level parallelism is exploited by using a data structure, called frame, which is allocated to each function instance. Intra-instance parallelism is exploited as multi-thread parallel processing. Fig.2 shows the overview of a frame. The *variable slots* area is used to manipulate local data. The *thread stack* is provided in order to dynamically schedule intra-instance fine-grain threads. When a thread becomes ready to run, or a *ready thread*, the entry address of the thread is pushed into the stack. A processor executes instructions of a thread in a serial order until it reaches its termination point. If the execution of the current thread terminates, a ready thread is popped from the top of the thread stack for the next execution. A processor get a ready thread from a thread stack and execute the thread repeatedly. If ready threads are exhausted, the processor switches to another frame.

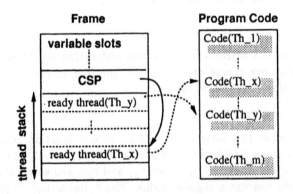

**Fig. 2.** Overview of a frame

As AP1000 does not support multi-thread execution, the compiler insert the code, which controls multi-thread execution according the patterns shown in Fig.3. Local Synchronized JUMP code(abbreviated as LSJ in the rest of this paper) is inserted when the last operation of a thread tries to activate another thread as shown in Fig.3(a). LSJ is a synchronized jump operation, and, in Fig.3(a), Th1 can pass the control Th2 if Th1 is the Th2's last predecessor which tries to activate Th2. If a thread, Th2, is activated by the operation in the middle of another thread as shown in Fig.3(b), Local Synchronized FORK(LSF) is inserted. LSF can make a thread "ready"(but does not pass the control immediately) in succeeding the synchronization. Message handler code, which handles the reply message from remote thread, is embedded in a thread at the point of split-phase operation, as shown in Fig.3(c).

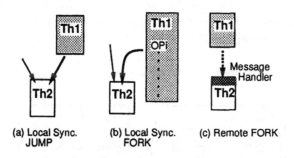

(a) Local Sync. JUMP     (b) Local Sync. FORK     (c) Remote FORK

**Fig. 3.** Execution controls between threads

Our implementation model is similar to Threaded Abstract Machine(TAM)[7]. TAM is also based on a thread-level dataflow model, and such dataflow graphs are constructed from Id programs. The execution model of TAM is an extension of a hybrid dataflow model. Our implementation also has its origin in an optimized dataflow, but it is an original one, Datarol[4], and our intermediate DVMC can be mapped onto the Datarol-II architecture.

The compiler partitions a Datarol graph at split-phase operation points, traces subgraphs along arcs in a depth-first way and rearranges nodes, in order to generate an efficient threaded code for conventional multi-processors. Since code scheduling strategy depends on the run-time costs of parallel processing of the target machine, the compiler uses machine dependent cost function to generate threaded code.

## 4   Implementation on a Distributed Memory Machine

On a distributed-memory machine, AP1000, an instance frame is created by using message passing. The message consists of data, PE ID, frame ID and thread ID of the target thread. Inter-PE Messages are stored in the system message buffer of the target node. Intra-PE Messages are stored in the local message buffer realized by software. When a PE finds that the current frame has no executable thread, the processor gets a message from its message buffers in the precedence of the local buffer over the global system buffer, and switches its context according to the message contents.

Fig.4 illustrates an example of a function invocation and message passing between two instance frames on different PE nodes. S1, ...,S4 and T0, ...,T2 represent thread labels. An arrow from a thread to another thread represents a message passing, and the contents of the message are shown with the arrow.

When PEi executes, GetFrame, an operation for instance creation(corresponding to a Datarol call operation) in the thread S1, one PE is selected to activate the new instance(In Fig.4, PEj is selected). An initializing thread, T0, is activated at the beginning of an instance creation. The initializing thread performs FrameAlloc to get a frame area. The address of the frame prepared in this execution is set into a message and sent back to the caller instance. This message tries to activate the threads S2.

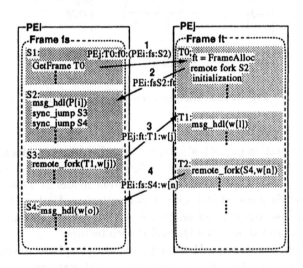

**Fig. 4.** Overview of inter-frame message passing

A remote_fork operation(corresponding to Datarol link operation) in the thread S3 will activate the thread T1. At the head of the thread T1, the message handler msg_hdl extracts the data from the message and stores it in the slots of the frame. Concurrently, S3 may proceed its computation and activate some threads successively. A return value is returned in a similar way from T2 in the callee frame to S4 in the caller frame.

# 5  Performance

## 5.1  Fine grain parallel processing

We report a preliminary performance evaluation of V on the AP1000 using 1 to 64 processors. Table 2 shows the elapsed time in seconds for the V and C programs, and the relative speedups of V programs compared with C programs. The C programs are written using the same algorithms as the V programs.

**Table 2.** Time comparisons of V (64CPUs) and C(1CPU).

| Program | Time (sec.) | | Speedup |
|---|---|---|---|
| | V | C | |
| | 64cpus | 1cpu | |
| sum(1, $10^6$) | 0.0385 | 1.47 | 38.1 |
| matrix(512) | 10.2 | 558 | 54.8 |
| nqueen(10) | 1.57 | 55.6 | 35.5 |

Fig.5 shows the speedups of V programs relative to the number of processors for each benchmark program. In the graph, the horizontal axis shows the number of used processors, the vertical axis the speedup, and the linear proportion line the ideal speedup.

As the AP1000 does not have special hardware, a sophisticated compilation technique is necessary for the lenient execution of a fine grain parallel language such as V. Our naive implementation showed that overheads of fine grain parallel processing are critical. We examined the cost of our runtime system, focusing on the cost-hierarchy compilation, especially trying to reduce the frequency of communication and to exploit locality. Fig.6 shows an improvement in the speed-up ratio for the 'nqueen' program. From Fig.6, we can conclude that a sophisticated exploitation of parallelism makes fine grain parallel language such as V feasible on stock parallel machine.

## 5.2  agent and field

We compare the cost of message passing communication and connected stream communication. As an example, we compare the number of the assembler instructions for a thread activation, including message construction in the sender instance, message queuing and dequeuing in the receiver instance. The number of the assembler instructions of connected stream communication is reduce to 84% compared with that of message passing communication.

In addition, information of stream connection enables implementation to map the partner instances onto the physically close location. In the special case, connected stream communication also enables efficient implementation of no buffering communication like message-oriented implementation of GHC[13].

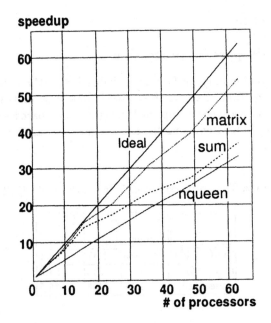

**Fig. 5.** Speedup graphs for V programs on AP1000

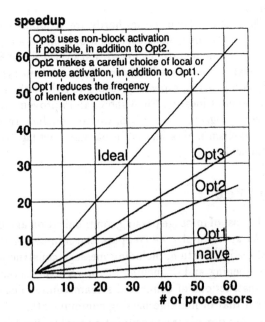

**Fig. 6.** Speedup improvement('nqueen').

We evaluate the effectiveness of exploitation of the explicit description using field, which expresses logical structure of the problem, using the example shown in section 2. We show the elapsed time in seconds in the Fig.7 using three types of mapping strategy: random mapping, 1-dimensional block clustering and square clustering, to compare the performance with/without the intelligent mapping exploiting the regularity of topology and communication.

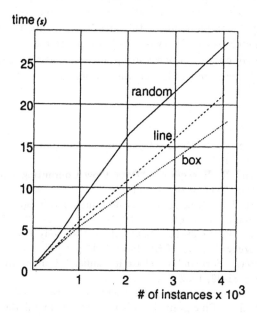

**Fig. 7.** Effect of instance mapping of a field whose agent instances communicate with four neighbors on **torus** template.

Elapsed times are random>line>box. The more number of instances there exist, the more the differences of elapsed time between three strategies increases. This shows the effectiveness of exploitation of the logical structure of the program.

## 6  Conclusion

We proposed a dataflow-based massively parallel programming language V, which minimizes the conceptual difficulties in writing massively parallel program. V has both merits of functional programming language and object-oriented programming language. We introduced object-oriented abstraction, *agent* to write concurrent processes naturally because object-oriented programming is appropriate in expressing problems in terms of communicating entities. Moreover, we introduced *field* which abstracts an ensemble of agents and its topology description in order to write massively parallel programs which reflect structure of problems naturally.

As V has its basis on a functional programming language originally designed for a dataflow architecture, it is easy to extract parallelism of various level. Implementation issues for the Sequent Symmetry and the Fujitsu AP1000 were discussed. Our implementations extract fine-grain parallel threads and schedule them to exploit as much parallelism as target machines provide. Our message-flow computation based on the dataflow computation scheme can be implemented effectively by implementing the message passing between in a similar way to the parameter passing between function instances. An agent instance is implemented as a concurrent process using a frame. Intra-instance parallelism is realized as multi-threads scheduled on the frame.

# References

1. G.A. Agha : "Actors: A Model of Concurrent Computation in Distributed Systems", MIT Press, 1986.
2. M. Amamiya and R. Hasegawa : "Data Flow Computing and Eager and Lazy Evaluations", New Generation Computing, Vol.2, p.p.105-129, 1984.
3. M. Amamiya, et al. : "*Valid*: A High-Level Functional Programming Language for Data Flow Machine", Rev. ECL, Vol.32, No.5, p.p.793-802, NTT, 1984.
4. M.Amamiya, and R.Taniguchi : "Datarol: A Massively Parallel Architecture for Functional Language", Proc. IEEE 2nd SPDP, p.p.726-735, 1990.
5. D.C. Cann : "Retire Fortran? A Debate Rekindled", Communications of the ACM, Vol.35, No.8, p.p.81-89, 1992.
6. A.A. Chien : "Concurrent Aggregates." The MIT Press, 1993.
7. D.E. Culler et al. : "Fine-grain Parallelism with Minimal Hardware Support: A Compiler-Controlled Threaded Abstract Machine" Proc. of 4th ASPLOS, 1991
8. R.E. Filman and D.P. Friedman : "Coordinated Computing", MIT Press, 1984.
9. C.A.R. Hoare : "Communicating sequential processes", Communications of the ACM, Vol.21, No.8, p.p.666-677, 1978.
10. T. Kawano et al. : "Datarol-II: A Fine-Grain Massively Parallel Architecture" Proc of PARLE'94, pp.781-784, 1994.
11. B. Meyer : "Object-Oriented Software Construction", , Interactive Software Engineering, 1988.
12. E. Takahashi et al. : "Compiling Technique Based on Dataflow Analysis for Functional Programming Language *Valid*", Proc. of SISAL'93, pp.47-58, 1993.
13. Ueda, K. and Morita, M. : Message-Oriented Parallel Implementation of Moded Flat GHC, Proc. of Int'l. Conf. on Fifth Generation Computing Systems 1992, pp.799-808, 1992.
14. A. Yonezawa, editor: "ABCL: An Object-Oriented Concurrent System – Theory, Language, Programming, Implementation and Application" The MIT Press, 1990.
15. A.Yonezawa and M.Tokoro : "Object-Oriented Concurrent Programming", MIT Press, 1987.

# Programming with Distributed Data Structure for EM-X Multiprocessor

Mitsuhisa SATO[1], Yuetsu KODAMA[1], Hirofumi SAKANE[1]
Shuichi SAKAI[2], Yoshinori YAMAGUCHI[1] and Satoshi SEKIGUCHI[1]

[1] Electrotechnical Laboratory
1-1-4 Umezono, Tsukuba, Ibaraki 305, Japan
[2] Real World Computing Partnership, Tsukuba Research Center

**Abstract.** The EM-X, a new generation of EM-4, is a distributed memory multiprocessor which has a dataflow mechanism. The dataflow mechanism enables a fine-grain communication packet through the network to invoke and synchronize the thread of control dynamically with very small overhead. In this paper, we present programming with a distributed data structure shared by threads, and its implementation for the EM-X multiprocessor. Threads may communicate and coordinate by leaving data in a global address space. A new distributed data structure, called the Q-structure, is introduced. This can be used as a shared queue in the context of thread-based programming in the parallel programming language EM-C. We also discuss related distributed data structures including Linda'a tuple space, synchronizing data structure in the dataflow computation model.

## 1 Introduction

The EM-X[6], a new generation of EM-4[9], is a distributed memory multiprocessor which has a dataflow mechanism. Dataflow processors are designed to directly send and dispatch small fixed-size messages to and from the network. Those messages are interpreted as "dataflow tokens", which carry a word of data and a continuation to synchronize and invoke the destination thread in another processor. The dataflow mechanism allows multiple threads of control to be created and efficiently interact. In the EM-X, network messages can also be interpreted as fine-grain operations, such as remote memory reads and writes in a distributed memory environment. Remote memory access operations can be thought of as invoking a fine-grain thread to reference memory in a different processor.

EM-C[10] is a parallel extension of the C programming language designed for efficient parallel programming in the EM-X multiprocessor. In EM-C, parallelism and synchronization of threads of sequential execution are described explicitly by the programmer. From the viewpoint of an executing sequential thread, the EM-X can be thought of as a memory-distributed multi-processor: each PE has its own local memory, and threads in the PE operate on the local memory. As a multi-threaded processor, each PE may have many sequential threads of control. To express parallelism explicitly, a set of operations and parallel constructs is provided to fork a new thread, send/receive messages between threads and share data by remote memory access.

EM-C also provides the notion of a *global address space* which spans the local memory of all processors. Using fine-grain remote read/write messages, the language supports direct access to remote shared data in a different processor.

In this paper, we present a distributed data structure called the Extended I-structure or Q-structure for thread-based programming in the EM-X, together with its implementation. We use the term "distributed data structure" to refer to a data structure that is directly accessible by many threads. This term was introduced in the parallel computation model, Linda. Our distributed data structure provides a restricted form of Linda's tuple space. From the viewpoint of thread-based programming, the Q-structure is used as the communication channel between threads. The feature of the Q-structure is that it allows its elements to be exclusively accessed to its element by different threads. From the viewpoint of the data flow architecture, the set of operations defined for the Q-structure is the same as the extended I-structure, formerly referred to a "the restricted I-structure"[11] proposed by the SIGMA-1 group at ETL, and implemented in SIGMA-1's structure elements (SE) unit. The I-structure and M-structure in the functional programming languages, Id, can be regarded as a kind of distributed data structure. We describe these structures in the context of thread-based programming, rather than in the context of functional programming. EM-X provides effective architectural support for the distributed data structure in thread-based programming.

In Section 2, we first present the EM-X architecture and runtime structure of EM-C programs. Section 3 describes our distributed data structure and its programming. The implementation details for EM-4 and EM-X are described in Section 4. In Section 5, we discuss related work. Section 6 is a brief conclusion.

## 2　The EM-X multiprocessor

### 2.1　Architecture

The EM-X and EM-4 are parallel hybrid dataflow/von Neumann multiprocessors developed in Electrotechnical Laboratory. The EM-X consists of single chip processing elements, EMC-Y, which is connected via a Circular Omega Network. EM-X is a distributed memory multiprocessor; each processing element has its own local memory. The EMC-Y is a RISC-style processor suitable for fine-grain parallel processing. The EMC-Y pipeline is designed to fuse register-based RISC execution with packet-based dataflow execution for synchronization and message handling support. The architecture of the EM-X including its instruction sets, clock and network interface is improved in order to achieve higher parallel performance than that of the EM-4.

All communication is done with small fixed-sized packets. The EMC-Y can generate and dispatch packets directly to and from the network, and it has hardware support to handle the queuing and scheduling of these packets.

Packets arrive from the network and are buffered in the packet queue. As a packet is read from the packet queue, a thread of computation specified by the address portion of the packet is instantiated along with the one word data. The thread then runs to its completion, and any live state in the thread may be saved to an activation frame associated with the thread. The completion of a thread causes the next packet to be automatically dequeued and interpreted from the packet queue. Thus, we call this an *explicit-switch thread*. Network packets can be interpreted as dataflow tokens. Dataflow tokens have the option of *matching* with another token on arrival — unless both tokens have arrived, the token will save itself in memory and cause the next packet to be processed. Each word has a seven-bit tag for storing matching status and data types.

For remote memory access, we use the packet address as a *global address* rather than specifying a thread. A global address consists of the processor number and the local address in the processor. The remote memory read generates a remote memory read packet, and terminates the thread. The remote read packet contains a continuation to return the value, as well as a global address. The result of the remote memory read packet is sent containing the value at the global address to the continuation which will receive the value. The remote memory write generates a remote memory write packet, which contains a global address and the value to be written. The thread does not terminate when the remote write message is sent. The EM-X provides two types of hardware support for remote memory access [7]. First, the remote memory access packet is handled in parallel with instruction execution. And the remote memory access is done with higher priority than other types of packets to reduce the latency of remote memory access.

The interpretation of packets can also be defined in software. On the arrival of a particular type of packet, the associated system-defined handler can be executed. This mechanism is used for allocating activation frames remotely.

In the EMC-Y processor, incoming packets are queued and served in FIFO (first-in first-out) order. Any communication does not interrupt the execution. Threads switch explicitly at a function call and return.

## 2.2 Runtime Structure of EM-C

EM-C is a parallel extension of the C language designed for EM-4/X. The current compiler compiles the program into several explicit-switch threads. The EM-X recognizes two storage resources, namely, the code segments and the operand segments (activation frames). The compiled codes of functions are stored in code segments. Invoking a function involves allocating an operand segment as the activation frame. The code segment is linked to associate codes with its activation frame, as shown in Figure 1. A continuation or an entry point is represented as an address in the activation frame. A packet invokes a thread which executes the code associated to the activation frame. The argument values are stored into locations within the frame. The caller allocates the activation frame, depositing the argument values into the frame, and sends its continuation as a packet to invoke the callee's thread. Then it terminates, explicitly causing a context-switch.

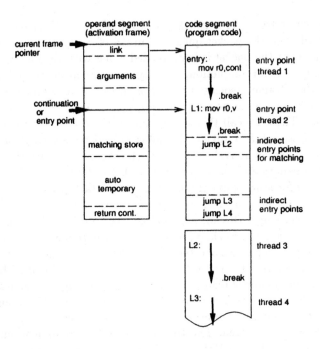

**Fig. 1.** Activation frame structure in EM-C

The first instruction of a thread operates on input tokens, which are loaded into two *operand registers.* The registers cannot be used to hold computation state across threads. The caller saves any live registers to the current activation frame before context-switch. The continuation sent from the caller is used for returning the result, as the return address in a conventional call. The result from the called function resumes the caller's thread by this continuation.

This calling sequence can be easily extended to call a function in a different processor remotely. When the caller forks a function as an independent thread, it is not suspended after calling the function. When using the parallel extension in EM-C, an executing thread may invoke several threads concurrently in other activation frames. Therefore, the set of activation frames form a tree rather than a stack, reflecting the dynamic calling structure, illustrated in Figure 2. All activation frames are fixed-size, and free frames are managed in a linked-list.

## 3  Distributed Data structure with the EM-X

In this section, we describe a set of operations on our distributed data structure in EM-C. Threads in a program may communicate and coordinate by leaving and removing data in the distributed data structure. We describe these operations on the distributed data structure as C built-in functions, which are expanded in-line into a few instructions at compile time.

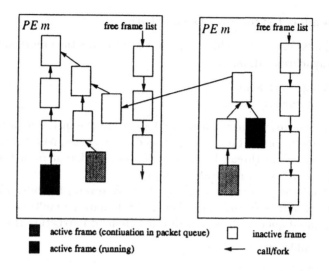

active frame (contiuation in packet queue) □ inactive frame

active frame (running) ← call/fork

**Fig. 2.** Runtime Structure in EM-C

## 3.1 Global Address Space in EM-C

In EM-C, data objects are allocated at the same local address as local objects in each PE as the default. Since all accesses to such objects are local, access can proceed without interference or delay.

EM-C provides a global address space and allows data in that space to be referenced through *global pointers*. A *global pointer* represents a global address, and is declared by the quantifier global to the pointer declaration:

```
int global *gp;
```

A global pointer may be constructed by casting a local pointer to a global pointer. The same object is referenced by different PEs through the global pointer. The compiler generates remote memory access code for the memory reference with the global pointer. Arithmetic on global pointers is performed on its local address while the processor address remains unchanged.

In EM-C programs, a new thread is created by the operation fork.

```
void fork(pe_addr,func,n,arg1,...,argn)
```

where pe_addr is a global address that specifies the PE where the new thread is executed. The created thread starts executing a given function with the following arguments. When the main function is returned, the thread being executed disappears. A thread can notify its termination by leaving data in the distributed data structure rather than executing a "JOIN" instruction.

## 3.2 Extended I-structure: Q-structure

For any address in a global address space, EM-C allows the programmer to access data with synchronization.

```
I_write(global_addr,word)
word = I_read(global_addr)
```

If a word has not yet been written by I_write at the specified location, I_read blocks the execution of the current thread. The subsequent I_write resumes the execution of the thread blocked by I_read. Different from the original I-structure[1], our I_read removes the data.

We extend the I-structure to share data by several threads. The structure memory at g_addr may contain either multiple data or multiple continuations in the associated queue. Thus, we call this extended I-structure the *Q-structure*.

```
Q_out(g_addr,word)
word = Q_in(g_addr)
```

Q_in is blocked until data is written by Q_out. Multiple Q_in operations also block the calling threads. The continuations of these threads are stored in the queue. Q_out resumes the corresponding waiting threads. The data written by Q_out is returned to the caller of Q_in. If multiple threads are blocked in Q_in, only the first thread is resumed and the remaining threads are still blocked in the waiting queue. If the memory already contains data, data written by multiple Q_out are buffered in the associated queue. Although this set of operations is similar to the operations on the M-structure of MIT, we developed these operations in the context of thread-based programming. For example, multiple Q_out operations allow structure memory to be used as a communication channel between threads.

```
word = Q_read(g_addr)
```

Q_read reads the data at g_addr, but does not get rid of the data. If the structure memory contains no data, Q_read blocks the calling thread as Q_in.

## 3.3 Q-structure with key

The Q-structure described above maps the distributed data structure to global address space. To support sparse distributed data structures, we introduce *Q-structure with key*, which associates data in the queue with a key.

```
Q_out_with_key(g_addr,key,word)
word=Q_in_with_key(g_addr,key)
word=Q_read_with_key(g_addr,key)
```

Q_out_with_key puts word with key key into the structure memory at g_addr. Q_in_with_key takes data associated with the given key from the queue. If such data is not found, Q_in_with_key blocks the calling thread, and its continuation is stored in the queue with the key. When data with the key is put by Q_out_with_key, the waiting thread is resumed, and returns with the data.

```
Q_out_with_any(g_addr,word)
word=Q_in_with_any(g_addr,&key)
word=Q_read_with_any(g_addr,&key)
```

These operations are the same as those of Q_out_with_key, Q_in_with_key and Q_read_with_key except that these operations match any key. For Q_in_with_key and Q_read_with_key, the key is returned with its data.

This example of *delay statment* uses the Q-structure with keys. While the Q-structure maps data structure into a global address space, we have to use keys of the Q-structure when the data structure to be mapped is unknown or sparse. The clock process (or thread) executes the following statement:

```
time_t global *clock;
```

```
Q_in_with_any(clock,&now);
Q_out_with_key(clock,now+1,0);
```

To read the clock, any thread can execute:

```
Q_read_with_any(clock,&now);
```

The function delay(d) delays the calling threads for (at least d) time units.

```
delay(d){
    int now;
    Q_in_with_any(clock,&now);
    Q_read_with_key(clock,now+d);
}
```

## 3.4  Fork operations for Distributed Data Structure

For a distributed data structure, the fork operation is extened by combining with the associated write operations to return the result of the forked function. The following fork operations create a new threads that store the return value of the function into the distributed data structure.

```
I_fork(g_addr,pe_addr,func,narg,arg1,...)
Q_fork(g_addr,pe_addr,func,narg,arg1,...)
Q_fork_with_key(g_addr,key,pe_addr,func,arg1,...)
```

where g_addr specifies the structure memory address. The new thread is executed in the PE specified by pe_addr, and terminated when the return value of func is "out"ed. If pe_addr is NULL, the thread is executed in the same PE as that where the structure memory is located,

These functions are useful for the live-data-structure program[3]. The live data structure is one of Linda's programming methods[3]: each element of this data structure is implicitly a separate process, which becomes a data object upon terminating. To communicate, they simply "refer" to each other as elements of some data structure. The following example, taken from Linda's programming, finds the prime numbers:

```
main()
{   int i;
    for(i = 2; i <= N; i++){
        Q_fork(prime_gaddr(i),NULL,is_prime,1,i);
    }
    .....
}

int is_prime(i)
{   int k,n;
    n = sqrt((double)i)+1;
    for(k = 2; k < n; k++)
        if(Q_read(prime_gaddr(i)) && (i%k == 0)) return FALSE;
    return TRUE;
}
```

The local function prime_gaddr maps the given number to the global address at which the result are stored.

A thread, after forking other remote operations, may continue to other work and waits at the distributed data structure to be 'outed' after the operations complete. The following simple example computes the fibonacci number:

```
fib(n)
{   int t1,t2;
    if(n <= 2) return(1);
    else {
        I_fork((global *)&t1,NEXT1,fib,1,n-1);
        I_fork((global *)&t2,NEXT2,fib,1,n-2);
      return(I_read((global *)&t1)+I_read((global *)&t2));
    }
}
```

Here, the variables NEXT1 and NEXT2 contains the addresses of the neighbor PEs in EM-X's Omega network.

## 4   Implementation Details

The system-defined handler plays an important role in implementing the distributed data structure in EM-4. The operations on the distributed data structure send the special packet to invoke the associated system-defined handler. In EM-4 and EM-X, every memory word has an additional tag field to store the synchronization status.

For a read (in) operation, the address part specifies the global address and whose data part specifies the current continuation. Then, the calling thread suspends until the packet from the handler resumes the thread. The read handler fetches the word at the location specified by the address part. If any data has not yet been stored, the continuation in the packet data part is stored in that location. Note that the continuation in EM-4/X is represented in one word. If other continuations have been already stored, the continuation is managed in a queue associated with that location in case of the Q-structure. If data exists at the location, that data is taken from the location to send to the continuation.

A write (out) operation sends the packet whose address part specifies the global address and whose data part specifies the data. The write handler fetches the word at the location specified by address part. If any continuations has not yet been stored yet, the data in the packet is stored at that location. If other data has already been stored, that data is managed in a queue associated with that location in case of Q-structure. If a continuation exists at the location, the continuation is taken from the location to invoke the waiting thread along with data.

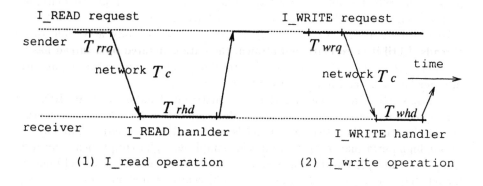

**Fig. 3.** Timing diagram of I_read and I_write

Figure 3 shows the timing diagram for I_read, I_write operations. In current EM-4 implementation, I_read and I_write requests take $T_{rrq} = 1$ cycle and $T_{wrq} = 4$ cycles respectively. $T_c$ is the time to transmit the packet through the network. The in operation handler takes $T_{rhd} = 8$ cycles if data already exists, otherwise 7 cycles. The write operation handler takes $T_{whd} = 8$ cycles if a readers already waits, otherwise 11 cycles. The Q-structure operations may take additional time to manage the queue if required. Note that the time for context switch is zero due to dataflow mechanism.

The EM-X provides hardware support for I-structure operations. The EM-X allows matching operations for the special packets to invoke the system-defined handler. It can be used to match the reader's packet and writer's packet at any location. The packet generation instructions are enhanced so that I_read and I_write requests take $T_{rrq} = 2$ cycles and $T_{wrq} = 1$ cycles respectively. Because matching operations can be executed in parallel with instruction execution, $T_{rhd}$ and $T_{whd}$ become zero unless both reader and writer have arrived. In this case, a continuation or data will be automatically saved by hardware. When both are arrived, the system handler is invoked to send the data to the continuation. So $T_{rhd}$ and $T_{whd}$ are only one cycle. To support Q-structure access, multiple writes or multiple reads causes a hardware exception to handle in software.

The other way to implement the operation is by using the remote procedure call. To call the function in other PEs, it needs to allocate the operand segment before passing arguments. Since more than three arguments cannot be passed to the handler by a packet and only one value is returned, some operations for the Q-structure with key are implemented by using the remote procedure call.

## 5 Related Work

Our Q-structure provides a restricted form of Linda's tuple space. As the computation environment "tuple space"(TS) provides the basis for Linda's communication model, the global address space is used as the communication environment of our computation model using distributed data structure. As in Linda, distributed data structure in global address space is equally accessible to all threads. Until it is explicitly withdrawn, the data generated by a thread has an independent existence, and is bounded to none. Data is exchanged in the form of a persistent object, not a transient message.

Linda's TS is more general than our distributed data structure. It is not concerned with processor allocation or data allocation for tuples. When using the Q-structure, the programmer needs to consider these issues explicitly to obtain high performance. Q-structures are simple enough to implement efficiently using the EM-4/X dataflow mechanism. Linda is inherently a shared-memory model. Supporting it in the absence of physically shared memory requires a coherence mechanism. Although TS has been implemented in software on many conventional multiprocessor, the Linda kernel will spend large amounts of time for communication.

In dataflow computation model, many types of synchronized data structure was proposed. Many of these come from in the context of functional programming languages. These structure memory data is assumed to be automatically reclaimed by the garbage collection in the language system. The I-structure[1] limits one writer to the same address. Multiple read operations can wait the data written by the writer. The M-structure was originally designed for making histograms in parallel. The major difference from the I-structure is that the write operation resumes a suspended read operation. This structure is found as Mutex-structure in [2].

Comparing with the M-structure, the Q-structure has a queue for written data. In addition to the functionality of the M-structure, this structure is also effective to implement the producer / consumer type synchronization mechanism, as described in this paper. This distributed structure can often be used for the task bag structure for load balancing.

The Q-structure operations are the same as that of Extended I-structure on the SIGMA-1, and similar to the operations on M-structure. Also it does not suspend the write operation. A precise definition of the operation of this structure is given in [11] as the restricted I-structure. This gives a detailed definition of access operations at the viewpoint of the data flow architecture.

In many parallel languages, the related synchronization mechanisms are proposed. Multilisp's *future*[5] enables synchronization points to be carried as a value, while our distributed data structure associates synchronization with the global address. The split-phase assignment in Split-C[4], and the join cells in Cid[8] support split-phase operations to wait for remote operations to complete. These mechanisms use a counter to synchronize with remote operations.

# 6   Conclusion

In this paper, we have proposed a distributed data structure that can be shared by several threads. The dataflow mechanism of the EM-X allows efficient implementation of the operations on the distributed data structure. The EM-C runtime structure is designed to enable threads to be created and managed efficiently in the EM-X architecture. Using the distributed data structure in EM-C, a programmer can create and coordinate multiple threads in thread-based programming. It also allows a programmer to control parallelism and data distribution in global address space of the EM-X. Different from the structure memory proposed in functional programming language, its can be used as parallel data structures such as the communication channels between threads and the task bag for load balancing.

## Acknowledgements

We wish to thank Dr. Ohta, Director of the Computer Science Division of ETL for supporting this research, and also thank the staff of the Computer Architecture Section for their fruitful discussion.

## References

1. Arvind, Rishiyur S. Nikhil, and Keshav K Pingali. I-structures: Data structures for parallel computing. *ACM Transactions on Programming Languages and Systems*, 11(4):598–632, October 1989.
2. Paul Barth, Rishiyur S. Nikhil, and Arvind. M-structures: Extending a parallel, non-strict, functional language with state. In *Proc. Functional Programming and Computer Architecture, Cambridge, MA, Springer Verlag LNCS 523*, pages 538–568, August 28-30 1991. Also: CSG Memo 327, March 1991, MIT Laboratory for Computer Science 545 Technology Square, Cambridge, MA 02139, USA.
3. N. Carriero and David Gelernter. How to Write Parallel Programs: A guide to the Perplexed. *ACM Computing Surveys*, 21(3):323–357, 1989.
4. D. E. Culler, A. Dusseau, S. G. Goldstein, S. Lumetta T. von Eicken, and K. Yelick. Parallel Programming in Split-C. In *Proc. of Supercomputing '93*, Nov. 1993.

5. R.H. Halstead. Multilisp: A Language for Concurrent Symbolic Computation. *ACM Trans. on Prog. Lang. and Sys.*, 7(4):501–539, 1985.

6. Y. Kodama, Y. Koumuara, M. Sato, H. Sakane, S. Sakai, and Y. Yamaguchi. EMC-Y: Parallel Processing Element Optimizing Communication and Computation. In *Proc. of 1993 ACM International Conference on Supercomputing*, pages 167–174, 1993.

7. Y. Kodama, Y. Koumuara, M. Sato, H. Sakane, S. Sakai, and Y. Yamaguchi. Message-based Efficient Remote Memory Access on a Highly Parallel Copmuter EM-X. In *Proc. of International Symp. on Parallel Architectures, Algorithms and Networks (ISPAN)*, Kanazawa, Japan, 1994.

8. R. S. Nikhil. Cid: A Parallel, Shared-MemoryČ for Distributed-memory Machine. In *Proc. of 7th Annual Workshop Language and Compilers for Parallel Computing*, Ithaca, NY, Aug. 1994.

9. S. Sakai, Y. Yamaguchi, K. Hiraki, Y. Kodama, and T. Yuba. An Architecture of a Dataflow Single Chip Processor. In *Proc. of the 16th Annual International Symposium on Computer Architecture*, pages 46–53, June 1989.

10. M. Sato, Y. Kodama, S. Sakai, and Y. Yamaguchi. EM-C: EM-C: Programming with Explicit Parallelism and Locality for EM-4 Multiprocessor. In *Proc. of the 1994 Parallel Archtectures and Compilation Technique (IFIP Transactions A-50)*, pages 3–14, Aug. 1994.

11. Satoshi Sekiguchi, Toshio Shimada, and Kei Hiraki. Sequential description and parallel execution language DFC II for dataflow supercomputers. In *Proc. of 1991 International Conference on Supercomputing, Cologne, Germany*, pages 57–66, June 17-21 1991.

# List of Workshop Participants

| | |
|---|---|
| Makoto Amamiya | Kyushu University |
| Kenichi Asai | University of Tokyo |
| Manfred Broy | Technishe Universitaet Muenchen |
| Robert H. Halstead, Jr. | DEC Cambridge Research Lab |
| Naofumi Harada | Tohoku University |
| Kohei Honda | Keio University |
| Yutaka Ishikawa | Real World Computing Partnership |
| Takayasu Ito | Tohoku University |
| Suresh Jagannathan | NEC Princeton Research Institute |
| Tomio Kamada | University of Tokyo |
| Max Kanovich | Tohoku University |
| Shin-ichi Kawamoto | Tohoku University |
| Shigetomo Kimura | Tohoku University |
| Naoki Kobayashi | University of Tokyo |
| Hiroki Konaka | Real World Computing Partnership |
| Satoshi Matsuoka | University of Tokyo |
| Susumu Nishimura | Kyoto University |
| Atsushi Ohori | Kyoto University |
| Benjamin Pierce | Edinburgh University |
| Vaughan Pratt | Stanford University |
| Christian Queinnec | Ecole Polytechnique |
| John H. Reppy | AT&T Bell Laboratories |
| Takahiro Saito | Tohoku University |
| Mitsuhisa Sato | Electro Technichal Laboratory |
| Ichiro Satoh | Keio University |
| Kenji Takahashi | Tohoku University |
| Junichi Tatemura | University of Tokyo |
| Kenjiro Taura | University of Tokyo |
| Atsushi Togashi | Tohoku University |
| Tomohito Uchida | Tohoku University |
| Kazunori Ueda | Waseda University |
| Tetsuya Ujiie | Tohoku University |
| Masayoshi Umehara | Tohoku University |
| Nobuyuki Usui | Tohoku University |
| Ken Wakita | Tokyo Institute of Technology |
| Ken-ichi Yamazaki | NTT |
| Akinori Yonezawa | University of Tokyo |
| Nobuko Yoshida | Keio University |
| Norihiko Yoshida | Kyushu University |
| Sen Yoshida | Tohoku University |
| Taiichi Yuasa | Toyohashi University of Technology |

Vol. 881: P. Loucopoulos, P. Constantopoulos (Eds.),
Entity-Relationship Approach — ER '94. Proceedings, 1994.
XIII, 579 pages. 1994.

Vol. 882: D. Hutchison, A. Danthine, H. Leopold, G.
Coulson (Eds.), Multimedia Transport and Teleservices.
Proceedings, 1994. XI, 380 pages. 1994.

Vol. 883: L. Fribourg, F. Turini (Eds.), Logic Program
Synthesis and Transformation — Meta-Programming in
Logic. Proceedings, 1994. IX, 451 pages. 1994.

Vol. 884: J. Nievergelt, T. Roos, H.-J. Schek, P. Widmayer
(Eds.), IGIS '94: Geographic Information Systems.
Proceedings, 1994. VIII, 292 pages. 1994.

Vol. 885: R. C. Veltkamp, Closed Object Boundaries from
Scattered Points. VIII, 144 pages. 1994.

Vol. 886: M. M. Veloso, Planning and Learning by
Analogical Reasoning. XIII, 181 pages. 1994.

Vol. 887: M. Toussaint (Ed.), Ada in Europe. Proceedings,
1994. XII, 521 pages. 1994.

Vol. 888: S. A. Andersson (Ed.), Analysis of Dynamical
and Cognitive Systems. Proceedings, 1993. VII, 260 pages.
1995.

Vol. 889: H. P. Lubich, Towards a CSCW Framework for
Scientific Cooperation in Europe. X, 144 pages. 1995.

Vol. 890: M. J. Wooldridge, N. R. Jennings (Eds.),
Intelligent Agents. Proceedings, 1994. VIII, 407 pages.
1995. (Subseries LNAI).

Vol. 891: C. Lewerentz, T. Lindner (Eds.), Formal
Development of Reactive Systems. XI, 394 pages. 1995.

Vol. 892: K. Pingali, U. Banerjee, D. Gelernter, A.
Nicolau, D. Padua (Eds.), Languages and Compilers for
Parallel Computing. Proceedings, 1994. XI, 496 pages.
1995.

Vol. 893: G. Gottlob, M. Y. Vardi (Eds.), Database Theory
— ICDT '95. Proceedings, 1995. XI, 454 pages. 1995.

Vol. 856: A. Oberweis, Modellierung und Ausführung
von Workflows mit Petri-Netzen. (to be published).

Vol. 857: G. Tel, P. Vitányi (Eds.), Distributed Algorithms.
Proceedings, 1994. X, 370 pages. 1994.

Vol. 858: E. Bertino, S. Urban (Eds.), Object-Oriented
Methodologies and Systems. Proceedings, 1994. X, 386
pages. 1994.

Vol. 859: T. F. Melham, J. Camilleri (Eds.), Higher Order
Logic Theorem Proving and Its Applications. Proceedings,
1994. IX, 470 pages. 1994.

Vol. 860: W. L. Zagler, G. Busby, R. R. Wagner (Eds.),
Computers for Handicapped Persons. Proceedings, 1994.
XX, 516 pages. 1994.

Vol. 861: B. Nebel, L. Dreschler-Fischer (Eds.), KI-94:
Advances in Artificial Intelligence. Proceedings, 1994. IX,
401 pages. 1994. (Subseries LNAI).

Vol. 862: R. C. Carrasco, J. Oncina (Eds.), Grammatical
Inference and Applications. Proceedings, 1994. VIII, 290
pages. 1994. (Subseries LNAI).

Vol. 863: H. Langmaack, W.-P. de Roever, J. Vytopil
(Eds.), Formal Techniques in Real-Time and Fault-Tolerant
Systems. Proceedings, 1994. XIV, 787 pages. 1994.

Vol. 864: B. Le Charlier (Ed.), Static Analysis.
Proceedings, 1994. XII, 465 pages. 1994.

Vol. 865: T. C. Fogarty (Ed.), Evolutionary Computing.
Proceedings, 1994. XII, 332 pages. 1994.

Vol. 866: Y. Davidor, H.-P. Schwefel, R. Männer (Eds.),
Parallel Problem Solving from Nature — PPSN III. Proceedings, 1994. XV, 642 pages. 1994.

# Lecture Notes in Computer Science

For information about Vols. 1–831
please contact your bookseller or Springer-Verlag

Vol 867: L. Steels, G. Schreiber, W. Van de Velde (Eds.), A Future for Knowledge Acquisition. Proceedings, 1994. XII, 414 pages. 1994. (Subseries LNAI).

Vol. 868: R. Steinmetz (Ed.), Multimedia: Advanced Teleservices and High-Speed Communication Architectures. Proceedings, 1994. IX, 451 pages. 1994.

Vol. 869: Z. W. Raś, Zemankova (Eds.), Methodologies for Intelligent Systems. Proceedings, 1994. X, 613 pages. 1994. (Subseries LNAI).

Vol. 870: J. S. Greenfield, Distributed Programming Paradigms with Cryptography Applications. XI, 182 pages. 1994.

Vol. 871: J. P. Lee, G. G. Grinstein (Eds.), Database Issues for Data Visualization. Proceedings, 1993. XIV, 229 pages. 1994.

Vol. 872: S Arikawa, K. P. Jantke (Eds.), Algorithmic Learning Theory. Proceedings, 1994. XIV, 575 pages. 1994.

Vol. 873: M. Naftalin, T. Denvir, M. Bertran (Eds.), FME '94: Industrial Benefit of Formal Methods. Proceedings, 1994. XI, 723 pages. 1994.

Vol. 874: A. Borning (Ed.), Principles and Practice of Constraint Programming. Proceedings, 1994. IX, 361 pages. 1994.

Vol. 875: D. Gollmann (Ed.), Computer Security – ESORICS 94. Proceedings, 1994. XI, 469 pages. 1994.

Vol. 876: B. Blumenthal, J. Gornostaev, C. Unger (Eds.), Human-Computer Interaction. Proceedings, 1994. IX, 239 pages. 1994.

Vol. 877: L. M. Adleman, M.-D. Huang (Eds.), Algorithmic Number Theory. Proceedings, 1994. IX, 323 pages. 1994.

Vol. 878: T. Ishida; Parallel, Distributed and Multiagent Production Systems. XVII, 166 pages. 1994. (Subseries LNAI).

Vol. 879: J. Dongarra, J. Waśniewski (Eds.), Parallel Scientific Computing. Proceedings, 1994. XI, 566 pages. 1994.

Vol. 880: P. S. Thiagarajan (Ed.), Foundations of Software Technology and Theoretical Computer Science. Proceedings, 1994. XI, 451 pages. 1994.

Vol. 881: P. Loucopoulos (Ed.), Entity-Relationship Approach – ER'94. Proceedings, 1994. XIII, 579 pages. 1994.

Vol. 882: D. Hutchison, A. Danthine, H. Leopold, G. Coulson (Eds.), Multimedia Transport and Teleservices. Proceedings, 1994. XI, 380 pages. 1994.

Vol. 883: L. Fribourg, F. Turini (Eds.), Logic Program Synthesis and Transformation – Meta-Programming in Logic. Proceedings, 1994. IX, 451 pages. 1994.

Vol. 884: J. Nievergelt, T. Roos, H.-J. Schek, P. Widmayer (Eds.), IGIS '94: Geographic Information Systems. Proceedings, 1994. VIII, 292 pages. 19944.

Vol. 885: R. C. Veltkamp, Closed Objects Boundaries from Scattered Points. VIII, 144 pages. 1994.

Vol. 886: M. M. Veloso, Planning and Learning by Analogical Reasoning. XIII, 181 pages. 1994. (Subseries LNAI).

Vol. 887: M. Toussaint (Ed.), Ada in Europe. Proceedings, 1994. XII, 521 pages. 1994.

Vol. 888: S. A. Andersson (Ed.), Analysis of Dynamical and Cognitive Systems. Proceedings, 1993. VII, 260 pages. 1995.

Vol. 889: H. P. Lubich, Towards a CSCW Framework for Scientific Cooperation in Europe. X, 268 pages. 1995.

Vol. 890: M. J. Wooldridge, N. R. Jennings (Eds.), Intelligent Agents. Proceedings, 1994. VIII, 407 pages. 1995. (Subseries LNAI).

Vol. 891: C. Lewerentz, T. Lindner (Eds.), Formal Development of Reactive Systems. XI, 394 pages. 1995.

Vol. 892: K. Pingali, U. Banerjee, D. Gelernter, A. Nicolau, D. Padua (Eds.), Languages and Compilers for Parallel Computing. Proceedings, 1994. XI, 496 pages. 1995.

Vol. 893: G. Gottlob, M. Y. Vardi (Eds.), Database Theory – ICDT '95. Proceedings, 1995. XI, 454 pages. 1995.

Vol. 894: R. Tamassia, I. G. Tollis (Eds.), Graph Drawing. Proceedings, 1994. X, 471 pages. 1995.

Vol. 895: R. L. Ibrahim (Ed.), Software Engineering Education. Proceedings, 1995. XII, 449 pages. 1995.

Vol. 896: R. N. Taylor, J. Coutaz (Eds.), Software Engineering and Human-Computer Interaction. Proceedings, 1994. X, 281 pages. 1995.

Vol. 897: M. Fisher, R. Owens (Eds.), Executable Modal and Temporal Logics. Proceedings, 1993. VII, 180 pages. 1995. (Subseries LNAI).

Vol. 898: P. Steffens (Ed.), Machine Translation and the Lexicon. Proceedings, 1993. X, 251 pages. 1995. (Subseries LNAI).

Vol. 899: W. Banzhaf, F. H. Eeckman (Eds.), Evolution and Biocomputation. VII, 277 pages. 1995.

Vol. 900: E. W. Mayr, C. Puech (Eds.), STACS 95. Proceedings, 1995. XIII, 654 pages. 1995.

Vol. 901: R. Kumar, T. Kropf (Eds.), Theorem Provers in Circuit Design. Proceedings, 1994. VIII, 303 pages. 1995.

Vol. 902: M. Dezani-Ciancaglini, G. Plotkin (Eds.), Typed Lambda Calculi and Applications. Proceedings, 1995. VIII, 443 pages. 1995.

Vol. 903: E. W. Mayr, G. Schmidt, G. Tinhofer (Eds.), Graph-Theoretic Concepts in Computer Science. Proceedings, 1994. IX, 414 pages. 1995.

Vol. 904: P. Vitányi (Ed.), Computational Learning Theory. EuroCOLT'95. Proceedings, 1995. XVII, 415 pages. 1995. (Subseries LNAI).

Vol. 905: N. Ayache (Ed.), Computer Vision, Virtual Reality and Robotics in Medicine. Proceedings, 1995. XIV, 567 pages. 1995.

Vol. 906: E. Astesiano, G. Reggio, A. Tarlecki (Eds.), Recent Trends in Data Type Specification. Proceedings, 1995. VIII, 523 pages. 1995.

Vol. 907: T. Ito, A. Yonezawa (Eds.), Theory and Practice of Parallel Programming. Proceedings, 1995. VIII, 485 pages. 1995.

Vol. 908: J. R. Rao Extensions of the UNITY Methodology: Compositionality, Fairness and Probability in Parallelism. XI, 178 pages. 1995.

Vol. 910: A. Podelski (Ed.), Constraint Programming: Basics and Trends. Proceedings, 1995. XI, 315 pages. 1995.